Major publications by Theodore Dreiser

NOVELS

> Sister Carrie (1900)
> Jennie Gerhardt (1911)
> The Financier (1912)
> The Titan (1914)
> The "Genius" (1915)
> An American Tragedy (1925)
> The Bulwark (1946)

STORIES

> Free and Other Stories (1918)
> Twelve Men (1919)
> Chains (1927)
> A Gallery of Women (1929)
> Fulfilment and Other Tales of Women and Men (1992)

AUTOBIOGRAPHY

> A Book About Myself (1923)
> Dawn (1931, 1998)
> American Diaries 1902–1926 (1982)
> An Amateur Laborer (1983)
> Newspaper Days (1991, 2000)

MISCELLANEOUS

> A Traveler at Forty (1913)
> A Hoosier Holiday (1916)
> Plays of the Natural and Supernatural (1916)
> The Hand of the Potter (1918)
> Hey Rub A Dub Dub (1920)
> The Color of a Great City (1923)
> Moods, Cadenced and Declaimed (1926)
> Dreiser Looks at Russia (1928)
> Tragic America (1931)
> America Is Worth Saving (1941)
> "Heard in the Corridors": Articles and Related Writings
>   by Theodore Dreiser (1988)
> Theodore Dreiser Journalism, Vol. 1: Newspaper
>   Writings 1892–1895 (1988)

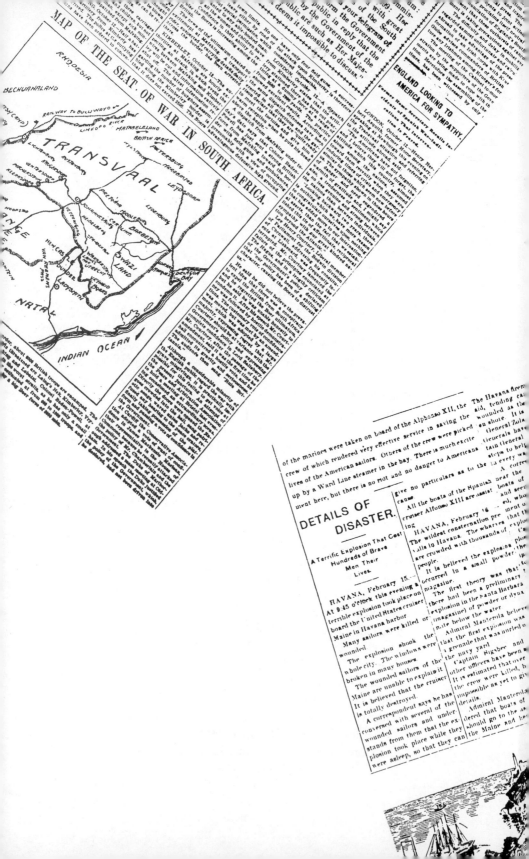

MAP OF THE SEAT OF WAR IN SOUTH AFRICA.

RHODESIA

BECHUANALAND

TRANSVAAL

MATABELELAND

RAILWAY TO BULUWAYO

LIMPOPO RIVER

SWAZI LAND

NATAL

ORANGE

INDIAN OCEAN

DELAGOA BAY

ENGLAND LOOKING TO AMERICA FOR SYMPATHY.

DETAILS OF DISASTER.

A Terrific Explosion That Cost Hundreds of Brave Men Their Lives.

HAVANA, February 15.— At 9:45 o'clock this evening a terrible explosion took place on board the United States cruiser Maine in Havana harbor. Many sailors were killed or wounded.

The explosion shook the whole city. The windows were broken in many houses.

The wounded sailors of the Maine are unable to explain it. It is believed that the cruiser is totally destroyed.

A correspondent says he has conversed with several of the wounded sailors and understands from them that the explosion took place while they were asleep, so that they can give no particulars as to the cause.

All the boats of the Spanish cruiser Alfonso XIII are assisting.

HAVANA, February 16.— The wildest consternation prevails in Havana. The wharves are crowded with thousands of people.

It is believed the explosion occurred in a small powder magazine.

The first theory was that there had been a preliminary explosion in the Santa Barbara (magazine) of powder or dynamite below the water.

Admiral Manterola believes that the first explosion was a grenade that was hurled to the navy yard.

Captain Sigsbee and other officers have been saved. It is estimated that over the crew were killed, but it is impossible as yet to give the details.

Admiral Manterola ordered that boats of the arsenal should go to the assistance of the Maine and bring aid, tending to care for the wounded as they reached the shore.

THEODORE DREISER

Newspaper Days

AN AUTOBIOGRAPHY

Edited By
T. D. NOSTWICH

BLACK SPARROW PRESS
Santa Rosa · 2000

NEWSPAPER DAYS. Copyright © 1991 by The University of Pennsylvania Press.

Black Sparrow Press books are printed on acid-free paper.

LIBRARY OF CONGRESS CATALOGING-IN-PUBLICATION DATA

Dreiser, Theodore, 1872–1945
    Newspaper Days / Theodore Dreiser : edited by T. D. Nostwich.
      ·p.   cm.
    Includes bibliographical references and index.
    1. Dreiser, Theodore, 1872–1945–Knowledge–Communications.
    2. Novelists, American–20th century–Autobiography.   3. Journalists–
United States–Biography. I. Nostwich, T. D., 1925- . II. Title.
      ISBN 1-57423-138-3 (paperback)
      ISBN 1-57423-139-1 (cloth trade)

CONTENTS

ACKNOWLEDGMENTS

Of primary importance in my preparation of this edition has been the influence of my good friend Neda Westlake, former Curator of the Rare Books Collection at the University of Pennsylvania. Her continuing encouragement and enthusiasm for the project have sustained me through years of arduous toil. Not only did she introduce me to the vast resources of the Van Pelt–Dietrich Library Center Dreiser Collection, but she has given generously of her time in reading my manuscript carefully and offering constructive criticism of it.

To Ingalill H. Hjelm, former managing editor of the University of Pennsylvania Press, I am indebted for her good-hearted support of this project in its initiatory stage.

Lee Ann Draud and Thomas P. Riggio have performed the grueling and thankless task of supervisory editing with wisdom and tact. I am sincerely grateful for the contributions these good friends have made to this edition.

My colleague Richard Herrnstadt kindly read my historical and textual commentaries in their early form and gave me the full benefit of his characteristically sage advice and good taste.

Karl E. Gwiasda and Douglas L. Stenerson generously gave of their knowledge and time to help me unravel some puzzling questions raised in Dreiser's text.

I thank the University of Pennsylvania for permission to quote from manuscript materials in its possession.

Publication of this book has been made possible through generous subventions provided by David Bright, Dean of the College of Liberal Arts and Sciences at Iowa State University, and by Frank Haggard, Executive Officer of the Iowa State University Department of English.

Preparation of this edition was facilitated by assistance in the form of released time and grants-in-aid from the Iowa State University College of Sciences and Humanities, the Graduate College, and the Research Foundation.

The Department of English at Iowa State University was especially considerate in providing me with research assignments and funds for the reproduction of printed and manuscript materials.

Three travel grants from the National Endowment for the

Humanities made it possible for me to do research at the Van Pelt–Dietrich Library Center.

I thank the following individuals and organizations for permission to reproduce the photographs in this volume: The Lilly Library, Indiana University (Theodore Dreiser in the early 1890s); The Chicago Historical Society (Eugene Field, 1893); Vera Dreiser and The Robert W. Woodruff Library, Emory University (John Paul Dreiser); and The Mercantile Library, St. Louis (Joseph B. McCullagh).

My labor in the preparation of this edition was greatly eased by the loving encouragement of my wife Ann, and to her I dedicate that portion of it which is my own.

NEWSPAPER DAYS

CHAPTER I

During the year 1890, and perhaps a little before that, I had been getting my first clear notions of what it was I wanted to do in life. There was one man who was writing on one of the Chicago papers, the *Daily News*, —Eugene Field, no less—whose work interested me greatly. For two years and more I had been reading "Sharps and Flats," a column which he wrote daily, and through this—the varied phases of life he suggested in a humorous, romantic way—I was beginning to understand that I wanted to write. Nothing else that I had read so far— books, plays, poems, histories—gave me quite the same feeling for constructive thought; for the subject of his daily notes, poems and aphorisms was Chicago and America, whereas nearly all the others dealt or concerned themselves with foreign lands.

But this local life, these trenchant bits on local street scenes, institutions, characters, functions all moved me as nothing hitherto had. For to me Chicago at this time had a peculiarly literary or artistic atmosphere. It is given to some cities, as to some lands, to suggest romance, and to me Chicago did that daily and hourly. It sang, or seemed to, and in spite of what I deemed my various troubles I was singing with it. These seemingly drear neighborhoods through which I walked each day, these somewhat ponderous regions of huge homes where new-wealthy packers and manufacturers dwelt, these curiously congested foreign neighborhoods of almost all nationalities, and lastly that great downtown area (surrounded on two sides by the river, on the east by the lake, and on the south by railroad yards and railroad stations, and set with these new tall buildings, the wonder of the western world) fascinated me. Chicago was so young, so blithe, I thought. Florence in its best days must have been something like this to young Florentines, or Venice to the young Venetians.

Here was a city which had no traditions but which was making them, and this was the very thing which everyone seemed to under-stand and rejoice in. Chicago was like no other city in the world, —so said they all; Chicago would outstrip every other American city, New York included, and be the first of all American if not all European or world cities. This dream many hundreds of thousands of its citizens held dear. Chicago would be first in wealth, first in beauty, first in art achievement. At this very time a great world's fair was being planned which would bring citizens from all over the world to see it. The Auditorium, the new Great Northern, the amazing (for its day) Masonic Temple—in sum, a score of public institutions—depots, theatres and the like—were being constructed. It was something wonderful, quite inspiring indeed, to see a world metropolis spring up under your eyes, and this was what was occurring here.

Nosing about the city in an inquiring way as I was and dreaming half-formed dreams of one and another thing I would like to do, it finally occurred to me that I might like to write of these things, if I could. I would like to describe a place like Goose Island, in the Chicago River, which, neglected and covered with shanties made of upturned boats sawed in two, seemed the height of the picturesque; a building like the Auditorium or the Masonic Temple, that vast wall of masonry, twenty-two stories high and then truly the largest building in the world; a seething pit like that of the Board of Trade, which I had once visited and which astonished and fascinated me as much as anything ever had. That roaring, yelling, screaming whirlpool of life. And then the lake with its pure white sails, the Chicago River with its tall grain elevators and black coal pockets, the great railroad yards covering miles and miles of space with their cars. How wonderful it all was! As I walked from place to place collecting, I used to improvise strange, vaguely formulated word-hashes or rhapsodies—free verse I suppose we would call it now—which concerned everything and nothing, but somehow expressed the seething poetry of my soul. Indeed, I was crazy with life— a little demented or frenzied with romance and hope. I wanted to sing, to eat, to dance, to love. My word-dreams or maunderings concerned my day, my age, poverty, hope, beauty, which I mouthed to myself, chanting them aloud at times. Sometimes, because I had heard the Reverend Frank W. Gunsaulus and his like spout rocket-like sputterings on the subjects of life and religion, I would orate, pleading great causes of one kind and another as I went. I imagined myself a great orator, thousands of people before me, my gestures and enunciation and thoughts perfect, poetic, and all my hearers moved to tears or demonstrations of wild delight. Some of these things I committed to paper, scarcely knowing what they were, and in a fever for advancement bundled them up and sent them to Eugene Field, at his house. In his column and elsewhere I had read how great geniuses were occasionally discovered by some chance composition or work noted by some one in authority. Although I waited for a time with great interest, but no vast depression, to see what my fate would be, no word came, and in time I forgot them and came to realize that they must have been very bad and were dropped into the nearest wastebasket. This did not give me pause or grieve me. I seethed to express myself. I bubbled. I dreamed. And I had a singing feeling, now that I had done this much, that someday I should write for sure and be very famous into the bargain.

But how? How? That was the great question, and to this I saw no immediate answer. My feeling was that I ought to get into newspaper work, and yet this was so nebulous that I thought it would never come to pass. I saw mentions in the papers, daily, of reporters calling to find out this or being sent to do that, and so the idea of being a reporter and being sent to write up something was gradually formulated in my mind, though how I was to get such a place I had not the slightest idea. Again, it occurred to me that, perhaps, reporters needed a special training of some kind, or that they had to begin as clerks behind the counter in the business office of papers—which made me very sombre, for those glowing business offices that I saw throughout the city here and there always seemed so far removed from anything to which I could aspire. Most of them—the great ones—were ornate, floreate, with onyx or chalcedony wall trimming, flambeaus of bronze or copper on the walls, lights in imitation of mother-of-pearl in the ceilings—in short, all the gorgeousness of the Sultan's court brought to the outer counters where people subscribed or paid for advertisements. Because the newspapers were always dealing with signs and wonders—great functions, great commercial schemes, great tragedies and pleasures—I began to conceive of them as wonderlands in which all concerned were prosperous and happy. Indeed, so brilliant did this seem—they and the newspaper world, as I thought of it—that I imagined if I could once get in it—if such a thing were possible—that I would be the happiest person imaginable. I painted reporters and newspapermen generally as receiving fabulous salaries, being sent on the most urgent, interesting and distingué missions. I think I confused, inextricably, reporters with ambassadors and prominent men generally. Their lives were laid among great people—the rich, the famous, the powerful—and because of their position and facility of expression and mental force they were received everywhere as equals. Think of me, new, young, poor, being received that way. How marvellous that would be. As a matter of fact this idea, once I had it, haunted me as a way out, the next step, if I made any at all; and I had begun to ponder even before I had left Mr. Midgely of the Lovell Manufacturing Company how I was to get into it, if at all, and when.

Imagine my intense delight and interest one day therefore when, scanning the "help wanted—male" columns of the Chicago *Herald* these pre-holiday hours, I encountered an advertisement which ran (in substance):

"Wanted. By the Chicago *Herald* a number of bright young men to assist in the business department during the Christmas holidays. Promotion possible. Apply to Business Manager between 9 and 10 a.m."

"Here," I said, as I read it, "is just the thing I am looking for. Here is this great paper, one of the most prosperous in Chicago, giving an opening to striplings like myself. Now if I can just get this, my fortune is made. I will rise rapidly. I will write wonderful things."

Therefore, I conceived of myself as already being sent on some brilliant mission and returning, somehow, covered with glory. I hurried to the office of the *Herald,* which was in Washington Street near Fifth Avenue, this same morning, and requested to see the business manager. After a few minutes' waiting I was permitted to enter the sanctuary of this great person, who, because of the material splendor of the front office (one of those onyx and bronze affairs I have described), seemed to me the equal of a millionaire at least. He was tall, graceful, dark, his full black whiskers parted aristocratically in the middle of his chin, his eyes vague pools of subtlety. His hair was curly and he seemed to breathe of a select social atmosphere only. "See what a wonderful thing it is to be connected with the newspaper business," I said to myself, and then, "I saw your ad in this morning's paper."

"Yes, I did want a half-dozen young men," he replied, beaming on me reassuringly. "I think I have nearly enough. Most of the young men who come here imagine that they are to be connected with the *Herald* directly. Now, as a matter of fact, it is not exactly that, though this may lead to something a little later. The *Herald* is conducting a free Christmas gift bureau this year, and we need a few young men with intelligence and discrimination to act as clerks. They have to decide whether the applicants are imposters or not and keep people from imposing on the paper. The business here is in need of one or two bright young men, and after the holidays are over we propose to select these from the young men who are employed now. We will give the others the first chance afterward, provided they prove worthy. This work will only be for a week or ten days, but you will probably earn as much as ten or twelve dollars in that time." (My heart sank.) "After the first of the year, if you take it, you may come around and see me and I may have something for you." When he spoke of the *Herald's* free Christmas gift bureau I vaguely understood what he wanted. For weeks past the *Herald* had been conducting a campaign for free Christmas presents for the poorest children. It had been importuning the rich and the moderately comfortable to give through the medium of its scheme, which was a bureau for the free distribution of all such things as could be gathered via cash or direct donation of supplies,—toys, clothing, even food for children. How successful its efforts had been I had no idea, but this call for help seemed to indicate an interesting experience.

"But I wanted eventually to become a reporter if I could," I suggested.

"Well," he said, with a wave of his hand, "this is as good a way to begin as any other. When this is over I may be able to introduce you to our city editor."

It was far from what I anticipated, but I took it joyfully. Thus to step from one job into another, however brief—and one with such prospects—seemed the greatest luck in the world. For by now I believe that I was actually hypochondriacal on the subject of poverty, loneliness, the want of the creature comforts and pleasures of life. The mere thought of having enough to eat and to wear and to do had something of paradise about it. Those long, fruitless searches for work which had previously afflicted me had marked me with a kind of horror of them. So I bustled about to the *Herald* Christmas Annex, as it was called—a building standing in Fifth Avenue between Madison and Monroe— and reported to a brisk underling who was in charge of the work of doling out these pittances to the poor. He put me behind the single long counter which ran across the front of the room and over which were handed all those toys and Christmas pleasure pieces which a loud tom-toming concerning the dire need of the poor and the proper Christmas spirit had produced.

Life certainly offers some amusing paradoxes at times, and with the best intentions in the world apparently, and with that gay insouciance which life alone can formulate and display when it is at its worst. Here was I, as I soon found, a victim of what socialists would look upon as economic error, almost as worthy of free gifts as any other, and yet lined up with fifteen or twenty other economic victims—as poorly off as myself—all out of a job, many of them almost out at elbows. All had taken this work in the face of a cheerless Christmas and to tide themselves over a very bitter period, and all of them were doling out Christmas gifts from eight-thirty in the morning until eleven and twelve at night, for the noble sum of ten or twelve dollars, and that to people who were not as bad off as, certainly no worse off than, they were themselves.

I wish you might have seen this chamber as I saw it for eight or nine days just preceding and including Christmas day itself. Yes, we worked Christmas day from eight a.m. to five-thirty p.m., no less, and very glad to get the money, thank you. There poured in here from the day the bureau opened, which was the morning I called, and until it closed Christmas night, as fine a line of alleged poverty-stricken souls as one would want to see. I am not saying that many of them were not deserving. As a matter of fact, I am willing to believe that most of them were—or that, deserving or no, dire poverty or not, they were still worthy of all they received here. Indeed, when I think that many of them, old women, old men, young women, young men, children, came miles, walking or riding, carrying slips of paper on which was listed all they desired Santa Claus to bring them, and that for all their pains in getting their minister or their doctor or the *Herald* itself to visé their request, they only secured a fraction of what they sought, I am inclined to think that all were even more deserving than their reward indicated.

For in the first place, the whole scheme, as I soon found in talking with others and seeing how it worked, was most badly gotten up. Endless varieties of toys and comforts had been talked about in the paper, but only a few of all the things promised—or vaguely indicated—were here to be had. In the next place, no sensible system of checking up either the gifts given or the persons who had received them had been devised. That is, the same person could come over and over and over on different days, bearing different lists of toys, and get them apparently, or a part of them at least, until some clerk with a

better eye for faces than another would chance to recognize the of-
fender and point him or her out. Jews—the fox-like Slavic type—and
the poor Irish were the worst offenders in this respect.

Again, the same family could send one child after another, the
parents having come singly first, until quite a number of trashy toys
must surely have been collected. Again, the *Herald* itself, which was
supposed to have kept all the applications for toys written by children
to Santa Claus, had not done so, or the applications had come so
numerously that it had been thought inadvisable or impossible to even
attempt to sort out those of the needy from those of the greedy or
frivoling or well-to-do. At any rate, hundreds claimed that they had
written a letter and received no answer, or that they had received an
answer and lost it. At the end of the second or third day before
Christmas it was found necessary, because of the confusion and uncertainty, to throw the doors wide open and give to all and sundry who
looked worthy—we haphazard, picked-up clerks being the judges.

In the face of this, the clerks themselves, seeing that no records
were kept and how without plan the whole thing was, notified poor
relations and friends, who descended on us with baskets, expecting
candy, turkeys, suits and the like, but getting only toy wagons, tin toy
stoves, baby brooms, Noah's Arks, storybooks and the like—the shabbiest mess of cheap things one could imagine. For the newspaper, true
to that canon of commerce which demands the most for the least, the
greatest show for the least money, had gathered all the odds and ends
and leftovers of toy bargain sales and had dumped them into the large
lofts above higgledy-piggledy, to be doled out as best we could. A
sensible division of suitable things, family for family, was therefore
impossible. We could not give a much desired thing to one person now
because we could not get at it or find it. A little later, another person
having applied and a lot of the same toys having been uncovered
somewhere, he or she would be supplied. The whole thing in many of
its phases was pathetic, ridiculous, asinine. And we clerks ourselves,
going out to lunch or dinner (save the mark!) and having no time to
travel the long distance to our respective homes, would seek some
scrubby little one-horse restaurant and eat ham and beans or crullers
and coffee or some other tasteless dish at ten or fifteen cents per head.
Hard luck stories, comments on the mess and botch and failure the
whole thing was, comments on the strange characters that showed

up,—the hooded Niobes, the dusty Priams with eyes too sunken and too dry for tears—were the order of the day. I met a man who was a newspaperman, young, gloomy, out at elbows, who told me what a wretched, pathetic struggle the newspaper world itself presented, but I did not believe him. He had worked in Chicago, Denver, St. Paul. "A poor failure," I said. "Some one who can't write and who now whines or who wastes his subsistence in riotous living when he has it!" So much for the sympathy of the poor for the poor.

But the *Herald* was doing very well, at that. Daily it was filling its pages with the splendid results of its charity, the poor relieved, darkling homes restored to gayety and bliss. Can you beat it? But it was good advertising, and that was all the *Herald* wanted, and that was what it got.

Hey, Rub-a-dub! dub! Hey, Rub-a-dub! dub!

CHAPTER II

I t was Christmas Eve, while I was still working for the *Herald,* that there came to our house to spend the next two days, which chanced to be Friday and Saturday, a Miss Lois Zahn, a friend and fellow clerk of my sister Claire's in one of the largest department stores in the city. Because this store kept open until ten-thirty or eleven at Christmas time and my task detained me until the same hour, we arrived at the house at nearly the same time, I a little later than the others.

For some reason by now—possibly because I was giving so much evidence of commercial activity in one way and another and bustling out evenings, when I had the opportunity, to see a young Scotch girl, Nellie Anderson, whom no member of the family as yet had seen, and because I was taking myself and my ambitions in a lofty spirit, talking of what I proposed to do in the future—I think my sister Claire for once had conceived rather highly of me—to the extent, for instance, of wanting me to meet her friends and join in on such social matters as she for the moment was interested in. At any rate, on this particular evening as I entered and was hurrying up the stairs to take a bath and then see what if any pleasures were being arranged for the morrow, I was intercepted by her with a "Hurry up and come down, won't you. I have a friend here—Miss Zahn—and I want you to meet her. She's awful nice."

At the mere thought of meeting a girl I brightened, for my thoughts were always on the other sex, and I was forever complaining to myself of my lack of opportunity and of courage, when I had opportunity, to do the one thing I most craved to do—make love. Although, at her suggestion of a girl, I pretended to sniff and be superior, yet I bustled to the task of embellishing myself, hoping intensely that she would prove to be pretty and that I would be attractive to her. Imagine my satisfaction then, on walking into the general living room on the parlor floor where a fire was burning in the one fireplace which the house possessed, to see a really pretty, dark-haired girl of medium height, smooth-cheeked and graceful. She seemed and really was guileless, cheerful, good-natured—a little stationery clerk, in so far as position in this world was concerned—and in her head, as I came to know, was nothing but innocent, colorful dreams of a remote, affectional supremacy which boded no ill to any one in the world. For quite a little while after meeting her I felt stiff and awkward, I am sure, for the mere presence of so pretty a girl in so close proximity to me was always sufficient to make me nervous and self-conscious. Yet from the look and manner of her, I read at once that I was at least not objectionable and that she was prone to make friends with me for my sister's sake. Ed, as I learned, had gone off early in the evening to join the family of some girl in whom he was interested. Al was out on some Christmas Eve lark with a group of fellow employes. The elder members of the family had disposed of themselves in ways and places which I have now forgotten. So here I was alone with Claire and this stranger, and doing my best to appear gallant and clever.

I recall now the sense of affinity and welcome which I felt for this girl from the start,—the sense of sympathy and interest. It must have been clear to my sister, for before the night was over she had explained, by way of tantalizing me I presume, that Miss Zahn had a beau. She herself referred to a banjo club to which she belonged and to a group of young men and women friends who lived in her vicinity and who came in and went out on the same trains mornings and evenings and who had organized among themselves various social proceedings by which they managed to brighten otherwise cheerless days and evenings. Later I learned that Lois was an orphan adopted by a fairly comfortable Irish couple who loved her dearly and gave her as many pleasures and as much liberty as their circumstances would permit, but who had made the mistake of letting her know, some years before, that she was only an adopted child—which gave her a sense of forlornness, I think, and a longing for close enduring love.

Such a mild and innocently vain and sweet little thing as she was. I never came across a more attractive or clinging temperament. She could play, as I soon learned, on both the banjo and guitar, for finding these instruments in this room where they always stood, she took first one and then the other and played a little. I remember marvelling at the dexterity and prettiness of her fingers as they raced up and down the frets and across the strings. Again, she had on a dark green blouse and brown corduroy skirt, with a pale brown bow about her neck to match, and her hair was parted on one side, man-fashion, giving her a sort of maidenish masculinity. I thought she was delightful. Better yet, I found her looking at me slyly now and then and smiling sweetly at some remark of mine as though she were pleased. I recounted the nature of the work I was doing, but confused it in her mind and my sister's with the idea that I was now regularly employed by the *Herald* as a newspaper man and that this was merely a side task. Subsequently, out of sheer vanity and a desire to appear more than I was, I let her believe that I was a reporter on this same paper, when I was not, of course.

One of the charms of the evening was that it was snowing and the ground was white. Outside we could see great flakes fluttering about the gas lamps. Across the street in a small cottage a large party of merry-makers was at play. Laughter was in the air, for people were coming from and going to places visiting their friends. Someone, I or Claire, proposed that we go out and get chestnuts and popcorn and roast them, and that we make snow punch out of milk, sugar and snow.

How gay I felt—how inspirited, hopeful. In a fit of great daring I took one hand of each of my companions and ran, trying to slide them over the snow. I remember that Miss Zahn's screams and laughter seemed disturbingly musical to me and that as she ran her little feet seemed fairly to twinkle under her skirts. She stopped at one corner where the nearest streetcar was and where all the stores, because it was Christmas Eve, were still brightly lighted, and did a little dance under the electric light that swung there, proving to me how charmingly graceful she was.

"Oh, if I could just have a girl like her—if I could just have her," I thought, forgetting for the moment that I was nightly, or nearly so, telling Nellie Anderson that she was the sweetest thing I had ever known or wanted to know.

At last bedtime came, with nothing save laughter and gayety up to the last moment. She was to sleep with my sister and preceded me upstairs, saying she was going to eat salt New Year's Eve in order to dream of her coming lover. That night I lay and thought of her, and the next morning hurried downstairs hoping to find her up before me, but she was not. There were Christmas stockings to be examined, which brought her, but before eight-thirty I had to be going in order to work this day from nine on. I remember waving them all a gay farewell and looking forward eagerly toward evening, for she was to remain this night and the next day.

That night I came home at five, and then it was—between then and seven—that I learned that she cared for me. When I arrived, dressed, as I had been all day, in my very best, Ed and Al were there endeavoring to entertain her, Ed to make love to her. His method was to press her toe in an open foolish way, which seemed to me at the time the height of dullness and lack of personal sensitiveness. Claire was there and some of the elder members of the family. I was offered candy and punch, and some game was played. I believe we had a Ouija board and tried to obtain spirit messages.

I fancied from the moment I entered that Lois had been waiting for me. She smiled at me so winningly and sat still sometimes when I was near, gazing romantically into the fire. Like those birds of plumage that strut before the females in the mating season, I posed about, Romeo-wise, lost, as I wished to seem, in moody gloom. At this date it is not possible to recall the trend of the conversation or what it was that drew us together. No matter. We were so drawn.

During this evening I watched her, again admiring every detail of her dress, which was somewhat different from that of the day before and even more attractive. She seemed infinitely sweet, and I persuaded her to play, flattering myself that I was preferred over my brothers who were present. What they said or how they acted, I have forgotten. I recall that after a time, we two being left together for some reason, she arose once and went into the large front room which looked out on the street through three large windows, standing and looking out in silence on the pretty homelike scene which our neighborhood presented. The snowing had stopped and a full moon was brightening everything. The little cottages and flat-buildings about glowed romantically through their drawn blinds, a red-ribboned Christmas wreath in every window. I recall pumping up my courage to a rather unusual point for me and, heart in mouth, following her and standing beside her.

She pressed her nose to the pane and then breathed on it, making a misty screen between her and the outside. Finally she inquired my initials and then, writing them, rubbed them out with her fingers and then, breathing on the window again, wrote her own. Still no clear memory of what was said—just that she turned and looked up at me, then down. Her face was like a wax flower in the moonlight—a moon flower. I had drawn so close, moved by her romantic call, that my body almost touched hers. I had just slipped my arm about her waist and was about to kiss her when I heard my sister's voice:

"Now, Lois and Theo, you come back."

"We must go," she said shamefacedly, and as she started I ventured to touch her hand, quite pleadingly. She looked at me, smiled and went on, and I waited, eager for other solitary moments.

There was no other opportunity this same evening,—the festivities were too general and inclusive—but the next morning, church claiming some and sleep others, there was a half-hour or more when I was with her alone in the front room, looking over the family album! And the family Bible! By now she had quite captured my fancy. I realized also that she was as drawn to me as I to her and that, as in the case of Nellie, I was master if I so chose to be. I was so wrought-up in the face of cold opportunity, however, that I scarcely had the courage to do that which I sincerely believed I could do. As we stood over the album looking at the pictures, I toyed first with the strings of an apron she had put on in which to help my sisters, and then later, finding no opposition manifested, allowed my hand to rest ever so lightly at her back. Still no sign of opposition or even consciousness. I thrilled from head to toe.

Then I closed my arm gently about her waist, and when it became noticeably tight she looked up and smiled. "You'd better watch out," she said. "Some one may come."

"Do you like me a little?" I pleaded, almost choking.

"I think so," she said. "I think you're very nice, anyhow."

I tried to kiss her cheek.

"You mustn't," she said. "Some one may come," and then, as I drew her to me, pretended to resist, but maneuvered her cheek against my mouth and pulled away.

She was just in time too, for my sister came in the back parlor almost unheralded, saying, "Oh, there you are. I wondered where you had gone to."

"I was just looking at your album," she said.

"Yes," I added, ambling out, as red as a beet, I presume. "I was just showing it to her."

"Oh, yes," laughed my sister cynically. "You and Lois—I know what you two were trying to do. You!" she exclaimed to me, pushing me. "And Lois, the silly. She has a beau already. You'd better look out."

She laughed and went off, but I was hugely satisfied with myself. Beau or no beau, Lois belonged to me. Youthful vanity over any feminine conquest was swelling my chest. I was always more of a personage, it seemed to me, for having it proved to me that I was not unattractive to girls—pretty girls—and Lois was certainly one.

CHAPTER III

What is it about sex conquests, I should like to know, that gives the average youth or man of strong sex proclivities such a wonderful estimate of himself as a man and even a hero? May it be perchance nature's idea of true dominance? Or is it just one of the many forms of power sought and contested for everywhere and gloried in when achieved? I, for one, am curious. Certain it is that in my case each triumph of this kind (this being only the second) gave me a sense of fitness and physical ability. I was not, therefore, I now said to myself, wholly unattractive. One type and another of girl obviously was drawn to me. In the case of Nellie Anderson the compliment was not all that it should have been, I argued, for while not ill-favored she was by no means chic nor did she carry herself with that air of consciousness of her own charm which so allured me in women—that air of smart disdain. On the other hand, Lois did, and for the reason that she knew herself to be really pretty, which she was. She had those little innocent airs and

nuances of temperament—pretences and make-believes—which belong to the attractive woman and which fascinated me and raised her
value in my estimation. Thus she talked of her social life—this and
that euchre party, this and that neighborhood dance, this and that drill
or performance of the banjo club—all trivialities of her little world and
all laid within the confines of the homes of clerks, small managers and
floorwalkers, but all of which made me feel that she must be very
popular just the same—for, after all, a world is a world. When I asked
when I should see her again, she suggested the following Tuesday or
Thursday and asked me not to say anything to my sister Claire, which I
was glad enough to do. She did not want her to know for some reason.
An honest little maid withal, for I had not been calling on her more
than a week or two before she confessed that there was another suitor, a
telegraph operator then working in one of the great railway stations of
the city, to whom she was engaged and who was still calling on her
regularly. When she came over to our house to spend Christmas it was
with no intention, so she said, of seeking a serious flirtation, though in
order not to embarrass the sense of opportunity we boys might feel if she
were not engaged, she had taken off her engagement ring. Also, she
now confessed to me, she never wore it at the store for the reason that it
would create talk and embarrass her position by making it seem as
though she were about to leave shortly, which she was by no means sure
that she would. In short, she became engaged thus early without being
really certain that she was in love.

Never were there happier hours spent by anyone than those I
spent with her, though at the time I was in that state of unrest and
change which afflicts youths who are endeavoring to discover what it is
that they are going to be able to do. With the end of work on Christmas
day my job was gone and the task of finding another before me, but now
this did not seem so grim either. I felt more confident. True, the
manager of the *Herald* had told me to call after the first of the year, and I
did so, only to find that his manner of suggesting something important
and valuable to come later had been merely a ruse to get eager,
industrious service for his bureau. With a princely air and smile he now
waved me aside, and when I suggested that I would like to be a reporter
he explained, "But, you see, I have nothing whatsoever to do with
that. You must see the managing editor on the fourth floor." When I
went there, it being early morning, no one was in. When I came

another day at three, only a few uncommunicative individuals—very distant and indifferent—were to be seen at desks, and I was informed that twelve and six were the best hours. When I observed those hours, the managing editor sent out word to find out what I wanted and, being told, replied, by messenger, no help needed. So I went away very crestfallen and rather frightened by the high and distant tone of the whole place.

Not actually to be put down by this, however, I went to other newspaper offices—great, thrashing worlds, as it seemed to me, the very epitome of this strenuous life in which I found myself, only to find the same and even colder conditions to be apparently prevailing. I began to feel that the newspaper world must be controlled by a secret cult or order. No one seemed to want me, or anyone, indeed. I recall one lithe, bony specimen of an editor with a pointed green shade over his eyes and dusty red hair, who, within the precincts of this graphic world where in the distance I could hear printing presses thrashing, looked at me much as an eagle might look at a pouter pigeon and asked, "Ever worked on a paper before?"

"No, sir."

"How do you know you can write?"

"I don't, but think I could learn."

"Learn? Learn? We haven't any time to teach anybody here. You better try one of the little papers—a trade paper maybe, until you learn how—then come back," and he walked off.

That gave me a definite idea of how I might begin, but it did not get me a position, just the same.

But, in the meantime, looking here and there and not having been arrested as yet by Mr. Midgely, I decided to try one of those other fly-by-night installment concerns of which, in one way and another, even while I was working for Mr. Midgely, I had learned. One, the largest of them all, as I soon discovered, was in this same Lake Street, not so far from Midgely's, and while I was trying to find some way of getting into the newspaper business I decided to try here. I was afraid that I would not get it—afraid, if I gave out that I had worked for Midgely, that he would explain that I had stolen from him. So instead I merely said that I had worked for Munger's Laundry and that I knew the city thoroughly.

Somehow at this place, as at Midgely's and elsewhere, my appearance seemed to commend me. The manager, a thin, straw-stuffed mannikin of the minor commercial life, wanted to know if I could give a bond for as much as three hundred dollars. They had just had one collector arrested for stealing sixty or seventy dollars. I told him I thought so, and decided to explain the proposition to my father and obtain his advice since I knew little about how a bond was secured. When I learned that the bond company investigated your past and held you responsible and prosecuted you for perjury and other things if you misstated or understated anything, I was terrorized. Besides, my father, on being told, scouted the idea with much vehemence. Why should they want a bond from me? he demanded to know. Hadn't I worked for Midgely in this same line? Couldn't they go there and find out? The idea—a three-hundred-dollar bond for so small a job, and me with so good a record! Let them go to Midgely, to Munger, to Conklin. At the thought of Midgely, I shook, and, rather than have an investigation, dropped the whole matter, deciding not to go near the place anymore.

But the strawy manager, taken by my guileless look, I presume, called on me one evening at our house, much to my curiosity and nervousness, determined to get me. It seems, for one reason or another, that they were in need of even more than one collector and that they were anxious to get hold of really trustworthy young men. Mr. Sypherstit had taken a fancy to me, he told me. I promised, he said, on my looks to be honest and industrious. He liked the neighborhood I lived in—our family appearance. He now proposed that I should go to one of the local bond companies which would give me a three-hundred-dollar bond for ten dollars per year, and that, if I wished, the Corbin Company (the name of the new concern) would pay for the bond out of my first week's salary, which, by the way, was to be only twelve dollars. This seemed to involve explaining concerning Midgely, but I decided to go to the bond company and refer only to Conklin and Munger, and see what happened. For the rest I proposed to say that school and college life had filled my years before this. If trouble came over Midgely, I would run away. So I argued.

But, as I soon found out, and much to my astonishment and delight, my ruse worked admirably. The following Sunday afternoon my new manager called and asked me to report the following morning, for at this company, instead of reporting only at evenings and starting out in the morning at what hour one pleased, as was the case at

Midgely's, one started out definitely from the office at nine, reporting only the next morning again at eight-thirty and keeping overnight what money one had collected.

Oh, those singing days in the streets and parks and showplaces of Chicago. Those hours when in bright, refreshing, or thick, artistic, lowery weather I tramped the highways and byways of this new Florence, dreaming chaotic dreams of all that was to, or might, befall me. Here, as I soon found, I had practically all my afternoons from one or two o'clock on to myself. The speed with which I worked and could walk would soon get me over the list of my customers, and then I was free to go where I chose. The spring was soon to be at hand, as I saw. Even now bright warm days appeared, which, to one briskly walking, seemed doubly beautiful. I was only twenty. Life was all before me. I had two girls in love with me; and the feel of plenty of money in my pocket, even if it did not belong to me, was a comfort. And then youth, youth,—that singing gayety of the blood which only youth knows. I felt most of the time as though I were walking on tinted clouds, among the highlands of the dawn.

But how shall I do justice to a period like this, which, for perfection of spirit—ease of soul, as it were—was the very best I had so far known, and one which promised much for the future? In the first place, due no doubt to months and months of exercise in the open air, my physical condition was about as good as it could be. I still had the notion that I was sexually impotent, or nearly so, and because of that thought was constantly being restrained from excesses which certainly would have drained me physically, I knew; but mentally I was not so despondent. Because of this newspaper idea which despite my rebuffs was now fixed in my mind, I was certain that I was to get somewhere. Again, the condition of our family was better than it had ever been in my time, for we four younger children were working steadily and advancing and apparently getting saner and more successful views of life all the while. Our home life, despite fearsome bickerings at times between Claire and Mame and between Claire and Theresa and between Theresa and Mame, was still pleasing enough. Al had gotten in with friends and elements which seemed to centre around the vaudeville stage and promise eventually to place him as a comedian—Irish, blackface, or Jew. Claire was reasonably contented with her work at the great department store, for a little while anyhow. Ed was still with one

Edwin Davis, a scene painter, now earning nine dollars a week and feeling very much set up about it. Altogether we were prospering, and my father was actually looking forward to a day when all the family debts would be paid and the soul of my mother, and his own, when it passed over, would be freed from too prolonged torments in purgatory!

But as for myself, life really was at the topmost toss. It was Chicago for one thing and my own temperament for the rest. I was, if I may so phrase it without seeming egotistic, like some bird that you may occasionally see poised on some topmost twig, teetering and fluttering on upstanding legs and ready for some distant flight. Again, I was like those high-flying hawks and buzzards that poise so gracefully on still wings above a summer landscape, seeing all the wonders of the world below. Again, I was like a song that sings itself, the spirit of happy music that by some freak of creation might be able to rejoice in its own harmonies and rhythms. Joy was ever before me—the sense of some great adventure lurking just about the corner and ready to take me in its delicious keeping—all life spread out like a great field of adventure which I was to have the privilege of reconnoitering without real harm.

To think, as I write now, that days like these are never to come again. To think that in all the endless dark or light no surety of their brothers is guaranteed. One ages—to what? One withers—to what? What has become of that swinging boy whose brain was compact of confused dreams of beauty, whose eye and heart were touched to a surging dizziness by every aspect of this blundering, blustering, articulate world? How I loved the tonic note of even the grinding wheels of the trucks and cars of the Chicago of that day; the clang and the clatter of its cable and electric lines. Its great beer and express wagons, its lurching surge of vehicles in every street. All had a tonic, rhythmic, symphonic import.

The palls of heavy, dark manufacturing smoke that hung low over the city at times like impending hurricanes; the storms of wintry snow or sleety rain; the glow of yellow lights in little shops at evening, mile after mile, where people were stirring and bustling over potatoes, flour, cabbages, or tobacco and papers, preparatory for their evening meal and after-dinner rest—were the substance of songs, paintings, poems, to me. I liked the sections where the hetaerae of the city were at noon still sleeping off the debauches of the previous night, or at night were preparing for those gaudy make-believes of their midnight day. Those sections crowded with great, black factories—stockyards, steelworks, Pullman yards, soap factories and the like—where in the midst of Plutonian stress and clang, men mixed or forged or joined or prepared those delicacies, pleasures and perfections for which the world buys and sells itself. Life was at its best here, its promise the most glittering. I liked those raw neighborhoods where in small, unpainted, tumbledown shanties, set in grassless can-strewn yards, drunken and lecherous slatterns and brawlers were to be found mooning about in a hell of their own sodden thoughts. And I liked for contrast those areas of great mansions set upon the great streets of the city, in spacious lawns, where liveried servants stood behind brocaded doors and windows, and carriages turned in spacious gates and under heavy porte cocheres to receive or return my lady shopping or calling, or to receive her perfumed guests, disdainful of the hard, constructive animality of this world outside.

Chicago seemed so aspiring at this time. Its bad was so deliciously bad—its good so very good—keen and succulent, reckless, inconsequential, pretentious, hopeful, eager, new. Here it lay, this great city of the West, and I was seeing it all. Wherever you found them, people were gay or at least somewhat dramatic in their misery, whereas, elsewhere, in other cities, they did not seem so much so. Nowhere was there any blank indifference to life. People cursed or raved or snarled, but they were never heavy or old or asleep. In some neighborhoods the rancidity of dirt or the bony stark bleakness of poverty fairly shouted, but if such neighborhoods were here, they were never still, decaying pools of misery. On wide bleak stretches of prairie swept by whipping winds, you could find men who were tanning dog or cat hides, or making soap, or sorting rags, or picking chickens, in a sort of hard, Marchy, acute realm of the commonplace or worse, while their wives were buying yellow plush albums and red silk-shaded lamps or blue or green rugs on time. Churches with gaudy altars and services; saloons with bars that were glistering symphonies of colored glass and mirrors; homes—miles of them all alike and all mildly comfortable—showing the last touches of those little things which men deem best for themselves and their children; vice districts and wealth districts hung with every enticing luxury that the wit of a commonplace or conventional mind could suggest—this was Chicago. In the vice districts I had even been paid by plump, naked girls striding from a bedroom to a chiffonier to get a purse, and in addition been offered the privilege of coitus for a dollar or its equivalent, a credit on their contract slip for that same amount—a courtesy which I fearsomely and gingerly refused! In the more exclusive neighborhoods I had been sent around to a side entrance by comfortably dressed women who were too proud or too sly to have it known in their neighborhood that they bought anything on time. Black negresses leered at me from behind shuttered windows at noon; plump wives drew me into risqué subjects on sight to entice me, as I supposed, into carnal relations with them; drunken, death-bereaved weepers mourned over their late lost in my presence—and postponed paying me. But I liked life. I was crazy about it. Chicago, as I viewed it then, was symphonic. It was like a great orchestra in the tumult of noble strophes. I was like a guest at a feast, eating and drinking in a delirium of delight.

CHAPTER IV

But if I was wrought up, if I may so phrase it, about the artistic aspects of the varying facets of the city, I was equally so about the delights of love which the arrival of Lois Zahn presented to me. Was I in love with her? No—as I now understand myself, I was not. Indeed, now that I look back on my life I doubt whether I have ever been in love with any one or with anything, save life as a whole. Twice or thrice I have developed stirring passions which bid fair to, and did, confuse my reason in regard to many things, but always there was a voice or thought within, which seemed to say over and over, like a bell at sea, "What does it matter? What does it matter? Beauty is eternal! Beauty will come again!" But this thing *life*, this picture of effort, this colorful panorama of hope and joy and despair which like a procession was adumbrating itself before my eager eyes—that did matter!

Beauty, like a tinkling bell, the tintings of the dawn, the whisperings of gentle winds and waters in summer days and Arcadian places, was in everything. The sting and appeal of this local life was in its eternal relations to perfect beauty. That it should go!—that I should go!—that never anywhere again after a few years might I see it more! That love should pass! that youth should pass! that I should soon stand old and grizzled, with age-filmed eyes contemplating joys and wonders whose sting and color I could no longer feel or even remember! Out on it for a damned tragedy and a mirthless joke! Soon—and this was the thing that I felt bitterly at twenty—soon I would be old. The opportunities that the world offers to each or any, I told myself, are few. The contest and struggle to take from you the little that you might gain was too great. And at that, the game was not fairly played. The dice were loaded. Vast favors were dispensed with such intense partiality.

For one woman that had the Circe gift of beauty ("beauty like a tightened bow"), for instance, ten thousand trod their shabby days in homely vacuity, only dully conscious of the infinite glory that had been denied them. For one man that had strength or wit or genius enough to wrest from the whirling maelstrom of life a brief but shining dominance, ten thousand—a hundred thousand—trod broken, peevish, hungry, hopeless ways. Oh, to be lifted out of this slough of the defeated and the hopeless. To rise where the light was,—the lustre, the music of happy events. To turn from bleak, unrewarded ways and unknown places to gorgeous chambers where a fanfare of applause would greet a great and yet most easily accomplished victory. Life! Life! this sweet, deep, intricate mechanism that had it in its power to do this for me, to give me splendid things. How could I appeal to it? If it but would, I said to myself, it could lift me in to Antonian splendors. It could give me love, place, fame, force, fascination, splendor. Where the crush of mighty things was—at their very apex—life could place you. But ah, the dice were loaded,—fortune was looking idly, romantically, capriciously here and there. With diabolic subtlety she was planning her artistries, her favors, her abstruse plots and her cataclysmic outcomes. Who would she favor? How long would the radiance of her smile endure? When, and for what trivial reason, would she turn the dark, condemning savagery of her glance?

But I was still young—but twenty—and all her favors could yet be bestowed,—love, wealth, fame, place. Would she, would she! deign to notice me? Out of her great casket of evanescent baubles would she take so much as one and toss it to me? "Not yet," I said—oh, thoughtless ingrate that I was—"has she given me one. Not one."

And yet fortune seemed to smile for a little while even then and even though I believed at the time—and in one mood and another— that she would not or could not or that I was beyond her ken. With supreme indifference to my praise or my blame or my longings, she smiled—a little—and I thought the whole world was before me to do with almost as I chose.

For one thing Lois proved to be desperately in love with me. She lived in a two-flat or apartment frame house in what was then the far middle-south section of the city—a region about 51st and Halsted. At that time the South Side L had newly begun operations—the first L road in Chicago—and I could reach her place by taking that to 47th Street on the South Side, and then taking a crosstown car which was there, and going west to Halsted Street, and then walking or riding south again from there to 51st Street, a distance of over half a mile. There were many suburban trains to be had around the rush hours at some nearby avenue and 51st Street, but mostly at such times as I wanted to go or come, few or none were to be had.

And again, it was only a moderately well-to-do working population which lived hereabout—clerks, floor managers, telegraph operators, cashiers, street car conductors and the like. Lois's foster-father was a railroad watchman—formerly a foreman, who had taken the latter place because of age. He had saved up a competence of a few thousand dollars by years of toil. This little apartment which they now occupied represented his expenditures plus her taste, such as it was. A simple little place with red plush curtains shielding a pair of folding doors which divided two large rooms front and back, lace curtains and white shades at the windows, a piano (a most soothing luxury for me to contemplate at the time), and then store furniture—a red velvet settee, a red plush rocker, several other types of new but badly designed chairs and the like.

Quaint little soul—how cheery and dreamful and pulsating with life she was when I met her. Her suitor, as I afterwards came to know, was a quiet, phlegmatic man of thirty-five or -six who had found in her all that he desired and was most anxious to marry her—as he subsequently did. He was wont to call regularly Wednesday and Sunday evenings and occasionally to take her to the theatre or to dinner downtown. When I arrived on the scene I must have disrupted all this, for after a time, and my manifesting some opposition—leaving her no choice, indeed—Wednesdays and Sundays became my evenings, and any others that I chose. For regardless of my numerous defects and no doubt asinine characteristics, she was in love and was willing to accept me on my own terms.

What a pathetic and dramatic thing is passion. Here was surely a case where a roving comet swept into the orbit of a minor planet and disrupted its simple and customary course completely. Once she pointed out Herbert Whipple, her intended, now assistant train dispatcher, through a depot window; and I saw in him, his face and body, the exact nature of the still, routine neighborhood life to which she was subsequently doomed. Here was no erratic, roving dreamer, but a placid, only slightly ruminating family man, a comfortable cog in the great mechanism of life. I could have sworn as I looked at him that all he ever read, if at all, was the Sunday newspapers. All that he knew, technically, was telegraphy and the details of his job. He was large, sleepy, pleasant looking.

But I—. No rooster stepping gingerly about, a high red comb on its head, one eye cast warily aloft for hawks, tail feathers superiorly displayed, was ever more conscious of individuality and possibility than I. Life was all one thrashing sea of possibility. Great adventure was just around the next corner. I wanted to see the world. Love was something—much—I was dying for affection. But adventure was almost more, and I would have sacrificed anything and anybody (as I almost uniformly did in a crisis) to advance nearer to that great something which seemed to be calling me, yet the nature of which I could not exactly detect—I mean the thing that I was eventually to be.

But Lois, I fancy, saw something that she wanted to—and thought she could—hold. She wanted to unite with me for this little span of existence, to go with me hand in hand into the ultimate nothingness. I think she was a true poet in her way, but minor and voiceless. When I called the first night, I remember that she sat primly for a little while on one of her red chairs near the window while I occupied a rocker. I had hung up my coat and hat with a flourish and stood about for a little while, examining everything with the purpose of estimating its and her value to me. It all seemed cozy and pleasing enough, a red-shaded lamp glowing in one corner, and curiously here I felt more at ease, even on this my first visit, than I did ever at the Andersons, much as Nellie made over me. There her thrifty, cautious, religious though genial and well-meaning mother, her irritable blind uncle and her more attractive young sister disturbed and tended to alienate me. I did not admire the background from which she sprung. Here, for weeks and weeks, I never saw Lois's adopted parents. When I finally was introduced to them, rather shamefacedly on her part, I think, for she was above her surroundings in her mood, they grated on me not at all, rather appealed to me, and they greeted me cordially—and disappeared. In these well-lighted double front rooms we were always alone. This first night she played a little on her piano, then on her banjo, and then because she was coming to seem especially charming to me I went over and stood behind her chair and, leaning over, decided to take her face in my hands and kiss her. Perhaps a touch of remorse and in consequence a bit of indecision now swayed her, for she got up before I could do it and moved away. On the instant my assurance became less, and yet my mood hardened for I thought she was trifling with me. After the Sunday previous it seemed to me that she could not do less than permit me to embrace her. Perhaps she had seen her fiancé in the meantime and decided to reform. At any rate she put up the banjo and I went to the window and looked out. I was deciding that the evening was about to be a failure, this whole adventure one, when she came up behind me and said, "Don't you think it's nice across there, between those houses?"

Over the way a gap between peaked-roof houses revealed a long stretch of prairie, now covered with snow, gas lamps flickering here and there in orderly rows, an occasional frame flat-house glowing cozily in the distance.

"Yes," I said, moodily.

"This is a funny neighborhood," she said conversationally. "People are always moving in and out in that row of houses over there."

"Are they?" I replied, not very much interested now that I felt myself defeated. There was a silence and then she laid one hand on my arm.

"You're not mad at me, Dorse?" she asked, using a sobriquet my sisters had given me.

The sound of it on her lips, soft and pleading, touched me. The spirit in which she said this was so different to the one in which she had gotten up—gracefully enough—and moved away. I saw that she had changed completely from the former mood.

"Oh, no," I replied loftily. "Why should I be?"

"Well, you came over here and looked out. I was thinking that maybe I oughtn't to do what I am doing. There's been someone else up to now, you know."

"Yes," I replied.

"I guess I don't care for him at all any more or I wouldn't be doing what I am."

"I thought you cared for me," I said. "Why did you invite me down here?"

"Oh, Dorse, I do," she replied, putting both her hands on my folded arms and looking up into my face with a kind of tenseness. "I know it isn't right, but I can't help it. I oughtn't to do it, but I do care for you and I don't care for him at all now. You're so wonderful, Dorse. You have such nice hair and eyes, and you're so tall. Do you care for me at all?"

"Yes," I replied, smiling cynically over my victory. "I think you're beautiful. You have such large soft eyes, and your hair and neck are so nice." I smoothed her cheek with one hand while I held her about the waist with the other.

"Oh, I know I'm nice that way," she replied. "But you might not really love me, you know, Dorse," she added sweetly, moueing with her lips and leaning against me, both hands on my breast and looking into my eyes. "I wish you could love me. I'm afraid you can't, but if you could—."

I thought at the time that it was because I seemed to be connected with the newspaper world and getting on so well that she was over-awed. Years, years afterward, I concluded that she was a better reader of character than I thought her.

"I can. I do," I said, enticed by her petite charms. She was the coziest, clingingest little thing. We sat on the red settee and I took her in my arms and held her and kissed her mouth and eyes and neck. She clung to me close and laughed and told me bits about her work and her pompous floorwalker and her social companions and even her fiancé. She got up and danced for me because I wanted her to, doing a running, overstep clog, sidewise to and fro, her skirts lifted to her shoe tops. She was sweetly feminine, in no wise aggressive or bold—really a most enticing figure. I staid on until nearly one in the morning—her fiancé's habit being to go at eleven-thirty—and then being reminded that she had to be at the store at eight-thirty (up at seven), I went away a little sorry. She looked so tired. I myself had all of nine or ten miles to go by owl cars, arriving home at nearly three. But I was not working at this time and so my rising time was my own. The thing that troubled me—a little—was what Nellie would think if she knew, which she never would, and how I could extricate myself from a situation which, now that I had Lois, was not a tithe as interesting as it had been before.

CHAPTER V

As the spring approached, this affair moved on apace. The work of the Corbin Company was no harder than that of the Midgely Company, if as hard, and I had if anything more time to myself. Because of an ingrowing sense of my personal importance and because I thought it was such a wonderful thing to be a newspaper man and so very much less to be a collector, I lied to Lois as to what I was doing. I told her that I was a reporter when, as a matter of fact, I merely hoped to be, and she believed it. You can imagine how determined I was to get into this world when I tell you that I lived in the thought of this change or improvement day after day and week after week. When would I be through with collecting—when would I be reporting? I cannot tell you how urgently my soul pressed forward to this something that I deemed better. Every intellectual and artistic thing—all great lines of effort that led to wealth, power or distinction seemed to be calling to me. I was eager now to know all about music, painting, sculpture, literature, and to be in those spots and places where life at its best—as I took it to be—was manifesting itself. I was regretful now that I had not made better use of my school and college days, and in my free hours, which were plentiful enough, I read, or visited the art gallery or the library, or, anxious to know, went to theatres and concerts when I could find that they were important. The free, intellectual churches or, better yet, ethical schools, as they should be called, were my favorite places on Sunday mornings. Of a weekday evening, if I could raise the money, I sometimes took Lois or Nellie Anderson to the Theodore Thomas concerts which were then being given in Chicago at the Auditorium, or to see the best plays and actors—Booth, Barrett, Modjeska, Fannie Davenport, Mary Anderson, Joseph Jefferson, Nat Goodwin—who were then in their heydey. Conceiving of myself as somebody with a future, I assumed a kind of cavalier attitude toward my two sweethearts, finally breaking with Nellie on the pretext that she was stubborn and superior and really did not love me, whereas I merely wanted to take privileges which she with her conventional notions could not permit and which I was not generous enough not to want. As for Lois, on the other hand, to show you the paradox of human character, she was perfectly willing to yield herself to me, with a view, I have always thought, of moving me to marry her. And here, having the opportunity and being deeply moved by her very obvious charms, I still did nothing—fear as to my impotence and the ridiculousness of showing myself incapable holding me back! I thought she would discover that I could not perform the sex act in a powerful, healthy way and so would scorn me when she really knew, whereas, if I had only known, I was capable enough, intensely so.

But oh, these spring nights when we two were truly maying. Chicago was so wonderful, the new ambitious life all about us so enticing. Once my work was done of an afternoon, I loitered over one thing and another, waiting for evening to come when I should see Lois again. She was so intensely sweet to me. Some women have a modeled roundness, soft and enticing, and Lois was one of these. Her eyes were so soft, so liquid, so unprotesting and so unresenting. She was customarily gay, with at times a suggestion of hidden melancholy. At night in that great stormy world of life which is the Chicago business heart, I used to wait for her in Dearborn Street, near Adams, which was close to where she worked. And together, once we had found each other in the surging crowds, and often in the dark, we would make our way to the great railway station at the end of the street where a tall clock tower held a single yellow clockface which was to be seen from where we stood.

If it chanced to be Tuesday or Thursday I usually went home with her, for these, together with Sunday afternoons and evenings, were my regular calling days. On other nights she would occasionally stay down with me to dinner, we eating in some simple, inexpensive place, or, she having an engagement, I would escort her quite to the door of her friends. I never knew until toward the end of the following summer, when things were breaking up for me in Chicago and seemingly greater things were calling me elsewhere, that during all this time she had never really relinquished her relationship with my predecessor. But

fearing my instability, no doubt, and by what necessary lies and innocent subterfuges I know not, she had held on to her first love against the
time possibly when I might not care for her any more. Was she unfaithful? No—I do not think so. At any rate she was tender, clinging and in
need of true affection. She would take my hand and hold it under her
arm or against her breast and talk of the little things of the day—the
strutting customers and managers, the condescending women of social
pretensions, the other girls who sometimes spied on or traitorously
betrayed each other. Usually her stories were of amusing things, for she
had no heart for bitter contention. There was a note of melancholy
running all through her relationship with me, however, for I think she
saw the unrest and uncertainty of my mental point of view. Already my
mind was scanning a far horizon in which neither she nor any other
woman had a vital part. Power, fame, applause—these were calling me,
and yet for this very reason this simple heart affection of hers was
doubly poignant to me. Once she said to me, her eyes looking longingly
into mine, "Do you really love me, Dorse?"

"Don't you think I do?" I replied evasively and yet curiously,
saying that I truly cared for her in my fashion, which statement was
true.

"Yes, I think you do, in your way," she replied, and the correct
interpretation shocked me. It hurt me. I saw myself as in a mirror, a
stormy petrel, hanging over the yellowish black waves of life and never
really resting anywhere. I could not. My mind would not let me. I saw
too much, felt too much, knew too much. What was I, what any one,
but a small bit of seaweed on an endless sea—flotsam, jetsam, being
moved hither and thither by what subterranean tides?

Ah, little Lois, you have gone this long while. Gone is your youth,
your beauty, that gentle, innocent smile that was as free of malice as a
flower. You deserved better of life than that I should have crossed your
path. I should never have taken your hands, kissed your mouth, told
you that you were sweet to me, as you were. A stable soul, in whom you
could have put all your faith safely, should have been yours. And yet,
knowing all, I wonder, had you it to do over again, would you do
differently?

Oh, Lois, dead or living, eternally sleeping or eternally waking,
listen to but these few true words. You were truly beautiful to me. My
strange, unfathomable heart was hungry. I wanted youth, I wanted

beauty, I wanted sweetness, I wanted a tender smile, wide eyes, a lovely form—all these you were. The winds of life were from the south, the air was balmy, youth was surging in my veins. Oh, pretty girl, pretty girl, have no vain regrets. Do you think I have ever been happy? That going on out of your life has brought me that which I was so hungrily seeking? No, no, no—a thousand times no. Here at forty I look back and onward into the dark, and I can say to you truthfully, for me there is no peace. My heart will not let me have peace. It is all a yearning and an endless uncertainty. But in this long gallery of adventures which is life there is a niche brightened by the halo-ing lamp of memory, and there you are.

Sweet, sweet, peace! I would not ask more for myself.

But this determination of mine to leave the Corbin Company was associated with other changes equally important and to me of much more emotional interest. For one thing the lines along which our home had been and was being conducted had early in this very same year become most unsatisfactory. The airs and plotting, the domination of my sister Mame—toward whom I had never borne any real affection— had become practically unbearable. As a matter of fact I disliked her greatly, for, being in a socially precarious or at least very individual position herself, she was nevertheless inclined to criticize or dogmatize as to the duty of others, a thing which enraged us all. Here she was, living with Brennan at such times and in such places as suited his convenience, getting scarcely enough from him to maintain herself in the state to which she thought she was entitled, contributing only a minor portion to the upkeep of the home, and yet setting herself and Brennan up as gods whose exemplary social manners might well be copied by us all. I cannot recall all, or perhaps even any, of the many instances which irritated me, but her whole manner from morning to night, day in and day out, was one of temperamental superiority. "I am Mrs. Austin Brennan, if you please," she seemed to say. "Austin is doing this. I am going to do so and so. It can scarcely be expected that we, in our high state, should have much to do with the rest of you." Yet whenever Brennan was in or near Chicago, he made our home his abiding place. Two of the best rooms on the second floor were set aside for his and Mame's convenience. The most stirring preparations were made whenever he was coming, the house swept, flowers bought, extra cooking done, and so on. The moment he was gone things fell to their natural and rather careless pace. Mame retired to her rooms and was scarcely seen for days. Theresa, who despised her heartily, would take fits of sulks and, when she thought the burden of family work was being shouldered on her, would do nothing at all. My father was left to go through a routine of duties such as fire building, furnace care, grocery marketing and the like, which in the ordinary run of things should have facilitated the housework generally, but in these quarreling conditions made it seem as if he were being put upon for nothing. Claire, who was anything but a peacemaker, added fuel to the flames by criticizing the state of everything to the younger members, Al, Ed and myself.

The thing that had turned me permanently against Mame and caused her to be an abomination in my eyes was that once, when I was still working for Conklin and my mother was alive, a letter came from my brother Paul from somewhere, enclosing a check for ten dollars and intended especially for Mother, I believe. Since he had sent it personally to her, she wanted to keep it a secret from the others and, trusting me to aid her, sent me to the general post office on which the check was drawn, with her signature filled in and me designated as the proper recipient. I showed her how to do this. I secured the money and returned it to her, but either because of her increasing illness or because she still wanted to continue to conceal the fact of its receipt from the others (Paul having mentioned in another letter that he had sent it), she said she had not received it. Then she died, and the matter of the money's whereabouts coming up, it was proved by an inquiry at the post office that the money had been paid to me. But I admitted this and asserted, which was true, that I had given it to my mother. Mame alone of all the family decided to make a row about this. For some reason—a love of contention, I fancy—she visited an inspector who was connected with the general post office—he being a friend of Brennan's— and persuaded him to make an inquiry, with a view, no doubt, to frightening me into better conduct in the future. The result of this was a formal government letter asking me to call at his office. I went, scarcely knowing what it was about, but suspecting, and on finding that he was charging me with the detention of this money and demanding its return on pain of my being sent to prison, I blazed. I talked distantly and savagely to him. I think I told him to go to the devil, or words to that effect. Anyhow, nothing more was ever said or done concerning it. When I reached home I was furious and raged and stormed. I called out my sister Mame and told her that she was a sneak, a liar, a loud-mouthed meddler. "You're a big noisy, nosey stuff," I said. "If you would only pay as much attention to your own morals as you do to mine, you would get along better."

At this she raged. "Well, I don't care!" she exclaimed. "The money's gone, you received it, and mother said you never gave it to her."

"Mother never said anything of the kind, you big liar!" I replied, but by now my father, my brother Al and others had interfered, and I was quieted down or persuaded to stop. For weeks and even months I had a burning desire to strike her. Whenever she passed me at first, I merely glared at her or did not see her at all. Later I asked her for anything I wanted, but always in a cold, distant manner. For over fifteen years the memory of this divided us completely, so much so that I hated the very thought of her, but after that, having risen—as I thought—to superior interests and viewpoints, I condescended to be friendly, always contemning her in private. To this day her general character has remained ridiculous in my eyes,—vapid, stormy, inchoate, ragbag, of no import to herself or anyone else.

Be that as it may, this first half of 1891 was the period of my greatest bitterness toward her. And in consequence when my sister Claire came to me with her complaints and charges, we brewed between us a kind of revolution based primarily on our opposition to Mame and her airs, but, secondarily, on the inadequate distribution of the family means and the character of the life the other sister, Theresa, was leading. According to Claire, who was most bitter in her charges, both Mame and Theresa were grossly immoral. Theresa was better than Mame in her eyes—indeed, Claire and Theresa were reasonably friendly at times—because the latter worked hard about the house and because she contributed much more of her means than Mame did. The latter, besides using the family as a convenience when she should not have sponged on it, did little if any of the very necessary work.

"At least Theresa helps all she can," said Claire, "and she doesn't bring Davis here in the house. Old Brennan comes here and struts about like a lord. Who is he, anyhow, I'd like to know? Nothing but a cheap, new-rich Irishman. And he doesn't care for her any more than if she were a dog. She's less than the dirt under his feet to him."

She was most acrid in her mood.

As a matter of fact, I cared as little for Claire and her woes in this crisis as for any of the others—less so, if anything. She was always too hard, narrow and selfish for me, a most unattractive type. But the thought of this home, dominated by Mame and Theresa and supported by us younger ones, with Father as a kind of pleading watchdog of the treasury, an aged Priam weeping in his beard and moaning over the general recklessness of our lives, was too much. Indeed, this matter of money, not morals, was the crux of the whole situation, for if there had been plenty of money or if each of us could have retained all our earnings, there would have been but little grieving over morals. As a matter of fact, money, or the lack of it, was the thing that was irritating Claire most of all. She was jealous of Mame and Theresa, the means with which their pseudo-marital relations supplied them, and although she was earning eight dollars and expected to earn more, she felt that the three or four dollars which she contributed to the household expenses each week was far too much. On the other hand, Al, who earned only ten and contributed five, had no complaints to make, and Ed, who earned nine and supplied four and a half of that, had nothing to say. I was earning twelve, later fourteen, and contributed only six, but I frequently begrudged much of this just the same. So between myself and Claire—little as we had in common, almost nothing in fact, being superior and critical toward each other—we brewed a revolution which ended really unsatisfactorily for us all.

The immediate cause of this was that between jealousies and arguments among the girls, there were days when all household duties were dropped because they could not agree as to who should do them, and nights when there was no dinner on the table, or scarcely any, because they could not agree as to who should get it. My father, religion stricken, aging by degrees and inclined by nature to worry over money and morals, was beside himself with grief over the stormy quarrels and bitter charges of immorality and social degradations which flew thick and fast. Hitherto, whatever he had thought of the conduct of the different girls, he had not believed that they were morally beyond the limits which he believed necessary for social approval or spiritual salvation. Now it came out in the charges they were making that Mame was not married, that Theresa was the mistress of the smug Davis who called here often, that there were secret entrances and exits after midnight, and the like. The hardest kind of words flew about. All we younger ones were really scandalized. Often Al and I, or Claire and I, took long walks and discussed it. Could we stand such goings-on? Wouldn't the home necessarily break up? My father, out of work and feeling too old to connect himself helpfully with anything, sat about brooding. Whatever he thought he ought to do, he did nothing. Perhaps religion and fear of personal want if he broke up this scheme of things deterred him. After all, where could he go? With which one of us or which group would he prefer to live? Theresa for all her alleged immorality was most thoughtful of him and made his way as easy as possible. Claire, Ed, Al and myself quarreled with him for being narrow, stingy, dogmatic, foolish. Would he join with us? Outside of Al, I do not think that any of us wanted him. Mame had no thought apparently for anyone but herself. I think these were among the most trying years of his life.

And now finally, late in March, a split actually came because of a bitter quarrel that sprung up between Mame and Claire. I do not know what it was all about, probably nothing of import, but it lacked none the less in feeling for that. Mame charged Claire with meddling, spying, being a talebearer and I know not what else. Claire declared that she would not live in this house any longer with such a foul-mouthed beast. Disliking Mame intensely because of what she had done to me, I sided with Claire. Together (it was her proposal, however), and with the aid of Al and Ed if we could get it, we proposed to either drive Mame from the house and take charge ourselves or rent a small apartment somewhere, pool our funds and run a rival home of our own, leaving this home to subsist as best it might. It was a hard and cold thing to have planned, and I wondered sometimes afterward, as I do now, why I shared in it. Yet it was a plausible thing to do, as I saw then, and appealed to us on that score. Besides, somehow it seemed to offer greater freedom both of means and action. I always felt here at home as though my actions and thoughts were being observed, studied and unpleasingly commented on.

Be that as it may, this to us very revolutionary programme was worked out to a definite conclusion. With Claire as the whip and planner and myself as general executive, a small apartment of four rooms and bath in Taylor Street, only a few blocks from where we were now, was first looked at, prices of furniture-on-time were studied, the general cost of food, light, entertainment was gone into. After a short lapse of time, we drew up a schedule of expenses which seemed simple enough—rent, twelve dollars per month or three per person; board, eight per week for all or two per week each, and so on. Claire, in her anxiety to bring her rage to cataclysmic conclusion, volunteered to do the cooking and housekeeping alone—and work as before. If each contributed five, as we first figured, we would have primarily a fund of over eighty dollars a month, from which we could be housed and fed and buy furniture on the installment plan into the bargain. Al was consulted first as to this and refused, saying (which was the decent thing to say, and characteristically Albertian) that we ought to stay here and keep the home together for Father's sake, he being old and feeble. Ed, on the contrary, always a lover of adventure and anxious to share in any new thing, agreed to go with us. We had to revise our programme, but even with only sixty dollars a month as a general fund, we fancied we could get along. And so we three, Claire being the spokesman, had the temerity to announce one day at a special conversation at which our father, Al and ourselves were present that either Mame should leave and permit the house to be run as we wished or we would leave. The ultimatum was not given in any such direct way. Charges and countercharges were first made. Long arguments and pleadings were indulged in by one side and the other. Finally, seeing that there was no hope of anyone compelling Mame to leave, Claire announced that she was going anyhow, alone or with others. I then stated that I would follow. Ed said he was coming, and there you were. I never saw a man more distressed than my father—more harassed by what he knew to be the final dissolution of the family. He pleaded, but his pleas fell on youthful, inconsiderate ears. I went and rented the flat, had the gas turned on and some furniture installed, and finally, toward the end of March, in blustery, inclement weather, we were actually ready to move, and did.

I never saw a home more gloomy, a man more distrait than my father during these last two or three days in which we were moving out. It was raw, blowy, sloppy, gray outside. Having completed all the details, Claire, Ed and myself were busy marching to and fro at spare moments, carrying clothes, books, nicknacks, some pictures and the like to the new home. There were open squabbles even now between Claire and Mame as to the possession of certain things, but these were finally adjusted without blows. Finally our last bundles were ready. Ed,

Claire and myself made our last adieus to Al and my father, in the order given. When it came my turn I marched out, with a hard, cheery, independent, inconsequential look on my face, whereas I was internally heavy with a sense of unfairness and brutality. Al and my father were the two I preferred over Ed and Claire. Al was always so warm and friendly to me—intellectually sympathetic. My father was so old and frail.

"Well," he said with a slight German accent when I came to say good bye, "you're going, are you? I'm sorry, Dorsch. I done the best I could. The girls—they won't ever agree, it seems. I try, but it don't seem to do no good. I have prayed these last few days . . . I hope you don't ever feel sorry. It's Tillie who stirs up all these things." He waved his hands in a kind of despairing way, and I, after uttering some uselessly mollifying phrases, went out. The cold March winds were blowing from the west. It was so gray and drear this evening. Tomorrow it would be brighter, no doubt, but tonight—

If I could compose, I would do in the strophes of a Schubert or a MacDowell the things that I then felt.

CHAPTER VI

This new home was nothing, an awful mess from the start. It was not built on any binding affection between any of us, and what kind of a home is that which is not? Claire, interested as she was to have a separate, independent abode, was no housekeeper as I soon found, at least at this time, and besides she was not interested in anything for anybody but herself. She was too entirely absorbed in herself—her needs, her rights, et cetera. After a few spasmodic efforts in the beginning to make things seem homelike, she gave up and became decidedly indifferent. No doubt it was too much to ask of her, working by day as she did. As for myself I was interested to do but little, having Lois to look after and feeling lonely and distant in this place. It seemed a terribly dreary place, especially at nights without my father, Al and the old family atmosphere. I realized when it was too late what fools we had all been. Ed, during the past six or seven months had wormed himself into the good graces of a certain Irish family, the one remaining daughter of which was almost a household pet, and there he spent quite all of his free hours, eating, spooning, even sleeping there on occasion. Evidently he was a youth after their own heart, the right man for their daughter, for though young he was received with all the honors and emoluments of a prospective husband. Nothing was too good for him, within the limited means of the De Goods. Indeed, in addition, his whole family was welcome on his account. Libby, his inamorata, was not very attractive, as I always thought. But what of that? Ed liked her. Claire, Al and myself, who had called there at one time and another, had looked down on them as not being sufficiently important socially— commonplace and Catholic, in sum—but they took no offence. Later when this other home broke up after many difficulties, they were even willing to have Ed and myself come and live with them, as we did, I in a lofty, condescending way, Ed as one of the star members of their circle. Is it not a haphazard world?

But this house or flat, of which I have been speaking, what a dreary place it was, to be sure. I think it lasted to the end of April, or the middle of May, at which time it broke up, Claire going to a rooming or boarding house in Ogden Place, facing Union Park, Ed and I going to the De Goods. The family, such as it was, was still in Flournoy Street, but, we having deserted so roughly, that did not last long either. Theresa and Mame falling out, the latter went East somewhere with Brennan for a time, Theresa on the advice of Davis took an apartment in Polk Street, to which Al and my father were invited. Mame having departed, Theresa and Claire made up their affairs, and the latter returned home. Al I believe also took up his abode there for a time, and Sylvia paid them an unwelcome visit from New York.

The thing that began to dawn on me at this time—even while I was living with Claire and Ed in this Taylor Street flat—was that I was now practically alone in this world. To my surprise I was finding that I had little in common with any single member of our family and with few if any people anywhere else. Indeed, by now I had deserted Nellie Anderson, largely because she was not interesting enough. Lois was sweet—intensely so—but even she, as I was beginning to imagine, was not enough to fill my life. I remember once, when I was still collecting and living in Taylor Street, that, having fallen out with some foster-aunt, who, by the way, was very fond of her but whom she disliked at times, she came over to Taylor Street one lovely April Saturday afternoon, having laid off from work on the plea of illness and, according to Claire, in whom she confided, with the hope of inducing me to marry her. By now Lois and I had become very intimate. In my crude, youthful scale I had weighed her and decided that she was not all that she should be,—not varied enough, not of a position or force which would offer me any real advancement. Something seemed to say to me, "Don't marry her, don't marry her." And besides, my meagre income, however cleverly we might manage, did not seem to warrant me in any such undertaking. I was dreadfully afraid of becoming financially stranded and of being compelled to endure many of the miseries which we had seen in our own home.

So when I came home and found her there, I was most elusive, Claire having whispered beforehand something of all I have just told. She was most enticing in a new spring dress of some simple, cheap material, having, as she had, the knack of planning individual things. It seemed to me she had never looked so pretty, and after a half hour here in the house we started for the nearest pretty park, the charming one called Union, which interrupted the progress of Washington Boulevard westward. I recall that the city had just newly built a wading pond for children, where in shallow water on a cement floor they could sail their boats, and here, on a bench, we watched them sending forth their minute argosies of white sails to the distant realms of childhood's fancy. Here, enjoying the sun and the new green leaves, she told me of this one family quarrel—the first I ever heard her relate—and also that she wanted to leave home. She did not ask me to marry her, but I could see she had some romantic dream of my taking her to a minister somewhere, having the ceremony performed and beginning a new life with her then and there.

Dear little Lois—the simple, colorful creature that she was. I can see her yet, as soft and rounded as a cherub and as pretty as any girl need ever be—actually beautiful in a simple way. Her mind was full of colorful, inconsequential dreams that rose like bubbles on wine in her young brain, cloudlands and misty pastures of light created by the rays of fancy playing on the fumes of temperament. Neither Lois nor I were living in any real world,—she in some gilded argosy afloat on a summer sea, I in mystic thought-realms and palaces of my own creation,— things which had no relation to the dull work-a-day about us, as many would have conceived it.

What I said I do not now recall, but it was to the effect that she was making a mistake, that her quarrel was not serious, as it was not, that I could not help her now, being uncertain of my position in life. She denied any intention of seeking aid and looked quickly with a different feeling on her home. We went on into the business heart after a time for something to eat, riding on the front seat of a grip car together, and then afterward south toward her home via the lake shore. In the moonlight, in the park, I held her hand and dreamed vague dreams and grieved that I did not have plenty of money and talked of my great success in life which was sure to come later. I was to rise in the newspaper world and be—I do not know what, president I think. In pathetic hope she clung to me, feeling no doubt that it was an insubstantial reed she was leaning on in her dreams.

As April advanced its sunny steps, I left the Corbin Company, determined to advance my condition, willy-nilly. At several points in my life I have done this, I am pleased to state. I was by now really tired of collecting, for this position offered no least variation from the work done for the Midgely Company—the same districts, the same kind of people, the same excuses, innocences, subterfuges. By degrees I had come to have a kind of contempt for the average mind which I had not had at first. So many people were so low, so shifty, so dirty, so nondescript. They were food for pictures and drama, little more.

And in addition to this, owing to my experience with Midgely, I had become very cautious in the matter of taking what did not belong to me—fear of the penitentiary deterring me,—and this meant that I should be compelled to live from week to week on my miserable twelve dollars, which did not please me at all. I was too unhappy with so little money. In addition this new phase of home living was becoming a horrible burden. Claire was of no least interest to me whatsoever, as I soon found. The house was badly kept and wretchedly supplied with meals. She could not really cook and did not want to. Beside being of a quarrelsome, fault-finding disposition, and not having Mame or Theresa to fight with, she now turned her attention to Ed and myself. We did not do this and that, the burden of the work was left to her, I must buy this and that, bring home this and that—things which I could not possibly do, not having the means. By degrees I grew to a revolting mood, and being told one April Friday that we needed this and that which I and Ed must supply, and having figured that I could not endure either this abode or my present task, I deliberately took fate by the horns the next day and resigned, having all in all, say, sixty-five dollars in my possession. I was determined now, come what might, never to take any other job save one of reporting unless I was actually driven by starvation, and in this mood returned home and announced that I had lost my position and that this place would therefore have to be given up. How glad I really was, as I thought of it. Now I would be shut of this new dull flat which was so colorless and burdensome that it was somewhat like a nightmare. Actually, as I see it now, my dear sister had figured that Ed and I as dutiful brothers should support her while she spent all her money on clothes. I came to dislike her almost as much as I did Mame and told her gladly this same day that I had lost my place and that we could not live here any longer. In consequence the furniture company was at once notified to come and get the furniture. Our lease of the place being only from month to month, it was easy enough to depart at once. Ed, having decided before that he would like to go to the De Goods to live, our home life here being so bare and cold, quickly made an arrangement this same day and invited me to come along. I was to share a good room with him for one dollar and fifty cents the week, and my meals would be charged to me at the rate of twenty-five cents per meal, according as I took them. The De Goods for some reason seemed to be delighted to have us both and welcomed us almost as members of the family.

Now, and here, as I have always noted with a kind of fatalistic curiosity, the last phase of my rather troublesome youth began. Hitherto, up to and even including this last move to Taylor Street, I had been intimately identified in spirit at least with our family and its concentrated home life. During my mother's life, of course, I felt that wherever she was, was home. Afterwards it was the house where she had been, as well as my father and those who had been connected with her and who now remained together to keep up in some manner the family spirit. When this, through bitter recrimination and the continuous development of individuality in all of us, began to go to pieces, this new branch home established by three of us seemed something of the old place and spiritually allied with it, but when it fell and the old home, as I have mentioned, broke up at about the same time, I felt completely adrift. Now what was I to do with myself, I asked myself. Where was I to go? Here I was, soon (in three months) to be twenty-one years of age and yet without trade or profession, a sort of non-descript dreamer without the power to earn a decent salary and yet with all the tastes and proclivities of one destined to share an independent fortune. My eyes were constantly fixed on people in positions and stations far above my own. The people who interested me were bank-ers, millionaires, artists, politicians, the real rulers of the world. Just at this time the nation was being thrown into its quadrennial ferment in regard to who should be the next president of the United States. The newspapers, egged on by the politicians and the various financial and social elements interested in government control, were publishing reams upon reams of information and comment, favorable and other-wise, in regard to this or that politician or element or private individual who might by some unforeseen turn of events be catapulted into the chief seat of the nation. David B. Hill of New York, Grover Cleveland of New York, Thomas B. Hendricks of Indiana, and others were being widely and favorably discussed by the Democrat party, whose conven-tion was to be held here in Chicago this coming June, now almost at hand. Among the Republicans Benjamin Harrison of Indiana, James G. Blaine of Maine, William B. Allison of Iowa, and others were very much to the fore. The convention of this party was to be held in Minneapolis, not far from Chicago.

If I have seemed to indicate by my devotion to minor matters that I was not interested in the general drift of public affairs, I have given an inadequate picture of myself. It is true that life at close range, as I have described it, fascinated me, but the general progress of both Europe and America and Asia and Africa was by no means beyond my intellectual inquiry. By now I was a reader of Emerson, Carlyle, Huxley, John Stuart Mill and others. The existence of Nietzsche in Germany, Darwin, Spencer, Wallace and Tyndall in England, and what they stood for, were well within the range of my feverish intuition if not exact knowl-edge. In America Washington, Jefferson, Jackson, Lincoln, the history of the Civil War and the subsequent drift of the nation to monopoly and so to oligarchy were all within my understanding and private philosophizing. American writers, American and European artists, American politicians and statesmen were like those stars which rise in the east at night to me. They were on the eastern horizon of my intellectual development and gradually rising and brightening into clear view. Indeed, the heavens of my intellectual night were already brightened by a galaxy of stars.

And now this national ferment in regard to political preferment and advancement, the swelling tides of wealth and population in Chicago, the upward soaring of names and fames in regard to wealth and place stirred me as do whips and goads the lesser animals. I wanted to get up—oh, how eagerly. I wanted to shake off these garments of the commonplace in which I seemed swathed and to step forth into the public arena where I would be seen and understood for what I was. "No common man am I," I was constantly saying to myself, and I would no longer be held down to this shabby world of collecting in which I found myself. The newspapers, the newspapers, somehow, by their general familiarity and intimacy with everything which was going on in the world, seemed to me to be the nearest and quickest approach to all this of which I was dreaming. Always an avid reader of them, it seemed to me now as I looked at them, anxious to make some one move which would truly advance me, as if I understood already all the processes by which they were gotten up. This matter of reporting, for instance, I said to myself, must certainly be easy. Something happened, one car ran into another, or a man was shot, or a fire broke out. You, as a reporter, ran to the scene, observed or inquired after the details, secured the names and addresses of those immediately concerned, and described it. To reassure myself on this point I went about looking for small accidents on my own account, or imagining them and then, taking pen and paper in hand, sat down and wrote out what I saw. The result to me, as contrasted with what I found in the daily papers, was quite satisfactory. I was satisfied after a few private efforts of this kind that I could and must report. Some paper must give me a place. I was out of work now, and I would never go back to collecting or anything else if I starved. I had saved up the very satisfactory sum of sixty-five dollars, and on this I proposed to subsist until I finally secured a place.

CHAPTER VII

Imagine a dreamy cub of twenty, soon to be twenty-one, long, lank, spindling, a pair of gold-framed specs on his nose, his hair combed à la pompadour, a new spring suit, consisting of a pair of light check trousers and bright blue coat and vest, with a brown fedora hat and new yellow shoes, starting out to connect himself with the newspaper press of

Chicago. At that time, although I did not know it, Chicago was in the heydey of its newspaper prestige. Some of the nation's most remarkable editors, publishers and newspaper writers were at work here—Melville E. Stone, afterwards managing editor of the Associated Press; Victor F. Lawson, publisher of the *Daily News*; Joseph Medill, editor and publisher of the *Tribune*; Eugene Field, managing editor of the *Morning Record*; William Penn Nixon, editor and publisher of the *Inter-Ocean*; George Ade, reporter; Finley Peter Dunne (Philosopher Dooley), reporter; Brand Whitlock, and a score of others subsequently to become well known. Indeed the local newspaper world was fairly seething with talent of all kinds, and if one made an impression here it was because of a definite ability for the work and nothing less.

Having no training and no one to introduce me I was still not without definite ability, as I was to find, but it was of a most incoherent, blundering and emotional character. Having made up my mind that I must be a newspaper man, I did not trouble to look for anything else but made straight for the various offices each day, asking if there was anything to do. By now I had learned the proper hours of inquiry— twelve noon and five-thirty or six at night. My Christmas experience with the *Herald* and its managing editor had taught me that. The chill advice of the latter in regard to experience had made me feel as though I might not be able to connect with any of the larger papers, but I was determined to see as to that. By degrees I made my way into the presences of the various city and managing editors of quite every paper in Chicago, with the result that they surveyed me with that cynical fishy eye which only newspapermen and financiers can boast and told me there was nothing. They did not seem to see me at all. One day in the office of the *Chicago Daily News* a tall, shambling, awkward-looking man in a brown flannel shirt (coat and waistcoat having been removed because of the warmth) and suspenders down was pointed out to me by an office boy who saw him slipping past the city editorial door, in which room I was expectantly loitering.

"Want to know who dat is?"

"Yes," I replied humbly, grateful for even the attention of office boys.

"Well, dat's Eugene Field. Heard o' him, ain'tcha?"

"Sure," I replied, recalling the bundle of incoherent manuscripts I had thrust upon him. I surveyed his retreating figure with interest and some nervousness and envy, feeling as though he might psychically detect that I was the perpetrator of unsolicited slush and abuse me then and there.

In spite of my energy, manifested for one solid week and longer between the hours of twelve and two at noon and five-thirty and seven at night—the hours in which assignments were given out—I secured nothing. It seemed to me as I went about now that newspaper offices were the strangest, coldest, most haphazard and impractical of places. Gone was that fine ambassadorial quality which had formerly seemed to surround them. These rooms were crowded with commonplace desks and lamps—the floors frequently strewn with newspapers. Office boys and hirelings generally gazed at you in the most unfriendly manner, wanting to know what you wanted and insisting that there was nothing—they who knew nothing. Some city editors came down at twelve, others at twelve-thirty, others at one. I was told by office boys to apply after one or two in the afternoon or after seven at night when all the assignments had been given out, but when I did so I was told that the city editor was not in, or that he had gone, or that there was nothing and would be nothing. I began to feel desperate.

About this time I had an inspiration. I determined that, instead of trying to see all of the papers each day and missing out on the most of them at the vital hour, I would select one paper and see if in some way I could not ingratiate myself in the good graces of its editor. I had by now the very sensible notion that a small or, rather, unsuccessful paper would probably receive me with more consideration than one of the great thriving ones, and in my thoughts I picked on the *Chicago Daily Globe,* a spindling, struggling affair financed by one of the Chicago politicians for political purposes only. It was then located in Fifth Avenue between Madison and Monroe and directly opposite the *Chicago Daily News,* and about it I decided to hang until I got something.

You have seen perhaps a homeless cat hang about a given doorstep for days and days, meowing to be taken in, or a dog following a given pedestrian and making humble overtures for adoption. That was me, exactly. I selected the *Chicago Daily Globe,* and like a homeless dog or stray cat I hung about its back door. The door in this case was a side door and gave out on an alley. Inside was a large, bare, colorless or smoke-colored room filled with a few rows of tables set end to end, with a railing traversing the northern one-fourth, behind which sat the city editor, the dramatic and sporting editors, and one editorial writer. Outside this and at a desk which was near the side door sat a large, fleshy, gelatinous, round-faced, round-headed young man who, like myself, wore gold-rimmed spectacles, and who had as hard and keen and cynical an eye as I have ever seen in anyone, and who seemed to me at first glance to be most vitally opposed to me and every one else. He was so silent, dour, indifferent. As it turned out, he was the *Daily Globe's* copyreader and a typical professor of that art. I did not see him the first few times I called, seeing that the first week I canvassed the papers I only came here between twelve and twelve-thirty. But after that, having planned a hangdog campaign of my own, which consisted in coming in at twelve or twelve-thirty, taking a seat in a far corner and staying until two or two-thirty or even three—until, indeed, the city editor went out to lunch,—I soon discovered him, for he usually arrived at two. Nothing was said by me to anyone at first save the city editor, a brisk young man of thirty who bore a most remote and uncommunicative attitude toward all his staff during assignment hours. By degrees some of the reporters began to talk to me, thinking that I was a member of the staff, which eased my position a little during this time, and afterward I noticed, as soon as all the reporters had gone, the city editor became most genial with the one editorial writer who sat next him, and the two often went off together for a bite.

Parlous and yet delicious hours! But they secured me nothing although I felt all the time as though I were on the edge of some great change, absolutely convinced of it indeed. Still no one seemed to want me. This city editor, when I came in each day—or rather, having been in long ahead of him, when I approached after all the others had gone—would shake his head and say, "Nothing today. I don't see a thing in sight." But not roughly or harshly, and therein lay my hope. For a time, upon this remark, I would go out and wander about the streets, or visit most of the other newspaper offices, more as a duty than with any feeling that I would get anything, but latterly I did not even do this, being convinced that my hope was here. So here then I would sit and read the various papers which were lying about, or, finding ample copy paper, would try and write out something I had seen. I was always on the qui vive for some accident or other which I might report to this city editor in the hope that he had not seen it, and thus win my way to his good graces.

The ways of self-advancement are strange—so often purely accidental. I did not know it but my mere sitting about in this fashion was really a card in my favor. A number of the employed reporters, of whom there were eight or nine (the best papers carried from twenty to thirty), seeing me sit about in this fashion from twelve to two, imagined that I was employed here and in consequence struck up occasional conversations with me. Reporters rarely know details of staff arrangements or changes. Some of them on finding that I was only seeking work ignored me, as is the fashion of so many. Others gave me a bit of advice. Why didn't I see Selig of the *Tribune* or Herbst of the *Herald*? It was rumored that staff changes were to be made. One youth learning that I had never written a line for a newspaper suggested that I go round and see the city editor of the Associated Press or the United Press, where the most inexperienced beginners were put to work at as little as eight dollars a week. But somehow this did not suit me at all. I felt that I could write. Anyhow, it was just as hard to get a place there as anywhere else.

Finally, however, my mere sitting about in this fashion brought me into contact with that copyreader whom I have previously described, one John Maxwell by name, who, although he did not care for me in particular nor anyone in general, still, out of mere curiosity as to who I was, once remarked, "Are you doing anything special for the *Globe*?"

"No," I replied.

"Just looking for a position?"

"Yes."

"Ever work for any paper before?"

"No."

"How do you know you can write?"

"I just feel that I can. I want to see if I can't get a chance to try."

He looked at me curiously, amusedly, cynically. "Don't you ever go round to the other papers?"

"Yes, after I find there is nothing here."

He stared at me and smiled.

"How long have you been coming here like this?"

"Two weeks."

"Every day?"

"Every day."

He laughed now, a genial, rolling, fat laugh. "Why do you pick the *Globe*? Don't you know it's the poorest paper in Chicago?"

"That's why I pick it," I replied innocently and with the best feeling in the world. "I thought I might get a chance here."

"Oh, you did," he laughed. "Well, you may be right, at that. Hang about. You may get something. This National Democratic Convention is going to open in June. They'll have to take on some new men then. I don't see why they shouldn't give you a show as anyone else. But it's a hell of a business to be wanting to get into."

He began taking off his coat and waistcoat as he always did these warm days, rolling up his sleeves, sharpening his blue pencils and taking up stacks of "copy" intended for the Sunday issue, I presume, while I merely stared at him, unable or unwilling to argue this point. The newspaper business seemed certainly good enough for me. Every now and then as he sat there he would look at me through his round, gold-rimmed glasses as though I were some strange animal. I grew restless and went out. After that, though, each day he greeted me in the most friendly fashion, and because he seemed inclined to talk I staid to talk with him.

What it was that finally drew us together in a minor bond of friendship I have never been able to discover, but so it was. One courtesy or geniality led to another. When other newspaper men occasionally drifted back after a fruitless assignment begun at twelve-thirty, or friends came in to see him and I was there, he introduced me. He seemed to take a liking to me from the moment of that first conversation and to include me in what I might call the *Globe* family spirit. He was interested in politics, literature and the newspaper life of Chicago. Bit by bit he informed me as to the various editors, who the most successful newspaper men were, how some reporters did police, some politics and some just general news. I learned merely from sitting about that on every paper was a sporting editor, a society editor, a dramatic editor and, here, a political man. There were managing editors, Sunday editors, news editors, city editors, copyreaders and editorial writers, all on what seemed to me wonderful salaries—thirty-five to sixty—and even more. I learned at once from him of all those clever men I have mentioned, the men with reputations, and also—which I had not fully realized before—that this newspaper world was a seething maelstrom in which clever men struggled and fought as else-where, that some rose and many fell, and that there was a roving element among newspaper men that drifted from city to city, many

drinking themselves out of countenance, others settling down somewhere into some fortunate berth. Before long he told me that only
recently he had been copyreader on the *Chicago Tribune* but had been
jockeyed or politicked out of his place.

CHAPTER VIII

I cannot tell you how thrilling even this profitless connection with
journalism was to me. I was delighted to know that, whether I had
gained a place as yet, I had achieved even so much as one friend at
court. Maxwell advised me to stick, after a few days. "You'll get on," he
said. "I believe you've got the stuff in you. When the time comes I'll
edit your copy for you. Maybe I can help you. You'll probably be like
every damned newspaperman when you get a start, an ingrate, but I'll
help you just the same. Hang around. That Democratic convention
will begin in three or four weeks now. They'll have to put some new
men on. I'll speak a good word for you, if you don't tie up with some
other paper before then."

And he was as good as his word—dear old cynical John. He must
have spoken to the city editor shortly after this, for the manner of the
latter changed markedly toward me. He was more smiling and less
brusque. He asked me where I came from and what I had been doing. "I
don't see that I can do a thing for you before the convention, but if
you'll come around then I'll see what can be done. Of course, you never
can tell. Something might break loose any day, and then if you were
here I would give it to you."

I decided to hang around just the same in the hope of that
problematical something. But before even a newspaper story appeared
for me to do, a new situation arose which tied me up closer with this
prospect than I had originally hoped for. It appeared after a little while
that the editorial writer of whom I have previously made mention, the
friend and intimate of the city editor, had just completed a small work
of fiction which he and the city editor in combination had had privately printed, I believe, and which they were very anxious to sell and
make money out of. It was a kind of fictional transposition of the
editorial writer's own school days here in Chicago. Only, as I recall it, it

was very badly done—an immature imitation of *Tom Sawyer* without any real charm or human interest, a type of book in which the two or three hundred schoolmates who knew the author in his Hyde Park School days might recognize a familiar atmosphere. He was a small, picayune individual, this editor, yellow-haired, meticulous, chaffering. He spent quite all of his time writing those biased, envenomed and bedeviling editorials which are so constantly required by purely partisan managements. Mr. Gissel, for that was his name, was your true henchman, or editorial mercenary, a "peanut" or "squeak" writer, as they were termed in those slangy days, and as such he amused and even interested me, though I could not like him. Whenever he had concocted some peculiarly malicious or defaming line or thought, he would get up and dance about in a kind of jack-in-the-box fashion, cackling and chortling in a, to me, disconcerting fashion. For the first time in my life I began to see quite clearly how party councils and party tendencies were manufactured or twisted or belied or smirched, and it still further reduced my estimate of humanity. Men as I was finding them out were small, irritable, nasty in their struggle for existence. This little editor, for instance, was not interested in the Democratic party, which this paper was supposed to represent, or indeed party principles of any kind. He did not believe what he wrote, did not care particularly, but receiving forty dollars a week, he was anxious to make as workmanlike a job of it as possible. Just at this time he was engaged in throwing mud at the national Republican administration, the local mayor and state governor, various local politicians and statesmen and, in short, all those whom the reprobate gambler and financier, whose money financed this publication and who was interested in gambling, contracts and houses of prostitution on a percentage basis, wished him to attack. I was of a distinctly democratic bias myself at the time, so I can scarcely be accused of holding a brief for the Republican party in this.

What a pitiful thing is journalism and an alleged free press anyhow! What a huckstering to and fro of this and that dishonest argument, what shabby, tricky backroom councils looking to public favors and fames which shall lead again to public contracts and financial emoluments! Journalism, like politics, as I was now soon to see, was a slough of muck, a heap in which men were raking busily and filthily for what they might uncover in the way of financial, social, political and publicity returns, such as those of fame or even passing applause. As a matter of fact, I was in the heart of America's political, social and financial counting room, only I did not know it. Here—in the hundreds of offices of this kind throughout the country—character, reputation, position were made or unmade. I looked at this dingy office and then at this little yellow-haired rat of an editor one afternoon as he worked, and it came to me what a desperately subtle and shifty thing life was. Here he was, this little runt of a man, thin, minute, ant-like, with scorpion-like tendencies, scribbling away busily, and above him were strong, dark, secretive men, never appearing in public but paying him his little salary privately—dribbling it down to him through a publisher and an editor-in-chief and a managing editor—in order that, for the miserable, untraceable sum which he received, he might be kept busy chaffering, misconstruing, lying, intellectually cheating.

Be that as it may, the plan which he had in connection with this book (and in which the city editor plainly concurred) was this: The graduating class of the Hyde Park High School of which he had been a member a few years before had numbered roundly about three hundred students. Of these according to his estimate, of which I was shortly to be made aware, about two hundred were girls, and of these he claimed to have known personally all of one hundred and fifty. One afternoon after all the assignments had been given out and I was preparing somewhat disconsolately to leave, the city editor called me over, and, being joined by this scheming little editorial writer, they began to explain to me a plan by which, if I carried it out faithfully, I could connect myself with the *Chicago Daily Globe* as a reporter. I was to take a certain list of names and addresses—all on the South Side—which they would provide me, and, armed also with as many copies of *The Adventures of Mickey Finn* (which was the name of the work) as I could conveniently carry, was to visit each one of these quondam schoolmates of Mr. Gissel at their homes and, recalling to their mind that he was an old schoolmate of theirs and that this book related to scenes with which they were all familiar, endeavor to get them to buy a copy at one dollar. My reward for this was to be ten cents a copy on all copies sold, and in addition—and this was the real bait—if I succeeded in selling as many as one hundred and twenty copies within the next week or so, I was to have a tryout on the *Globe* as a reporter at fifteen dollars a week. After that if I succeeded in writing to suit them and doing the work as planned, I was to be retained. If not I was to be dropped, but I was certainly to have a tryout during the two weeks in which the great convention would be assembling, which work would begin just about the time I would be through with my canvassing.

I took the list which they had already prepared and, gathering up an armful of the small, thin, green cloth-covered volumes, and, fired by the desire to thus definitely make certain my entrance into the newspaper world, set forth. I cannot say that I was very much pleased with the eleemosynary character of my mission, or that I did anything but intellectually contemn this method of foisting one's work on one's friends for cash and because of old time associations, but my necessity or aspiration or what you will was so great that I was glad to do it just the same. I was a little nervous and shamefaced as I approached the first home on my list and rang the door bell, and I cannot say that throughout my entire list I did anything but suffer pains and aches in my vanity and my sense of the fitness of things, but I felt that I had to do it.

"Me a book agent," I said. "Me a wretched canvasser."

The only salve I could find in the whole thing was that Mr. Gissel actually knew these people, or claimed to, and that I could say I came personally from him, as a friend and fellow member of the *Globe* staff. It was a thin subterfuge, but it went down apparently with some—these pretty, unsophisticated girls who were still busying themselves, as I soon found, with social enjoyments of one kind and another.

But what a contrast this proved to be to that world in which I had previously been collecting from door to door. By far the greater majority of these homes were in the best residence sections of the South Side, some of them mansions of the truly rich whose democratic parents had insisted on their children going to the local high school. In each case, upon inquiring for a specific girl and being wise enough to combine my inquiry with the remark that I came from Mr. Gissel of the *Globe*, I was received into the family parlor or reception room and told to wait. Presently some singing, cheerful or remote or curious type of Chicago girl would come bustling in and, after looking me over, would listen to my tactful story, smiling contemptuously perhaps at my shabby mission or opening her eyes in surprise or curiosity.

"Mr. Gissel? Mr. Gissel?" said one girl simply. "Why I don't even recall such a person"—and she left, leaving me to make my way out as best I might.

Another exclaimed, "Harry Gissel! Has that little snip written a book? Yes, I remember him. The nerve—to send you around to sell his book! Why do you do it? I will take one because I am curious to see the kind of thing he'll do, but I'll wager right now it's as silly as he is. He's invented some scheme to get you to do this because he knows he couldn't sell the book any other way."

Others there were who were much more friendly. Some remembered him and seemed to like him. Others remembered him vaguely but bought the book because he was a member of their class. There were others who struck up a genial conversation with me, curious as to my personality, and bought the book to detain me, I think. I may say I had prepared the best costume I could for this work, feeling that the more spruce and presentable I was the less reason my customers would have for thinking me a pitiable book agent. At the same time it took all the courage and even effrontery that I could command to make my way into these various homes, some of them the acme of comfort or prosperity, and make this catchpenny errand seem an important one.

But in spite of my distress at having to do this from some points of view, from others there were compensations. It gave me a last fleeting picture of that new, sunny prosperity which was the most marked characteristic of Chicagoans of that day, and contrasted sharply and well with the scenes of poverty and limited earnestness which I had so recently seen. In this region, because of the particular season of the year, newly and fully fledged collegians, only recently returned from the colleges of the East and Europe—young men and young women of Chicago's best families—were disporting themselves about the lawns and open-windowed chambers of the parental roof. Traps and go-carts filled the best of the South Side streets where social calls were being made. The lawn tennis suit, the tennis game, the lawn party and the family croquet game were everywhere in evidence. I think, at this time, Chicago (and by Chicago I mean its new-rich and most ambitious citizens) was peculiarly susceptible to the airs and manners of older and more pretentious regions of the world. Almost like actors they were bent on interpreting their new wealth in terms of a de rigueur luxury and as they had observed it somewhere else. Hence the strutting youths in English suits with turned-up trouser legs, swagger sticks and flori-colored ties and socks to suggest the spirit of London, as they imagined it to be; hence the high-headed girls, in flouncy, lacy dresses, their cheeks and eyes bright with color, who here imagined themselves, no doubt, to be great ladies, princesses at the least, and who carried themselves before all with an air of almost remote disdain. This region, in particular, which was one of the best in Chicago, seemed to be buzzing with an intense social life, so self-conscious that to me it was highly disturbing, even painful. These young people all thought so intensely well of themselves. In sum, the whole thing seemed to be staged, the homes, the lawns, the movements of the people, this region a stage in itself in which something new and, in its way, altogether lovely but highly artificial was being enacted. To me in my life-hungry, love-hungry state, this new-rich prosperity with its wealth of loveliness in the way of women was almost too much. It set me to riotously dreaming and longing, made me ache to lounge and pose after this same fashion, a thing that was obviously never meant for me at all.

CHAPTER IX

In due course of time—a week or ten days at the least—I having performed my portion of the contract well and truly, as the law papers run, it now became the duty of these two gentlemen to fulfill their agreement with me. Every day now for all of ten days or more I had been turning in orders or, rather, the cash for from five to fifteen books, thereby establishing my reputation for industry, sobriety and the like with these two, who, at the beginning, I think, were inclined to imagine that I was not much good for anything and might be frightened off by this proposition. As a matter of fact, as my daily order kept up and the list of unchecked names grew shorter and shorter, these two seemed to acquire a kind of respect and even affection for me. Mr. Gissel was most anxious to know at the end of each day whom in particular I had seen and how the mention of his name was received. Instead of telling him how many sneered or laughed or bought a book largely to get rid of me gracefully, I gave him flattering reports which set him up in his own estimation. Quite recently, too, by way of reward I presume, he had taken to reading me the—to him—cleverest passages in his editorials—a thing which in turn set me up in my estimation. Mr. Sullivan, the city editor, confided to me one day that he was from a small town in central Illinois, not unlike Warsaw, the character of which I had roughly and jestingly sketched, and from then we were fairly good friends. Conceiving me to be unusually talented, he dug up a number of poems from out his desk and granted me the favor of reading them. A number of them were almost as good as similar ones to be found in Whittier and Bryant, after whose work they were obviously modeled. Today I know them to be very bad or rather mediocre. Then I thought they were excellent and grieved to think that anyone should be going to make a reputation as a great poet, whereas I, the only real poet extant (although I had nothing wherewith to prove it as yet), was remaining unrecognized.

I did not know, however, that for all their geniality and present favor, I would have managed to secure a place even now, so numerous were the applications of rather clever and experienced newspapermen, had it not been for the hearty favor and influence of my friend John Maxwell, who by now had come to conceive a most feeling regard for me. One cannot explain such things or why they arise, but for one reason or another, my errant youth perhaps, he was most interested in my future and anxious to see me get a start. Out of the tail of his eye from the sunny corner of the room in which he worked, he had been watching the goings-on in regard to this same work of fiction by Mr. Gissel. At such times as I arrived of an evening, when there was no one present to receive me, he was not averse to inquiring what it was that I was doing and, by degrees, although I had been cautioned not to tell, extracted from me the whole story. I even loaned him a copy of the book, which he took home one day and read. Meeting me the next evening in the office when it was still empty, he handed it back, exclaiming, "Piffle! rot!" and then adding, "They ought to be ashamed of themselves, sending you out on a job of that kind. You're better than that." But being friends of theirs also, and in a way desirous of standing well with all newspapermen, particularly the successful ones, he said nothing.

Just the same, as the end of my task drew near and I was dreading another uncertain wait between it and my promised place, he put in a "good word" for me, as I learned afterwards, commenting on my brightness and alertness, my hopefulness and the like. Even then, so shifty and uncertain are all things mortal that, if it had not been for the convention work which was rapidly drawing near and making a number of extra men really necessary, I doubt if I should have received a trial. These two were not particularly interested in me—certainly not enough to give me the room of a more experienced man. But having seen what had been done by me and how I had been used, Maxwell was, I think, fully determined that these twain should not escape without giving me a trial. He was not above asking them in my presence, "Why don't you give this kid a chance? He may be a little wild, but he looks as though he would do as well as any other," which I suppose eventually turned the tide in my favor. At any rate, on the day the various newspapers were beginning to chronicle the advance arrival of various district leaders and the like from all parts of the country, I was taken on at fifteen dollars a week, for a week or two anyhow, and assigned to watch the various committee rooms in the Hotels Palmer, Grand Pacific, Auditorium and Richelieu. There was another youth who was set to work with me on this and who gave me some slight instruction, and over us again was a political man by the name of Gerald Davis, who commanded other men in different hotels whose presence I scarcely noted or knew of until the convention was nearly over.

If there was ever a youth who was cast utterly adrift and made to realize that he really knew nothing at all concerning the thing he was so eagerly aspiring to do, that youth was I. No sooner had I been given this place than I realized quite clearly that I did not know what to do or how to do it—how or where to begin, what to ask, what to say. "Cover the hotels for political news," was my complete instruction. But what the devil was political news was the great question with me. What did they really want me to do, what say or write? Who see? At once, and that speedily, I was thoroughly terrified by this opportunity that I had so eagerly sought, for now that I had it I did not see how I was to write or make anything clear. It seemed to me as if I knew absolutely nothing at all about anything. For the first day or two or three I wandered about the various hotels mentioned like a lost soul, trying to find out where the various committee rooms were, who and what the men in them were, what they were trying to do, and trying to imagine the import, if any, of the various goings-on in their secret chambers. No one seemed to want to tell me anything. Various country congressmen and politicians brushed past me in a most secretive manner and, when I hailed them with the information that I was from the *Globe*, waived me off with the information, "I am only a delegate. You can't get anything out of me. See the chairman." Well, what was a chairman? I didn't know. When I sought to discover who the chairman was, I did not even have experience enough to know that there had been printed lists published in all the papers, my own included, giving the information which I was now so eagerly and wastefully seeking and which would have saved me hours of time.

Worse than this, I had no real understanding of politics or the political situation, either local or national. I did not know who the various state leaders were, who all the prospective candidates were, why one candidate might be preferred and another not. The machinations, for instance, of such an institution as Tammany Hall or the interests that are called monied—property interests—were almost entirely beyond me as yet. My mind was too much concerned with the poetry of life to busy itself with such minor things as politics. I knew for one thing that, in so far as this Democratic convention was concerned, there was a bitter feud on between one David Bennett Hill, the then-governor of New York, and Grover Cleveland, then ex-president of the United States, both candidates for nomination on the Democratic ticket, and that the Tammany organization of New York City was for Hill and bitterly opposed to Cleveland. Again, I knew that the South was for any good Southerner as opposed to Cleveland or Hill and that a new element in the party was for one Richard Bland, better known as "Silver Dick," of Missouri. I also knew by reputation only, of course, many of the men who had been in the first Cleveland administration, which began in 1885.

Imagine a raw youth like myself who really knew nothing of the political subtleties of America trying to gather even an inkling of what was going on in such a maelstrom of politics as this. Both the nation and the city were full of strange political trafficking in regard to the nomination, but of it all I was nearly as innocent as a babe. The second day I was working, the hotels were literally crowded with delegates and their friends and Democratic marching clubs from all parts of America. Aside from secret conferences held morning, noon and night behind closed doors in the various hotels, the lobbies and bars of the hotels were full of inconsequential, spouting delegates who drank, swore, sang and orated at the tops of their lungs. Never before had I seen such a storm of what I might call backwoods life. These swinging Southerners and Westerners in their long frock coats and wide-brimmed hats amused me. They were forever pulling their whiskers or mustachios, drinking, smoking, talking or looking solemn or desperate, as the case might be. They had not in many cases much more knowledge of what was really going on than I had. If I had only known, the thing had really been adjusted long before by the monied interests of the East, and Cleveland was to be the nominee. But I was told to watch the movements of one Benjamin Ryan Tillman, senator from South Carolina, and report any conclusions or rumors of conclusions as to how his delegation would vote in the national convention. If you will believe me, I had a very hard time finding where his committee was, in the first place, and when if ever it sat in deliberation, but once I identified my man, I never left him. I located his room and dogged his steps until, finally becoming very much aware of me and irritated by this constant espionage, he turned on me the second afternoon as he was going out of the Palmer House and, fixing me with his one fiery eye, exclaimed, "Young man, what is it you want of me, anyhow?"

"Well, you're Senator Tillman, aren't you?"

"Yes, sir, I'm Senator Tillman."

"Well, I'm a reporter from the *Globe,* and I've been told to learn what conclusion your delegation has reached as to how it will vote in the convention."

"Well, you and the editor of the *Globe* be damned," he replied irritably, "and I want you to quit following me wherever I go. Just now I am going for my laundry, and I have some rights to privacy. I don't want you at my heels all day long. The committee will decide when it's good and ready, and it won't tell the *Globe* or any other paper. Now you go 'way from me and let me alone. Follow somebody else."

Needless to say, I went—for the time being anyhow.

But of all these wild plungings to and fro, and my first feverish attempts at writing, I remember only this: that I came back to the office the first evening at five-thirty and sat down to write, the wild impression in my head that I must describe the whole political situation as it then existed in Chicago—everything! I had no notion at that time that there was a supervising political man who, in conjunction with the managing editor and editor-in-chief, understood all about current political conditions and could much better theorize on it than I could. I imagined what was wanted from me was some general description of this whirling maelstrom in which I had been all day, not the particular facts, if any, which I had been set to discover; and with this fiery thought in mind, I sat down and began to try to describe (in words and phrases such as I had seen employed in other newspapers in regard to politics in the past) all that I had seen.

"The political pot," I began most exuberantly, "was already beginning to seethe yesterday. Around the lobbies and corridors of the various hotels hundreds upon hundreds of the vanguard of American Democracy—" et cetera, et cetera. I do not think I had scrawled more than eight or nine pages of this mush before the city editor, curious as to what I had discovered, no doubt, and wondering, since it was apparently so important, why I had not reported it to him, came over and, picking up the various sheets which I had turned face down, studied them and then exclaimed: "No! no! no! You mustn't write on both sides of the paper. Don't you even know that? And all this stuff about the political pot boiling is as old as the hills. Every country-jake paper for four thousand miles east or west has used it for years and years. You're not to write general stuff. You're not to write the lead. Davis will tend to that. Here, Maxwell, see if you can't find out what Dreiser has found out and show him what to do with it. I haven't got time." And he turned me over to my gold-spectacled friend, who eyed me very severely, afraid perhaps that I was a flash in the pan after all, some over-enthusiastic jackanapes who had betrayed this reasonably capable organization into the notion that there was something to me, journalistically.

Nevertheless, he sat down and took my copy in hand, examining it with partially knitted brows. He had a round, meaty, cherubic countenance which seemed all the more ominous for that he could scowl fiercely and because his eyes could blaze with a cold, examining, mandatory glance.

"He's quite right," he said, as he read the first page. "This is old stuff. You want to try to forget that you're the editor of this paper and just consider yourself a plain reporter sent out to cover some hotels. Now where'd you go today?"

I told him.

"What'd you see?"

I described as best I could the whirling world in which I'd been.

"No, no—I don't mean that," he replied. "That's literature—not news stuff. Did you see any particular man? Did you find out anything in connection with any particular committee?"

I confessed that I had tried but failed. I had not been able to find any particular man who seemed to know anything.

"Very good," he said, "you haven't anything to write," and he took my precious nine pages, tore them up and threw them into the wastebasket. "You'd better sit around here now until the city editor calls you. He may have something special he wants you to do. If not, watch the hotels for celebrities—Democratic celebrities—or committee meetings, and if you find any, try to find out from some one what's going on. The great thing now is to discover beforehand who's going to be nominated, do you see? You can't tell from talking to four or five people, but what you find out may help piece out what somebody else has pieced out. When you come back, see me. And unless you get other orders, come back by eleven. And call up two or three times between the time you go out and eleven."

Because of these specific instructions, I felt somewhat encouraged, although, my first attempt at writing having been thrown in the wastebasket, I was beginning to have cold chills for fear that I might not be able to write anything which would suit anybody. However, I sat about until nearly seven, when I was given a certain address and told to find John G. Carlisle, ex-secretary of the treasury, and see if I could get an interview on the political situation and probable outcome of the convention's deliberations. Failing this, I was to "cover" the Grand Pacific, Palmer House and Auditorium and report all important arrivals and delegations.

If I had secured the desired interview, I am sure I should have made an awful botch of it, knowing as little as I did of the ins and outs of public affairs, but fortunately I could not get it. But what between dodging to and fro between the various hotels mentioned and running back and forth between this address and the business heart, this evening soon passed, and I had not had any dinner either. The truth was I was so excited over being a really, truly reporter that I scarcely cared to eat until midnight brought exhaustion, and, besides, by now my funds had begun to run so low that I felt called upon to husband my means in the extreme. Ten or fifteen cents for breakfast, ten or fifteen cents for lunch, and no more than twenty cents for dinner was all that I felt that I could afford, so that these nervous bursts of strength were merely money in my pocket. Only one thing of interest developed for me, and that was the presence of a Democratic United States Supreme Court justice at the Grand Pacific, who, upon being intercepted by me as he was going to his room for the night and told that I was from the *Globe*, eyed me genially and whimsically.

"My boy," he said, "you're just a young new reporter. I can see that, or you wouldn't waste your time on me. But I like reporters because I used to be one years ago. Now this hotel and every other hotel is literally full of delegations and leaders and statesmen, discussing this question as to who's to be president. I'm not discussing it because, first of all, it wouldn't become a justice of the United States Supreme Court to do so, and in the next place I don't have to. My position is for life. Politics for me is over. I'm just stopping here one day on my way to Denver, where my wife is, to see a few old political friends. Now if you want to write that up you can, but your editor won't want it. He's too much interested in other things. Now you go round to these committee rooms and see if they can't tell you something"—and smiling, and laying one hand on my shoulder in a genial, fatherly way, he dismissed me.

"My!" I thought, "what a fine thing it is to be a reporter. All I have to do is to say I'm from the *Globe* and even a justice of the United States Supreme Court is smiling and agreeable to me. How I have come up in the world overnight. How fast I shall rise if I can only write."

I hurried to a phone to call up the office and explain, but Maxwell, who was there, said, "He don't count. Write a stick of it if you want to when you come in, and I'll look it over."

"How much is a stick?" I asked eagerly and curiously.

"About one hundred and fifty words," he replied. So much for a United States Supreme Court justice in election days.

CHAPTER X

I cannot say that I discovered anything of import either this night or the next or the next, though I secured various interviews. After he had wrestled with my spirit and made hard, intelligent, frank statements (for which I can never be too grateful), John Maxwell managed to whip them into shape for fillers.

"The trouble with you, Dreiser," he said, the first night when I attempted to write out what the Supreme Court justice had said to me, "is that you haven't had any training, and you're trying to get it now when we haven't any time. You can write, but you don't know how to tell your story. Over in the *Tribune* office they have a sign which reads, 'Who or what? How? When? Where?' All those things have to be answered in the first paragraph, do you hear?—not in the last paragraph or the middle paragraph, or anywhere but in the first paragraph. Now come here—gimme that stuff." And he cut and hacked and slashed, running thick, cold lines of blue lead right through my choicest thoughts and restating in a line or two all that I had thought necessary to express in ten. As he did it, though, he occasionally looked up, a sardonic smile playing about his fat mouth, and I saw by his twinkling eyes that he felt that it was good for me. At the same time, as I leaned humbly over his shoulder, liking him and being grateful for his interest in me, the idea came to me at last that what was wanted was terseness, the bare facts, and these stated in as clear and orderly a way as possible. This I had not been doing.

"News is information," he went on as he worked. "People want it quick, sharp, clear—do you hear? Now you probably think I'm a big stiff—chopping up your stuff in this fashion," and he slashed some more and smiled the fat, sardonic smile, "but if you live and hold this job you'll thank me. As a matter of fact, if it weren't for me you wouldn't have this job now. Not one copyreader out of a hundred would take the trouble to show you," and he looked up at me with hard, cynical and yet warm goggle eyes and laughed, I presume, at my temporary discomfiture.

But though I found nothing these first few days and was wretched with the thought that I should be immediately dropped once the convention was over, yet I bustled here and there, anxious to find something which would endear me to the management. Of a morning from as early as six a.m., when I arose, until noon, I studied all the papers out at the De Goods, trying to discover what all this fanfare and enthusiasm was about and just what it was that was expected of me. By degrees the thought began to soak into my head that the one great thing to find out (in advance, of course) was who was to be nominated and to enumerate the delegations or individuals which or who would support the successful candidate. How was this to be done? I asked myself. Where could I get the information? I talked to John Maxwell the third day at noon, and as a favor he got out a paper in which a rough prognostication was made and showed me that the choice lay really between David Bennett Hill and Grover Cleveland of New York, with a third man—one Senator————, long since forgotten, I presume—as a dark horse. Southern sentiment seemed to be centreing about him, and in case no agreement could be reached by the New York delegation as to which of its two imposing candidates it would support, its vote might (this was only a rumor) be thrown to this third man and so start a boom for him which would bring about his nomination.

Naturally this was all very confusing to me, for my bump of politics was not very large. I did my best to get it straight and, learning that the Tammany delegation, two thousand strong, was to arrive from New York this same day, and that the leaders were to be quartered at the Auditorium, I made my way there, determined to get an interview with no less a person than Richard Croker, who, along with Bourke Cockran, the Tammany orator of the occasion, and a certain hard-faced, beefy individual by the name of John F. Carroll, seemed to be the brains and mouthpiece of the whole Tammany organization. In honor of their presence, I presume, the great Auditorium was decorated with flags and banners, some of them crossed with tomahawks or Indian feathers, and above the onyx-lined bar was placed a huge tiger with a stiff, projecting tail which when pulled downward, as it was every few seconds by one bartender or another, caused the papier-mâché image to emit a deep-voiced growl. This caused, or seemed to, the assembled Tammany host and their friends the utmost delight, and after each roar I noticed there would be an extra round of drinks purchased by somebody, and the tinkling and clinking of glasses. Red-faced men in high silk hats and long frock coats slapped each other on the back and bawled out their joy or threats or prophecies, frequently into the eyes and teeth of their hilarious companions.

It was some excitement. Actually this hotel for at least thirty-six or forty-eight hours was a seething cauldron of conferences, friendly greetings, secret meetings and hilarious drunkenness. On the first floor above the office of the hotel, occupying a whole floor, were Richard Croker, his friend and adviser John F. Carroll, and Bourke Cockran— as it were, in state. About them seethed endless delegations, friends and visitors of import. The weather was clear and warm, even sultry, the sky faultless. I remember, as I hung about this chamber or general reception hall where a few guest tables and chairs were scattered about, looking out through great arched windows over the blue lake where white sails were to be seen and thinking how pagan and Roman it all was. To begin with, the Auditorium, because of its massive architecture, suggested both Egypt and Rome. These heavy arched windows opening to the sky and giving out on a grey granite balcony permitted such an enchanting view of the lake and of the glittering sunshine outside. On this balcony again were seated some of the Tammany leaders and their friends. In the centre of this room, on a huge red plush divan sat, for the major portion this first afternoon, Croker, Carroll and Cockran, receiving and talking.

As a representative of the *Globe,* a cheap nickel star fastened to one of the lapels of my waistcoat and concealed by my coat of course, my soul stirring with the privilege I felt of being thus permitted to mingle in affairs of great import, I finally made my way to the footstool, as it were, of this imposing group and ventured, after stating who I was, to ask for an interview with Croker himself. Short, stocky, most carefully—almost too carefully—dressed in a smart, dark, striped suit and bright tie, his face the humanized replica of that of a tiger, the great man looked at me in a genial, quizzical, condescending way and, waving one hand, said—"No interviews." I remember, as it were yesterday, the patent-leather button shoes with the gray suede tops, the heavy gold ring on one hand and the heavy watch chain across his chest.

"You won't say who is to be nominated?" I asked nervously, bringing all my physical strength to bear to seem at ease.

"I wish I could," he grinned genially. "I wouldn't be setting here trying to find out."

He smiled again and repeated my question as a joke to one of his companions. They all looked at me with a smiling condescension, and I beat a hasty retreat, confident that I had lost my one great chance. Nevertheless, defeated though I was, I decided to write out the little scene, largely to prove to the city editor that I had actually seen him and been refused an interview.

To show you how fortune often comes to one who sleeps and that life when it wills can dish up success out of failure, I went down to the bar, curious to view the interesting scene which was being enacted there once more, and in a way anxious to console myself with so simple a thing as a lemonade. While I was standing there, one of those curious lulls which come over men, scenes, events, even ages, occurred. A number of the drinkers left the room, for the moment leaving it thinly populated. Two men next to me (Westerners, by the way) were arguing as to who would be nominated, Cleveland, Hill or some third person, not the one I have mentioned at all. When one of the strangers mentioned the third man as the most likely choice, I, bursting with my new political knowledge and longing to air it, solemnly shook my head, as much as to say, "You are all wrong."

"Well, who do you think, then?" inquired the stranger, who was short, red-faced, intoxicated.

"———, of South Carolina," I replied, feeling as though I was stating an incontrovertible truth.

A tall, fair-complected, dark-haired Southerner, in a wide-brimmed white hat and flaring frock coat, whose full-bosomed white silk shirt was showily exposed in a most summery fashion, paused in his hurried passage through the room and looking at the group exclaimed, "Who does me the honoh to mention my name in connection with the presidency? I am Senator——— of South Carolina, and hearing it just now, I am a little curious. No intrusion, I hope?"

The other two stared, confused, I presume, for the moment.

"None whatsoever," I replied with an air, thinking how interesting it was that this man of all people should be passing through the place at the time. "I was. These gentlemen here were saying that ——— of ——— would be nominated, and I was going to say that sentiment is running more in your favor."

"Well now, that is most interesting," he exclaimed, flattered, I fancy, by the outcome of his question. "And who are you, may I ask?"

"My name is Dreiser," I replied. "I represent the *Chicago Globe*."

"Oh, do you," he replied. "That makes it doubly interesting. Won't you come along with me to my rooms for a minute. I want to get some papers, and there we can sit out on the balcony. To tell you the truth, you interest me greatly. You're a most likely young man, it seems to me. How long have you been a reporter?"

"Oh, for nearly a year now," I replied grandly, lying out of the whole cloth.

"And have you ever worked for any other paper?"

"Yes, I was on the *Herald* last fall," I replied.

He seemed peculiarly elated by his discovery. I have often thought since that he must have been one of those swelling nonentities, flat-tered silly by this chance discussion of his name in a national conven-tion atmosphere. I do think that, aside from the aimless complimentary palaver that goes on in all national conventions, he had not the least chance for being even seriously considered. Some non-troublesome nondescript from the South had to be mentioned as a compliment more than anything else, and this man was fixed up as the least likely to prove disturbing later. At any rate, he bustled out onto a shady balcony overlooking the lake, ordered two cocktails, and wanted to know more specifically on what I based my calculation.

In order to justify myself and not seem a fool, I now went over my conversation with John Maxwell as though we two had quietly seated ourselves at this difficult political hour to figure out who would be nominated. I spoke of different delegations and their complexions as though these conclusions in regard to them were my own. As a matter of fact, I was quoting Maxwell verbatim. My hearer seemed surprised at my intelligence and complimented me.

"You seem to be very well informed," he said genially, "but I know you're wrong. The Democratic party will never go to the South for a candidate—not for some years anyway. I am pleased by all this talk, and I can frankly say that I wish I were as popular as I seem, but I'm not. Just the same, since you've been good enough to champion me in this public fashion, I would like to do something for you in return. I suppose your paper is always anxious for advance news, and if you bring it, you get the credit. Now at this very minute, over in the Hotel Richelieu, Mr. William C. Whitney and some of his friends—Mr. Croker has just now gone over there—are holding a conference. He is the one man who holds the balance of power in this convention. He represents the monied interests, and he is heart and soul for Grover Cleveland, and he is going to do his best to have him nominated. As a matter of fact, I am satisfied that he will be nominated. Now if you want a real beat, you go over there and hang about, and you may get something after the conference is over. Mr. Whitney is sure to make a statement sometime today or tomorrow. See his secretary, Mr.——, tell him I sent you, and he will do anything he can for you."

He smiled and I thanked him profusely, certain at last that I had a real piece of news. This conference, if true and conclusive, was the most important thing that would or could take place in the whole convention. I was so excited by it that I wanted to jump up and run away, leaving him where he was, but he detained me most easily.

"It will keep," he said. "No other newspaper man knows of it as yet,—I am sure of that. The secretary just spoke to me over the phone. Nothing will be given out yet for several hours because the conference won't be over before that time."

"But I want to phone my office," I said, "anyhow."

"All right, do that, if it will do you any good, and then come back."

I jumped up and ran to the nearest phone—an implement very much scarcer in those days than it became later. Indeed, they were almost exclusively to be found in hotels and drugstores. Getting the city editor on the phone, I explained to him my beat, and, anxious lest I be not able to cover it, asked him to inform the head political man. He was all excitement at once, congratulated me, and told me to follow up this conference until I received a different word. Then I ran back to my senator.

"I see," he said (and as I recall the scene it seems like something out of a play), "that you are a very industrious and eager young man. I like to see that. It's a good sign that you are going to get along. I do not want to say anything which will set up your hopes too much because things don't always work out as one would wish, but did anyone ever suggest to you that you would make a good private secretary?"

"No, sir," I replied, flattered and eager.

"Well, from what I have seen here today I am inclined to think you would. Now I don't know that I shall be returned to the Senate after this year—there's a little dispute in my state—but if I am, and you want to write me after next January, and will be good enough to mention this little incident, I may be able to do something for you. I may not have anything myself, and I may. Or in the interim I may hear of something. You seem to be a most likely boy, and I'd like to do something for you. I've seen a lot of bright young fellows come up in the newspaper profession and a lot go down. If you're not too attached to it, perhaps you would like this other better."

He smiled serenely, and I could have kissed his hands. At the same time, if you please, I was already debating whether one so promising as myself should leave the newspaper profession where all seemed so hopeful!

Ah, those halcyon summer days!—that balcony over the lake, the comfortable senator in his good clothes sipping his cocktail. It seemed to me as though I had suddenly fallen upon some sunbeam path and was treading it upward to a glorious zenith! Was I?

Ah, that halcyon summer—that balcony over the lake—and youth! and hope! and all the wondrous things that we dream!

CHAPTER XI

The senator let me go with a handshake and a promise, and I tore to the Richelieu, intending to hang about its plush-covered corridors until this conference was over. The secretary, who was closeted in some thickly carpeted room on the second floor, at the mention of Senator ———'s name, was good enough to see me. He told me not to wait, but to return at six-thirty, when he was sure the conference would be over and a general statement would be issued to the press. If I wished, I might come at five-thirty. This dampened my joy in the thought that I had something exclusive, though I was cheered later by the fact that I had probably saved my paper from defeat anyhow. For, being too poor, we did not subscribe to the general news service which would have brought us this statement, and, as the news was only sent out by the service as exclusive to the affiliated members, we might not have got it at all or at least not until too late for our first editions. As a matter of fact, my early information was a great comfort to and wonder in the office, the political man coming down himself late in the night to discover how I had learned so soon. I spoke of my friend Senator ———and other sources as though I had known of him and them a long while. The political man merely looked at me and said, "Well, you ought to get along in politics on one of the papers, if nowhere else."

The capture of this one fact, as I rather felt at the time, was my making, newspaperly speaking. As requested, I was on hand at five-thirty, and true to his word the secretary did outline verbally exactly what conclusions the conference had reached. He brought out a type-written statement and read from it such facts as he wished me to have. Cleveland was to be nominated. Some other man, Adlai Stevenson of Illinois, of whom I had never heard, was to be nominated for vice-president. There were other details, so confusing I could scarcely grasp them, but I made some notes and then ran to the office and tried to write out all I had heard. I believe now that I made a very bad job of it and that if it had not been for Maxwell I would have been thrown out as incompetent anyhow after the convention, merely on the grounds of inability to get my material in shape. But Maxwell, heaven fend him, worked so hard and so genially that he saved me. From one source and another—through newspaper friends and other papers—he confirmed or modified my statements, wrote an intelligent introduction and turned it in.

"You're one of the damnedest crack-brained loons I ever encountered," he said at one place, cutting out a great slice of my stuff, "but you seem to know how to get news just the same, and you're going to be able to write—I can see that. If I could just keep you under my thumb for four or five weeks, I believe I could make something out of you."

At this, being flattered by his remarks, despite their severity, I ventured to lay one hand over his shoulder in an affectionate and yet partially appealing way. But he only looked up frowningly and said: "Cut the gentle con work, Theodore. I know you. You're just like all other newspapermen, or will be—grateful when things are coming your way. If I were out of a job or in your position, you'd do just like all the others—pass me up. I know you—better than you know yourself. I know all the others. Life is a God-damned, stinking, treacherous game, and nine hundred and ninety-nine men out of every thousand are bastards. I don't know why I do this—" and he cut some more of my fine writing to revenge himself, I presume—"but I like you, in spite of yourself, and so I'll let it go at that. I don't expect to get anything back. I never do. People always trim me when I want anything. There's nobody home if I'm knocking. But I'm such a God-damned fool I like to do it. But don't think I'm not on, or that I'm a genial ass that can be worked by every Tom, Dick and Harry." And after visiting me with that fat superior smile, he went on working while I stared, nervous, restless, resentful, sorrowful,—trying to justify myself to life and to Maxwell. "If I had a real chance," I said, "I would show him."

As a matter of fact, I knew intuitively that I would do as he said—that is, I would take time and condition into consideration— and that the mood of the moment would govern. It is always so. We try to believe otherwise and to flatter ourselves that life runs along grooves of justice, mercy, tenderness and the like. It doesn't anything of the kind, and these are songs we sing, pictures we paint, dreams we dream, to make an ultimately too grim struggle seem palatable. And let no leisurely student in the ease of a leather-covered sanctum based on a seemingly indestructible income say me nay.

The convention opened its sessions the next day, and now because of my seeming cleverness, I was given a front seat in the press stand where I could hear all the speeches, observe the crowd, trade ideas with the very best newspapermen in the city and the country. In a day, if you will believe it, and in spite of the fact that I was only getting fifteen dollars a week, my stock had risen so that, in our office at least, I was looked upon as a newspaperman of rare talent, an extra-bright boy sure to carve out a future for himself, and one to be made friends with and helped. Here in this press stand I was being coached in the abstrusities of convention life, for I knew next to nothing about it, and, aside from the color, cared less. I was not really fitted mentally as yet to paint a general picture of its import and drift, and I was too nebulous minded to gather the facts which would have permitted me so to do. But fortunately I was not called upon to paint more than a color picture of the convention as a whole, which to the best of my ability I tried to do. Here, in this press stand, for the first time I was introduced to two other members of our staff who were supposed to be experienced men, both of them small, clever, practical-minded individuals, well adapted to the work in hand. One of them, Harry L. Dunlap, followed my errant fortunes for years, securing a place through me in St. Louis and rising finally to be the confidential advisor of one of our presidents of the United States—William H. Taft, a not very remarkable president to be advisor to, at that. The other, a small brown-suited soul, one Brady by name, came into my life for a very little while and went—I do not know where. I never saw him but once after I left the Globe.

But this convention—how it thrilled me! To be picked up in this fashion and tossed into the very vortex of national politics at a time when the country was seething politically over the possible resuscitation of the old Democratic party to strength and power was something like living, I thought. I listened to the various speeches, those dully conceived flights and word gymnastics and pyrotechnics whereby, in American conventions, backwoods statesmen, district leaders and personality followers seek to foist their own personalities as well as those of the particular individuals whom they admire on the attention of the country. Although by now it was generally known and conceded that Cleveland was to be nominated and there was no use in naming anyone else—the money power of America having fixed on Cleveland—still as many as ten different "statesmen"—or great leaders, saviors and the like—were put in nomination in language the most flowery. If you could have believed each speaker, each man so mentioned was the beau ideal of a country's savior, a natural-born leader, statesman, patriot, lover of liberty and the people, and so on and so forth ad infinitum. Hearing this in itself was a liberal education and slowly but surely opened my eyes. I watched with amazement the convention's love of fanfare and noise—the way in which various delegations and individual followings loved to shout and walk up and down waving banners and blowing horns. Different states or cities had sent large delegations, or, as in the case of New York, a marching club two thousand strong, all of whom had seats not on the convention floor exactly but in the hall, and all of these were plainly instructed to yell and demonstrate at the mention of a given name. Whenever either the name of David Bennett Hill of New York, or Grover Cleveland of New York was mentioned, the convention, or rather the audience, seemed to rise en masse and yell and scream until it was hoarse. The one thing I did hear which seemed rather important at the time—beautiful because of the man's voice and gestures—was a speech by that same Bourke Cockran of New York, whom I had seen at the Auditorium a day or two before, exhorting the convention to nominate his candidate, David Bennett Hill, and save the party from defeat. Indeed, his speech, until later I heard some of those made by William Jennings Bryan, seemed to me the best I ever heard—clear, sonorous, forcible, sensible. He had something to say apparently, and he said it with art and seeming conviction. Not that I thought his voice was beautiful—it was not—nor that it had in it any of that emotional appeal, which, as in the case of a great actor, so many deem all-essential, but it had a sort of vibrating resonance, which sent the sentences and words cannonading to the uttermost parts of the convention hall, as clear as though you were immediately in front of him. Again, his sentences had a rounded brevity and symmetry and compactness which struck me as most useful in carrying his logic and his theories to his hearers. He had presence too—a sort of Herculean, animal-like effrontery which seemed to defy indifference. He made me sit up and pay particular attention to him, when, as a matter of fact, I was much more interested in the general character of the convention. I even tried to take notes on what he said until one of my associates informed me that the full minutes of his speech could soon be secured from the shorthand reporters—which was true.

But being in this great hall, cheek by jowl with the elite of the Chicago reportorial world, thrilled me as no workaday experience ever had before. "Now," I said to myself, "truly I am a newspaperman, and if I can but get interesting things to write about, my fortune is made." At once, as the different forceful reporters of the city were pointed out to me—George Ade, Finley Peter Dunne, "Charlie" Seymour, Charles D'Almy—my neck swelled as does a dog's when a rival of any kind appears on the scene. Already, at the mere sight of them, I was anxious to try conclusions with them, individually or collectively, on some important mission to see which of us was the better man. Actually, I said to myself as I looked them all over, "I am as good as any of these," and I sniffed and scratched, looking for contest. I think I have always, until these very late middle years, conceived a deadly opposition to anyone who even looked as though he might be able to try conclusions with me in anything, and, if I have not haughtily stared them out of countenance, it has been for no lack of willingness or intention. Spiritually my lip was curling, my neck feathers bristling. I was ready for a row or an insult, believing, once I had got only this far, that I was destined to be one of the greatest newspapermen that ever lived!

But this convention brought me no additional glory such as I had already won. I did write a flowery description of the convention as a whole, a part only of which was used. I did get some details of committee work, which were probably incorporated in the political man's general summary. The next day, Cleveland being nominated, convention interest and work fell off tremendously. Hundreds, and possibly thousands, packed their bags and departed. I was used for a day or two about hotels, gathering one type of item after another, but I could see that there was no import to what I was doing, and I began to get terribly nervous lest, ere many more days had gone, I should be summarily dropped. I spoke to Maxwell about this, pleading in an humble way with my eyes for a longer show, and once more his foolish interest in me got the better of him.

"Do you think they'll drop me?" I asked.

"Not by a damned sight," he replied contentiously and feelingly. "You've earned a show here, it's been promised you, you've made good, and they ought to give it to you. Don't you say anything. Just leave it to me. There's going to be a conference here tomorrow as to who is to be dropped and who kept on, and I'll have my say at that time. You saved the day for us on that nomination stuff, and that ought to get you a show, and there's nobody can deny it. You may be a raw cub yet and all that, but I know you can write. You ought to get a show. Just leave it to me."

I went out as cheered as a cuddled baby.

The next day this conference evidently took place as scheduled, although I was not there, staff work having fallen off tremendously. Of the five men who had been taken on to do extra work during the convention, I and one other—a youth by the name of Bullitt—were the only ones retained, and we at the expense of two former reporters dropped. At that, I truly believe that if it had not been for Maxwell, I would have been let go for the simple reason that the editors' friendship for others was stronger than their temporary interest in me. The convention was over, the books were sold, and—. But Maxwell, who was in spirit a kind of cross between Don Quixote and Jean Valjean, both of which characters he greatly admired, came to my rescue and that most valiantly. As I have said, he had been present during most of the transactions concerning Mr. Gissel's book, and I think he thought I deserved work on that score alone, to say nothing of my subsequent efforts. He was even ready to make trouble since there was no overplus of love in this office, and his was the kind of disposition inclined to look on the book transaction as unprofessional and un-newspaper-like. I think he disliked the little editorial writer very much. At any rate when this conference began, Maxwell, according to Dunlap who was an eyewitness and subsequently revealed the matter to me, sat back, a look of contented cynicism on his face, not unlike that of a fox about to devour a chicken. Several names of the new men were proposed as substitutes for the old ones when, not hearing mine mentioned and assuming, I suppose, that the situation was becoming critical, he inquired, "Well, what about Dreiser?"

"Well, what about him?" inquired Sullivan, the city editor. "He's a good man, but he lacks training. These other fellows are experienced."

"I thought you and Gissel sort of agreed if he sold that book for you to give him a show?"

"He smirked," said Dunlap, "as much as to say, 'I wouldn't drop him if I were you.'"

"No, I didn't," replied Sullivan. "I only promised to give him a tryout 'round convention time if I could. I've done that."

"But he's the best man on the staff today," insisted Maxwell. "He brought in the only piece of news worth having. He's writing better every day."

He bristled, according to Dunlap, and Sullivan and Gissel, taking the hint that the quarrel might be carried higher up or aired inconveniently, changed their attitude completely.

"Oh, well. Let him come on," exclaimed Sullivan genially. "I'd just as leave have him. He may pan out."

And so "on" I came, at the remunerative sum of fifteen dollars the week, and thus my newspaper career was begun in earnest.

CHAPTER XII

This change from the seeming insecurity and inconsequence of being a collector to being an accredited newspaperman was one of the most delightful that ever befell me. For a little while—a year or so, or more—it seemed to open up a clear, straight course which, if I followed it energetically, must lead me to great heights. The thing that disappointed me most was that whereas I had anticipated most comfortable salaries for everyone, I was finding that beginners (at least on this paper) were very badly served. Salaries ranged from fourteen to twenty-five dollars for reporters, and as for those important missions and trips for newspapermen about which I had always been reading—those fine, ambassadorial commissions—they were not even thought of here. The best I could learn of them in this office was that they did exist, for some people, on other papers. Young men were still sent on missions abroad or to the West or to Africa, like Stanley, but they had to be men of proved merit and budding genius and connected with papers of the greatest importance. How did one prove oneself to be a budding genius? And how connect oneself with a "greatest paper"?

Salary—scarcely a decent one to live on—or no salary, however, I was still now officially a newspaperman and with the opportunity, as I thought, of eventually making a name for myself. Having broken with the family and with Claire, I was now quite alone in the world, free to go anywhere, and I was already getting sick of the De Good ménage with which I was still connected, for, be it written of my finicky tastes, they did not keep house to suit me. They were not clean, in my estimation, and they were not of my order of intelligence. De Good senior, or "old man De Good" as he was known thereabouts, I believe, was a small contracting mason, having a tiny shop somewhere, and in addition was a scummy, sweating vegetable who bathed once or twice a month, let us say, and sat about the house in his shop clothes these hot nights (minus a coat and waistcoat, however) and perspired and smoked a vile pipe, thereby emitting a concatenation of smells. Mrs. De Good, a large, rosy, good-natured, smiling, greasy soul, seemed to live in a yellowish-brown wrapper which she rarely washed. The breakfast, luncheon, and supper tables were invariably mussy and allowed to stand by the hour uncleared while the flies rioted. My bed linen was none too clean—changed once the week or so—and I suspected bedbugs, although my brother Ed did not seem to mind. I argued these conditions with him some, urging possible hints at improvement via his sweetheart, who was not so objectionable herself—a rather energetic girl, indeed—but he was the soul of contentment, cradled as he was, so to speak, in Libbey's arms. There was one sister whose husband was a trainman somewhere, a younger replica of her mother, who during the several weeks I was looking for a place, or rather besieging the office of the *Globe*, used to come to her mother's home and spend the day on an average of two or three times a week, bringing a child or two with her. Although married and possessed of two children, one and three years of age respectively, she laid siege to me, or encouraged me in so direct a way that my passions were aroused, and yet so great was my fear of my fancied impotence that I would not allow myself to be entrapped in such a way that I could not conscientiously—and with some show of reason—retreat and not press the relationship too far. One sunny morning, for instance, no one but ourselves being at home, and I having nothing better to do, I remember helping her clear the dishes, while she bustled about with nothing but a thin undershirt over the upper half of her very plump body. She had big soft arms and swelling breasts, and after a while, as she worked and we scuffled over one thing and another, I found myself pinching and feeling of the latter, without much resistance from her. We played about until we reached a divan on which she toppled, and I lay on her, pretending to hold her down. Instead of concluding the arrangement as it should have been, however, and as we both intensely wished, fear as to whether I could give her satisfaction and not be exposed as a sexual weakling overcame me, and I desisted. Believe it or no, this is true. If anyone of my readers has ever been in the same ridiculous or nervous state, he will know how true it is.

But aside from this—my pathetic failure in connection with this and the untidiness of the place, which nauseated me at times—there was the new matter of hours to consider. Hitherto when I worked for one and another of the various business houses I had been connected with, I had been rising at eight and leaving at eight-thirty in order to reach the office by nine. Now I did not need to leave until eleven-thirty or noon, arriving at the office at twelve-thirty, but my hours were anywhere from twelve-thirty to one, two and even three a.m. I was nearly always given the late watch; I was made to stay for possible fires. I was even called out at nine a.m. to attend queer police court sessions, and I was expected to do Sunday specials in the bargain. I did not know it then, but these Sunday specials were to help my onward progress greatly.

But this matter of late hours, which meant disturbing Ed when I came in, the unclean food and all, determined me. I would leave the De Goods and Ed and go somewhere by myself. He did not want to move, I found. Claire did not particularly want me where she was in Warren Avenue, so I found a front room in Ogden Place, overlooking Union Park (in which area I afterwards placed one of my heroines), and congratulated myself on the fact that at last I was wholly free, out in the world alone, and much nearer my work. I could walk from here to the office in a little over twenty-one minutes, which was mostly a pleasure. My route lay through either Madison Street or Washington Boulevard, west of the River, and morning and night I had ample opportunity to speculate on the rancid or out-at-elbows character of so much that I saw—sections and people. Both Washington and Madison Streets from Halsted Street east to the River were lined with vile dens and tumble-down yellow and gray frame houses which kept my mind busy with the sloven, rancorous, unsolved and possibly unsolvable misery and degeneracy of so many who were here—whole streets of degraded, dejected, miserable-looking souls. Always I was intensely curious about these things—the why thereof. Why didn't society do better by them, why didn't they do better by themselves? Was government to blame? Or they? Or who? Always the miseries of the poor—the scandals, corruptions and physical deteriorations which trail folly, weakness, uncontrolled passion and the like—fascinated me. I was never tired of looking at it, as saddening and frightening as it was, and as I walked here and there through these truly terrible neighborhoods—Chicago's vast collection of riffraff from all parts of the world—I peered through open doors and patched and broken windows at this wretchedness and squalor, much as a man may tread the poisonous paths of a jungle, curious and yet fearsome and evasive.

It was this nosing and speculative character, however, that helped me most, as I soon found. Journalism, even in Chicago, was still in that curious, discursive stage, which loved long-winded yarns upon almost any topic. Nearly all news stories apparently were padded to make more of them, especially as to color and romance, than they really deserved. America, or the Middle West rather, was just beginning to awake apparently to its literary possibilities. All specials were being written in imitation of the great novelists, particularly the late Charles Dickens, of England, who was the beau ideal of all newspapermen and editors and, I presume, magazine special writers. (How often have I been told to imitate Charles Dickens in thought and manner!) The city editors wanted not so much bare facts, as became the rule later, as feature stories—color, romance—and although I did not myself see it clearly at the time, I was their man. Write!—why I could write reams on any topic, once I discovered that I could write at all. Someone one day—Maxwell I suppose—from hearing me talk of what I was seeing, suggested that I do an article on Chicago's vilest slum, the one that lay between Halsted and the River, Madison and Twelfth Streets, and this was as good as meat and drink for me. I begged for the opportunity. Once I got it, in a kind of frenzy of perception and composition I visited this region on several nights between one and four in the morning, wandering about its clattering boardwalks, its vile, dark alleys, its gloomy mire-and-muck atmosphere. I have said before that Chicago's wretchedness was never utterly tame, disconsolate or hangdog, whatever else it might be. Rather, it was strident, savage, bitter, or at best larkish and impish. This region which I now re-examined was no exception but the reverse. These vile slovens, slatterns, prostitutes, drunkards and drug fiends who infested this region all led a strident if beggarly or horrible life. Aside from saloon lights and smells and lamps gleaming smokily behind broken lattices and below wooden sidewalk levels, the accordian, the harmonica, the jew's-harp and the clattering tin-pan piano or stringy violin were forever going. These paintless tumbledown rotting shacks, where seemingly only the lowest of the low and the poorest of the poor would think of harboring themselves, were always resounding with a kind of noisy blasphemous life between twelve and four a.m. Oaths, foul phrases, a walking to and fro at all hours of prostitutes, drunkards, drug fiends and I know not what other bedlamic types and villains were common things. In addition a Hogarthian shamelessness and reconciliation to filth were everywhere apparent. Although there was a closing-hour law—either one or two a.m., I believe—there was none here, wherever it was deemed worthwhile to keep open. Only at four and five in the morning did a heavy peace seem to descend, and even this seemed as wretched to me as the heavier vice or degradation that preceded it.

Yet as I have often thought since and said, vice to me, as I view it now from the vantage point of a long period of observation, is little more than a difference in temperament or chemical composition. Some people are bright, some dull; some sprightly in their physical texture, some lethargic. Some are like hogs or alligators that require a wallow, and could scarcely be content without one. Some are spruce and separate like deer and pea fowls. Filth is fatal to them. In contemplating regions of this kind, at that time, owing to Christian and moralistic traditions, I was rather of the opinion that these people could, if they would, take themselves in hand, think better, do better, forsake their evil or slimy ways and make themselves over into something lighter, sweeter, more attractive. A longer observation of humanity, freed as it finally was from asinine Christian and moralistic traditions, has led me to the conclusion that humanity does as it is physically and mentally constructed. From somewhere in the universe are flowing strange and even conflicting currents of energy, finding representation here in all forms of animals and men. Are they moral? Are they helpful socially? Who can say? Are they to be made over by puny man? I for one doubt it, whatever his necessity for self-protection may be. A silk purse cannot be made out of a sow's ear, and a model, conventional home-loving citizen cannot be made out of an individual whose physical or psychic composition craves swinish debauches. There are fires built in souls, the origin and satiation of which have nothing to do with earthly moralistic thought. People come, born saints or sinners, as the terms go,—ascetic or libidinous and lecherous, and these temperaments no earthly training will overcome. Jails break some, disease and crime destroy others, but as they come so they go. It is useless to say, as some will, that the light-fingered thief will become by effort the banker, or the luster after women the poet. A poet may perchance be, and no doubt is, a luster after women in a refined, selective way, and a commercial master may have many of the attributes of a thief—but the thief and the lecher, per se, are lacking in the commercial and poetic qualities or they would not remain thief and lecher, and nothing more. Like drifts to like, birds of a feather flock together, and in every community or state or nation these little pools of individuality—obscene, spiritual, criminal, social, or merely dull or commonplace—will be found. Little can be done—little is ever really done in spite of all the clamor for betterment and the moral uplift. One might well destroy the worst specimens perhaps, but new ones will arise. There is a sower somewhere. Is he a planet, gas, element or a ball of fire? He gardens and sows these things. What is his plan and why does he?

But at this time I still think that I thought that a little something might be done possibly. At the same time I rejoiced in the thing as a spectacle and a contrast to the more conventional types of life about me. It was all so bad, so bitter, so scummy, so nondescript. I smiled as I thought of my father's attitude as opposed to all this. Here he was out on the west side, demanding that all creatures of the world return to Christ and the Catholic church—see clearly, whether they could or not, its grave import to their immortal souls—and here were these sows and termagants—wretched, filthy, greasy, swining things. And the men—save the mark! These low-browed, ill-clad, rum-soaked, body-racked specimens. Mere bags of bones, so many of them, blue-nosed, scarlet-splotched, diseased—if God could really get them, what would He want with them? On the other hand, in the so-called better walks of life, there were so many strutting, strident, contentious, self-opinionated swine-masters whose faces were maps of gross egoism and whose clothes were almost a blare of sound.

I think I said a little something of all this—not much—in the first newspaper special I ever wrote. It followed swiftly on my convention experience and before any really worthwhile assignment of a strictly news character was given me. It seemed to open the eyes of Maxwell, who read these things and edited them, and brought about a somewhat different attitude on his part.

As Maxwell read it the next morning between one and three a.m. (for I had poured it all forth in one mass between eight a.m. of the day after I had returned from my speculative wanderings and slept a little, and midnight this same night), he said, "You know, Theodore, you have your faults, but you know how to write in a way, and you get a new angle on this stuff. It's pretty good. I think maybe you're cut out to be a writer and not just an ordinary newspaper man after all." He lapsed into silence, and then at periods as he read he would exclaim, "Jesus Christ!" or "That's a hell of a world!" and then he would fall foul of some turgid English and, with a kind of malicious glee, cut and hack and restate and shake his head despairingly until I was convinced that I had written the truckiest rot in the world. At the close, however, he got up, dusted his lap, lit a pipe, shoved his hands in his pockets which ornamented fat swelling thighs and said: "Well, I think you're nutty, but I believe you're a writer just the same. They ought to let you do more Sunday specials." And then he began to tell me of phases of Chicago he knew, and how vile it was in one section of San Francisco, where he had once worked.

"A hell of a fine novel is going to be written about some of these things one of these days," he remarked, and from now on he took me on such terms of absolute equality as made me think I must be a very remarkable man indeed.

CHAPTER XIII

But this world of newspapermen who, on account of Maxwell and the city editor (who now became very friendly), received me on terms of social equality—how they affected me! Earlier in this self-analysis, I mentioned the liberalizing or unbinding effects of the public schools of Warsaw after the chill terrorism of the Catholic ones of Evansville. Similarly, this stepping out among men who saw life from a purely opportunistic and yet in the main sentimentally imaginative viewpoint broadened me considerably, and in a way, I may say, finally liberated me. I found here, within a week or so—perhaps longer—youths who had never been troubled at all by the moralistic and religionistic qualms which had disturbed me. So many of them were hard, gallant adventurers without the slightest trace of that nervousness and terror of failure which agitated me. They talked of life in a broad, cynical and iconoclastic spirit. They had been here, there, everywhere—some of them—San Francisco, Los Angeles, New York, Calcutta, England. I cannot relate here even a tithe of all the stories and incidents which came swiftly in the course of newspaper gossip and work, or the interesting types of men I soon met, but suffice it to say that I met many, most interesting men all, and in so doing, I can say that roughly everything I heard was tonic, revealing, instructive. Most of these men had worked in other cities than Chicago, many of them had worked on other papers here. They knew the ways of the newspaper world and to a limited extent the workings of society at large. The sober, dull or conventional minded would have called them brash, impracticable, impossible—largely because they knew nothing of trade, I suppose—the great American standard of ability and force. Even so, they were far nearer the really important ideas than those hodden-minded creatures who swallow the moralistic mouthings of newspaper publishers as they appear in the biased editorial columns of a money- or success-seeking press. Most of them, as I soon found, were like John Maxwell, radically free of notions of how people were to do and what they were to think. They were not the victims by any means of dull, stark, religious and moralic notions. To a certain extent, it is true, they were confused by the general American passive acceptance of the Sermon on the Mount and the Beatitudes as alleged governing principles, but in the main they were nearly all mistrustful of these things and of conventional principles in general. They did not in the main believe, as I still did, for instance, in spite of all my wanderings and errantries, that there was a fixed moral order in the world which one contravened at his peril. Heaven only knows where they had been or what they had seen, but they misdoubted the motives, professed or secret, of nearly every man. No man apparently was really utterly and consistently honest—that is, no man in a powerful or dominant position—and but few were kind, or generous, or truly public spirited and so on. Many of them translated life in terms of gross animality only, and as I sat in the office between assignments or forgathered with them at dinner or at midnight in some one of the many small restaurants frequented by the newspapermen of our staff and as frequently by those of others, I heard interesting tales of all sorts of scandals—robberies, murders, fornications, incendiarisms and the like—not only in low but in our so-called high life. Most of these young men that I met, and I think I speedily became familiar with about eight or ten, looked on life as a fierce, grim struggle in which no quarter was either given or taken and in which all men laid traps, lied, squandered, erred through illusion, and the like—a conclusion with which I now most heartily agree. The one thing I would now add is that the brigandage of the world is in the main genial, and that in our hour of success we are all inclined to be more or less liberal and warm hearted.

But at this time I was still sniffing about the Sermon on the Mount and the Beatitudes, expecting ordinary human flesh and blood to do and be those things. Hence their point of view still seemed somewhat horrific to me, even as it does at times to this day, though my intelligence compelled and still compels me to perceive that earthly advantages and positions lie more with cunning and selfish courage than anywhere else. I was constantly looking out for myself with single-minded zeal, the while I was constantly looking to others for those mercies, tendernesses and beatific traits which I myself did not possess and did not dream of practising except possibly in a very minor and unimportant way.

Thus John Maxwell would sit and expatiate for a half hour at a time in his spare moments on the subject of sex liberty and sex vagaries, a topic with which I was not nearly so familiar as later I became. He seemed to think it nothing harmful that all men should run around with other men's wives, or that youths should seduce girls, or that a man should have a wife and a mistress, or two or three or four of the latter, if he could maintain them. As a matter of fact, he talked as if this were a matter of course—that all attractive, passionate men and women did it and that only the dull and religionistic were caught by the rules of sobriety and virtue.

"People make laws for other people to live up to," he once said to me, "and in order to protect themselves in what they have got. They never intend those laws to apply to themselves or to prevent them from doing anything that they want to do. Never believe that Christ knew what he was talking about. He never lived at all. Read Schopenhauer, Spencer, Voltaire—then you'll get a line on this scheme of things."

He told me of a mistress whom he was keeping on the West Side, and how she would lie by the half hour looking at his penis and testicles, and then—the thought provoking him—he would lie back in his chair and guffaw until any one chancing to pass would pause to inquire why so much laughter. And even now I can not help laughing long and loud at the spectacle he presented narrating it.

There was another youth who had a wife who believed that he did not drink, whereas he had an appetite in this direction which frequently left him white faced and comatose, a condition which caused one to imagine him ill rather than anything else. This tendency to get sick instead of boisterous and cantankerous permitted him to "put over" the illusion that he was really sick and not drunk at all. On two occasions within six weeks I was sent, as a rather pleasing envoy perhaps, to inform his wife that her husband had been suddenly taken ill with indigestion and would soon be home. Then Maxwell and the youth by the name of Brady, previously mentioned, or some one else would bundle him into a hack and send him off, some one or two of us going along to assist him in getting into the house. And so solemnly was this all done and so well did we play our part that his wife believed it for a while—long enough for him to pull himself together a year later and give up drinking entirely. There was a third youth by the name of Gilchrist who boasted that he was syphilitic but was curing himself with mercury, a fourth whose joy it was to sleep in a house of prostitution every Saturday night, and so on. I tell these things, not that I am rejoicing in them or that I wish anyone to go and do likewise—I do not—but merely to indicate the atmosphere into which I was thrown, and to cause my readers to understand that the thought that was coming to me was that neither sobriety nor continence nor incontinence was a compelling or preventive cause of either success or failure, or had anything to do with true newspaper ability; but rather that men succeeded because of something which was not intimately related with any virtue or vice, but rather with the skill or taste to achieve something which the world desired. If you could do anything which the world really wanted very badly, it would not trouble itself so much about your private life—only you must learn to save yourself whole in the matter of finance and health, otherwise no one would want anything to do with you.

And at the same time there was another change which was now being daily brought about in me due to my growing experiences in this new world, and this was that which related to my personal opinion of myself, the feeling which I was now swiftly getting that after all I amounted to something, was somebody—and, if you please, a rather extraordinary somebody as contrasted with the rank and file. A special or two which I wrote following the one edited by Maxwell, and thanks largely to his careful schooling, brought me to the forefront among those of the staff who were writing for the Sunday supplement. News stories—not many, but a few—fell to my lot, and I handled them with a freedom or, perhaps, unconscious ease which won me praise on all sides. I even essayed a few parables of my own—mild, poetic commentaries on I scarcely recall what—which John Maxwell scanned with a suspicious and even scowling eye at first but a little later deigned to publish, affixing the signature of "Carl Dreiser" as opposed to my own name because he had decided to nickname me Carl, and so had the advantage of being able to put his humor into type. This grieved me because I was dying to see my own name in print, but when they appeared, I had the audacity to call on the family and show them, boasting of my sudden rise in the world and saying that I had used the name Carl as a compliment to the little unsanctioned waif whom Sylvia and her lover had brought into the world.

In the meantime, again, I was taking a very lofty hand with Lois because of my sudden rise in the world, unmindful of the fact that I had been boasting for months that I was connected with one of the best of the local papers and that I had then given her to understand that I did not think it so wonderful. But now I began to think that I was to be called to much higher realms, and I solemnly asked myself if I wanted to get married at all. A number of things helped seriously to formulate this question in me, for, for one thing, I had no sooner been launched into general assignments than one afternoon, in seeking for the pictures of a group of girls who had taken part in some summer night's festival, I encountered one who seemed to take an interest in me. Always on the lookout for new encounters and experiences, I looked at each and every girl who appealed to my fancy with an eager and propitiating glance. This one—a little blonde of a little less than my own age, very sleek and dreamy, living in a very comfortable residence on Wabash Avenue near 31st Street—reciprocated my somewhat timid advances when I called on her and condescended to smile as she gave me her photo. We talked of I do not know what. I only recall that I drew persuasively close to her and attempted a flirtation. She was not at all averse, and on parting I asked if I might call some afternoon or evening, imagining that I might crowd it in between my other work. She accepted, and for several Sundays and week nights I was put to my utmost resources to keep my engagements and do my work, for, as I soon found, the newspaper profession tolerates neither weekdays nor Sundays off. I had to take an assignment and shirk it in part—a very dangerous proceeding indeed—or phone (and her home was fortunately blessed with a phone) that I was delayed or could not come. Twice I took her to the theatre, once to an organ recital and once for a stroll in Jackson Park, by which time she seemed inclined to yield to my blandishments to the extent of permitting me to put my arms about her and kiss her, protesting always that I was wanton and froward and that she did not know whether she cared for me so much or not. For my part I can honestly say that, charming as she was, graceful, young and very good looking— beautiful, I thought—I did not feel that outside of a temporary sex gratification, if that could ever be achieved, I should care for her so very much. She was too lymphatic, socially well mannered—too carefully reared. Her mother, for instance, on hearing of me, looked into the fact of whether I was truly connected with the *Globe* and then cautioned her daughter to be careful of whom she countenanced. I soon saw that I was not very welcome at that house, her parents chilling me with distant looks, and my Clarissa told me that she was compelled to tell her mother that she had met me at a church social and thereafter to meet me slyly. I think I might have triumphed in this case had I been so minded and possessed of a little more courage. But fancying that I should have to undergo a long courtship with marriage at the end of it if I really wished to win her, my ardor cooled, and a few months later, being out of the city and having new interests, I ceased writing. But at this time because, in contrast to Lois and Nellie, she was new and comfortably stationed and better dressed than either of them had ever been, I esteemed her more highly, made invidious comparisons from a material point of view and wished that I could marry some such really wealthy girl without, as it were, assuming all the stern obligations of matrimony. Ah, if I could just marry a really rich girl, I said to myself—one truly rich and truly beautiful!

Ah! Oh!

Again there arrived on the scene, about the second month of my work on the *Globe*, a man who was destined to have a very marked effect on my career. He was a tall, dark, broad-shouldered, slender-legged individual of about forty-five years of age, with a shock of curly black hair and a burst of ruffian-like whiskers which gave him, to me, a decidedly Western and yet somewhat Olympian cast of countenance. He was a truly Bret Hárte or gold-miner type—queer, sloven, red eyed at times, but amazingly intelligent and genial, reminding me a little of my brother Rome in his best hours. The first time I saw him and indeed all the time I ever knew him, he wore a long dusty brownish-black frock coat and a pair of black trousers, so specked, gummed, shined and worn by tobacco, food, liquor and rough usage as to make them seem rather grievous, and it seemed grievous too that he should be compelled to wear them at all. In addition to this, the swirl of Jovian locks and beard about his forehead, ears and face was surmounted by a wide-brimmed black hat such as Kentucky Colonels were once wont to affect, from under which his curly black hair protruded. His generous feet were encased in wide-toed shoes of old "boot leather" variety, and, in addition, his nose and cheeks were tinted a somewhat fiery red from much drinking, the former organ having already assumed a slightly veinous, bulbous, even mottled and strawberry texture from his having, as one of the members of the staff used to express it, "his nose full" so often.

This individual was none other than John T. McEnnis, a well- and favorably known newspaperman of the Middle West—truly a brilliant writer whose sole fault, in so far as I could make out, was that he drank too much. Originally from St. Louis and the son of a well-known politician there, he had espoused journalism as the most direct avenue to fame and fortune. Imagine the gloom of his soul therefore when at forty-five or eight he still found himself a mere hanger-on in this not infrequently successful procession, tossed about from job to job on account of his weakness, his skill equaled if not outrivaled by that of younger men. His dreams of a literary or social pre-eminence had of course long since gone glimmering. His conscience compelled him to admit that drink had defeated him at every step. At once a lover of women and the bottle, it had come now truly that he loved the bottle more than anything else. It was commonly said, sometimes in his praise, I presume, by his more riotous companions, that he could drink more and stand it better than any newspaper man in Chicago. "Why, he can't begin to work unless he's had three or four drinks to limber him up," Harry Dunlap once said to me, and again, "He has to have six or seven more to get through till evening." He did not say how many he required to carry him on until midnight, but since nearly all drinking newspapermen, as I found later, deemed it a right to relax somewhat in favor of liquor as the evening wore on, I fancy he must have consumed at least a half dozen more. At any rate, as I came to observe him more narrowly later on, I took it that he was in a constant state of semi-intoxication, though often rather well and even skillfully concealed.

Be that as it may, the second month that I was on the *Globe*, this same individual, whom I had seen bustling in and out on one errand or another for some time now, was made city editor vice Mr. Sullivan, gone to a better paper. A little later he was made managing editor even. He was famous (so I now learned from Maxwell and others) about Chicago for his wit, his trenchant editorial pen and the fact that once he had been considered the most brilliant newspaper editor in St. Louis. He had a small, spare, intellectual wife, very homely and very dowdy, who still adored him and who had suffered God knows what to be permitted to live with him. When I first saw him sitting in the city editorial chair one afternoon—the going of young Sullivan had not been communicated to me—I was very much afraid of him and of my future, seeing that he looked so hyperborean, raucous and uncouth and, as Maxwell dourly informed me, that new editors usually bring in new men. As it turned out, however, and much to my astonishment as I can tell you, he took an almost immediate fancy to me which rapidly ripened into a kind of fatherly affection and even—if you will permit me to humbly state a fact—a kind of adoration. Indeed, to use a phrase current at the time, he "swelled my head" by the genial, hearty manner in which almost at once he took me under his protection and guidance—why, I have never been able to think—and furthered my career as rapidly as he could, the while that he borrowed a goodly portion of my small salary wherewith to drink. I have never been able to decide whether it was because of my youth or innocent unsophisticated appearance, but so it was, and in addition I wish to say here that I never was able to look on his borrowing from me in any but a friendly and even grateful way. Indeed, he did not borrow so much at that—he could not, seeing that I made so little—and in addition my one grief is, as I think of him, that I had so little to give him for the very, very great deal that he did for me. His was a broad, generous, albeit dispirited soul, and wherever he now rests in the sightless substance of things, he will know that in my mind and heart is nothing but the kindliest recollections and the warmest gratitude.

Be that as it may, I do not think that either he or Maxwell, who still remained here and who championed me as heartily as ever, was under any great illusion as to my various and sundry defects. But I do think that in spite of my manifest faults, which were due more to inexperience than anything else and which no one seemed to hesitate to criticize, they must have seen something in me which drew them, for it was as plain as anything that they were as fond of me as one man can well be of another. McEnnis, the first day he took charge of the office, called me over and asking me a little about myself, gave me an assignment which was of no import but which, because of the ominous nature of all changes of administrations, I pursued to the utmost reaches of its possibilities, getting nothing to write about. That night he gave me another, and that proving abortive, let me go at eleven. The next day he gave me a German picnic to report, the general details of which as I indicated them must have amused him, for he smiled on me thereafter, assuming, presumably, that I had some sense of humor. He said nothing, but he plainly was friendly.

Things drifted in this fashion from day to day for a while, I blundering through one type of assignment and another, each day learning a little bit more of the nature of the work I was trying to do, until one day he gave me a small clipping concerning a girl on the near southwest side, who, as I soon found on looking it up, had run away, or been kidnapped, from one of the dreariest homes it has ever been my lot to see. I wrote a story which pleased him very much. In the first place he had asked me, in one of those weary indifferent tones which newspaper men can so effectively assume, to see if there was anything in it. "I don't want a sex story altogether," he said, blowing a snort into a great white handkerchief almost a yard square which he always carried, "but there may be some other features to tone it up. See if you can make anything out of it. We're awfully short of good news stories today."

I bustled forth, eager to make something wonderful out of this, as I wished to do in truth with everything that was given me, and was soon engrossed in one of those pathetic, shabby back-street romances which have always had, I must say, an intense fascination for me.

There was nothing very much to this story, as I may as well explain in the first place. It concerned a hardy, sexy Irish girl of about sixteen or seventeen who had run away with a neighborhood street boy who had taken her to some wretched dive in South Clark Street and seduced her. Her mother, an old, much troubled Irish Catholic washwoman, whom I found bending over a washtub at the time that I called, was greatly exercised as to what had happened to her daughter, for since her disappearance she had heard nothing. The police had been informed, and from clues picked up by a detective who had been assigned to the task, I later learned the facts first mentioned. But the mother did not know—had never been taken into her confidence by the girl—and in addition had suffered many disturbing blows of fate during the past few years. Her husband had died of some illness, a boy had been injured in some way so that he could not work, and now this girl, her last hope, was gone—and she cried into her wash as she told me of her troubles, very simply and innocently.

From a newspaper point of view there was not so much to the story, as I decided even at the time, knowing Maxwell and Sullivan's opinion of romance and sentiment, but still I decided to follow it up and in the course of few hours get the thread of the story rather clear and straight. I found the house where the girl and the youth had been—only they had just decamped. I found the parents of the youth, simple, plain, working people who knew nothing of his whereabouts— had not been able to do anything with him for a long time. Something about the wretched little homes in both instances, the tumbledown neighborhood, the poverty and privation which would ill become a pretty, sensuous girl, decided me to write it out as I saw it and felt it. I hurried back to the office between four and five of the afternoon, having gathered all the data I wished, and scribbled out a kind of slum romance which in the course of the night seemed to take the office by storm. Maxwell, who read it, scowled at first, then said it was interesting—then fine.

"Carl," he interpolated once, jestingly, as he was reading, "you're letting your youthful romantic mood get the best of you. This will never do. This will never do. Read Schopenhauer, my boy, read Schopenhauer."

The city editor when he returned picked it up, intending, I presume, to see if it had any sign of interest in the general introduction, and finding it moving, I presume, followed it up swiftly and interestedly even as he sat there. When he had done, he looked over at me and then came over into the corner where I was.

"I just want to say to you," he said, "that you have just done a fine piece of writing. I don't go much on this type of story—don't believe in it as a rule, for a daily paper—but the way you have handled it is fine. You're young yet, and if you'll just keep yourself well in hand, you have a future."

He had a way of sniffing and punching at his nose with his large white handkerchief which always amused me, and this he did now. Thereafter he became very friendly, asked me out one lunchtime to have a drink, borrowed a dollar and told me some of the charms and wonders of doing journalistic work in St. Louis and elsewhere. It was his thought that the *Globe* was too small a paper for me, that I was wasting my talents, that I ought to get on a larger one, preferably in a different city, and he suggested how valuable would be a period of work in St. Louis, for instance, on a paper like the *Globe-Democrat* (of which he had once been city editor), seeing that then it was being conducted by one of the most famous editors in America.

"You haven't any idea how much you need all this," he said at the time. "You're young and inexperienced. The mere sight of a man like McCullagh, his point of view, his ideals, would do wonders for you. A great paper like the *Globe-Democrat* or the New York *Sun* starts a boy off right. It understands him—does something for him. I would like to see you go first to St. Louis and then to New York. It wouldn't hurt you to work in different cities for a while, but don't settle down anywhere yet, don't drink, and don't get married, whatever you do. A wife will be a big handicap to you. I believe you have a future, and I am going to help you if I can."

Then he borrowed another dollar and left me.

I meditated on all this and what he could do for me and whether he really would or not, believing truly that he would if he could. My salary was too small as yet to permit me to lay up enough to even start traveling, and if I did, how would I get a job on the *Globe-Democrat* without his aid? But I returned to the office just the same, dreaming great dreams and wishing (although with not as much enthusiasm as I might, considering my inherent affection for Chicago and all its scenes) that the beginning of this outer-world campaign were already upon me!

CHAPTER XIV

The thing which brought my newspaper life in Chicago to a close, and indeed that whole period which I may call my guileless, fumbling youth, was a series of assignments or rather a campaign to close a group of so-called "fake auction shops" which were then licensed by the city and from which the police themselves—the superior officers of the force—were deriving a very handsome revenue. The task of exposing these shops to the public and so compelling the police to act was placed in my hands as a regular daily assignment, and I was supposed not to relinquish it until the police backed down and the places were closed.

Campaigns of this kind are occasionally undertaken in a spirit of righteousness, I make no doubt, and I have known newspapers that undertook them for no worse object than to increase circulation and popularity; but in this case no such laudable or excusable intent could be alleged.

This paper, as I now soon learned, was controlled by one Michael C. McDonald, a celebrated local politician, gambler, racer of horses, and the owner and manager of a string of local houses of prostitution, saloons and gambling houses, all of which combined netted him a handsome income and made him one of the most influential men politically in the city. Recently, owing to one political accident and another, he had fallen on comparatively difficult days. His reputation as a shady character had become too widespread. The pharisees and influential men generally who had formerly profited by his favor found it expedient to go by on the other side. Public sentiment against him had been aroused by political attacks on the part of one newspaper and another which did not belong to his party; the last election had been lost to him, and the police and other departments of the city were now supposed to work in harmony to root out his vile though profitable vice privileges.

Everyone knows how these things work.

Some administration attacks were made upon him, or rather his privileges, whereupon, not finding suitable support in the papers of the city which were of his own persuasion, they having axes of their own to grind, he started a paper of his own. This was the *Globe*—the one with which I was connected. He had brought on a capable newspaper man from New York, so I understood, who was doing his best to make an interesting paper which would satisfy Mr. McDonald's desire for influence and circulation in this respect the while he lined his own pockets as best he could against a rainy day. For this reason, perhaps, our general staff, though fairly capable, was underpaid. During my stay the police and other departments, under guidance from Republican politicians and newspapers, were making an attack on Mr. McDonald's preserves; to which he replied by attacking his rivals' preserves as best he might through the medium of the *Globe*. Among these were these large numbers of mock auction shops in the downtown heart, which were daily fleecing hundreds by selling them fake watches, jewelry, diamonds and the like. Evidently the police or some of their friends were deriving a direct revenue from these shops, but since the administration was now anti-McDonald—and these were not Mr. McDonald's property—nothing was said or done by either the newspapers or the police to stop this traffic, though victims hourly appeared before the latter to explain that they had been swindled and to ask for restitution.

I can scarcely recall now what it was about my treatment of these particular institutions, unless it was the vivid realism of my descriptions of what went on in them from day to day, which aroused so much interest in the office and made me into a kind of *Globe* hero. Mentally I was practically innocent of all knowledge of the complications I have described above when I started and almost as innocent when I concluded. Daily now at ten o'clock in the morning I went to one or another of these institutions and listened to the harangues of the noisy "barkers," as they were called. I saw tin-gilt jewelry, watches and the like "knocked down" to unsuspecting yokels from the South and West, who stood open mouthed and whiskers up, watching the hypnotizing movements of the fake auctioneer's hands as he waved a glistering gem or watch in front of them and expatiated in pyrotechnic language on the beauties and perfections of the jewel or watch he was compelled to part with for a song. The worst thing about these places was that they were not only deceptions and frauds in the matters of what they pretended to be and what they sold, but that in addition they were gathering places for thieves, pickpockets, footpads and the like, who, finding some poor deluded bystander to be possessed of a watch, pin or a roll of money, there and then robbed him by some sly legerdemain or, following him into a dark street at night, knocked him down and took his purse and valuables away. Chicago was notorious for this sort of procedure at this time and later, and it was openly charged in the *Globe* and elsewhere that the police connived at and thrived by the transactions.

Be that as it may, my descriptions of what was going on seemed to please Mr. McEnnis far and beyond anything I had previously done. He was enthusiastic and laughed and swore over the pictures I transcribed, as did Maxwell and others. I was cautioned against detection and being "beaten up" by those whom I was offending, for I noticed after the first day or two that the "barkers" of one shop or another occasionally studied me curiously or ceased their more shameful effronteries in my presence and presented something of more value—or some one followed me as I left, to see where I went, no doubt. They could not be sure, however, because my wanderings were devious and erratic, and after a time they would leave me and resume their work, I suppose. The facts which the articles presented in a rather realistic way finally began to attract a little attention to the paper. Because either the paper sold better or this was an excellent club wherewith to belabor his enemies, the publisher finally decided to call the attention of the public to what was going on in our columns via the billboards, and McEnnis himself undertook to frighten the police into action by swearing out warrants against the different shops and compelling the police to take action.

For the first time in my life I now became the centre of a semi-literary, semi-public reform hubbub. The principal members of the staff were agreed in assuring me that the articles were forceful in fact and color and highly amusing, to say the least. One day via the license bureau and the aid of McEnnis I secured the names of the alleged owners and managers of nearly all of these shops and thereafter began to attack them personally, by name describing them just as they were, where they lived, how they made their money, et cetera. In company with a private detective and several times with McEnnis, I personally served warrants of arrest and accompanied the sharpers to police head-quarters, where they were immediately released on bail. Then I ran to the office and wrote out my impressions of all I had seen, repeating conversations as nearly as I could remember, describing uncouth faces and bodies of crooks, police and detectives, and by sly innuendo indicating what a farce and a sham the whole seeming interest of the police was. They were so plainly on the side of the crooks.

One day as McEnnis and I were personally calling on the chief of police, demanding to know why he was so indifferent to our crusade and the facts we put before him, the latter actually shook his fist in our faces and exclaimed, "You can go to the devil and so can the *Globe*! I know who's back of this campaign and why. It's Mike McDonald, and he's sore because we've been bothering him. Well, go on and play your game. Shout all you want to. You're not going to make a mark out of me, and you're not going to get me fired out of here for not performing my duty. Your paper is only a dirty political rag, and it hasn't any influence."

"Hasn't it?" exclaimed McEnnis. "Well, you wait a little while—I think you'll change your mind as to that, Mr. Superintendent," and we marched solemnly out.

And in the course of time he did change his mind. Some of the auction fakers had to be arrested and fined and their places closed up, and the longer we talked and exposed, the worse it became for them. Finally one dealer approached me one morning and offered me an eighteen-carat gold watch, to be selected from any jewelry store in the city by me and paid for by him on the spot, if I would leave his particular store out of the discussion. I refused. Another, a dark, dusty, most amusing and serious-seeming little Jew offered me a diamond pin, insisted on sticking it in my cravat and said, "Go see! go see! Ask any jeweler vot he thinks if that isn't a real stone. If it ain't, if he says no, bring it back to me, and I'll give you one hundred dollars in cash for it. Don't you mention me no more now. Don't say I got any store. Be a nice young feller now. I'm a hard-working business man just like any other—I run a honest place."

I had to laugh. I carried the pin to the office, gave it to McEnnis and reported what had happened. He stared at me in amazement. "Did you take this?" he asked. And when I said, "Yes, I thought it would be good as evidence," he laughed loud and long and then said, "If I didn't have faith in you, Theodore, in your face, I'd think maybe these fellows had already corrupted you. You haven't taken anything else, have you?"

I declared stoutly and truthfully that I had not.

"Well," he went on, "you shouldn't have taken this. It may get the paper in trouble. They may have had witnesses as to this, but perhaps not. Perhaps this fellow is just trying to protect himself. At any rate don't take anything more—money or anything—always refuse. If I didn't think you were honest in this I'd fire you right now, but I know you're honest, and I'll see you through."

He took me into the office of the editor in chief, a short, stocky, dressy, silent man, who looked at me with still, gray-blue eyes and listened to my story. When I had done he dismissed me and conversed with McEnnis for a while. When the latter came out, he exclaimed triumphantly, "He sees that you're honest, all right, and he's tickled to death. Now we'll take this pin back, and then you write out this whole story just as it occurred." At the same time we went somewhere—a magistrate's court—to swear a charge of attempted bribery against this individual, and later in the same day I went with the detective to serve the warrant. To myself I seemed to be swimming in a delicious sea of life. I had no malice toward anyone, not even these thieving "auction" dealers. It was all a gay, peculiar, amusing, delicious picture of living. I liked even the detectives, slimy things that they were, the truculent police lieutenants and captains, the "dealers" who tried to ingratiate themselves via bribery. "What a fine thing life is," I thought. "Here I am getting along famously because I can write. Soon I will get more money, and maybe some day soon people will begin to hear of me. I will get a fine reputation in the newspaper world. Maybe I will be sent on some big commission like Stanley (who had been sent to Africa by the New York Herald) or George Kennan (who had been sent to Russia to ferret out the horrors of the exile system by the Century Magazine)." Already the distant city New York, with its now famous elevated road, its world of great hotels and theatres and mansions, was calling to me, but as yet it was a dim call. Thanks to this vigorous campaign of which McEnnis was the inspiration and guiding spirit, all these shops were eventually compelled to close, and in so much at least, Michael C. McDonald had achieved a slight revenge.

But as for me, I felt as though there must be some serious and favorable change impending for me, so warm was McEnnis's espousal of my cause, so constant was his genial companionship, and, true enough, within a fortnight or so after this, the change came. As this auction campaign had progressed, I had noted that McEnnis had become more and more friendly. He introduced me to his wife one day when she was in the office and told her in my presence what splendid work I was doing. Often he would take me to lunch or a saloon for drinks (for which I would pay), and then he would borrow a dollar or two or three, no portion of which he ever returned. He lectured me on the subject of study, urging me to give myself a general education by reading, attending lectures and the like. He wanted me to look into the matter of painting, music, sculpture, in order that I should know what was going on in the world esthetically. As he talked the blood used to swirl in my head, and I kept thinking to myself what a brilliant career must be awaiting me. One thing he did do was to secure me a place on the *St. Louis Globe-Democrat*, and this in a manner so genial, affectionate and profitable for me that as I looked back on it in after years, it seemed as though it were something which had not happened at all. The way of it was this—

Just at this time there chanced to come to Chicago one Henry C. Millerand, the Washington correspondent of the *St. Louis Globe-Democrat*, who was there to report the preliminary preparations for the great World's Fair which was to open the following spring. Already the construction of the great buildings in Jackson Park by the lake had begun, and the newspapers throughout the country were on the qui vive as to its progress, its problems, import and the like. Immense sums of money had been voted for it. Powerful individuals in Chicago and elsewhere were its friends. This man, a cool, capable observer and writer, chanced to be an old-time friend of McEnnis—one of his cronies—and before he had been in our office an hour, he introduced me to him and made an impassioned plea in my behalf and in my presence for an opportunity for me to do some writing for the *Globe-Democrat* in St. Louis under his direction. The idea was to get this man to let me do some World's Fair work for him—on the side, as it were, and in addition to my work on the *Globe*.

"As you see," he said, when he introduced me, "he's a mere boy without any experience, but he has the makings of a first-rate newspaper man. Now, Henry, as a favor to me, I want you to help him. You're close to Mac (Joseph B. McCullagh, editor in chief of the *St. Louis Globe-Democrat*), and he's just the man this boy ought to get his training under. You remember the splendid things he did for us—the inspiration he was. Dreiser here has just completed a fine piece of journalistic work for me. He's closed up the mock-auction shops here, and I want to reward him. He only gets fifteen dollars a week here, and I can't do a single thing for him here or anywhere else in Chicago just now. But you can, and I think he ought to go to St. Louis anyhow. I want to write and ask Mac to put him on down there, and you write and tell how I feel about it. You're going to have some of that 'Heard in the Corridors' stuff done here, and I want you to let him do it. He needs the money, and it will show you what he can do."

The upshot of this was that I was immediately taken into the favor of Mr. Millerand and given some easy gossip writing to do, which netted me sixteen dollars the week for three weeks straight running in addition to my fifteen dollars earned from the *Globe*. At the end of that time, some correspondence having taken place between the editor of the *Globe-Democrat* and his two Chicago admirers, I one day received a telegram which read:

"You may have reportorial position on this paper at twenty dollars a week beginning next Monday. Wire reply."

I stood in the dusty little *Globe* office when it came and stared at it, wondering what so great an opportunity and change portended. Only six months before, I had been jobless and hanging about this back door, agonizing about my future and my life. Here I was tonight with as much as fifty dollars in money in my pocket, a suit of good clothes on my back, good shoes, a good hat and overcoat. I had learned how to write and was already classed here as a star reporter. I felt as though life were going to do wonderful and beautiful things for me. I thought of Lois, for one thing, of whom I was truly fond, and how now I should have to leave her and all this familiar and now comfortable Chicago atmosphere, and then I went over to McEnnis to ask him what he thought I ought to do. At the sight of the telegram he turned on me and said, "This is one of the best opportunities that could possibly come to you. You're going to have the opportunity of working on one of the greatest papers and under one of the greatest editors that ever lived. Make the most of your chance. Take it? Of course you will. Work hard and save up your money and don't drink and be faithful and don't ever shirk an assignment. In ten years if you keep on doing serious work, you'll look back to this afternoon and thank yourself and me. Go? Of course go. Let's see. It's Tuesday now. Our regular week ends Friday. You hand in your resignation now to take effect then, and go Sunday. I'll give you some letters that will help you"—and he immediately turned to his desk and wrote out a series of introductions and recommendations which he later gave me. For my part I wrote out a formal resignation which he sent in to the publisher. I forget what I said.

That night, and for four days after until I took the train for St. Louis, I was in a state of enthusiasm. I walked on air. All my life seemed new and brilliant to me. I was going away. I was going out in the world to make my fortune. No knight ever mounted his faithful steed or set his lance at rest, facing an unknown adventure, with more ease and cheer of mind than did I just at this time. I was your true adventurer, meditating the wonders of a distant unknown world which was calling to me with a voice that was of purest music. And withal I was touched by the pathos of the fact that life and youth and everything which now glimmered about me so hopefully was, for me as well as for every other living, breathing individual, insensibly slipping away.

CHAPTER XV

This sudden decision to terminate my newspaper life in Chicago involved the problem of what I proposed to do about Lois. All during the spring and summer days, up to and after I had connected myself with the *Globe,* I had been amusing myself with Lois, imagining sometimes, because of her pretty face and figure and her soft clinging ways, that I was in love with her, at other times convincing myself that it was all a make-believe and that I really did not care.

By the lakes and pagodas of Chicago's parks, on the lakeshore at Lincoln Park where the white sails were to be seen, in Lois's cozy little rooms with the windows open, and the lights out, or of a Sunday morning when her parents were away visiting friends and she was getting me my breakfast and flouring her nose and chin in the attempt—how happy we were! How we frisked and kissed and made promises to ourselves concerning the future. We were like two children at times, blissfully happy. For a while I half decided I should like to marry her. It was so pleasing to have won so pretty a girl and to have her hang on my arm in this devoted fashion. In a very little while we were going everywhere together—the parks, the theatres, those places within my limited means—and she was planning her wedding trousseau, the little fineries she would have when we were married. We were to live on the South Side near the lake somewhere, in a tiny apartment—anything to be together. She described to me the costume she was going to wear, which was to be of satin of an ivory shade, with laces, veils, slippers and stockings to match. Like all the birds of spring, she was chirping over the charms of her future nest.

But as the spring wore on and I grew so restless and finally connected myself with the *Chicago Globe*, I began to think not so much less of Lois as more of myself. I am absolutely honest when I say that I never saw her as anything but beautiful, tender, delicate, an absolutely perfect creature for some one to love and cherish. And I sincerely wished her to be happy—was pained, if you will believe it, to think that she might not be and that I would probably be the cause of it, and yet I felt constrained to leave her. Even early in this year before I got my new place and was worrying so intensely about my future, I was convinced that I should never marry her, and yet I was not willing to give her up.

Once I remember we went hand in hand over the lawns of Jackson Park of a Sunday afternoon. She was enticing in a new white flannel dress and dark blue hat—additions to her wardrobe which must have taken the last penny of her earnings. The day was so warm and clear. A convoy of swans was sailing grandly about the little lake, whose shore we skirted for a time. We sat down and watched them and the ducks, and the rowers in green, blue and white boats, and the white pagoda in the centre of the lake, reflected in the water. All was so placid, gay, like a canvas by Watteau.

"Oh, Dorse," she said at one place with a little gasping sigh which moved me by its pathos, "isn't it lovely?"

"Beautiful."

"We are so happy when we are together, aren't we?"

"Yes."

"Oh, I wish we were married. If we just had a little place of our own. You could come home to me, and I could get you such nice things."

She hung on my arm affectionately. I promised her happy days to come, but even as I said "yes, yes, yes," I knew it could not be. I did not think I could build a life on my salary—I did not feel that I wanted to. Life was too wide and full. She seemed to sense something of this from the very start and clung close to me as we walked, looking up dumbly into my eyes, smiling almost sadly. As the hours slipped away into dusk and the hush of evening suggested change and the end of many things, she sighed again.

"Oh, Dorse," she said, as we strolled homeward and sat on her little doorstep, "if we could just always be together and never part."

"We will be," I said, but I did not believe my own words.

It was on this night, in the flush of spring, sitting in her little parlor after the others of her family had gone, that she attempted to persuade me, not by words or any great craft but merely by a yielding pressure, to take her and make her fully mine. I think she hopelessly imagined that if she yielded to me physically and found herself with child, sympathy would cause me to marry her. We found some pillows after a time and threw them on the floor, and there in my arms she kissed and hugged me, begging me to truly love her, but I had not the courage. The silly belief I have previously mentioned deterred me, and, again, I had a conscientious scruple about taking her even though I could. It would not be fair to take her and then leave. But at that, had I not been troubled by this persistent thought of inefficiency, I should have united with her this night and possibly subsequently taken her with me, though I am not sure. I am satisfied that she was grieved by her failure to succeed.

After this we drifted along for a few weeks without going further, for it was in this period that I was attempting to connect with and finally did succeed in joining the *Globe*. My duties and my enthusiasm for them compelled me to neglect Lois at first, which she immediately noticed, complaining that I was changing. I was not able to explain it on a truthful basis for the simple reason that I had been saying all along that I was working for a newspaper, and since that fact had not interfered before, why should it now? Besides, it was not so long after that I encountered Miss Winstead of Wabash Avenue, and this complicated my desires in regard to sex and made me temporarily uncertain as to whether I really wanted Lois or no.

The pathetic part of it from her point of view was that I still continued with her, but making love on my own terms and in my own way. Since I could no longer go by day or evening very well, either Sundays or at any other time, she agreed that I should come after eleven or twelve at night, and since she had the free run of the forepart of the house after nine at night as a rule, this was easy enough. Accordingly, when I was through with my work at eleven or twelve, and if it did not chance that I was compelled to do the late watch, I would journey down to her place, arriving as late sometimes as one o'clock. At that hour or earlier I would usually find her sleeping—the front door unlocked and a small light in her bedroom to guide me. Invariably she made herself up in some charming way to tempt me, lying snuggled up in a pink or blue nightie, a book under her arm, the soft glow of the red-shaded lamp falling over her. Sometimes I think she pretended to be asleep in order that she might have the pleasure of being waked. At other times she was soundly enough asleep, and only much hugging and kissing would cause her to unclose her drowsy eyes. Invariably she would slip her arms about my neck and sigh, "Oh, Dorse—I'm so glad. I've been wishing you would come." Instead of indulging in those happy unions so dear to the sybarite, I would merely fondle and talk to her, staying until three or four in the morning before I took my way homeward. Instead of taking a room in her immediate vicinity, as I easily could have and which would have facilitated matters greatly, I still chose to live on the West Side because I had always lived there and because our family—in part—was still there.

But after this change of work and hearing Maxwell talk and longing savagely as I always was for sex satisfaction, I finally screwed up my courage to the place where I decided that I would take Lois. Instead of using her home as a convenience, I decided that it would be more delicious if she came and stayed with me somewhere, and to this end I took a room in South Halsted Street, where I thought her coming in with me some evening would be taken for granted—or at least without comment. Previous to this, however, I had foolishly inquired at a certain hotel in Dearborn Street—a very third-rate affair—whether I could reserve a room for myself and wife for later in the day. Since I had no baggage and looked exceedingly nervous, I presume, the clerk no doubt decided that this was a mere sex affair, but of some doubtful character, and quietly said no. I retreated very much abashed and flushing furiously. The least tact and skill would have solved the problem for me easily.

But after this defeat I rented the room in question, and telling Lois that I wanted her to come, met her at a certain downtown restaurant where we had dinner and later went to this chamber. It was a difficult and unsatisfactory evening for her, however, for twice between eight-thirty and eleven I was compelled to leave her, not having the courage or forethought to beg the evening off from McEnnis, who had then become city editor. Work was running very light at this time, and as a rule there was very little to do, so I thought that it would be as well to say nothing and get off as early as possible. As luck would have it, he came very near sending me on a late assignment but at eleven-ten, the second time I reported, changed his mind and permitted me to go for the night.

It was then—at the age of twenty-one—that I started to take the first woman I had ever been attractive to or courageous enough to persuade to the hymeneal couch. Little Lois was nervous and tired, but happy to be with me. She clung to my arm as we went, pale and almost too nervous to talk. In the dark areaway of the cheap brick building in which I had my room, I fumbled for my key and then guided her into the nondescript room which presumably was to be her bridal chamber. In the glow of a cheap lamp I held her close and there eagerly helped undress her and, divesting myself of my own clothing, climbed in beside her. The bed was nothing, a creaky yellow-pine contraption, the bedclothing none too clean, but in my arms was Venus Aphrodite. I felt her sweet soft lines and smoothed her curly black hair and kissed her mouth and eyes and breasts. I fondled her until I was almost broken with desire, and then finding her pressing me close, endeavored to enter. She cried out softly with pain, begging me to stop, and when I would, saying, "But I don't mean to cry—I can't help it." In the excitement I found myself ejaculating heavily, which I took to be proof positive that I was impotent! Because she had begged me to stop the moment before, I now withdrew and spilled into a handkerchief which was near at hand, pretending the while that it was because of her cries that I had ceased. I reasoned with myself in an unbelievably asinine way that each time that I attempted this connection it would be the same, that she would soon discover that I could not satisfy her and have done with me. I decided to pretend that it was her sufferings that deterred me, and so instead of forcing an entry and taking the bliss that was in our hands, I merely trifled about the surface until the mere feel of her body plus this slight friction was sufficient to cause me to ejaculate, when I would withdraw, never letting her know that my "impotence" was again manifesting itself!

In this fashion, after three separate efforts and without opening the matrix or giving her the happiness she was entitled to, I finally fell asleep—convinced that my life was a failure. I have often wondered what it was that Lois thought—whether she blamed her own pretty whimpering or me, or the two of us?

Be that as it may, this union drew us closer together, and I am satisfied that I should have impregnated her if I could have but convinced myself that I was not sterile and without power to perform the act successfully. We arose in the morning and went out to breakfast— she subsequently to her work, I back to my couch. I grieved all day, and for days, over my condition. The horrors of a life of impotence haunted me. I went out to see her the following Wednesday after midnight and, now convinced that I was helpless, only did as before. One night as I was only trifling with her, wishing that I could do more, she said: "Dorse, I think you're the most bashful man I ever knew, but I love you just the same." A little later we made another appointment for a hotel and restaurant, and after much trepidation because I had not courage or sense enough to bring a bag and register the two of us as man and wife, I managed to smuggle her into my room—which might possibly have ended badly for the two of us, so moralistic was this Western world. On this occasion I merely held her close all night, afraid to try! But still we kept close in affection thereafter, though I half believe that she imagined that I did not want to—did not want to involve myself!

Let that be as it will, it was after this that the upward turn of my fortune began. I was involved in the mock-auction war for over three weeks and for two weeks following that with my buzzing dreams of leaving Chicago and becoming a great man. I can scarcely explain how it happened save that in this rush and paying some attention to Miss Winstead I neglected Lois shamefully, going over ten days once without calling at the house or the store or writing her a note. One Sunday morning, troubled about me and no doubt heartsick, she attended the ethical culture lecture in the Grand Theatre where I most regularly went—instead of going out to see her. On coming out she met me and I greeted her affectionately, but she only looked at me with sad, reproachful eyes and said, "Oh, Dorse, you don't really care any more. You're just a little sorry when you see me. Well, you needn't come any more. I'm going to go back to Harry. I'm only too glad that I can."

This started a discussion as to her former beau, and it appeared that misdoubting me she had never really dropped him entirely, but had kept him calling occasionally, he sometimes having left at ten-thirty on the same night that I called at twelve or one a.m. This angered me a little and I said to myself—"What is she, that I should worry over her?" But this suggestion of double-dealing cut me to the quick, although I had been doing as much and more; only so constituted is the individual that as a rule he sees but his side, not the other, though, when I thought, I knew she was entitled to protect herself against so uncertain a love as mine. Even now I could have taken her—she practically asked me to—and ended all her doubts, but I offered reasons and excuses for delay. I went away both angry and sad, and the following Tuesday the telegram from the editor of the St. Louis Globe-Democrat arrived. I left Chicago without notifying her, being mixed in my own feelings as to what I should do. Indeed, I had trifled about on this score, debating with myself until Saturday night, when McEnnis asked me to come to dinner with him and I could not refuse; afterwards when I hurried to her home she was not there. This angered me groundlessly, even though I knew that she never expected me any more of a Saturday night. I returned to my room on the West Side, disconsolate and gloomy, packed all my belongings, decided once that I would go back after midnight and knock at her door or window,—then bethinking me that my train left at seven-thirty a.m. and that she was probably off with my rival, I decided to punish her. After all, I could come back if I wanted to, or she could come to me. I sat down and penned her a note, then went to bed and slept fitfully until six-thirty, when I rose and hurried to make my train. At eight o'clock I was off, speeding through those wide flat yards which lay adjacent to her home and, my nose against the window, a driving rain falling outside, I could see the very windows and steps by which we often sat. My heart sank and spiritually I ached—for when, ever, was I not the romanticist? I decided at once to write her more fully when I should reach St. Louis and beg her to come—not to be my wife perhaps, but my mistress. I brooded gloomily all day as I sped southward, picturing myself as a lorn youth, without money, family, love, anything. I railed at life even in this my hour of pseudo-intellectual triumph. I almost tried to be sad, thinking at the same time what wonderful things might not be going to befall me. But I was leaving Lois! Chicago, my early home,—all that was familiar and dear. I felt as though I could not stand it—as though when I reached St. Louis I would take the next train and return.

CHAPTER XVI

It is interesting to me, at this late date, thinking of my entrance into St. Louis, to realize how nebulous I was, how blazing with desire for experience, how important my future seemed to me, how painful the danger of its non-fruition, how the air and the sky were full of pictures of what I might be, pleasures I might enjoy, things I might see and do. Without visualizing in particular any one thing, unless perchance it might be love, the actual contact with some new and charming girl, my mind was full of possibilities of professions, labors, connections by which I might rise and profit. Journalism even at this early date was no *end* to me. Barely in, I was seeing clearly that I might soon want to get out. Its topmost honors, unless it might be ownership—or control— did not tempt me. To be an editor-in-chief was something, but clearly it meant that I would have to stay in one place, accept routine without complaint, understand all the intricacies of journalism and politics, and while these were something, still the wide untraveled world was better. Perhaps I did not formulate all that is here set down so clearly— but in some vague, disturbing way, it was all in my mind.

The time was November 1892. St. Louis, as I stepped off the train of a Sunday evening, having left Chicago in cold, dreary state, seemed a warmer clime. The air was soft, almost balmy, although St. Louis could be cold enough too, as I soon discovered. The station, then at 12th and Poplar (the new Union Station at 18th and Market was then merely building), an antiquated affair of brick and stone, with the tracks stretching in rows in front of it, and reached by board walks laid

at right angles with them, seemed unspeakably shabby and inconvenient to me after the better ones of Chicago. Such mild standards of
comparison as I had thus far acquired were being brought vigorously
into play—and to the disadvantage of St. Louis, of course. It was not as
good as Chicago, I said to myself, as dynamic, as interesting. Chicago
was rough, powerful, active. St. Louis was sleepy, slow. This was
because I entered it of a Sunday evening and all its central portion was
still. I made my way to the Silver Moon Hotel, recommended to me by
my mentor and sponsor, John T. McEnnis, and found it all he had said
it would be, a simple, inexpensive affair—a room for a dollar, a meal for
twenty-five cents. I recall the strangeness—the loneliness.

When you are twenty-one and romantic and eager to see the world
and vigorously avid of life and healthy, still you can have mental aches
and pains—terrible ones. I was born with a fox gnawing at my vitals—
the fox of desire for life or love or pre-eminence or dominance or
wealth—only, unlike the Greek boy, I cannot be sure to this day
whether I was ever successful in concealing it or not. Actually, I think
not.

But this Middle Western city, compounded almost entirely of
trade and the things which related to it, what a wonder world it
seemed—even at night and during these first few hours. I was in a
strange city! I was out in the world now, actually—away from my family
and all kith and kin. Outside of Mr. McCullagh and one Edmond
O'Neill—the former editor of the *Republic* and now the president of a
wholesale plumbing company to whom I bore a letter—there was no
one to whom I might even commend myself. Did I care? Not in the
least. My care then, as now, was for life, this singing, rhythmic, mystic
state in which I found myself. Life the great sea! Life the wondrous
colorful riddle! After eating a late bite in the almost darkened restaurant, I went out into Pine Street, the thoroughfare in which this hotel
stood, and stared at the new-to-me street cars—yellow, red, orange,
green, brown—labeled Choteau Avenue, Tower Grove, Jefferson Avenue, Carondelet. My first care was to find the *Globe-Democrat* building
of which McEnnis had spoken, a prosperous eight-story brownstone
and brick affair, standing, as the signs on the corner of the building
indicated, at 6th and Pine. (Already in 1892 St. Louis and Chicago
were largely lighted by electricity, whereas New York City—Manhattan Island—was not really so lighted until 1916. Evansville, Indiana,

one of my hometowns, was so lighted—and adequately in 1882!) I stared at it in the night, looking through the great plate glass windows at an onyx-lined office and counter, and finally went in and bought a Sunday paper.

It was not long before I wearied of this dark downtown heart and returned to the hotel, which was in it but more cheerful. I went to my room and slept, thinking of my coming introduction in the morning. I was awakened by what seemed an endless clangor outside—countless cars passing. And going to the stationary washstand to bathe my face, I was struck at once by the yellowness of the water, a dark, yellowish-brown, which in a glass, as I saw, immediately deposited a yellow sediment—river water, I presumed. Was that all St. Louis could afford, I asked myself in youthful derision. I drank it just the same, for it was cool, went down to my breakfast and then out into the city to see what I should see. At once I bought a paper—the morning *Globe-Democrat* (a Republican party paper, by the way—an anachronism of age and change of ownership), and then a *Republic*, the one morning Democratic paper—and then walked up to that selfsame corner of 6th and Pine to have another look at the building in which I was to work, if I could retain my place. Behind me was Chicago, my now-seeming distant youth. Would I ever see Lois any more? Would I ever return to Chicago?—or soon at least? I wandered along Broadway, once I found it, and 4th Street, the street of the old courthouse, sought out the Mississippi and stared at it—that vast river, lying between unprepossessing banks of yellow mud—then back to the office of the *Globe-Democrat*, for it was nearing the time when its editor in chief might choose to put in an appearance. I had learned from McEnnis, his staunch admirer, that he always went to work at eleven, or thereabouts.

This same Joseph B. McCullagh ("Little Mack" of Eugene Field's verse) was, as I found later, a short, thick, aggressive, rather pugnacious and defensive-looking person of Irish extraction, who looked when I saw him as though he were quite capable of editing this and a dozen other great papers at one and the same time. He was so short, so sturdy, so Napoleonic, so ursine rather than leonine, that he pleased and yet frightened me. I was instantly drawn and thrown back by his stiff reserve. A negro elevator boy had waved me along a marble hall on the seventh floor to an end room where I was greeted by a uniformless office boy, an amazingly pliable and cheerful lad, who took in my name and then ushered me into the great man's presence. I found him at a roll-top desk in a minute office, the desk and his swivel chair almost completely buried in discarded newspapers. I learned afterwards that he would never allow these newspapers to be moved save on state occasions—when he, being all but crowded out, personally commanded it. I was racked with nervousness. Whatever high estimate I had conceived of myself till now had oozed out as I approached along the hall. I was surveyed by keen grey Irish eyes from under bushy eyebrows.

"Um, yuss! Um, yuss," was all he deigned after I had given my name and the fact that he had telegraphed for me. "See Mr. Mitchell in the city room—the city editor. Your salary will be—um—um—twenty dollars to begin with" (he was chewing a cigar and mumbled his words), and he turned to his papers.

I was disappointed, of course, at not receiving a more demonstrative welcome. Not a word, not a sign, that he knew I had ever written a line worthwhile. After my pyrotechnic career in Chicago, I expected twenty-five dollars at the least, and a few kind words, but what would you? I returned to a handsome city room—one of the best I had seen anywhere so far in my career—and found only empty desks. The city editor was not here yet. Not knowing what to do, I sat down and waited fully three quarters of an hour, examining old papers and staring out of the windows over the roofs of this, my new city, before the city editor arrived. Like his employer he was thickset also, a bigger man physically, but vastly less attractive. He had a round, closely cropped head—convict style—and a thick neck with several wrinkles at the back, and as severe and scowling an expression to his face as one would care to see. He reminded me of schoolmaster Squeers, in *Nicholas Nickleby*, the brutal master of Smike. A savage fat man—can anything be worse? He went to his desk with a quick stride when he entered, never noticing me, and when I approached and explained who I was and why I was there, scarcely gave me a glance. "The afternoon assignments won't be ready until twelve-thirty," he commented drily. "Better take a seat in the next room. I'll call you when I want you."

It was only eleven-thirty then.

I went into that same next room and sat down. It was empty, but deliciously warm on this chilly day, and so clean and polished. What a severe man, I thought. How different to McEnnis. And if a city editor didn't like you, it was quite plain he could make your work seem more or less unsatisfactory. Decidedly, being called to a newspaper by tele-gram was not to be interpreted as auguring that you were to lie on a bed of roses. A little bit afraid to leave for this hour in case he might call, I hung about the two windows in this room, staring at the new city. How wonderful it seemed—strong and forceful in this November air. The streets and sky overhead were full of smoke. There was a clangor of street car gongs below and the rumble of endless trucks. A block or two away arose a very tall building of the older order—twelve stories at least—the Equitable. Most of the buildings were small—old family dwellings turned into stores. The high-building craze had not even begun here. I wondered intensely about the life of the city, its charms, its prospects. What would it hold for me? How long would I stay here? Would this paper afford me any real advancement? Could I make a great impression and rise?

As I was thus meditating, several newspaper men came in. One was a short, bustling fellow with a golden-brown mustache and a shock of curly brown hair, whose name I subsequently learned was Hazard—a good name for a newspaper reporter. He had on a minute fedora hat, a short cream-colored overcoat which had many wrinkles around the skirts where he was evidently accustomed to sit on it, and rather noticeable striped trousers. He came in with a brisk air, slightly skip-ping his feet as he walked, and took a desk, which was nothing more than a segment of one great long desk, fastened to the wall and divided by varnished partitions of light oak, where he immediately opened a drawer and took out a pipe. This he briskly filled and lighted, after which he began to examine some papers he had in his pockets. I liked his looks.

There sauntered in next a pale, diaphanous creature in a steel-grey suit of not too new a look, who took a seat directly opposite the first comer, back to back as it were against the other wall, and took some papers out of a drawer, which he began to examine. His left hand, gloved with a brown glove, hung suspiciously at his side, and I saw at once that there was something the matter with it. Apparently it was of wood or stuffed leather.

Latterly there came a negro of very intellectual bearing, who took a seat next to the second arrival, and then a stout, phlegmatic-looking soul with dark eyes, dark hair and dark skin, which gave me a feeling of something saturnine in his disposition. He took a seat on the side where the negro and the man with the wooden hand were, and stared idly at the door.

In a little while there came a small, skippity soul, bustling about like a little mouse and having somewhat of a mousey look in his eyes, who seemed to be attached to the main city editorial room in some capacity. He came in from that room where the solemn city editor sat and, bustling up to the young man who had first come in, whispered something in his ear.

The other laughed and said, "That's right." I looked at this midget and liked him also. He was apparently so guileless and good natured. "Just a harmless little chatterbox," I thought, and waited to see who else would show up.

They came, a curious company, fourteen or fifteen all told, each one with his special characteristics. I gave up trying to catalogue them and turned to look out the window. The little bustling creature came through the room several times and finally put his head in at the door and fairly whispered to the attendant group, "The book's ready." Then there was an immediate stir, and one by one the men went into the next room. Assuming that they were going to consult the assignment book, I followed, but my name was not down. In Chicago my city editor had usually called each individual to him in person, and in consequence, when I found that each one here was supposed to discover his assignment from a written page, it seemed cold, distant. Also, when I found my name was not down, I returned to the reporters' room to wait, being in doubt as to what I would be used for.

The procession had not long disappeared before I was sought for by the mouse—one Hugh Keller Hartung, no less—who whispered, "The city editor wants to see you." And then for the second time I faced this gloomy Cerberus whom I had already begun not only to dislike but to fear. He seemed such a potent creature for evil if he wished to be. He was dark and savage in his mood, to me at least—whether unconsciously so or not I do not know. His broad face, set with a straight, full nose and a wide, thin-lipped mouth, gave him a frozen Neroic outline. He seemed a queer, unliterary type to be attached to so remarkable and journalistic a soul as McCullagh.

"There's been some trouble down at this number," he said, handing me a slip of paper on which the address was written. "A fight, I think. See if you can find out anything about it."

I took it and hurried out. To get outside into the fresh air and the new city was an immense relief. To get outside anywhere, at any time, has always been so consoling to me, but particularly in my youth. There has always been something friendly, intimate, consoling, about the outdoor world. By one form of inquiry and another I finally made my way to the place, only to find a vacant lot. There wasn't any such number. Then, thinking there might be some mistake, I went to the nearest police station and inquired. Nothing was known. Fearing to fail on my first assignment, I returned to the lot but could learn nothing. Gradually then it began to dawn upon me that this might be merely a trial assignment, one of the frowning fat man's bright ideas—a bearings finder. I had already conceived a vast contempt for him, a mere stumbling block in my path, I thought. No wonder, as I learned afterward, he came to hate me.

By degrees I wandered back through the city, looking at the strange little low houses—it was the region between the river and north Broadway about a mile above the courthouse—and marveling at the darksome character of the stores. Never in my young life had I seen such old buildings, I thought, all brick and all crowded together, with solid wooden or iron shutters and windows composed of such very small panes of glass. Their interiors were so dark, so redolent of an old-time life—European, I thought. The streets, too, appeared old fashioned with their cobblestones, and I felt as though the people must be different. Else how could they accommodate themselves to this distinctly antique and un-Chicagoesque atmosphere?

I was not long in getting back to the office, but Mr. Mitchell was gone. The little mouse-like individual whom I had heard whisper, "The book's ready," was at one of the parti-divisions of the wall desk, near Mr. Mitchell's big one, diving into a mass of copy. He had all sorts of compositions before him, one of which he was reading industriously, the while he scratched his ear, or trifled with his pencil, or jumped mousily about in his seat. He seemed to be troubled with some nervous disorder—like the whirling white mice—and I was struck with the ridiculousness of this in connection with him, though I tried not to show it.

"Mr. Mitchell's not around, is he?" I inquired.

"No, he isn't," replied the other briskly. "He never gets in much before four o'clock. Anything you want to know? I'm his assistant." He did not dare say assistant city editor. There was no such person. His superior would not have tolerated one.

"He sent me out to this place, but there isn't any such number. It's a vacant lot."

"Did you look all around the neighborhood? Did you inquire next door?"

"Yes," I replied.

"Sometimes you can get news of these things in a neighborhood, you know, when you can't get it right at the spot. I often do that."

"Yes," I commented, critically looking at him. "I inquired all around there."

"That would be just like Tobe to send you out there even if there wasn't anything there, just to break you in," he went on feverishly and timidly. "He does things like that. You're the new man from Chicago, aren't you?"

"Yes," I replied.

"Dreiser—that's the name, isn't it, eh?"

"Yes," I said, "But how did you know?"

"He said you were coming," he replied, lowering his voice respectfully and jerking his left thumb over his left shoulder. "He told me to put your name down. My name's Hartung. Hugh Keller Hartung."

I could not help smiling—he was so respectful, almost fearsome in his references to his superior. Now that I had my bearings I did not feel so keenly about Mr. Mitchell. He seemed dull.

"I'm glad to meet you, Mr. Hartung," I said grandiosely and took his hand.

"I'm glad to meet you. I suppose you'll find St. Louis a little slower than Chicago at first?"

I made some equivocal reply. St. Louis seemed pretty large and lively, I said.

"It's big enough for any newspaperman, sometimes," he boasted. "We have some of the biggest newspaper stories you ever saw here. St. Louis is famous for that. You remember the Preller Trunk Mystery, don't you, and that big Missouri-Pacific train robbery last year?"

I recalled both distinctly.

"Is that so?" I commented, thinking of my shining career in Chicago and its possible duplication here.

Peculiarly weighty steps were heard in the hall just outside, and then Mr. Hartung jumped to his work like a frightened mouse. His head, on the instant, was fairly pulled down between his shoulders and his nose pressed over his work. He seemed fairly to shrivel and shrink, and I wondered and would almost have liked to ask him why, though I could see that further conversation, for the present at least, was not desired. I turned and went in the next room, just as Mr. Tobias Mitchell came in.

I returned after a few moments and explained that there was no such number. He merely looked up at me quizzically—suspiciously, I imagined.

"Couldn't find it, eh? Some one must have given me the wrong tip. Take a seat in the next room. I'll call you when I want you."

I returned to that empty room, where, sitting alone, I could hear the industrious pencil of Mr. Hartung and the occasional throat-clearing cough of Mr. Mitchell, brooding among his papers.

CHAPTER XVII

This same reporters' room, for all its comfortable and handsome furnishings, never did acquire an agreeable atmosphere to me. It was too gloomy—and solely on account of the personality next door. I have often thought of that—how a single individual can give a horrible atmosphere to a whole institution. Tobias Mitchell (what a name!) was one such. No one had come in to turn on a light, and there was no one present. An old drunken railroad reporter with a red nose came in after a time and sat himself down at a corner seat but took no notice of me. I confined my mind to the items of the morning paper and waited.

Presently the others began to come in, and the room was soon full of those I had seen at noon and some I had not. The little man whom I had first admired for his brisk jovial manner returned to his desk about five-thirty and, after turning on his light, wrote industriously. All the others did the same. I felt very much out of tune. A reporter's duty at this hour of the night, I had long since learned, was to write.

However, I made the best of the time reading, and finally went out to supper alone, returning as quickly as possible and taking an assignment to look up a Chicago minister who was visiting in the city, in order to obtain his views. My name was on the book this time, and I thought by the choice of the subject this city editor deemed that it would be easier for me to interview a Chicago minister than any other. I felt foolish being given a thing so trivial—for I fancied that even if I secured an interview, it would not be used. I went out into the night again, hunting among the jumble of cars for the one which would take me nearest to my destination, and finding the man after a blunder or two, knocking at wrong doors, got nothing worth a stick—religious drivel—and finally returned with my story.

It was not much of an interview. The minister talked of what he considered a significant religious revival of the time, but the public was not interested, and I knew it. I wrote it up, however, an account which made five hundred words, and turned it in. It was then about ten p.m.

While I was doing this, the youth of the Jovian curls returned from some assignment on which he had been, hung up his little wrinkled overcoat and sat himself down in great comfort. His evening's work was apparently futile, for he took out his pipe, rapped it sonorously on his chair, lighted it and picked up an evening paper. The dark-haired, dark-eyed, dark-bodied reporter, who I subsequently learned was an Englishman, born of English parents but in India, and who had already been written up locally for a joke as a Hindu, was also back and was working in his corner.

"What's doing, Jock, up at police headquarters?" called the little man to him over his paper.

"Nothing much, Bob," replied the other without looking up.

"By jing, you police reporters have a cinch," retorted Bob, jocularly. "All you do is to sit around up there at headquarters and get the news off the police blotters, while we poor devils are chasing all over town. We have to earn our money." His voice had a peculiarly healthy, gay and bantering ring to it. It was delicious, friendly.

The other chuckled.

"That's no joke," put in a long, lean, spectacled individual who was sitting in another corner, near the westernmost of the two windows, and who looked as though he might be very nearsighted. He had the rawboned appearance of a countryman combined with what might be termed the outlines of a student. "I've been tramping all over south St. Louis, looking for a confounded robbery story."

"You've got long legs, Benson," retorted the jovial Hazard. "You can stand it. Now, I'm not so well fixed that way. Bellairs there ought to be given a chance at that. He wouldn't be getting so fat, by jing!"

The one called Jock answered also to the name of Bellairs.

"You people don't do so much," he replied, stopping and grinning broadly and cheerfully. "If you had my job you wouldn't be sitting here reading a newspaper. It takes work to be a police reporter."

"Yes? Is that so?" queried the little man banteringly. "You're proof of it, I suppose! Look at him! That's good. You work? You never did a good day's work in your life."

The other only grinned genially.

"Give us a match, Bob, and shut up. You're too noisy. I've got a lot of work ahead of me to-night."

"I got your work," replied the other banteringly, handing him out a match. "Is she over sixteen? I wish I had your job."

The other only folded up some copy paper and put it in his pocket, the while he smiled enigmatically. Then he walked into the next room where the little assistant was toiling away over the night's grist of news. Some conversation occurred there, accompanied by laughter. Then he went out.

I still sat looking wearily on.

"It's pretty tough," said the spirited Hazard, turning to me finally and including me genially in his remarks—he knew that I was a stranger and just "put on" here; his manner showed it—"to go out on an assignment and get nothing. I'd rather work hard over a good story any day, wouldn't you?"

"That's the way I feel about it," I commented. "It's not much fun sitting around. By the way, do you know whose desk this is? I've been sitting at it all evening."

"It doesn't belong to anyone at present. You might as well take it if you like it. There are three or four others around here that no one is using. That one over there next to Benson's vacant."

He waved toward the tall, awkward scribe in the corner.

"This is good enough," I replied contentedly. "I'd just as leave sit here."

"Take your choice. There's no trouble about desks at present. The staff's way down anyhow."

He lapsed into silence at this and turned to his paper. In a few moments he wheeled around, however, and added, "You're a stranger here, aren't you?"

"Yes, I only came down from Chicago yesterday."

"What paper'd jeh work on up there?"

"The *Globe* and *News*," I replied, lying about the latter in order to give myself a better standing than I thought that otherwise I would have.

"They're good papers, aren't they?"

"Yes, pretty fair. The *News* has the largest evening circulation."

"We have some good papers here. This paper's one of the biggest. The *Post-Dispatch* is pretty good, too. It's the biggest evening paper."

"Did you ever hear just how much circulation this paper has?" I inquired.

"Oh, about fifty thousand, I should say. That's not so much compared to Chicago circulation, but it's pretty big for this country. We have the biggest circulation of any paper in the Southwest. McCullagh's one of the greatest editors in this country—outside of Dana in New York, the greatest of any. If he was in New York he'd be bigger than he is, by jing!" I was ready to agree with that after one look at him.

"Do you run many big news stories?"

"Sometimes. Not often. The *Globe* goes very light on local news. They play up the telegraph end here. We use $400,000 worth of telegraph news every year."

I opened my eyes and thought of this dubiously in relation to my own work. It did not promise well for a big feature on which I might "spread myself," as the phrase ran.

We talked on, becoming more and more friendly as we did so. In spite of the wretched city editor I now began to like this place, although I could feel, if I could not see as yet, that these men were more or less browbeaten by this man—held down and frozen. The every action of most of them indicated as much. The room was much too silent for a healthy, Western reportorial room. The atmosphere was too thick.

We talked of St. Louis—its size, 450,000—its principal hotels, the Southern, Lindell and Laclede (I learned that its oldest and best had recently been torn down and was going to be rebuilt someday)— what the chief lines of news were. It seemed that fires, murders, defalcations, scandals were here as elsewhere the great things, far overshadowing most things of national and international import. Recently a tremendous defalcation had occurred, and this new acquaintance of mine had been working on it—had "handled it alone," as he said. Like all American citizens he was anxious to say a good word for his own city: he was pro-St. Louis. The finest portion of it, he told me, was in the west end—all the wonderful new residences and places. I should see those. There was a great park here—Forest—over fourteen hundred acres in size, a wonderful thing. A new bridge was building in north St. Louis and would soon be completed—one that would relieve traffic on the Eads Bridge and help St. Louis grow. There was a small city over the river in Illinois—East St. Louis—and a great Terminal Railroad Association which controlled all the local railroad facilities and charged each railroad six dollars a car to enter—and each passenger twenty-five cents. "It's a great graft and a damned shame, but what can you do?" was his comment. Traffic on the Mississippi wasn't so much anymore—owing to the railroads that paralleled it, but still it was a good deal, and interesting.

The already familiar noise of a roll-top desk broke in on us from the next room at this point, and then I noticed a hush to fall on the room. "What an atmosphere," I thought. Then, after a few moments of silence, my new friend turned to me and whispered very softly— "That's Tobe Mitchell, the city editor, coming in. He's a proper son of a bitch, as you'll find."

He smiled wisely and began scribbling again.

"He didn't look so very pleasant to me," I replied as softly.

"I've quit here twice," he went on whispering. "The next time I go I'll not come back. I don't have to stay here, and he knows it. That's why he's civil to me. I can get a job any day on the *Chronicle* and not have to work so hard. That's an evening paper. I stay here because I like a morning paper better. There's more to it. Everything's so scrappy and kicked together on an evening paper. But he doesn't say much to me, though, you can bet, although he doesn't like me. You'd think we were a lot of kids and this place a schoolroom." He frowned.

We dropped into silence again. I did not like to have this thought of difficulty thrust upon me. What a pity a man like McEnnis wasn't here.

"He doesn't look much a newspaperman to me," I observed.

"He isn't either," replied Hazard. "McCullagh keeps him because he saved his life once in a fight somewhere—down in Texas, I think— or that's what they tell me. I don't know whether it's so or not, but I've never liked the big stiff."

We sat and read while the clock ticked audibly, the sound of city life having died out below, and you could hear the scratching of reporters' pens.

Assignments were written up and turned in, and then the reporters idled about, dangling their legs from spring-back chairs, smoking pipes and cigars, and whispering. As the clock registered eleven-thirty the stout, round body of Mitchell appeared in the door, his fair-tinted visage darkened by a faint scowl.

"You boys can go now," he said solemnly.

All arose, I among them, and went to a closet where were our hats and overcoats. I was tired and this atmosphere had seriously depressed me. "What a life," I thought. "Have I come down here for this?" The thought of the small news end which the local life received depressed me. I could not see how I was to make out.

"Well, I'll be going," Hazard said to me as he left. "Good night."

"Good night," I replied.

I went down a small rear elevator, which was the only one running at this time of night, and into the dark street, where a carriage was waiting. I assumed at once that this must be for the famous editor. It looked so comfortable and sedate, waiting patiently at this door in the dark for an editor who, as I learned later, might not choose to leave until two a.m. I went on to my room at the little hotel, full of nebulous ideas of how someday I would be a great editor and have a carriage waiting for me—very likely. Yes—I felt I was destined for a great end. For the present I must be content to look around for a modest room where I could sleep cheaply—and bide my time and opportunity.

CHAPTER XVIII

My next experience, as I recall it, was the securing of a room which should cost me much less than I was paying at this hotel—a dollar a day for my room and about as much for my food. I was quite hungry enough nearly always to be willing to pay so much for food. But a room! At most I should not pay more than two-fifty or three dollars a week. (The room renting business—what a commentary that is on the social and financial condition of the mass!)

I found one the next morning in Pine Street, only a few doors from this hotel but on the opposite side of the street between 7th and 8th and only a block from my new office. It was a hall bedroom—one of a long series that I was to occupy—and dirty or, if not that exactly, grimy. I recall it still with a kind of sickening sense of unsatisfactoriness, and yet as I recall it, its cheapness and griminess did not trouble me much, for did I not have the inestimable boon of youth and ambition which made most material details, however crude, unimportant? Some drab of a woman rented it to me. Outside was the continuous line of street cars previously mentioned—those red, yellow, blue, green and orange cars, clanging and roaring and wheezing by, quite all night long. They never really stopped. Inside were four narrow gray walls, a small wooden bed, none too clean sheets and pillow cases, a yellow wood washstand and I presume—at least I suspected—bedbugs. But what would you? I wasn't going to stay here always. I went to the hotel and carried over my humble bag, arranged "out" the few necessaries I felt that I need not keep under lock and key, and returned to the office, or to the streets rather, for I need never bother about the office until twelve-thirty, when the assignments were handed out—or rather "the book," as Hartung reverently called it, was laid out for our inspection.

And now spread out about me for my inspection and entertainment was the new (to me) great city of St. Louis, and life itself as it was manifesting itself through this city. As a light on my character and the nature of my mind, I give you my solemn word that this was the most important and the most interesting thing to me—not my new position. Positions? Well, they were important enough, heaven knew, considering the difficulty I had had in times past of getting one. And what was more, I was always driven by the haunting fear of losing this or any other position that I ever had, of not being able to find another,—a leftover fear, I think, due to the impression poverty made on me in my extreme youth—although one might have thought that a young man in his twenties and in the best of health and spirits would not be so haunted. Just the same, the city came first in my imagination and desires, and now I began to examine it with care—its principal streets, shops, hotels, its residence district and the like. What a pleasure to walk about, to stare, to dream of better days—great things to come to me. Fortunately, my work was such that in the course of time I would naturally be carried into every portion of the city, but I was impatient to see it. One could never tell. I might not be in St. Louis so long.

And fortunately, also, it appealed to me in my youthful mood and ambitions. Just at this time it seemed to be upon the verge of change and improvement, and this appealed to me. An old section of mansions bordering upon the business heart was rapidly giving way to a rabble of small stores and cheap factories; and in addition the excellent car service led out to astonishingly attractive residence portions. There was the stir of things changing. Already several new buildings of the Chicago pattern of skyscraper were either contemplated or in process of construction, and there was a new club, the Mercantile, the largest in the city, composed entirely of merchants in the downtown section, which had just been opened and about which the papers, as I could see, were making a great stir. There was a new depot contracted for, one of the finest in all the country, so I was told, which was to house all the roads in the city; and a new city hall—an enormous thing to be—was being talked of. Out in the west end, where progress seemed the most vital, new streets were being laid out and some truly magnificent residence "places" so called, parked and guarded areas—the first I had ever seen—in which were ranged the residences of the ultra-rich, the new rich of this comparatively young city. The first time I ever saw one of them I was staggered really by their richness—their air of newly manufactured exclusiveness.

You should have seen them—great grey or white or brownstone affairs—bright, almost gaudy, with wide verandas, astonishing door-ways, flights of stone steps, heavily and richly draped windows, immense carriage houses, parked and flowered lawns, carriages and pairs of the most polished and finished character.

To say that I was impressed was putting it mildly. Because I was young and poor, with scarcely enough to carry me from weekend to weekend as I saw it, to look into these immense homes, the gaudy trappings of luxury, was enough to set up a kind of material longing which was then almost too painful to endure. Why was I born poor? Why couldn't I just as well have been born rich? Why had life and nature been so cruel to me? Think, even now I might be a member of some such home, riding in a carriage, wearing the best of clothes, traveling, attending all those wondrous affairs, which, solely because I was so inexperienced, so green, seemed wondrous. The illusion of exclusiveness! How it traps the average human mind. Mine must have been very average, indeed, to have been so cut and bitten by this wondrous picture of luxury.

And then the trade and poor sections of the city! At once, by being sent hither and yon, I encountered them all—or nearly all. Great throbbing wholesale streets, already crowded with large, successful companies—and then a mill area, along the waterfront and elsewhere, backed up by wretched tenements, as poor and grimy and dingy as any I have ever seen anywhere. And then the long, long streets of middle-class families, all alike or nearly so, all with white stone doorsteps or windowsills, or both, and tiny front yards or no yards, and thousands upon thousands of commonplace fathers and mothers and sons and daughters, trudging or street car riding to and fro between their homes and the big stores and shops downtown! How strange it all seemed—how wonderful and how commonplace. All the time my mind was dimly asking itself how came it to be so. Why were we born? Why were there such things as dogs and horses and pigs and chickens and men? Was there a heaven really? Was there a hell? Would I be damned eventually for not believing in the Catholic church?—for not being good (whatever that might be)?—for being bad? And what was good? And what was bad? Was being rich a sign of being good—or what? Was being poor a sign of being bad? Were fornication and adultery such terrible crimes, and if so, why was everybody so lustful— woman- or man-hungry?

As I bustled to and fro on one assignment and another, day after day, my mind was busy with these various and intricate problems. Needless to say, I never solved them—but, oh, the sweet tangle and welter of it all! To be alive! To want to live! To have indissoluble problems to tinker over! To be life-hungry, sex-hungry, love-hungry, wealth-hungry—fame-hungry!

Something, don't you think?

St. Louis, as I have said, was not as large as Chicago, but it was a great city and one that had a personality all its own. I could not help thinking of the Mississippi as I had seen it the first day I entered, and the maze of tracks at the old depot, also Broadway and Olive Street, as well as 6th and Pine and Washington Avenues, which I found to be the principal brisk commercial thoroughfares—very impressive in spots. The great breweries—Anheuser-Busch and Lemp—I had heard of and proposed to visit, but never during all my stay did I do so, and never, curiously, did I have a reportorial call so to do.

Just at this time also the atmosphere of the *Globe-Democrat* peculiarly appealed to me, for, as I have said, it was dominated so completely by that robust personality of McCullagh, which I could not help admiring and feeling the dignity and distinction of, even though I knew so little about him. The air of St. Louis was actually redolent of his personality. Men actually came to St. Louis from the South, West and elsewhere to see his great office—the place where he sat. I have often thought of him since in that small office, surrounded waist deep by his heaped-up papers, his heavy head sunk on his pouter-like chest, his feet incased in white socks and low slipperlike shoes, his whole air one of complete mental and physical absorption in his work; and I have rejoiced in the distinction and worth which truly able brains give a man. And he was able, and sweet and kind into the bargain. A few years later, out of sheer weariness, he committed suicide—tired of an inane world, I presume. I did not learn until a long time after, when I was much better able to judge him and his achievement, what a wonderful thing it was he had really done here—built up a journal of national and even international significance in a region which one would have supposed would have never supported anything more than a mediocre panderer to trade interests. But as I soon learned, he had built up something which had long since far transcended the wildest dreams of most American editors. As Hazard, as well as his telegraph editor later, proudly informed me, the annual bill for telegraph news alone was $400,000—a sum which, in the light of subsequent journalistic achievements in America, may seem insignificant but which at that time surely must have been a great deal. He seemed to have a desire to make the paper not only good (that word is much used in connection with papers), but great, and from my individual memory and impression I can testify that it was. It had, as one could gather at a glance, an editorial solidity and news catholicity which were impressive. The whole of Europe as well as America was accurately reflected each day in its pages. You could read carefully edited telegraph news of curious as well as scientific interest from all over the world. Its editorials were in the main wise and kind and jovial—frequently beautifully written by the editor himself. Of assumed Republican tendencies in so far as politics was concerned, it was much more of a party leader than follower, both in national and in state affairs—daring as frequently to dictate to its party as to follow, to threaten and cajole as to plead.

The rawest of raw youths, I barely and dimly sensed this at the time—and yet I did too. I felt the wonder and beauty of it all. Later it became a fact of some importance to me that I had ever been called to a paper of so much true worth and at so young an age, by a man so wise—so truly able.

But there was one drawback to all this at first, and that was, as I have said before, that I was intensely lonely. Those great houses in the west—how often I wished I might be a happy inmate of one of them at evening—a part of a luxurious family. In Chicago, as I have indicated, in spite of the gradual breakup of our home and the disintegration of the family, I had managed to build up that spiritual or imaginative support which comes to all of us via familiarity with material objects. I had known Chicago, its newspaper world in part at least, its various sections—its places of amusement, some dozen or two of newspaper men. Here I knew no one at all.

And then, back in Chicago there had been Lois and Nellie and Katharine, whereas here—who had I? This matter of Lois was destined to prove quite a thorn—a living pain, really, for years, for in my erratic way I was really fond of her. She had appealed to me in so many ways. I am of that peculiar constitution—due perhaps as much as anything to a strongly retentive memory as well as an extremely impressionable emotional nature—which will not let memories of old ties and old pleasures die easily. I suffer, or have at least in the past, for things which might not give another a single ache or pain. In Lois (as I have elsewhere indicated) I had found someone who had come extremely close to me. Now she was gone. Without any reasonable complaint save that I was slightly weary (did not care for her as much as I had) and that my mind was full of the world outside and my future, I had left her, never really to see her again—not as she was then, anyhow. It had not been over three or four weeks since I had visited with her in her humble little *parlor* in Chicago, sipping of those delights in which only youth and ecstatic imagination can indulge. Now I was three hundred miles away, and her kisses and the warmth of her hands seemed more important—very important, indeed. At the same time there was this devil or angel of ambition, as you will, which, quite in spite of myself as I see it now, was sweeping me onward to a destiny which I but dimly felt at times, yet at other times of which I was most sure. I fancied some vast Napoleonic ending for myself which I have never been able to realize—have not even wanted to. I could not have gone back to Chicago then, even if I had wanted to. It was spiritually not possible to me. Something within kept saying "On—on," and besides, it would have done no good. The reaction would have been more irritating than the pain it satisfied. As it was, I could only walk about the city in the chilling November days and think and wonder about myself and Lois and Nellie and Katharine and my own future. What an odd beginning, I often thought to myself, scandalous, perhaps, in one so young—three girls in as many years—and two of them deeply and seriously wounded by me—the latest, Lois.

"I shall write her," I thought. "I shall ask her to come down here. I cannot stand this. She is too lovely and precious to me. It is cruel to leave her so. Oh, woe is me."

There was this to be said for me in connection with the fact that I did not immediately carry out this programme: I was decidedly uncertain in my own mind as to the financial practicality of it. In Chicago some time before, I had been telling her of my excellent position—boasting youthwise that I was making really more than I was. So long as I was there and not married, the pretence could easily be sustained. Here, three hundred miles away, and where she would not and could not come unless I was prepared to support her, it was a different matter. To ask, or rather persuade, her now meant a financial burden with which at the time I did not feel able—or at least willing—to cope. I could have supported her, no doubt, on twenty dollars a week, and had I been desperately swayed by love, would have done so. I could have even had her, had I so chosen, on conditions which did not involve marriage. She was timid, but had I insisted that love demanded it, she would have come. But I was so peculiarly minded in regard to myself and even her that I could not bring myself to do this. I did not think it was quite fair. Besides, I felt, instinctively I think, that if I did—why then, Lois would have a just claim on my continuing the relation with her. And outside was the wide world. In one scale Lois. In the other the world. Did I want her?

I don't think I ever answered myself that direct. I did not need to marry her to obtain possession of her body—I had had that practically, and with no loss to her. And I said to myself that I would marry her if I had money. Again, if she had not been of a soft yielding type herself, she could easily have entrapped me, for I was a perfect mark in so far as the blandishments of the fair were concerned. But she had not chosen so to do—for a lack of ability, perhaps. Anyhow, here I was and here I staid—meditating betimes over the tragedy of it all.

And there was an element of tragedy in it, of course—not so much for me as for her, I am sure. Subsequent events proved as much. She was one of those sweet, soft little creatures, without the age, the wisdom or the experience to know what she was doing, but with a heart to love. In my angular corporeal frame I represented a higher type of being to her. Strangely enough, I was a god in a way, no doubt—not a strong powerful one, but one whom she loved. When I left, as she wrote me afterwards, she stood by her window and looked out on the night, feeling all the bitter helpless pangs of longing. She had only received my note that I was going when I was already gone, and she could scarcely endure it. She clasped her hands and wrung her fingers, endeavoring by force of will to modify the tugging sensation she felt at her heart. The need to explain to her family was something. Not that she had been seduced—I do not mean that—but that she had been deserted, and after she had deserted a more suitable man for me. When it was scarcely endurable, she turned to her little room to find something to do, passing a wretched night and a more wretched day, and then many such days. This was for me the first deep lesion in connection with sentiment and inherited sense of right feeling, and it has cut deep. Think as I will, I have never been able quite to eradicate the sting of it—the pity of it.

There is this to be said for me at that time: that we are dealing not with an ethically correct and moral youth who answered to all the important moral, social and religious conceptions of the day, but with a sentimental boy of a considerable range of feeling, who in the confusion of evidence of life thrust upon him was not prepared to accept anything as final. I did not know then and could not say, as yet, whether I believed that the morality and right conduct preached by teachers of the world were important or not. I had been told so. For as long as I could remember, the religious and social aphorisms of the day on these subjects had been impressed upon me, but they did not stick.

Something whispered that there was an easier way than the straight and narrow path in all matters except money, and even there, in the larger realms of finance, this was true. I would not perhaps have deliberately lied about anything if a question had been put to me direct, at least not about important matters, and I would not under ordinary comfortable circumstances perhaps have stolen. Beyond this I could not say how I would act under given circumstances. All depended. If anyone had been put in difficulty or great danger from my acts, I would have been very sorry; and furthermore, had poverty appealed to me, my heart would have leaped in tearful sympathy. Time and again I have suffered undue agonies over the ills of others which had no basis in fact—my brothers and sisters in particular. Beyond this, I was not conscious of any clear line of moral rectitude to which I must adhere, and I was not certain that I would willingly do so. Women were not included in my moral speculations as among those who were to receive strict justice—not pretty women—and in that perhaps I was right. They do not always desire it. I was anxious to meet with many of them, as many as I might, and I would have conducted myself as joyously and libertinely as their own consciences would permit. That I was to be in any way punished for this, or that the world would severely censure me for it, I did not as yet believe. Other boys did it. They were constantly talking about it. The world, the world of youth at least, seemed concerned with libertinage. Why should not I? Why not, indeed?

CHAPTER XIX

My progress in St. Louis was not as meteoric as the little excitement which had attended my departure from Chicago might have indicated. Of late years I have often been interested to think how important each of our lives is to us—how amazing its successes and disasters, particularly in youth—and how completely this enthusiasm ebbs with age, and the whole thing becomes unimportant, or at least our part in it anyhow. However minute, infinitesimal, in the general scheme of things, still anything we wish or do in youth is the most amazing thing in the world. I recall how intensely I felt about everything in connection with myself. I made so much of my life, my dreams.

You do of yours because it is significant to you, as mine is to me, but in a little while the fanfare of strength, of passion, of interest even within ourselves dies, and then what is left? We nearly all have our friends, our admirers, our well-wishers, our relatives, but beyond these, a time-thinning circle, how utterly unimportant we are. Your average manager of a shop, your clerk in a store, how thoroughgoingly they take themselves here and now; how briskly they stride and parade, and yet how soon their strength fails. What a little time it is in any case, a few years at most, before a germ seizes on their lungs or their blood. The years deteriorate their puny architecture, and then like the wasp or the bee or the fly of this spring they are dusted over or worn down and thrown aside by nature as one might cast down a broken tool. The young are born blind and deaf to experience and failure. The old scarcely live long enough or gain sufficient wisdom or experience to see what a vast force it is that controls them—what tools and fools they have been. How truly ridiculous, in the face of the great forces of nature, all strutting by a man or a woman is.

And yet how we strut!—how have not I, as much as any? And truth to say, there is a charm in it, even when it is no more than a rooster on a heap of dung flapping his wings lustily and vainly, or a child that "crows" or a man that swaggers and "talks big." There is so little to swagger about actually—and yet—?

No picture of these, my opening days in St. Louis, would be of the slightest import if I could not give a fairly satisfactory portrait of myself and of the blood moods or so-called "spiritual aspirations" which were animating me in those days. In *Dawn* I have given a very fair pen portrait of myself, I think, allowing for the fact that no one can see himself as others see him or truly remember and report the things which relate to himself. We are all so biased in our own favor—so poetically inclined to "color up" our side of the story.

Be that as it may, at that time I had already attained my full height, six feet one-and-one-half inches, and weighed only 137 pounds, so you can imagine my figure. Aside from one eye—the right,—which was turned slightly outward from the line of vision, and a set of upper teeth which because of their exceptional largeness were crowded and so stood out too much, I had no particular physical blemish except a general homeliness of feature to which I freely admit. It was a source of woe to me all the time because I imagined that it kept me from being interesting to women, which apparently was not true—not to all women at least. This same protrusion of the teeth, by the way, was cured a few years later by the loss of one of them, which gave the others freedom to spread.

In *Dawn* I have narrated the peculiar delusion I had that, because of a short period of masturbation practised between my fifteenth and sixteenth years, I had seriously injured myself—a delusion which, as I have said, was fostered more by much reading of quack "diseases-of-men" advertisements, with their long lists of aches and pains and their predictions of untold horrors to come, than anything else. Actually, as I have indicated before, I was exceedingly, troublesomely virile. That was the principal difficulty with me. I had too much sex vitality, not too little. Up to this time, however, aside from an exciting trifling with Lois which came to no definite fruition or complete contact, I had had no physical contact with women. And by that I mean actual copulation. Into Lois I had actually partially inserted my penis on several occasions, but never sufficiently to rupture the maidenhead and never sufficiently to prove to myself that I was as virile as I really was. Although in these contacts I ejaculated copiously and much too quickly, no doubt, for any comfort to the girl, owing to the fact that the sensation to me was so amazingly keen, still I half imagined that I was impotent due "to youthful errors" and that I was thus early bordering on senility! Imagine such a silly notion—due to what, pray? an over-working imagination possibly. If anybody can explain the reason for these peculiar vagaries of the human mind, I wish they would. I can think of no immediate parallel, save that of the ultra-religionist who imagines he is close to heaven and yet is at the same time a cold, narrow, grasping skinflint. The two states seem somehow reasonably well related.

Again, as I have written of myself, I was the sum and substance of what might be called a poetic melancholiac crossed with a vivid materialist with a lust for life. I doubt if any human being, however poetic or however material, ever looked upon the scenes of this world, material or spiritual so-called, with a more covetous eye. My body was blazing with this keen sex desire I have mentioned, as well as a desire for material and social supremacy—to have wealth, to be in society et cetera—and yet I was too cowardly to make my way with women readily. And at the same time I doubt sometimes whether my so-called passion—vigorous as it was—was not much more a thing of the mind than of the body. Love of beauty as such—feminine beauty first and foremost, of course, but in addition to that all natural forms which were somehow included with and supplemented the feminine lure—was the dominating characteristic of all my moods: joy in the arch of an eyebrow, the color of an eye, the flame of a lip or cheek, the romance of a situation; spring trees, flowers, evening walks, the moon; the roundness of an arm or a leg, the delicate tracery of an ankle or a foot; spring odours, moonlight under trees, a lit lamp over a dark lawn—what tortures have I not endured on account of these! Not even music at its zenith, or color at the end of a master's brush, or the poignant phraseology of a de Maupassant, a Flaubert or a Daudet (vide *Sapho*) has ever expressed for me the sweet agonies that I myself have endured, contemplating the charms—the public, conservative, fashionable charms, if you will—of those enticing flowers, girls, in their delicious setting, the beauty of life itself. Nature—all its sights and sounds, its tragedies, enticements, comedies—was but a symphonic accompaniment to the lilt of this central lure. My mind was riveted on what love could bring me once I had the prosperity and fame which somehow I foolishly fancied commanded love. And at the same time I was horribly depressed by the thought that I should never have them—never—and that thought, for the most part, has been fulfilled. At the same time I was filled with an intense sympathy for the woes of others—life in all its helpless degradation and poverty—which it would be unfair to myself not to indicate. Actually, the unsatisfied dreams of people, their sweaty labors, the things they were compelled to endure—nameless impositions, curses, brutalities, the things they would never have, their hungers, thirsts, half-formed dreams of pleasure, their gibbering insanities and beaten resignations at the end—touched me as only the great symphony of life should move one. I have sobbed dry sobs looking into what I deemed to be broken faces and eyes of human failures—eyes that suggested despairing or broken hearts. A shabby tumbledown district or doorway, a drunken woman being arraigned before a magistrate, a child dying in a hospital, a man or woman injured in an accident. The times unbidden tears have leaped to my eyes and my throat has become parched and painful over scenes of the streets, the hospitals, the jails are too many for me even to guess at their number. I have cried so often that at times I have felt myself to be a weakling. At other times I have been proud of them and of my great rages against fate and the blundering, inept cruelty of life. If there is a God, conscious and personal, and He considers the state of man—and the savagery of His laws and His indifference—how He must smile at little insect man's estimate of Him. It is so flattering, so fatuously unreasoning, that only a sardonic devil could enjoy it. To return to myself, what I was really seeking in spite of all this was swift and intimate contact with life in many forms—beautiful women and all the materialistic and exotic trappings which beauty plus a high disdain is able to command. The pleasures of prosperous love were first in my thoughts. After that came all other things and ways in which a man might honor and pleasure himself.

In regard to this city and my work and possibilities, I was happy enough—intensely interested—only I was also despondent, as I have indicated, lest all the pleasures that can come to youth via health, courage, wealth and opportunity should elude me while I was working and trying to get somewhere. I had health, really, yet I imagined I had not because I was not a Sandow, an athlete, and was troubled with an irritated stomach due to an undiscovered appendix problem and with that amazing "loss-of-manhood" notion previously referred to. As a matter of fact, I was teeming with nervous energy—amazing energy really. Again, as to courage, when I examined myself in that direction I fancied that I had none at all. Would I slip out if a dangerous brawl were brewing anywhere? Certainly. Well, then, I was a coward. That was self-evident. Could I stand up and defend myself against a man of my own height and weight? I doubted it—particularly if he were well trained. In consequence, I was once more a coward. There was no hope for me among decently courageous men. Could I play tennis, baseball, football? No—not successfully. Assuredly I was a weakling of the worst kind. Nearly everybody could do those things. Nearly all youths were far more proficient in all the niceties of life, manners, dancing, knowledge of dress and occasions. Hence I was a fool. The dullest athlete of the least proficiency could overcome me. The most minute society man, if socially correct, was infinitely my superior. Hence, what had I to live for?

And when it came to wealth and opportunity, how poor I seemed—and no girl of real beauty and force would have anything to do with a man who was not a success, wealthy, athletic, handsome— and so there I was, a complete failure to begin with.

Ah, the aches and pains that went with all this—the amazing depression—all but suicidal, I thought; only, truth to say, suicide was never farther from any mortal. How often, as I have said, I have looked into comfortable homes and wished some kindly family would give me shelter, or through the windows of some successful business or manufactory and wished I had achieved ownership—or a position similar to that of any of the officers and managers inside. Actually nothing in the world seemed so remote to me at this time—so impossible of achievement as to be the president or vice-president of something, some great thrashing business of some kind. The mills, the stores—how superior official work of any kind in them seemed to that which I was doing. (And yet if I had only known how centrally controlling the tool of journalism can be made.) Even a secretaryship of any kind in a corporation! Great God, how sublime it seemed! Ah, me. It mattered not that I was doing fairly well as it was, all things considered, that most of my employers had been friendly to me and solicitous of my welfare, that the few girls I had approached had responded freely enough. Still I was a failure. I knew it. Through what doorways, over what splendid lawns have I not looked, saying to myself how cruel it was, at least now in my youth when I could enjoy them, that I was shut out from these perfections. Curses! Curses! Curses! And here I was by no will of my own, and onward I had to go in labor and poverty whether I would or no.

Well, messieurs, there is something to the argument in many, many cases, only I think that in mine it was not, perhaps, as much justified as I had supposed or as would be the case with many others.

In regard to the *Globe-Democrat* itself, I became rapidly familiar with the city news-gathering end of that organization and what it required. Its needs, aside from great emergencies, were truly simple enough: interviews, the doings of conventions of various kinds (wholesale grocers, wholesale hardware men, wholesale druggists), the plans of the various city politicians when those could be discovered, the news of the courts, jails, city hospital, police courts, the deaths of well-known people, the goings-on in society, special functions of one kind and another, and then the customary fires, robberies, defalcations and the like. For the first few weeks that I was there nothing of importance seemed to happen. I was given the task evenings of looking in at the North 7th Street police station—a slum district—to see if anything had happened, and was naturally able to add to my depression by contemplating the life about there. It was pathetic, as well as dreadful.

Again, I attended various churches to hear sermons, interviewed the Irish boss of the city—one Edward Butler, an amazing person with a head more or less like that of a great gnome or ogre, who immediately took a great fancy to me and wanted me to come and see him again (which I did once) and who, as I discovered later, held the political fortunes of the city in his right hand. I wrote up a fire or two, a labor meeting or two, and at one of these first saw Terence V. Powderly, the head of that astounding, albeit mushroom, organization known as the Knights of Labor.

It was in a dingy hall at 9th or 10th and Walnut, a dismal region and a dismal institution known as the Workingman's Club or some such thing as that, which had a single red light hanging out over its main entrance. This long, lank leader, afterwards so much discussed in the so-called "capitalistic press," was sitting on a wretched platform surrounded by local labor leaders and about to discuss the need of closer union between all classes of labor, as he subsequently did.

In regard to all matters which related to the rights of labor and capital at this time, I was ignorant as a mongoose. Although I was a laborer myself, in a fair sense of the word, yet I was more or less out of sympathy with these individuals, not as a class struggling for their "rights" (I did not know truly, what their *rights* or *wrongs* were) but rather as individuals. I thought, I suppose—I cannot remember what I did think, but it comes back to me in this way—that they were not quite as *nice* as I was, not as refined and superior in their aspirations and therefore not as worthy, perhaps, or at least not destined to succeed as well as myself. I understood, or let me say felt, then dimly what subsequently and after many rough disillusionments I came to accept as a fact: that some people are born dull, others shrewd, some wise and some undisturbedly ignorant, some tender and some savage, ad infinitum. Some are silk purses and others sows' ears and cannot be made the one into the other by any accident of either poverty or wealth. Just at this time, however, after listening to Mr. Powderly (a significant man in connection with that movement) and taking notes on his speech, I came to the conclusion that all laborers had a just right to much better pay and living conditions, and in consequence had a great cause and ought to stick together—only I was not one of them. Also I concluded that Mr. Powderly was a very shrewd man and something of a hypocrite—very simple seeming and yet not so. Something that he did or said—I believe it was a remark to the effect that "I always say a little prayer whenever I have a stitch in my side" (he had been seized with some pain or other)—irritated me. It was so suave, so English-chapel-people-like; and he was an Englishman, as I recall it. Anyhow, I came away disliking him and his local labor group and yet liking his cause and believing in it—and wrote a comment which, as I recall it now, was neither favorable nor unfavorable. Our paper was not pro-corporation exactly—at least I did not understand so—and yet it was not pro-workingman either. It merely gave the barest facts and let it go at that.

In regard to that same Edward Butler who, as I have previously mentioned, took a great fancy to me, he has always stuck in my mind as one of my odd experiences in life as well as in St. Louis. He was such an amazing creature, more like a great hog than anything else—and I am not saying this roughly or cynically—and yet with a manner as soft and ingratiating as that of an Italian courtier. He lived in a small red brick family dwelling just beyond the prostitution area of St. Louis, which stretched out along Chestnut Street between 12th and 22nd. He was at once the city's sole garbage contractor (out of which he was supposed to make countless thousands) as well as one of its principal horseshoers, having many blacksmithing shops—and was incidentally its Democratic political boss, a position he retained until his death, never having been successfully ousted.

When I first saw him, it was at a political meeting of some kind during these my first few weeks in St. Louis, and the manner in which he arose, the way in which he addressed his hearers—quite like a lord—the manner in which they listened to him, and his outré visage all impressed me greatly. Subsequently, being sent to his house, I found him in his small front parlor, a yellow plush album on the marble-topped centre table, horsehair furniture about the room, a red carpet, crayon enlargements of photographs of his mother and father—the usual concomitants of commonplace life.

But in the man—what a difference! What force! What reserve! What innate gentility of manner and speech! He seemed more like a prince disguised as a blacksmith than anything else.

"So ye've come to interview me," he soothed. "Ye're from the *Globe-Democrat.* Well, that paper's no particular friend of mine, but ye can't help that, can ye?" and then he told me whatever it was I wanted to know—things about the conduct of the city—giving me no least true light, you may be sure. At the conclusion he offered me a drink, but I told him that I did not drink, which was literally true at that time. I could not. Then as I got up to go he surveyed me pleasantly and tolerantly, as one might a young horse or colt.

"Ye're a likely lad," he said, laying an immense hand on one of my lean shoulders, "and ye're just startin' out in life—I can see that. Well, be a good boy. Ye're in the newspaper business where ye can make friends or enemies just as ye choose, and if ye behave yerself right ye can just as well make friends. Come and see me once in a while. I like yer looks. I'm always here of an avenin', when I'm not attendin' a meetin' of some kind, and that's not often—right here in this little front room or in the kitchen behind with me wife. Come an' see me some Sunday afternoon. I'd like to taalk to ye. I might be able to do somethin' fer ye at some time or other—remember that. I've a good dale ave influence here. Ye've heard that. Well, come and see me, and remember that I want naathin' aave ye. Ye'll have to write what ye're told, I know that, so I won't be offended. So come and see me," and he gently ushered me out and closed the door behind me.

But I never went—not for anything for myself at least. I was nebulous and uncertain of what I wanted to do. I had the idea that he wanted to get me a small position politically—or would have, had I requested it. But did he? Just the same, the one time when I asked him for a position for a friend who wanted to work on the local street cars as a conductor, he wrote across the letter asking for the place which I gave the man, "Give this man what he wants," only it was wretchedly scrawled—barely legible (the man brought it back to me before presentation)—and was signed "edward butler." But what was more to the point, the man was given a place and at once.

Incidentally, although Butler was an earnest Catholic, he was supposed to control and tax the vice of the city—which charge may or may not be true. One of his sons owned and managed the leading vaudeville house of the city—a vulgar burlesque theatre, at which Frank James, the brother of the amazing Jesse, who terrorized Missouri and the Southwest as an outlaw at one time and has filled endless "dime novels" since, was ticket taker. As dramatic editor of the *Globe-Democrat* later, I often had my curiosity in regard to his appearance satisfied. Also this same son, a more or less stodgy type of Tammany politician, popular with a certain element in St. Louis, was later elected to Congress from his district. But all this is merely in passing and had little or nothing to do with me—a commentary on the political and social state of the city at that time.

CHAPTER XX

Personally my connection with the *Globe* had many aspects, chief among which was my rapidly developing consciousness of the significance of journalism and its relation to the life of the nation and the state, a thing which had not been quite as clear heretofore as it might have been. It must be remembered that my journalistic career had only begun five months before in Chicago and that preceding that I had had no newspaper and certainly no literary experience of any kind. The most casual youthful reader of a newspaper had been as good as myself in many respects.

Here though, for some reason, I began to sense the significance of it all—the power of a man like McCullagh, for instance, for good or evil; the significance of a man like Butler in this community; the difference in states and their separate interests; the import of the union in relation to all of them. Still, I had a lot to learn—the extent of graft in connection with politics in a city such as this, which somehow first seemed to dawn on me here, the power of a newspaper to make sentiment in a state and so help carry it for a governor or a president. I think the political talk I heard about these rooms on the part of one newspaper man and another, "doing politics," as well as the leading editorials in this and the other papers, which just at this time were concerned with a coming mayoralty fight and a feud in the state between rival leaders of the Republican party, served to clear up my mind on this subject.

I was new to the community. All its facets and peculiarities were interesting to me. Hence I listened to all that was being gossiped about in this connection, read the papers rather more carefully than I would have in Chicago, wondered over the personalities and the oddity and novelty of state governments in general in connection with our national government. Just over the river in Illinois everybody was concerned with the administration of John P. Altgeld, who was governor there at the time, and whether he would pardon the Chicago anarchists whose death sentences had been commuted to life imprisonment. Here everyone was interested in the administration of one William Joel Stone, who was governor. A man by the name of Cyrus P. Walbridge was certain to be the next mayor if the Republicans won—and they ought to win because the city needed to be reformed. The local Democratic board of aldermen (I believe there were two bodies like the Senate and House at Washington, which jointly ruled the city) was supposed to be the most corrupt in all America. (How many cities have yearly thought that, each of its particular governing body, since the nation began?) And a man like Edward Noonan, the reigning mayor, was supposed to be the lowest, the vilest, creature that ever stood up in two shoes. The chief editorials of the *Globe* were frequently concerned with blazing denunciations of him. He had joined with corporations and the councilmen, as I understood it, in helping to steal, sell franchises, and the like. With the police he had joined in helping bleed the saloons, gambling dives and houses of prostitution. Gambling and prostitution were never so rampant as now, I understood. The good people of the city should join and help save the city from destruction.

It all sounds rather familiar, doesn't it? Well, this was in 1893, and I have heard the same song every year since, in every American city in which I have ever been. Gambling, prostitution, graft et cetera, with politicians preying upon them, until I was finally compelled to believe that they were among our national weaknesses,—our normal condition.

At the same time, in so far as this particular office and the country about St. Louis were concerned, Joseph McCullagh, our editor, was of immense significance to his staff and the natives—a great political force. Plainly, he was like a god to many of them. For the farmers and residents in small towns in states like Texas, Iowa, Missouri, Arkansas and southern Illinois, where his paper chiefly circulated, he was their political light and beacon, for they came to the office whenever they were in the city to get a glimpse of him. And if he was not always able to check vice, plainly he was able to preach virtue—which he did most sonorously.

If ever an editor had a more adoring or more humbly believing and faithful group of followers anywhere, I never heard of or saw it. "The chief says," "the chief thinks," "the old man looks a little grouchy this morning—what do you think?" "Gee, the old man would be sore about that!" "Lord, wait'll the old man hears about that—he'll be hopping!" "Maybe the old man didn't see it, eh?" or "Maybe he won't." "That ought to please the old man. He likes a bit of good writing." How often have I heard one and all of those expressions in connection with this, that and the other fact, item, event, accident, success.

Yet for all this verbal clatter, in so far as I could see, "the old man," as he was reverently and truly affectionately called, never seemed to notice much of anything or have very much to say to anyone, except possibly to one or two of his leading editorial writers and his telegraph editor. If he ever conferred for more than a moment with his stout city editor, I never saw it—nor heard of it—and if anything seen or heard by anybody was not whispered about the reportorial room before night-fall or daybreak, it was a marvel of concealment. Everybody talked—a little. Everybody brought news from somewhere, to somebody. Then soon it was whispered in your ear or retailed with gusto over a restaurant table. Occasionally he might be seen ambling down the hall to the lavatory or across it to the room of his telegraph chief, but most always it was merely to take his carriage or walk, possibly, to the Southern Hotel at one o'clock for his lunch—his derby hat pulled over his eyes, his white socks showing, a cane in his hand, a cigar between his lips. If he ever had a crony I never saw him. If he ever went with anybody it was not known or believed. He was a solitary or eccentric and a few years later committed suicide, or so it was said, by leaping from the second-story window of his home where he lived in as much privacy and singularity as a Catholic priest—only a housekeeper officiating.

"The old man thinks—" or "The old man said—" or "Say, did you hear the latest? The old man is going to do thus and so."

Always "the old man" or occasionally "J.B." No one else was ever mentioned apparently. No one counted. There were silent figures slipping about—one Captain King, a chief editorial writer; one Casper S. Yost, a secretary of the corporation, assistant editor and what not; several minor editors, artists, reporters, the city editor, the business manager—but there was no one of them nor all of them collectively that seemed to amount to a hill of beans. "J.B." "J.B." "J.B." "J.B."

And as I went along I felt truly, and not merely because I was overawed, that he was worthy of it. The paper had a character, a succinctness, a point, both in its news and editorial columns, which was refreshing. Although it was among the conventional of the conventional of its day—what American paper of that period could have been otherwise?—still it had an awareness about it which made you feel that the "old man" knew much more than he ever wrote—the true inwardness of things, for instance. He seemed to love to have it referred to as "the great religious daily," and often quoted that phrase, but with the saving grace of humor behind it. It was anything but that, of course.

In addition he seemed to understand just how to supply that region with all it desired in the shape of news. Was it mere news, gossip, oddities about storms, wills, accidents, eccentricities? Somehow you could always find them briefly and collectively presented, and in quantity for the smalltown areas, so that the idlest store lounger would have plenty, and all of them had humor, naiveté, or pathos. Was it politics? Somehow the drift of things was always presented in leaders in such a way that even I, a mere stripling, began to get a sense of things national and international. Those adjacent states, in particular the ones supplying the *Globe*'s circulation, were given a special news attention which need never bother the general reader and yet which he could follow if he chose. The editorials, sometimes informing, sometimes threatening and directive, sometimes mere folderol and foolery, and intended as such, had a delicious whimsy in them. Occasionally "the old man" wrote one himself, and then everyone sat up and took notice. You could easily single it out for yourself, even if it had not been passed around, as it nearly always was. "The old man wrote that. Have you read the old man's editorial in this morning's paper? Gee! read it!" Then you expected brilliant, biting words—a strangely luminous phraseology, sentences that cracked like a whip, and you were rarely disappointed. The paragraphs exploded at times. At others the whole thing ended like music—the deep, sonorous bass of an organ—or burst like a torpedo or a rocket. "The old man" could write—there was no doubt of that. He also believed, apparently, what he did write, for the time being anyhow. That was why his staff, one and all, really revered him. He was a real editor—a great one,—one who could write, as contrasted with your namby-pamby "businessman" masquerading as an editor. That was the true reason, if you want to know it, why his staff adored him. They knew he understood writers (or reporters and editors), their whimsies, moods, difficulties. He had been a great reporter and war correspondent himself in his day—one of the men who was with Foote on the Mississippi and with Sherman and elsewhere during the great Civil War.

There was an old, red-faced, fat-faced, red-nosed German, very protuberant as to stomach, very genial as to expression, dull and apparently unimportant, who wandered about the building a great deal and who, as I was subsequently informed, was the owner of the major part of the corporate stock of the *Globe* and was therefore its real owner. (Daniel M. Houser was his name.) But apparently he never dared to pose as such. He was a mere underling—a nobody in so far as the staff and their great editor were concerned. And a more apologetic mien and a more obliging manner were never worn by any mortal, especially when he was in the vicinity of the same McCullagh's office. He was as urbane and smiling as a calf as he stood in the great editor's doorway from time to time and looked in and greeted that solitary genius. For the most part he wandered about the building like a ghost seeming to wish to be somebody or to say something. He owned it, but his visits to his editor and partner were never for any length of time—I noted that. He seemed always to be wishing to say good morning or something to somebody and never having sufficient courage to do it. The short, stout Napoleonic editor ruled supreme.

By degrees I made friends with a number of those who worked here—Robert Hazard, or "Bob" as he was familiarly known, Jack or "Jock" Bellairs, son of the Captain Bellairs who presided over the City Zoo, Charles or "Charlie" Benson, and a long list of others whose names now escape me entirely—all in that tentative way in which those who work for any great corporation have of making friends. Of all those on the city staff I was inclined to like Hazard most, for he was a personage—a true character, quick, gay, intellectual, literary—a really forceful and brilliant person in his way. Why he never came to greater literary fame I do not know. He seemed to have all the flair and feeling necessary for the task. He was an only son of some one who had long been a resident of St. Louis and was himself well known about town. He lived with a mother and sister in southwest St. Louis in a small neat cottage which always appealed to me because of its hominess, and supported them in the most loyal, son-like fashion. I wasn't on the paper many weeks before I was invited there to dinner, and this in spite of a rivalry which was almost immediately and unconsciously set up between us the moment that I arrived. And it endured in a mild way even after our more or less allied literary interests had drawn us socially together. There was also that same "Jock" Bellairs previously mentioned, a most curious compound of indifference, wisdom, literary and political sense and a hard social cunning, who had a capacity for what, as some one in the office once phrased it, was a "lewd and profane" life. He was the chief police reporter at a building which was known as the "Four Courts," an institution which housed among other things four judicial chambers of differing jurisdiction, as well as the county jail, the city detention wards, the office of the district attorney, the chief of police, chief of detectives, the city attorney, and a "reporters' room" where all the local reporters were permitted to gather and where they were furnished, forsooth, paper, ink, tables and the like.

A more dismal atmosphere would be hard to find than that which prevailed in this same building and, for that matter, about similar institutions in all of the different cities in which I ever worked. In Chicago it was the City Hall and County Court House, with its police attachment; in Pittsburgh the County Jail; in New York the Tombs and Criminal Courts Building, with Police Headquarters as a part of its grim attachment. I know of nothing worse. I think these places, essential as they are, are, or at least always have been in my experience, low in tone—vile—and defile nearly all they touch. They have or had a more or less corrupting effect, not only on those with whom they come in contact but on those who are employed to administer law or so-called "justice" within them as well. Harlots, criminals, murderers, buzzard lawyers, political judges, detectives, police agents and court officials generally—what a company! I have never yet had anything to do with one of these institutions in any way in any city, either as a reporter, a plaintiff or an assisting friend, without sensing anew the essential brutality and even horror of these whirlpools of so-called legal administration. The petty tyrannies that are always practised by underlings and minor officials—how they always grated on me! The "grafting" of low, swinish brains! The tawdry pomp of ignorant officials! The cruelty and cunning of so-called agents of justice! "Set a thief to catch a thief." Verily. And clothe these officials as you will, in whatsoever uniforms of whatsoever splendor or sobriety, give them desks of rosewood and walls of flowered damask and entitle them as you choose—High and Mightinesses This and That—still they remain the degraded things they have always been, equivalents of the criminals and crimes they are supposed to do away with.

It cannot be helped. It is a law of chemistry—of creation. Offal breeds maggots to take care of it—nullify its stench. Carrion has its appointed buzzards, carrion crows and condors. So with criminals and these petty officials of the lower courts and jails who are set to catch them. Essentially they are of the stuff with which they are in contact, else were they never there—depend on it.

But this is a wandering paragraph and has little to do with this same "Jock" Bellairs, save that he was of and yet not of this particular atmosphere. From the first time I ever laid eyes on him until the last, I felt compelled to study him, for he seemed somehow to suggest this atmosphere to which he was appointed as reporter. From twelve-thirty to five-thirty, from seven to eleven at night, he was supposed to be at his station in this building, noting all the small incidents which might make items of a few lines or more, covering larger ones up to that point where they would make, say, a half a column of type, and then immediately notifying the office when anything larger—not to be covered in so little space—occurred or "broke loose," as the phrase had it.

Bellairs, it appeared, was just the man for this purpose. He could do this excellently well. On all occasions when anything of real import broke loose he was always apparently present, in close touch with it and the police and detectives who were his cronies, and ready to telephone the office in case anything happened which was beyond his power to manage. On more than one occasion, some "mystery" occurring, he would telephone the office, and I, who by then had risen to some importance, was then appointed to handle it, the supposition being that it was likely to yield a large story—larger than he could write or spare time for, being a court fixture. On such occasions I would seek him out at the Four Courts and be "given" what he knew, whereupon I would begin investigating on my own account. Nearly always I found him lolling about with other reporters and detectives, a chair tilted back in the reporters' room, possibly a card game going on between him and other employes of other papers, a bottle of whiskey in his pocket, "to save time" as he once amusingly remarked, and a girl or two present—friends of one or other of these newspaper men, their "dollies." On these occasions, if he knew anything at all he would rise and explain to me just what was going on, take me aside and whisper confidentially in my ear the name of the principal person who could give me information, the name of some other newspaperman who had been put on the case by one of the other papers, ask me possibly to mention the name of some shabby policeman or detective who had been assigned to the case, one who was a "good fellow" and who could be depended upon to help us in the future.

I was often compelled to smile. He was so naive—and yet so truly wise in his position—so matter of fact and commonplace about it. He was so secretive and quiet in his way. Sometimes he would give me the most befuddling information as to how the news got out. He and John somebody or other were down at Maggie Sanders' place in Chestnut Street the other night when somebody—some detective or other—was telling somebody else, who told somebody else—and so——. Then he would get me to the prisoner if there was one, or tell me where the body was to be found if there was a body. Then, I having gone about my labors, he would return, I suppose to his card game, his girl and his bottle. There were stories constantly afloat of midnight—"after-hours"—outings with these girls, of the using of some empty room in this same building somewhere for immoral purposes—with the consent, no doubt, of complaisant officials. And then all around him and it, of course, the atmosphere of detained criminals, cases at trial, hurrying parents and members of families, weeping mothers and sisters—an awful mess.

On an average of once or twice a month regularly during my stay in St. Louis, if not oftener, I was called to this building on one errand and another—and always I went with a kind of sicky and sinking sensation, and always I came away from it breathing a sigh of relief. To me it was a horrible place, a pesthole of suffering and error and trickery, and yet necessary enough, I know—one whose services could not possibly be dispensed with.

CHAPTER XXI

In connection with this same "Four Courts," the peculiarly low mayor, the grafting city council et cetera, I have often thought since (although it did not occur to me at the time) what a fine commentary all this presented to the wearisomely reiterated "high moral tone" of the city and of the nation to be found in the daily papers of that day and ever since in America. I recall so distinctly how low and undeveloped all European nations were considered to be, at that time, as contrasted with America—how high and pure our standards were and what a light we were to all the world. This same *Globe-Democrat*, as well as all other American papers that I ever came in contact with, teemed with this idea. Some of the daughters of our rich—many of them indeed—were marrying "effete foreigners," "titled snobs," "worn-out" aristocrats and the like. American girls with their high notions of purity, virtue and the like were immeasurably too good for them. As a matter of fact, as I gathered from my reading at that time, nearly all European nations were backward as compared to ourselves—slow, ignorant, et cetera. At the same time, as I might have known had I known anything of current history, those same nations—the most forward-looking ones at least— were slowly taking over and developing most portions of the backward world with which we were not connected—Asia and Africa, to wit. And many of the others, after long steps forward, were merely intellec- tually tired for the time being—quiescent. But what was I to discover of that in America?

At the same time here locally, in this perfect land, as I soon discovered (although, as I say, the contrast between our professions and our deeds was by no means as obvious to me then as it has since become), was all this teeming chicane, vice, adultery and what not in as free and, if you choose, as revolting a form as could be found anywhere, I am sure. Here in St. Louis, as in London or Paris or Vienna—those effete European cities—girls walked the streets for hire, and the section where they walked, Olive Street between 6th and 12th and about the post office, was quickly pointed out to me by my fellow craftsmen, who were youthfully interested in these matters. Again there was a truly amazing bagnio district, stretching from 12th and Chestnut to 22nd or 23rd and Chestnut, occupying both sides of the street and literally lined with "houses" where the sexually restless and unsatisfied were free to repair and for a comparatively modest price satisfy their needs. There is no moral pretense or pharisaical "better- than-thou" gesture in my statement that I never used one of these houses for any such purpose—lack of money, a slight hesitancy relative to so public a procedure, a feeling of revulsion at being one of many to slake my thirst at the same fountain held me back. A bit of a snob, as you may guess.

At the same time I was intensely interested in the atmosphere which these houses created as well as the physical charm of some of the women, and later in my stay visited many of them in the company of newspapermen and friends of theirs—men of money and position about town, who did not seem to be above the delights which these same places offered. Of a spring and summer evening, walking out Chestnut Street on one errand or another, I have seen scores of these women—most diaphanously, or I might even say gorgeously, arrayed— seated on their doorsteps, at the windows or walking up and down the sidewalk, not necessarily soliciting, although they may have been, but rather, I think, taking the evening air after a hot day in the house. (And it could be stifling in St. Louis, as I can testify.) In spite of all my yearnings in the direction of pleasure of this kind, my willingness to visit these places in a sniffing prurient mood, still my puritanic conscience, due to my religious upbringing, could not but indulge in a few qualms over the degradation and horror of all this—a condition of mind which now makes me smile. Positively there is not only something ridiculous but abominable, sickeningly shabby, about some of the transitional moods of human nature. It can be so small—so self-deceiving, so ignorantly self-misunderstanding.

And at this point I cannot refrain from a commentary on the noble, the almost religiously elevated atmosphere of the remaining portions of the city of which this was a part. Of course husbands, sons, cousins, fathers, daughters made possible this region (I am talking of the "tenderloin" as it was then already known); but behold the perfection of their outlying homes, their absolute insistence on the non-existence of such things—or, perchance, such things being true, the non-relationship of them to their kith and kin. No husband, son, daughter or father of theirs would be guilty of any relationship with anything of this kind.

Be it so. I am not anxious to make over the natural subterfuges of nature which may spring, for all I know, from a great and shrewd desire on the part of the master or masters of all this to build up differences, and hence from a healthy, moving, constructive interest in this mortal scheme. All I wish to point out here is this—and this is nothing new (Lecky, in his History of European Morals, has pointed it out before me)—that in the large, uneven, poorly adjusted (or is it?) mechanism of life, the prostitute or common whore of the bagnio is a godsend, a haven of grace. With all the fires of daring and erotic youth, and in many instances besotted manhood, persistently let loose on the common virginity of the world by nature itself, how many of the truly innocent, the morally simple and pure, do you suppose would escape unharmed if there were no streets of prostitutes, no walking places of girls? How safe would most marriage beds be? How rifled would most families and how very common would seduction and, what is more, rape become? After all, these places do satisfy a restless number and without harm to many others. If they did not, where would these men and women go? We talk about establishing morality by law or, better yet, by religious or moral suasion. I am willing if it can be done, but I seriously doubt whether it can be, observing nature as I have. I should say that the only thing that will cure this thing will be the cooling of the earth itself—the dying down of those fires lit in the very chemistry of man and which spring from what sources we know not—the sun, the moon, the stars, the juices of this planet. Cure nature itself first, or better yet arrange life—our life—according to the dictates of nature— that is, accept nature according to her own rules, and there will not be so much moral agony. The Japanese as well as the French and Russians and others with their segregated women districts understand and arrange these things better.

We rage against and harry so-called vice and vice regions, militating against the natural tendency to segregate, and then consider the question solved. But is it? As I write I am in a simple farming region, in a highly religious part of America, where labor and duty and the struggle for a living are as sharp and compelling as they are anywhere, and yet here amid rich fields and green and blue hills, the lust of man is as rampant as ever and quite as unregulated. Tales, tales, tales of girls seduced, of boys who have run away after the crime of seduction—of family shames, concealments, pretences. This is no doubt conditional with a state of ignorance, and ignorance will always be—a measure of it, I fancy, anyhow. The truth is, the whole thing comes down to a desire on the part of all families to succeed and to avoid failure. When a girl or boy goes wrong—more particularly a girl than a boy—it is, I assume, locally considered a failure on the part of this particular family. Hence the shame, the disgrace, the rise of morality, the horror of districts. Even so. But is it correct? Speaking for the individual, to whom alone we can address ourselves, is it not meet that he should rise above such petty considerations? Prostitution is not destructive, scarcely even injurious. The Rockefeller Commission, which in 1912 investigated vice conditions in Europe and here, concluded that 85 per cent or thereabouts of the women who entered upon this career of so-called shame, instead of dying in the gutter of disease or drink or a morbid conscience, left the business, married and became comparatively respectable and successful citizens—with probably (this my own conclusion) a penchant for denouncing vice on account of its hardships. I am not jesting. I know women who, having so retired, are comparatively successful and have this very point of view.

What would you? Are we not here to *reform* nature?

I was walking down the marble hall of our editorial floor one day not long after I arrived when I noted on a door at its extreme west end the words "Art Department." The only paper I had ever worked on before had no art department that I ever discovered. If so it had escaped me entirely. And, forsooth, this was a world that interested me greatly. The mere word *art*, although I had no real understanding of its import, I think, was fascinating to me. Was it not on every tongue? A man that painted or drew was an artist. Doré (!) was one, for instance, and Rembrandt. I classed the two together—so much did I know about art. Bouguereau and Raphael or any celebrity, indeed, would have been tumbled into the same bag by me, I presume. In Chicago I had known, of course, that each paper had an art department, and that interested me in this one. What were artists like? I had never known one. They must be interesting.

Another day I was on my way to the lavatory and discovered that I had come away without the key—a duplicate of which every department possessed. The art department door being nearest, I entered to borrow its. Behold, three distinctive, if not distinguished, looking individuals at work upon drawings laid upon drawing boards. Two of these, those nearest me, looked up—the one nearest with a look of criticism in his eye, I thought—and at once I took an impression of something different and interesting, a world that was pleasing to me. One of the men—the one who answered me, by the way, when I inquired for the key and arose with alacrity to secure it for me—was short and stocky with a bushy, tramp-like "get-up" of hair and beard, a full and efflorescent growth of the latter, so much so that any Western mountaineer or French cabinet minister might have been proud of it.

There was something that flavored of opera bouffe about it, and yet, as I could see, this individual took himself seriously enough, although perhaps with a grain of salt. There was something so pleasing in his voice, too, as he said, "Certainly. Here it is," and smiled.

The other one, who looked up at first and frowned but made no move, was much less cheery but as much of a type as this first, though far more of the conventional or, rather, the Quartier Latin type than anything else. To this hour I can clearly recall the long, thin, sallow face—Dantesque in shape; the coal-black hair, long and coarse, which was parted most carefully in the middle and slicked down at the sides and back over the ears until it looked as though it had been oiled, as it well may have been; and the eyes, black and small and querulous and petulant (as was the mouth, with drawn lines at either corner) as though he had endured much pain, which he had not. And that long, loose, flowing black tie, and that soft white or blue or green or brown linen shirt—would any Quartier Latin denizen have done without them? He had pale, thin, almost bony hands—small and graceful— and an air of "touch thou me not, O defiled one." The man appealed to and repelled me at a glance, appealing to me much more afterwards than at the time he dawned upon me, however, and remaining ever after a human humoresque—something to coddle, endure, decipher, laugh at. Surely Dick Wood—or "Richard Wood, Artist," as his card read—might safely be placed in any pantheon of the unintentionally ridiculous and delicious.

But I run past my story. This single visit provided a mere glance. On returning the key, I may have said something. I forget. At any rate, I was given no encouragement. A little later, however, when, owing to various minor assignments entrusted to me, my ability to write had been fairly established, I was given a rather large order for one so new— namely, a double-page spread with illustrations, for the Sunday issue which was to concern nothing less than the new depot now under construction: its great iron and glass train shed to house thirty-two tracks, and its locally amazing station proper with a separate clock tower 222 feet high. This seemed quite an honor to me since it was to carry drawings, and I went about it with an energy and an enthusiasm which only a gay youthfulness could summon. At the same time I was told gruffly by that same Mitchell, who was my mentor in this, to look to the art department for suitable illustrations.

Evidently the art department knew all about it before I came there, the idea and the order having originated in the front office, but this took me to that department once more, and upon inquiry I found that P. B. McCord, he of the tramp-like hair and whiskers, was the one who had been scheduled to make the pictures. His manner pleased me. He was so cordial, so ingratiating, so helpful. Several conversations were necessary. We visited the depot together, and a few days later he called upon me in the reportorial room to ask me to come and see what he had done. Being mutually agreeable and having in regard to most things the same point of view, we were soon the best of friends. As a matter of fact, a more or less affectionate relationship was then and there established, which endured until his death sixteen years later. During all of that period we were scarcely out of touch with each other, and through him I was destined to achieve some of my sanest conceptions of life.

CHAPTER XXII

It has been one of my commonest experiences, and one of the most interesting to me, to note that nearly all of my keenest experiences intellectually, my most gorgeous rapprochements and swiftest developments mentally, have been by, to, and through men—not women—although, as I say, there have been several exceptions to this. Nearly every turning point in my career has been signalized by my meeting up with some man—not woman—of great force, although, as I wish again to reiterate, there have been exceptions to this rule. I have had too many splendid reactions to women of great force and taste not to make a point of it. But just the same, to as few as a half-dozen men,—eight at the most,—I owe some of the most ecstatic intellectual hours of my life—hours in which life seemed to bloom forth into new aspects, took on splendid prospects and colors, glowed as with the radiance of a gorgeous tropic day.

These men I can easily name from my youth up: my brother Albert, with whom only occasionally I had the privilege of sojourning,—a remarkable temperament; my brother Paul, wondrous lamp of sentiment and humor that he was; the Reverend H. W. Thomas of

Chicago, aged, trembling humanist whom I never met but only heard preach; P. B. McCord, "the only Peter" as I have often styled him; "Dick" Wood, quaint illustration of urgent, seeking failure; Arthur Henry, critic, student, philosopher, dreamer; Henry L. Mencken; John Cowper Powys. Who else?

A not very extended list, as you see—yet how significant to me! Some men do this for you—they act as wire to carbon, tow to fire. Meet but once and you sputter and blaze as an arc lamp newly brought into contact with its circuit—one or both do. It is as though an X ray or a searchlight were suddenly provided and turned upon life (all that you know), and you see it as under a glistering ray—revealed in all its thinness or its rich color.

From time to time this has been my most fortunate experience. I have turned a corner idly—and, behold, a man, a friend, an admirer, a very present help in a dreary world. One hears occasionally of the thinness of friendship, and in minor cases this may be true. But those that I have experienced have been for the most part of a gorgeous and enduring character. For instance, this with Peter (joy to his flaming spirit) was one of the best of all.

I cannot recall now exactly how it was that it developed,—a thing of bits and moments at first, as all friendships no doubt are—a word, a look, a smile, a feeling of aura and atmosphere. And certainly if ever a man had the latter, he had it for me. There are certain natures, even in this humdrum, puritanic American world, that seem to be born free— pagan—gloriously and yet unconsciously so. Peter was one such. I have never seen a better. About my own age at this time—a year more or a year less, I forget which—he was blessed with a natural understanding which was simply princely. Although like myself he was raised a Cath- olic and still pretended in a boisterous, Rabelaisian way to have some reverence for that faith, he was amusingly sympathetic to everything good, bad, indifferent—but going, as he said, to confession and com- munion annually "in case there might be something in it. You never can tell." Still he had no least interest in conforming to the tenets of the church and laughed immoderately at its pretensions to solution, preferring his own theories to any other. Nothing amused him so much apparently as this same thought of confession and communion—of being shrived by some stout, healthy priest as worldly as himself and preferably Irish like himself. At the same time he had a hearty affection for the Germans—all their ways, conservatisms, their breweries, food and the like—and finally wound up by marrying a German girl who could speak no word of English when he met her. As far as I could make out, Peter had no faith in anything except nature itself, and very little faith in that except as to those aspects of beauty and accident and reward and terrors with which it is filled and for which he had an awe if not a reverence, and in the manifestation of which in every way he took the greatest delight. Life was all a delicious, brilliant mystery to him, horrible in some respects, beautiful in others—a great adventure. Unlike myself at the time, he had no least trace of any lingering puritanism and wished to live in a lush, vigorous, healthy, free, at times almost barbaric way. The negroes, the ancient Romans, the Egyptians, tales out of the Orient and the grotesque Dark Ages, our own vile slums and evil quarters—how he reveled in these! He was for nights of wandering—endless investigation, reading, singing, dancing, playing in any way possible. He loved mysteries, rituals, secret schools, ancient history, medieval inanities and atrocities—a most singular, curious and wonderful mind. And murders, lusts, terrible barbarities—the details of them seemed to fill him with an immense and amused delight. His family—at least his parents—were at once both extremely religious and moral. This troubled him no whit. Even at his age he did not consider that they were suitable judges of these matters, ignorant, in short, although he was very fond of them. Already at his age he knew many writers,—a most astonishing and illuminating list to me: Maspero, Froude, Rawlinson, Froissart, Hallam! The list of painters, sculptors and architects with whose work he was familiar, and books about whom or illustrated by whom he knew, is too long to be given here. His chief interest, in so far as I could make out in these opening days, was Egyptology and the study of things natural and primeval—all the wonders of a natural, groping, savage world.

"Dreiser," he would exclaim with a gusto that was at once delicious and infectious, his bright beady eyes gleaming with an immense human warmth, "you haven't the slightest idea of the fascination of some of the old beliefs. Do you know the significance of a scarab in Egyptian religious worship, for instance?"

"A scarab. What the devil's a scarab? I never heard of it," I probably exclaimed.

"A beetle, of course. An Egyptian beetle. You know what a beetle is, don't you? Those things burrowed in the earth—the mud of the Nile—at a certain period of their season to lay their eggs, and the next spring, or whenever it was, the eggs would hatch and the beetles would come up. Then the Egyptians imagined that the beetle hadn't died at all—or if it had, it also had the power of restoring itself to life, possessed immortality. So they thought it must be a god and began to worship it"—and he would pause and survey me with those amazing eyes—as bright as glass beads—to see if I was properly impressed, as I nearly always was.

"You don't say?"

"That's right. That's where the worship came from," and then he might go on and add a bit about monkey worship, the Zoroastrians and Parsees, the sacred bull of Egypt—the sex power as a reason for its religious elevation—and of sex worship in general; the fantastic orgies at Sidon and Tyre, when enormous images of the male and female sex organs were carried aloft before the multitude.

Being totally ignorant of these matters at this time—no least rumor of them having reached me as yet (think how ignorant we can remain of the most obvious and tremendous facts of life)—I was greatly surprised, amazed. No hint of all this had reached me as yet in my reading, and yet I knew it must be so. It fired me with a keen desire to read—not the old orthodox emasculated histories of the schools but those other books and pamphlets to which I knew he must have access. Eagerly I inquired of him where, how. He told me that in some cases they were outlawed, banned—not translated correctly—in most instances by the puritanism and the religiosity of the day, but he also gave me titles and authors to whom I might have access and the address of an old-book dealer or two who could get them for me. These I was always promising myself that I would get. At the same time I was postponing it on the ground that I had so many other books that I wanted to read first—studies in particular subjects that I wanted to make—and then there was my daily work with hours and tasks exacting enough, as well as the splendid, hourly singing panorma of life itself.

In addition he was interested in ethnology and geology, as well as astronomy. Also he had a love of the bizarre and the eccentric as contributing to the humor of life—and indulged in them on every occasion and at his own expense, as when he allowed his hair and beard to grow in this amazing fashion, only to appear not so many moons after with his hair neatly trimmed and his face shaven as smooth as a monk's. Once he had his scalp tonsured for the sheer ridiculousness of it. He was addicted to chewing as well as smoking and expectorating freely after the backwoods fashion, and another time, although an iron cuspidor was provided for each office desk, he purchased a most amazing frilled and decorated brass spittoon which—having removed the old one and with the most elaborate formalities placed the new one in its accustomed spot—he would permit no one to use, declaring that it was too precious. At the same time, he himself for weeks expectorated all about this perfect ornament, making a brown circumference for it, saying that it needed something like that to set it off.

At that time he was already making the, for him, comfortable salary of thirty-five dollars a week, and, living as he did at home and having some very little money of his own, he was already indulging in rare books and prints, Chinese plates and pottery, and also making a collection of historical matter relative to Egypt. One of the first things he ever fascinated me with was an accurate description of some of the tombs and temples of Egypt, their purpose, the probable import of their mysteries, the number and character of the gods worshipped and the prevalence in ancient days of sex worship—Priapus, the sex trinity, Astarte and the remaining evidences of this ancient worship in our modern signs and symbols. I never dreamed of doubting him—he was too wonderful, too absolutely convincing and sincere—and, of course, I grew rapidly by mere contact with him.

Well, Peter is dead now, in his thirty-eighth or thirty-ninth year, with few if any of the great riddles solved, and he was so eager to know. Let us hope that the flame of him is not dead and that it is brooding over new data elsewhere.

And then the amazing Wood—Dick, as we both familiarly called him. I have never encountered another like him, possibly because for years I have not been associated with young people, who are frequently full of eccentricities. A more romantic ass than Wood never lived—nor one with better sense in many ways. In regard to newspaper drawing he was, I believe, only a fairly respectable craftsman, if so much—nothing to boast of, McCord being better, but in other ways he was fascinating enough, amazing really. Both of these men were compelled to use at that time the old chalk plate process then generally in vogue in newspaper offices for much of their hurried work, a process which required the artist to scratch with a steel upon a chalk-covered surface, blowing the chalk away from his outlines as he made them. This created a dust which both McCord and Wood complained of as disagreeable and "hard on the lungs." Wood, who pretended to be dying of consumption at the time—and, as a matter of fact, he did die of it sixteen years later (within a month of his friend McCord, by the way)—made an awful row about it. Although as a matter of fact if he had chosen, he could easily have done much to mend matters by taking a little exercise and keeping out of doors as much as possible, which he never would, preferring to hover over a radiator or before a fire. Always, however, on every occasion, he was given to playing the role of the martyr—a thing which he heartily enjoyed, I am sure.

Spiritually, however, he was chronically morbid like myself— only, as I firmly believe, he let it show much more in his manner. He had much the same desire as I had at the time—that is, to share in the splendors of marble halls and palaces and high places generally—and like myself he had but little chance. Fresh from Bloomington, Illinois, a commonplace American town of perhaps forty thousand, he was enamored—quite obsessed, I believe—with the rather commonplace dream of marrying rich and by the all but imaginary splendors of that west-end life of St. Louis, which was so interesting to both of us. Ah, those great houses in the west end near Forest Park with their spacious lawns and parked courts—how they weighed on him, as on me! And the great commercial organizations which are ruled by presidents, vice-presidents and secretaries. The wonder of their interiors, of their resources, of their functions supposedly held! Far more than myself, I am sure—and I have the keenest desire to be just in this matter—he seemed positively to be seething with an inward rebellion against the fact that he was poor, not of these, not included in their exclusive and recherché pleasures. At the same time he was glowing with a desire to make other people imagine that he was or that he soon would be.

What airs! What nuances of manner! What a splendid dream he really lived in all the time, I am sure. Positively, the world he lived in was not real—anything but. In regard to the same mansions and their so-called functions, I have the gravest doubts as to whether they were of any import socially, and even if they were, neither of us could have told you how. But what matter? They were better, different, more costly, more sought after than anything we had—hence, for the time being, and in this region, they were the all-desired.

Wood, as I have said, like myself was forever dreaming of some gorgeous maiden—rich, beautiful, socially elect, who was to solve all his troubles for him, although from another point of view, from mine purely, there was this difference between us. Dick, being an artist, rather remote and disdainful in manner, and decidedly handsome as well as poetic and better positioned than myself, as I fancied, was certain to achieve this gilded and crystal state, whereas I (these were my own deductions at the time), not being so handsome, nor an artist, nor sufficiently poetic perhaps—certainly not yet—could hardly aspire to so gorgeous an end. I might perchance arrive at some such goal if I sought it eagerly enough, but the probabilities were that I would not— or I would have to wait a long while. And besides my dreams and plans varied so swiftly from day to day that I couldn't be sure what I wanted to do, whereas Wood, being so stable, and this, that and the other—all the things I was not—was certain to do so quickly, any day now, as it were. Sometimes, around dinner time, at the office (this was the succeeding spring after my arrival), when perchance I would see him leaving, arrayed in the latest mode, as I assumed—a dark-blue suit, patent leather boots, a dark, round, soft felt hat, a loose tie blowing idly about his neck, a neat thin cane in his hand—I was firmly convinced that this much anticipated end had arrived already, or was certainly about to arrive—this very evening perhaps—and that I should never see him more, never be permitted to speak to him even. Somewhere, out in the west end, of course, was *the* girl, wondrous, rich, beautiful, whom he was to marry or elope with and be forgiven for doing so by her wealthy parents. Ah, me! Even now he was on his way to see her, whereas I, poor oaf that I was, was moiling here over some trucky task. Would my ship never come in?—my great day never arrive?—my turn? Unkind heaven!

And Wood, may I remark in passing, was just the kind of person who would take an infinite delight in creating just such an impression. It was, in the main, I think, why he stalked thus nobly forth, Hamlet-like—if to nothing more than an adjacent beanery. A few years later (ten to be exact) when McCord and I were in the East together and Wood was still in St. Louis, we were never weary of discussing this histrionic characteristic of his, laughing sympathetically with him and at him—his desire to give just such an impression of himself. Subsequently he actually married—but I will not anticipate. Mentally, I am sure, at this time he was living the dream—and in so far as possible acting it—of what he sought, the part of some noble Algernon Charles Claude Veer de Veer, heir to or fiancé of some maid with an immense fortune which was to make him and her eternally happy and allow him to travel, pose, patronize as he chose. A laudable dream, verily.

As for myself, I confess I was bitter with envy. What, never to shine thus? Never to be an artist? Never to have beauty grovelling at your feet or laying endless treasures in your lap? How terrible! And at the same time, there were additional stings which were as sharp as serpents' teeth. Dick had a wristwatch, for instance, the envy of my youthful days, and wore it (oh, wondrous watch!); also a scarfpin made of some strange stone, brought from the Orient and with a cabalistic sign or word on it (enough to entice any heiress); a boutonniere of violets—his favorite flower. He was never without that!

And in addition that sad, wan, reproachful, dying smile!

And that mysterious something of manner which seemed to say, "My boy! My boy! The things you will never know." And yet Dick condescended to receive me after a time into his confidence and into his "studio"—if I may take a look forward—a very picturesque affair, this latter, situated in the heart of the downtown district. And also he condescended to bestow upon me some of his dreams as well as his friendly presence—a thing which quite exalted me, being so new to this art world. I was *permitted*—note the word—to gather dimly, and as a neophyte from a priest, the faintest outlines of these same wondrous dreams of his and to share with him the hope that they might be realized. Actually, I was so set up by this great favor—its import—that I felt certain that great things must flow from it. Assuredly we three could do great things if only we would stick together. But was I worthy? There were already—by degrees, of course—rumors of books, plays, stories, poems, to come from a certain mighty pen. As a matter of fact, it was already hard upon the task, writing some of them—the stories, for instance, which were to set the world aflame (by and by) and make us all realize how wonderful he was. Certain editors in New York were already receiving them and sending back deep, dark insinuations in regard to mysterious but necessary changes which would perfect them and so inaugurate the new era. Moreover, Dick knew certain writers, certain poets, certain playwrights were already better than any that had ever been, the best ever, in short. And I was allowed to share this knowledge with him—to be thrilled by it.

Great Dick! Amazing Dick! Amusing Dick! Delicious Dick!
Where, aside from the master portraits of a master humorist—a
Cervantes perhaps—will your equivalent ever be found?

CHAPTER XXIII

Once the ice was broken with Peter, via the double-page depot
spread, my intimacy with these twain ripened fast. Although I
never became as friendly with Dick as I did with Peter, largely because I
could not think him as important as the other, still, because of our
mutual liking for Peter and Peter's growing friendship for me, he could
not very well have excluded me, I suppose. Wood had some of the characteristics of a woman, I think. He could be jealous of anyone's interest
in Peter or, more particularly, Peter's interest in anyone else. He was
large enough at times to see the folly, or rather the smallness of this,
and be anxious to rise above it, but at other times probably he could not
quite help it. Years after, when we were in New York together, McCord
confided to me in the most amused way how first when I appeared on
the scene, Dick had—almost unconsciously, Peter thought—begun to
belittle me and to resent my presence and my obvious desire "to break
in," as he phrased it—these two, according to Dick, having established
some excluding secret union.

This last, however, was not quite the case. The union was not
exclusive in so far as McCord was concerned. It appears that shortly
after my arrival young Hartung had begun running into the art room
with (so Peter told me) amazing tales of the new man, his exploits in
Chicago and elsewhere. I had been sent for to come to this paper—that
was the great thing. I was vouched for by no less a person than John T.
McEnnis, one of the famous ex-newspapermen of St. Louis, a former
city editor of this paper and well known to Hartung. Also by a Mr.
Somebody, the Washington correspondent of the paper, for whom I had
worked in Chicago—helped on World's Fair work. According to him I
had already written four or five minor items which seemed to agree with
his sense of important reporting. As a matter of fact they were nothing,
mere bits of description—a funeral of some big Mason, the first skating
at Forest Park, a fire picture—the easiest of all to do. On several

occasions he had come to me, I recall well enough, and complimented me on several bits of color which he said McCullagh was certain to like. Then, evidently, he had hurried to the art department with this same intelligence, wishing, I fancy, to be on friendly and on happy terms there. As it was, however, Dick considered Hartung's judgment as less than nothing—himself as an upstart, a mere office rat. To have him try to introduce anybody to them was too much. And then to have me appear on the scene and under his very eyes make friends with Peter— his beloved—was even worse. At first he received me quite coldly; then finding, I suppose, that I was better than he thought, likely to succeed—anyhow above the average—he hastened to make friends with me.

This last came about in various ways. Not infrequently Peter and Dick would dine together at some downtown restaurant at seven, Peter preferring that to his home; or, if a rush of work was on and they were compelled to linger, a late supper was at times indulged in, or at least sandwiches and beer in some German saloon where cards and tenpins or billiards and pool were to be had. It was Peter who first invited me to one of these late séances, and subsequently Wood did the same, only this last was based on another development in connection with myself which it is fit that I should narrate here.

The office of the *Globe*, as it chanced, proved an ideal sprouting-bed for incipient literary talent. Hazard, as it turned out, some fifteen or eighteen months before, in company with some newspaperman of whom I later heard amazing things but who had since died, had written a novel entitled *Theo*, which was plainly a bog fire created by those blazing suns, Zola and Balzac. It was laid in Paris (imagine two Western newspapermen who had never been out of America writing a novel of French life!) and had, as I recall it (I was later given the pleasure of reading it), much of the atmosphere of Zola's *Nana*, plus the delicious idealism of Balzac's *The Great Man from the Provinces*. Never having read either of these authors at that time, I could not then recognize the similarity, but two years later, coming across the latter work in Pittsburgh, I saw the similarity at once and recognized the origin. Either one or both of the authors had fed up on the French realists of the time to such an extent that they were able to create the illusion of France, for me at least, and at the same time fire me with a desire to create something in a literary way—possibly a novel of this kind—but preferably a play. (My first love among the artistic forms—the one I first seriously attempted—was that of the play.) At any rate, it seemed intensely beautiful to me at the time—wonderful—with its frank pictures of raw, greedy, sensual human nature, and of indulgence in vice.

The way the discovery of Hazard's book came about was interesting, but I would not narrate it save that it had such a marked effect on me. I was sitting in the city reportorial room late one gloomy afternoon in December, having returned from a fruitless assignment, when the office boy who attended on the wants of the editors delivered me a letter. It was postmarked Chicago and was addressed in the handwriting of Lois. Up to now, as I have said before, I had allowed matters to drift—having written but one letter, in which I had apologized rather indifferently, I suppose, for having come away without a word. At the same time my conscience had been paining me so much that now when I saw her handwriting I started. She was really so simple, so sweet, so altogether desirable—that was what troubled me most. I tore it open and read her remarks with a sense of shame. Here it is—out of an old letter file:

Dear Theo:

I got your note the day you left, but then it was too late. I know what you say is true about your being called away and I don't blame you. I'm only sorry our quarrel (there hadn't been any save of my making) didn't let you come to see me before you had to go away. Still that was my fault too, I guess, in part. I couldn't blame you entirely for that.

Anyhow, Theo, that isn't what I'm writing you for. You know that you haven't been just the same to me as you once were for a while back. I know how you feel. I have felt it, too. I want to know if you won't send me back the letters I wrote you. You won't want them now and I wouldn't want you to keep them in the future. It might cause trouble. Please send them to me, Theo, and believe I am as ever your friend,

Lois.

There was a little blank space on the paper, and then:

I stood by the window last night and looked out on the street. The moon was shining and those dead trees were waving in the wind. I saw the moon on that little pool of water over in the field. It looked like silver. Oh, Theo, I wish I were dead.

I jumped up as I read this and clutched the letter in my hands. The pathos of it cut me to the quick. I went to the window and looked out on this other scene where amid smoke and grey shadows another world of labor, such as that of which Lois was a part in Chicago, was going forward. To think that I should have left her so. To think that I should be here and she there. Why had I not written? Why had I shilly-shallied these many days? Of course she was broken-hearted. Of course she wished to die. And I—what of me?

I went over the situation in detail and tried to figure out just what I could do. I was in no position, as I reasoned then, to return to Chicago, since, before coming here, I had never received enough money to save any—at least, I had never felt that I had—and here I was no better off. Twenty dollars a week, as I viewed life then, was little to go on. I wished to keep myself looking well, to have a decent room—which I did not have—and clean linen, and to eat three reasonably fair meals; and I was finding that twenty dollars did not go very far. A room cost me three dollars; my board—eating as I did, here, there and everywhere—was never less than six dollars and sometimes a little more. I had a laundry bill of never less than seventy-five cents a week; and my baths (not obtainable at my present abode), shaves and private carfare added another dollar and a quarter. That made a total of eleven dollars for legitimate expenses. Outside of this, but coming regularly enough, were shoes, hats, clothing, haberdashery and an occasional bit of jewelry such as I longed to own. Then my new friendships with Wood and McCord as well as these newspapermen, nearly all of whom liked to drink for sociability's sake if nothing more, were costing me something extra. I could not associate with them and not buy an occasional drink. And I did not see where I was to save much, or how, if I wished to get married, I could support a wife. It was a serious problem.

In addition there was the newness of my position here to be taken into consideration—its promise. I could not very well leave it now, having just come from Chicago. By nature I was timid anyhow, little inclined to battle for my rights or desires, and consequently not often getting them. I was in a trying place mentally, really, for I had always, as I have said, let it appear to Lois in Chicago that I was doing much better than I had been, that money was no object really. With much of the natural vanity of youth, I had always talked of my good salary and comfortable position, and now that this salary and this comfortable position were to be put to the test I did not know what to do about it. Honesty would have dictated, of course, a heartfelt confession. A regard for my word would have carried me back to the place where I would have assured Lois that I would marry her as soon as I was able. In a burst of youthful desire I had fallen in love with a pretty face, and although I now realized, dimly enough perhaps, that that had been a mistake for me, still I should have done the straightforward thing— told her exactly how things stood.

As a matter of fact I did no such thing. Instead I wavered between two horns of an ever-recurring dilemma. Sympathizing effectually with the pain Lois was feeling and alive to my own loss of honor and happiness, still I hesitated to pull down the fine picture of myself which I had so artistically built up—to reveal myself for what I was, a man incapable of marrying a woman on his present salary.

If I had loved Lois more, if I had really respected her, or if I had not looked upon her as one who might be so easily put aside, I would not have allowed things to remain so. My natural tendency, however, was to drift in these matters—to wait and see, suffering untold agonies myself in the meanwhile. And this I was preparing to do now. I did not see how I could do otherwise.

These mental calamities were enough to throw me in a soulful mood, however, and I looked out the window now on the "fast-widowing sky" with an ache which rivaled in intensity those touches which we sometimes find in the most sensitive music. My heart was torn by the inextricable problems which life seemed to present to me and others, and I fairly wrung my hands as I looked into the face of the hurrying world. How it was hastening away! How my own life was slipping by. The few sweets which I had thus far tasted were always accompanied by bitter repinings. No pleasure was unalloyed with pain. All my days thus far I had been seeing this, and yet life offered no solution. Only silence and the grave ended it all.

I went to my desk, turned on the incandescent light, and took my pencil in hand. My body was racked with a fine tremor, my brain ached. I sat and looked at my hands before me, looking into the face of the tangle as one might look into the gathering front of a storm. Words moved in my mind. They bubbled. They marshalled themselves in curious lines and rhythms. I put my pencil to paper and wrote line after line, rhyming each second with the first preceding it, and dividing the resulting array into four. Presently I saw that I was writing a little poem, but that it needed polishing and modifying. It seemed very crude. I stopped for a moment here to change a word and there to substitute an ending. I was in a great fever, however, as I did so, eager to go on with my idea, which was about this same tangle of life, and desirous of ignoring those defects as much as was possible. I became so moved and interested that I was almost forgetting Lois in the process. When I was done I went back again and read it, changing more and more, for it seemed but a poor reflection of the thoughts I had felt—the great, sad mood I was in. I changed and reworded it, finally getting it into a shape reasonably satisfactory to me. Then I sat there, dissatisfied and unhappy, resolving to write Lois and tell her all.

I took a pen and composed a letter telling her that I could not marry her now, that I was in no position to do so. Later on, if I found myself in any better shape financially, I would come back. I told her I did not want to send her her letters—I did not want to think that our love was at an end. She was hasty. She would change her mind. I had not meant to run away. I closed by telling her how I still loved her and that the picture that she had painted of herself standing at the window in the moonlight had really torn my heart. However, I could not write it as effectually as I might have, for the reason that I was haunted by the idea that I would never fulfill my word, for all I was saying. Something kept telling me that it was not wise—that I really did not want to. This was something which I could not conceal. Any girl who felt as deeply as did Lois concerning me would have detected it—as she did, later events proving it.

While I was writing, Hazard came in. He glanced over my shoulder to where the poem was lying and saw what it was. It must have stirred his own restless literary ability deeply, for he exclaimed, "What are you doing, Dreiser? Writing poetry?"

"Trying to," I replied a little shamefacedly. "I don't seem to be able to make much of it, though." The while I was wondering at the novelty of my being taken for a poet. It seemed such a fine thing to be.

"There's no money in that sort of thing, though," he observed helpfully. "You can't sell 'em. I've written tons of 'em, but it don't do any good. You'd better be putting your time on a book or a play."

A book or a play! I sat up. This sort of a discussion appealed to me immensely. To be considered a writer, a dramatist—even a possible dramatist—raised me in my own estimation greatly. Why, at this rate I might become one—who knows? I began to feel I might do something when the time came. The time might be coming right now. Why not?

"I know it isn't profitable," I said. "Still it might be if I wrote them good enough. I'd like to write them, just to be writing them, if I could. It would be a great thing to be a great poet."

Hazard smiled sardonically. From his pinnacle of twenty-six years such aspirations seemed ridiculous. I might be a good newspaperman—I think he was willing to admit that—but a poet!?

"There are very few of those," he rejoined simply and truthfully. Only I didn't believe him. Seriously, I half imagined by now that I was a great one—or at any rate probably destined to be.

The discussion now took the turn of play and book writing. He had written a book in connection with another newspaperman. Recently he had been having a play in mind. He expatiated on the money there was to be made out of plays, the splendid name some playwrights attained. Look at Augustus Thomas, who had once worked on the *Star*. He was a great playwright. One of his pieces was then running in St. Louis. Look at Henry Blossom, once a St. Louis society boy, and one of whose books was now in local bookstore windows. Think of Alfred Robyn, whose music for an opera had recently been accepted, and the opera being tried out here. All around he cited instances. To my excited mind the city was teeming with brilliant examples. Indeed, and truly enough, it had been the quondam stamping ground of much now-successful talent—artists, playwrights and the like. Eugene Field had once worked here—on this very paper. Mark Twain had idled about here, drunk and hopeless.

I returned to my desk after a time, greatly stirred by the knowledge which I had thus received. Hazard had promised to let me read his book—would bring it the next day, indeed. This world was a splendid place for talent, I thought. I began to see that now. It heaped beauty and honor upon those who could succeed. Plays or books or both were the direct entrance to every joy which the heart could desire. Something of the rumored wonder and charm of the lives of successful playwrights came to me, their studios, summer homes and the like. Ah, here was the equivalent of Dick's wealthy girl. I sat thinking about plays, somewhat modified in my grief over Lois for the nonce, but nonetheless aware of its tremendous sadness. I reread my poem and it seemed good—beautiful even—for the moment. I must be a poet! I copied it and put the duplicate in Lois's letter. Then I folded my own copy and put it in my pocket, close to my heart. It was my first poem since my budding maturity—my very first. It seemed as though I had just forged a golden key to a world of beauty and light where sorrow and want could never be. Never!

CHAPTER XXIV

The heroine or central character of Hazard's book was an actress, young and very beautiful. Her lover was a newspaperman. He was deeply in love with and yet not faithful to her—in one instance, anyhow. This brought about a Zolaesque scene in which she spanked another actress with a hairbrush. There was treacherous plotting on the part of somebody in connection with a local murder, which brought about the arrest and conviction of the newspaper man for something with which he had nothing to do. This entailed a great struggle on the part of Theo to save him, which resulted in her failure and his death on the guillotine. A priest à la the Romanist in *Henry Esmond* figured in it in some way—grim, Jesuitical.

It was the second creative work of anybody's that I had ever come in direct contact with (the first being a silly, boy book by two editors in Chicago, so trivial as not to matter), and in consequence, as I have said, I was deeply stirred. Youth brings such a glamour to anything it touches, anyhow. Streets old and wearisome to the aged are paradises to the young and inexperienced—refreshing beyond words. This book being my first look-in upon the methods of the French Realists, even if at second hand, and they being fascinating to me, it was tremendously impressive. To this day four or five of the scenes come back to me as having been most forcefully done—the fight between the two actresses, a feast with several managers, the gallows scene, a confession. The name of the newspaper man who collaborated with Hazard on this work escapes me entirely, but the picture of his death in an opium joint painted for me by Hazard—and the eccentricities of his daily life—

stand out even now as Poe-like. He seems to have been blessed or cursed with some such temperament as that of Poe—dark, gloomy, reckless, poetic.

Be that as it may, this borrowed and posthumous work, never published, in so far as I know, was the opening wedge for me into the realm of literature. It has always struck me as curious that the first original novel written by an American (or Americans, as it chanced in this case) that I ever came in contact with and was interested in and fired by was a book which by the inherent state of the times was banned. So thick was the self-delusive puritanism of the hour that these fascinating newspaper men—fresh, forceful, imbued with a burning desire to present life as they saw it—were completely overawed by the moral state of the times and had not even ventured to send it forth to a New York publisher. Or perhaps they had and had received a crushing letter in reply. At any rate, my recollection of the situation is that Hazard was deeply impressed with the futility of attempting to do anything with that kind of a book. The publishers wouldn't stand for it. You couldn't write about life as it was. You had to write about it as somebody else thought it was—the ministers and farmers and dullards of the home. Yet here he was, as was I, busy in a profession that was hourly revealing to both and all of us the fact that this sweetness and light code—this idea of a perfect world which contained neither sin nor shame for any save vile outcasts, criminals and vagrants—was the veriest lie that was ever foisted upon an all too human world. Not a day, not an hour, but what the pages of the newspapers, which we were helping scribble and fill, were full of the most incisive pictures of the lack of virtue, of honesty, of kindness, of even average human intelligence, not on the part of a few, but in the course of time and by and large on the part of nearly everybody. Not a business apparently, not a home, not a political or social organization, or an individual, but what or who, in the course of time, was guilty of an infraction of some kind of this seemingly perfect and unbroken social and moral code. All men were honest—but they weren't. All women virtuous and without evil intent or design—but they weren't. All mothers were gentle self-sacrificing slaves, sweet pictures of the songs and Sunday schools—only they weren't. All fathers were kind, affectionate, saving, industrious—only they weren't. But when you were writing for a newspaper, however—unless perchance you were describing actual facts for the news columns, which you most often were if you were a reporter—you weren't allowed to indicate these things. Alongside of the most amazing columns of crimes—robberies, adulteries, political trickeries, social badgerings on the part of one and another, a whole newspaperful nearly—would be the most amazing other columns of sweet tales about love undying and sacrificial, editorials about the perfection of the American man, woman, child, his or her home, their sweet deeds, intentions and the like—a wonderful dose. And all this last in the face of the other which was supposed to represent the false state of things—those news columns. They were merely passing indecencies, accidental errors that didn't count. In the main, as usual, all mankind was honest, kind and true—all women as pure as driven snow. If a man like young Hazard or myself had ventured at that time to transpose a true picture of facts from the news columns of the papers, from our own reportorial experiences, into a story or novel—what a howl. What scoundrels we would have been. Ostracism would have followed much quicker in that day than it does in this—for today turgid slush that approximates some facts at least is tolerated. But then—a true picture! Never. It couldn't be done, and Hazard, having a book in hand, really didn't seriously think of it. Years later—all of fifteen—he told me he still had it buried in a trunk somewhere, but by then he had turned to adventure fiction. And the next year he committed suicide, without much reason apparently—blowing his brains out.

But what a marked impression his novel made on me! It gave me a great respect for Hazard—made me seriously fond of him. And in addition it fixed my mind definitely on this matter of writing, not a novel, curiously—I did not think myself capable of that—but a play, a form which from the first seemed easier for me and which I still consider so, one that I work in with great ease as compared to the novel.

Nothing came of my ambition, however, at once, save this. It was a thought, an impressive one. And I mentioned to Wood and McCord that Hazard in conjunction with some newspaperman had written a novel and that he had allowed me to read it. I must have enthused over it for both were impressed, and in addition I seemed to gain standing, especially with Wood. Hazard was an important man on the paper—one of the best reporters in the city, it was generally admitted. To be admitted to his confidence in this way seemed to be a significant thing to Wood, who knew him but slightly and, I think, rather admired him.

In addition I had another thing to tell which seemed of considerable importance to them—McCord at least, who seemed to know something of the conditions surrounding the situation. There was a column on the editorial page of the paper entitled "Heard in the Corridors," which was nothing more than a series of imaginary interviews with passing guests at the various hotels, which were supposed to result in a series of tales. These when condensed daily made about six tales (the length was fixed by the management), one at least credited to a guest at each one of the three principal hotels, the others scattered among these and the remaining hotels, private homes, or the Union Station. Previous to my coming here this column had been written by a man who subsequently became very famous as the editor of a brilliant radical paper published at Waco, Texas—W. C. Brann, no less, the editor of the *Iconoclast*. By the time I arrived, however, Brann had departed. The column, so I was told by Hartung at the time it was turned over to me, had sagged. Hazard was doing a part of it, Bellairs another, still others others—but they were tired of it, apparently, and were not doing very well. It was suggested—by the front office, I presume, since it was this sort of work that had first attracted the editor's attention to me—that the column be turned over to me to fill.

At first, when I considered it—a little *extra* thrown in on top of my daily reporting—it seemed an impossible thing to do, but after a trial I discovered that it gave free rein to my wildest imaginings, which was exactly what I desired. One could write any sort of story one pleased,—romantic, realistic or wild—and credit it to some imaginary guest at one of the hotels, and if it wasn't too improbable it went through without comment. It was not specifically stated by the management that the interviews could be imaginary—the management gave me no instructions direct save one, and that via Tobias Mitchell, Esq., who said to me one Sunday evening, "You've read our column 'Heard in the Corridors'?"

"Yes, sir."

"See if you can't get me a few stories for that tonight."

"Yes, sir."

After that a hurried re-examination of the column in question, and then Hartung slipped in.

"Don't let that worry you very much. You did that sort of stuff before you came down here, didn't you—about the World's Fair?"

"Yes."

"I thought so. I edited it. Just any good story you can remember will do. Bob never tried to get actual interviews except once in a while. Of course, if you come across anybody it would be a good thing to interview 'em." His voice was so low I could scarcely hear him.

I went forth to the hotels to get names—personages stopping at the hotels. I inquired for celebrities. The clerks could give me no information concerning such or were indifferent. They seemed to take very little interest in having the hotels advertised. I returned and racked my brains, scribbled six marvels forthwith and attached fictitious names. The next day they were published and nothing said. That same day I was informed that I should do the column regularly plus my regular assignments—such and such an assignment, so the book ran, "and Heard in the Corridors."

I was lost. My efficiency had won me a new task, without any increase in pay.

However, it seemed an honor to me at that time—quite an honor to have the whole column assigned to me, and this *honor* I communicated to McCord and Wood, which, as I say, impressed them greatly. (It was McCord or Wood who informed me that Brann had done it—and written snake stories for the paper. Peter had illustrated them. He was "official snake artist" as he said.) That very night I was invited by Dick to come with Peter around to his room—*the* room, the studio.

I would not make so much of this *honor* at this time if it were not for what it meant to me then. I was so green in all that related to artists and studios. It was a large dark room, centered directly in the business heart on Broadway between Market and Walnut, one flight up—with the cars jangling below. It had a great white bed in it, a long table covered with the papers and literary compositions of Mr. Richard Wood no less, and was decorated and re-enforced with that gentleman's conception of what constituted literary insignia. On the walls were dusty engravings representing the death of Hamlet and the temptings of Mephistopheles. In one corner, over a chest of drawers, was the jagged blade of a swordfish, and in another a most curious display of oriental coins. The top of the wardrobe was surmounted by a gruesome-shaped head of papier-mâché representing some half-demented creature, commonly known in England as Ally Sloper. A clear space, at one corner of the table, held a tin pail for carrying beer in, and the floor, like the walls, was covered with some dusty brown material which once might have been a clean carpet, but which was now faded from all semblance of anything new. Owing to the darkness of the furnishings and the brightness of the fire, together with the cleanness of the bed, the room had a very cheery aspect, and I was delighted to be invited into it.

"Say, Dick, did you notice where one of————'s plays has made a great hit in New York?" inquired McCord. "He's made a big strike with this one."

"No, I didn't," replied Dick solemnly, at the same time poking among the coals of the grate and drawing up a chair. "Sit down, Dreiser. Pull up a chair, Peter. This confounded grate smokes whenever the wind's in the south. Still, there's nothin' like a grate fire to me."

We took him at his bidding and drew up chairs. I was revolving in my mind the subtle charm of the room and a vision of greatness in playwriting. These two men seemed subtly involved with the perfection of the arts. They were of it. In the atmosphere of such a room, with such companionship, I felt that I could accomplish anything, and soon.

"I'll tell you how it is with that game of playwriting," observed Dick sententiously, keeping the flow of conversation to himself. "You got to have imagination and feeling and all that, but what's more important than anything of that kind is a little business sense, to know how to get in with them fellers." (Dick was heavily inclined to slang and what in our parlance was known as *rube* or country-joke pronunciation. We all considered it amusing—witty.) "You might have the finest play in the world in your pocket, but if you didn't know just how to dispose of it—the ropes—you understand, w'y what good would it do you? None at all. You got to know that end first."

He reached over and secured the coal scuttle, pulling it into position as a footrest, and looked introspectively at the ceiling.

"The play's the thing," put in Peter, before he was quite through. "If you could write a real good play, you wouldn't need to worry about getting it staged."

"Ah, wouldn't I? Ah, listen to that now," Dick replied, irascibly. "I tell you, you don't know anything about it." (He straightened up.) "Say, now, did Campbell have a good play in his pocket? Did he? Ah, yah betcher neck he did!" (This latter quite fiery.) "And did he get it staged? No, you betcher boots he didn't!" (This last most emphatically stated.) "Don't talk to me. I know."

You would have thought by his manner that he had a standing

bone to pick with Peter, but this was only his way. I could see this. It made me laugh.

"Well, the play's the first thing to worry about, anyhow," I observed. "I wish I were in a position to write one."

"Why don't you try your hand at it?" suggested McCord. "You ought to be able to do something in that line. I'll bet you could write a good one." He stared at me approvingly.

We fell to discussing dramatists now. Peter, with his usual eye for gorgeous effects, costuming, and the like, immediately began to describe the ballet effects and scenery of a comic opera laid in Algeria which was then playing in St. Louis.

"You ought to go and see that, Dreiser," he urged. "It's wonderful. The effect of those balconies in the first act, with the muezzins crying the prayers from the towers in the distance is great. Then the harmony of the color work in the stones of the buildings is something exquisite. You want to see that."

I felt myself growing. This intimacy of conversation with men of such marked artistic ability in a room which was the reflection of an artist's personality raised my sense of latent ability to the highest point. Not that I felt that I was not fit to associate with these people; I felt that I was more than fit, their equal at the very least, mentally and every other way. But it was something to come in touch with your own, to find real friends, to the manner born, who were your equals and able to sympathize with you and appreciate you in your every mood. These were men to know—to cultivate and cherish. A man who found such friends as these need never worry.

"I tell you what I propose to do, Peter, while you people are talking," observed Dick, who had but now been gazing at the ceiling. "I propose to go over to Frank's and get a can of beer. Then I'll read you that story."

This suggestion of a story was something new to me. I had not heard of Wood as a storywriter before. I looked at him more keenly. A little flame of envy leaped up in my soul. To be able to write a short story—or any kind of a story! That was a long way along the road which led to that fairyland of which I was beginning to dream.

Wood got up in his quick wiry way and went to his wardrobe, from whence he extracted a medium-length black cape of broadcloth which he threw around his shoulders, and a soft felt hat which he drew over his eyes, took his tin pail and a piece of money from a plate, after the best fashion of the artistic romances of the day, and went out. I looked admiringly after him, touched by the romance of his figure. Such a face—drawn, waxen, sensitive, with deep burning eyes, and such a frail body. That cape! that hat! that plate of coins! He looked the artist, and yet he was so free and easy. This was Bohemia! This was that middle world which was better than wealth and more heavenly than simple poverty. It was the serene realm in which moved freely talent, artistic ability, noble thought, ingenious action, and, coupled with them, absolute freedom of thought and conduct! These people could do as they pleased! No one knew them, the great city was not aware of their existence!

I talked of the character of the room and the character of its occupant in a roundabout way to Peter until the former returned, when the charm of the original circle was restored. Wood then poured out the beer. Incisively he noted some of the leading traits of the German who sold his beer.

"Get your story now, Dick," said Peter, finally and with an air of authority. "I know you're dying to read it. You don't know him yet, Dreiser, but you will. He's an awful poseur! Awful! You'll get on to that after a while"—to all of which Wood paid not the slightest attention unless perhaps to cast an amused and condescending smile in our direction. Then he picked up his story from what I now observed to be a mass of them scattered idly in disarray in a heap.

"I don't want to inflict it on you, Dreiser," he said sweetly and apologetically to me. "We had planned to do this before you came around."

"That's the way he always talks," put in Peter badgeringly. "Dick loves to stage things."

"Oh, it isn't an infliction. I'll be glad to hear it," I said.

And then opening it and drawing up his chair to the table and adjusting a green-shaded table gas lamp (a commonplace figure of a swashbuckling nobleman, holding up his right arm to support the light) close to the table's edge, he began to read. He read, I noted, in a low, well-modulated, semi-pathetic voice, which appealed very effectively in the more sentimental passages. Reverently I sat and listened. This was Bohemia, beyond question. This was one of the realms I had dreamed of. I could be happy here with these people. I was positive of it.

CHAPTER XXV

From now on my life in St. Louis took on a much more cheerful aspect. Hitherto, in spite of the work I had to do and the natural interest of a wholly strange city (for me at least), it had had its intensely gloomy moments. All things considered, I could be as morbid at times as any human being, I think. By opposing my actual condition to what might be, my desires or dreams to my actual possessions, I could always manage to be as unhappy as any and to look on the darkest side of things. One of my favorite pastimes when I was not busy or when I was out on some assignment was to walk the streets and, viewing the lives and activities of others and their varying states, think how hard life was for some and how gay and flowery for others; how the lightning of chance was always striking in somewhere and disrupting somebody's plans, leaving destruction or death in its wake. Occasionally I would vary this by returning to the lobby of one or other of the three principal hotels. My favorite was the Lindell because of a long line of great arm rocking chairs which extended from one end of the lobby to the other. Here I could sit and rock in peace and watch the crowd of strangers—drummers, country men, politicians and the like—amble to and fro or hurry off, and think of my own lone state—my lack of friends, a girl. The manager of this hotel, as I recall, was a brisk, rather interesting American, who seeing me sit about every afternoon between four-thirty or five and six, and knowing that I was from the *Globe*, finally began to greet me and occasionally to ask if I didn't want to go up to dinner. (I often wonder how lonely or forlorn I must have looked.) On Thanksgiving and Christmas afternoons, seeing me idle there (there was no news to compel me to work), he came over and asked me to be his guest, which I accepted, not knowing much what else to do. To make it seem like a real invitation apparently, he came after I was seated at the table assigned me and sat down with me a few minutes, talking about nothing in particular—hotel life et cetera—and then left, but returned once or twice during the meal to see how I was getting along. I remember feeling a little peculiar about it, but he was so charming and the hotel so brisk and crowded that I felt at home and welcome, and so I staid. I don't think he was interested in anything save that I was lonely and needed cheering up.

And naturally, being in the newspaper profession and in the department which dealt with the news of the day, the mere routine of my work provided ample proof of my suspicions that life was grim and sad, from one point of view anyhow. Now and again it would be a murder, now a suicide, now a failure or a defalcation which I was assigned to "cover." The same afternoon or the same day it would be an important wedding, a business or political banquet, a ball or something of that sort, which provided just the necessary contrast I needed to prove that life could be cruel to some, lavish in its attentions to others—if I really needed proof. Clad in an ordinary business suit and possibly—the weather compelling—a rain- or overcoat, or perchance with a mere umbrella, I would travel from one to another in the same afternoon or evening, looking first possibly into the face of some grisly horror or weariness or hunger or despair. Then I would hurry by a crosstown line, let us say, to some hall or residence of great import where, as I say, a banquet or a dance or a wedding or social function of some kind was being given or some person of affluence or position was speaking. Here, tolerated by the thinnest courtesy, I would be allowed to gather names of those present and make notes on silly speeches or the gifts heaped upon some sillier bride and groom, in a world whose attention seemed wholly riveted to pleasure and success.

The effrontery of life!—I was fond of thinking. Its coarse and vulgar distinctions! Mere money—so often unworthily inherited or made by such shabby methods—seemed, in this second Western city that I was examining, to throw such commonplace and even wretched souls into such glittering and condescending prominence. The indifferent characters of some of the men who were successful! Their crass ignorance and vanity! The airs of the new rich—and the old rich, for that matter! Their patronizing ways! The snobbery of parvenus in a land scarcely more than a hundred years old. These local pooh-bahs and high-and-mighties generally—what pangs they cost me. As one who was called upon to visit and question some of the *leading* families of the city as well as some of the most wretched, I was constantly impressed by the airs of the socially prominent, their craving for show and pleasure, their insane craving for personal mention, their hearty indifference to anything but money, plus a keen wish to seem to despise it and fame, and yet their marked indifference to anything which did not contribute to these. I remember going one evening to some imposing residence where a function was being held, of course—sent by my suave city editor to get a list of names—and of being met by an ostentatious butler who exclaimed most nobly, "My dear sir, who sent you here? The *Globe* knows we never give lists to newspapermen. We never allow reporters in," and stiffly shut the door on me. I reported as much to the city editor, who remarked, "Very well," and gave me something else to do. The next day, however, a list of names of guests at this function was published—and in this paper. I wondered at it and naturally made inquiry of Hartung, who exclaimed, "Oh, yes. That's right. The society editor must have turned that in beforehand. Tobe didn't know it probably. He often makes mistakes like that. These society women send in their lists beforehand and the society editor sends them up, and then they say they don't receive reporters."

Another time it was at the residence of the Catholic Archbishop of St. Louis, a very shrewd but ōld man whom, so it was rumored in newspaper circles, the local priests—an inner ring of them—were plotting to make appear infirm and weak-minded in order that a favorite of theirs might be made coadjutor and so themselves advantaged. (I am merely giving you inner newspaper gossip.) I was sent to inquire after the health of the Archbishop—to see him if possible and so ascertain by direct observation and question the state of his health. It seemed a legitimate enough inquiry to me, seeing that he was a high public dignitary, in a way obligated to the public. At the door of the archiepiscopal residence, however, I was met by a sleek dark soul who inquired what I wished and, learning, assured me that the Archbishop was too feeble to be seen.

"But that is exactly why I am here," I insisted. "The *Globe* wishes to inform the public of his exact condition—to testify to it. There appears to be a belief on the part of some that he is not as ill as is given out."

"What! You accuse us of concealing something in connection with the Archbishop! This is outrageous," and he quietly but firmly shut me out.

It seemed to me at the time that this was anything but fair, that the simple frank thing would have been to let me meet or look at the Archbishop. He was a public official, the state of whose health was of interest to thousands. But no—mere official control regulated that. Shortly afterward he was declared too feeble to perform his duties, and a coadjutor appointed. Whether any other newspaperman was permitted to see him, I do not recall.

Again, I was sent to a decidedly fashionable west end hotel once to interview a visiting governor who was being entertained there. He was, as we understood it, leaving the next day.

"My dear young fellow," a functionary connected with the entertainment committee charged me, "you cannot do anything of the sort. This is no time to be coming around for anything of this kind. You must see him some other time."

"But he is leaving tomorrow."

"I cannot help that. You cannot see him now."

"Well, how about taking him my card and asking him about tomorrow?"

"No, no, no. I cannot do anything of the sort. You cannot see him"—and once more I was shunted briskly forth. This was one of my commonest experiences wherever wealth, position or authority were concerned, nearly always to be snubbed or shut out firmly, until I began to think that the newspaper profession—the reporting end of it—was the roughest, most degrading, most disheartening of any—going about and begging for information which none seemed willing to give.

But the sharp contrasts of life! One state with another and my own as a third or middle one—how they weighed on me! I remember being called upon one evening to attend a great public ball of some kind—The Veiled Prophet's, possibly (I cannot recall)—given in the general selling room of the great stock exchange, following a huge autumnal parade of some kind, the purpose of which was to give the elite of the city an opportunity to pleasure themselves in this way. My presence there was due to a desire on the part of my city editor for a general view, or pen picture, which was to be used as an *introduction* or opening to the full story, which others would do piecemeal. So far along was I already in my reporting work. For this occasion I had to rent a dress suit, which cost the paper three dollars (I not owning one myself). And I remember being greatly impressed and disturbed beforehand, not only by my own appearance, never having previously worn a dress suit or owned one, but also by the estimate of myself in it which the various members of the staff would take on seeing me. And I was not wholly disappointed.

"Say, look at our friend the millionaire, will you?"

"Who is he, boys? I don't seem to remember him myself." This from Bellairs.

"Those pants come darned near being a fit. Hanged if they don't." This from Hazard who had already laid hold of the side lines of the trousers as I entered late in the evening.

Alas! alas! I couldn't make up my mind whether I was startlingly handsome or a howling freak fit to be exhibited.

But the thing which weighed on me most at the time was the picture of local luxury this ball presented, the assumed happiness I credited to all present, contrasted of course with my own ignoble state. It seemed wholly wonderful, gorgeous, the quintessence of luxury— indulged in by all-but-plethoric sybarites whereas I, I—et cetera, et cetera.

Just the same, after spending three hours there, bustling about and examining the flowers, the decorations, getting names, details of costumes, and drinking various drinks with various officiating floor masters whose sole duty it seemed was to look after "the press" so-called and see that they got all the details right, I had to return to the office and sit down and pour forth a glowing—I might as well say pyrotechnic, for that was what was really desired—account of just how beautiful it all was, how gorgeous: the women how perfect (sirens), their costumes how marvellous; or the men, how gracious and graceful (save the mark); and in addition how oriental or occidental or Arabic—I forget which—the decorations were (outdoing the Arabian Nights, of course, or the fabled splendors of the Khalifate). Who does not know this indiscriminate newspaper tosh, poured forth from one end of America to another for everything from a farmers' reunion or an I.O.O.F. Ladies' Day to an Astor or a Vanderbilt wedding? It makes little difference.

At any rate I did as I was told, or was doing so, my head whirring with all the nearly purely imaginary splendors of the occasion, when I was informed by my city editor (and he had a cold, urgent look when he said it) that when I was done I had better go out to such and such a number in south St. Louis where only an hour before, or less, apparently, a triple or quadruple murder had been committed. And I had "better hurry" and "cut it short" (referring to my "introduction"). And I was to go out on a street car, and if I couldn't get back in time that way, most cars ceasing to run save hourly after twelve or one, I was to get a carriage somewhere and drive back at breakneck speed in order to get it into the last edition of the paper anyhow. The great fear on all these occasions was that the rival paper—the *Republic*—might have it, whereas *we* wouldn't. It appeared that some other reporter, Bellairs I believe, had been sent out ahead of me, but I was to go and get *the color* or the principal details and once more write the "introduction" and possibly the principal phases of the story.

What a harum-scarum wild-eyed enthusiast I must have then seemed to my superiors to be thus regularly and quickly assigned to these principal but always flamboyant items!

But so it was. St. Louis, just at this time appeared to love turgid color—the daring, bizarre, rather loose and colorful style of newspaper description then in vogue there. And I, fortunately or unfortunately, seemed to have the power to write it. Just the same, my head full of what had appeared to me to be the most glorious luxury, pleasure and comfort—and my eyes full of pearls, diamonds, silks, satins, laces, nearly all white and glistening, as well as a world of flowers and light—I was now bustled out along the dark, shabby, lonely streets of south St. Louis to the humblest of humble cottages in the humblest of humble streets, where among little paintless shacks, with lean-tos at the back for kitchens, was one which contained this story.

And when I arrived, what a scene! An Irish policeman, silent and indifferent, was already at the small dark gate in the dark silent street, and another inside, just beyond the door, which stood partially open— while a few horrified people had gathered on the sidewalk beyond. A word of explanation and I was admitted. The mere word *Globe* was an open sesame. Once inside, a faint glow from a small smoky glass lamp illuminated the front room darkly, as well as one or two others which brought up the rear. It seemed, as I soon discovered, that some simple kindly Irish-American of about fifty-five, who had been working by the day hereabouts before, had recently been ill and out of his mind with brain fever; and on this night, only about an hour or so before, had arisen from his sickbed where he had been tossing in a fever, and, the others being asleep, had seized a flatiron from an ironing board left standing and, creeping into the front room where his wife and two little children slept in one bed, had brained all three of them with it, and then returning to the rear room where his daughter slept on a couch beside him, had first felled her in the same way and then subsequently cut her throat with a butcher knife! Murderous as the deed seemed and possibly premeditated—due to a quarrel, maybe—it was still apparently not so. The policeman who stood at the gate informed me of as much when I came and also that the father had already been taken to the Four Courts and that a hospital ambulance (of all things—all being dead) was due any minute now.

"He's out av his mind," he insisted blandly. "I'm sure av it. He's crazy, sure, or sick av the fever. No man in his right sinses would do that. He's been workin' here for twenty year. I tried to taalk to him meself, but he couldn't say naathin'—jist mumble, 'twas all.' "

The wretched front room presented a sad and ghastly disarray in the dim smoky flame cast by the lamp—the cheap bed awry and stained red, the mother and two children lying in limp and painful disorder on it, the bedding dragged half off the bed. In the back room was the daughter—on the floor. Apparently a struggle had taken place. A chair and table were upset, the ironing board thrown down, a bureau pushed sidewise and the bed also. The rooms were so small that they were inconvenient and stuffy. And so dark. It appeared, as I say, that the father had been sleeping on the bed in this room while the daughter lay on a couch improvised as a bed. Poverty and paucity of ideas were written all over the place, and yet it was plain also that the place was clean, neat, and that order had prevailed. Both mother and daughter, lean and overworked as they were, were cleanly looking, and the two dead children were healthy enough—quite chubby.

Shocked beyond measure, yet with an eye to color only—knowing the zest of the public for picturesque details—I examined the three rooms with care, the officer in the house following me. Together we looked at the utensils in the kitchen, what was in the cupboard to eat, what was in a closet to wear. I made notes of various things—the contents of the rooms, their cheapness—asked all manner of questions, then went to the neighbors on either hand to learn if they had heard anything, which they had not, or knew anything, which they did—a little. Then in a stray owl car—no carriages being available—I hurried to the Four Courts, several miles cityward, to see and talk with the criminal if possible—to find out whether he really were crazy or no. As the officer had told me, he was old, pale, sick, thin, a man who to look at him would not be capable of planning such a crime. He was too decent looking—and so moving. Walking up and down in his small iron cell, he was plainly out of his mind, the picture of hopeless, unconscious misery. His hands trembled idly about his mouth. His shabby trousers bagged about his shoes. He was unshaven and weak-looking, and all the while he mumbled to himself some unintelligible sounds.

I tried to talk to him, of course, that being the first duty of a news-paper reporter, but could get nothing. He seemed not even to recognize that I was there, so brainsick was he. Then I questioned the jail attendants—those dull wiseacres of the law. Had he talked? Did they think he was sane? With the usual mental acumen and delicacy of this tribe, they were inclined to think he was shamming. You never can tell, they said. He looked desperate. Criminals, all, were so cunning any-how—such shrewd conniving dogs and swine. Personally, I couldn't believe them. He looked too old, too worn, too sick, too sad.

I hurried back through dark streets to the office. In a reportorial room—almost empty, save for Mitchell, Hartung and Hazard who, coming in late, had been dragooned to help if necessary—I scribbled my dolorous picture. And what writing! With the feverish impetuosity of youth and curiosity and sorrow and wonder, I told it all—the terror, the pity, the inexplicability. As I scribbled each page it was removed at once by Hartung, edited and sent up. Then having done a column or two or two and a half—I cannot recall (Bellairs had arrived with various police theories)—I was allowed finally to amble out into a dark street and seek that same dark, miserable little room with its small creaky bed, its dirty coverlets, its ragged carpet and stained walls, my evening's work done. And yet, believe it or no, I was not unhappy—quite the contrary. I recall that I was rather pleased with myself over my fine assignments and my industry—my two "introductions"—and the fact that I must be thought an exceptional man to be picked in this way for two such difficult tasks in the same evening. I stopped at a small all-night "beanery" so-called—a little cubbyhole of a stand stuck between two buildings in Pine Street—and feeling hopeful and even gay over my future, had two fried eggs and a cup of coffee in honor of the occasion. Yes, I was saying to myself at this time, I was some reporter—there was not doubt of that. I must be.

Then, as I say, I returned to that same dark dingy little room, in front of which the cars squeaked and ground all night—centering there from various streets—and stretching myself out to rest, thought of life and its accidents and tangles and miseries, illustrated by this terrible tragedy—as well as its gauds and glories, illustrated by the ball during the earlier hours. Those girls—how beautiful they were! Those rich young men! If I could only be as rich as one of them! If you will believe me, although I had cried in writing my last story and tingled with silly envy and enthusiasm and self-commiseration in writing my first, I now lay down with a kind of high pride and satisfaction over my lot. I was not so bad. I was getting along, by George. Certainly I was. And life wasn't so bad either, in the face of this. It was just higgledy-piggledy— catch-as-catch-can, that was all. If you were clever, like me, or lucky, it was all right. You might get a lot out of it. I might.

It was true the feverish crime of the old man was a terrible thing. It had blotted out four lives without rhyme or reason, but had it not given me a good story to do and showed once more that I was a good reporter—one of the best, I thought? And as for that ball—well, its magnificence and the beauty of its women were depressing to one who was eager to take part in the pleasures of life and hopelessly debarred by necessity, apparently, but hadn't I written a fine introduction? I had so, and no one could do it better—believe me. (I am quoting my youthful thoughts.) And so I went to sleep dreaming of a raise, perhaps, or eventual fame anyhow—or something. And the next morning I arose and I took my dress suit back and had a good breakfast the while I read my fine pictures, and the world seemed very good indeed. And then going to the office, and Hazard and some of the others who had read my stuff casually (not Peter, however) remarking that they thought it was "pretty good," I was beside myself with glee and strolled about as though I owned the earth, pretending simplicity and humbleness but actually believing that I was "the finest ever" and that no one could outdo me at this game of reporting—it did not matter who he was or where he came from. And for a day or two this served to make me feel that way, if you please. Of such strange contrasts are the joys and ills of this world compounded.

CHAPTER XXVI

But all this was a mere incident—a mere "bag of shells," as one of my cronies used to remark in regard to anything negligible. Things relatively interesting, contrasts nearly as sharp and as well calculated to cause me to pause and meditate on the wonder, the beauty, the uncertainty, the indifference, the cruelty and the rank favoritism of life were almost daily, if not hourly, put before me. Now and again, as I say, it was a murder, now a social scandal of some kind—often of a gross and even revolting kind in some ultra-respectable neighborhood—now a suicide of some peculiarly sad or grim character. Again it would be a fine piece of chicane, as when a certain "board-and-feed" stable owner of the west end, about to lose his property because of poor business and anxious to save himself by securing the insurance, set fire to it and destroyed seventeen healthy horses as well as one stable attendant who was burned to death. His plan had evidently been to save the horses and the man, but his plan miscarried. In interviewing him for the *Globe* I suspected as much and put some pertinent questions to him but could get no admissions or errors on which to base a charge. He was a shrewd, cold, commercial type, vigorous and semi-savage, who in another sphere might have made a good farmer. He evaded me most blandly and, finding myself baffled, I had to write it up as a sad accident, thus really aiding him to get his insurance, the while I was convinced that he was guilty—a hard-hearted, conniving scoundrel. It was so often this way with many cases in the newspaper world.

Another thing which began to come to me very clearly at this time was the fact that your average newspaper reporter was a far better detective in his way than your legitimate official detective, and not nearly so well paid—an infinitely higher type in every way. Your average so-called "headquarters man," as I now found here in St. Louis at least, was a loathsome thing—as low in the main in his ideas and methods as the lowest criminal he was set to trap—and duller, perhaps. Red-headed, freckled, with big hands and feet, store clothes, squeaky shoes—why does such a picture of an average detective come back to me? And yet it does. Popeyed, stary, with a ridiculous air of assumed mystery and profundity in matters requiring neither, dirty, offensive, fisheyed and merciless, he floundered about in difficult cases without a grain of humor. Whereas your average reporter was, by contrast anyhow, amazingly intelligent or shrewd, cleanly (nearly always) if at times a little slouchy, inclined to drink and sport perhaps (not always), but genial, often gentlemanly, a fascinating storyteller, a keen psychologist (nearly always one of the best), widely and frequently tastefully read, humorous, sympathetic, amusing or gloomy as the case might be, but generally able and to be relied on in emergencies for truly skillful work.

Naturally there was some enmity between the two: a contempt on the part of the newspaper man, a fear and dislike and frequently secret opposition on the part of the detective whenever the two chanced to come in contact, which was not often. Your average newspaper man could go forth on a mystifying case and, as a rule, in a short time, or given time enough, literally solve it; whereas the police detectives would tramp about, frequently trailing the reporters, reading the newspapers to discover what they had discovered and get some clue which, followed, might lead up to the grand moment of arrest, which was always the police officer's or detective's great moment. Again, these latter were constantly playing into the hands of newspaper reporters (police reporters as we called them) in unimportant matters during periods between great cases, doing them little favors, as they phrased it, helping them in small cases in order, when a great case came along, to get favors done unto them. Most important of all was it, of course, that their names should be in the papers as being engaged in solving the mystery or having done thus and so, whereas in all likelihood some newspaper man had really done it. I am not exaggerating this in the least.

Sometimes (nearly always) the "tip" as to where the criminal was likely to be found was furnished by the papers and latterly credited to the police—their excellent work! Sometimes the newspaper men would lash the police, sometimes flatter them; but always they (the newspaper men) were seeking to use them, you may depend on it, and in the main succeeding. At times the police would grow stubborn, recalcitrant, and defy the papers, but not for long. They loved publicity too much. In sum, your average newspaper reporter could be far more safely depended upon in any real emergency to ferret out a crime than the police or detectives, providing of course that your newspaper or papers would take a diligent interest in the matter and trouble to put really good reporters to the task. It was nearly always my experience in these opening days of my youthful journalistic work that the newspapers—which meant the reporters, of course, plus an efficient city editor and possibly a managing editor—would be the first to worm out the psychology of any given case and then point an almost unerring finger at the criminal. Then the police or detectives would come in and do the arresting and, as I said before, they were frequently given the credit, although as a matter of fact the reporters might know that they were dull and had failed utterly. Even then they were willing that this should be done in order that they might obtain favors in future cases—police aid in one way and another—favors that were never much of anything at that, the merest trifles of friendship.

Another thing that impressed me greatly at this time was this same kaleidoscopic character of newspaper work, which in my case, at least, its personal significance cannot be too much overemphasized. One day or one afternoon or evening, or for a series of days even, it would be many crimes or one crime of a lurid or sensational character, and the same day or hour perhaps it would be a lecturer or religionist with some finespun theory of life—some theosophist like Annie Besant, who in passing through St. Louis on a lecture tour would be at one of the best hotels of St. Louis, usually the Southern, and need to be interviewed. Or some mountebank or quack of a low order—a spiritualist, let us say, or mind reader or third-rate religionist like the Reverend Sam Jones who was then in his heydey, or the arrival of a prizefighter-actor like John L. Sullivan, then only recently defeated by Corbett, or a novelist of the quack order, such as Hall Caine.

Verily, these various individuals, including such excellent lecturers as Henry Watterson and Henry M. Stanley, or else a musician as excellent as Paderewski, or a scientist of the standing of Nikola Tesla, kept me busy, for, curiously enough, in odd moments, along with assignments to German or French social circles, I was sent to interview them, to get their views on something—anything or nothing really, for Tobias Mitchell seemed a little cloudy as to their significance, and I certainly had no clear insight into the matter as yet. One of my favorite thoughts, as I ambled forth to see one or the other of them, was to ask them what they thought of life—its meaning—since this was so much uppermost in my mind at this time, and I think I asked it of everyone from John L. Sullivan to Annie Besant.

And what a jangle of doctrines! What a noble burst of ideas! Annie Besant I recall in a cool silken grey dress, one January afternoon, in a room at the Southern delicately scented with flowers. She informed me that the age was material, that wealth and show were an illusion based on nothing at all (I wrote that down without understanding what she meant), that the Hindoo Swamis had long since solved it all—Madame Blavatsky being the most recent and greatest apostle of wisdom in this matter—and that the great thing to attain in this world or the next was Nirvana, a word which I had to look up in the dictionary afterwards, not knowing what it meant and not finding out during this interview. (When I told Dick Wood about her afterward, he seemed greatly impressed and said, "Oh, there's more to that than you think, Dreiser. You're not up on that stuff yet," and looked very wise. I am satisfied now, of course, that the great mystics see many things we do not even guess at—but I was not then.)

And then Henry Watterson. Imagine me at the age of twenty-one trying to interview him when he was in the heydey of his fame and mental powers. Short, stocky, protuberant as to stomach, slightly grey as to hair, he was accompanied by his rotund wife. He was gruff and simple in his manner and joyously secure in his fame and prime (he had just said the preceding summer that Cleveland, the Democratic candidate of the hour and later elected, was certain to "walk up an alley to a slaughter-house and an open grave"—and had seen his prediction fail, of course). He was convinced that the country was in bad hands, not likely to go to "the demnition bow-wows" but in for a bad corporation-materialistic spell. And when I asked him what he thought of life:

"My son, when you get as old as I am you probably won't think so much of it, and I won't blame you. It's good enough in its way, but it's a damned ticklish business, to say the least. You can say Henry Watterson said that if you want to. Do the best you can, and don't crowd the other fellow too hard, and you'll come out as well as anybody, I suppose." (I'm quoting from an old clipping.)

And then John L. Sullivan, raw, red-faced, big-fisted, broad-shouldered, drunken, with a waistcoat and tie pyrotechnic in the extreme, and rings and pins set with enormous diamonds and rubies— what an impression he made! Entirely surrounded by local "sports" and politicians of the most rubicund and material and even degraded char-acter (he was a great favorite with them), he seemed to me, sitting in his "suite" at the Lindell, to be the apotheosis of the humorously gross and vigorous and material—and he appealed to me accordingly, even at a glance. Cigar boxes, champagne buckets, decanters, beer bottles, overcoats, collars and shirts littered the floor of his suite, and he was lolling back in ease and splendor—a sort of prizefighting J. P. Morgan.

"Haw! haw! haw!" I can hear him even now after, having invaded his circle, I had asked my usual questions about life, his plans, the value of exercise (!), et cetera. "He wants to know about exercise! You're all right, young feller. Kinda slim, but you'll do. Sit down and have some champagne. Have a cigar. Give 'im some cigars, George. These young newspapermen are always all right to me. Exercise! What I think? Haw, haw! Write any damn thing yuh please, and say John L. Sullivan said so. I know it'll be all right. If they don't believe it, bring it back here an' I'll sign it, an' I won't stop to read it, neither. That suit ya? Well, all right. Now have some more champagne and don't say I didn't treat ya right, 'cause I did. I'm ex-champion of the world, defeated by that little dude from California, but I'm still John L. Sullivan—ain't that right? Haw! haw! They can't take that away from me, can they? Haw! haw! Have some more champagne, boy."

I adored him. I would have written anything he asked, and I got up the very best interview I could and published it, and I was told afterwards that it was fine.

One of the other things that was interesting me about this time in connection with newspaper work, in addition to its haphazard and kaleidoscopic character, was its pagan or unmoral character as contrasted with the heavy religionistic and moralistic point of view seemingly prevailing in the editorial office proper—the editorial page, I mean—as well as the world outside. While the front, or editorial, office might be writing the most flowery or moralistic or religionistic editorials regarding the worth of man and his progress, the glorious value of character, religion, morality, the sanctity of the home, charity and the like, the business office and news rooms were concerned with no such finespun theories, by any means. The former was all business, you may depend on it, with little or no thought of anything save success. And in regard to the city news room—if I may use a rough phrase—the mask was off and life was handled in a rough-and-ready manner, without gloves and in a catch-as-catch-can fashion, although it may not have been consciously handled in just this spirit. Many times we do things without knowing or seeing just how or why we do them. Get the news!—that was the cry in the city editorial room at least. Don't come back without it! Don't "fall down." Don't let the other newspapers "skin us"—that is, if you value your job. And write—and write well. If any other paper writes it better than you do, you're beaten anyhow and you might as well resign. No newspaper will tolerate a bad writer. It needs and will get fluent and agreeable ones if possible. The public must be entertained by the writing of reporters—as well as informed. Don't let finespun theories or delicacy of mood and the like defeat you in getting the news. Such were the tables of the law in St. Louis, when I was there at least.

But the methods and the effrontery and the callousness necessary at times in the getting the news were a great shock to me, even though I realized in a way that they were conditional with life itself. You had to be at most times so hard, cold, jesuitical—that is, if you secured any news. For instance, there was one problem that early troubled me and to which there was no solution save one—accept the working conditions as you found them or get out! You could not say when you went to a man or woman suspected of some misdeed or error that you came as an enemy or one bent on exposing him or her. That would have been the height of folly and would have lost you your news and your position into the bargain. You had, in the main, to approach as a friend, to pretend, perhaps, an interest or a sympathy you did not feel—to appear to be someone else even, or to lay the oil of flattery to the soul. To do less than this was to lose your news, and while a city editor might, even readily, forgive your trickery, he would never forgive your failure. Cheat and win, and you were all right. Be honest and lose, and you were fired. To appear wise when you were ignorant; dull when you were not; disinterested when you were interested; brutal or severe when as a matter of fact you might be quite the reverse—these as I rapidly discovered were the commonest and most essential tricks of the trade. You could scarcely get any news otherwise. "Be ye as wise as serpents—as gentle as doves." Jesus must have known something concerning the conditions surrounding newspaper reporters.

At the same time, being sent out every day—afternoon and evening—and loafing about the corridors of the various hotels at different times, I soon encountered other newspaper men who were as shrewd and wily as ferrets and who apparently had but one motive in life, and that was "to trim" (as the phrase went) their fellow newspapermen in the matter of news or the public that provided the news. There being only two morning papers here, the *Globe* and the *Republic,* and these suffering an intense rivalry, the reporters of each loved each other not—or if they were inclined to be friendly, as many of them were, they did not dare allow it to extend to their work. Meet a reporter of the *Republic* or the *Globe* "on a story"—he might be friendly enough or bantering, but he would tell you nothing. He wanted either to shun you or, if not that, worm your facts out of you, and was trying so to do all the while. Meeting in the lobby of the Laclede, where by common consent in the wintertime most seemed to gather, or in spring, summer and fall at the corner drugstore outside, each would be friendly with the other, trading tales of life, accompanying each other to a saloon for a drink or to "the Beanery" (a famous eating place between Fourth and Broadway on Chestnut) for a bite of something to eat, or perchance borrowing a dime, a quarter or a dollar "until pay day"—but no news "tips" were exchanged. Never. Many of them borrowed from me small amounts and seemingly became my intimates, but they had no use for me on a story.

The counsel of all of these men as I soon found was to get the news in any way that you could, by hook or by crook, and don't be long in theorizing about it. If a document was lying on an official's table, for instance, and you wanted to see it and he would not give it to you—if he turned his back, take it, or at least read it. If a picture of somebody was desired and they would not give it, and you saw it somewhere—take it, of course, and let them complain afterwards if they would. Your city editor was supposed to protect you in such matters. Any sensible fair-minded city editor would. If anybody who by all the conditions of the situation should be so foolish as to talk, and you knew that by his or her talking they would bring real harm to themselves, and in addition if you knew that they did not know how serious their words were to them—or to some one they might hold dear and desire to protect— still it was your duty to "pump" them, let the lightning of publicity blast them ever so heavily afterwards. You might know, for instance, of certain conditions of which a public official was not aware and the knowledge of which would have caused him to talk in one way, whereas lack of that knowledge would cause him to speak in another. Privately you might think it your duty to tell him, but certainly not as a news- paper man if you valued your place or the news. It was your duty to your paper and the news to sacrifice him. If you didn't, some one else would. Hence you first secured a statement from him, then contrasted it in the paper with the facts which he did not have, thus making "a mark" of him in the best sense of that phrase. I was not long in learning all this, and while in a way I appreciated its necessity, still I resented having to do it. I told myself at times that I would not, that I was better in this respect than other newspapermen, but when the test came I found I was as vulnerable as the others, as eager to get the news. Something akin to a dog's lust of the chase would in critical moments seize upon me, and in my eagerness to win a newspaper battle I would forget or ignore nearly every tenet of fairness and get it. Then, victorious, I might sigh over the sadness of it and decide that I was going to get out of the business—as I eventually did, and for very much this reason—but at the time I was weak or practical enough.

A case of this kind happened to me the first six weeks I was in the city. I was sent to interview the Democratic candidate for mayor—an amiable soul who conducted a wholesale harness business and who was supposed to have an excellent chance of being elected. When I entered his place to question him about something—I forget what—he was in the front part of the store discussing with several friends or politicians the character of St. Louis, its political and social backwardness, its narrowness, slowness and the like; and for some reason—the personality of his friends possibly—he was very severe. Local religionists among others came in for a good drubbing.

For some unexplainable reason I assumed at once that the man talking (I did not know him) was the candidate for mayor. Again I instinctively knew that what he was saying, if published, would create a sensation if credited to him. Again I knew that he was not talking for publication—and certainly would not talk so to me. The lust of a hunter stalking a wild animal immediately descended on me. What a beat to take down what this man was saying! What a stir it would make. Without appearing to want anything in particular, I stood by a case and examined the items of harness within. Presently he finished his tirade and coming over to me said, "Well, sir?"

"I'm from the *Globe*," I said. "I want to ask you—" and then I asked whatever question it was.

On hearing that I was from the *Globe* he became visibly excited. "Did you hear what I was talking about just now?" he asked.

"Yes, sir."

"Well, you know I was not speaking for publication."

"I know."

"And you're not to report that."

"I understand you."

What else happened I can't recall. Just the same I returned to the office and wrote up the incident just as it occurred. My city editor took it, glanced over it and departed for the front office. I could tell by his manner that he was excited. The next day it was published in all its cruel reality, and the man was ruined politically. There were furious denials in the rival Democratic papers. A lying reporter was denounced, not only by Mr. Bannerman, the candidate, but by all the other papers editorially. At once I was called to the front office to explain to Mr. McCullagh in person. I did so with the greatest frankness. I repeated just what I had heard—what he had said. "He said it all, did he?" he inquired, and I insisted that he had. "I know it's true," he said, "for other people have told me that he has said the same things before."

The next day there was a defiant editorial in the *Globe* defending me—my truthfulness—asserting that the truth of the interview was substantiated by previous words and deeds of the candidate. Various editors on the paper came forward to congratulate me, to tell me what a beat I had made; but to tell the truth I felt queer, shamefaced, dishonest, unkind. The man had not given me any such interview. To be sure I had stated the circumstances quite frankly, but still it seemed an unfair thing to do, and to this day it does still. I was an eavesdropper. I had taken an unfair advantage and in something which made no real difference to me. I benefitted by it not at all, or only very slightly. But I killed that man politically as certainly as ever a man was killed. Youth, zest, life, the love of the chase—that is all that explains it to me now. What sort of a boy was it that could gaily do such things at twenty-one—and then regret them afterwards?

CHAPTER XXVII

The room I had taken in Pine Street was retained only long enough for me to see that I was likely to retain my position and possibly do better in the future, when, conscious of its lacks, I decided to get something better. It was costing me two dollars and fifty cents the week, and I decided that now I could pay as high as four dollars if necessary, wishing so much, as I did, to be in a more congenial atmosphere. I hadn't very much time to search, liking to sleep later after my late hours and seeming to have no time afternoons and evenings. But in reporting in various parts of the city, I had seen several neighborhoods that I liked and, recalling one, about twenty minutes out in the Choteau Avenue district, which had seemed to me charming, decided to look there. It was the quondam abode of the well-to-do but was now decayed and full of old, red, square, brick houses, evidently the former homes of families of some means. Here and there these were occupied by people who let rooms.

I went out one morning and examined into this, finding finally a large, square, front room, with a porch outside, some leafless trees in the yard, and a sense of cleanliness and comfort which seemed to suit me exactly. It was charming—old, sad, reminiscent. It seemed slightly mysterious and romantic—a place about which to write a story. The house mistress was a short, stout, unromantic and comely creature, of no particular brains, and perhaps thirty-eight or forty years of age, with black hair and eyes and an olive skin,—very brisk and talkative. Shortly after I had taken it at three dollars and fifty cents the week, this woman began to shower me with attentions of the most personal and, to me at the time, unsatisfactory character. As eager as I was for love, my mind was packed with very different, relatively far more romantic, dreams and elegancies, and to have this more or less commonplace soul thrust upon me was a little too much.

Unfortunately for me also, she was not easily put in her place. To my surprise, after I had been there a few days she began to show me marked attentions, invading my room at odd moments with scarcely a knock or call, with towels, soap, the morning paper, coffee and rolls. She looked after me in my bath and seemed to wish to start a conversation there, telling me about her husband and son, the former a consumptive and of no use to her, as she said, the latter working out somewhere and seldom coming home. She seemed to wish to annex me in some capacity, affectional I feared, and I disliked her greatly.

I was overwhelmed. Somehow, although she was by no means objectionable to look at, there was still something about her that I did not like. She seemed to me to be the least bit untidy or unclean, her hair being frequently awry and her dress and apron soiled or mussy. Also at the very first I gathered in some indefinite way that she was disturbingly and aggressively sensuous. Even as I was lying in bed of a morning she would invade my room after a slight tap, inquiring after my health and wanting to know if I wouldn't let her bring me rolls and coffee now—that she would love to wait on me; and then she would proceed to straighten my pillows and coverlet and sit down beside me and talk to me, laying at times what I thought was a bold if not sacrilegious hand on my arm or side. This was a little too much, I thought, and I think I blushed like a girl.

As a matter of fact I was greatly shocked. Aside from the few girls I had known in the past, all young and pretty, I was totally inexperienced in this middle-aged art of love. It sickened me slightly, and one evening, having previously looked up another place, I quietly packed my belongings and slipped out unseen, leaving the lady surprised, no doubt, but not any the worse for any rent.

My next experiment was of a somewhat more pretentious character, but so much better at that, all things considered. By now having seen the wonder of Dick's studio and the kind of life he and McCord led,—very wonderful to me, as I thought—I was all for a studio existence, a life of much this same bohemian character. I wanted a studio such as his was, only, if possible, in a more bizarre neighborhood. His was on Broadway, in the heart of what might have been looked upon at the time as the theatrical and restaurant district—a very limited affair at best. I wanted a room, if possible, in a more picturesque, bizarre or broken-down neighborhood where an artist, such as I was beginning to feel myself to be, might appear strange, remarkable. I went, first, to look at the riverfront—that long stretch of levee which faces the Mississippi at the business heart—but finding it too dark at night and too disreputable by day, a most neglected region albeit with a striking view, I decided to content myself with a much more sober, if wholly unconventional, neighborhood.

It was at 10th and Walnut, the room I finally selected, where in a region of stables, odd stores and nondescript loft buildings of a very small size—one, two and three stories at best—I found over a tinsmith's shop just the room of my mood. It was odd, queer-looking, without and within. A large, rusty tin coffee pot of enormous size, a coffee pot so large that it might have boiled coffee for a hundred people, swung out in front overhead. By day various drainpipes, guttering, sheets of tin and zinc ornamented the sidewalk, but at night this vicinity was clean and deserted and still. A Bohemian peasant woman of perhaps thirty-one or two, a very attractive creature for her years and birth as I found (a widow with two children), occupied the top floor of this three-story building, which consisted of three rooms, and sublet the lower, which consisted of two. The room I saw and desired was the front one on the second floor, for it was large, high-ceilinged, the walls fortunately painted a light brown, the floor a dark one. It contained four windows, two front and two on one side, a large closet and a bath at the rear, which I rarely used, preferring to patronize those of the larger barbershops in the business heart, which seemed to cater to this form of public need—many of them in a most pretentious manner. There was, in addition, a fireplace that filled the room with cheer and warmth by the judicious use of little soft coal, which the house mistress seemed perfectly willing to provide (all for the modest sum of three dollars a week). It was fast drawing near to early spring, however, in St. Louis, and I required but very little fire.

Here, again, once I was properly installed, I rapidly became a favorite—why, I cannot say, for I never, to myself at least, seemed to have the least charm. Always the contrary. Whether it was due by now to the fact that I was beginning to array myself in rather garish clothes—having recently purchased a heavy grey winter suit of a very pronounced pattern, shirts of somewhat the hues I saw Dick wearing, and a hat and shoes of styles I thought most becoming to me—I cannot say, but certain it is that from the very first of my stay here, Mrs. Zernouse (or some such outlandish name) was plainly attracted to me and anxious to do me any little intimate favors that she might. It was not a week—or two at the most—before she learned that I was never likely to arrive home before midnight or be in my room after twelve noon. In consequence I was never suffered to be annoyed by overhead noises before that hour in the morning, and when I arrived at twelve at night or a little later, there was always a newly trimmed fire, a pitcher of fresh drinking water, sometimes a bit of pastry she had made. One of the things that attracted me to her from the first—as a housekeeper, of course—was that she was scrupulously clean, immaculately so. My floor had no carpet but was well painted, and she washed it twice a week. The windows facing a sometimes dusty street were always bright, the bed linen perfect. I had a sense of being looked after.

And so here again, in something less than a month, I began to note that I was the object of affectional attentions, only in this case the woman was far more attractive to me—in no wise really so objectionable as the other. She was rather large, quite buxom in fact, but well formed and decidedly well featured, possessing the strong, even features of the young European peasant—or at least workingman's wife—type. She had startlingly clear and bright black eyes and plenty of hair. There was something really clean and interesting about her. Far from being educated in the American sense, she still had a shrewd peasant's wit and intelligence which amused me. By degrees she began to drop in of a morning just before I was leaving, or I would find her on the stairs as I went out. Or when I called to pay my rent or to get something—a towel possibly or more coal—she would do her best to detain me and maneuver me into a conversation with her. Soon I knew considerable of her history, where she had come from in Bohemia, how her husband had been killed in some factory, the fact that she was struggling to give her two little children an education, American style. It was not long before she frankly confessed that she was going to get married again one of these days, but only for the sake of the children.

"I have chances enough," she added, "but it is not so easy to find the right one. I am good looking—I know that—but I am not a silly girl any more, you see. I want a good home now."

Mrs. Zernouse never planned to annex me for that purpose, I am satisfied, but she may have been filled with a kind of wonder and curiosity at the manner in which I lived. I had done considerable to try to brighten up this dull room and give it what I considered an artistic tone, and she was anxious for a passing flirtation with a young man such as me. From somewhere—some sale to which Peter had called my attention—I had by now secured four pieces of faded tapestry cloth of a rather grotesque character and draped the windows therewith, taking down the cheap lace curtains that had brightened them before. From an old print shop I secured a few prints, very wonderful to me then— Chinese, Japanese and Hindoo—largely because of what I had heard Peter say anent these things, and at once considered myself a connoisseur in such matters! A shelf which I had a carpenter install to one side of the fireplace I loaded with a few books representative of my then supposed superior (!) taste—*Ben-Hur, The Fair God, Ernest Maltravers, The Sketch Book, The Chronicles of Spain, Dombey and Son*—things that I had picked up for a few pennies at the various old-book stores around town, an execrable collection. I even went in for statuary, finding a plaster nude of some kind somewhere—a bathing Venus, I presume— and putting it on the mantelpiece, soon aroused the keen interest of Mrs. Zernouse thereby, who saw in this a very fair vehicle for banter and of approach. It was a nude—therefore, in her mind at least, a thing to be concealed and to be more or less ashamed of. To me, on the other hand, it was an object of more or less lascivious delight—fascinating. I had never owned one before. I was getting along, artistically. When she referred to it gaily, with the desire to arouse my male emotions, no doubt, I was more or less confused. I hardly knew what to say. I would have liked to have had it appear that I was a man of the world, used to all these little details of sex and the nude in art, and a connoisseur of art into the bargain, as well as one to whom sex was an old story and an easy matter. And yet I was half inclined to take advantage of it and make love to her, as I thought she wished. Only I was a little afraid she might resent me, so I did nothing much for the time being—took her by the arms once or twice when she teased me. But the statue spelled little but sex charm to either of us, and as for being a man of the world, I had no more courage for an affair than a mouse—if as much.

Just the same, the appearance of the room (after a time), my odd hours, the fact that there were soon late sessions here with Dick and Peter, as well as Hazard, Bellairs, myself and several newfound acquaintances, and empty beer bottles and bits of cheese and sandwiches and cigarettes and cigar stubs left on the floor the following morning, seemed to confirm Mrs. Zernouse in her feeling that I was a person of some daring or interest—a dull suspicion—and she redoubled her attentions. After cleaning up after us the following day (she soon made it a point to come in to clean just as I was about to leave), she affected to believe that I was a very bad young man—in the charming, attractive sense—one who was a very devil among the women and who would stop little short of nothing in his efforts to satisfy his pagan desires if he was interested. Oh, she knew, she would exclaim gaily. She could tell. Didn't I ever bring any of the wonderful girls that I must know up here? If she were a man, she would. She heard me. Yes, she did! What was all that laughing and singing again last night? A girl or two with us, she warranted. Oh, these young men! these young men! Still when one was young and happy and well-to-do, one couldn't blame one for having a good time and sowing a few wild oats. My male friends must be important also in that way, real devils, roysterers like myself!

And then she would dust the nude or hold it aloft and look at it, and smile a wise smile, as who should say, "Ah, these wild reckless boys and their girls." Actually she made me feel at times as though I might and should, in truth, achieve the most wonderful liaisons, and here, in this very room—that I was foolish for not doing it.

What brought this rather naive flirtation to a point of decision was an entirely different matter. One evening Dick Wood and myself were sent upon an assignment which required both an artist and a reporter, some religious meeting, which, if I recall aright, was of the Sam Jones variety. The words of some pyrotechnic speaker had to be taken down—his mannerisms illustrated. This was in a church at 18th and Pine. On our way out of the church after the services, we encountered two girls of a rather attractive type who smiled at us and seemed to wish to indulge in a flirtation. One of them, a plump roguish creature of perhaps nineteen or twenty, took my fancy at once and to such an extent that she set me quivering inwardly with nervous excitement. The other, a somewhat thinner, older person, did not appeal to me in the least, but that did not bother me—I was eager to attain to my choice. More adroit than myself apparently in these matters, Wood had already smiled back and then turned towards where they seemed to be lingering in the foyer before ever I had made up my mind what to do. I followed, of course, and, screwing up my courage to the sticking point and resolving to do or die, began a vigorous if ridiculous conversation, which resulted in our leaving arm in arm, while Dick, perforce I suppose, was compelled to accept the other. Fortunately for me, as it turned out, the girl I had selected seemed interested or rather pleased with me. She allowed me to take hold of her hand and laughingly accompanied me up the poorly lighted street, toward the *Globe* office. En route we discussed the meeting and why I was there and why she was there. Nearing 10th Street where my room was, I finally boasted that I had a studio and wanted to know (it was a most daring, throat-choking venture for me, as I can tell you) whether she didn't want to come up and see it. There was a parley on the corner of Pine and 10th. Laughingly she exclaimed, "Oh, no, I couldn't do that," but something in her manner seemed to indicate that she could and would, if I pressed her. This I did. She then walked with me to the room door and laughed at the huge coffee pot swinging aloft, but she would not go in with me. She could not, she said. She had never done that sort of thing before, et cetera, et cetera. Finally she added:

"You don't understand how it is. I have to be home by eleven tonight, sure. I live with my family, and they know where I went. If you'll be good though and let me go now, I promise you faithfully that I'll meet you any night you say. Truly I will. Any night after Thursday. As sure as I'm standing here. I know you won't believe that, but I will."

My countenance as well as my spirits fell at this, for had I not done wonders in achieving as much as I had—and now to lose her in this fashion! I knew that I had done more than I had really ever done before in my life in a flirting way in having done this. And now to be turned down! It was terrible, the cruelest blow that could possibly be inflicted on an eager, seeking youth such as I was!

She must have noticed it, for she took my hands and said, "Truly I will. Honest! You don't believe it, I know, but I will. Won't you believe me? I've told you why I can't go tonight, and that's true, but if you say any day after Thursday" (it was Tuesday then), "I'll come."

I was finally compelled to accept her terms, and we separated after I had accompanied her to a car and after I had convinced myself that it was all over and that I should never see her anymore. She was too nice—too clever for me. That was the trouble. She really did not like me. Worse yet, she had not given me her address and would not, but had agreed to meet me the following Friday evening at one of the entrances to the local post office building—a grey affair in Olive Street—and to stay all night with me if I wished, which I did very much. I didn't believe it—she was so very attractive—and I went back to the office feeling as usual that I was a failure, of no least interest to women.

The next Friday, however, more out of curiosity or a very thin hope rather than anything else, I went to see. To my utter astonishment there she was at the appointed place and hour, waiting. I had explained before that owing to my late working hours it would have to be a late meeting, and this had not seemed to trouble her. Nor did it, apparently. Now she took me by the arm, said she knew she oughtn't do this, that she was a bad girl, and that if her parents knew, there would be the deuce to pay—and walked with me to the room. En route my heart was fairly jumping with combined delight and fright. Owing to her ruddy health and buxom proportions and pretty face, I was really immediately terrified by my old fear that I would not be equal to the occasion, that I was all but sexless(!), having lost my virility years before, of course, by my "youthful errors and excesses"—so the advertisements ran. In a more or less trembling state (by all the virtues of Allah, I am not exaggerating one whit), I accompanied her up the stairs, unlocked the door and let her in, and then in a foolish way, I suppose, did my best to amuse her and make myself agreeable until the moment for our mutual agreement should arrive. To make the occasion more pleasing if possible, for her anyhow, I had previously brought in beer and wine—a few bottles of the former—and some sandwiches, but she refused my humble hospitality when I offered it, which seemed to me forthwith a bad sign. So, she didn't think much of my place. But, on the other hand, she seemed to like to sit and look at the fire, and she amusedly announced that she did like the room.

Eager and fearsome—feeling at one and the same time, if you please, that my hour of triumph as a masterful, maiden-controlling male, and my shameful and horrible exposure as a sex failure was at hand—I took her in my arms and gradually persuaded her to undress. It was a delicious contest, made all the more so by a real or assumed bashfulness, take your choice, which made her contest every point and wish "to wait," and plead please not to "do that" or to "leave that on." Finally it was accomplished,—all but the removal of one small tight-fitting slip, and to the removal of this she absolutely refused to consent, although eventually it was rolled to the thinness of a rope. From then on matters took their natural course, the eager kisses and embraces, the worshipping and enslaved fondlings and the half-silent, half-vocal ecstasies over every line and curve. To think that this rather commonplace linear formula—the feminine figure—should prove such a powerful psychic reagent to the mind of man. Not chemistry alone but rather a geometric design, a formula of line and curve, is the thing nature has invented to insure race propagation!

Whether I acquitted myself well or ill on this occasion is to this day, to me, a mystery. I do not know. That I personally passed an ecstatic, a delicious night—save for the haunting thought that I was miles from being as effective as the average man and that, of course, she must have detected it and was despising me accordingly—may be taken for granted. Personally, I was convinced that I was not long enough enduring in these happy unions, although she did not seem to notice this or to lack delight, in so far as I could judge. One of my disturbing thoughts was—this night and the next day—that I should be or should have been able to indulge in the sex act many many more times than I did—something, I suppose, which might be fixed by law or a committee of weights and measures. At any rate the night was passed, partially in wakeful thoughts and partially, for me at least, in feverish dozing. At last, the dawn breaking and I being very very tired, I fell asleep and did not wake again until I heard her stirring—getting up—which convinced me more than ever that I was a failure. She was planning to leave me without a word! She had been bored, not satisfied. In vain she assured me that she was late and that she had to hurry. I did not really believe her. I tried to induce her to stay, but she would not—saying she could not. Neither would she indulge me in a final union, but hurried out, leaving me convinced that the whole thing had been a horrible fiasco and that I was forever doomed to a ghastly sex loneliness. One thing she did do, however, and that was to leave me her address, saying I should write her sometime and make another appointment, but something either in her manner or my perfervid conviction as to my own inefficiency convinced me that she was really not interested in me, that I had proved dull and that she had not enjoyed herself. Thus my worst suspicions were once more confirmed in my own mind. I was a failure, sexually. I could never really look her in the face again, however much I might want to. In consequence, although often during the next few days and weeks I thought of writing her—of trying to make another appointment—I could not. Try as I might, I could not bring myself to do it. I was too sensitive, and all the time I was haunted by the feeling that, if I did, I would be turned down,—that she would not answer me or that she would not come. Also, as I say, that I would scarcely have the courage to look into her face again if she did—after my great failure!

Other matters intervening, I did not write, and curiously enough she did not write me—I doubt now whether she even took my name, the whole thing having been so casual. It is so hazy now that I cannot recall. But at any rate, this is the sum and substance of this my first true liaison, and as such you may decide whether I was a success or not. Actually, the girl seemed charming, delicious, physically and every other way, and as for me—was I or was I not a success?

CHAPTER XXVIII

The aftermath of this, perhaps not strangely, was more of the same thing, only in this instance with Mrs. Zernouse. As I recall it, it followed rather swiftly. Discovering several hairpins in the room or in the bed the next morning, as well possibly as other telltale evidences, she made such pointed comments and seemed to take it as so very natural and desirable even that I felt called upon to trifle with her, and in a very few moments she had surrendered, and in the same place, though in by no means so tempting a way. Mrs. Zernouse was, as I have said, of peasant origin, or nearly so. There was something the least bit coarse and, to me at that time, disturbingly practical about her. Her clothes, Americanized after a fashion, were peasant's clothes, her body a peasant's body—healthy, animal, fairly attractive, but not gratifying from the point of view of delicacy of limb and torso. She was too robust.

Just the same, at the time, she seemed interesting enough to me— a not wholly unworthy conquest. Curiously, it was she and no other who first and definitely, although not entirely so, established in my own mind the idea that I might not be as weak as I thought I was. She was decidedly passionate, and, in addition, it is entirely possible that she had been without any companionship of this kind for some time. The point that impressed me was that her transports, although vigorous and noisy, decidedly so, were yet very quick to end. She seemed to see nothing awry in her brief blazing orgasms, and over and over congratulated me enthusiastically, in the moments of action, of course, on my sex power. This naturally flattered my male vanity. I could scarcely believe my ears. Here was one woman who was plainly healthy enough, who had borne and reared, thus far at least, two robust little girls— certainly the product of some form of healthy sex labor—and yet she deemed me efficient, seemed to think, in short, that I was especially so. Then, how, I immediately asked myself, could I be as weak as I thought I was? The two situations were scarcely compatible. I detracted as much as possible from my joy in discovering that I was not as weak as I had thought I was by deciding that she was abnormally vigorous—a freak, in short—and that the average woman would not respond in this tempestuous and swift way.

However, the fact remained that she was entirely and obviously satisfied, and this was not easy to get over. Object as I might, it built me up in my own esteem. For all of two months thereafter, possibly three—well into warm weather—I was in the habit of returning at twelve or one, and, if the mood was on, of going upstairs to the third floor and opening her front-room door with the key with which she had provided me. She slept in a rear room with her two little girls close beside her—one or occasionally both of them in the same bed. When I would tap at this other door she would nearly always stir and come out, but occasionally she would be sleeping so soundly that she would not hear, and at these times I would go in on tiptoe and touch her gently. Always she would motion me silently to go away and then would soon rise and follow. During this period, in spite of the fact that I thought very little of her and saw almost as little—an hour or two a night once or twice a week—I was still constantly being improved in my own estimation, ridding myself of the delusion that I was a sexual failure. By degrees, but rather swiftly at that, owing to the growing feeling that she was gross and very much beneath me mentally and in every other way, I began to tire of her. After I had been with her a few times, the act itself became more and more repulsive, and I began to make my calls fewer and my stays briefer, until she began to complain, when I decided that there was but one thing left. I would have to move. It would not do to go on this way. She would make my life a burden. Accordingly I once more sought still another room, my fourth, and soon finding it in a much more conventional neighborhood, I moved, securing this new room first and then, by degrees and silently, moving my belongings. Nothing was left save the curtains, prints and plaster nude, when late one evening I made a clean sweep of all of these and departed, owing her nothing save an apology for my rude behavior. My feeling at the time was that an explanation would be both disagreeable and useless, and I was in no particular mood to lie or to put her boldly aside, so this other method seemed best.

In the meantime, other things had been happening to me which had definitely altered my views in other ways. I had been becoming a somewhat more important person to myself and for various reasons, all of which seemed to dovetail into and support each other. For one thing, my standing as a local newspaperman seemed to grow by leaps and bounds—I am not exaggerating in the least. Certain almost fortuitous events (how often they have occurred in my life!) seemed to assist me far above my willing or even my dreams. Thus one morning, when I was still in the house in the Choteau Avenue district, I had come down to the *Globe* city room to get something—a paper or a book I had left—before going to my late breakfast, when a tall, broad-shouldered St. Louisan, wearing a slouch hat and looking much like a typical Kentucky colonel, hurried into the office and exclaimed: "Is the city editor here?"

"He isn't down yet," I replied, seeing that no one had arrived, and added, "Anything I can do for you?"

"I just stopped to tell you there's a big wreck on the road up here, near Alton," he exclaimed. "I saw it on the train as I passed coming down from Chicago. A half-dozen cars burning. If you people get a man up there right away you can get a big lead on this. All the papers are sure to have it."

I grabbed a piece of paper, for I felt instinctively that this was important. Some one ought to attend to this, right away—some one ought to go out on it without any consultation with anyone, if that meant delay. I looked around to see if there was anyone to appeal to, but there was no one.

"What did you say the name of the place was?" I inquired.

"Wann," replied the stranger, "right near Alton. You can't miss it. There are a half-dozen cars burning there now. Better get some one up there quick. I think it's something big. I know how important these things are to you newspaper boys. I used to be one myself, and I owe the *Globe* a few good turns anyhow." He smiled at me and bustled out.

I did not wait to see the city editor. I felt in a way that I was taking a big risk, going out without orders, but I also felt that something terrible had happened and that the occasion warranted it. I had never seen a big wreck. It must be wonderful. The newspapers always gave them so much space. I wrote a note to the city editor in which I explained that the wreck was reported as large, and added that I felt it to be my duty to go at once. Perhaps he had better send an artist after me. (Imagine my advising him!) This I placed under the writing leaf of Tobe's desk and took my leave.

It was a bright, sunny morning, with little or no suggestion of a winter temperature in the air. Days like these came even in February in St. Louis at times. The grass was brown and faded, but the warm wind stirring gave the day a suggestion of spring. On the way to the depot I thought of what I must do: telegraph for an artist if the wreck was really important, and then get my story and get back. It was over an hour's run. On the way out I looked out the window, meditating on the fortunes of life. Here was another example of that indifferent fate which would choose a day like this to maim a score of people perhaps. I got off at the nearest station, St. Louis-ward of the wreck, and walked the remaining distance, which was little more than a mile. As I neared it, I saw a fair-sized crowd of people gathered around what were evidently the smouldering embers of a train, and on the same track, not more than a hundred feet further on, were three oil-tank cars, evidently those into which the passenger train had crashed. These were the cars that were surrounded by people, who were staring at them as the fire blazed about them. Their platforms were evidently burning. As I learned afterward, a fourth oil-tank car had been smashed and the tank's content of oil had poured out about these others of the oil group as well as the passenger train itself. The oil had taken fire and consumed the train although no people were killed, and it was now, as I learned afterwards, blazing brightly about the oil tanks.

The significance of the scene had not yet quite dawned upon me, however, when for the second time in my life thus far I was privileged to behold one of those terrific catastrophes which, I presume, it is given to few of us to see. The oil-tank cars, about which the crowd gathered, having become overheated by the burning oil beneath, all at once exploded with a muffled report which to me (I was no more than fifteen hundred feet away) sounded more like a deep breath exhaled by some powerful person than anything else. The ground seemed to tremble slightly. The heavens instantly appeared surcharged with flame. Fiery tongues seemed to fly like great yellowish sheets of light and to descend like red licking tongues. The crowd, which I had only a moment before seen solidly massed about the cars, was now hurled back in confusion, and I beheld men running, some toward me, some from me, their bodies either already on fire or being momentarily ignited. I saw flames descending toward me, long, red, licking things, but realizing the danger and in a kind of panic, I turned and ran as fast as I could, never stopping until I deemed myself at a safe distance. Then I halted and gazed back, hearing at the same time a chorus of pitiful wails and screams which tore my heart.

Death, I said to myself, is here! I am witnessing a great tragedy—a horror. The part of the great mysterious force which makes and un-makes our visible scene is here and now magnificently operative. But, first of all, I am a newspaperman. I must report this—run to it, not away—and see it. As I thought and looked, I saw dashing toward me a man whose face I could not make out clearly, for at times it was partially covered by his hands, which at other times were waved in the air like flails. His body was apparently being consumed by a rosy flame which was partially enveloping him. His countenance, whenever it became visible as he moved his hands to and fro, was screwed into a horrible grimace, something like those grotesque masks so often seen painted in theatres. Unconscious of me as he ran, he dashed like a fiery force to the low ditch which paralleled the railroad nearby and, hurling himself down, rolled and twisted like a worm.

I could scarcely believe my eyes or my senses. My hair rose on end. My own hands twitched convulsively. I ran forward, and pulling off my coat, threw it over him to smother if possible the spots of flame, but it was of no use—my coat began to burn also. With my bare hands I tore grass and earth from the ground and piled it upon the sufferer. For the moment I was beside myself with a combined terror and misery and grief. Tears sprang to my eyes, and I half choked with the sense of my own helpless misery. When I saw my own coat going, I snatched it off and stamped the fire out. Then I gathered more earth.

The stranger was burned beyond recovery, however. The oil had evidently fallen in a small mass upon the back of his head and shoulders and his back and legs. It had consumed his clothes and his hair and seized on and cooked the skin. His hands were scorched black, his neck and ears and face also. Even as I watched him screaming futilely for help, he presently ceased to struggle and lay still, groaning heavily but unconsciously. He was alive, but that was all.

Oppressed by the awfulness of it, I looked about for help, but seeing many others in apparently the same plight I realized the futility of it and of further labor here. I could do nothing more. I had stopped the flames in part, the man's rolling had done the rest, but to what end! Hope of life was ridiculous. I could see that plainly. I turned, like a soldier in a battle, and looked after the remainder of the people.

To this hour I can see it still—people running over the fields in the distance away from the now entirely exploded cars, and about the fallen victims other people approaching. A house, standing a little way beyond the wreck, was burning. A small town, not a thousand feet away, seemed blazing in spots, bits of blazing oil having fallen upon the roofs of some houses. People were running hither and thither like ants, bending over and examining prostrate forms. Evidently this wreck had become a holocaust.

My first idea, now that I had recovered my senses, was that I must get in touch with my newspaper and get it to send an artist—Wood, probably (I was always so impressed by him)—and then get the news. These people who were gathered here would do as much for the injured as I could, and more. Why waste my newspaper's time on them? I ran to a little road-crossing telegraph station a few hundred feet further on, and encountering the agent who was hurrying out, demanded to know what was being done.

"I've sent for a wreck train," he replied excitedly. "I've telegraphed the Alton General Hospital. There ought to be a train and doctors here pretty soon, any minute now." He looked at his watch. "What more can I do?"

"Have you any idea how many are killed?"

"I don't know. You can see for yourself, can't you?"

"Will you take a message to the *Globe-Democrat*? I want to telegraph for an artist."

"I can't be bothered with anything like that now," he replied roughly when he heard I was from the *Globe*. I felt an instant antagonism and caution envelope him. He hurried away.

"How am I to do this?" I thought, and then I ran, studying and aiding the victims wherever aid seemed of the slightest use—wondering how I should ever be able to report all this—and awaiting the arrival of the hospital and wrecking train.

CHAPTER XXIX

It was not long before the wreck train arrived—say, forty-five minutes—a thing of flatcars, boxcars and cabooses and coaches of an old pattern, with hospital cots made ready en route and a number of doctors and nurses who scrambled out with the usual air and authority of those who are used to scenes of this kind. Meanwhile, I had been wondering how long it would be before the wreck train would arrive and had decided before its arrival that it would be better to get my information as soon as possible, as once the doctors and authorities were on the scene, it might not be so easy. Accordingly I bustled about the task—a kind of scavenger or condor of the news. Names were what were wanted most, I knew, names of the injured and their condition, and I now started running from one to another of the different groups that had formed here and there over one dying or dead, asking who he was, where he lived, what his occupation was, and how he came to be at the scene of the wreck. Some, I found, were passengers, some residents of the nearby villages of Wann or Alton, who, having heard of the wreck of the morning, had hastened over to see it. Most of the passengers had gone forward on a train provided for them. Some of those injured were laborers with families, some men of moderate importance who lived in St. Louis or Chicago. There were no women, a fact which struck me as odd.

I had a hard enough time getting any information, even from those who were able to talk. Citizens from the nearby town and those who had not been injured or too much frightened by the catastrophe were lending a hand to do what they could. They were not interested in reporters or their needs. Some who were carrying the injured to the nearby crossing platform resented my intrusion, and others who were searching the meadows about for those who had run far away and had then fallen were too busy to bother with me. Still I pressed on. I went from one to another asking who they were and receiving in some cases mumbled replies, in other cases merely groans. With those laid out on the platform awaiting the arrival of the wreck train I had not quite so much difficulty. They were helpless and there was no one to attend them.

"Oh, can't you let me alone!" one man whose face was a black crust remarked. "Can't you see I'm dying?"

"Isn't there any one who will want to know?" I returned softly. It struck me all at once that this was a duty these people owed to everybody, their own families and friends included.

The man seemed to see the point.

"You're right," he replied with cracked lips after a long silence, and gave his name and an account of his condition and experiences.

I went to others. To each who was capable of understanding, I put the same proposition. It won me considerable news and the respect of those who were watching me finally. All except the station agent seemed finally to see that I was entitled to do this, and if I had thought, I could have soothed him with a bribe. This method of approach rarely occurred to me in my earliest newspaper work.

While I was working, the wreck train rolled in. It consisted, as I have said, of two or three flatcars, several cabooses, and old-fashioned passenger cars. Surgeons and nurses from the nearby hospital leaped down, and men brought litters to carry away the wounded. In a moment the scene changed, as I had feared. The authorities of the road showed a frowning face to inquiry, and I was only too glad now that I had thought to make my inquiries early.

Nevertheless, I managed in the excitement to install myself in the train just as it was leaving, and so reach Alton with the injured and dead and witness the transfer. Some died en route—others moaned in a soul-racking way. I was beside myself with pity and excitement, and yet I could only think of the way in which I would describe, describe, describe, once the time came. Now I scarcely dared to make notes.

At Alton the scene transferred itself gradually to the Alton General Hospital, where, in spite of the protests of the railroad officials, I demanded as my right that I be allowed to enter and was finally admitted. Once in the hospital I completed my canvass, being now assisted by doctors and nurses who seemed to like my appearance and to respect my calling, possibly because they saw themselves mentioned in the morning paper. Having canvassed every injured man and noted his condition and obtained his name and address where possible, I finally went out, heartsick and weary, and at the door encountered a great throng of people—men, women, and children—who had gathered betimes and were weeping and clamoring for information. One glance and I realized for all time what these tragedies of the world really mean to those dependent, affectionally or otherwise. The white, drawn faces, the liquid, appealing eyes—tragedy written in large human characters. It appealed to me intensely.

"Do you know whether my John is in there?" cried one woman, grasping me by the arm. "Do you know? Can you tell me?"

"Your John—" I said sympathetically, "will you tell me who your John is?"

"John Taylor," she replied. "He works on that road. He was over there."

"Wait a minute," I said, and reaching down in my pocket I drew forth a pad and consulted the names. "No, he isn't here," I said.

The woman heaved a great sigh.

Others now crowded around me. In a moment I was the centre of a clamoring throng. All wanted to know, each before the other.

"Wait a moment," I replied, as an inspiration seized me. "Wait a moment."

I raised my hand, and my voice—as sonorously as I could—at the same time.

A silence fell over the little group.

"You people are looking to know who is injured," I called. "I have here a list which was made over at the wreck and here. It is almost complete. If you will be quiet I will read it."

A hush fell over the crowd.

I stepped to one side where a broad balustrade ran and, mounting it, held up my paper.

"Edward Reeves," I began, "224 South Elm Street, Alton. Arms, legs and face seriously burned. He may die."

"Oh!" came a cry from a woman in the crowd.

I decided at once not to say whether any one was seriously injured.

"Charles Wingate, 415 North 10th Street, St. Louis."

No voice answered this.

"Richard Shortwood, 193 Thomas Street, Alton."

No answer.

I read on down through the list of forty or more, and at each name there was a stir and in some instances cries, but my audience seemed to be satisfied. It was waiting for this, and I had satisfied it. As I stepped down, two or three people drew near and said, "Thank you." A flush of gratification swept over my face. For once I felt that I had done something which I could be honestly proud of.

The rest of the afternoon was spent in gathering outside details. I hunted up the local paper which was getting out an extra and secured permission to read its earliest account. I went down to the depot to see how the trains ran, and by accident ran into Wood. In spite of my inability to send a telegram, Mitchell had seen fit to take my advice and send him. He was one excited artist, intensely wrought up over how to illustrate it all. I am satisfied that my description of what had occurred did not tend to ease him much. I accompanied him back to the hospital to see if there was anything there he wished to illustrate, and then described to him the horror as I saw it. Together we visited the morgue of the hospital where fourteen men had already been laid out in a row, and there the nothingness of man seemed to become coldly manifest. They looked so commonplace, so unimportant—so like dead beetles or flies. Curiously, now the burns which had killed them seemed in some cases pitifully small—little patches cut out of the skin as if by a pair of shears, revealing the raw muscles below. Some of the patches were no larger than peas—or postage stamps—others as large as your two hands or your hat. All these dead were stark naked—men who had been alive and curiously gaping two or three hours before. For once Dick was hushed. He did not theorize or pretend. He was silent, pale. "It's hell, I tell you," was all he said.

On the way back on the train, having secured a large pad of paper before I entered, I wrote. I asked the brakeman for a writing board and secured it. In my eagerness to give a full, brilliant account, I impressed the services of Dick himself, who wrote for me such phases of the thing as he had seen. At the office I reported briefly to Mitchell, giving that old salamander a short account of what had occurred. He ordered me to write it at full length, as much as I pleased. It was about seven in the evening when we reached the office, and at eleven I was still writing— and not nearly done—and writing fast. I asked Hartung to look out for some food for me at about midnight, and then went on with my work. By that time the whole paper had become well aware of the importance of the thing I was doing. I was surrounded and observed at times by gossips and representatives of out-of-town newspapers who had come here to get transcripts of the tale. The city editor came in to say that I could have all the space I wanted. The telegraph editor came in to get advance pages of what I was writing, in order to answer inquiries, and told me he thought it was fine. The night editor called to ask questions, and all the other reporters sat about and eyed me curiously. I was a lion for once, a big one in this office, if I might never hope to be one anywhere else again. The realization of my importance set me up. I wrote with vim, vanity, a fine frenzy. By George, I would give them a great story, and it is barely possible that I did. If I ever kept a copy of the paper or re-read it, I have forgotten.

By one o'clock I was through, and Hartung had the restaurant man, a dark Sicilian caterer who ran a little lunch for the employees of the paper in the back of the building on the floor above, spread my food before me on my desk in the city room. Then the boys gathered about me—Hazard, Bellairs, Benson, Hartung, David, the railroad man and several others—and listened attentively to what I had to say, the details of what had happened.

"This is going to be a great beat," said Hazard generously. "We've got the *Post* licked, all right. They didn't hear of it until two o'clock this afternoon, but they sent five men out there and two artists. It was over then, though. The best they can have is a *cold* account. *You* saw it."

"That's right," echoed Bellairs. "You've got 'em licked. That'll tickle Mac, all right. He loves to beat the other Sunday papers." It was Saturday night.

"Tobe's tickled sick," confided Hartung cautiously. "You've saved his bacon. He hates a big story because it always worries him, but he knows you've got 'em beat. McCullagh'll give him credit for this."

"Oh, that big stiff!" I said scornfully, referring to Tobias.

"That's right, somebody always saves him," echoed Hazard bitterly. "He plays in luck, by George. He hasn't any brains."

I got up after a time and went in to report to my superior, however. I told him, very humbly, that I thought I had written all I could down here, but I believed that there was considerable more up there to cover and that I ought to go back.

"Very well," he replied gruffly. "Don't overdo it, though."

"The big stiff!" I thought to myself as I went out.

That night I stayed at a downtown hotel, seeing that I was charging everything to the paper, and after a feverish sleep arose early and started out again. I was as excited and cheerful as though I had suddenly become a millionaire. I stopped at the nearest corner and bought myself a *Globe*, a *Republic* and a Sunday *Post-Dispatch* and contrasted the various accounts, scanning the columns to see how much my stuff made, and measuring the atmosphere and the quality. To me, of course, mine seemed infinitely the best and, if you please, much longer than the others. There it was, occupying the whole front page, with cuts, and nearly all of the second page, with cuts! I could hardly believe my eyes. But Dick's illustrations, I am sorry to say, were atrocious—a mess—no spirit or meaning to them at all. He had lost himself in an effort to make a picture of the original crumpling wreck, which he had done very badly. He fell at once in my estimation as an artist. But, I kept asking myself vainly, had I, single-handed, really written so much?—all mine?—and between the hours of five and midnight! It seemed astonishing. I picked out the most striking passages and read them first, my throat contracting uncomfortably, my heart beating proudly, and then I went over the whole of the article, word for word. It seemed to read amazingly well to me, very impressive indeed. I felt at the time that it was full of fire and pathos and done in the right way, with facts and color. This same paper contained an editorial calling attention to the skill of the *Globe-Democrat* in handling these matters and commiserating the helplessness of the other journals under such trying circumstances. The *Globe* was always best and first, according to this statement. I felt now, at last, that I had justified the opinion of the editor in chief in selecting me.

Bursting with vanity, I returned to Alton. Despite the woes of others, I could not help glorying in the fact that nearly the whole city—a good portion of it, anyhow—must be reading my account of it. It was anonymous, of course. They could not tell who I was. Still, I had done it, just the same. This was something. This was the opportunity I had been longing for, and I had not failed.

This second day at Alton was not nearly so important as I had fancied it might be, but it had its phases. On my arrival I took one more look at the morgue, where thirty-one dead bodies were now laid out in a row, and then began to look after those who were likely to recover, hearing what they had to say. I visited some of the families of the afflicted, and talked of railroad damages. At my leisure I wrote a full account of just how the case stood, and wired it. I felt that to finish the case up properly, I should stay still another day, which was really not necessary, and decided to do so without consulting my editor.

But by nightfall, after my copy had been filed, I realized my mistake, for I received a telegram to return, which added that the local correspondent could easily attend to all the remaining details. In consequence I did so, beginning en route to feel a qualm of conscience in regard to my conduct. Perhaps, after all, I had not done right in attempting to do this! The case did not require it, really. Had I not been taking a great deal for granted in thus attempting to act without first consulting with my superior? Perhaps he would think I was getting bold, a "swelled head," and so complain to McCullagh. Or perhaps he had. I knew he did not like me. And this gave him a good reason to complain. Besides, my second day's story, now that it was gone, did not appeal to me as important—I might as well have carried it in—and there was the extra expense of telegraphing it. I felt that I had failed in this and also that mature consideration might decide that I had failed on the first story also, the big Sunday story. The *Post-Dispatch's* account had struck me as being very interesting in spite of my desire to belittle it. The five men had done very well, even if there were five, as Hazard had said, and, besides, its illustrations were infinitely better—splendid, really. I began to think that, by my own attitude, I had managed to work up all the excitement in the office that Saturday night, and that on Sunday, when the paper had been read, everybody, perhaps, had thought less of it. Suppose, when I got back now, McCullagh had become dissatisfied and would discharge me. I began to think of my various follies and of my other work of the past here to see where I had written poor matter. Perhaps now, since I had made this last error, my sins were to find me out. "Pride goeth before destruction," I quoted, "and a haughty spirit before a fall." It was now, perhaps, my turn to fall.

By eight o'clock, when I reached the office, I was thoroughly depressed—afraid even—and hurried in, expecting the worst. The train was late, of course—had to be on this occasion—and I did not reach St. Louis in time to take an evening assignment. This was another offense, I thought. Mitchell was out when I did get to the office, which left me nothing to do but worry. Only Hartung was there, and he seemed rather glum. The excitement was all over. Why, I asked myself, had I been so silly, so self-hypnotized, so bold! I secured an evening paper and retired gloomily to a corner to wait. At about nine Mitchell arrived, but he did not call for me at once. He saw me, but said nothing. As I was about to go out and get something to eat, Hartung came in and said, "Mr. Mitchell wants to speak to you."

I arose in great depression. My heart sank. My feet were cold. I felt that a reprimand was now coming—a stiff one at the very least. I went in and stood before him.

"You called for me?"

"Yes. Mr. McCullagh wants to see you."

"It is all over," I thought. "I can tell by his manner. He is very sour. What a fool I was to build such high hopes on that story."

I went out in the hall and walked nervously to the editor-in-chief's office. Actually, I was so depressed I could have cried. To think that all my fine dreams were to have such a sudden end. That dignitary was sitting Napoleon-like in his little office, his chin on his chest, a sea of papers about him. He did not turn the moment I entered, but waited. My heart grew heavier. He was angry with me! I could tell it. At last he wheeled.

"You called for me, Mr. McCullagh," I murmured.

"Mm, yes, yes," he mumbled in his thick, gummy, pursy way. His voice always sounded as though it were being obstructed by something leathery or woolly. He seemed to pause for a moment, took me in with a single glance, then added, "I wanted to say that I liked that story you wrote very much—very much indeed. A fine piece of work, a fine piece of work. I like to recognize a good piece of work when I see it. I have raised your salary to twenty-five dollars, and I would like to give you this." He reached down in his pocket, drew out a roll, and handed over a yellow twenty-dollar bill.

I could have dropped where I stood. The reaction was tremendous—especially after my great depression. I felt as though I should burst with joy, but instead I stood there, awed by this generosity and heart-touched. I did not know what to say. Coming so fast on the heels of my depression, I felt upset by it.

"I'm very much obliged to you, Mr. McCullagh," I finally managed to say. "I thank you very much. I'll do the best I can."

"It was a good piece of work," he repeated mumblingly, "—a good piece of work," then slowly wheeled about.

I turned and walked briskly out.

CHAPTER XXX

The glory of an achievement of this kind was sufficient to last me for days. I walked on air. The fact that I had gained the notice of a man as important as McCullagh, a man about whom a contemporaneously famous poet had written a poem, was almost more than I could stand. I returned to the city room, satisfied that I had a great future. What luck—what a triumph! In spite of my triumph, however, I was listed for only "Hotels & Heard in the Corridors," as usual. What of it? I went out and walked the silent streets of the downtown section, convulsively digging the fingers of each hand into its respective palm and shaking myself with delight. This *was* an achievement for me. This was something worth talking about. Now, by George, I was a real newspaper man. I had beaten the whole town, and in a new city too—a city strange to me. Think of that!

Having nothing to do, practically, and my excitement cooling some, I was able to return after a while to the art department and report on what had happened. I was so set up that I not only told of my raise in salary but also of the fact that I had been handed a twenty-dollar bill by no less a person than McCullagh himself—an amazing thing, of course. This last was received with mingled feelings by the department. Mc-Cord was pleased, of course—delighted, I could see that. He was so generous. On the contrary Wood was inclined to be glum. His own part had been so unsatisfactory. McCord, as I now discovered, had been twitting him about his work on this occasion—did so in my presence. "Dick must have been seeing things when he made that biggest picture," he commented. Wood admitted it frankly, saying that he had not been able to collect himself. "You know I can't do those things very well," he insisted, "and I shouldn't have been sent out on it. That's Mitchell for you." Possibly it angered him to think that he should have been so unfortunate and that I should have been so signally rewarded. Anyhow, he did not show anything save a generous side to me at the time, although latterly I began to feel that it was the beginning of a renewal of that slight hostility, based on his original opposition to me. At any rate, he complimented me, albeit smiling enigmatically, and added, "You've done it this time. I'm glad you've made a hit, old man."

That night, however, I was not invited to his room as I had hoped, although he and Peter went off together, as usual.

The days now settled down into their old routine for me, days which because of this petty, temporary triumph seemed duller than ever—"Heard in the Corridors" and petty assignments of one kind and another. I had ample time to reflect on the worthlessness of newspaper reporting as a profession, which I did. However, I was again urged by Hazard to do a novel with him—a thing which flattered me intensely, for had he not done one, and to me a splendid one? I considered this seriously for a few days, inviting him down to my room to talk it over and arguing the details of the thing for hours, but it came to nothing. Plays, as I kept feeling at this time, were more in my line, and poems, although I could not think of any plot about which to build a play. Finally I gave the idea up for the time being and contented myself with writing poetry which was very bad, as I can tell you, mere jingling slush. Since writing that first poem, a month or so before, I had busied myself from time to time, scribbling down the most mediocre rhymes relative to my depressions and dreams and imagining them to be great verse. Truly, I thought I was to be a great poet—one of the very greatest—and so nothing else really mattered for the time being. Weren't great poets always lone and lorn, like myself? It was about this time, having received that gift of twenty and a raise of five, that I began to array myself in the what seemed to me especially smart manner previously described, indulging in a new suit, shoes, a light silver-gray hat and the like. About this time also I moved into my 10th Street room.

Curiously (and fortunately for me, as it eventually turned out) a change in the personnel of the staff occurred which had a direct bearing upon my ambitions. A man by the name of Carmichael, who had been accustomed to do the dramatics on the paper and had been considered very efficient in that field, had been called to a better position in Chicago, and the place which he had occupied here was therefore temporarily vacant. As I learned afterward, Hazard was really the logical man for the place and should have had it indeed, since he had held this position before in connection with one or more of his periods of work for the paper. He was older and much better qualified in every way, I am sure. However, as I say, I did not know this at the time, and besides I imagined I was just the person for this place. Why not? Was I not an excellent reporter—one of the best? As may be imagined, I was in a very appropriate mood for it, or for trying to get it, having only recently begun to think of writing a play. And besides, I was crazy for advancement of any kind—to rise and be somebody. Accordingly the moment I heard of it I was on the qui vive as to how I should get it— eager to make a plea for it myself, yet afraid to approach McCullagh in person, who reserved these higher appointments for himself, and not dreaming really that I would get it. The fact that my city editor was opposed to me, as I thought, was also a serious handicap. My sole qualification, as I see it now, was that I was an ardent admirer of the stage and one who, because of his dramatic instincts (I thought), ought to make a fairly good critic! I did not know or realize at that time that I was neither experienced nor cool enough for this work—to provide a balanced judgement of the art of others. I was too ignorant really and too flamboyant, although for some of the purposes here demanded (to write a little two-stick notice of each new play, mostly favorable, and to prepare a weekly announcement of all the new performances) I was perhaps not as poorly equipped as some might have been. At the same time my recent triumph in writing up the wreck at Wann had given me such an excellent opinion of myself—made me think that I stood so well in the eyes of Mr. McCullagh—that I decided to try for it. "Why not?" I thought. It was nothing so wonderful. I could do it—certainly I could. It might not mean any additional salary. But then think of the honor of it! Dramatic Editor of the *Globe-Democrat* of St. Louis! Ha! I decided to try.

There were two drawbacks to the position as I learned a little later once I began to look into this. One of these was that although I might be dramatic editor I would still be under the domination of Mr. Tobias Mitchell, as the previous man had been—a thing which irritated me very much and took much of the savor of the task away. Also, although I might be dramatic editor, still, on this paper at least, I would have to do general reporting into the bargain whenever the exigencies of the occasion required. The truth was there was not enough dramatic news to require the services of a single individual, and in addition Mr. McCullagh would not permit space for an important display, so there was not so much to it after all. Still, as I argued, there was the title and the right to visit the various theatres free and see all the important shows, which was something. Could I not say that I was a dramatic editor? And would it not give me free entrance to the theatres? Verily.

Consequently, I began to lay my plans for getting it. Mitchell was so obviously opposed to me that I knew that if I appealed to him I would never get it. Mr. McCullagh might give it to me. I thought of asking him direct, but that was going over Mitchell's head, and he would never forgive me for that. How should I do? I debated a day or two; then recalling that my principal relations had been with Mr. McCullagh, I decided to go to that worthy direct. What matter? Let Mitchell be angry if he would. If I made good he could not seriously harm me.

Accordingly, I began to lay my plans or rather screw up my courage to go and see Mr. McCullagh. He was such a chill and distant figure to me that I had a kind of horror of doing it. I could see his inquisitorial eyes. The facts that he had built up such a powerful paper of national and world-wide significance in so moderate-sized a manufacturing city like St. Louis, that he was a genius, that he was constantly referred to as having the most trenchant pen in the country, and that hundreds visited the city annually just to come and look at the paper as the seat of a great editor were sufficient to overawe me dreadfully. At the same time, as I was beginning to realize, this man who was the object of so much reverence was apparently and obviously one of the loneliest persons imaginable. He was not married. He had no children. A little niece, whom I had recently heard of, was but a year old. Day after day he came to this office alone, sat alone, ate alone, went home alone, for he had few friends, apparently, to whom he would condescend to unbend. This appealed to me greatly. He was too big, I thought, too lonely. This Western town was too small for him, and I knew it.

This knowledge drew me sympathetically toward him and made me imagine, if you please, that he ought to like me. Was I not his protégé? Had he not brought me here? Instinctively I felt that I was one who could appreciate him and, incidentally, one whom he might secretly like. I felt it. The only trouble was that he was old and famous now, whereas I was a mere boy, but he would understand that too. Under other conditions, with the disparity of ages removed, I told myself, he might even have become friends with me. Of such is the vanity of youth. I decided to ask him at the first opportunity.

Accordingly, the very next day after I had made up my mind, I came down early, before anyone else, and loitered in the long corridor which led to his office and through which he would soon have to pass. I did not want to infringe on the old man's distinction by invading his office, and I wanted to make out that I was encountering him accidentally, as it were, and that the idea of appealing to him had come to me as a sudden inspiration.

I had often noticed him in the past, shouldering along the marble wainscoting of this same hall as he entered in the morning, his stout little Napoleonic frame cloaked in a conventional overcoat, and his broad, strong, intellectual face crowned by a rather wide-brimmed derby hat. He was invariably smoking a short, fat cigar, and he looked exceedingly solemn, forbidding even. Every time I heard the elevator click on this particular morning I dodged into the city room, only to reappear in time to meet him, accidentally as it were, and to appear to be going to the toilet.

At about eleven he did arrive. At the sight of him I lost my courage for the moment and was for walking past him without a word. At the exact spot opposite him, however, I halted, controlled by a reckless, eager impulse.

"Mr. McCullagh," I exclaimed, without further ado, "I want to know if you won't make me dramatic editor. Mr. Carmichael has resigned, I hear. I thought you might like to try me. I think I can do it." I flushed and hesitated.

"Very well," he replied simply and gruffly. "You're dramatic editor. Tell Mr. Mitchell to let you be it."

I started to thank him but had time only to exclaim, "I'm very much obliged," before he was gone. The stocky little figure moved indifferently away.

I went back into the city editorial room tingling to the fingertips. This great man's consideration for me was certainly portentous, I thought. Plainly he liked me. That was the great thing. He was fond of me, else why should he do this? If I only did well enough now, if I could bring myself seriously to my labors, I had a great opportunity. This man would stand by me. I felt it deeply. He would make a great newspaper man of me. Ah, me! Ah, me! It was something to be the favorite of a great editor-in-chief, a very great thing indeed.

CHAPTER XXXI

The days which followed this stand out as among the most amusing, satisfying and halcyon of my life. And yet as I also recall I was scarcely any more satisfied then than I was before or after—barring, of course, occasional moments of self-gratulation and joy in my current opportunities. At first I could scarcely believe that I was dramatic editor, so important did the task seem and so sudden and unexpected my elevation. Here I was on the paper scarcely three months and yet this position had been thus summarily given me. On explaining to Mr. Mitchell what had happened, he looked up at me rather oddly. Then thinking, I suppose, that I must have some secret hold on Mr. Mc-Cullagh or at least his high favor, he gave me a wry smile and said that he would have a letter of introduction to the local managers made out for me. This last was shortly after laid on my desk by Hartung, who, after congratulating me exclaimed, "Gee, I'll bet you could have knocked Tobe over with a straw. He doesn't understand yet, I guess, how well you stand with the old man. He must like you, eh?"

I could see by his manner that my new honor made a considerable difference in his already excellent estimate of me.

Armed with this letter I visited the various managers of the different theatres, all of whom received me cordially. I can see myself on the morning that I did it, very gay and enthusiastic, sure that I was entering on a task of the utmost importance to me. It was all such a wonder-world, the stage, such a fairyland that I fairly bubbled with joy as I went about, thinking how amazing it was that I had this slight connection with it. To be a real dramatic critic—think of it—a person of weight and authority in this perfect realm! There were seven or eight theatres in St. Louis at the time, as I recall it, three or four of them of that better sort that play only the "first-class attractions." The others catered to melodrama, vaudeville and burlesque.

One manager, of one of the two best theatres, the Grand, a short, thick-set, sandy-complexioned individual of most jovial mien (Mc-Manus was his name—the father of the well-known cartoonist of a later period and the prototype of at least two of his most humorous characters, Mr. Jiggs and Mr. Newlywed), exclaimed on seeing me: "So you're the new dramatic editor, are you? Well, they change around pretty often over there, don't they? First it was Hartridge, then Albertson, then Hazard, then Mathewson, then Carmichael, and now you, all in my time. Well, Mr. Dreiser, I'm glad to see you though. You're always welcome here. I'll take you out and introduce you to our doorman, and Mr. Dugmore of the box office. He'll always recognize you. We'll give you the best seat in the house if it's empty at the time you come."

He smiled humorously, and I had to laugh at the way he rattled off this welcome. He was so gay, direct. An aura of badinage and humor encircled him—quite the same as that which makes Mr. Jiggs delightful. This was the first I had heard that Hazard had once held this position, and now I felt a little guilty of having cut him out of it.

"Did Bob Hazard once hold this position?" I asked familiarly.

"That's right. That was when he was on the paper the last time. He's been on and off the *Globe* three or four times, you know." He smiled clownishly. I laughed.

"We'll get along, I guess," I said.

At the other theatres I was received less informally, but with uniform courtesy. Everyone seemed most anxious to be agreeable to me. They all assured me that I would be welcome at any time and that if I ever wished tickets for a friend or anyone else on the paper, I could get them if they had them. "And we make it a point to have them," said one box clerk, good-humoredly.

I felt that this was quite an acquisition of influence. It gave me considerable opportunity to be nice to any friends I might acquire; and, then, think of the privilege of seeing any show that I chose whenever I chose—to walk right into any theatre without being stopped and be pleasantly greeted en route. It was a great joy.

The character of the stage of that day, as I recall it, in St. Louis and America I mean, as contrasted with what I know of it now—its history in the world in general—is a curious and an interesting thing to me. Although now as I look back on it it seems inane, then it seemed wonderful. It is entirely possible that nations, like plants or people, have to grow and obtain their full development regardless of the accumulated store of wisdom and achievement in other lands, else otherwise how explain the vast level of mediocrity that maintains in some countries and many forms of effort—the stage for instance, here in St. Louis, at this time? Surely the stage in other lands had already seen a few tremendous periods—in Greece, France, England, Germany. Even here in America the mimetic art was no mystery. A few great things had already been done in acting at least—Booth, Barrett, Macready, Forrest, Helena Modjeska, Fannie Davenport, Mary Anderson, to name but a few. I was too young at the time to know or judge the import of their art or the quality of the plays they interpreted—aside from those of Shakespeare perhaps—but certainly their fame for a high form of classic production was considerable. Still, here during the few months I was dramatic editor and the following year when I was a member of another staff and had entrée to these same theatres, I am satisfied that with but one or two exceptions, if so many, I never saw but one or two actors worthy of the name and scarcely a single performance of anything which now, at this period, I can deem serious. Richard Mansfield and Felix Morris stand out in my mind as having been excellent, and DeWolf Hopper as an amazing and delightful comedian, but who else? Comic and light operas, with a heavy intermixture of straight melodrama, and comedy dramas were about the only things which managers ventured to essay in this region. Occasionally a serious actor of the calibre of E. S. Willard would appear on the scene, but even his plays were of a more or less melodramatic character—highly sentimental, emotional and unreal. In my short stay here of about a year and a half as dramatic editor and otherwise, I saw Joseph Jefferson, Sol Smith Russell, Salvini junior, Wilson Barrett, Fannie Davenport, Richard Mansfield, E. S. Willard, Felix Morris, E. H. Sothern, Julia Marlowe and a score of others, more or less important or unimportant as you will but too numerous to mention—comedians, light opera singers and the like—and although at the time I was mightily entertained and moved by some of them, I now realize that in the main they were pale, spindling lights scarcely worthy of the name of actors. America just then, apparently, was entering upon its grandest period of stage sentiment or mush. Charles Frohman of "Mr. Frohman, Presents" was rapidly rising to his lonely high height. I remember staring at his colorful three-sheet lithos and thinking how beautiful and perfect they were and what a great thing it was to be on the stage. Ah, to be an author, an actor, a composer, a manager. Ah! The Empire and Lyceum theatre companies with their groups of perfect lady and gentleman actors were at their height—the zenith of stage art—Mr. John Drew, for instance, with his wooden face and manners, Mr. Faversham, Miss Opp, Miss Spong. Such excellent actors as Henry E. Dixey, Richard Mansfield or Felix Morris could scarcely gain a hearing.

I recall sitting one night in Hagan's theatre at 9th or 10th and Pine Streets and seeing and hearing Richard Mansfield order down the curtain at one of the most critical or tense points in his most famous play, "Baron Chevreul" or some such name, and then come before it and denounce the audience in anything but measured terms. It had applauded at the wrong time in that asinine way which only an American audience can when it is *there* solely because it thinks it ought to be *there*. By that time Mansfield had already achieved a pseudo-artistic following. He was slowly but surely becoming a cult. On this occasion he explained to that bland gathering that they were fools, or worse— that American audiences were usually composed of such and dull beyond belief. That they were not there to see a great actor act, but to see a man called Richard Mansfield who was said to be a great actor. He pointed out how American audiences uniformly applauded at the wrong time, how truly immune they were to all artistic virus, how wooden and reputation following. Some of them, incensed at his tirade, arose and left. Others seemed to enjoy it and remained. A few hissed. But I also recall that having finished his speech he ordered up the curtain and proceeded with his act as though nothing had happened—as though the audience were not there really. I rather liked him for his stand, and yet I did not quite realize the import of it all, or know whether he was right or wrong. I think that I decided that he was really right but wrote it up in an apologetic way as though he had grossly insulted his audience—a body of worthy, respectable St. Louisans. If I am not mistaken some one, Hazard or some one, suggested that it would be good policy so to do—and being green to my task, I did.

The saccharine strength of the sentiment and mush we could gulp down at that time and still can and do to this day—in the movies, for instance—is to me beyond belief, although I was one of those who in my time did the gulping. It may seem odd to say it, but I was one of the worst. Ah, me, those perfect nights when as dramatic critic I strolled into one theatre or another—or two or three possibly in an evening—and observed (critically, as I thought) the work of those who were leaders in the fields of dramatic or humorous composition and our leading actors!

I remember my thoughts concerning Mr. Drew—his polished work—and how wonderful I thought some of the plays of Henry Arthur Jones and Pinero to be! The cruel overlords of trade—how cruel they were! The virtues of the lowly working man and the betrayed daughter, with her sad cast-down expression! The moral splendor of the young minister who denounced heartless wealth and immorality and cruelty in high places and reformed them, by George, or made them confess their errors! I can see him yet: slim, simple, perfect, that wonderful thing, a truly good man. Mind you, I do not say that phases of these things are not true. All great art deals with them. But the manner in which they were handled here! And the splendid reforms effected—and the wrongs righted—in plays! Don't laugh. You can still see them in any movie house in America. Do you know, there is no such thing as a reckless unmarried girl in any movie exhibited in Philadelphia. They're all married.

But how those St. Louis audiences applauded! Right was always appropriately triumphant. Wrong was always properly drummed out, as it should be. Our better selves invariably got the best of us in the end, and there was little of evil that went before which could not be straightened out in the last act.

Just the same, the spirit of these plays (the kind which I most preferred) captivated my fancy and elevated me into a world of unreality which fell in, unfortunately, with the wildest of my youthful imaginings. Love as I saw here set forth, in all those gorgeous or sentimental trappings wherewith the mimetic art is wont to invest it, was the only kind of love worthwhile—dramatic love, violently demanding and rewarding love. Fortune, also, as gilded in that showy way in which fortune always appears on the stage was the only fortune worthwhile. Ah, to be rich, elegant, exclusive—how these words and this atmosphere appealed to me. According to these worthy plays which I saw, love and youth were the only things worth discussing. The gorgeous trappings of the Orient, the social flare of New York, London and Paris, the excited sex imaginings of such minds as Dumas junior, Oscar Wilde, who was then in his heydey, Jones, Pinero and a number of other current celebrities were all paraded before us, clothed in that showy framework of which the stage alone is aware. The dreary humdrum of actual life outside was carefully shut from these pieces. The simple delights of ordinary living, if they were used at all, were exaggerated beyond sensible belief—although not to me, then. Elsewhere—outside my life, in the East, New York, London, Paris—were all the things that were worthwhile, not here. If I wanted to be happy I must go to those places. Yes, indeed. There were the fine clothes and the fine personalities (physically and socially speaking). And vice and poverty (painted in such peculiar colors that they were always divinely sad or repellant) only existed in these great cities also—or in England. Imagine!

Having decided that these various things were true, or that if they weren't they ought to be, I now began to dream more than ever of establishing some such perfect atmosphere for myself somehow, somewhere, but never in St. Louis of course. That was too common—too Western—too far removed from the real wonders of the world. Love, as I have said, and mansions and travel and saccharine romance were the great things, but they were afar off—in New York principally—and life was worthless without them. (It was around this time, by the way, that I was establishing the atmosphere of the so-called "studio" in 10th

Street.) Nothing could be so wonderful as love in a mansion, a palace, or in some oriental realm such as was indicated in the various comic operas in which DeWolf Hopper, Thomas Q. Seabrooke, Francis Wilson, Eddie Foy and Frank Daniels were appearing. How I raved over some of these poetic stage scenes with McCord and Wood as my companions, or occasionally Hazard, or Rodenberger, a new friend introduced to me by Wood and known as Rody, a most amazing person as I will latterly relate. As I say, I now visited as many theatres as I could conveniently, if for no more than an act or an hour, and drank in the wonder or delight of particular scenes that had appealed to me—the denunciation scene for instance in *The Middleman* or the third act of nearly any of Henry Arthur Jones' plays. The light operas of Reginald De Koven and Harry B. Smith, as well as those compendiums of nondescript color and melody, the extravaganzas such as *The Crystal Slipper, Ali Baba, Sinbad the Sailor,* fascinated me beyond words—set me beside myself. Young actresses such as Della Fox, Mabel Amber, Edna May, forerunners of a long line of comic opera soubrettes and who somehow suggested Lois to me, held me spellbound with delight and admiration. Here was the kind of maiden I was really craving—an actress of this hoyden, airy temperament—and here was I, as I told myself, attempting to content myself with so commonplace a creature as Mrs. Zernouse. Pah!

Speaking of this, I remember one night, at the close of one of Mr. Willard's performances at the Olympic, *The Professor's Love Story* I believe, in which he was appearing with an almost equally popular leading woman whose name I forget. I was asked by the manager to wait a few minutes after the performance and he would introduce me. It appeared that he was taking them to supper and thought I might like to accompany them—an 'honor which I declined, however, more out of fright or bashfulness than anything else. When they finally appeared, however, in the foyer of the theatre, the young actress, who was very beautiful after her kind, soft and clinging and gotten up regardless (in the most impressive manner of the stage) and hanging most tenderly on her star's arm (she was his mistress I understood), I was beside myself with envy and despair, nervousness. Such beauty, I told myself! Such grace! Such vivacity! Could anything be so lovely? Think of having such a perfect creature to love you, to hang on your arm! Ah! And here I was, a mere reporter, a nobody, one whom such a creature—this creature for instance—would not deign to glance at a second time. Mr. Willard himself was full of the actor's heavy hauteur, which made the scene all the more impressive to me. I glanced at her bashfully, side-wise, pretended to be but little interested while really I was dying of envy and despair. Finally, after a few idle words and a few sweety-sweet smiles cast in my direction, I was urged to come with them, but instead hurried away, pleading necessity, which was really true, and cursing my stars and my fate. Think of being a mere reporter—a nobody—at twenty-five a week while others were thus basking in the sunshine of success and love! Ah! Ah! Ah! Why should not I have a maiden so beautiful?

Why not indeed?

It is a fact, though, that if I had been of an ordinary, sensible, everyday turn of mind with a modicum of that practical wisdom which puts moderate place and position first and sets great store by the saving of money, I might have succeeded fairly well here—much better than I really did anywhere else for a long period after. Unquestionably Mr. McCullagh liked me. I think in some amused saturnine way he may have been fond of me, interested to keep such a bounding, high-flown dunce around the place. For a year or two or three at least I might have held this position and made it a stepping-stone to something better in the same line or different, but constituted as I was, I could not. Instead of rejoicing in the work and making it the end and aim of my daily labors for the time being, I looked upon it as a mere bauble, something that I had today but might not have tomorrow; and anyhow there were better things, apparently, than working day by day even at this as I was, and living in a small room. Life ought certainly to bring me something truly splendid, I argued. It must. I deserved it. Every window into which I looked, glimmering at night in those fine mansions of the West End, which I so much admired, was confirmation of the truth of the scenes I saw in these plays and that one might rise swiftly and per accident. Had I not, so far? I thought so, at least. People were intensely happy, somewhere. Fine homes and fine clothes, with pretty women and strikingly clothed men, produced happiness and should be the port of all, or at least of myself. It must be so. All the pain and misery of the world were caused by people not having these things. I had this theory salted down in my mind as a fact, and nothing that I saw in my daily life about me could alter or displace it. In a way I was ready to accept socialism in order to get what I wanted, while not ready to admit that all people were as deserving as I was by any means. The sad state of the poor workingman was a great and constant thought with me, but incidentally I was nearly the greatest and poorest and most deserving of all working men. I believed that what I thought on this subject was so.

This view naturally tended to modify the sanity of my work. Any youth who, with a modicum of imagination, gets imbued with this idea and still expects to succeed in some avenue of the world's ordinary labors has a long road to go. Taken from the point of view of ordinary labor it is a false idea and tended to unfit me, at least for solid practical service. Even in that most imaginative of all professions—the literary—the possessor of such a notion is utterly debarred from accomplishing anything until he gets over it. It is a peculiar illusion of youth, given apparently to some of the finer minds in its worst form and by them retained until, with rough experience, it is either knocked out of them or they are destroyed utterly in the process.

One of the things which this point of view did for me at this time was to give my writing a peculiar turn of melancholy and to allow me to paint the ideal (of which the performances I was witnessing were full) in most glowing colors. I could describe the most commonplace of scenes in sentimental plays or elsewhere until you would imagine that it was beautiful. I let this imaginative turn run away with me at times, and probably only the good sense of the copyreader or the indifference of a practical-minded public saved the paper from appearing utterly ridiculous.

On one occasion, for instance, I went to report a play of mediocre quality, which was running at the Olympic, and was so impressed with a love scene, which occurred under the customary moonlight surroundings, that I was blinded for the time being to all the faults of construction which the remainder of the play showed. I wrote it up in the most glowing colors, a mere paragraph, of course, but one which smacked of the idealism of which my nature was full. The copy reader, little Hartung, read it, but was too weary that night I suppose or too inattentive to capture it, and so let it go. The next day some of the other newspaper men in the office noticed it and commented on it to me, or to Hartung, saying it was rather high-flown as it was, especially to all of those who knew anything about the play, or who were imbued with the workaday atmosphere of a workaday world. But no bad result came of it. It was just a case of being slightly ridiculous—passed over, of course, because I was young.

A little later a negro singer, a young woman of remarkable vocal ability who was being starred as the Black Patti, in compliment to herself and another woman of that name, was billed to appear in St. Louis. The manager of the auditorium which was presenting this attraction called my attention by letter to the wonderful ability of this woman, and by means of clippings and notices of her work published elsewhere had endeavored to impress me favorably. I was an easy victim. I read these notices couched in the glowing phrases of the press agent and decided beforehand that she was something exceptional. I called for two seats and, inviting McCord for the evening in question, proceeded to the theatre where I was given a box.

The young woman was a sweet and impressive singer—there was scarcely any doubt of that—possessing into the bargain an engaging and magnetic manner. She could really sing. I listened to the programme of a dozen pieces, including such popular favorites as "Swanee River" and "Comin' Thro the Rye," and being greatly moved for some reason, returned to the office and wrote an account, which was fairly bubbling with the idealism of my nature. I did not attempt to analyze the quality of her art, which I could not, knowing nothing of even the rudiments of music, but plunged at once into that wider realm which involves the subtleties of nature itself.

"What is so beautiful as the sound which the human voice is capable of producing," I wrote in part, "when that voice is itself a compound of the subtlest things in nature? Here we have a young girl, black, it is true, who comes up from the woods and fields of her native country, blessed with some strange harmony of disposition which fits her to represent in song that which we know to be most lovely. The purling of the waters, the radiance of moonlight, the odour of sweet flowers, sunlight, storm, the voices and echoes of nature, all are found here, trilling forth over lips which represent in their youthfulness only a few of the years which wisdom requires. And yet here they are. You may sit and hear Miss Sissieretta Jones—" (that was the lady's name)"—sing, and as you do the charm of all these things comes to you. She is a compound of them—youthful, vivacious, the elemental sweetness of nature itself."

To understand the significance of a statement like this in St.

Louis, one would have to look somewhat into the social and political conditions of the people who dwelt here. To a certain extent they were Southern in temperament and feeling, representing the vigorous anti-negro spirit which prevailed for so many years after the war. They were also intensely practical. A bit of idealism of this character, especially when indulged in in connection with a negro, would naturally fall on dense ears, and would appear ridiculous. A negro the compound of the subtlest elements in nature! And this stated in their favorite paper.

By some strange chance, it went through, Hartung having come to look upon most of my work as the outpourings of some strange genius who could do about as he pleased. Neither Mitchell nor the editor-in-chief saw it, perhaps—or if they did, gave it no attention. The editors of the various rival papers, however, saw it and knowing the sensitive-ness of our editor in chief to criticism of his own paper (though he was free enough to point out the errors of others and in a lofty tone), as well as his own personal dignity, set to work to make something out of it. Of all editors in the West, of course, McCullagh was the easiest to target in this way. He was then a shining light in the editorial field and a man who was extremely conspicuous in his own neighborhood. Anything that he said or did was always the subject of local newspaper com-ment, and when any little discrepancy or error appeared in the *Globe-Democrat* it was always charged to him personally. Thus if an error in grammar was made, it was charged to him—"This is the way Mc-Cullagh speaks." Consequently this fervor over "Black Patti" was im-mediately credited to him personally. It was too good a thing to be lost sight of.

"The erudite editor of the *Globe-Democrat*," observed the *Post-Dispatch* editorially, "last night visited one of our principal concert halls. It is not often that that ponderous intellect can be called down from the heights of international politics to contemplate so simple a thing as a mere singer of songs, a black one at that, but when true art beckons, he can be depended upon to answer. The 'Black Patti' beck-oned to him last evening and he was on hand, as his magnificent penmanship testifies. None but the grandiloquent editor of the G.D. could have looked into the subtleties of nature as represented by the person of Miss Sissieretta Jones, and there discovered the wonders of music and poetry, such as he openly confesses to have seen. We have here a measure of that great man's insight and feeling, his love of art, music, poetry such as has not previously been provided, and we hasten to make representation of it, that others may not be deprived of the great privilege."

Here followed the quotation originally given. After it came more of the same gay raillery, with here and there a reference to "the great patron of the black arts," and the joy of being able to appreciate "the purling of the waters." It was gentle satire, not wholly uncalled for seeing that the item had appeared in the *Globe,* and directed of course at the one man who could least stand that sort of thing, sensitive as he was to his personal dignity. At that it may not have irritated him as much as we all thought, though it was generally assumed locally that it had.

At any rate I was blissfully unaware that any comment had been made on my effusive acknowledgement of the Black Patti's ability until about five in the afternoon of the next day, when the *Post-Dispatch* had been out several hours. A number of people on the paper had already read the article, inquiries had been made, of course, and I had been discovered as the guilty perpetrator. When I entered the office at five, comfortable and at peace with myself in my new position, excited comment was running about the office as to what "the old man" would think and say. He had not returned as yet from some afternoon expedition. He had gone to the Southern Hotel for lunch at two and was staying out late. Wait till he saw it! Oh, me! Oh, my! Wouldn't he be hopping! Hartung, who was reasonably nervous as to his own share in the matter, was the first to approach and impress me with the dreadfulness of it all, how savage "the old man" could be on such occasions. Even as they talked, he passed up the hall.

"Oh, you've put your foot in it," he exclaimed excitedly, after McCullagh had passed. "It's fine. I thought it was all right, but it won't do out here. You shouldn't write so fulsomely, old man. You should curb yourself. The other papers are always looking for just that sort of thing so that they can make fun of him."

I saw my dramatic honors rapidly dwindling. What if I should be fired now?

"Here," I exclaimed, pretending a kind of innocence—even at this late hour. "What's this all about? What's the row, anyhow?"

"Didn't you see the editorial in the *Post-Dispatch?*" inquired Hartung gloomily. It was his own position that was troubling him.

"No, what about?"

"Why, that criticism you wrote about the Black Patti. They've made all sorts of fun of it. The worst of it is they've charged it up to the old man."

I smiled a sickly smile and paled. I felt as if I had committed some great crime. Why had I attempted to write anything fine? Why couldn't I have a little sense about these things? I was always trying to do that sort of thing, hang it all! Perhaps this would be the end of me. He was so excitable, anyhow.

Hartung brought me the paper and showed it to me. I read it eagerly but with a sinking sensation—my stomach seeming gradually to retire to my backbone. Why had I done it? Why wouldn't the other newspapers let me alone? This was a ridiculous comment, unfair, even though possibly well deserved. Why had I written it?

As I was standing there, near the door which looked into the main city room where Tobe had his desk and where I could see him now scribbling dourly away, I saw McCullagh enter and walk up to the stout city editor. He had the *Post-Dispatch* crumpled roughly in his hand, and on his face was gathered what seemed to me a dark scowl. It may not have been. I was in no position to judge. Evidently he was in no mood for banter. I could see that.

"Did you see this, Mr. Mitchell?" I heard him say.

Tobe looked up—then closely and respectfully at the paper.

"Yes," he said.

"I don't think a thing like that ought to appear in our paper. It's a little bit too high-flown for our audience. Your reader should have modified it."

"I think so myself," replied Tobe quietly.

The editor turned and walked out. Tobe waited a sufficient length of time for his footsteps to die away, then growled at Hartung:

"You shouldn't have let that stuff go through," he said. "I've always warned you against that sort of thing. Why can't you watch out?"

I could have fallen through the floor. I had a vision of Hartung burying his head in his desk, scared and mute.

After the evening assignments had been given out and Tobe had gone out to dinner, the former crept up to me.

"The old man was as mad as the devil," he began. "Tobe gave me hell. He won't say anything to you but he takes it out on me. He's a little afraid of your pull with the old man."

Then he gave me the most exaggerated details.

CHAPTER XXXII

The chill which this untoward reception threw over my idealistic tendencies was for the time being sufficient to frighten me into a condition of caution. I felt no immediate desire to write anything more so high flown, and it gave me my first keen perception of the fact that idealism is not an everyday commercial quantity. The world uses very little of it. It sometimes stamps it out as unnecessary. Idealists are generally, and to a certain extent properly, looked upon as negligible quantities; and life, that grim struggle, which is involved mostly with the movement and control of material quantities, casts aside the fine feelings of most people as unimportant. Nevertheless, the idealist persists. He gives to the brown earth its softer appearance. He gathers of its mists and its dews, its sunlight and its moonlight, and weaves into garlands of enduring firmness those beautiful fancies wherewith he decks the world. Art, literature, music—these are his. Who shall say of his treasures that they are not valuable?

In spite of this little mishap, which apparently did me no great harm, there was a marked improvement in my affairs in every way as I saw it. I had a better room, not as good as I wished, by any means, but a room of some small charm; a mistress of sorts; various friends—Wood, McCord, Rodenberger, Hazard, Bellairs, a new reporter by the name of Johnson, another by the name of Walden Root (a nephew of the senator); and the growing consideration, if not admiration, of many of the newspapermen of the city. This latter was one of those curious growths not easy to explain—mouth-to-mouth chatter among the local newspapermen solely, and not extending to the public by any means. I was beginning, as I found, to be looked upon as a man of some importance in this small local world. I say this by reason of certain mention latterly thrust upon me. Wood, for instance, condescended sufficiently now to take me about with him to one or two Chinese restaurants of the most beggarly description in the environs of the downtown section—hangouts for crooks and thieves and disreputable tenderloin characters generally (of such was the beginning of the Chinese restaurant in America)—and to introduce me to a few of his Celestial friends, whose acquaintance apparently he had been most assiduously cultivating for some time past and with whom he was now on the best of terms. He had the happy knack of persuading himself that there was something vastly mysterious and superior about the whole Chinese race, that there was some Chinese organization known as the Six Companies, which, in so far as I could make out from him, was ruling very nearly (and secretly, of course) the entire habitable globe. For one thing, it had some connection with great constructive ventures of one kind and another, supplying, as he said, thousands of Chinese laborers to any one who desired them anywhere. And, although they were employed by others, it ruled them with a rod of iron, cutting their throats, for instance, and burying them head down in a bucket of rice when they failed to perform their bounden duties; or transferring their remains quietly to China in coffins made in China and brought here for that purpose whenever they died, supposing they had acted well and fulfilled the letter of their obligations. The Chinese who had worked for the builders of the Union Pacific had been supplied by this company, as I understood from him.

Again, there were the Chinese Freemasons, a society so old and so powerful and so mysterious, in so far as I could make out, that one might only speak of it in whispers for fear of getting into trouble. This, indeed, was the great organization of the world—in China and everywhere else. Kings and potentates knew of it well enough and trembled before its power. If it wished, it could sweep the Chinese Emperor and all European monarchs off their thrones tomorrow. There were rites, mysteries, sanctuaries within sanctuaries in this great organization. As yet, as Wood assured me, he himself was a mere outsider, snooping about, as it were, and, by degrees and peradventure, but slowly and surely, worming its secrets (its lowest organization mysteries only, of course) out of these Chinese restaurant-keepers and laundrymen here in St. Louis, whereby he hoped to profit in the following way. He was going to study Chinese, he said. He was going to China. There he was going to get into this marvellous organization through the influence of some of his Chinese friends here—no less!—via letters, wise pleas or commands. Then he was going to "get next" to some of the officials of the Chinese government, the leading ones, of course, and being thus highly recommended and thought of, come back here eventually to Washington as an official Chinese interpreter, attached perhaps to the Chinese legation at Washington. How he was to profit by this so vastly I could not see, but he seemed to think that he would. Naturally, I listened, but I must say I was by no means seriously impressed.

Then, again, there was his literary work, which he was always dreaming about and, in so far as I could make out, slaving over—his art ambitions, into which I, now, by degrees, was being permitted to look. I was becoming important myself, you see—therefore I must be a reasonably fair judge, I supposed. His great dream or scheme, in so far as I could make it out at the time, was to study the underworld life of St. Louis first hand—those horrible, grisly waterfront saloons and lowest tenderloin dives and brothels where, listening to the patois of thieves and pimps and lechers and drug fiends and murderers and outlaws generally, he was to extract from them, aside from their stories, some bizarre originality of phrase and scene, which, so he seemed to think, was to stand him in good stead in the composition of his tales. He was going to make stories out of them, show the horror, the pathos and the ridiculousness of their lives.

Well and good. I think myself that a great deal might have been done with it. Only at the time he seemed to me to be much too romantically inclined for the task (his great admirations being Loti and Percival Pollard!), but he was contenting himself with making notes— jotting down scraps of conversation heard at bars, in sloppy urinals, cheap dance halls and I know not what. Actually, with a little more time and a little more of that slowly arriving sanity which comes to most of us eventually, I am inclined to think he might have made something out of all this—a little something, anyhow. He was so much in earnest, so patient; only, to me, as I say, he was full of an almost impossible idealism and romance which threw everything (far beyond its just deserts, I am sure) into the arabesque and the grotesque. His dreams were too wild, his mood too utterly romantic, his deductions far beyond what a sane contemplation of the facts warranted.

And relative to this period I could other tales unfold. He and Peter, long before I had arrived on the scene, had surrounded themselves with a company of wayfarers of their own: down-and-out English army officers and grafting younger sons of good families; a Frenchman or two, one of whom was a poet; several struggling artists of both less and more years than themselves, who "grafted on them," as the phrase then went; and a few weird and disreputable characters so degraded and nondescript that I could scarcely make out what the charm was. At least two of their peculiar friends had rooms, where, in addition to Dick's and mine, we were now accustomed to meet. Poems, on occasion, were read. Dick's stories, as Peter invariably insisted, were "inflicted"; the "growler" or "duck"—a tin bucket of good size—was "rushed" for beer and cheese and crackers; and "hot crawfish," sold by old ambling negro men and women on the streets after midnight, were purchased and consumed with gusto. Captain Simons, Captain Sellar, Toussaint, Benét—these are mere names of figures that are now so dim that they are mere wraiths, ghosts ranged about a smoky, dimly lighted room in some downtown rooming house. Both Dick and Peter had reached that distinguished state where they were center of attraction as well as supports and props to these others, and between them got up weird entertainments—knockabout Dutch comedian acts, which they took down to some wretched dance hall somewhere and staged—Dick and Peter and sometimes Captain Sellar and Toussaint "doing a turn," as it were. The glee over the memory of these things as they now narrated them to me! The honor and exclusiveness in which their relations to these various individuals were held!

Physically, Wood was so thin, and yet mentally so vigorous, seeking, dreamful, that he was fascinating to look at at times. He had an idea that this bohemianism of his and his story-work were so important—far more important than anything else in the world. I have seen him enter a dirty, horrible saloon in one of St. Louis's lowest dive regions and, sitting down at a small sloppy table on a sanded or sawdusted floor (of such was this section), transcribe from memory whole sections of conversations he had heard elsewhere—outside on the street, for instance—trying to remember the exact word and phrase. Unlike myself, he had a knack of making friends with these shabby levee and underworld characters—syphilitic, sodden, blue-nosed bums mostly, whom he picked up from heaven knows where. And how he seemed to prize their vile language and viler thoughts! We think of the universe as moral. Our preachers and puritans shut themselves off in small, well-furnished sections of our cities and talk about morality and virtue and saving the world for Christ. They truly imagine that because a certain section, or a few sections even, are reasonably well swept and well ordered that all the world is so. I wish they would consider some of the things I have seen—which any reasonably curious soul can see in nearly any city in some such atmosphere as this—the horrible dens, the bedraggled souls, the truly evil and murderous spirits abroad. In this very upper southside section of St. Louis, bordering on the business heart, where Wood and McCord were fondest of roaming, I myself have seen of a snowy night a large, powerful Irish policeman dragging an old gray-headed harridan of, say, fifty or sixty along the street by her hair—along the gutter really, while he walked on the sidewalk—and the natives thinking nothing of it, or too cowardly to interfere.

"You Goddamned bitch, I'll show you! You won't come, will you? You Goddamned old whore—well, I'll fix you—." And because she was yelling and grabbing at his legs, he turned and struck her over the head two or three times with a long, oak nightstick such as policemen in the West were wont to carry in these sections at night.

"What do you want to hit that old woman with a club for?" I complained, being the brash newspaperman of twenty-one, and very vain of my position.

"Who the hell are you? What do you want to stick your nose in this for?" And then he paused long enough in the dragging and beating to survey me contemptuously and savagely.

"Well, I'm from the *Globe-Democrat*, and I know Murphy, the Chief of Police, all right," and then I stared at him.

"Well, now looky here, Charlie. Maybe y'are who you say. I'm willing to believe you, all right. But suppose you worked down here among these Goddamned cattle. Here's a Goddamned drunken bitch, that, drunk every night of her life. She's no Goddamned good. She's a Goddamned drunken, fucking old whore, that's what she is. She hangs around these barrelhouses until she gets a little booze in her, and then she begins to fight. I've had trouble with her before—ever since I've been here. Drunk or sober, she'd just as leave cut me as not. And I'm not hurting her by pulling her by her hair. She's been pulled that way before. I can't make her come any other way, almost. She's like a Goddamned wild cat. I believe you're from the *Globe*, all right, but now listen to her. She thinks she's got a friend!" (She was weeping and moaning and swearing at the same time—no polite oaths either, as I can tell you.) "Any one around here can tell you about Slippery Annie—that's what they call her—Slippery Annie. She's a Goddamned fighting cat, and say—" (this to Slippery Annie herself) "if you don't get up on your feet and walk with me to that box, I'll club you some more, you Goddamned old bitch. Don't you think you can put anything over on me."

She was drunk and cantankerous. I could see it. There was a slight drizzle of snow falling, causing the cobblestone streets to take on a Christmas-night atmosphere. From the low two- and three-story red brick houses about glowed illicit and profane lights. Here was an officer, a youngish man whom one would have assumed to be a rather decent sort, and yet here he was, beating an aged crone over the head in the snow, and those perfect home neighborhoods of the city not more than a mile or so away at the most. That is what I was always discovering for myself these days and wondering about—dregs cheek by jowl with alleged perfection. I was sick to my marrow.

"Ah, come away, Dreiser," counseled Wood. "Whaddya want to fuss for? She's drunk, can't you see? What else can he do?"

The policeman beamed cheerfully on Wood.

"You're right, sport," he said. "She ain't no damned good. Y' can see that yerself. Still, I won't hit 'er no more, but she's got to come along just the same—."

And by her arms, her neck and the back of her dress he partly pulled and partly shoved the wretched, staggering, smeary-faced creature to the nearest patrol box, about a half a block away, and pulled the handle.

Of the moralists and the churches I would like to ask, "Where do you suppose all these creatures come from? Is poverty or inherent tendency to blame, and, if so, who is to blame for either or both—God or man? If man, who is to blame for man?

Or—

'Tis a foolish question, I suppose.

CHAPTER XXXIII

And then there was McCord, bless his enthusiastic materialistic heart, who seemed to take fire from this joint companionship and was determined to do something, he scarcely knew what—be a painter, poet, collector or something. He was also a lover of this region, but in a different way. Peter's idea of a *grand* evening—at times (not always or very often even)—was to find some black house of prostitution, of which there were many in St. Louis, and entering (having made friends with some one before, the mistress or some girl) have one or two or three of the inmates come out and, while he played a flute and some one else a tambourine or small drum, dance naked in some weird savage way that took me instanter to the central wilds of Africa. I know not how he achieved these acquaintances—so strange they were. I was never with him when he did. He knew them, I presume, before ever he met me. But when I think of the shabby, poorly-lighted, low-ceiled rooms, the absolutely black or brown girls with their white teeth and shiny eyes, the absolutely unexplainable, unintelligible love of rhythm and the dance, the beating of a drum and the sinuous, winding motions of the body, I marvel. What is this? I have often asked myself since. How? Why? Who or what in the chemic or psychic depths of things loves the dance, rhythm, this aimless rum-tum-tum of a drum? For two or three hours of a night after working hours, from midnight to dawn nearly, I have sat with Peter and these blacks trying to be gay, feeling really that I was low, a criminal, and yet staring with all my eyesight and enjoying it intensely—feeling a strange, almost impossible reaction to it which then I was almost inwardly ashamed to acknowledge, but which since has come to have, to my mind at least, a dynamic something to it which is anything but evil. That way, as I now know, lies a better and saner interpretation of nature and the constructive forces of life. Our theology is too narrow. A God of this world, if there be one, is at once a compound of all our evil and all our good. The so-called forces of law and order and morality are probably indebted to these very shames, so-called, for their continued existence. Our God is our old devil plus our old God, only he is neither—something we haven't the brains as yet to comprehend.

Oola, boola, boola! Tum! tum! tum!
Oola, boola, boola! Tum! tum! tum!

So goes the ancient rune of the drums and the dance.

Who loves it? And why?

But to return to McCord. His mind was so wrought up by this rich pattern life was weaving before his eyes that he could scarcely sleep o' nights. Instead he was, as I say, for prowling about with us, Wood and myself, these winter days and first slowly warming ones of spring, and looking at the dark city after work hours. Or we would take a banjo, a mandolin and a flute,—McCord could perform on the latter and Dick on the mandolin—and, sallying forth in Forest Park or one of the minor parks on the south side, make the night hideous no doubt with our carollings until some solid policeman, assuming that the public had rights, would interfere and suggest that we desist. Our invariable retort was that we were newspaper men and artists and as such entitled to courtesies from the police, which the thick-soled minion of the law would occasionally admit. But more often he suggested, sometimes rather cantankerously we thought, that we be a little more careful. Or we would go to Dick's or my room and chatter and sing until dawn nearly, when, somewhat subdued, we would usually seek out some German saloonkeeper whom either Peter or Dick knew and, rousing him out of his slumbers at such an unholy hour as half-past four or five a.m., demand that he come down (they seemed always to live over the saloon) and supply us with ham and eggs and beer. On one of these occasions there was a loud argument which ended in our being driven away. In other cases mine host kindly enough came down and served us, assuming I suppose that youth and spirits would have to be considered.

One of the developments of my life at this time, due to my stage critical work, was the renewal of my desire—a fever it became at this time—to write a play or a comic opera on the order of *Wang* or *The Isle of Champagne,* two of the reigning successes of that day, or the pleasing *Robin Hood* of De Koven, which ran for a week or two during my period as a critic. In this idea I was aided by the fact that the atmosphere of the *Globe* office, as well as of St. Louis for that matter (for me anyhow), was both inspirational and creative. There were so many about here apparently who were destined to do things and were so anxious to begin— Wood, McCord, Hazard, a man by the name of Bennett who was engaged in sociologic propaganda of one kind and another, and still another, Albert Johnson by name, who before I came to St. Louis had resigned from the *Globe* and gone over to the *Chronicle,* and who according to Hartung, Hazard and others was a genius of the purest ray. I had only recently met him and, being greatly impressed, was moved to ambitious dreams by him—he was so captivating and inspirational a young man, with a life-urge and a poetic flare which were positively thrilling—like one of those young men whom Balzac was so fond of describing as coming to the great city to make their fortune. He was so fair haired, blue eyed, gay, wise, with a charming profile and figure. About him was much of an Apollo and not the least trace of any current convention—one who in the rumored mythical day of Pan would have run naked with that great god in the woods.

Somehow, at this time, to me at least, all St. Louis seemed to breathe of achievement in the arts—literary, musical and otherwise. It was a rich, thick, heavy atmosphere—an alchemist's menstruum. I have mentioned the wonderful W. C. Brann who preceded me in writing "Heard in the Corridors" and subsequently stirred America with the *Iconoclast*. There was in the city at this time Alfred Robyn, whose *Answer* had caught the emotional musical fancy of America and who was writing an opera already announced for local trial. I have described Hazard's novel and Dick's stories. Johnson, so we were all told, was surely destined for great literary fame. He had a dream of being a poet, a real one I think. And William Marion Reedy, then comparatively young and enthusiastic, an ex-*Globe* reporter, was already stirring the city with his newly issued *Mirror*. So it went.

Somehow all this, plus the fact that Augustus Thomas—a reporter on the *Post-Dispatch*—had come from here and that I was now seeing one of his plays, *In Mizzoura*, among others, moved me to the point where I finally thought out what I considered a fairly humorous situation or plot for a comic opera, which I decided to call *Jeremiah I*. It was based on the idea of transporting an old Indiana farmer of a most cantankerous, irritable and inquisitive disposition back into the era of the Aztecs of Mexico by a process purely magical—the result of striking a mythical Aztec stone on his farm. Owing to a religious invocation then being indulged in for the purpose of discovering a new Aztec ruler, he was assumed to be that same, and from beginning as a cowardly refugee in fear of his life, he was slowly, by the process of worship and adulation indulged in by the natives, changed into an amazing despot who eventually had all of three or four hundred ex-viziers in a cell, awaiting poisoning. He was only dissuaded from carrying out his rueful purpose by his desire for a certain Aztec maiden who, because of his crimes, avoided him and eventually persuaded him to change the form of government to that of a republic, with himself as a candidate for president.

There was nothing much to it. Its only humor was that evoked by the sight of a cranky, curious, critical farmer superimposed upon ancient architecture and forms of worship. Everything was, of course, turned upside down and inside out. Purely imaginary Aztec processions, dances, a court idiot and the like were a part of it. Having once thought it out, however, and being pleased with it, I worked at it feverishly nights when I was not out on an assignment or at the theatre, and in a week or less had a rough outline of it, lyrics and all, in my mind, which I first hinted at and then told to McCord and Wood with a great deal of satisfaction. As I looked at it then, it seemed amusing—very. It made me smile—sometimes laugh outright. I chuckled as I worked. Here was the way out of my various difficulties, I thought—the path to that great future I desired. I would become an author of comic opera books. There was an intense satisfaction in that. Already I saw myself in New York, famous, rich—possessed of every comfort and pleasure.

But one cannot write without encouragement, and having barely roughed it out, I now burned for assistance in developing it in detail—piecemeal as it were. Hazard had seen me writing and inquired what I was doing, but somehow I did not take any satisfaction in the thought of telling him. At best and as much as I liked him, Hazard was a rival—he was always talking about writing plays himself. His attitude when I had shown him the poem had chilled me. So I did not take him into my confidence fully.

But McCord, that warm, robustious enthusiast—he was the person I naturally gravitated to. McCord was an artist. He had, apparently, no ambition to be a playwright. He furnished a fine, hearty, generous comprehension. I decided to show it to him first, and to Wood, of course, at the same time.

Accordingly, I went into the art department one evening just at eight, when I thought I might catch Peter alone. He was there, hard at work over some additional snake picture—some marvellous triumph in Africa—and was evidently pleased with his labor. I can recall him even now, the gleam of cheerful satisfaction in his eye.

"Come in, old man. How are things?"

"Fine," I said.

"Anything new out your way?"

"Nothing except that I'm writing an opera."

"An opera!" His eye lighted. "Really?"

"Fact. I've been working on it all this week. I've almost finished it now."

"You mean the book, of course. You can't write music."

"Sure, the book," I replied.

"You don't say! That's fine! I don't like to be inquisitive, but if you care to tell me I'd like to hear about it."

"I'm only too glad," I said, and then roughly outlined my plot.

Peter was interested—very much so. He seemed to relish the whole idea hugely, so much so that he made the whole thing seem far more amusing to me than it had been before. Enamored of costumes and gorgeous settings, he appeared to be intensely interested in the opportunity which it offered for these same and immediately began to suggest possible color schemes which he thought would be effective. I was lifted to the seventh heaven. To think that I had worked out something in the operatic line which he would consider interesting.

Later in the same evening, at Peter's suggestion and with his aid, I outlined portions of it to Wood. He also apparently was strongly inclined to believe that it was good. He insisted that there must be an evening either at his room or mine when I would read it all to the two of them. Accordingly, a week later because of their enthusiasm I had worked it out complete in rough form and had had it typewritten. Then I read it to them, to much applause if you please—a veritable riot of success. A little while later, on one of our happy outings at night, it occurred to McCord that he would like to design costumes and stage settings for it, with which, plus the manuscript and music, it was to be presented to some manager. He even went so far as to suggest that he would love to act the part of Jeremiah I, and forthwith began to give us imitations of the proposed king's mannerisms and characteristics. Whatever the merit of the manuscript itself, certainly we imagined Peter's characterizations to be funny and laughed accordingly, and later he brought me as many as fifty designs of costumes and scenes in color, taken from the book, which amazed me by their charm. He had evidently worked for weeks—nights after hours, mornings before coming to the office, and Sundays. I was so thrilled I could scarcely believe my eyes. To think—to think that I had written the book of a real comic opera and that it was within the range of possibility that it might be produced.

Amazing. I certainly began to feel myself a personage, and yet into the bargain I can frankly state that I was not outwardly vain. At bottom I mistrusted the reality of it all. Fate could not be that kind. Not so swift. I would probably never get it produced anyhow—and so, unlike the man in the fable who, dreaming great dreams, kicked his tray of glassware over, I did not do so but went about my work as nervously and as enthusiastically as ever, hoping that I might have such great good fortune but not seriously depending on it. Perhaps it would have been better for me if I had.

CHAPTER XXXIV

The atmosphere of this world in which I now deemed I was moving was one of those delightful things which was, on a mind like mine, certain to leave a marked impression. It all seemed so wonderful, so rich with experience. We are inclined to think that emotions and feelings of certain periods are fleeting things which leave no deep impression, but this is not always true. There are certain conditions under which temperaments and atmospheres are joined and welded irretrievably, and this was one of them. I had come across an atmosphere and condition which suited my mental state precisely, and I felt vastly in love with it. This was the state for me, I thought—none better.

And these were some of the things which I considered that this state represented: Absolute immunity from thought or want of money. A fine liberty as to personal conduct—to go when one chose, to stay when one chose, and to do as one chose. One was not to be hampered by thought of personal morality except in so far as it was necessary to keep oneself sane and clean. Religion as preached by the churches had already lost its significance. Family life was a splendid thing if you had a lovely wife and loved her dearly, but you must have plenty of money to support her on, and your marriage must not interfere with your general conception of personal liberty. Art was really more important, the first thing in the world—art and your personal fame. You must really hold yourself in a dignified, silent reserve, but in such delightful ways (as did, for instance, Mr. Dick Wood) and bide your opportunities. When fame and money came, you might do as you please. Meanwhile you might solace your poverty and lonely hours with any such charming figures—male or female—as were artistically suitable. In my case it would have preferably been female. The cultivation of poetry, painting, literature, every form of art, and the beauty of the world as the source of all was, of course, the object of all men worth their salt. Such was the creed of Bohemia, as I understood it.

At the same time, as those who have experienced such things may know, I was not necessarily as blissfully happy as I may seem, for I had still so much work of a routine reportorial character to do that I was exceedingly annoyed. By contrast with this critical work which I liked very much, the other, outside of the largest news features, now seemed trivial or irritating, and yet it didn't either, exactly. For it must be remembered that the general news as I was helping dig it out from day to day was always suggesting to me dramas and tragedies which might be done in play form. Or, better yet, slowly revealing with a definiteness which could never be subsequently eradicated the absolute meaninglessness of life in so far as the individual was concerned—its essential tragedy as well as comedy. There might be, as I often said to myself even at this time, some divine far-off event to which the whole creation was moving, but in so far as the individual was concerned he was no very significant part of it. He was too casual, too purely accidental. No one really cared whether the individual lived or died, however much he might think of a nation or race or life in general. One of the things that grieved me intensely, as I have previously pointed out, was the sight of bitter poverty and failure. And also, by contrast, that I was not, among other things, one of those solid commercial figures of some kind— manufacturer, owner, grower—who, as I could see on every hand or thought I could, were free of apparently all danger of want and failure and were making a great success of their various commercial ventures. St. Louis was full of such men at this time—all American cities were, in fact. They filled the great hotels, the clubs, the mansions, the social positions of importance. They were the prominent people of all these inland cities and were most talked about. They were free to indulge in all those luxuries and pleasures which, as I so sadly saw, the poor were not privileged to indulge in—myself included. There was something about an immense factory of any kind, its exterior simplicity and bareness, the thrash of its inward life, its suggestion of energy, true force, compulsion and need, which moved me greatly. At the same time, the control of it somehow at this time always seemed essential to a man if he were to have any force or dignity in this world, and the fact that I was not in control of one (doing something which I, or the world anyhow, considered really serious) made me sad also, terribly so. Only such men, strong commercial types in this Western material world anyhow, were apparently to be considered. To be a pale sprout of a newspaper man, or even an editor or author, seemed at times wholly unimportant.

Naturally, at times this state of mind tended to make me irritable and even savage—by contrast with being sad. I thought that my benefactor, the great McCullagh, whom I by now truly revered, ought to see what an important man I was and to be good enough to give me the dramatic editorship free and clear, or at least to complicate my position with something over and above mere reporting. I ought to be allowed to do editorial or special work only. Why include the various minor news items of the day—including hotel registers and such—when there was nothing else to do, instead of leaving me to my proud critical labors? Besides, as I have perhaps not previously pointed out, my mind, although largely freed of Catholic and religious dogma generally and the belief in the workability of the Christian ideals as laid down in the Sermon on the Mount, was still—in my everyday life at least—constantly thinking of and repeating to itself those same highflown and idealistic maxims of Christ. And, being what by far the great majority of Americans are, an unconscious hypocrite, I contrasted the maxims with the seeming selfish materialism of the day (my own *not* included) which, while professing a faith in Christ and the following of His teachings, was sharply at variance with Him in practice and ideas. The strong men at the top, so comfortable, so indifferent, so cruelly dull, how I flailed them with these words of Christ. The faces of the poor were everywhere about me. Those large districts south of the business heart along the river and elsewhere—crowded as I thought with the unfit, the unsuccessful, the unhappy—how they haunted me and how I attempted, in my mind of course, to comfort them with the beatitudes, "—blessed are the poor, et cetera." At times, thinking of what Christ said and interviewing one important citizen and another, I gained the impression that some of them actually hated poverty, anyone who was poor, and that they did not care what became of them. This attitude seemed very terrible because, having been raised a Christian and taught to believe that there was a great deal to the Sermon on the Mount—a workable code, no less—I thought they ought to care.

"Lay not up for yourselves treasures upon earth, where moth and rust doth corrupt, and where thieves break through and steal: But lay up for yourselves treasures in heaven, where neither moth nor rust doth corrupt, and where thieves do not break through and steal: For where your treasure is there will your heart be also."

Imagine bothering with that in St. Louis in 1892!

"Take no thought for your life, what ye shall eat, or what ye shall drink; nor yet for your body, what ye shall put on. Is not the life more than meat, and the body than raiment?" (They may be, as I now think, but they seem to disappear without meat and raiment—here, at any rate.)

"Behold the fowls of the air: for they sow not, neither do they reap, nor gather into barns; yet your heavenly Father feedeth them. Are ye not much better than they?" (But they do sow or, the equivalent of it, toil and reap also. The frozen bird on the wire—the starved birds in bad seasons—how about their heavenly Father and them?)

"Consider the lilies of the field, how they grow; they toil not, neither do they spin: And yet I say unto you, That even Solomon in all his glory was not arrayed like one of these." (But they do toil and they do spin; the struggle underground is often pathetic—read Maeterlinck—and they often die for want of a reasonable result to their efforts.)

"Resist not evil; but whosoever shall smite thee on thy right cheek, turn to him the other also.

"And if any man will sue thee at the law, and take away thy coat, let him have thy cloak also.

"And whosoever shall compel thee to go a mile, go with him twain.

"Give to him that asketh thee, and from him that would borrow of thee turn not thou away.

"Love your enemies, bless them that curse you, do good to them that hate you, and pray for them which despitefully use you, and persecute you.

"Ask, and it shall be given you; seek and ye shall find; knock and it shall be opened unto you: for every one that asketh receiveth; and he that seeketh findeth; and to him that knocketh it shall be opened.

"And when thou prayest, thou shalt not be as the hypocrites are: for they love to pray standing in the synagogues and in the corners of the streets, that they may be seen of men. Verily I say unto you, they have their reward. But thou, when thou prayest, enter into thy closet, and when thou hast shut the door pray to thy Father which is in secret; and thy Father which seeth thee in secret shall reward thee openly.

"Judge not, that ye be not judged. For with what judgement ye judge, ye shall be judged: and with what measure ye meet, it shall be measured to you again.

"Not every one that sayeth unto me, Lord, Lord, shall enter into the kingdom of heaven, but he that doeth the will of my Father which is in heaven."

Statements like these, professed to be believed in by so many, and in contrast with the sharp, hard facts of life everywhere about me, pained me greatly. I could not see why it was that things could not be arranged better. Why didn't the world do something about it? Why didn't people reform? (!)

I forgot to note that already, in spite of my unhappiness, Mr. McCullagh had begun sending me out of town on various news stories of import, which was in itself the equivalent of a traveling correspondentship and might readily have led to my being officially recognized as such a correspondent if I had remained here long enough. Trials of murder cases in St. Joseph and Hannibal, threatened floods in lower Illinois, and train robberies between either St. Louis and Kansas City or St. Louis and Louisville—a common occurrence at this time in this region—made it necessary for me on occasion to make arrangements with either Hazard or Wood or both to carry on my dramatic work while I departed on these tasks, a necessity which I partly relished and partly disliked, being uncertain as to which task was the more important to me. But they most generously undertook the dramatic work for me and without recompense of any kind.

However, as I say, I was still not satisfied. Mentally I was too restless and dissatisfied—born so. Life, life, life—its contrasts, disappointments, lacks, enticements—was always irking me. Unlike the king in Baudelaire's distinguished poem who was master of only a rainy kingdom, I was a thrall in an unsatisfying one. The sun might shine never so brightly, the winds of fortune blow never so favorably. Though enjoying them with my eyes and rejoicing in them with one part of my mind, there was always this undertone of something that was not happiness. I was not placed right. I was not this, I was not that, rich, loved, happy and the like. Life was slipping away fast, I always said to myself. By the hour I could see the tiny sands of my little life's hourglass sifting down, and what was I achieving? True, I was still young but soon I would be old. Soon the strength time, the love time, the gay time of color and romance would be gone, and if I had not spent it fully, joyously, richly, what would there be left for me then? Disappointment and despair only. The joys of a mythical heaven or hereafter played no part in my calculations. When one was dead, one was probably dead for all time, hence the reason for the heartbreak in failure here and now— the awful tragedy of a love lost, a youth never properly enjoyed. Ah, me! Ah, me! Think of living and yet not living to the best of what life had to offer! Think of seeing this tinkling phantasmagoria of pain and pleasure—beauty and all sweets—go by and yet be compelled to be a bystander, a mere onlooker, enhungered but never satisfied! Was my cup full? By no means! Was life giving me a fraction of what I desired? Oh, no, no, no! Who would have the effrontery to say so? In this mood I worked on, doing sometimes self-amazing work because I was temporarily fascinated and entertained—at other times grumbling and dawdling and moaning over what seemed to me the horrible humdrum of it all.

One day, in just such a mood as this it was that I received the following letter from Lois, from whom I had not heard now in months (I have taken it from an old file):

Dear Theo,

Tomorrow is my wedding day. Tomorrow at twelve noon. This may strike you as strange. Well, I have waited, heaven knows how long—it has seemed like years to me—for some word, but I knew it was not to be. Your last letter showed me that. You said we must wait, but you did not say how long. Of course I understood. I knew that you did not intend to return, and so I took up again with Mr. Williams. I had to. What else have I to look forward to? You know how unhappy I am here with my family now that you are gone, in spite of how much they care for me.

Oh, Theo, you must think me foolish for writing this. I am ashamed of myself. Still I wanted to let you know and to say good-bye, for although you have been indifferent I cannot bear any hard feelings toward you. I will make Mr. Williams a good wife. He understands that I do not love him, but that I appreciate him. Tomorrow I will marry him, unless—unless something happens. You ought not to have told me that you loved me, Theo, unless you could have stayed with me. You have caused me so much pain.

But I must say good-bye. This is the last letter I shall ever write you. Don't send my letters now—tear them up. It is too late. Oh, if you only knew how hard it has been to bring myself to this.

Lois.

I sat and stared at the floor after reading this. It was in the office of the *Globe* where all my mail came. The pain I had caused—was causing—was a heavy weight. The letter really touched my heart (such as it was), and made me suffer. The implication that, if I would still come to Chicago before noon of this day (I did not get the letter until her wedding day) or wire possibly for her to delay, I still might have her was too much. I thought, what if I should go to Chicago, as she evidently wishes, and bring her away—then what? To her it would be a beautiful thing, the height of romance, saving her from a cruel or dreary fate. But what of me? Would I be happy? Permanently? And if I was not, eventually would she be with me? Was this profession of which I was a part—or my present restless and uncertain state of mind— anything on which to base a marriage? Instinctively I knew it wasn't and, incidentally, that Lois, in spite of my great sadness and affection for her, was really nothing more to me than a passing bit of beauty, charming in itself, but of no great import to me. I was sad for her and for myself, verily, saddest because of that chiefest characteristic of mine and of life which will not let anything endure permanently—love, wealth, fame. I was too restless, too changeful, but so is life itself, I told myself. Before me at this time rose a picture of my then finances as compared with what they ought to be, and what I desired, and of any future in marriage that I might have based on them. Actually, as it looked at the time, it seemed more the fault of life than of me. I was, as I have said, now getting twenty-five dollars a week. But what was that?—enough to support a wife on? Certainly not. Could I travel? Suppose I lost my position here . . . I had no money saved up. And then the working hours I had to put in here—no newspaper man should ever marry, working such hours. He had no time to marry or to give to a wife after he was married.

This conclusion, balancing with the wish I had for much greater advancement, caused me as usual to hesitate. I was in no likelihood of doing anything, even if I could have, for the reason, as I have said before, that I felt no great impelling passion for Lois. It was more sentiment than anything else, growing more and more roseate and less operative as the likelihood of my doing anything about it grew less and less. I would not have gone—any one knowing me might have told that. I groaned inwardly, but the night came and sleep and the next day, and I had not answered. The day before at noon Lois was married, as she afterward told me—years afterward, when the fire was all gone and this romance was ended forever.

During the next few weeks thereafter I dawdled about the city, wondering what should become of me. I was not making any marked progress, I thought. My dramatic work, interesting as it was from some points of view, was so trivial from the point of view of space or public attention given it that, although I received free theatre tickets and saw many plays, I felt that I was wasting my time doing it. What good was it all to me? Where was I getting by it, truly?

"I must do something," I told myself. "I must make some move to get out of this hopeless profession." Otherwise I would rot in it—be an awful failure.

CHAPTER XXXV

Curiously, circumstances were bringing about an onward, if not upward, step whether I wished it or no. My own restless, querulous temperament was the cause of it, as I will show. I was becoming daily, as I have said, so restless and incensed and unhappy that it would have been strange if something had not happened. To think that there was no more in this dramatic work for me than now appeared and that, in addition, without any consideration for the work involved, Mr. Mc-Cullagh was allowing Mr. Mitchell to give me afternoon and night assignments when, as I saw it, I had fairly important theatrical performances to report! As a matter of fact, they were not important and Mr. McCullagh was really right, but no matter. Mr. Mitchell had no consideration for my critical work, however, and that was the thorn. He continued to give me not only one, but two or three things to do on nights when I felt that I ought to be permitted to spend the entire evening witnessing a single performance. I take it he was overdoing it some. This was to pay me, I suppose, for having gone over his head. At any rate, instead of going over his head once more and complaining to McCullagh direct, I took it out in private rages and despairs. The reason for this was that I did not wish to appear to be "a knocker," as the phrase went, or a complainer in Mr. McCullagh's eyes. I was too much afraid of him as well as fond of him, and I did not wish to lower myself in his estimation. Besides, again, I had too much respect for his many duties. If he gathered the idea that I was restless and complaining, he would probably not help me at all. In consequence, I remained silent, but the result was that I grew more and more resentful and finally, per accident, this, as I deemed it, inconsiderateness on the part of Mitchell brought on a catastrophe, laughable to a degree from one point of view and yet ultra-serious from another. The details were as follows.

It happened that one Sunday night late in April three shows were scheduled to arrive in the city and open, the performances being in each case worthy, as I thought, of special attention. Nearly all new shows opened in St. Louis on Sunday night. Of course, I could not attend them individually on the same night, and it was also true that owing to the sometimes pressing duties of the other reporters I could not, as I thought, always get a suitable man to help me. In this case I might have given both Dick and Peter tickets and asked them to help me, but I decided, since this was a custom which had been practiced by my predecessor at times, to write up the notices beforehand, the facts being culled from various press-agent accounts which were invariably sent in beforehand, and then possibly comment on the plays more succinctly later in some notes which I published midweek. It was my intention to go about afterward, a little while to each one, and verify these press-agent impressions.

It so happened, however, that on this particular evening Mr. Mitchell had other plans for me. Without consulting me as to my theatrical duties, he handed me a slip of paper at about seven in the evening containing a notice of a street car holdup in the far western suburbs of the city which required additional information.

"You go out there and see what you can find out about that."

I was about to protest, but concluded that there was no use. He would merely advise me to write up the notices of the shows as I had planned or, worse yet, tell me to let other people do them. I thought once of protesting to Mr. McCullagh, but went my way finally, determined to do the best I could and protest later. I would hurry up and get the details as quickly as possible and then come back and visit the theatres.

However, when I reached the scene of the supposed holdup, there was nothing to guide me. The people at the carbarns did not know anything about it, and the crew which had been held up was not present. I visited a far outlying police station, but the sergeant in charge had no more information than that which had been sent to headquarters, which was that the alleged crime was not so very important—a few dollars stolen. Then I went to the exact spot, but there were no houses in the neighborhood—only a barren stretch of track lying out in a rain-soaked plain. It was a gloomy, wet night, and I decided to return to the city. Plainly there was no news of any importance to be extracted.

But when I finally reached a car line and a car, it was late. The long distance out and the walks to the carbarn and police station had consumed much time. I found as I neared the city that it was all of eleven o'clock, and would be eleven-thirty before I reached the office. What chance had I to visit the theatres then, I asked myself angrily— to know even whether the shows had really arrived? There had been heavy rains all over the West for a week past. Many washouts had occurred—a common occurrence in that country, entailing serious delays to trains at times. It was entirely possible that the shows had not arrived. Instead of arranging to discover this exactly before going out, or phoning from somewhere during the evening to find out, I had neglected it, thinking to get back in time or work it out somehow. As it happened, however, I didn't, you see.

"I ought to go around and see about those shows," I thought dismally. "Some one of them might not have got in." But at the same time I was so irritated by the task that had unnecessarily, as I thought, been imposed upon me that I told myself I really did not care whether they had arrived or not. This was not true. I was worried.

I got off finally in front of the nearest theatre and went up to the door, but it was silent and dark. I thought of asking the drugman, who occupied the corner of the building, but that seemed a rather silly thing to be doing at this hour, and I neglected to do it. Nevertheless, something kept telling me afterwards that I should have done so. I had, as it were, a psychic hunch. Then I thought of phoning the rival morning paper, the *Republic,* when I reached the office and asking the dramatic man, but when I reached the office I had first to report to Mitchell, who was just leaving, and then, irritated and indifferent, I put off doing so for the moment. Perhaps Hartung, I told myself, would know.

"Do you know what time the first edition goes to press here, Hugh?" I asked of him at a quarter after twelve.

"Twelve-thirty, I think. The telegraph man can tell you."

"Do you know whether the dramatic stuff I sent up in the afternoon gets in that?"

"Sure. At least I think it does. You'd better see the foreman of the composing room about that, though."

I went upstairs. Instead of calling up the *Republic* at once or any of the managers of the theatres who had phones, or knocking out the notices entirely as I should have, I thought to inquire how matters stood with the first edition—to find out how much time I had. I was not sure that I had any reason for wondering about my shows, though something kept telling me to make sure. What held me back was one of those unkind evil spirits, I suppose.

Finding that the first edition had already been closed with the notices in it, I went to the phone and called up the *Republic.* The dramatic editor had gone. Then I tried to reach another of the theatres, but there was no response. The clock registered twelve-thirty a.m. by then, and I weakly concluded that there was no use to be alarmed. Things were probably all right.

I went home and went to bed but slept poorly, troubled by the thought that something might be wrong and wishing that I had not been so lackadaisical about it all. Why hadn't I phoned earlier? I kept asking myself. Why couldn't I attend to things as I should at the proper time instead of dawdling about in this fashion? It was true that Mitchell was imposing on me, but still if anything went wrong now, I would get the blame. I sighed and tried to sleep, but I couldn't.

There is a curious tendency in some natures to hesitate and delay—a tendency which is due partially to timidity and partially to an overpowering sense of obstacles to overcome. Such natures are not exactly lazy—they are at once optimistic and careless. The thought that things may come out right consoles them. They linger, hesitate, and delay all the more when a little pride or sense of injury besets them, and then when the calamity falls, they stare in dumb amazement. "Why did I not do so and so?" they are wont to ask of themselves. "Whatever possessed me to neglect that detail?" The more mystical of spirit are inclined to attribute their indiscretions to malign, opposing forces. They see in nature a crowd of unfriendly spirits besetting them to their harm. This was myself to a dot. Supposing one of the shows had by some dire chance not reached the city!

The next morning I arose and went through the two morning papers very eagerly and nervously the first thing. To my utmost horror and distress, there in the *Republic* on the first page was an announce-ment to the effect that owing to various washouts in several states, no one of the three shows which had been scheduled to arrive the night before, and which I had written up as having appeared, had arrived! And in my own paper, to my great pain and distress, on an inside page was a full account of their having been staged and of the agreeable reception accorded them!

To say that I was tortured is putting it mildly. "Oh, Lord," I exclaimed as I now viewed my amazing statements—amazing in light of the fact that the shows had not arrived at all. "What will McCullagh say?" What would the other newspapers say? The perspiration fairly burst from my forehead as I read that "a large and enthusiastic audience had received Mr. Sol Smith Russell" at the Grand and that the gallery of a certain performance at Pope's Theatre, which I deemed unworthy, "was top-heavy." I began to speculate at once as to what newspaper criticism, if any, would follow this last performance, remembering Sissieretta Jones and my tendency to draw the lightning of public observation and criticism. "Great God!" I thought. "Wait till he sees this! This is certainly the last straw." And I was nearly ready to weep, so depressed I was. At once I saw myself not only the laughingstock of the town, but discharged also. Think of my being discharged now, and that after all my fine dreams as to the future.

In anticipation of possible disaster I now went to the office and removed my few belongings, resolved to be prepared for the worst, whatever happened. In anticipation of disaster also, but more with a feeling that I owed Mr. McCullagh an explanation than anything else, I sat down and composed a letter to him in which I explained from my point of view just how the thing had happened. I did not attempt either to attack Mr. Mitchell or to shield myself, but merely illustrated how I had been expected to handle my critical work in this office—but all this without bitterness and, as I thought, exactly as it was. I told him also how kind I thought he had been, how much I had valued his personal regard, and asked him not to think too ill of me, that really I had not meant to do him an injury—as I had not. This letter I put into an envelope addressed to "Mr. Joseph B. McCullagh, Personal," and going forward to his private office before any one had come down, laid it on his desk. Then I retired to my room to await the afternoon papers and think.

They were not long in appearing and, as I had feared, neither of the two leading afternoon papers had failed to note the faux pas. It was mutton for their gravy.

With the most delicate, laughing raillery they had seized upon this latest error of the great *Globe* as a remarkable demonstration of what they affected to believe was its editor's lately acquired mediumistic and psychic powers. I have forgotten to note that the *Globe* was regularly given to writing up various séances, slate-writing demonstrations and the like in St. Louis and elsewhere—things in which Mr. McCullagh was interested—and this was now professedly looked upon as a fresh demonstration of his development in that line. He was becoming a great medium himself. "Oh, Lord. Oh, Lord," I groaned when I read this.

"To see three shows at once," observed the *Post-Dispatch*, "and those three widely separated by miles of country and washed-out sections of railroad in three different states (Illinois, Iowa and Missouri) is indeed a triumph, but to see them as having arrived and displaying their individual delights to three separate audiences of varying proportions assembled for the purpose is truly amazing—one of the finest demonstrations of mediumistic, or perhaps we had better say materializing, power yet given to science to record. Indeed, now that we think of it, it is an achievement so astounding that even the *Globe* itself may well be proud of it—one of the finest flights of which the human mind or its great editor's psychic strength is capable. We venture to say that no spiritualist or materializing medium has ever outrivaled it. We have always known that Mr. McCullagh is a great man—none greater. The illuminating charm of his editorial page is sufficient proof of that. But this latest essay of his in the realm of combined dramatic criticism, supernatural insight and materialization is one of the most perfect things of its kind—a great feat—and can only be explained by genius of the purest form. It is psychic, supernatural, spooky." Then it went on, as did the *Evening Chronicle,* to explain how ably and interestingly the spirit audiences and actors had conducted themselves, doing their part without a murmur—although they might as well have been resting at the time, not having (the actors at least) any contract which compelled their subconscious or psychic selves to work. Incidentally it was explained that in the future it would be unnecessary to have any dramatic critics at all at the *Globe.* Why have one? Was not the psychic mind of the editor sufficient? And, anyhow, the human race was plainly fast reaching that place where it could perceive in advance that which was about to take place without stirring from its chair; and in proof of this it pointed, of course, to the noble mind which now occupied the editorial chair of the *Globe-Democrat,* never moving from his seat but seeing all this just the same.

To say that I was agonized as I read this jesting is to say really nothing at all. Sweat rolled from my forehead. My nerves shook from sheer shame. And to think that this was the second time within a month or so that I had made my great benefactor the laughingstock of a great city! What must he think of me? I could see him at the moment reading the editorial himself! Who would endure it? Why should he? Naturally he would discharge me—and he ought to.

Not knowing what to do, I sat there and waited. There was a little clock in my room, and I can almost hear it tick yet as I sat and brooded. Alas, for all my fine dreams, my great future, my standing in this man's eyes and on this paper! What was to become of me now? Who would have me here in St. Louis or elsewhere? I saw myself returning crestfallen to Chicago to do what—hide away from my benefactor there? What would Peter, Dick, Hazard, Johnson, Bellairs—all my newfound friends—think? Alas, alas. For a day or two after this I could scarcely eat or sleep for thinking. Instead of going boldly to the office and seeing my friends who were still fond of me, if laughing at my break—or Mr. McCullagh, who subsequently showed me that he was sorry and wanted me to come back—I slipped about the city to cheap restaurants and the like, meditating on my fate and wondering what I was to do. Where was I to go now? To whom apply for a position? Would anybody have me after this terrible break?

For at least a week, during the idlest hours of the morning and evening, I would slip out and get a little something to eat or loiter in an old and but little-frequented bookstore in Walnut Street, which I had come to like, and so keep myself out of sight and out of mind, I hoped. Sad! Kind heaven, how sad I really was! Words will never convey it. Now in a spirit of intense depression, I picked up a few old books, deciding to read more, to make myself more fit for life since, as I now felt, I was so very deficient, scarcely worthy to work anywhere, and in need of education and likely to endure a long spell of leisure.

Again, I decided that I would have to leave St. Louis, as no one would have me, and began to think of Chicago and whether I could stand to return there or whether I had better drift on to a strange place. If I went on, how would I live or travel since I had but little money— very little indeed, having wasted it, as I now thought, on riotous living, fixing up this room, eating occasionally with Dick and Peter and buying new clothes! (Alas, alas, for the unhappy end of a spendthrift!) After mooning about for a day or two more and weeping in my beard, as it were, I finally concluded that since I was so short of cash I would have to move and, what was more, that I could not very well leave St. Louis right away without earning a little more somehow—I scarcely knew how. In consequence, I now decided that I had better try my luck here again—try for a place on one of the lesser papers. They might not refuse me. It was entirely possible that, if I explained my state, they would allow me to work for a few weeks. In consequence, one morning, without venturing near the *Globe*, and giving the principal meeting places of reporters and friends a wide berth, I ventured into the office of the old *St. Louis Republic*, then thriving fairly well in an old building at 3rd and Chestnut Streets—in one of the darkest and most dilapidated portions of St. Louis. And here with a heavy heart I awaited the coming of the rival of the *Globe*'s city editor, one H. B. Wandell, no less, of whom I had heard a great deal but whom I had never seen.

CHAPTER XXXVI

The appearance of the *Republic* office, exteriorly and interiorly, after that of the *Globe* with its eight stories, its marble halls and pleasingly finished editorial rooms, was a blow to me—a sad comedown, as I thought—especially since the *Globe* was so much more impressive in every way and centrally situated. And the *Republic*, as I have said, was in a tumbledown old building in a fairly deserted old neighborhood at the outskirts of the business heart, in that region near the waterfront from which the city proper had been steadily growing away for years. This paper, if I am not mistaken, had been founded in 1808. It was to a former editor of it that I had brought my principal letter of introduction. It was so altogether old and rattletrap that it was discouraging at first sight. The elevator as I had discovered on entering was a slow and wheezy box, bumping and creeping as it ran, and suggesting immediate collapse. The boards of the entry hall as well as the city editorial room squeaked under my feet. The city reportorial room, where, if I secured a place now, I would work, was larger than that of the *Globe* and higher ceiled if anything—once an imposing room—but beyond that had no advantage. The windows were tall but cracked as to their panes and patched with now faded and even yellow copy paper, and the desks, some fifteen or twenty all told, were old, dusty, knife-marked, smeared with endless ages of paste and ink, and altogether in a disreputable condition. There were wastepaper and rubbish on the floor. There was no sign of either paint or wallpaper about the place. If there ever had been wallpaper, it had long since disappeared. The only windows of any import—those facing the east—looked out into a business court or alley, where trucks and vans creaked all day but which at night was as silent as the grave, as was this whole neighborhood. The buildings directly opposite were decayed wholesale houses of some unimportant kind, where, in slimpsy rags of dresses or messy trousers and shirts, girls and boys of fourteen to twenty or thereabout—tenement girls and tenement boys—worked all day. The girls' necks were, in the summertime at least, open to their breasts, and their sleeves rolled to their shoulders; the boys, in armless undershirts and with tousled hair, flirted with them, or they with the young and avid reporters of our local staff, who seemed not at all averse to their slimpsy charms—I among the others. But I am getting ahead of my story.

The city editor, one H. B. Wandell, whom I shortly after encountered, was one of those odd forceful characters who, because of my youth and extreme impressionability perhaps and his own vigor and point of view, succeeded in making a deep impression on me at once. He was such a queer little man—so different to Mitchell and McCullagh—jumping, restless, vigorous, mouse-like, with piercing eyes that reminded one vividly of those of a hawk, and a dark, swarthy skin somehow made all the more emphatic by a large, humped, protruding nose pierced by big nostrils. His hands were small, wrinkled and claw-like, and he had large yellowish teeth which showed rather fully when he laughed. And that laugh! I can hear it yet—when he was amused, a cross between a yelp and a cackle. Somehow it always seemed to me to be a mirthless laugh, insincere, and yet somehow also it had an element of appreciation in it. He could, as it were, see a point at which others ought to laugh without sincerely enjoying it himself. One of the things which impressed me at the time and still sticks in my mind was that he was at once a small and yet a large man mentally—wise and incisive in many ways, petty and even venomous in others—a man to coddle and placate should you chance to find yourself beholden to him, one to avoid if you were not; but on the whole a man above the average in ability, or a few miles from the borderline of greatness, as it were.

And he had the strangest, fussiest, bossiest love of great literature of anyone I have ever known, especially in the realm of the news-papers—although that is where you find true greatness so often appreci-ated, by the underlings at least. Zola, as I recall it now, was at this time his beau ideal, and after him Balzac and Loti (the latter just then admitted to the French Academy). He seemed to know them well and to admire and even love them after his fashion. Zola's vivid descriptions of the drab and the gross and the horrible—how they appealed to him! And Balzac's and Loti's sure handling of the sensual and the poignant! How often have I heard him refer to them with admiration, giving me the line and phrase of certain stark pictures, and yet at the same time there was a sneaking bending of the knee to the Middlewest conven-tions of which he was a part, a kind of horror of having it known that he approved of these things! (Pathetic America.) Incidentally, he then had the reputation of being one of the best city editors in the city—far superior to the late loggy Tobe, of whom I was now free. Previously he had been city editor of the *Globe* for many years, having left a record for achievement still favorably spoken of in that office. Also, sometime after I had left St. Louis, he returned to the *Globe* and became once more its guide and selector in the matter of local news.

But that is neither here nor there in so far as I am concerned, save as it illustrates what is a cardinal truth of the newspaper world, and that is that the best of newspapermen are occasionally to be found on the poorest or worst of papers—temporarily anyhow—and vice versa.

Just at this time, as I understood, he was here because the *Republic* was making a staggering effort to build itself up in popular esteem, which it finally succeeded in doing after McCullagh's death, becoming once more the leading morning paper as it had been years before the *Globe* arose to power under McCullagh. Just now, however, in my despondent mood, it seemed an exceedingly sad affair, and I a very sad example of how not to get on.

Mr. Wandell, as I now soon learned, had heard of me and my recent faux pas as well as some of the other things I had been doing.

"You say your name is Dreiser," he commented when I approached him and explained.

"Yes, sir."

"Been working on the *Globe*, have you? What did they pay you?" I told him.

"When did you leave there?"

"About three days ago."

"Why did you leave?"

I told him. "Perhaps you saw those notices of three shows that didn't arrive in town. I'm the man who wrote them up."

"Oh, ho! ho! ho! Ha! ha! ha!" He began eying me drily and slapping his knee. "I saw those. Ha! ha! ha! Ha! ha! ha! Yes. That was very funny. Very." (His manner seemed to belie it entirely.) "I know all about that. We had an editorial on it. And so McCullagh fired you, did he?"

"No, sir," I replied indignantly. "I quit. I thought he might want to, and I put a letter on his desk and left."

"Ha! ha! ha! Quite right! That's very funny. I know just how they do over there. I was city editor there myself once. They write them up in advance once in awhile. We do here. Where do you come from?"

I told him.

He meditated awhile, as though he was uncertain whether he needed any one. "You say you got thirty there. I couldn't pay anybody that much here, not to begin with. We never give anyone more than eighteen to begin with. Besides, I have a full staff just now and it's summer. I might use another man if eighteen would be enough. You might think it over and come in and see me again sometime."

Although my spirits fell at this mention of so great a drop in salary, I hastened to explain that I would be glad to accept eighteen. I needed to be at work again. "Whatever you would consider fair would be satisfactory to me," I added.

He smiled. "The newspaper market is slow just now. If your work proved satisfactory I might raise you, a little later." He must have perceived that he had a soft, more or less unsophisticated boy to deal with. He was most superior in his tone and indifferent.

"Suppose you write me a little article about something, just to show me what you can do," he added.

I went away, insulted by this last request and despairing, but realized that I would not get the place if I did not write an article and that most certainly I would if I did. In spite of all he said, I could feel that he wanted me, only I had no skill in manipulating my own affairs. A cleverer man might have done better. To drop from thirty dollars and a position as dramatic editor to eighteen and a mere job as a reporter once more was terrible. With a grain of philosophic melancholy, I faced it, however, feeling that if I worked hard I might yet get a start in some way or other. I would work and save my money and then, if I had not bettered myself later on, would leave St. Louis. My ability must be worth something somewhere. It had been on the *Globe*. Who knows? This new man might take a fancy to me and promote me. I went home, wrote the article—a mere nothing about some street scene—and returned and left it. The next day I called again.

"All right," he said. "You can go to work."

I went back into that large shabby room and took a seat. In a few minutes the place filled up with a staff, most of whom I knew and all of whom eyed me curiously—reporters, special editors such as the dramatic, sporting, railroad, religious and the like—and the city editor and his assistant, a Mr. Williams, of blessed memory (peace be to him wherever he is), one-eyed, sad, impressive, intelligent, who had nothing but kind things to say of what I wrote and who was friendly and helpful to the day that I left.

In a little while I was called, or rather, as on the *Globe*, the assignment book was put out, with the task I was to undertake written out,—something of no great import. Before I left I was called in and advised concerning it. What it was I have forgotten. I went out, looked into it, whatever it was, and reported later in the day when, having

written it, Mr. Williams took it and later edited it and "sent it up."
When I asked him nervously later whether it was all right, he said,
"Yes, I think so. It reads all right to me," and then gave me a kindly
one-eyed smile, if you can imagine such a thing. I liked him from the
first day, a better editor really than Wandell,—one with more taste and
discrimination and one who subsequently rose to a higher position
elsewhere later, as previously he had held one somewhere else. Meanwhile I strolled about thinking of my great fall. It seemed as though I
should never get over this, but in a few days I was back into my old
reportorial routine, depressed but secure as to this salary and convinced
that I could write as satisfactorily as ever and for any newspaper.

Oh, charming days on this antique and yet still young and vigorous paper! Oh, glorious breath of tangled and complex life pouring in
fresh each day, so rich, so non-understandable, so tantalizing, so stirring. You hours spent here in hot days, or out in the hotter streets of the
city, pursuing and attempting to unravel the endless unravelable tangles of endless pleasures and pains. Will I ever forget you? The hot
crowded streets of the "downtown" heart, the long wide thoroughfares
of comfortable homes in the west end where people sat in rocking
chairs of an evening and smoked or sang or conversed in idle laughing
ways—"safe," conservative, self-centered homes where all the conventions of our Midwestern life of that day were observed or pretended to,
regardless of what anguishes and tragedies their simple walls might
conceal. The hot, packed, treeless thoroughfares of the waterfront and
the slum regions—dirty, smelly, hopeless, and only a few miles away
from the comfortable other section, and yet so amazingly far apart in
every way, spiritually and otherwise. How wonderful it all was! The
loving, spooning, dreaming atmosphere of the parks, the exclusiveness
and hard ambitious character of the great mansions in the west end.
How I saw, sensed, mooned, yearned over it all!

For the romance of my own youth was upon me and my ambitions
and my dreams, coloring it all. Does the gull sense the terrors of the
deep, or the butterfly the traps and snares of the woods and fields?
Neither I. Roaming this keen new ambitious Midwestern city, life- and
love-hungry and underpaid, eager and ambitious, I still found so much
in the worst to soothe, so much in the best to torture me. In every scene
of ease or pleasure were both a lure and a reproach, in every aspect of
tragedy or poverty a threat or a warning. I was never tired of looking at

the hot, hungry, weary slums any more than I was at the glories of the mansions of the west end. Both had their lure, their charm, one because it was a state worse than my own, the other because it was a better—immeasurably so, as I thought. Amid it all I hurried, writing and dreaming, half-laughing and half-crying as I might, with now a tale to move me to laughter and now another to bottomless despair. But always youth, youth, and the crash of the presses of our paper in the basement below me and a fresh damp paper laid on my desk of a morning with "the news" and my own petty achievements or failures to cheer or disappoint me—so it went, day in and day out, day in and day out.

The *Republic*, while not as successful as the *Globe-Democrat*, was in some ways, as I found a little later, a much better paper for me to work on, at any rate. For one thing, it took me out, as I have said, from under the domination of Mr. Mitchell, a man who was really a wet blanket upon me, if not upon newspaper talent in general, and put me under one who, whatever may have been his defects (and I cannot say that they were many), gave me far greater latitude in which to write and supplied a far better judgement as to what constituted a story and a news feature than did the other. Now that I think of him, Mr. Wandell was far and away the best judge of news from a dramatic or story point of view of anyone I ever worked for. Unlike the city editor of the *Globe* he had a passion for drama.

"A good story, is it?" I can see him smirking and rubbing his hands miser- or gourmet-fashion as over a pot of gold or a fine dish. "She said that, did she? Ha! ha! That's excellent—excellent. You saw him, did you? And the brother, too! By George—that'll make a story. Be careful how you write that now. All the facts you know—just as far as they will carry you—but we don't want any libel suits, remember. We don't want you to say anything we can't substantiate, but I don't want you to be afraid either. Write it strong, clear, definite. Get in touches of local color, if you can. Ever read Zola or Balzac? Well, you should. Bare facts are what are needed in a case like this, with lots of color as to the scenery or atmosphere—the room, the other people, the street and all that. You get me, don't you? You need raw color at times of that sort—lots of it, like Balzac or Zola give it to you."

I recall him now, lecturing like a stage director.

And truly, truly, he was a great city editor, as time proved to me, even if I secured but little cash out of it. For I always felt—perhaps unjustly, who knows—that he made but small if any effort to advantage me in any way except that of writing. He was nearly always enthusiastic over my work, in a hard bright waspish way, quite as he was nearly always excited about the glittering realistic facts of life which this Midwestern world was fairly determined that it would not see. He must have known—I suppose he did well enough—what a sham and a fake most of the Midwestern pretensions to sanctity and purity were, and yet if he did, and was irritated by them, he said little if anything to me, nothing in fact. Like most Midwestern and other Americans of the time he was probably confused by the endless clatter concerning personal perfection—the Christ ideal as opposed to the actual working details of life. He could not decide for himself which was true and which false—the Christ theory or that of a Zola or both. At the same time, when things were looking up from a news point of view, and great strong realistic facts were coming to the surface regardless of local sentiment,—facts which utterly contradicted all the noble folderol of the puritans and the religionists—he was positively transformed. At such times there was something gay and even appealing about him. In those hours when the loom of local life seemed to be weaving brilliant dramatic or tragic patterns of a realistic Zolaesque character, he was positively beside himself with gayety, trotting to and fro in the local room, or between it and the front or editorial offices, leaning over the shoulders of scribbling reporters and interrupting them to ask details or to caution them as to certain facts which they must or must not include, beaming at the ceiling or floor, whistling, singing, rubbing his hands—a veritable imp or faun of pleasure and enthusiasm. Deaths, murders, great social or political scandals or upheavals, and the like, those things which presented the rough raw facts of life as well as its tenderer aspects seemed to throw him into an ecstasy—not over the woes of others but over the fact that he was to have an interesting paper tomorrow and that the real grim facts of life were at last coming to the surface, regardless. "Ah, it was a terrible thing, was it? He killed her in cold blood, eh? You say there was a great crowd out there, do you? Well! Well! Well, write it all up. Looks like a pretty good story to me,— doesn't it to you? Write a good, strong introduction for it, you know— all the facts in the first paragraph—and then go on and tell your story. You can have as much space as you want for that—a column, column and a half, or two, just as it runs. Let me look at it before you turn it in."

Then he would begin whistling or singing—very badly, I must say—or would walk up and down in the city room rubbing his hands in obvious satisfaction. It was wonderful! Wonderful!

And that reportorial room—how it seemed to thrill or sing at such hours, between five and seven at night when the stories of the afternoon were coming in, or between ten-thirty and midnight when the full grist of the day was finally being ground out. How it throbbed with human life and thought, quite like a mill room full of looms or a counting house in which endless records and exchanges were being made. Those reporters—eighteen or twenty of them about me—how they bent over their desks, scratching and thinking, their hands to their brows, puzzling, their minds lost in the mazes of arrangement and composition.

Wandell had no least tolerance for any but the best of newspaper reporters, as you may well imagine, and would discharge a man promptly for falling down on a story—especially if he could connect it with the feeling that the reporter was not as good a newspaperman as he should be, even though it might not always be his own fault. He hated commonplace men and would often ask me in a spirit of unrest if I knew of any especially good ones anywhere with whom he could replace others, a thought which jarred me but which did not prevent me from telling him. Somehow I had an eye and a taste for exceptional men myself. It was not so very long—perhaps a month or two or three at the most and despite my newness and my meagre salary—before he began to rely on me to supply him with suitable men, so much so that I soon began to get the reputation of being a local arbiter of jobs—one who could get men in or keep them out—a thing which did me a little harm later, made me some enemies. In the meanwhile, while he was trying me out to suit himself, he had been giving me only routine work, the North 7th Street police station afternoons and evenings, where one or two interesting stories might be expected every day—crimes or sordid romances of one kind or another,—or occasional crime stories elsewhere. And I, handling these to suit him, was at once pushed into the topnotch class and given only the largest of stories, as they might appear, of what might be called crime or sensation.

I cannot pause to narrate the character of these here, but what was more important to me at this time was that his opening method of making me come out right was correct, and that was to pile all the big assignments he could on me in order to keep me in working form. With a ruthless inconsiderateness, as I thought at the time, he filed story after story for me to do, and when none of immediate import was supplied by the daily news, created new ones himself, studying out interesting phases of past romances or crimes in the city which he thought it would be worthwhile for me to work up and then publishing them on Sunday. Without cessation, Sunday and every other day, he called upon me to display sentiment, humor, or hard, cold, descriptive force as the case might be, now quoting Hugo, now Balzac, now Dickens, and now Zola to me to show just what was to be done.

In a little while, despite my reduced salary and the fact that I had lost my previous place in disgrace as it were and was not likely to get a raise soon, if at all, I was as much your swaggering newspaper youth as ever, strolling about the city with the feeling that I was somebody and looking up all my old friends, with the idea of letting them know that I was by no means such a failure as they might have imagined. Two of these—the very first, and they soon after I had achieved my first feeling of recovery—were Dick and Peter, who late one hot night received me with open arms.

"Well, you're a good one," yelped Dick in his high, almost fal-setto, voice, after I had timidly knocked at his door and he had called, "Come in." I could see he had been sitting before his open window which commanded Broadway below, and where he had been meditat-ing in philosophic style. "Where the hell have you been keeping yourself? We've been looking for you for weeks. Why didn't you ever come around here? You're a dandy, you are. We've been down to your place a dozen times, but you wouldn't let us in. Ah, you're a good one, you are. McCord has some more of those opera cartoons done. Why didn't you ever come around, anyhow?"

"I'm working down on the *Republic* now," I replied, blushing, "and I've been busy."

"Oho!" laughed Dick, bending over and slapping his knees. "That's a good one on you. I heard about that. Those shows written up and not one in town. Oho! That's a good one." He indulged in a consumptive cough or two and then relaxed.

I laughed with him.

"It wasn't really all my fault," I ventured apologetically.

"I know it wasn't. Aw, dontcha think I know it wasn't? Don't I know the *Globe*? Didn't Carmichael get me to work that same racket? Ask Hazard. He can tell yah. It wasn't your fault. Sure it wasn't. Sit down. Peter'll be here in a little while. He said he'd be around. Then we'll go out and get something."

I took a chair.

"But it was my fault in part," I insisted, now bravely. "I should have gone around after I got back, or called up the *Republic*. I did call up the *Republic*, but I didn't ask for anybody but the dramatic editor."

"Ah, I know. Dontcha think I do? You needn't explain to me. But you're a dandy!—to stay away like this. You certainly are. How do you like your new place?"

I told him, making my new position rather plain.

We fell to discussing the attitude of the people on the *Globe* after I left and what some of them said. Wood had not heard much, he insisted. He knew instinctively that Mitchell was glad I was gone, as he might well have been—a youth so restless and uncertain as myself. Hartung had reported to him that McCullagh had raised Cain with Mitchell and that two or three of the boys on the staff had manifested relief.

"You know who they'd be," continued Wood, "the fellows that can't do what you can do, but who would like to."

I smiled. "I know about who they are," I said.

We then fell to talking about the world in general—literature, the drama, current celebrities, the state of politics—all seen through the medium of youth and aspiration and inexperience, coupled with the bias of optimism or pessimism according to our respective temperaments. While we were talking McCord came in. He had been to his home in south St. Louis, where he preferred to live in spite of his zest for Bohemia, and with him with us the ground had all to be gone over once more.

"Well, by heck, if here ain't Dreiser," he exclaimed as he came in, chuckling and snuffling. "Ha! Ha! You're a bird. Where have you been all this while? Why didn't you come round?"

I told him.

"Oh, he's explained," put in Dick excitedly. "He's just told me how it happened. Oh, ho! ho! Was there ever anything funnier?"

The whole story was once more gone over amusedly by the three of us, and then we settled down to an evening's enjoyment. Dick went for beer. Peter lit a rousing pipe. Accumulated poems and short stories were produced and plans for new ones recounted. Incidentally at one point McCord exclaimed, "You know what I'm going to do, Dreiser?"

"Well, what?" I asked.

"I'm going to study for the leading role in that opera of yours. I can play that, and I'm going to do it, if you don't object. Do you?"

"Object! Why should I object?" I replied, doubtful however of the wisdom of this. Peter never struck me as quite the actor type. "I'd like to see you do it, if you can, Peter."

"I can do it, all right," he replied. "That old rube appeals to me. I'll bet if I ever get on the stage I can get away with that."

He eyed Dick for confirmation.

"I'll bet you could, too," replied Dick loyally. "Peter makes a dandy rube. Oh, will you ever forget the time we went down to the old Nickelodeon and did a turn? Oho! We told Dreiser about that, though, didn't we?"

After a while McCord and I were compelled to leave, but I could see that I was, if anything, stronger in their favor than ever before. My escapades and mishaps, coupled with the attention and discussion which my name evoked among local newspaper men, made me an interesting figure. I was well beloved by them, as such youthful affections go, and I reciprocated that feeling. My transfer, then, had not done me so much harm, except in so far as it had reduced my salary. This was a great blow at present, but it was one which might be remedied. I might make some such strike as I had on the *Globe*.

CHAPTER XXXVII

In the meantime the new city appealed to me even more, if anything, than it had before. Somehow, its business heart with its throb of trade and show, smacking more of a Southern than a Northern city—with its sprinkling of wide-hatted, long-coattailed Southerners with their goatees and flowing mustachios and their pretence to a distinction and a superiority which I doubt if they themselves felt really—attracted me as being kindly, gently sober, a good place to be in.

For now, once more, it was spring in St. Louis, May and June, and the trees and flowers were all in bud or leaf and bloom. At odd moments, in vagrom hours, I could go down to the Mississippi—that vast yellow current which bounded the city to the east, receiving the Missouri but a few miles above the city, and which fascinated me intensely. I stared at its silent and serene current coming from what distant places I could only guess, bearing on its bosom the remnants of a once vast traffic now slain by the railroads; and I mooned over the lackadaisical water life which seemed to sing far more of human sim-plicities—idleness or the love of it, love of pleasure and romance—than of trade.

Or, perchance, as I often did these spring and summer days, I would rise early and go to Forest or Tower Grove or O'Fallon Park (on the north side) or the woods proper at the extreme edge of the city. And there all alone—or accompanied by Dick, Peter, or both, or by my brothers Al or Ed, both of whom later, for a time at least, I induced to come from Chicago with a view to finding work and staying here—I would idle about under the trees, examining the flowers and listening to the birds. How wonderful life seemed to me then—how perfect. Actually it seemed tingling with a strange promise for me—someday, someday. Someday surely something wonderful, beautiful beyond all belief, delightsome would happen to me. I felt it, believed it, knew it.

And then that splendid west end, with its long streets of better and even pretentious homes basking in a sleepy regularity, which made one feel that idleness or calling or mere possession and show was by far the most important thing in the world—how it appealed to me! I longed so to be of it. There was a panic on at the time, or an approach to one—the great depression of 1893—brought about by the banks attempting to establish the gold standard, as I understood it. Trade was at a standstill, or nearly so. When I first went on the *Republic*, factories were already closing down or slowing up, and discharging men or issuing scrip of their own wherewith to pay their men until times should be better, and some shops and stores were failing entirely. It was my first experience of a panic that I could remember, and my early duty, among others, was to visit some of the owners of these factories and shops and ask the cause of their decline and whether better times were in sight. Occasionally I read long editorials in the *Republic* or the *Globe* on the subject which I could in no wise understand. I can remember the heavy gloom in some streets and shops and how solemnly some of the manufacturers spoke of the crises and the hard times yet in store. There were to be bad times for a year or two or three. I recall one old man at this time, very prosy and stiff and conventional, "one of our best business-men," who had or had had a large iron foundry on the south side "for fifty years," as he said, who now in his old age had to shut down for good. I found him, after searching in various places, within one of the silent wings of his empty foundry, walking about alone, examining some machinery which was also still. I asked him what the trouble was and if he would resume work again soon.

"Just say that I'm done," he said. "This panic has finished me. I might possibly go on later with a little luck, I suppose, but I'm too old to begin all over again. I haven't any money now to speak of and that's all there is to it."

I left him meditating over some tool he was trying to adjust, and, as for myself, I meditated over what his end would be.

One of my most interesting experiences during this summer was in connection with that same North 7th Street police station I previously mentioned, to which I was now regularly assigned for a time. It seemed, as I now discovered, that this was a great centre of news. All sorts of really amazing stories originated here, as I might indicate,—rapes, riots, murders, fantastic family complications of all kinds. It was at once the centre of a mixed ghetto, slum and negro life, which at this time at least was appalling to me in some of its aspects. It was all so dirty, so poor, so stuffy and even starveling. There were in it all sorts of streets, Jewish, negro and rundown American or plain slum—the latter the worst of all—the first crowded with long-bearded Jews and their fat wives so greasy, smelly and generally offensive that they sickened me— ragpickers, chicken dealers and feather sorters all. In their streets the smell of these things—picked or crated or barreled chickens, many of them partially decayed, decayed meats and vegetables, half-sorted dirty feathers and rags and I know not what else—was sickening in hot weather. In the negro streets, or rather alleys—for they never seemed to occupy any general thoroughfare—were rows of stuffy one-, two-, three-, and four-story shacks or barns of frame or brick, crowded into back yards with thousands of blacks of the most amused, idle and shuffling character hanging about. In these hot days of June, July and August they seemed to do little but sit or lie in the shade of buildings, swap yarns or contemplate the world with laughter or in silence.

Occasionally, of course, there was a fight, a murder or a love affair among them which justified my existence here. Again, there were those slum streets of soggy, decayed Americans, much more terrible than either of these others, and filled with so low and cantankerous a population of whites that they were a kind of a terror to the police themselves. These latter here traveled in pairs, and whenever an alarm from some policeman on his beat in this region was turned in, a sergeant plus all the officers in the station at this time would set forth to the rescue, as it were—sometimes as many as eight or ten with orders, as I myself have heard them given, "to club the God-damned heads off them," or "break their God-damned bones but bring them in here. I'll fix them." In response to which, then, all the stolid Irish huskies would go forth to battle, returning frequently with a whole vanload of combatants or alleged combatants, all much the worse for the contest which they had recently endured.

But, oh, those streets! And the tang of the life here, rich, complicated, mystic.

There was an old, fat Irish sergeant of about fifty or fifty-five here—James King by name—who used to amuse me greatly. He ruled here like a potentate under the captain, whom I rarely saw. With King, if I remember correctly, I became great friends. His place was behind the central desk, in the front of which were two light standards and on the surface of which were his "blotter" and reports of different kinds. Behind the desk was his big tilted swivel chair with himself in it, stout, perspiring, coatless, vestless, collarless, his round head and fat neck beady with perspiration, his fat arms and hands moist and laid heavily on his protuberant stomach. According to him at this time, he had been at this work exactly eight years, and before that he had "beat the sidewalk," as he said, traveled a beat.

"Yis, yis, 'tis a waarm evening," he would begin when I would arrive, warm and a little weary of my job—very weary at times, seeing, as it appeared to me, that the rest of the world was busy about much more delightful things than this. "But there's nothing for you, me lad. Ye might just as well take a chair and make yerself comfortable. It may be that something will happen, and again maybe it won't. Ye must hope for the best. 'Tis a bad time for any trouble to be breakin' out now, though, in all this hot weather," and then he would elevate a large palm-leaf fan which he kept near him and begin to fan himself.

Here he would sit then, answering phone calls from headquarters or marking down reports from the men on their beats or answering the complaints of people who came in here, hour after hour, to complain that they had been robbed or their houses broken into, or that some neighbor was making a nuisance of him- or herself in some way or other, or their wives or husbands or sons or daughters wouldn't obey them or stay in at nights.

"Yes, and what's the matter here?" he would begin when one of these would put in an appearance.

Let us say it was a man who would be complaining that his wife or daughter would not stay in nights, or a woman complaining equally of a husband, son or daughter.

"Well, me good woman" (or "man" as the case might be), "I can't be helpin' ye with that. This is no coort ave law. If yer husband doesn't support ye or yer son doesn't come in of nights and he's a minor ye can get an order from a judge at the Foor Coorts compellin' him perhaps. Then if he don't mind ye, and ye want him arrested or locked up, I can help ye that way, but not otherwise. Go to the Foor Coorts."

Sometimes, in the case of parents complaining of a daughter or son not obeying them, he would relent a little in case the situation appealed to him and say, "See if ye can bring him around here. Tell him" (or "her") "that the Captain wants to see him. Then if he comes I'll see what I can do for ye. Maybe I can frighten him a bit fer ye."

Let us say they came, a shabby, overworked mother or father leading a recalcitrant boy or girl. When the latter was the case, the sergeant would assume a most ferocious air and, after listening to the complaint of the parent as if it were all news to him, would demand, "What's ailin' ye? Why can't ye stay in at nights? What's the matter with ye that ye can't obey your mother?" (or "father?") "Don't ye know it's against the laaw fer a minor to be stayin' out after ten at night? Ye don't? Well, it is, and I'm tellin' ye now. D'ye waant me t' lock ye up? Is that what ye're lookin' fer? There's a lot ave good iron cells back there waitin' fer ye if ye can't behave yerself. Ye know that, don't ye? Well then, what are ye goin' to do about it?"

Nine chances out of ten instead of responding favorably or being overawed, the victim would sulk or stand silent and defiant.

"I'm given ye warning now," the sergeant would proceed, grimly. "Ye've got a good hard-workin' mother (or "father") here. Why can't ye behave yerself? Don't ye know it's fer yer own good she's wantin' ye to stay in? Ye don't? Ye don't want to sit in the house aall of the time? Ten o'clock isn't late enough fer ye to be gallivantin' the streets? It ain't? Ye don't stay out any later than that often? Well, you oughtn't to be out that late at all. It's naat good fer ye. These streets are no place fer a girl—especially these streets around here, full ave toughs and thieves and drunks. If I let ye go home now, will ye be after behavin' yerself or shall I lock ye up now—which is it?" Possibly by now the one in error would relent a little and begin arguing with the mother or father, charging unfairness, cruelty and the like. "Here now—don't ye be taalkin' to yer mother like that. Ye're not old enough to be doin' that. An' what's more, don't let me catch ye out on the streets or her complainin' to me agin. If ye do, I'll send one of me men around to bring ye in. This is the last now. D'ye want to spend a few nights in a cell? What? Well, then! Now be gittin' out of here and don't let me hear any more concernin' ye. Not a word. I've had enough now. Out with ye."

And he would glower and grow red and popeyed and fairly roar, shoving them tempestuously out—only, after the victim had gone, to lean back in his chair and wipe his forehead and sigh. " 'Tis tough—the bringin' up of children, hereabouts especially. Ye can't be blamin' 'em fer wantin' to be out on the streets, and yet ye can't let 'em out either exactly. It's hard to tell what to do with them. I've been talkin' like that fer years now to waan and another. 'Tis all the good it does. Ye can't do much for them hereabouts."

CHAPTER XXXVIII

How many of the interesting stories I reported or evolved here under Wandell's direction between May 1893 and February or March 1894, when voluntarily and much against his wishes I left him, I cannot now recall. But suffice it to say that of all of my newspaper days, which covered a period of only three years, as well as of my earthly experiences, which have been considerable, this short period of nine or ten months sticks in my mind as one of the most interesting and even exotic—a stirring, forceful, painful period of mental development from

brooding semi-Christian or religious doubt to a deep and abiding ag-
nosticism which has remained with me to this day. While mentally
discarding all faith in the so-called future rewards of an honest sacrific-
ing life, I still retained some faith in moral punishment—an odd
situation, to say the least. Somehow nature seemed to me to be balanced to this extent: that if you didn't take very good care of yourself—
complying at least outwardly, and even inwardly after a fashion, to the
average person's theories of right and wrong—you were likely to go on
the rocks. There was much in the commonplace, guarded, narrow,
conventional life, according to my feelings then, which was very
important. It seemed to suit the mental states of so many, and because it
did that I concluded, by what logic I cannot now recall, that it ought
necessarily to suit mine. Vox populi, vox Dei, I suppose. One had
better be good because the conventionalists wouldn't like you if you
weren't and would have nothing to do with you. Imagine the horror of
being ignored by the average home! Not much of the laughing superman in that, is there? At the same time, so swift and colorful were the
facts forced upon me, so demonstrative of the uncertainty and brutality
of life as well as of its beauty and lure, coupled with a riant cynicism and
gross and unjustifiable favoritism, that I was completely staggered and
compelled to readjust my viewpoint from one of whining religiosity or
dependence on the good intentions of God or moral order to one of
helpless acceptance of the blows of fate, which left me horribly sad at
times, and at others, never having been of an utterly despondent or
suicidal turn, preternaturally gay and hopeful.

For, as I figured it, life in spite of all its aches and pains was nearly
all before me. It was a game of chance at best, and with a little luck I
might finish it in splendor, who knows? Many did. I might have been
born under a lucky star. At the same time, love or the thought of it was
always before me—just around the corner, as it were—love the great
comforter, the phrenetic, ravishing enchantress with eyes of fever and a
smile that could pile the little streets upon the great. Somewhere, you
see, there was to be a girl—or many of them.

And then, incidentally, this was a period of meeting men, newspaper men especially—that flotsam and jetsam company to be found
about all successful and unsuccessful newspaper centres. Newspaper
men were so intelligent and definite from many points of view as to
seem worthy of any position or station in life, and yet so indifferent and

errant too at times or so poorly placed in spite of their seeming efforts and capacities as to cause me to despair for the reward of merit any-where (intellectual merit, I mean). For some of these men, while mentally fascinating, were the rankest kind of failures—drunkards, drug fiends, hypochondriacs. Many of them had staid too long in the profession—which is a young man's game and nothing other—and others had wasted their opportunities, dreaming of a chance fortune, no doubt, and then taken to drink or dope. Still others, young like myself, were uncertain as to the future and just finding out what an unprofitable maelstrom the newspaper game is, cynical, ironic, waspish at times.

I am not familiar with many professions, so I cannot say whether any of the others abound in this same wealth of eccentric capacity or understanding, or offer as little opportunity for reward or any real grip on successful productive results of any kind, but if so I would like to know of them. Certainly all the newspaper offices I have ever known fairly sparkled with these exceptional brains, few of whom ever seemed to do very well, and no paper I ever worked on paid wages anywhere commensurate to the services rendered or the hours exacted. It was always a hard, cold, driving game—with the ash heap as the reward for the least weakening of energy or ability. At the same time these newspapers were constantly spouting editorially about kindness, jus-tice, charity, a full reward for labor, and were getting up fresh-air funds and this, that, and the other for others not half as deserving as their employes which were likely to bring them increased circulation (which was the point). In the little while that I was in the newspaper profession in St. Louis and elsewhere, I met many of these men who seemed to me to be thoroughly sound intellectually, quite free for the most part from the narrow cramping conventions of their day, and yet they never seemed to get on very well. For the most part they were so poorly paid and so shabbily equipped physically as to cause me to wonder at once why it was that life could treat them so badly, whereas others in other fields far less capable mentally than themselves were so much more fortunate and acclaimed. Since then I have had many, many long, long thoughts on this subject, to the end that it has become perfectly plain that material rewards follow most largely in the wake of the gross supplying of some material need, and since most human needs are purely material—tea, coffee, bricks, furniture—it is not to be wondered at that minds which dwell in the realm of ideation are but thinly supplied with material rewards. Even in the newspaper business, while it is literally true that brains and imagination are necessary to the construction of a great paper, still the ordinary mechanical methods of preparation and distribution are nearly always looked upon as equally if not more important, and the business end as the great thing. It is also true that while it is generally assumed that great ideas are involved in the construction of large material fortunes, this is not necessarily the case by any means, as a careful examination of the methods of great fortune builders will readily show. Nearly always a few ideas plus a dominant, mechanical insistence on distribution and sales are what have built up our largest fortunes, and the possessors of them usually present sufficient evidence in themselves of the truth of this.

I remember one newspaperman, however, by the name of Clark, who literally fascinated me during this time—he was so able and sure of touch from an editorial and reportorial point of view and yet financially and in every other way such a failure. He came from Kansas City or Omaha while I was on the *Republic* and had worked in how many places before that—heaven only knows where. In appearance he was a stocky, dark, clerkly figure who when he first came to the *Republic* seemed surely destined for a rapid rise, if such a thing were possible, and who seemed to wish nothing so much as to be let thoroughly alone. He was a hard worker, sober and many other things which are usually admired in successful workers. At the same time he always appeared to me to be a sad man—lonely, remote. Once I gained his confidence, he gradually revealed to me a tale of past positions and comfort which—verified as it was by Wandell and Williams—was startling when contrasted with his present position. Although he was not much over forty—forty-one or two at the most—he had been in times past, so I was told, editor or managing editor of several papers of import in the West but had lost them through some primary disaster which had caused him to take to drink and through his subsequent inability in recent years to stay sober for more than three or four months at a stretch. Life pressed on him so heavily, apparently, that he could not endure persistent sobriety. Once, somewhere, as I was told, he had had a wife and two children who were now no longer in his charge. In some other city he had been an important factor in politics. Here he was, still clean and spruce (when I first saw him, at any rate), going about his work with a great deal of energy, writing the most satisfactory newspaper stories, as I understood it, and yet after two or three months' labor was no longer one of us— gone for weeks before I missed him, so busy was I myself. When I inquired of Williams and Wandell as to his whereabouts, the first stared at me with his one eye and smiled—then lifted his fingers in the shape of a glass and up-ended them before his mouth.

"Whiskey, my boy! Good old booze."

Wandell merely remarked, "Drunk, I think. He may show up and he may not. He had a few weeks' wages when he left." I have often wondered since whether persistent underpayment was not a factor in his despair.

I neither heard nor saw anything more for a period of, say, three or four weeks thereafter, perhaps longer, when suddenly one day, in the sombre, dusty, grey days of late fall in that wretched section of St. Louis beloved of Dick and Peter as a source of literary material, I was halted by a figure which on the instant I assumed to be one of the lowest of the low. A short, matted, dirty black beard concealed a face that bore no resemblance to anyone I knew. A hat that looked as though it might have been lifted out of an ash barrel was pulled slouchily and defiantly over longish uncombed black hair. His face, ears, neck, and hands (what little of the first was visible) were dirty as were his clothes and shoes, filthy beyond belief—slimy even. What impressed me most about him at the time was that the old reddish-brown coat he had on (originally a wine-colored cloth, no doubt) was actually marked by a greenish slime across the back and shoulders—slime that could only have come there from some gutter or other where he had lain.

"You know me, don't you, Dreiser?" he queried in a deep, rasping voice—a voice so rusty that it sounded as though it had not been used for years—"Clark, Clark of the *Republic*. You know me—." And when I stared in amazement he added shrewdly, "I've been sick and in a hospital. You haven't a dollar about you, have you? I have to rest a little and get myself in shape again before I can go to work."

"Well, of all things," I exclaimed in amazement and then, "I'll be damned!" Incidentally, I laughed after a few moments. I could not help it. He looked so queer—impossible almost. A stage tramp could scarcely have done better.

"Sick, are you?" I said and gave him the dollar which I needed badly enough myself. "What in the world are you doing, drinking?" and then, overawed by the impression his past efficiency and force had made on me, I could not go on, but merely stared. It was too astonishing.

"Yes, I've been drinking," he admitted, "but I've been sick, too—just getting out now. I got pneumonia there in the summer and couldn't work. I'll be all right after awhile. What's news at the *Republic?*"

"Nothing," I told hm.

He said some words about having played in bad luck, that he would soon be all right again, he thought, then ambled up the wretched rickety street and disappeared.

I bustled out of that vicinity as quick as I could. Actually, I was so startled and upset by this that I hurried back to the lobby of the Southern Hotel—my favorite cure for all despondent gray days—where all was warm, brisk, colorful, gay, in fact. Here was no least sign of poverty or want, but only of comfort and luxury. Here everyone was at least apparently prosperous—busy about one money-making scheme or another—or enjoying the peace of this atmosphere. In order to be rid of the sense of failure and degradation which had just crept over me, I sat down to think. That anyone as interesting as Clark could fall so low in so short a time was beyond me! To think that a handsome, reticent, well-ordered man could change so. Perhaps I might get that way someday myself, I thought to myself—who knows? The strongly puritan and moralistic streak in me was shocked beyond measure, and for days I could do little but contrast the figure of the man I had seen about the *Republic* office with that I had met in that street of degraded gin mills and tumbledown tenements. Could people really vary so greatly and in so short a time? And what must be the nature of their minds, pray, I asked myself, if they could? Was mine like that? Would it become so? For days thereafter, in spirit at least, I was wandering about with this man from gin mill to gin mill and lodging house to lodging house, seeing him drink at scummy bars and lying down at night on some straw pallet in some wretched hole. It was too much.

And then there was Rodenberger—strange amazing Rodenberger—poet, editorial writer, feuilletonist, who when I first met him had a little weekly editorial paper for which he raised the money somehow (I have forgotten its name) and in which he poured forth his views on life and art and nature in no uncertain terms—beautiful, I thought. Gracious, how he could write. (Incidentally, he was connected with some drug company or other by birth, marriage, or I know not what, which may have helped to sustain him. I don't know. I never knew anything definite concerning his private life.) As I view him now, Rodenberger was one of those curious geniuses of the Poe, Mangan, Baudelaire, De Quincey, Villon order—that is, a man in whom imagination and logic exist in such a confusing, contesting way as to induce fatalism and, from a worldly or material point of view, augur failure. Their kingdoms are not of this world. He was constantly varying between a state of extreme sobriety and vigorous mental energy and the most Clark-like degradation—debauches which lasted for weeks and which included drink, houses of prostitution, morphine, and I know not what else.

Once, for instance, one sunny summer morning in June I found him standing at the corner of 6th and Chestnut, outside the Laclede drugstore, quite stupefied with drink or something.

"Hello, Rody," I called when I saw him. "What's ailing you anyhow? You're drunk again, are you?"

"Drunk," he replied with a slight, sardonic motion of the hand and an equally faint curl of the lip, "and what's more, I'm glad of it. I don't have to think about myself or St. Louis or you when I'm drunk. And what's more," and here he interjected another slight motion of the hand and hiccoughed, "I'm living down here in Chestnut Street with a God-damned fucking whore, and I'm glad of that. She's as good as anybody, and so am I—" and he hiccoughed again. "And what's more," and here he waved a very feeble finger under my nose, "I'm taking dope, and I'm glada that. I got all the dope I want right here in my little old vest pocket, an' I'm goin' to take all I want of it—" and he tapped that significantly and then in a boasting, contentious spirit, I suppose, drew forth a white pillbox and slowly opening it, revealed to my somewhat astonished gaze, say, thirty or forty small white pills, two or three of which he at once extracted and began to lift toward his mouth.

In my astonishment and sympathy and righteous horror, I suppose, I decided to save him if I could, so I struck his hand a smart blow, thus knocking the pills and pillbox from it and scattering the pills all over the sidewalk. Without a word of complaint save a feeble, somewhat comic "Zat so?" he dropped to his hands and knees and began to pick up the pills and put them into his mouth, crawling here and there after them as fast as he could, while I, equally determined although laughing, began jumping here and there and crushing them under my feet.

"Rody, for God's sake! Aren't you ashamed of yourself? Get up!"

"I'll show you," he called determinedly if somewhat ridiculously, "I'll eat 'em all," and he swallowed those that he found as briskly as possible.

By now I was frightened rather badly, I think, for I imagined the aftereffects of too much morphine to be absolutely fatal.

"Here, Johnson," I called to another of his and my friends who came up just then. "Help me with him, will you."

"What's the trouble?" he asked, standing over him.

"He's drunk and he's got a box of morphine pills and he's trying to take them and I knocked them out of his hand and now he's eaten a lot of them!"

He lent a hand.

"Here, Rody," he called, pulling him to his feet and holding him against the wall, "stop this." And then to me he added, "Maybe they're not morphine after all. Why don't you ask the druggist. If they are, we'd better get him to the hospital."

"They're morphine, all right," gurgled the victim. "Donchu worry. I know morphine, all right—an' I'll eat 'em all," and he began struggling with Johnson.

Per the latter's suggestion I hurried into the drugstore, the proprietor and clerk of which were friends of all of us, Rody included, and inquired. The former assured me they were morphine and, what was more, that we had better get the victim to a hospital at once—or call a doctor—this after I assured him that Rodenberger had probably swallowed a dozen. "Well, well," he exclaimed. "We'd better hurry." It so happened that one Dr. Heinie Marks, head physician of the St. Louis City Hospital, was another friend of all newspaper men—their devoted ally. (What free advertising we used to give him! His name was in most of the hospital news of every day, day after day, year in and year out, per our friendship—he giving us fancy hospital stories in return.) And to him I now turned for aid, calling him up and explaining.

"Bring him out, bring him out," he called, for he knew Rodenberger also. "Wait, I'll send the wagon." And in the meanwhile Johnson with the aid of the clerk and the druggist had brought him inside and seated him in a chair in the backroom, where we anxiously surveyed him for any signs of his approaching demise. He was very pale and limp and seemed momentarily, as we thought, to grow more so. To our intense relief, however, the city ambulance soon arrived, a smart young interne in white propped up behind, and with his aid and that of Johnson and myself and the druggist's clerk and a policeman—also known to all of us, he being the officer of this beat—we bundled Rodenberger into it and saw him hauled away, to be pumped out and detained for days. As I was told afterwards by the doctor, he had taken enough of the pills to safely end him had he not been promptly pumped out. As it was he was soon on his feet again—fate in the shape of myself and Johnson and Marks having intervened—and turned up at our old corner one morning as sound and smiling as ever.

"Yes," I exclaimed scornfully, if somewhat affectionately, "so here you are again. You're a bird, you are."

"All in the day's wash, my boy," he assured me blandly when I ventured to reproach him for his shameful conduct. "If I was so determined to go, you should have let me. Heaven only knows what trouble you have stored up for me now by keeping me here when I wanted to go. That may have been a divine call! But Kismet! Allah is Allah! Let's go and get a drink."

And forthwith inside at Phil Hackett's Laclede Bar, surrounded by fellow bibbers and looking out through cool lattices to the hot street outside, we fell to discussing the vagaries and cruelties of life while we drank something—a pleasant drink, whatever it was. I should add that Rodenberger's end was not at all commensurate with his early career, basing it as one might on the usual moralistic judgement of deeds such as this. In fact ten years later he had completely reformed his personal habits and entered the railroad business, having attained to a considerable position in one of the principal roads running out of St. Louis.

At this time, however, I was of such a puritanic turn as to augur from this his certain death in the gutter and a pauper's grave. I did not know that in some natures imagination tempered by logic seems to tend to just such states as this. Surrounded by a dull, conventional, moralistic world, they still dwell in a consciousness of that hinterland of space and time and eternal substance from whence, apparently, all things take their rise and where phantoms of an amazing character are easily erected, which is likely to render them morbid. On the other hand, logic filtered through imagination seems to lead scientifically to the same place, only it is not so much concerned with creating phantoms as with puzzling over the riddle of existence, finding in all the visible and invisible scene neither reason nor vast phantoms but only a grave or sad uncertainty. And curiously, as a rule, a combination of these two forces augurs fatality to this extent, that a man who is in its power (controlled by some thing much stronger than his will) ends poorly from a material point of view, however glorious may be his art contribution to life, as for instance in the case of Poe and many others. Such a man is apt to be a sad man, lonely, suspicious of his fellows or their import; and, since imagination makes for sensitiveness or a highly nervous organization, easily pained and reduced by the mishaps of life, he may readily take refuge in a drug or drink or both—vide Poe, Baudelaire, Dostoievski, De Quincey, Coleridge, Villon, Mangan—finding in one or both an anesthetic for the blows and bruises of ordinary existence. Your moderately dull man, as we all know, is stimulated by liquor or a drug, raising himself thereby to heights and moods he could not possibly aspire to in ordinary life. Not so your genius or highly organized temperament. It is from too much of these that he flees.

Rodenberger, I take it, was some such man as this. When sober he was utterly charming and wise, kind, gracious, helpful. When drunk— due to his despair, I presume—he was quite the contrary. In my ignorant and brash youth I was for criticising him severely at this time, as much as I liked him—solving all these delicate matters by rule of thumb and saying to the drunkard "Drink not" and to the drug user "Dope not." Since then I have learned many things, among them the amazing gradations and fluctuations in temperament, and how ills or fortunes of one period or of one's internal organization quite as much as any of external life aid so often in steering or wrecking our frail barks, and of what small use are maxims and wise saws and precedents and examples to one whose vision contemplates and whose organism senses so much of all that the trashy vulgarian with his press and pulpit school of morals and his *averages* never even dreams. At this time Rodenberger was certainly in the painful grasp of his wide imagination and his stern logic, and the only refuge for him I suppose was in drink and other forms of intoxication.

This same Laclede, as I have perhaps before indicated, was nearly the centre of all gossiping newspaper life at this time—at least that part of it of which I knew anything. Here by turns or in idling groups during the course of any single morning, afternoon or evening might appear Dick or Peter or both, Rodenberger, Clark, Hazard, Johnson, Root, Johns, Davis—a long company of excellent newspaper men who worked on the different papers of the city and who, because of a desire for companionship in this helter-skelter world and the certainty of finding someone here, were certain to be found hanging about for a little while between eleven and twelve or four and five or seven and eight or eleven and midnight, hoping to encounter someone else. You may recall those favored cafes of Paris, where the aristocracy of the arts or the younger aspirants to their honors were, on occasion, accustomed to meet and discuss life. Similarly, the Academy of Plato at Athens may have had some such origin—a simple, natural meeting place for discussion. At any rate, here in the Laclede, per accident and custom, there had sprung up in my day this casual meeting of reporters and newspapermen generally, where, if one chose, one could "get in on" a highly intellectual or diverting conversation of one kind or another at almost any time. Here we formed groups, strolled off to dinner together or traded news. Nearly always there were one or two newspaper men about, anyhow. So many of these men had come from distant cities— New Orleans, San Francisco, Denver, New York, Boston—and knew them much better perhaps than they did St. Louis. As a rule, being total strangers and not inclined to remain here for long, they were inclined to sniff at conditions as they found them here and boast of those they had met with elsewhere—especially the men from New York, Boston, San Francisco and Chicago. I was one of those who, knowing only Chicago and St. Louis and wishing to appear wise in these matters, boasted vigorously of the transcendent importance of Chicago as a city, whereas such men as Root of New York, Johnson of Boston, Ware of New Orleans and a few others merely looked at me and smiled.

"All I have to say to you," young Root once observed to me roughly if genially enough, after one of these heated and senseless arguments, "is wait till you go to New York once and see for yourself. I've been to Chicago, and it's a way station by comparison. It's the only other city you've seen, and that's why you think it's great." There was a certain amount of kindly toleration in his tone which infuriated me.

"Ah, you're crazy," I replied. "You're like all New Yorkers. You think you know it all. You won't admit that you're beaten when you are."

The argument proceeded through all the different aspects of the two cities until finally we succeeded in calling each other "damn fools" and leaving in a huff. Years later, however, having seen New York, my one thought, if ever I met him again, was to apologize. The two cities, as I then learned, individual and wonderful each, were not to be contrasted in that way. But how sure I was of my point of view then. Nearly all of these young men, as I now saw, presented such a sharp contrast to those I had known in Chicago—or, at least, the character of the work in this city and my own changing viewpoint made them seem different. Chicago, to me, at that time had seemed so full of exceptional young men in the reportorial world, men who somehow or other had already achieved considerable local repute as writers and coming men—Finley Peter Dunne, George Ade, Brand Whitlock, Ben King, Charles Stewart, and many others. Some of them even in that day were already signing their names to some of their contributions or, failing that, had achieved such a reputation for worth that they stood out clearly in the local reportorial mind, whereas here in St. Louis, from lack of size perhaps—as much that as anything else—few if any of us had achieved any local distinction of any kind. No one as yet had created a personal or literary following. No one was hailed as a sure genius certain to stir the world. In regard to our lives and our knowledge of each other, we formed little more than a weak scholastic or professional union, recognizing each other genially enough as worthy fellow craftsmen, perhaps, but not offering each other much consolation in our rough state beyond perhaps a mere class or professional recognition as working newspaper men. Yet this Laclede was at times a kind of tonic bear garden or mental wrestling place, where unless one was very guarded and sure of himself, one might come by a quick and hard fall, as I soon discovered, as when once in some argument in regard to a current political question and without knowing really what I was talking about, I made the statement that sociology indicated so-and-so, whereupon one of my sharp confreres suddenly took me up with, "Say, what is sociology, anyhow? Do you know?"

I was completely stumped, for I didn't. It was a comparatively new word, outside the colleges, being used here and there in arguments and editorials, and in that spirit I had glibly taken it over myself. I floundered about and finally had to confess that I didn't, whereupon I endured a laugh for my pains, a thing which left me wiser and much more cautious.

But this in itself, in my raw ignorant state, as I saw later, was a very great help to me. So many of these men were intelligent and informed to the cutting point in regard to many facts of life of which I was extremely ignorant. Many of them had not only read more but seen more—much—and took my budding local pretensions to being somebody with a very large grain of salt. In many of the casual meetings, where at odd moments reporters and sometimes editors were standing or sitting about and discussing one phase of life and another, I received a backhanded slap which sometimes jarred my pride, but invariably widened my horizon.

CHAPTER XXXIX

The thread of love or romance during this period was thin indeed, or at least it seemed so to me. At the time that I left Mrs. Zernouse in 10th Street, which was not so long after I secured my new position on the *Republic*, I took up my residence in a rather attractive neighborhood, as I judged it then, out in Chestnut Street just beyond Jefferson Avenue, in a rooming house managed by a petite, dark, rather attractive young widow. Not unlike Mrs. Zernouse and the rooming-house keeper before her, she took a friendly and kindly interest in me from the first. As a matter of fact, having been moving about now from room to room ever since our family had broken up in Chicago a little over a year before, following my mother's death the previous year and just before I entered the newspaper business, I was becoming an expert in this matter of selecting a room. Not incuriously, owing to my previous experiences, it was coming to be connected now with the thought of a possible romance. What would I find? Might there not be here, as there had been at the two places previous, a woman or girl who would be interested in me and, since hope springs eternal in the human breast, better than the last? Besides, I was now reaching the place in my understanding of living—so few really ever do reach it—where I desired an atmosphere of some charm to envelope me, a thing rather difficult of achieving in an ordinary rooming house and for the money I was able to pay. Still there were certain things which one could look for in this world, and that with some slight hope of finding them: trees or flowers, for instance, or both, a building that in itself had a kind of poetic charm, let us say, a neighborhood that was not run down in the shabby sense, or, if so, had achieved a kind of outré charm of its own, a room that was not ungraceful in its appointments, not small and stuffy and generally shabby.

How I hunted before finding this one. I visited various neighborhoods in various parts of the city, calculating the distance from the office and the quality of the lives of the people by whom I was to be surrounded. Finally this one, with its tall white stone-trimmed windows and doors (after the fashion of those houses in Philadelphia, Baltimore and other cities which reflect the South), took my fancy and I knocked. As it turned out, in this instance the woman who operated the place was as pleasing to look at as the house. She could not have been more than thirty-three or four years of age at the most, if so much, pretty, active, pert or bird-like in manner with chestnut hair and brown eyes. Although we subsequently became intimate, I have forgotten her name. There was something very self-possessed and experienced in the way in which she looked me over very incisively, I thought, and decided whether she wanted me or no. After a few moments she appeared to be satisfied that she did, and admitted me. The room she showed me on the second floor turned out to be so large and redolent of a much older and better state of things that I was charmed by it. Besides, it was clean and tastefully furnished with an old four-poster bed and a mahogany-veneer bookcase. A tall gilt pier mirror between the two back windows suggested that it might have been part of a full-floor drawing room. I accepted it at once, paying the price asked, and, as I have said, began transferring my few effects from Mrs. Zernouse's place by degrees.

It is odd how particular atmospheres affect one. This one which so appealed to me then has lasted intact for years. As I found shortly after my arrival, I was looked after by her in a most cordial manner—a manner which I appreciated all the more because I was lonely and she was attractive. It soothed an intense sense of neglect which I suffered the moment I was off duty and alone. As I see it now, looking back after this period of years, I was of an intensely uxorious nature and the feminine ministrations were what I needed more than anything else. She was constantly running into my room after the first few days, especially in the morning or the afternoon, if I chanced to come in for a moment, to see if I needed anything. My shelf of books, my prints and my curtains, which I now doubled and threw over an old lounge which stood against one wall, interested her.

In spite of my recent experiences, however, perhaps because of them, I was intensely shy. In addition, my whole point of view will be much clearer if it is understood that I was never really looking for this kind of a woman but an ineffable poetic something which had nothing to do with age or meanness or the ordinary crotchets of individuals, male or female, but some perfect girl such as I had seen in passing here and there,—a paragon without flaw, not necessarily identified with either prosperity or poverty, but partaking of some charm or spell, which neither poverty nor prosperity could supply, I presume. Is it youth? Yes. Is it understanding? No and yes—a kind of material and mental, though by no means articulate, en-rapport-ness with all beauty—the charm of the skies, the colors and odours of the flowers, the hue and scent of the earth, the glory of form, the perfection of imagination. A clown or a clod could not have it. Youth and beauty might be utterly devoid of it. Age might possibly conceal it under a wrinkled or repulsive exterior, but with me it was nevertheless identi-fied with youth and beauty in the female form. Only so much youth, even where attractive, as I saw, was so utterly devoid of it. I might look at the dancing figure of a girl on a lawn playing croquet or tennis or dancing and laughing, and in one sense—one phase at least—here was the thing I was seeking, of which I was dreaming, but in actual contact with this, any given material girl, it was so easy to be utterly disillu-sioned. The stiffness, the dullness, the shallowness! Now and then in some of my peregrinations, reportorial and otherwise, I had come in contact with someone who seemed to embody much of what I was seeking—a delicacy and sweetness and dreamfulness which was like to throw me into the utmost fever of self-dissatisfaction and longing—or this may have been an illusion also, probably was. But the ideal which dominated me and which in this crude fashion I have been seeking to express was so real that it stood as a marble pattern might, by which all things were to be measured.

"You want me to compete with a wraith, an illusion, a phantom?" a very clever and beautiful woman once said to me, with a measure of deserved sarcasm. "Well, it can't be done, and I don't propose to try."

And she didn't.

And she was right.

Only in fleeing the contest she achieved a measure of that ideal which I vaguely fancied that she did not have.

We are on treacherous ground. It is thin air, perhaps, that I am discussing and trying to make real. Be it so. The point that I am emphasizing here is that in my mind at this time was this last or pattern of the ideal, an ineffable, poetic something which no woman could hope to realize perhaps, least of all a woman like Mrs. X or Mrs. Zernouse, neither of whom had the first essential—youth—let alone some of the others.

But what matter? Have I made my point?

Not knowing in the least how to respond to the attentions of any woman of any kind, and feeling all the while that I was in danger of presuming or, in case I did, of being taken for a fool, my general tendency was to freeze up and say nothing—not knowing what to say.

Yet in spite of myself—quite—an affectional relationship finally sprung up between us, and that in part due to another piece of good fortune which I had in nowise anticipated and which came as it were out of a clear sky.

It so happened that at this time, as for years past, the *Republic* had been conducting a summer charity of some kind—a fresh-air fund, if I am not mistaken—in support of which every summer it attempted to invent and foster some quick money-raising scheme which this year had taken the form of that musty old chestnut, a baseball game to be played between the fattest men of the Owls and the leanest men of the Elks, two local fraternities. The idea of the *Republic*, of course, was to work up local interest in this startlingly novel situation by a humorous handling of it and so draw a large crowd to the St. Louis baseball grounds on the occasion when it should be played, which would, of course, produce large gate receipts.

But before ever having been given to me, it had been assigned to two or three others—a new man each day—in the hope of extracting fresh phases of humor, but so far apparently with indifferent results.

One June noon I was handed a clipping concerning this proposed game which had been written the preceding day by some other member of the staff. It was headed "Blood on the Moon," and purported to narrate the preliminary mutterings and grumblings of those who were to take part in this contest. It was not so much an amusing picture as a news item, and I did not think very much of it, but since I had been warned beforehand by Williams that I was to be called upon to produce the next day's burst and that it must be humorous, I was not inclined to judge it so harshly. The efforts of your predecessor always appear more forceful as your own threaten to prove inadequate. I was told by Wandell when he handed me the clipping most of the conditions which surrounded this contest and was then asked to do something really funny. "See if you can't get some fun into it. Make us laugh," he commented with a dry, almost frosty smile. "Laugh," I thought. "Yes," and then, "Good heavens, how am I to make anyone laugh? I never wrote anything funny in my life."

Nevertheless, here was my assignment for the afternoon (fancying, I suppose, that I might have a hard time he gave me no other), and being the soul of duty in these matters I took it and went to my desk and pondered over it. Not an idea came to me. Actually it seemed that nothing could be duller than this—a fat and lean men's baseball game! But if I didn't write something, it would be a black mark against me—a distinct failure on my part—and if I did and it proved a piece of trash I would sink equally low, if not lower, in the thoughts of my superior. Without going out of the office therefore, I took my pencil and began scribbling introductions at haphazard, thinking of one possible situation or humorous scene and another, and that if I could but once get a start it would come out all right. After scribbling rather aimlessly for over a half-hour, I finally took the same tack as my predecessor—the only avenue apparently which the situation warranted—only instead of describing the aspirations and oppositions of the two presumably rival organizations in general terms, I assumed a specific interest and plotting on the parts of their chief officers, who in different buildings in different parts of the city were even now, as it were, spending days and nights devising ways and means of outwitting the enemy. Thoughts of rubber baseball bats, baskets and nets in which flies might be caught, secret electric wiring under the diamond between the bases to put "pep" into the fat runners all occurred as having some faint trace of humor in them, and these I now introduced as having been suggested at these dark and secret meetings by these various officers and their friends. As I went on, building up purely imaginary characteristics for each and every one involved (I did not know any of them), I began to get interested about as one might in pure fiction—and then amused. It seemed to me that I was writing humorous stuff, only when I had finished this particular scene and started to reread it I was struck with a disturbing sense of the coarse horseplay of it all—the slush and balderdash! "This will never get by," I thought, but having by now come to a rather friendly understanding with Williams, the assistant city editor and copyreader who worked here invariably during the afternoons, I took it over to him and asked him for a preliminary opinion. "Tell me whether it's any good, will you? If it isn't, I'll tear it up and try again."

He took it, eyeing me rather sympathetically with his one eye, and then leaning back in his chair began to look it over. At first he did not appear much interested, but after the first paragraph, which he examined with a blank or weary expression, he smiled and then finally, reading on about half way, chortled and added, "This is pretty good stuff—you needn't worry about. it. Leave it with me." Later on in the afternoon, after I had gone out and returned and Wandell had come in to give out the evening assignments, I saw Williams gather it up and go into him. After a time he came out smiling, and in a little while Wandell himself called me in.

"Not bad, not bad," he said, tapping the manuscript lightly. "You've got the right idea, I think. I'll let you do that for awhile afternoons until you get stale in it." Then he gave me some particular task for the evening.

Curiously enough, this trifling bit of work which I undertook in a spirit of great dissatisfaction and uncertainty proved for me the most fortunate thing I had undertaken here as yet. If you will believe it, this rough horseplay almost immediately made a great strike, at least with the *Republic* readers. Apparently it amused and interested the proposed participants, for very shortly afterward—almost at once—I was the center of a certain amount of local attention and blandishment or favor, all intended to secure a certain amount of free advertising or mention of this, that and the other person in connection with it. No doubt it was just crude or common enough to appeal to the current local intelligence and appetite for baseball humor. At any rate, and in a trice, I was lifted into another atmosphere of journalism—one of which previously I had had but a taste, if so much—that of personal popular esteem. Before three days had gone our local staff was aware that I was making a hit of this local assignment, and in less than a week the alleged participants in this proposed contest, whose names I was using freely and indiscriminately, were congratulating the city editor on his comedy and me personally, writing me or arranging with some third person—Wandell or others—to meet me. I was informed by Wandell personally that this, that and the other citizen of some local distinc- tion—all proud to have their names bandied about in this idle but not unflattering manner—"was tickled nearly to death." He also began to give me the names of one and another who might be mentioned, if I chose, and in a little while because of these personal mentions, I suppose, a well-known Congressman, a brewer, the division passenger agent of one of the trunk lines entering St. Louis, as well as hotel managers and wholesale dealers (all assumed members of the great teams) had signified their desire to meet me. I was told by fellow newspaper reporters of what this, that and the other person thought of what I was doing. Newspaper men at the Laclede bar laughed and drank with me, and at the expense of the proprietor if you please, whose name I had several times mentioned. I felt myself to be moving all at once in a light, amusing, superior world. In short, as the days went on, I was told that owing to my efforts the game was sure to prove a great success and that it would net several thousand dollars for the fund.

For a very brief period of four or five weeks now—no more—it seemed to me as if I was walking on air. Life was so pleasant here these hot, bright days, with everyone apparently pleased with me, and my name as a clever man—a humorist, if you please (imagine it)—being bandied about among one person and another. Some of my new ad- mirers were so pleased with me that they asked me to come to their homes to see them or, failing that, would meet me at the bar of the Southern or some downtown cafe and talk about the eccentricities of work and life and character. I was becoming a personage in my small way, and I felt it. Phil Hackett, of the Laclede, asking casually where I lived one day, surprised me at my room with a large wicker hamper full of champagne, whiskey and cordials. I transferred it to the office of the *Republic* for the reportorial staff, with my compliments.

In the meantime, also, owing to this very assignment I have always thought, I reached an understanding with my landlady which proved highly diverting and delicious, to say the least. Very pleased with my work, no doubt, and satisfied that it would be unwise to burden me with other duties, at least during the afternoon when I was supposed to be composing these flights, Wandell, for almost the entire period in which I was conducting this campaign, gave me scarcely anything else to do, especially in the afternoons. At one o'clock the assignment book invariably read "baseball story" and at night, lest I become entangled perhaps in some large story which would carry over into the next day, I was assigned to the North 7th Street Station or sent on some matter which could produce but a few sticks at most.

Naturally, this made an ideal writing period for me, and one which contributed greatly to my leisure. As current reporting went, it was pleasant, to say the least. As I found, after my third or fourth day's attempts at composition I could get up my story in just about an hour, no more, and have an excellent time doing it into the bargain. Fearing, of course, that it would be noted how easy it was for me, I never did it at the office after the first day, but immediately retired to my room, where, seated before a table placed at one of my two large rear windows which commanded the rear lawns and trees of the houses of this block and shaded by the branches of one which came close to my window, I composed at my leisure. Incidentally, there were various pretty girls in this block, who at this time of the year, in summer frocks and tennis shoes, were playing croquet or tennis, and over whom I could dream at my leisure.

Looking back on this period during subsequent and less comfortable days, I can only say that it has a lustre which smacks of the ideal. This house was so large and cool, a solid brick affair, with graceful windows and hardwood floors. After a week or two of residence here and because she was coming to fancy me, I suppose, my landlady came in one morning and announced that since no one was occupying the front room at present I might as well have the use of it, and forthwith threw open the large folding doors which separated mine from the front room and gave me a clear sweep, straight through from front to back with two shaded windows in the side walls. In addition, she told me that I might use either bed. And thus settled in this quiet street with pleasant views, front, side and back, and usually a breeze fluttering the curtains, I idled here as much as possible in these hot June or July days—I forget which—reading, dreaming, going out to Forest Park occasionally before I went down for my assignment, sitting on the green grass at the side of the house where a rustic bench had been placed, and counting myself as comfortably placed for the time as any newspaper man in the city.

And in addition, as I have said, my landlady, who had shown considerable interest in my comings and goings up to this time, now found that it was agreeable apparently to drop in during the afternoon or morning and see how I was getting on. Apparently she was a bit curious over my method of living and working, or she was just interested in me, for she would loiter here a half-hour at a time, especially in the afternoon, leaning over my writing table and listening to explanations of my work or talking about her other boarders. All the time I felt a coming out of something from her to me. She was so very genial and good natured where anything which related to me was concerned. Finally, after this baseball game assignment had grown to be a feature, and my composition of it a thrilling labor of love, she came up nearly every afternoon at three, hung over my shoulder and wanted to know how I was getting on. By now I had explained to her all about it and showed her each day's result. In consequence we came to be rather intimate, without my having the courage to go much farther.

She would tap at my door—or look in, for the reason that, desiring the draft which it created, I nearly always left it open—and coming over would look over my shoulder and say, "At it again? Don't you ever get tired?" or "It must be nice to be a reporter and sit here where it's cool and write." By degrees I began to feel more and more strongly that her interest was by no means platonic, and feeling her hand laid rather caressingly on my shoulder one day, I looked up and, noting the odd, provocative smile about her mouth, reached up and took it in mine.

"Sweet boy," was all she said—enough for many, I suppose, but nervous and bashful always, I took it as no final proof but merely held her hand, not knowing quite what to do, until with her free hand she stroked my hair. Then I pulled her down and kissed her and, feeling an appropriate response, ventured to feel her breasts. She broke away, saying the neighbors could see, and ran into the front room, which merely took us into greater privacy. Here I held her until feeling keenly that she was drawing me on, I first shut the rear door, and then—

But who have not had their passional experiences? Only in those days mine were so very simple and bashful—always heavily admixed with a sense of shame, degradation, sin and I know not what else. Even here I was doubtful whether I was vigorous enough for her and unhappily nervous lest she should consider me a sex failure.

CHAPTER XL

Mrs. X, as I shall have to call her, for I have entirely forgotten her name as well as the number of the house, was entirely different to the two or three women I had known thus intimately heretofore. She was so small, well formed, pretty, chirpy, with a pagan practicality and directness which was tonic to me at this time, but, for all that, with distinct signs of her thirty years about her. I liked her very much indeed. As it was, however, I still had such a snivelling and sniffy attitude in regard to all sex relations that I considered myself very much of a wastrel, if not a deep-dyed villain. Say what one would, according to my point of view at that time, due to my raising, of course, fornication was a crime—a mortal sin, as the Catholics say—but alas, somehow vastly delicious and humanly unescapable. No one should really do it—it was not right—but still, if one could and never be found out—. You know the American point of view. In addition I was dreadfully fearful lest I be led into a life of crime or shame by this, or disease—the various diseases springing from this relation being so very much discussed all the time. And I was always fearful lest (she being promiscuous and I not!) I would acquire some contagion, so that I was for purifying myself with the greatest care, afterwards. I fancy, due to her American or Midwestern bringing-up, of course, that she may have entertained, or had in the past, many notions to the same end. Still, compared to myself, she was a creature of the world and probably noted and was amused by many of my shy puritan ways. The mere act of silent secretive friction was sufficient for me, whereas I recall now that I was quite shocked—deliciously so of course (even if I looked on it as evil)—at some of her expressions in process, the direct vigorous way in which, after the first two or three times, she approached this pleasure.

"You like that?"

"You like to do it to me?"

And the way she bit my neck and cheek, in lieu of love-savageries which I should have indulged in, I presume. She was so small, and curled herself about me so tightly and pinched and uttered such muffled screams when her orgasm was upon her that I was astonished, even if pleased. And then the way she would pretend a shyness afterward—"You lie here now and don't look while I run," but if I did look, which I did, she would giggle elfishly, listening at the door which led out into the hall and then, hearing no one, slip out into the bath—rarely if ever returning then, sometimes not for hours or until the next morning. It was after the third or fourth time, I think, that she showed me where her room was on the ground floor and then later asked me to stop in one night on my way home. I did so, only to find her in bed, which resulted in my remaining there until dawn, when she suggested that it would be best if I went upstairs.

A curious thing about this relation, as well as the one preceding, although not the first one, was the fact that although it was delicious and in its own peculiar way broadening, it was so utterly incapable of fulfilling what some might call a spiritual (but which I would prefer to distinguish as a poetic) ideal. At the time and for many years after, I would not have been able to make this distinction, and it bears no least relationship to anything religious or moral (I am most anxious that that should be clearly understood). As I accept life now, it has long since been swept clean of all religious and moral interpretation. I accept success and failure in many ways as obvious, self-evident facts, but not based on anything religious or moral as we have understood those things but as something different—Darwin's unmoral fitness to survive, no less—man's strength, subtlety, cruelty, quickness of wit, as well as his geniality, generosity, understanding and charm. Various men succeed or fail in various ways, but in my lexicon there is no specific God to care, punish or reward, but only large laws or methods which, seized upon or accidentally and per adventure fallen in step with, produce those sometimes colossal successes and failures which we see, and all the puny ones besides. I have no spiritual ideal in the old sense. I never have had, but in its place there existed at this time, as I have previously indicated, that poetic something, a type or pattern not necessarily identified with either prosperity or poverty which, as I have said, was holding me as if in a spell. It extracted much of the pleasure I might have gotten out of this—for, alas, it was not the ideal! Somewhere that must be awaiting me!

What I did get out of this though was a further proof of my own sexual potency—although, if you will believe it, I still doubted. Better yet, I extracted a strong suspicion of the general American moralistic assumption that all women are pure as driven snow, or should be. In my limited experience, you see, I was not finding it so. In future years I was to discover that there was little true intellectual growth for either man or woman outside a certain amount of sexual experimentation. Under strict monogamy the mind seems to wither and take on working formulaes. Be that as it will, this relationship continued with considerable force and enthusiasm until a few weeks later when another change came which brought it to a quick, sad end—for me, anyhow.

It turned out, as I say, that this fat-lean baseball was a great success, for me, anyhow. While it brought me no more money, it certainly established me as a feature writer on my paper and, if you will, as having a fine sense of humor! Before it was quite concluded, another newspaper feature with which I was destined to be connected hove into view. Unnoticed by me, a voting contest which embraced the whole state and concerned the question as to which twenty school teachers, the favorites of any twenty districts in the state, were to be sent to Chicago to see the World's Fair for two weeks or more was then running in the *Republic*. The teachers with the largest number of votes, indicated by coupons printed in the *Republic* and from it clipped and presented or mailed to the business management, were to be permitted to visit the World's Fair, all expenses paid and in the best manner. All transportation, Pullman service, hotel bills, entrance to the Fair, and chaperonage were to be furnished by the paper, which undertook to see that everything was carried out properly. And in addition a reporter, or traveling correspondent if you please, was to be sent with the party to report its daily doings—pleasures, views and the like.

By this time, as I have said, my baseball campaign having proved such a great success, I was, in all modesty, easily the most eligible candidate for the place. I was not seeking it, to be sure, but, according to Wandell, who was selecting the man for the management, I was the one most likely to give a scintillant picture of the great Fair as well as render the *Republic* a service in picturing the doings of these teachers. An agent of the business manager was going also, to look after the practical details, as well as the city superintendent of schools. Out of a clear sky and while I was still busy with my baseball assignment and enjoying it hugely, I was informed by Wandell that I might have to go. The opportunity for seeing the World's Fair, which was then in its heydey and filling the newspapers, was of the greatest import to me. In the light of that, *having* to go appeared amusing. It appeared that the editor-in-chief, as well as the managing editor and business manager, had seen my work or had had it called to their attention, and when a man for the expedition was spoken of, I was at once decided upon. Mr. Wandell had the satisfaction of telling me.

"I don't mind telling you," he observed to me a few days before the final account of the game was to be written, "that your work on this ball game business has been good. Everybody is pleased. Now there's a little excursion we're going to send up to Chicago, and I'm going to send you along on that, for a rest. Mr.————, our business manager, will tell you all about it. You see him about transportation and expenses, and he'll fix you up."

"When am I to go?" I asked.

"Sunday. Sunday night."

"Then I don't get to see the ball game."

"Oh, never mind about that. Any one can write it up. You've done the important work."

I smiled. This was indeed a compliment. I went downstairs and hearing what it was, and what the paper was to do, congratulated myself. Now I was to have a chance to visit the World's Fair, which had not yet opened when I had been compelled to leave Chicago. All my expenses were to be paid. I could look up my father, whom it seemed to me that I had neglected since my mother's death, as well as such other members of the family as were still resident in Chicago, although I must say it did not seem that I was on very friendly terms with them. Also go around to the office of the *Globe* and "blow" to my old confreres about my present success. In addition I was to have none of the bother of attending to the commercial details. All I had to do was to go along and observe what the girls did and how they enjoyed themselves, and write it up—about eight hundred words a day. It was too easy. The reward was really more than I deserved, I thought. Still, clever work was worth while.

I went up the street humming and rejoicing and finally landed at the "Art Department" of my friends.

"I'm going to be sent to Chicago to the World's Fair," I exclaimed on entering."

"Bully for you," was the unanimous return. "Let's hope you have a good time."

Then light-heartedly and with a slight element of exaggeration I told them all about it. Also later in the night I returned to my rooms in

Chestnut Street. Mrs. X was there to receive me. I told her, rather gaily, saying that I should be back in three weeks. I did not explain, however, that I was helping chaperon a score of girls. Somehow I felt that the details of that were beneath me, but the trip and the chance to sightsee struck me as wonderful. Curiously, I was not the least moved to go and see Lois. I thought of her, rather wistfully, but she was married now and perhaps I had best let well enough alone.

Perhaps?!

CHAPTER XLI

As the time drew near, the thought of being a sort of literary chaperon to a lot of school teachers, probably all of them homely and uninteresting, was not as cheering as it might have been—I was getting such a fine estimate of myself. The attitude of the business manager and the managing editor, whom I now met, as well as the editor-in-chief or publisher, Mr. Knapp, was enough to convince me that whatever I thought of it, I was plainly rising in their esteem. Although no least word was said about any increase in pay, which I still consider the limit of a beggarly, penny-wise policy, I was taken in by Wandell and introduced to these magnificos, who smiled and congratulated me on my work and then turned me over to the gentle ministrations of the business manager who had the financing of the trip in charge. He reminded me a good deal of a banker and a church elder—small, dark, full-whiskered, solemn, affable—and assured me that he was most pleased over my success and that I was to be sent on this trip. After asking me to go and see a certain Mr. Soldan, superintendent of schools of St. Louis, who was also to be of the party, a guest of the *Republic*, he said he would send me a Mr. Dean, who was to be his agent en route to look after everything—baggage, fares, hotels, meals—and that I would be more comfortable if I kept in touch with him. The latter came and at once threw a wet blanket over me—and to a certain extent the trip. He was so utterly dull and commonplace, although if I had only thought so at the time, he probably contained delightful literary material at that. His clothes, his shoes, his loud tie and lower-middle-class trade instincts all irritated me beyond measure. Something he said—"Now of course, we all want to do everything we can to please these ladies and make them happy"—irritated me beyond measure. The usual pastoral, supervisory stuff, I thought, and at once I was beside myself with opposition.

"What! Did this horrible bounder assume that he was regulating my conduct on this trip—or that I was going out of my way to accommodate myself to him and his theory of how this trip should be conducted or to accept him as a social equal? 'We must!' indeed," I thought, "me—Theodore Dreiser, the well-known newspaper writer of St. Louis. The effrontery! Who was he to speak of himself and myself as 'we'?" I thought. I liked that! Well, he would get scant attention from me, and the more he let me alone—kept out of my way—the better for him and for all of us.

And then Wandell irritated me also latterly by extending me minute instructions as to just what was wanted and how I was to write it, although as I understood it, I was now working for the managing editor who would have the material edited in the telegraph department. Besides, as I argued, I was entitled by now to a little leeway and discretion in the choice of what I would report. The idea of making it all advertising for the *Republic* and myself a literary wet nurse to a school party was a little too much.

However, I arranged my affairs, and on the evening before the great day when the baseball game was to be played, bustled down to the train which was waiting to carry this party of blushing damsels to Chicago and the World's Fair—a solid Pullman affair which left St. Louis at eight-forty-five in the evening and arrived in Chicago early the next morning. It consisted, as I found, of the customary combination baggage car and smoker, and after that Pullmans only, strung in a long and shining row. The fifth of these, the *Benares,* was reserved to carry only the school teachers and their chaperons, Mr. Dean the business manager's representative, Mr. Soldan the superintendent of public schools, and myself. It stood in the dim and noisy sheds of the old depot at 12th and Poplar when I came down, wondering what the pleasures of this temporary companionship with so many girls might be. They were all prize-winners, I knew, but my pessimistic mind had registered a somewhat depressing conception of the ordinary schoolmistress, and I did not expect too much.

For once in my life, however, I was most agreeably disappointed.

The car when I arrived was practically empty. I had come down after a pleasant session with several of my newspaper friends in the cafe of the Laclede, and I was on a plane of comfortable thought not often attained by me. The world was going very well then, and I knew it. All I lacked to make me perfectly happy, I thought, was a satisfactory income. But this, in my happy mood, I thought might shortly follow now. I looked on Chicago as a distant world to which I was returning after many triumphs. The World's Fair, with its amazing displays and fascinating spectacles which the papers were daily reporting, would be of immense interest to me. Hundreds of thousands of people were longing to go who would never get there. I wondered what Lois was doing and what she would think if she could see me now. This was like some of the fictitious errands I had painted for her delectation in my earlier courtship. I was not inclined to crow over her. The memory brought an honest pang. I merely wished, with all my heart, that such a thing as this might have been true at the time I previously narrated it in a rather prophetic and anticipatory spirit.

As I sat there in the gaudy car, with its rosewood panels, bevel-edged mirrors and stuffy carpets and cushions, it seemed to me that I was doing very well indeed. Then the door opened and the Pullman porter carried in the luggage of the firstcomer, a pretty, rosy-cheeked, black-haired girl of perhaps twenty-four. I looked up in surprise. This was a good beginning, anyhow, I thought. At least there was one who was not homely. Thereafter—I am quoting from a much earlier attempt to portray all this—there came a tall, fair girl, with light brown hair and blue eyes, who fixed herself in a distant corner of the car very reservedly. Others came now more rapidly, through both doors. There were blondes and brunettes, with various grades and intermediate types of both persuasions, until the car was full, and in the shuffling and hurrying of friends I lost track of them. I did not see from this quite how I was to get in with them or make myself agreeable. I began to be overcome by a sickening sense of inefficiency and inappropriateness for an occasion of this kind. Why had they sent me? What could I do with twenty girls? Perhaps the business manager's representative or the superintendent would not come at all on this train, and I would be left to introduce them. I would have to find out their names, and I had not thought to inquire at the office. Horrors! I would find myself wretchedly outclassed by this bevy of beauties.

Fortunately for my peace of mind, while I was still thinking, a large, corpulent, rather showily dressed man, with big, soft, ruddy hands decorated with several rings, and a full oval face tinted with health, entered by the front door and beamed cheerily before me. He had big blue-grey eyes and light corn-colored hair, parted debonairly in the middle, I noticed.

"Ah, here we are now," he began, cheerily and with an impressive air of regularity and authority, beaming on the first maiden he saw. "I see you have arrived safely, Miss Cordon. I'm glad to see you again. We are all going to have a very nice time, I'm sure. How are you?"

"Oh, quite well, thank you," the girl replied, flushing slightly.

"And here is Miss Wetherill," he exclaimed, advancing to a second and beaming. "Well, I am glad. How do you do, Miss Wetherill? I am really delighted to see you. I read in the *Republic* that you had won."

"Yes, I succeeded, Professor," I heard this girl reply, though I could not see her. She was behind me. "I never thought I would, though, up to yesterday. There were so many others in the contest."

I realized at once that this was that Professor Soldan, superintendent of schools, whom I had been asked to meet. I liked him.

"And here is Miss McGanahan. Well, I'm glad to see you."

"Oh, here's Professor Soldan," called some girl in the rear of the car. "Genevieve, here's Professor Soldan."

There ensued a chorus of voices which drowned the possibility of hearing anything definitely. An engine went puffing and clanging by on a neighboring track. I gazed out of the window. It seemed that it was essential for me to begin to do something, and yet I did not know what. Suddenly the large jeweled hand was laid on my shoulder from behind, and the figure of the Professor stood before me.

"This must be Mr. Dreiser, of the *Republic,* I think. Your business manager, Mr. ——— of the *Republic,* phoned me this morning that you were coming. You must let me introduce you to all these school misses. I think I know most of them, or I will before I am through. We want to get the formalities over and be on easy social terms."

I bowed. The professor began at the end of the car and introduced me and, when he did not know them, himself first very informally, after which in these cases he explained who I was and what I was to do. I was flushed and yet delighted by his geniality and the fact that he was helping me over a very ticklish situation. I wished sincerely that I had as much ease and self-possession.

After all these formal introductions I found that I had still not met all who were to go, but the professor did not trouble himself any more. He betook himself elsewhere, leaving me to converse as best I might with a pretty, black-haired Irish girl, whose name I had forgotten but whose eyes made me wish to be agreeable. I struggled desperately for bright things to say, and managed to make a few remarks, of what quality I haven't the slightest memory. The girl helped me of course by briskly discoursing on the nature of the contest and the difficulties she had. It made matters much more comfortable.

By and by several others joined in the conversation, and then before I realized it, the train began to move. The porter came in to close the windows for the long tunnel; the girls threw themselves into comfortable attitudes in the seats. There was a general air of relaxation and good nature. As the environs of the city began rolling swiftly by I found myself more and more at ease. Before East St. Louis had been reached a general conversation was in progress, and by the time the train was a half-hour out, a party of the most select spirits had gathered in the little bridal chamber, or private compartment, which was at the rear end of the car, and were having a gay time laughing and talking. But myself and the girl I was now talking to were not of it.

"Why don't you come back here, Myra?" called a voice.

The girl to whom I was talking looked about. "Having lots of fun back there?" she called.

"Yes, come on back."

It was such an open bid, I could easily see which of us was wanted. I stood up.

"We might as well go back," she said. "Come on."

I followed uncertainly. At the door I stopped and looked in. It was full of pretty girls, my own partner of the moment before chattering lightly among them.

"There is room for one more," said a blooming blonde, more daring than the rest, making a place beside herself.

I could not refuse this challenge.

"I'm the one," I said lightly, as I entered. I had the feeling that I was being examined with coquettish interest. Possibly I was not, to outward appearances, bashful, although my feeling was that I appeared so and that they saw it and, besides, that I was so physically unattractive that I would not long be amusing to them. That I couldn't be.

"Isn't train-riding just glorious?" exclaimed one bright-faced girl exuberantly. "I just love to travel. I wish I could travel all the time."

"Hear! Hear!" I echoed smiling genially. "I'd like to travel too."

"Oh, would you?" demanded the girl who was sitting beside me and whom I had scarcely noticed.

"If I could have the proper surroundings," I declared stoutly.

"What do you call proper surroundings?" put in a new voice, drawing my attention to limpid blue eyes, a sweet cupid's bow mouth and a wealth of sensuous corn-colored hair.

"These, for instance," I declared gallantly, gazing about the compartment and at my companions. A burst of applause followed.

"You mean that we are ideal?" inquired the girl who had said that she loved to travel, laughing.

"Of course! Of course!"

"Oh, why should you make him fib?" put in the one beside me, cynically and with the light of roguery in her eye. "He can't help himself. It's not fair."

I was bewildered by the bouquet of faces around. Already the idea of the dreary school teacher had been dissipated. These were prizewinners. I had forgotten that. Look where I would, I seemed to see a new type of sweetness confronting me, and so closely. I was in the toils of those nymphs so artistically pictured in the *Ring of the Nibelungen*, and I no more wished to escape than those loving heroes of the mythical ages. I gazed spellbound and with a sense of intoxication at the pretty eyes of various colors, the short retroussé noses, the pink cheeks, the smooth white foreheads, and the small ears. They were all so becomingly dressed, so gay in spirit, so wilful in their abandon and good humor. They were out for a lark, I was the only man available, and they were making the most of me.

"If I had my wishes now I'd wish for just one thing," I declared conclusively, expecting to arouse curiosity.

"Which one?" said the girl with the brown eyes and piquant little face, who wished to travel continuously. Her look was exasperatingly significant.

"This one," I declared, running my finger around in a circle to include them all, and yet stopping at none. I had them interested for the moment.

"We're not one, though," said the same girl peevishly, punning on the word *won*.

"Couldn't you be?" I asked smartly, as I smiled at her.

"Not all at once, could we?" she asked, speaking for the crowd now.

"It will seem all at once," I returned quickly, "when it happens. Isn't it always so sudden?" I added. I was surprising myself.

"Aren't you smart!" said the blue-eyed girl beside me.

"Oh, that's clever, isn't it?" added the girl with the sensuous hair.

I gazed again in her direction. Beside her sat a maiden whom I had but dimly noticed heretofore. She was in white, with a mass of sunny red hair. Her eyes were almond-shaped, liquid and blue-grey, her nose straight and fine, her lips sweetly curved and ruddy. As I looked her mouth was open in a smile, showing dainty pearl-like teeth, but she seemed bashful and somewhat retiring. At her bosom was a bouquet of pink roses but one had come loose.

"Oh, your flowers!" I exclaimed.

"Let me give you one," she replied laughing. I had not heard her voice before, but it appealed to me.

"With pleasure," I said. Then gaily, to the others, "I'll take anything I can get." She drew a rose from her bosom, and held it out toward me.

"Won't you put it on?" I asked smartly.

"Yes, indeed," she replied, and leaning over began to fasten it.

As she did so I looked down. She worked a moment and then looked up, making as I thought a "sheep's eye" at me.

"You may have my place," said the girl next to me, feigning to aid her. She took it.

The conversation waxed even freer after she had pinned it on for me, but for the time being I felt that it had taken a definite turn. I was talking for her benefit. We were still in the midst of it when the conductor passed through—and after him my Mr. Dean, middle-aged, dusty, assured, advisory.

"These are the people," I heard him say. "They are all in one party."

He passed on through and then the conversation turned on him,—his manner of grouping us. I was annoyed by him, his methods and presence.

I wished he had not come. He came back after a time and, after signalling me, sat down beside me and began explaining cheerfully and volubly the trouble he was having keeping everything in order. "I'm looking out for the baggage and the hotel bills and all," he said. "In the morning we'll be met by a tally-ho," he explained, "and will ride out to the hotel." I was thinking of my splendid bevy of girls and the delightful time I had been having. Being called away this way broke it up for me.

"That's nice, isn't it?" I said wearily.

"Oh, we have it all planned out. It's going to be a delightful trip."

I evinced no desire to talk, but he still kept on. He wanted to meet the teachers, and blundering in my introductions, I showed him about. After this, fortunately, he became interested in one small group of three and I sidled away, only to find my original group considerably decimated. The original atmosphere and hilarity had evaporated. Some had gone to the ladies' dressing room. Others were arranging their parcels about their unmade berths. The porter came in now and began busily letting down the berths for the night. I looked ruefully about me.

"Well, our little group has broken up," I said at last to the girl of my choice, as I sidled up to where she was sitting.

"Yes, they have gone to get ready for bed. It's getting late. I must be going soon."

We dropped into an easy conversation, and I learned that she was from Missouri and taught in a little town not far from the city. She explained how she had come to win, and I responded by telling her how ignorant I had been of this whole affair up to four days previous. Friends, she said, had bought hundreds of *Republics* and clipped the coupons. It seemed a fine thing to me for a girl to be so popular. She had a way of talking that seemed to me ought to draw friends.

"You've never been to Chicago, then?" I asked.

"Oh, no," she said. "I've never been anywhere really. I'm just a simple country girl, you know—not much like the others that way. I've always wanted to go, though."

Somehow her telling me that she was just a country girl fascinated me. She seemed so direct, truthful, good natured, sympathetic.

"You'll enjoy it," I said. "It's worth seeing. I was in Chicago at the time the Fair was being built. My home is there."

"Then you'll get to stay with your home-folks, won't you?" she said, using a word for family to which I was not accustomed. It touched a chord of sympathy. I was not in touch with my family much anymore, but the way she seemed to look on hers made me wish that I was.

"Well, not exactly. They live over on the west side. I'll get to see them, though. I'll go over two or three times."

"I don't know anything about Chicago," she returned by way of apology. "I've only been to one city—St. Louis—you know."

"Is that all?" I asked, amused by her simplicity and directness. "Well, you'll like Chicago then, even better."

My mind was running on the fact that now that I had her out of that sparkling group she seemed even more agreeable than before. Her dress and hair and general look were the same and yet she was sweeter, more subdued and homelike. Her qualifications apparently were now those of a retiring home girl,—the kind I always imagined I was seeking.

"Well," I added at last, "we'll soon be there. Just a few hours' sleep now." My mind was full of the thrilling wonders of the Fair, all to be seen for nothing and at my leisure. The trip was to endure for two weeks.

She arose to leave me. The porter was lowering her berth.

"I want to get at some of my things before he puts them away," she explained.

I stepped out of her way.

"Good night," I said.

"Good night."

She tripped gracefully up the aisle and I looked after her, fascinated. There seemed to be a bond of sympathy between us. Our temperaments and mental points of view seemed to have much in common. Both of us had been raised apparently under circumstances which had excited a great longing for a wider, freer life in our bosoms. I felt an intense something about her which was concealed, however, by an air of supreme innocence and maidenly reserve. I went out into the smoking room, where I sat all by myself looking out of the window.

"What a delightful girl," I thought, with a feeling of intense satisfaction. "And think, I have the certainty of seeing her again in the morning!"

CHAPTER XLII

The next morning I was awake early, stirred by the thought of Chicago, the Fair, Miss White (my favorite), as well as the group of attractive creatures who formed a sort of background to her. And, in addition, there was the fact that I was now in a position to visit all my old scenes and familiars or friends—Maxwell, Dunlap, Brady, Hutchinson—a considerable group of local newspapermen, as well as my brothers Al and Ed who were here employed somewhere, and my father and several sisters, who were living in different parts of the city. One of the characteristics of my own youth—as it is, perhaps, that of many others—was to invest every place that I had ever been and left for even a brief time with a romance and strangeness such as might have attached to something abandoned a thousand years ago and now seen for the first time since. I always expected to find it greatly changed in architecture and people—nearly all done over—and in addition I invested it all with an intense melancholy at the passing of things, those things of which I had been a part a few years before and that now never, never, never would return again.

And so it was now with Chicago, that rapidly advancing and changeful city. Only two years before we had buried my mother in a miserable little Catholic cemetery on the north side and the family had once and for all been irretrievably broken up. In addition, advancing years and growing differences in temperaments and ambitions had caused all of us to look at one another with a certain amount of skepticism, or at least I thought so. In this respect, while I was perhaps the loudest in complaint of the views, conduct and moods of the others, I was certainly as little fitted as any by reason of temperament or anything I had ever done, kind or helpful, let alone by any perfectness of conduct or mental standards, to say anything at all. Just the same, owing to an irritable, restless, critical, ambitious and even domineering temperament at times, I was convinced that my older sisters and brothers were not sufficiently appreciative of me, were not doing as well as they should, were not as wise or as successful or as interesting as I thought they ought to be, and in addition were not living their lives as I would have them live them. In short, they were not good enough for me, and I complained of their being selfish, distant and the like, whereas I was the warm, genial, helpful soul, et cetera, et cetera.

On the contrary, as for my father, who was by now seventy-two or three years of age, I had, all of a sudden, the greatest sympathy. At home, up to my seventeenth or eighteenth birthday—before I got out in the world and began to make my own way—I had found him fussy, cranky, dosed with too much religion; although, in spite of all this and the quarrels and bickerings which arose because of it, always in my relations with him there had been, outside of Catholicism, something so colorful and tender in his views, charmingly poetic and appreciative, that I was drawn to him in spite of myself. I felt sorry for him—could not help it. A little while before and after my mother's death it had seemed to me, then in the worst period of my adolescence, that he had become unduly wild on the subject of the church and the hereafter, was annoying with his persistent preachments concerning duty, economy, and the like—the need of leading a clean, saving, religious life. Now after a year out in the world, however, with a broadening knowledge of very different things, I had an entirely different view of him. While realizing him to be irritable, crotchety, domineering, almost impossible to live with, for me at least, still he had suddenly become just a broken old man, whose hopes and ambitions were a failure, whose religion, impossible as it was to me, was still a comfort and blessing to him. Here he was: alone, without any one much to look after him, his wife dead, his children not very much interested in him any more. What would he do without his religion now, I thought. Now that I was entering Chicago again, I felt intensely sorry for him, anxious to do a little something, seeing that I had been away a year and done nothing at all—barely kept the present address of the different members of the family. I decided, once I had arranged my other affairs and was well launched upon this task, to go over on the west side and look him up and bring him out here and let him see the Fair, which as yet, no doubt, he had not seen. For, as I well presumed, his saving, worrying, almost penurious disposition would not let him. He had had too much trouble getting enough money to live on in these latter years ever to permit him to truly enjoy himself in any instance where it cost anything. I could hear him saying, "No, no. I cannot afford it. We have too many debts"—unpaid installment furniture bills left by my mother, and the like. He had not always been so, but time and many troubles had made the saving of money almost a mania with him.

Poor, tottering, broken soul. I can see him yet amid the storm of difficult circumstances that seemed always to assail him in these later years: thin as a grasshopper; brooding sadly with those brown-black German eyes, like one of those old men Rembrandt has so magnificently portrayed (ah, the weary eyes of those men of the Dutch master); his peculiarly German hair and beard combed and brushed as much like those of Rembrandt's old men as may be; his clothes loose and ill fitting, always purchased for durability, not style, or—more characteristic still—usually made over from abandoned clothes of my brother Paul who, realizing his desire for them, sent them home; an old carefully preserved derby hat, given to him also I believe by my brother Paul, pulled over his eyes; a Catholic prayer book under his arm, fluttering along to church in the sharp winter days (every morning regularly toward the last), going to pray before some saint or altar as dead or helpless as his own past.

And the thinness of his hands! The tremulousness of his inquiries! The something of appeal in his sad resigned eyes, where all power to compel or convince had long since gone. In the vast cosmic flight of force flowing from what heart we know not but in which as little corks our suns and planets swim, it is possible, I sometimes think, that there may be some care, an equation, a balancing of the scales of suffering and pleasure—want and the opposite thereof. I hope so. If not, I know not the reason for tears or those emotions with which so many of us salve the memory of seemingly immedicable ills. If immedicable, why cry? Or if not, is not that in itself all the more so then an augur that in universal energy from which we plainly take our rise there lurks a pity which is in itself the augur of an equivalent, a readjustment somewhere, a paying back or out? Or, if not, then is this pity in us the last, sad emanation of that for which there is plainly no help? Dark thought. Peace to him, then, wherever he is.

In the train, however, riding into Chicago I found Miss White up before me, dressed and beside her section window before ever I came from the washroom. She was gazing at the vast flat dreary prairie which constitutes the northern part of Illinois, and she looked very inviting. I was about to go and talk to her when my attention was claimed by other girls. This bevy could not very well afford to see the attention of the only man on board so easily monopolized. Others spoke to me and I sat down with them, unwilling to admit any early preference. There were so many pretty faces among them that I wavered. There were some who were much more sophisticated and assured, I thought as I looked at them, than the one I had chosen, but none more appealing. I talked idly among them, interested to see what overtures and how much of an impression I might make. My natural love of womanhood made them all inviting.

In the meantime, the train had drawn into the Union Station on the west side of Chicago, and there we were met by a tally-ho which the obliging Mr. Dean had been kind enough to announce to each and every one of us as the train stopped.

"We want to stay together," he called, appearing very briskly from I did not know where. "There'll be a tally-ho here to meet us. I'll find out whether it's on hand."

Personally, the idea of riding to the World's Fair in a tally-ho, only a few of which I had ever seen and in no one of which I had ever ridden, and with this somewhat conspicuous party of school teachers, was slightly antipathetic to me. Being very conscious of my personal dignity in the presence of others at this time, an American of the Middle West and therefore new to these persistently derided toys and pleasures of the effete East and England, I was inclined to look upon them as out of place in Chicago—lugged in by the ears, as I thought, and of no good or useful purpose here! It was fashionable—that was true—even in some circles here, but still it did not seem quite right in connection with a company such as this, so untutored in ways social—and even in connection with myself, experienced by now as I thought myself! A sign on the coach advertising the expedition seemed spiritually involved with the character of Mr. Dean. I wondered how the sophisticated and well-groomed superintendent of schools of St. Louis could lend himself to any such thing when plainly it was to be written up in the *Republic,* but he did not seem to mind it in the least. In fact he took it all with a charming gayety and grace which eventually succeeded in putting all my own silly provincialism and pride to rout—sitting up in front with me and the driver and discussing philosophy, education, the Fair, a dozen things, during which I made an immense pretence at wise deductions and a wider reading than ever I had indulged in. Besides, the remainder of the party were by no means so hypercritical or persnickety. They seemed to enjoy it hugely.

Once clear of the depot and turning into Adams Street, we were off behind six horses through the interesting business heart with its high buildings—the earliest and most numerous in America—and its mass of congested traffic, a lackey in livery at the back blowing long and exhilarating carols on his trumpet. It was such a drive—so perfect in its charm and views: Michigan Avenue with its splendid vista of the lake, whipped to cotton-tops this bright morning by a fresh wind, and then the long residence-lined avenue to the south with its wealth of new and pretentious homes, its smart paving and lighting, its crush of pleasure traffic, particularly at this time, hurrying townward or Fairward, the clear bright warm light, and this crisp lake wind whipping about us. At the hotel, which was a comfortable enough affair, hastily constructed for the occasion, no doubt, but close to the grounds—so many hotels were erected for just the period of the Fair, being subsequently changed into flats—we were all quickly assigned to our rooms, and then breakfast was served.

Although it has been twenty-five years since this occurred, I recall nothing in my life which contains anything more of freshness, color, beauty than these views of Chicago and the Fair on this first of our days here. Chicago was so interesting to me then, so crisp, so ambitious, so generally inspiriting. One wall of this hotel, as I now discovered, faced a portion of the fairgrounds, and from its windows, two of which were in my room, some of its classic facades, porticoes, roofs, domes, lagoons could be seen—a spectacle than which I have never seen anything more moving, more etherealizing, if I may say. Here all at once, as it were, out of nothing, in this dingy city of six or seven hundred thousand, which but a few years before had been a waste of wet grass and mud flats, and by this lake, which a hundred years before was but a lone silent waste, was now this vast and harmonious collection of perfectly constructed and snowy buildings, containing in their delightful interiors, and with an easy appeal for the mind, the artistic, mechanical and scientific achievements of the world to date. Nothing, I think it will be generally admitted, was ever more speedily or better done, nothing of either intellectual or artistic import forgotten. Not only were the sciences and the arts of the total countries of the world represented—and delightfully so—but the current color and romance of these lands as well, their ethnology and political economy. Greece, Italy, India, Egypt, Japan, Germany, South America, the West and East Indies, the Arctics, how well they were represented. I have often thought since how those pessimists who up to that time had imagined that nothing of any artistic or scientific import could possibly be brought to fruition in America anywhere, and especially in this Middle West, must have opened their eyes, as I did mine, at the sight of this realized dream of beauty, this splendid picture of the world's own hope for itself. I have long since marveled at it myself, its splendid Court of Honor with its monumental stateliness and simple grandeur, its peristyle with its amazing grace of columns and sculptured figures, the great central arch with its triumphal quadriga, the dome of the Administration Building with its free, daring nudes, the splendid groupings on the Agricultural Building, as well as those on the Manufacturers' and Women's Buildings—how they all come back to me even yet as comprising a world of beauty and poetry of the utmost significance. My particular stay endured but two weeks, during which time I was considerably employed with many things not exactly of the Fair, but in that period I seemed gradually to come to understand what had been done here. It was not, as I thought then, as if many minds had labored separately or, for that matter, collectively and with boundless wealth toward this great end, or as if this great raw city which did not quite understand itself as yet had endeavored to make a great "show," but rather as though some brooding spirit of beauty, inherent possibly in some directing oversoul, had waved a magic wand quite as might have Prospero in *The Tempest* or Queen Mab in *Romeo and Juliet*, and lo, this fairyland, this dream out of the Periclean Age of Athens.

One night, gliding in and out of the various lagoons, quite as in Venice, in one of the electric launches, accompanied by two or three or more of these eager maidens anxious to see all, a feeling of the true dreamlike beauty of it all came to me, at first only as a sense of intense elevation—not wonder, but elevation at being permitted to dwell in so Elysian a realm—quite as the new-dead faithful might feel on contemplating the Garden of Allah. It was all so lofty, so murmurous of joy, and yet so serene! The lights! the water! a summer moon! the mystic whiteness of the buildings! From somewhere over in that gay polyglot region known as the Midway came the sounds of those muffled oriental drums and cymbals so characteristic of the East—the flutings of their sad, complaining wind instruments. At first, as I say, only a sense of intense elevation held me as from a narcotic. Then followed an abiding wonder at so much beauty, a deep and exquisite feeling of contentment at having seen it, so that one might say, "At last! at last!" It was a mood which I am sure youth will understand, for want of which maturity languishes and dies: a sweet, calm expansion of the spirit, a sense of the complete unimportance of all dull everyday struggling, having and holding—the slavery and brutality of it all. Now, here and now, was heaven—beauty—a paradise for the soul. Here and now were color, light, the ultimate significance of sound and charm. We drifted deliciously for an hour or more in this world of glorious sights, an hour or more of dreaming over the arches, the reflections in the water, the statues, the shadowy throngs by the steps of the lagoons moving like figures in a dream. Was it real? I sometimes wonder, for it is all gone. Gone the summer nights, the air, the color, the form, the mood. In its place is a green park by a lake, still beautiful but bereft—a city that grows and grows ever larger, but harder, colder, grayer. Its quondam dream is ended. By command of a fairy thought, perhaps, it came—by as ruthless or casual a whim it went again. But many saw it—I among them—under circumstances most gracious, in summer under its winds and stars, and to this hour I have never forgotten it, a thing of gossamer and eiderdown, a crystalline bubble hovering on the borders of a dream. I saw and I have never been able to forget. The brightness and freshness of this first day; the romance of an International Fair idea in America and particularly in this Middle West; the snowy whiteness of the buildings which somehow against the morning sun, a blue sky and bluer lake, and with the lagoons weaving in and out and the brown earth and green grass providing a contrasting base, achieved a lightness and an airiness wholly at war with anything which this Western world presented as yet—possibly it was something of this which caused me to be swept into a dream from which I did not recover until sometime after, months really. Looking out of my hotel window this first morning, I was so deeply moved by it that I was ready to clap my hands for joy. I wanted to fall to versifying or describing it—a mood which youth will understand and maturity smile at, one of those things which cause the mind to sing, to set forth on fantastic pilgrimages.

Below in the dining room a little while later, I fell in with Miss

White, who, like myself, was among the first to come down. In my absence she had been joined by a sister of about her own age—a little younger—who had come on a separate train and who was paying her own way, as I understood it, merely to keep her company. I was promptly introduced, and we sat down at the same table.

It was not long before we were joined by the others, and then I could see by the exchange of glances that it was presumed that I had fallen a victim to this charmer of the night before.

However, just at this moment the personality of the sister was appealing to me quite as much as, if not more than, the firstcomer. She was so radiant of humor and gaiety—freckled, plump, laughing and with such an easy and natural mode of address, free of affectation or quilly reserve—that I was taken by her at once. Unlike her sister, she had the atmosphere of one who understood life. My favorite's hair was of an electric and yet rusty red, and very thick, whereas her sister's seemed to falter between red and brown—looking now one and now the other—but more plentiful if anything. They seemed almost perfect examples of American animal health and charm, and together made an excellent team.

After breakfast the company broke up into groups of twos and threes. Each had plans for the day, though there was a general consensus of opinion that the company should start out together and then break up afterwards as might suit the plans of those involved. While they were planning, I walked away a little space with my friend of the night before, learning more of her home and teaching environment. As I viewed her now, she seemed more and more natural, winsome, inviting—a girl to make a contest for, but one not easily to be taken. She was apparently so simple and straightforward, in no way affected as I thought, and with a tolerance and understanding that I had not as yet found in others. Patience seemed to be one of her chief characteristics—a quiet and restful and undisturbed patience.

I took to her with the greatest avidity. She seemed from the first to offer me an understanding and a sympathy which I had not previously realized in anyone. She smiled at my humor, appreciated my moods. She told me one or two innocent little school book yarns, such as parents tell their children, which amused me greatly. Her temperament seemed much like mine in many ways, as no doubt it was.

We started off finally for the Fair gate, and on the way I had an opportunity to study some of the other members of the party and make up my mind as to whether I really preferred her above all the others. Despite my leaning toward Miss White, I now discovered, as I looked about, that there were several whose charms under observation were greater than I had imagined, whereas those of some of the others who had attracted me the night before were being modified by little traits of character or mannerisms whose distinctness in the first blush of the parlor car excitement was not apparent. Among the former was one rosy Irish girl whose solid beauty attracted me very much. She was young and dark and robust. There was the air of a hoyden about her. Her name, as I recalled now, was Annie Ginity, one of the girls who had spoken to me in the car the evening before. I looked at her, quite taken by her snapping black eyes, but nothing came of it for the moment. We were all so lost in contemplating the wonders of the Fair itself.

CHAPTER XLIII

This first day, as so many of the others that followed, was spent in wandering about the Fair from building to building and exhibit to exhibit, the general exterior effect of the buildings far outrivaling in appeal, for me at least, anything which the interiors had to offer. The latter were astounding enough as to size and fascinating enough as to particular exhibits, where one could understand them, educational and broadening to a degree; but since machinery, electricity, textiles, and some phases of agriculture and architecture were in the main Greek to me, only the simpler and more surfacy things appealed—the first railroad trains, the largest engine, the latest marvels of electricity. All that an enormous display like that in the Machinery Hall had to say to me was—that I knew nothing about machinery and never would. Ditto electricity. Ditto textiles, mining, mineralogy and the like. It has since become perfectly plain to me that because of certain mental defects, I have missed whole worlds, not being able to comprehend abstrusities of one kind and another, but as one is, so is he. Mathematics, mechanics, physics, except in their larger sweeps and conclusions, have always been able to do but one thing for me—that is, give me a profound headache.

When it came to the surfaces and forms of things—their colors, tones, motions and groupings, harmonies—these, as I then saw clearly, talked to me in another language, giving rise to thoughts of a deep and serious character. They were by no means meaningless. The moment I ceased attempting to grasp the details of these very intricate displays and turned my eyes to the general scene, then, and not until then, was I happy and at rest—cogitating in ways agreeable to me. Just to wander and gaze, to think of something and feel its beauty,—the arch lines of the buildings themselves, the movement of the wind upon the water in the lagoons, the crowds massing or melting as shreds of gay color— these offered the facts for a philosophy of beauty. Somewhere near the Machinery Hall was a bandstand. In it occasionally, mornings and afternoons, I think, in fair weather, was so good a band as Sousa's, for instance. From the steps of the Machinery Hall, one could catch glimpses of the blue lake over green grass and through trees as green. Red flowers, gay sunshades, white buildings, the blue water—and then all at once the wind wafting strains of this open-air orchestra. It was heavenly.

As for my school teacher charges, after the first day or two I was spared any great pains in connection with them, for as I soon discovered, and in spite of anything which the officious Dean could do, they were bound and determined to go their own way regardless, and this they did—splitting up into pairs or threes at most as the mood dictated and wandering off by their lone. After considering for a moment that it raised a new problem in regard to how I was to report their collective doings, I solved this by deciding that I would interview them at night at dinner or whenever I chanced to meet them, extracting as much of their views and pleasures as possible, and so condense these into the next day's story. This was not so difficult, as I speedily found, and it gave me ample leisure for any private ventures of my own which I might wish to undertake. I was quick enough to seize upon this, going off to see my father, my friends at the *Globe* office and elsewhere, and bringing my father and several of my sisters and brothers to the Fair—Al and Ed among the number—and ad interim devoting myself to whatever individual or group of our party struck me as likely to prove the most attractive for the day.

One of the most interesting of these side trips was this same which I took to see my father, traveling over to the west side where he lived with one of my sisters. Naturally he was surprised and glad to see me, although I had sent no word,—so anxious to know (and this at once) if I still adhered to the Catholic faith and went to confession and communion regularly. In the old days this had been the principal bone of contention between us—as it was between him and some of the other children.

"Tell me, Dorsch" (that was his sobriquet for me), he inquired not two minutes after I arrived, "do you still keep up your church duties—confession and communion?" When I hesitated for a moment to reply, uncertain what to say, he went on, "You ought to do that, you know. You should never neglect it. If you should die at any time in a state of mortal sin—"

"Yes, yes," I hastily interrupted, making up my mind to give him peace on this score whether it were true or no—it would make him so much more comfortable and could do me no harm. "I always go right along,—certainly—once every month or six weeks anyhow."

"You really do that, do you?" he replied, eyeing me more in appeal than doubt, though I think, judging by my obstinate past, he must have doubted. "I'm glad of that. I worry so. I think of you and the rest of the children so much. You're a young man now and out in the world, and if you neglect your religious duties—" He paused as if in a grave quandary. "When you're out like that I know it's hard to think of the church and your duties, but you ought to tend to them—you shouldn't neglect them. It's all right when you're young, you think, but when you're old like me—" He shook his head sadly.

"Oh, Lord," I thought, "now he's off again. This is the same old story—religion, religion, religion."

"But, I do go," I insisted. "You mustn't worry about me. I go regularly."

"I know," he said with a sudden catch in his voice, "but I can't help it. You know how it is with the other children. They don't always do right in that respect. Paul is away on the stage. I don't know whether he goes to church anymore. Al and Ed are here in the city, but they don't come near me so much—I haven't seen them in—I don't know how long—months—"

I resolved to speak to Ed and Al when I saw them.

He was sitting in a big armchair, facing a rear window, and now he took my hand and held it, and soon I felt hot tears wet it.

"Pop," I said, pulling his head against me and smoothing it. "You mustn't cry. Things aren't so bad as all that. The children are all right. They'll come out all right. Why should you cry? We'll probably all be able to do more for you than we have ever done."

"I know, I know," he said after a little while, overcoming his emotion, "but I am getting so old, and I don't sleep much anymore— just an hour or two. I lie there and think. In the morning I get up at four sometimes and make my coffee. Then the days are so long."

I cried myself. The long days! The fading interests! Reading but a poor help during hours and hours of waking! Mother gone. The family broken up.

"I know," I said. "I haven't acted just right. None of us have. I'll write you from now on when I'm away and send you some money, once in awhile. I'm going to get you a big overcoat for next winter. And now I want you to come over with me to the Fair. Get your hat and cane and come on now. I've tickets and you'll enjoy it. I'll show you everything. I'm a press representative now—a traveling correspondent."

Then I went on to explain just what I was doing and how I had prospered.

He seemed pleased and cheered for the moment, or diverted, and after due persuasion finally secured his hat and stick and came with me. We took a car and an elevated road which finally landed us at the gate. And then, for as long as his strength would endure, we wandered about—he with his stout stick which he always carried now—looking at the enormous buildings, the great Ferris Wheel, several hundreds of feet high, the caravels *Nina*, *Pinta* and *Santa Maria* in which Columbus sailed to America, the Convent of La Rabida, which, because it related to the Trappists, fascinated him, and finally the German Village on the Midway, as German and "ordentlich" as ever a German would wish, where we had coffee and little German cakes with caraway seed on them and some pot cheese with red pepper and onions. He was so interested and amused by the vast spectacle that he could do little but exclaim "By crackie! That is now beautiful" or "That is now wonder-ful." And in the German Village he fell into a conversation with a buxom German frau who had a stand there and hailed from some part of Germany about which he seemed to know—and then all was well indeed. It was long before I could get him away.

These delightful visits were repeated only about four afternoons or evenings during my stay, at the end of which time he admitted that he had enough—that it was too tiring and that he did not wish to see any more. "It is all very fine, but I get too tired."

Incidentally, I looked up my brother Ed, who was driving a laundry wagon somewhere on the south side at the time, and got him to come out evenings and Sundays, and also Al, who was connected with an electric plant in the same region as assistant of some kind. He, too, was delighted to see me and took immediate advantage of the free passes that I offered him. I recall now, with an odd feeling of confusion as to the significance of relationship and family ties generally, how keenly important his and Ed's interests were to me then, and how I suffered because I thought they were not getting along as well as they should, and because I feared that they wouldn't in the future. Looking in a shoe window in Pittsburgh the following summer, I actually choked with emotion because I thought Ed was possibly not able to earn enough to keep himself looking well, and I wanted him to be able to do that. (I worried intensely over him and his future.) It was always the same with Al. He never seemed really hopeful, but more or less thwarted in his ambitions and sad; and whenever I saw him, as on this occasion, I felt sad because I seemed to realize that, like so many millions of others in this world, he had never had a real chance. Life is so casual and luck comes to so many who sleep. In the case of Al—not quite so much so with Ed, my younger brother—it always seemed to me as if here were one who under slightly different or more advantageous circumstances would have done so well. He was naturally so wise, if slightly cynical, full of a laughing humor and of fun. His taste for literature and artistic things in general was high, although entirely untrained. Besides, like myself, he had a turn for the abstrusities of nature, and was constantly wondering why this or that and seeking the answer in a broader knowledge. But long hours of work and poor pay seemed to handicap him a great deal in his search. Naturally, his condition immediately reflected itself in me, and I was sad beyond words, but urged him to come to St. Louis and try his luck there, which he subsequently did.

Another thing I did at this time was to visit the old *Globe* office in Fifth Avenue downtown, only to find things in a bad way there, although Brady, Hutchinson and Dunlap were still there. The paper was not paying and was, so they informed me, in danger of almost immediate collapse. Michael C. MacDonald, its financial backer or angel, having lost a fortune in trying to make it pay and win an election with it (he was currently represented as the master of nearly all local saloons, gambling houses and other institutions of vice), was about ready to quit or had already done so, and the paper was on its last legs. Could I get them a job in St. Louis? Maxwell had gone to the *Tribune* and was now a successful copyreader there. In my new summer suit and straw hat, with my various credentials upon me, I felt myself quite a personage. How much better I had done, indeed, than my friends thus far—these men who had been in the business longer than I had. Certainly I would see what I could do. They should write me. Incidentally, I was out at such and such a hotel.

The sweets of success!

But, although I describe myself thus gaily, it is not to be taken too seriously. These moments of triumph were but few and of brief duration. I was never really successful in the newspaper business for any important length of time. And in truth, at bottom, I was never able to think as well of myself as these passing moments of self-glorification would indicate. Always, always, there was an undercurrent of sad philosophy which dealt with the nothingness of everything. "You are but playing a part," it seemed to say. "You will not be here so very long. Your little body is very frail—a mere nothing in the sweep and substance of things. This city is nothing—the world is nothing. You may strut and stare if you wish for a little while, but soon, soon, it will all be gone. Like all things it is moving, moving, running away."

A fellow newspaper man of St. Louis, Archie Edmonstone by name, a fleshy heaving soul who was police headquarters man for the *Republic* at the Four Courts, now arrived on the scene on his own hook—on a leave of absence, and lacking companionship. I introduced him to my new friends and from him managed to extract occasional bits of news which were of use to me. Incidentally, my feeling for Miss White developed rather swiftly, blotting out all thought of Lois for the time being, but somehow not interfering very much with my relations toward the remainder of the group, as I propose to show.

Thus, this first day, after wandering about with them through various collections and listening to their comments, I left them at two, nervous as to the preparation of my first article and the method of transmitting the same from here. I first sought out the Newspaper Press Association offices in the Administration Building, and finding many desks commanding a great view of its rotunda, sat here and formulated my story. Then after filing it, I returned to the hotel, a little weary of sight-seeing, and finding an upper balcony which commanded a pleasing view of a part of the Fair, sat here in a rocker awaiting the return of some of the party.

They were not slow in coming after four. They were tired and anxious to rest and wished apparently to get into the seclusion of their rooms for the time being. I did not see any of them enter, but presently, as I was resting and humming to myself, there came down to the parlor, which was adjoining this, that Miss Ginity who had attracted me so in the morning. She seemed to be seeking this place to sing and play a little at the piano. She was dressed in a close-fitting suit of white linen, which set off her robust little figure to perfection. Her heavy, oily black hair was parted severely in the middle and hung heavily over her white temples. The rounded fulness of her cheeks, touched with a damask glow, offered a pleasing contrast to her full lustrous black eyes. Her arms and bust were full and plump and her hands round and soft. She had a rich-blooded, healthy, aggressive look, not unmarked by an atmosphere of desire.

I saw her through the window as she came in. I was just beginning to wonder if she would come to the window and discover me, when she did. She smiled, and I waved to her to come out. The exact details of the conversation that followed time has long since effaced. It probably concerned the beauty of the Fair and her enjoyment of it, as well as the charm of this particular scene which impressed me so much. Finally I recall her asking me where I had gone after I had left them, and my replying to find the telegraph office, write my description and file it. This aroused her curiosity as to what I had said, whether I had mentioned names—hers, for instance. I replied that I had mentioned them all, or nearly all—hers particularly.

"Oh, I'll look there tomorrow and see what you did say."

I looked at her admiringly and smiled. She laughed in return, nervously. On the instant it occurred to me—why, I cannot say—that she liked me and that I could influence her if I chose; that if I wished, and that very quickly, I could make her like me very much. It was something about her eyes and smile—the way she turned from my glance—which excited this feeling in me.

"What has become of your friend, Miss White?" I recall her asking with a touch of malice, born, I suppose, of a desire to gainsay and refute my look.

"I don't know. I haven't seen her since I left you. Not since this morning, really. What makes you say that?"

"Oh, I thought you rather liked her," she said boldly, throwing up her chin and smiling.

"And what made you think that?" I asked calmly. It was in my mind that I could master and deceive her as to this, and I proposed to try.

"Oh, I just thought so. You'd seemed rather to like her company."

"Not any more than I do any of the others'," I said, with the greatest assurance. "She seemed to me to be very interesting, that was all. I didn't think I was showing any particular preference."

"Oh, I'm just joking," she laughed. "I really didn't think anything about it. One of the other girls made the remark."

"Well, she's wrong," I replied indifferently.

Then I looked at her.

I could see that she wasn't joking. I could also see that I had relieved her mind. My attitude of indifference had quelled her feeling that I was not wholly free. As far as her affections were concerned, I was still an open proposition.

We sat and talked until dinner. Several others of the party came down, but not Miss White. She had apparently been overtaken by weariness due to too much walking, and was resting in her room. Most of the others seemed tired also, but Miss Ginity was apparently as fresh and strong as she had been in the morning.

"Would you like to go for a little stroll in the park?" I said to her after dinner.

She was looking so fresh and rested. As for me I was nervously keyed up by the idyllic atmosphere in which I was moving. My whole nature was yearning for the satisfaction which comes of idling, not in the lap of luxury but of affection. If I could only have such a girl as this to idle and dream with in this moonlight, providing that she cared for me. She looked to me at this moment, standing out on the piazza of the hotel, with the soft radiance of the windows shining on her face, like some nymph of an older day. Her ruddy, material, rather matter-of-fact temper was made appealing by the soft atmosphere of romance which overshadowed this trip.

"I don't mind," she said, and, taking her arm, we walked into the park.

The air was soft and balmy and the moon just rising over the treetops in the east. A faint odour of fresh flowers and fresh leaves was abroad in the air, and the night seemed to rest in a soothing stillness. From the Midway, not so far distant, came the sounds of those muffled drums and flutes, so redolent of the passion of the East. Before us were the wide stretches of the park, dark and suggestive of intrigue in places where groups of trees were gathered in silent, motionless array; in other places silvered by a fairy brightness which suggested a world of romance and feeling.

"In such a night," I might have quoted, "Troilus, methinks, mounted the Trojan walls and sighed his soul toward the Grecian tents, where Creseide lay that night.

"In such a night did Thisbe fearfully o'ertrip the dew and saw the lion's shadow o'er herself and ran dismay'd away.

"In such a night stood Dido with a willow in her hand upon the wild sea banks and waft her love to come again to Carthage.

"In such a night Medea gathered the enchanted herbs that did renew old Aeson."

Instead, I walked silently on with her, flooded with a voiceless feeling of delight. She seemed to like me—that was the great thing. Now I was surely proving to myself that I was not entirely helpless in the presence of girls. See how I had handled her! This time of idleness and moonlight was in such smooth consonance with my most romantic wishes. She was not so romantic herself—I feared that she was not so— but the ardent luxury of her nature answered to a romantic call in mine.

"Isn't this wonderful?" I said at last, seeking to interest her.

"Yes," she replied almost practically. "I was wondering why some of the girls wouldn't come over here tonight. I suppose they're too tired."

"They're not as strong as you are, I suppose. You are a vigorous girl. I was thinking today how healthy you look."

"Were you? I am healthy. I don't think I've ever been sick a day in my life. I was thinking just now what my mother would say if she knew I was out here alone."

"Would she care so much?"

"Would she! I should hate for her to see me," she gurgled in a soft, defiant, coquettish way. "Oh, dear, I'd never hear the last of it."

"She's not as bad as that, surely."

"Indeed, she is. I have to mind my P's and Q's when I'm at home. She'd never dream of my walking out like this with a total stranger."

"You told me you lived in St. Louis, I think?"

"Yes, out in the north end. Near O'Fallon Park."

"Oh, well, then I'll get to see you when you go back," I laughed.

"Oh, will you?" she returned coquettishly. "How do you know you will?" She laughed.

"Well, won't I? I hope I will, anyhow."

The thought flashed across my mind that once I had been in this selfsame park with Lois before on a moonlit night, and we had sat down under a tree, near a white pagoda which I could see from here, silvered by the moon, and listened to music played in the distance. I remembered how I had whispered sweet nothings and kissed her to my heart's content. Just now my mind was sincerely troubled for thinking of my fickleness these few moons later. What was I thinking of doing tonight? What was I wishing to do? It troubled me so much that I deliberately forced the thought out of my mind.

"Well, you may, if you're good," she replied to my hope.

I began jesting with her now, a little, exchanging those idle quips at which some boys and girls are so clever. I deliberately descended from the ordinary reaches of my intelligence to struggle with such thoughts as I thought would please her, anxious to match her own interests with some which would seem allied. I wanted her to like me, although I felt all the time that we were by no means allied in temperament. She was too commonplace and unimaginative, although so attractive physically.

"Let us sit down here," I said at last, as we neared a rustic bench by a little lake. "We can look at the water."

I sat down and drew her close beside me.

"Just look how that water sparkles!"

She sat and looked, and then by force of my own mood possibly, I induced her, I think, into an allied mood.

"It is pretty," she replied.

We sat there in silence for a time, and then pressing her arm I looked into her face, quite waxen in the moonlight, and slipped down my hand and laid hold of her fingers. She did not stir, pretended not to notice, although I felt that she was thrilling like myself. Our acquaintance was so brief. The night was so lovely, it seemed as though under the circumstances it might not be altogether wrong.

"You asked awhile ago about Miss White," I said. "What made you do that?"

"Oh, because," she replied. "I thought you liked her. Why shouldn't I?"

"It never occurred to you that I might like some one else?"

"No, certainly not. Why should I?"

I pressed her fingers softly.

She turned on me at once a face on which was written a feeble attempt at inquiry, but even more a strong suggestion of the feeling she now felt. It was as if she were almost breaking under an intense nervous strain which she was attempting to conceal. Her eyes looked strained.

"I thought you might," I replied daringly. "There is some one, you know." I was surprising myself.

"Is there?" Her voice sounded weak, uneven.

She did not attempt to look at me now, while I was wondering what I would say next, how far I would go.

"You couldn't guess, of course?"

"No. Why should I?"

"Look at me," I said quietly.

"All right," she replied with a little indifferent shrug of her shoulders. "I'll look at you. There now, what of it?"

Again that intense nervous strained look. Her lips were parted in a shy frightened smile, showing her pretty teeth. Her eyes were touched with points of light where the moonlight, falling over my shoulder, shone upon them. It gave her whole face an eerie, almost spectral, paleness, something mystical and insubstantial, which spoke of the brevity and non-enduringness of all these things. She was far more wonderful here than ever she could have been in clear daylight.

"You have beautiful eyes," I remarked.

"Oh," she shrugged, mock contemptuously, "is that all?"

"No," I said, "you have beautiful teeth and hair. Such hair."

"You mustn't grow sentimental," she commented, still letting me retain her hand.

"No?" I inquired feelingly, and loosing my fingers, slipped my arm about her waist.

She moved nervously.

"You mustn't," she pleaded, struggling.

"Oh, yes," I replied, and held her close. She protested feebly and finally desisted.

"And you still can't guess who?" I said finally.

"No," she replied, keeping her face from me.

"Then I'll tell you," and putting my free hand to her cheek, I turned her face to me.

"Don't you know?" I repeated.

"No," she indicated with a sidewise movement of her head.

I studied her closely, and then in a moment the last shred of reluctance and coquetry in her seemed to evaporate. During the major portion of this conversation she seemed to have been in a troubled state, feeling a certain instability of emotion and desire. Now at the touch of my hand upon her cheek she seemed to change. I could feel it. The whole power of her ardent nature was rising in my favor, I presume. I felt a passionate surge in her, half yielding, half withdrawing. I could not understand why she should like me,—I was surprised myself, intensely so, by her obvious emotion. At last she seemed to be yielding completely, and I put my lips to hers and kissed her warmly, then pressed her close and held her.

"Now, do you know?" I asked after a time.

"Yes," she nodded, and for a pro-offered kiss returned an ardent one of her own.

I was beside myself with astonishment and delight. It seemed impossible that I had won her so quickly. Could it really be, I asked myself. Was I so much of a charmer?

For a time we sat in the moonlight thus, I holding her hand and pressing her waist. For the life of me I could not explain to myself how it was that I had achieved this result so quickly. Something in the idyllic atmosphere, something in the temperaments of myself and her, I fancied, made this quick spiritual and material understanding possible. But I wanted to know how. I could not say now that I really liked her beyond the charm of her physical appearance, but that was enough at present. Physical beauty, with not too much grossness in the mental development, was all I asked at present—youth, a measure of innocence, and beauty!

We sat talking for awhile, and during this period I learned all about her home surroundings in St. Louis, where she lived, what church she attended, whom she knew. I pretended to have a real feeling for her and to be struck by her beauty, a thing which was not wholly untrue. My feelings, as I well knew, however, were of so light and variable a character that it seemed almost a shame to lure her in this fashion. Why had I done it? My love was not for her in particular. More likely it was for many girls—the sex beauty in general. The female form, its most beautiful expression—I was in love with that. My love had its shrine in many a varying maid. It was decidedly unfortunate for her, I now thought, that we two should ever meet under the same roof as in the present instance, and with Miss White and others perhaps making a third, fourth or fifth, but then I anticipated no troublesome results. I could keep them apart. Anyhow, if I could not, my relationship in either case had not become earnest enough to cause me to worry. I hoped, however, to make it so, in the case of Miss White. Miss Ginity I knew from the first to be only a momentary and passing flame.

CHAPTER XLIV

As I anticipated, there were really no ill effects from this little diversion, affectionate and compromising as it had been, although by now I was so interested in Miss White that I felt a little unfair to her, and, besides, I could not but look upon it as offering a problem which might prove difficult of solution, particularly in case she should get wind of it. As a matter of fact, as I look back on it now, I can imagine no greater error of mind or temperament than that which drew me to her, considering my own definite varietistic tendencies and my naturally freedom-loving point of view, but since we are, in the main, blind victims of chance and given to far better hind- than foresight, I have no particular complaint to make. It is quite possible that this was all a part of my essential and necessary destiny, or development—one of those storm-breeding mistakes by which one grows. Certainly it is curious that the most astounding characteristics of a decidedly conventional temperament should not have troubled me in the least, but then perhaps I would never have known that kind of a nature at all if I had not been drawn to follow her up. As it was, life seemed thus casually to thrust upon me an experience which was to prove as illuminating as any

NEWSPAPER DAYS • 325

I ever endured. Some of these difficulties and their result I have long since outlined in The "Genius," but even those are but a fragment and so modified by invented atmosphere and experiences as to scarcely give a true picture. In the main, I fancy I have been a far different creature to Witla—less pliable—more direct and even aggressive at times.

Were I to try even now to describe the woman who then accidentally moved into my ken, I doubt whether I should be able to do it. It is the things of which we really know most that elude our rapid-fire, cocksure interpretations. It is easy to say "conventional" or "unconventional," "passionate" or the reverse, "frank" or "designing." But the modifying and almost interchangeable qualities present in so many— what of them? In the main, a brisk, alive human being is almost indescribable—as elusive as radium or life itself.

Still, if I were to attempt a vague characterization, I should say that, in addition to being part and parcel of a family and a community as religiously and morally illusioned as ever existed anywhere in the world (our own dear Missouri Middle West), she was on the border line of considerable capacity—mentally, emotionally and in every other way. Frankly, she was as passionate and seeking as any girl might well be, but with all the firm small-town religious convictions as to how, where, when love is to be indulged in—under what favorable circumstances—the wife and mother to be in control always. As I have since thought it out, life presents itself to all such people as a very stable round of duties which one must perform willy-nilly under the strict guidance of those sacred rules laid down by the church, the state and a Midwestern country community. They are completely under the spell of such elusive words as honor, duty, truth, virtue, humility, self-sacrifice and the like, these being words by which they most frequently encouraged themselves in the face of the grim injustice or indifference of nature itself, its creatures—animal and social—who so accurately reflect it. As I look back on it all now, I am moved by mixed feelings of humor, sympathy, admiration, contempt—in sum, very mingled emotions—for it is so hard to say what state, if any, is more important than another. But then it was all very different to me. She was beautiful (to me),—very magnetic and very desirable physically and mentally, and I could think of nothing more desirable than to have her there and then.

But, as I soon discovered, she was by no means as easily to be taken as Miss Ginity. The daughter of a rather exceptional Missouri farmer and his wife, one of ten children who had all been brought to maturity under, as I afterwards judged, the most difficult conditions, she was as shy of the lures and wiles of this world as well as of the uncertain affections of man as ever a maid might be. She did not attempt to lure or win me in the least, although quite plainly I could see, or rather feel, at times that she liked me. Her general evasiveness, as I have since often thought, was due no doubt to that ingrowing sense of the import and even terror of social error of any kind, as well as of the marriage or sex relationship which seems to dominate the whole Middle West—or did at this time. Nothing was so degrading apparently in this region as error in this respect—not poverty, not even crime of other sorts. I doubt whether even murder in Missouri or Indiana was as terrifying to the average family as the loss of virtue in a daughter. Is this a blessing or a curse? Certain it is, in so far as I was able to make out, that her very interesting and capable family had scarcely, if ever, enjoyed what many would consider a warm, broadening prosperity. Neither had they ever suffered any of what they (and I myself for that matter at the time) would have considered the degrading phases of poverty, which come when—in addition to poverty or by reason of it (which is more likely)—the conventional notions of the time are set aside and the children indulge in sex relations not sanctioned by the local social code. This, in this Midwestern world, was the last straw under which conscious rectitude broke and sank to defeat, although, as I say, other crimes—such as dishonesty, murder, a hard, unyielding variation from the current standards of belief, et cetera—might also help pull one down on occasion. Hers was a strictly religious family; and owing to an unyielding "rectitude" or conventional acceptance of and insistence on the moral and social code as locally understood—by the mother in this instance, not nearly so much by the father—this family, seven girls and three boys, were strictly everything which their community could desire them to be. They were honest, religious, moral, ultra-conservative and careful of appearances. No least breath of scandal had ever blown upon any of them, and none ever would. In addition, which was more in their favor, with me at least, they were far from being dull, a life- and fun-loving group. In Sara, or Sallie, the girl I found myself interested in, was a variation in the direction of a sad brooding or melancholy at times, which was relieved by a love of the humorous and ridiculous, within the bounds, of course, that she set for herself. At this time, of course, I had not the faintest idea of what those bounds were, or how, subsequently, they were to affect me—or, better yet, I understood neither myself nor her. I imagined, as I have indicated before somewhere, that all these conventions of this Middle West region were true and of the utmost importance to the individual as well as humanity—only somehow all individuals were not able to abide by them, myself among these latter. That thus ridiculously imagining one thing and privately doing another I should come sniffing around a charming puritan of this character would fall well within the bounds of poetic justice, had it not in the long run worked out rather disastrously for her. But of that more, much later.

To follow the thread of my narrative, I saw Miss Ginity at break-fast, but she did not appear to be aware that we had been out together the previous evening. She showed no signs of either bashfulness or inti-macy. For that I was truly grateful. Instead, she went on her way rather briskly, seeming not to wish me to follow her and just as though nothing had happened, and this made her rather alluring again in my eyes.

At the same time, Miss White came down again, and at the sight of her I suffered a slight revulsion of feeling. She was obviously so fresh and innocent, as I thought, seemingly so spiritually and mentally above any such quick and compromising relationship as that which I and my new acquaintance had indulged in the night before. Because I felt sure she would object and have nothing further to do with me, I decided to be more circumspect in my relations with Miss Ginity and to pay more attention to her. She was worth it.

This plan was rather more facilitated than not by the way in which the various members of the party now grouped and adjusted them-selves. Out of compatibility of temper and relationship, I suppose, Miss White and her sister made a pair and preferred to go about together, with me as an occasional third; and on the other hand, Miss Ginity and several of her new acquaintances made a second company, with whom I occasionally walked. Then several others, somewhat older in years and quieter in mood, and accompanied by Edmonstone, preferred to go by themselves. So it came that after the first day, beyond a general ex-change of greetings in the mornings and an occasional meeting in the grounds, we did not really associate. Therefore, the varied distribution of my attentions was in no danger of immediate or even subsequent detection, and I went gaily forward.

A peculiar characteristic of me at this time, as well as during later years, was that I never really expected any of these relationships to endure. Marriage might be well enough for the average man, and I myself expected to indulge in it at some time or other, but somehow it never seemed to me that I should endure in it or, if I did, that it would permanently affect my present free relationship with the world. I did not feel that it could. As for my varied relations at any given moment—these two, for instance—as much as I might imagine for the moment that I desired them, still there was that in my disposition which told me clearly enough that they would not endure. I might be exceptionally grieved at times in a high emotional way because they could not, but that was rising to heights of sentiment which puzzled even myself. One of the things which troubled and astonished me, viewing, as I was, life through the conventional dictates of the time, was that I could like two, three, four and even more women at the same time—like them very much indeed. It seemed strange that I could yearn over them—now one and now another, as the thought struck me—and, of course, it seemed evil. A good man, I told myself, would not do this. It would never occur to him, or if it did, he would repress the thought sternly. As for me, I must be a weak, washy, evil thing who could not possibly make up his mind as to what he wanted or, if he did, could not keep it made. At the same time, the vast spectacle of life with its endless inflow of personalities, nearly all tempting, puzzled me too, for why should I be yearning over so many—going out to them,—their beauty and gayety? Why should various types of beauty appeal to me at one and the same time if it was not intended that it should be so? Or, obviously, if not profoundly evil, I was a freak and had best keep my peculiar thoughts and desires to myself, elsewise good people would promptly have nothing to do with me. I would be entirely alone or even seized upon by the law. To this hour, I suppose, there are millions who, chancing upon a confession such as this, would lift their eyes and hands in amazement. Or am I mistaken? I wonder. If there are, I can only ask that they examine more closely into the character of life itself—its working. All the facts are plainly not before them. Or if they are and they still lift their eyes, what an amazing number of hypocrites there must really be, seeing that the churches and the moral shouting places are so full.

During the next two weeks I saw much of both Miss Ginity and

Miss White. By day, as I have said, I was usually wont to accompany Miss White and her sister from place to place about the grounds, and of an evening to stroll with Miss Ginity when the opportunity offered. I was rather anxious not to have the two meet any more, but I was not troubled much in that respect either. Miss White, who was not very strong physically, nor hoyden enough to flirt ardently, kept to her room a good part of the time or stayed in the parlor with her sister, while I was left to wander in the park or the fairgrounds with Miss Ginity, wondering at times whether Miss White really liked me, whether her present feeling was likely to turn to something deeper, or whether she would let it. Curiously, I felt a very definite point of view there, very different to mine. She had none of the variability or varietism of myself. If ever a person was definitely fixed in conventional views, it was she. One life, one love, would have answered for her exactly. She could have accepted any condition, however painful or even degrading, providing that she was bolstered up by what she considered the moral law. "To have and to hold, in sickness and in health, in poverty and in riches, till death do us part." I think the full force of those laws must have been imbibed by her with her mother's milk.

On the other hand, in regard to Miss Ginity I was congratulating myself on having achieved an affectional triumph. She may not have been particularly impressed with the sum of my physical attractions, as I thought at the time, but there certainly was something about me nevertheless which seemed to hold her as if in a spell. At all times I seemed able to command her to do about as I wished, and even my vicinity seemed at times to induce a nervous excitation which was amazing. I recall that she always wanted to see me for a little while before bedtime every day—and that regardless of whether we had been together during the day or not. She had so many friends that she did not seem to be able to manage to be alone much—as much as she desired it. After a few days she had removed to the apartment of some friends or relations she had found not very far from the hotel—very strict Catholics, I presume—to whom she had to pay considerable attention. But in my box, nights or mornings if by any chance I had not seen her, I would regularly find notes explaining where I would find her at such and such an hour in the evening—usually at a drugstore near the park and her new apartment, from where we could take a few minutes' stroll together in the park. Such a fever of emotion as she displayed at times and as she evoked in me! The crude eager force of her. "Oh, dear!" she would exclaim in an intense, hungry way on seeing me. "Oh, I could hardly wait!" And then, once in the park, she would throw her strong, young arms around me and, holding me, kiss me in a fiery, hungry way.

"You don't know what you've done," she said to me once. "I don't seem to know myself—but, oh, I don't care. Why should I? We may not be able to see so much of each other when we get back to St. Louis. My parents are so very strict, and I have so much work to do."

What did we do? Well, nothing so very much. It never came to a forthright sex relation, very largely, I suppose, because I did not have the courage to push my advantage to the utmost. It was fast nearing that stage when she was compelled to leave for Michigan with some relative who came along. There was one last transport between eleven and midnight, one night—the night before she left—during which, if I had been half the Don Juan I longed to be, we would have united in the moonlight or in my room. As it was, for sheer lack of courage on my part and inexperience on hers, we remained caressing, kissing, until it was literally too late and she had to go. Even then, I fancy, I might have detained her perforce.

As it was, when I saw her again in St. Louis—

But that is still another story.

CHAPTER XLV

The days sped swiftly and ecstatically by. For once in my life I seemed to be truly and consistently happy, and that in this very city where but a year or two before I had suffered such keen distress. Nothing arose to mar the color of it during all my stay. It was only toward the middle of the second week that Miss Ginity left, and then I had Miss White all to myself, as it were. And by now I had come to feel an intense interest in her—an elation over the mere thought of being in her company, than which I have never felt any thing keener, more indescribably and sweetly pervasive. She was like a narcotic to me—something inspiring, provocative of dreams for the future. Besides, all my mind and body seemed to be responding at this time in some ecstatic fashion to Chicago and the Fair as a whole—the romance and color of it all, the wine-like quality of the air in the city, its raw, fresh, young force, so vividly manifested in its sounding streets, its far-flung lines of avenues and boulevards, its towering new buildings, than which I had never seen anything more imposing; and by contrast with these, its vast regions of middle- and lower-class poor. When we were living here as a family, I had always thought that poverty was no great hardship—not in the Argonautic atmosphere which seemed to characterize the city. The poor were poor enough, in all conscience, but, oh, the singing hope of the city itself, its spirit. Up, up and to work! Here were tasks for a million hands! In spite of my attachment to the Fair and Miss Ginity and Miss White, I was still often lured cityward,—to the west and north and southwest sides where we had lived or where I had walked so much in the old days—mere journeys of remembrance. I wanted to see the places I had seen, to feel once more the atmospheres in which formerly I had been either gay or sad.

But most of all as I wandered about, I realized that the city was not my city anymore really. I had no home here now. And also what a baseless, shifting thing life itself was: how uncertain and unstable were all our ties; how that which we held with joy today, like my mother's presence, for instance, is tomorrow gone and will come no more; how seemingly brisk organizations such as the *Globe* here in Chicago, and some others I had been connected with, could wither, or disappear completely; how our own family had been scattered to the four winds. I felt an intense sense of loneliness and homesickness, for what I could scarcely say,—each and every one of all the old, past pleasant moments, I presume, here and elsewhere. Our abandoned house in Flournoy Street, now rented to another, my old desk at the *Globe*, Lois's former home on the south side—all, all gone spiritually, although still present in wood or stone. I was gloomy indeed over having no fixed abode of any kind, no intimates worthy the name here who could really soothe and comfort me in such an hour as this, for instance. Curiously enough, at such moments I felt an intense leaning toward Miss White, who seemed somehow,—far more than the restless, vigorous Miss Ginity, or my housekeeper in St. Louis—to answer with something stable and abiding. I am at a loss now to describe it, but so it was, and it was more than anything else a sense of peace and support which I found in her presence—a something which seemed to suggest durability and warmth—possibly the whole closely knit family atmosphere which was behind her and on which she relied. At any rate she seemed always to represent durability, personal convictions and an atmosphere against which one could lean—at the same time being quick to see, subtle to feel. She listened, apparently with avidity, to all my youthful and no doubt braggadocious accounts of my former newspaper experiences here as well as in St. Louis, which, with a kind of bravado or silly vanity born of her sympathy and interest, I painted in high colors, myself as a newspaper man deep in the councils of my paper! Going to the Fair one night to see the illumination, I desired to take her hand, but so overawed was I by her personality, so respectful of it, I could scarcely muster up the courage so to do. When I did try it she merely shyly withdrew it, pretending not to notice.

It was the same an evening or two later, when, Miss Ginity having gone to Wisconsin or Michigan, I persuaded her and her sister to accompany myself and Edmonstone to Lincoln Park on the north side, where was not only a band concert but the playing of a colored fountain given by the late C. T. Yerkes to the city, and then looked upon as one of the sights of the city. I can recall now so very well the character of the evening—warm and clear, with an electric sky in the west. I can recall our coming downtown on the newly built "Alley L," so called because no public thoroughfare could be secured for it, and getting off at Congress Street, where the enormous new store of Siegel Cooper and Company had only recently been opened, and of then taking a surface cable line to Lincoln Park—the hurrying crowds, the freshness of the wind from the lake, and the electric blue evening sky making a gala atmosphere of it all. When we reached the park it was barely dusk, but the bandmen were already assembling. The fountain did not play until nine, but pending its colored wonders, Arabian in their quality, we walked along the shore of the lake in the dark. Fancying that we desired to be alone, I presume, her sister and Edmonstone early lost us, disappearing in the great crowd.

Once near the lake in the dark we were secluded enough—quite alone. For once in my life I found myself desperately interested, without really knowing how to proceed. It was a state of hypnosis, I fancy, in which I felt myself to be rapturously happy, because more or less convinced of her feeling for me, and yet gravely uncertain as to whether, liking me or no, she would ever permit herself to be ensnared in love and yield. She was so self-poised and serene, so stable and yet so tender. I felt foolish, unworthy, somehow like a juggler who is attempting a hazardous feat and is yet uncertain of his skill. Would she ever really have me? That was the great question. Were not the crude brutalities of love too much for her? She might like me now, but the slightest error in word or mood or deed on my part would no doubt end it all and drive her away—and I would never see her any more. I was so fearful of this that I was unhappy also—like one who tastes sweet and salt at the same time. I would have liked to put my arm about her waist or hold her hand, but it was all beyond me then—she seemed too remote, a little unreal. Finally, the music beginning in the distance, and moved by the idyllic quality of it all, I left her and strolled down to the very edge of the lake where the water was lapping the sand. It was all dark lakeward, save for stars and lights of ships and lighthouses. The great lake wall had not been built here then. I had the feeling that if she really cared for me she would follow me—that she would see how much moved I was by her and, sympathizing with me, testify to her regard in this way. However, she did not, but waited sedately on the rise above, while I stood below, although I seemed to feel all the while that she was drawing toward me intensely and holding me as in a vise. Half angry but still fascinated I returned, anything but the master of this situation—unable to say that I was happy and yet too fascinated to say that I was not. In truth, she had me as completely in tow as any woman could wish and was able consciously or unconsciously to regulate the progress of this affair to suit herself. At the same time, I have often doubted whether it was so much a conscious as an unconscious process on her part—far more likely an unconscious response to all the theories and methods of a thousand countryside wooings.

Nevertheless, nothing came of all this then, save a deeper feeling on my part as to her exceptional charm. I was more than ever moved by her grace and charm. What sobriety! What delicacy of feature! Her big eyes, as soft and appealing as those of a doe, her small red mouth, her abundance of red hair, were a constant enticement.

Before leaving for her home in that section of Missouri, which she insisted was so very country, one of the inland counties about ninety miles from St. Louis, all that was left of the large party, which was not very many, paid a visit to St. Joe on the Michigan shore, opposite Chicago. It is not my purpose to describe this trip, pleasing as it was, but to narrate a curiosity in connection with it which has remained in my mind for years. It was a wonderfully bright Sunday—warm, and the lake really delightful. The steamer was comfortable and the beach at St. Joseph perfect, as it seemed to me—a long coast of lovely white sand with blue waves breaking over it. En route, because of the size of the party and the accidental arrangement of friends, I was thrown in with Rose, the sister of my adored one, and curiously, in spite of myself, I found myself being swiftly drawn to her, desperately so, and that in the face of the strong attachment for her sister. There was something so cheering and whole souled about her point of view, something so provoking and yet elusive, a veritable sprite of gayety and humor— "the R. W. mantrap," I used to call her. She had a fund of stories as well as of amusing expressions and the general air of a young scapegrace who would not be taken. For some reason she devoted herself to me, on the boat and in the water, until I think she suddenly came to realize what was happening, not only to me but to herself.

Then she desisted, and I saw her no more, or very little of her, but the damage had been done. I was intensely moved by her, dreaming even of changing my attentions, although I realized that it could never be done—she was too fond of her sister. From then on, however, she avoided me but, as I could see, with the sole intent of not injuring her sister. I saw it in her eye. We returned at night, I with the most troubled feelings about the whole affair. It was only after I had returned a day or two later to St. Louis—the party having gone its way by separate routes—that the old feeling for Miss Sallie, or "Jug," as I heard her called, returned, and I began to see and think of her as I had that night in Lincoln Park. Then her charm somehow seemed to come with full force, and for days I could think of nothing else—the Fair, the hotel, the evening walks, and what she was doing now. At the same time, it was mixed with the most jumbled thoughts of Rose and Miss Ginity. I leave it to those who can to solve this mystery of the affections. From both Miss White and Miss Ginity I had obtained their local addresses. Only, as I have said, Miss White was not in St. Louis at all, but at her home in Montgomery County, ninety miles away, and not returning until later in the fall to teach in an aristocratic suburb about twenty miles out from St. Louis, whereas Miss Ginity was little more than a half-hour's ride from my local abode.

I soon settled down to my customary routine duties, but with what longing backward thoughts toward Chicago and the Fair, all the glamor of the latter sinking and rising before my eyes as in a dream—my father, my brothers and sisters, this gay company of girls, my old newspaper associates. Only, as I now ruefully thought, I had not troubled myself to look up Lois, although once she had meant so much of Chicago and of happiness to me. What kind of a person was I, I often asked myself, to become thus easily indifferent and then grieve over it? Why?

CHAPTER XLVI

To return and take up the ordinary routine of reporting after these crystal days of beauty and romance was anything but satisfactory. Gone was the White City with its towers and pinnacles and the wide blue wash of lake at its feet. After the Fair and the greater city, nearly twice as large as St. Louis, the latter place seemed prosaic indeed. Still, I was getting along here, I argued with myself—much better than I had been in Chicago before I left the first time—and in the presence of Mrs. X, who welcomed me cordially enough on my return, I felt that I had at least someone who took a little interest in me. I found her, when I walked in one weekday morning, stirring about in one of the rooms on the second floor. She seemed as pleased as ever to see me and, following me into my room where I was unpacking my grip, listened to some of the details of my trip, and then—

Later I went down to the office, where I found Wandell, poring as usual over scores of current papers. He was always busy scribbling and snipping, like a little old leathery Punch, in his mussy office. The mere sight of him made me wish that I were done with the newspaper business forever. It brought all the regularity of the old days back. When would I ever get out of it? When would I get a chance to have my evenings to myself? I asked myself. When would I be able to idle and dawdle as I had seen other people doing in Chicago, traveling for pleasure? I did not realize how few the leisure class really comprises. I took the evidence of one or two passing before my gaze, and the clatter the newspapers made over them, as really indicating a vast company. I was one of the unfortunates who were shut out. I was one whose life was to be made a wretched tragedy for want of means to enjoy it now when I had youth and health!

"Well, did you have a good time?" he asked, smiling at me in a way which reminded me of a caricature.

"That's right," I replied, somewhat dolefully. "That's a great show up there. It's beautiful."

"Any of the girls fall in love with you?" croaked my city editor good-humoredly.

"Oh, it wasn't that bad."

"Well, I suppose you'll be ready to settle down now to hard work. I've got a thing or two here for you."

"Well, I guess I'm as ready as I ever will be. I'm not so very much for work just now."

Wandell cackled. "We'll see," he added afterward. "Get yourself something to eat, and show up at one."

I went out, depressed with the truth that I was once more in the harness, and after lunching, returned to take up my customary tasks. It seemed to me as if an idyllic chapter of my life had been closed forever.

For some time thereafter, as the news dictated, I undertook one interesting assignment after another which continued that exact education as to the working of life which tended to shatter my idealism and cause me to see the hard reality underlying all romance. For, cloud itself over as life will with dreams, there is always at bottom this substratum of fact. Now it was a great murder mystery over in Illinois, perhaps, that transported me to and kept me stationed in a small county seat for days, my expenses paid by the paper, following up the ramifications of an ancient crime; now, again, it was a great train robbery in the centre of the state that took me into the heart of a truly rural region where nothing but farmers and small towns were and set me to following almost imaginary clues which always came to nothing. One day it would be a change of train service which permitted the distribution of St. Louis newspapers earlier than the Chicago papers in territory which was somehow disputed between them. And because of this I would have to make the trip between midnight and dawn, riding for hours just behind the engine in the mail car, and subsequently describe fully this supposedly amazing special newspaper service, which was to make all the inhabitants of this particular region wiser, kinder, richer because they could get the St. Louis papers before they could those of Chicago! A famous mind reader, coming to town and desiring to advertise his skill, requested the *Republic* to appoint a man or a committee who would ride with him in a carriage through the crowded downtown streets of the city while he, blindfolded but driving, followed the directing thoughts of the man who should sit on the seat beside him and *think* where to go. And amusingly enough, I was ordered to get up the committee,—Dick, Peter, Rodenberger and myself—and sit on the seat and do the thinking while he, blindfolded, raced in and out between cars and wagons, turning sharp corners, escaping huge trucks by a hair only, to finally wind up at Dick's door, as my thoughts directed him. And there alighting, dashed up the one flight of steps and into the room, the door being left open for the occasion, and climbing up on a chair next a wardrobe, took down that peculiar head of Ally Sloper, previously mentioned—the most unusual and different bit in Dick's room—and handed it to me. When written up as true, which it was, it made a very good story indeed. In fact, this once and for all cleared up my thoughts as to the power of mind over so-called matter, and caused Dick, Rodenberger, Peter and myself to enter upon experiments of our own with hypnotists, spiritualists and the like until we finally satisfied ourselves as to the import of these things. Only, having established the truth of them to ourselves, we found no method of doing anything with our knowledge. It was practically useless and in addition taboo.

Again, it was a spiritualist—a fat, slug-like Irish type—who, coming to town about the same time and proving immensely successful in getting up large public meetings and charging so much admission, turned out to be so sensuous and gross that soon, in spite of his success, there were ugly rumors as to the orgiastic character of some of his meetings and especially of his home, where he was receiving interested spiritualists in private, and where he was soon supposed to be indulging in the most pagan and unnatural relations with his devotees. Not without intelligence on the part of Wandell, I was set to ferret all this out, describe it in detail, if possible—and in addition, in case I could get sufficient evidence, to drive him out of town.

Why?

Well, because Mr. Wandell, responding to the local sentiment of the hour, perhaps considered him a real menace to St. Louis—its morals. Only really and truly, and this was the amusing part of it all,

Mr. Wandell cared no more for Mr. Wallace or the public or its sub-surface morals than he cared for the politics of Beluchistan or Dahomey. In the heart of St. Louis, in Chestnut Street, as I have previously stated, was a large district devoted to just such orgies—and worse—as Mr. Wallace was supposed to be perpetrating. But these streets—or this area—were somehow never in the public eye, and you could not, for your life, put them there. The public apparently did not want them persistently attacked, or, if it did, there were forces sufficiently powerful to keep it from obtaining its wish. You couldn't write newspaper articles about them as such or arouse any particular interest—or you didn't dare to, I don't know which. The police were supposed to extract regular payments from one and all in this area—Rodenberger frequently so charged in his weekly. The most amazing social complications of the most disrupting order occasionally led directly to one or another of these houses—to some woman or other in one of them—but no comment was ever made on the peculiarity of the presence of the large area as a whole or its persistence. Local commercial houses made excellent money out of it, no doubt. In fact, I am sure they did, and rightly so, only—. Some such thoughts as these occurred to me at the time I was set to drive Mr. Wallace from his present ease and comfort in St. Louis.

Naturally enough, I had but little success at first. He had a large following and many defenders whose curiosity or gullibility, or both, led them to look upon him as a personage of great import. Again, he was a shrewd and able manipulator—really one of the finest quacks I have ever seen. The manner in which he would race up and down among the members of one of his large audiences, his fat waxy eyelids shut, his immense white shirtfront glowing, his evening dress coattails flying like those of a bustling butler or headwaiter, the while he exclaimed, "Is there anyone here by the name of Peter? Is there anyone here by the name of Augusta? There is an old white-bearded man here who says he has something to say to Augusta. And Peter, Peter—Peter—your sister says not to marry, that everything that is now troubling you so much will now come out all right!"

He would even open these meetings with spiritual invocations of one kind and another and pretend to the profoundest religiosity and spirituality himself.

As a matter of fact he was really a fakir of the most brazen character. As I learned afterwards from Wandell, he had been driven from one city and another—usually cities very far apart, so that the news of his troubles might not spread too quickly. His last resting place before coming to St. Louis had been Norfolk, Virginia, and before that he had been in Liverpool, San Francisco, Sydney, New South Wales and such widely scattered spots. Always, apparently, he had been immensely successful, immediately drawing large crowds, taking up collections and doing a private séance business which must have netted him a tidy sum. Indeed, in private life, as I soon found, he was a gourmet, a sybarite and a riant amorist, laughing in his sleeve at all his touts and followers.

Be that as it may, for a long time after he had arrived and begun to take in his easily earned money—nightly drawing large crowds to his temple—I seemed unable to gather any evidence which would convict him of anything in any direct and final way. He said there were spirits present at all his meetings. Well, maybe there were—I'm sure I don't know. And that he talked with them and received cheering messages. Possibly he did. Anyhow, his victims all believed him. At any rate, once he found the *Republic* to be unfavorable and attempting to ridicule him, he became distinctly pugnacious and threatened to assault me personally if I ever came near him or his place or wrote up things which he deemed untrue. On the other hand, Mr. Wandell was equally determined to have him followed up and exposed. I was therefore compelled to hang about his meetings and his house, trying to find someone who would tell me something more definite than I could get from his believing followers. Chancing one afternoon to call at his house when he was at a meeting or elsewhere, I managed to meet his landlady, who, thinking I was a visitor for him, was about to close the door, saying he was not there, when I stayed her by saying that I was from the *Republic* and that I did not particularly care to see him, but that I wanted to know something about him—his visitors, private conduct and so forth. In some of my previous attempts to see him, this same woman had come to the door, but on those occasions she would have nothing to do with me, merely answering me yes or no, whether Mr. Wallace was in.

On this occasion, however, for some reason—I have always thought since that there must have been a tiff or occasion for pique between her and her tenant—she asked me to come in. And having escorted me very secretly to a room on the second floor, where she shut and locked the door, she there and then began a long story concerning the very peculiar relations which existed, according to her, between Mr. Wallace and some of his male and female disciples, which interested me greatly. She was, although not exactly homely, tall and bony, but dressed in rather agreeable clothes. She had, she finally admitted, after arousing my curiosity to the highest pitch without really explaining anything, been watching through a keyhole giving into Mr. Wallace's rooms—just where, she did not say. There had been during weeks past various peculiar and intimate visitors whose comings and goings had meant nothing to her until they became so regular and Mr. Wallace so particularly engaged with them. But since Mr. Wallace's fame had been spreading, and the *Republic* had begun to attack him, she had been most watchful, and, to further perfect her information in regard to him, she had been most recently engaged in looking through a keyhole which gave into his room and there studying him at her leisure. What was her righteous horror then, on several occasions, to discover that he was indulging in relations with some of his visitors, especially two or three women ranging in age between twenty and forty and several young men—in relations, she repeated, which were "not natural." Just what those relations were she at first refused to state; but later, when I pointed out to her that unless she could furnish me with rather convincing proof as to just what these relations were, together with names and addresses or a sight of the orgies themselves, her mere statements would be of small value. She unbent sufficiently to fix on one particular woman, whose card once left for Mr. Wallace and a note addressed to him, which she had evidently purloined from his room, she now produced and showed, and in addition stated that on more than one occasion, when she had been looking through her keyhole, she had seen this particular woman, bared to the waist, and, even more, on her knees before Mr. Wallace, who was also partially disrobed, and that there and then, as the law says, they were indulging in the relation which she was content to describe as "unnatural."

Naturally, I was rather surprised, if not vastly shocked, more at my good fortune than anything else, at so suddenly coming upon this interesting information, and at the same time slightly envious of the gentleman or, rather, his sybaritic pleasure. Think of him having all these interesting women, as the landlady insisted he had—not one but many—and he a gross soul to look at, fat after the manner of Maxwell, with a heavy sensual jaw and cheeks, baggy eyes, a white, pasty complexion—whereas I . . . The idea of such a gross specimen being permitted such luxuries and at the same time pretending to be in communion with what at that time I took to be *pure* spirits was a little too much.

However, I was still not so far advanced toward the accomplishment of my object—or I felt, at the time, that I was not—unless I could obtain from this peculiar moralist the card and the letter of the lady involved. At first she did not want to give them up, endeavoring to compromise by saying that I might have the name and the address, which was in one of the best portions of that west end I so much admired, but I persisted, explaining that the paper was powerless without these. And after assuring her that I would eventually return them and leave her out of the matter entirely, I finally managed to secure the card and the letter—the latter rather compromising, considering that the writer of it was married, as the card showed. Armed with these I immediately proceeded to that further west end, where I so loved to walk and where I soon found the house in one of those palatial residence streets I have previously described. Now feeling rather strong in possession of the evidence I had, I debated with myself just how I would go about this.

Supposing I should ring the bell and her husband should appear, or I should send up my card and the husband, not the wife, come down. Or supposing that I charged her with what I knew—or rather hinted at it—and she called some one to her aid. To tell the truth, I did not know exactly why I wanted to see her, except possibly that there might be a dramatic scene of some kind, and then I should have something especially remarkable to report. When I reached the house, however, I went rather nervously up the steps and rang the bell, whereupon a footman who proceeded to stare me out of countenance opened the door.

"Who is it you wish to see?"

I told him.

"Have you an appointment with her?"

"No," I said, "but I am from the *Republic,* and please say to her that it is very important for her to see me—very. We have an article about her which we propose to publish in the morning, and I think she will want to see me about that."

I stared at him with a great deal of effrontery, I suppose, and he eyed me, not knowing what to think, I presume. Then he shut the door, leaving me outside, but presently returned and opening it said, "You may come in here."

I walked into a large, heavily furnished reception room, representing the best Western taste of the time, I suppose, and in which I nosed about—thinking how fine it all was and wondering how it was that I was to proceed about all this once she appeared. Supposing she proved to be a fierce and contentious soul well able to hold her own, or there was some mistake about this letter or the statement of the landlady. I felt that I should have to be decidedly cautious in what I said lest she refuse to discuss the matter with me at all and order me out. Indeed, once inside this way, my own effrontery rather frightened me, and fearing as I did to state frankly what it was that I knew, I was at a loss to know just what it was that I would say. As I was walking up and down, however, quite troubled in my own mind as to just what I would say, I heard the rustle of silk skirts, and on the instant a rather vigorous and well-dressed woman of, say, thirty-three or four swept into the room. She was rather smart, as I thought at the time, bronze haired, pink fleshed, not at all nervous or disturbed.

"You wish to see me?"

"Yes, ma'am."

"About what, please?"

"I am from the *Republic*," I began. "We have a rather startling story about you in connection with this Mr. Jules Wallace, the spiritualist and medium, who is holding meetings here at this time. It appears that his place has been watched and that you—"

"A story about me," she interrupted with an air of considerable hauteur, not seeming to have the least idea to what I referred. "And a Mr. Who? Wallace, you say? What is this? What kind of a story is it? Why do you come to me about it? Why, I don't even know the man."

"Oh, yes, but I think you do," I replied with an unbelieving smile, thinking of the letter and card in my pocket. "As a matter of fact, I know that you do. At the office we have a card and a letter of yours to Mr. Wallace which the *Republic* proposes to print along with some other matter unless some satisfactory explanation as to why it should not be printed can be made. We are conducting a campaign against Mr. Wallace, as you probably know."

All at once a most startling change came over this situation. Just what it was that happened at this time I cannot now quite clearly recall. I have a rather faint recollection that there were a few additional exclamations as to blackmail, that she would inform her husband, that I would be put out of the house and so forth, when, possibly owing to the fact that I replied that we positively had her letter to Mr. Wallace in her own handwriting and that there were witnesses who would testify to what had transpired between her and Mr. Wallace—that she had been watched through a keyhole—her whole demeanor suddenly changed. From one of extreme bravado and tempestuousness, I saw a decidedly healthy and vigorous woman drop to her knees before me, seize my hands and coat and begin pleading in an agonized voice and with tears. "But you wouldn't do that! My husband! My home! My social position! My children! My God, you wouldn't have me driven out of my own home! He doesn't know a thing! If he came here now! Oh, my God, tell me what I am to do! What is it you want? Tell me that you won't do anything like—the *Republic* won't. I'll do anything you ask. I'll give you anything you want. Oh, you couldn't be so heartless. Maybe I have done wrong—but oh, my God, think of me, please!—of what will happen to me if you do this!"

I stared at her in amazement. Never in my life before had I been the centre of—to me—such a peculiar scene. The nervous tension of it! And my reaction to it! It was astonishing really. On the instant I felt mingled feelings of extreme triumph and extreme pity, as well as curious thoughts as to whether the *Republic* would have the cruelty to expose this woman, whether she could be made to pay blackmail, and the like. Always I was hearing of this latter in connection with newspaper work. Personally, I never knew a single newspaper man who ever admitted to having taken or made a single cent out of a situation of this kind, or ever took one, although I have known many of them to pay for information or help. I myself have done so—worked on people's cupidity. But on this occasion I thought of nothing much save what Wandell or the *Republic* would do, whether he would now proceed to drive Wallace out through her, and the like. Personally, I doubt now whether my pity was anywhere as great as my sense of having achieved another newspaper beat. Now assuredly, if it chose, the *Republic* could make this very erratic individual move on. Through this woman or the landlady or others—just how I wasn't sure—we could drive him out. On the instant, though, I made it perfectly plain that I personally was helpless, a mere reporter, who of himself could do nothing. If she wished she could see Mr. Wandell, who could help her if he chose, I was sure, and I gave her his home address, knowing well that he would not be at his office at this time of day.

"Oh, I'll go to him at once, at once," she exclaimed. "He must have pity on me—he must help me." And in this mood she raced up her stairs for her hat, I suppose, while I made my way out of the house as best I could. Once out I meditated on my effrontery and the hard cold work I was capable of doing. Surely this was a dreadful thing to have done. Was it my business so to do? Was I doing right in doing it? Supposing I had been the victim? Still, I could not help feeling that I had done a very clever piece of work and that I would be rather highly complimented for it, as I was in an indirect way, afterwards.

In the meantime, the lady must have proceeded at once to my city editor and found him at home, for I returned to the office at six-thirty, and when Wandell came in he immediately called to me.

"Great God!" he exclaimed, cackling and chortling in his impish way as I came into his office, "What have you been doing now? What are you up to anyhow? You certainly are the Goddamnedest man I ever knew. You can get me into more trouble in a half hour than any man I ever saw before could in a year. Here I was sitting peacefully in my home reading, and up comes my wife telling me there is a weeping woman in the parlor who has just driven up in a carriage, and that she wants to see me. Down I go and there she was, and she grabs me by the hands, falls on her knees and begins telling me about some letters we have, and that her life will be ruined if we publish them. Great God, man, do you want to get me sued for divorce?" And he cackled again, delighted with his position as an arbiter and a social power, however humble. "What letters are they anyhow?" he went on. "What is this story you've dug up? Who is this woman? You're the damnedest man I ever knew! I had to promise her that we wouldn't do anything to hurt her before she would let me go." And he cackled again.

He was pleased beyond measure for some reason, as I could well see.

I produced my letter and told my story. He was intensely interested, but seemed to meditate over its contents for some time as though surprised, although I really think that from what the woman herself had told him, he had gained all he wished to know. What had happened in connection with her and himself I was never able to make out, but after a few moments he continued—

"All right—you leave this with me and just drop this end of the story for the present. Don't do anything more about her. There are other ways to get Wallace." And sure enough, in a few days thereafter Mr. Wallace suddenly left town.

In the meantime, however, I had been "taken off" the meetings, and another man—a strange reporter from Salt Lake City and San Francisco—had been put to reporting. It was a curious procedure to me, all told, but Mr. Wallace was soon gone—and—

But figure it out for yourself.

CHAPTER XLVII

Two other reportorial incidents in connection with my newspaper work at this time impressed me rather sharply as throwing a clear light on social crimes and conditions which cannot always be discussed or explained. One of these related to an old man of about sixty-five years of age who was in the coffee and spice business in one of those old streets which bordered the waterfront and who was charged with—but perhaps I can tell this story in a slightly more entertaining way.

One mid-afternoon in mid-August there chancing to be very little if anything to do in the way of reporting, I was hanging about the office waiting quite idly for something to turn up. Wandell after receiving a telephone message from somewhere handed me a slip of paper and said, "You go down to this address and see what you can find out about this fight or something that has taken place down there. A crowd's been trying to beat up an old man and the police have arrested him—to save him, I suppose. If you go around to the 7th Street Station afterward, you can probably find out all about it."

I took a car and soon reached the scene of the alleged trouble, a decayed and tumbledown region of small family dwellings now turned into tenements of even a poorer character. At this time St. Louis had what so large a life centre as New York, for instance, has not: alleys or rear passageways to all houses by which trade packages, waste and the like are delivered or removed; and facing these occasionally old barns, sheds and even tumbledown warrens of houses or flats of one kind and another occupied by poor whites or blacks or both, as the case might be. In one of these alleys—and in an old half-decayed and vacant brick barn which, however, when I reached the scene of action gave no evidence of any difficulty of any kind, all being warm and peaceful— there had been quite a furious scene, and that only several hours before. An old man whose name I was not able to learn at the time—"a gray-headed old bastard," as one of the local "laboring" men of the region informed me—had been caught in this barn with a little eight or nine year old girl whom he was endeavoring to induce, or had induced, for a few pennies or some candy, to perform what Maxwell used to describe with his fat, cynical smirk as "French massage." However, just as the crime was about to be performed—and with no evidential objection on the part of the child, apparently—some other children or laborers or neighbors happened in, who, being shocked or alarmed and the perpetrator starting to leave, informed the child's parents or friends and a chase ensued. In a few moments the criminal had been sur- rounded by a group of irate citizens who threatened to kill him. As a matter of fact, he was just beginning to be struck and pummeled by some when, as I learned, the police had arrived on the scene and, beating off the crowd, had escorted the old man to that same station previously referred to, on North 7th, where I had long done duty and where supposedly he was locked up unharmed to await the legal ad- judication of his case.

When I arrived at the station, however, and began to look over the "blotter," which contained a public record of charges made and which it was my custom, as well as that of every other newspaper man, to look over at his pleasure, with a view to discovering what disposition had been made of this case, there was no least evidence, apparently, of any such offense having been committed, or at least brought here. No mention of any case in North Levee Street or that vicinity was to be found.

"What became of that attempted assault in North Levee Street?" I inquired of the sergeant, who was drowsily reading a newspaper. "I was just over there and they said the man had been brought here."

He looked up at me wearily, not seeming to be very much inter- ested in my inquiry, and apparently knowing nothing about it. "What case is that?" he inquired. "It must be down there if it came in here. What case are ye taalkin' about? Perhaps it didn't come here."

I looked at him curiously, struck all at once by an atmosphere of what I imagined to be concealment about the place. The case had not been recorded—that was plain. This sergeant seemed just a little different to his usual natural self. He was not so friendly. There could scarcely be any doubt in my mind that he had something to conceal. The man had been brought here. The people of the vicinity had distinctly stated that the man had been taken here, but evidently the officers of the station did not wish me to see him, or some other disposition had been made of the matter.

"That's funny," I said. "I've just been over there, and they told me he had been brought over here. Some of the people said they came here and that you locked him up. Are you sure it would be put on here? Were you here an hour or two ago?"

All at once and for the first time since I had been coming here, this individual grew the least bit truculent.

"Sure," he said, "I don't know anything about it. If it's not on there it's not on there, and that's all I know. If you want to know more than that ye'll have to see the captain."

At the thought of the police attempting to suppress a thing like this, and particularly in the face of my direct knowledge, I grew decidedly irritable and bold myself. "Where's the captain?" I asked.

"He's out now. He'll be back at four, I think."

I sat down and waited—then decided to go and call up the office for further instructions. Fortunately Wandell was there, but he couldn't understand why I hadn't obtained the name of the criminal at the scene of action. When I made it clear that no one seemed to know, he exclaimed, "Well, call up Edmonstone at the Four Courts. See if it's recorded there. If it isn't, go back and tell them you want the facts, or we'll make trouble at headquarters."

I returned and found the captain in. He was a stout, taciturn person who had small use for reporters at any time and particularly now, apparently.

"Yes, yes, yes," he kept reiterating as I asked about the case— reiterating the facts and requesting to know what the culprit's name was and what disposition had been made of the matter.

"Well, I tell you," he said finally after a long pause, seeing that I was determined to know, and during which he eyed me silently, "he's not here now. I let him go. I thought it best that I should. No one saw him commit any crime. He's an old man with a big wholesale business in 2nd Street, never arrested before, and he has a wife and grown sons and daughters. To be sure, he oughtn't to be doing anything of that kind, but still he claims he wasn't. Anyhow, no good can come of writing it up in the papers now. Here's his name and here's his address," and he opened a small book which he kept on his person and showed me just that—the name and address. "Now you can go talk to him yourself if you want to, but if you take my advice ye'll let him alone. I see no good in pulling him down if it's going to hurt his family and many others. However, that's as you newspaper people see it—"

I could have sympathized with this stocky Irishman more if we had not all been suspicious of the police concealing cases to their own profit and if, where they had anything to conceal, they were not so uniformly truculent and cynical. I decided to see this old gentleman myself, curiosity and the desire for the details of a good story controlling me. I hurried to a car and rode out into that same west end, where, in a decidedly well-built street and a house of fair proportions if no great taste, I found this same probably much troubled individual sitting on his front porch, possibly awaiting some such disastrous onslaught as this, and anxious no doubt to keep it from his family as long as possible. He got up as he saw me coming in his gate and began to make his way down the steps and walk. He was tall and angular with a grizzled short, round beard and a dull, unimportant face, a man who looked all of his years and had a kind of vulpine carefulness into the bargain. He had deep-set grey eyes with marked crow's-feet at the side. Apparently he was well past—or at least as these Midwestern Americans would have thought—the time when passions of any kind should have troubled him, well into that period when one is supposed to settle down into a serene old age and forget all that he ever knew as youth. At any rate, I rather thought so myself as I eyed him coming down the walk and then inquired whether a Mr. Nelson lived here. He replied that he was Mr. Nelson.

"I'm from the *Republic,*" I went on, "and we have a story regarding a charge which has been made against you today in one of the police stations."

As I talked, I recall his eying me with a kind of nervous uncertainty which was almost tremulous. He did not seem to be quite able to speak at first, but just walked slowly and nervously toward the gate. "Not so loud," he said finally. "Come out here," and then, "I'll give you ten dollars if you won't say anything about this"—and he began to fumble nervously in one of his waistcoat pockets.

"No, no," I said righteously, quite with an air of profound virtue. "I can't take money for anything like that. You mustn't offer it to me. I can't stop anything the paper may want to say even if I wanted to— you'll have to see the editor about that." At the same time I was thinking how like an old fox he was, and that if one did have the power to suppress a story of this kind what a very fine opportunity for black-mail was here. Plainly he might have been made to pay a thousand or more. At the same time, also, I could not help sympathizing with him a little, considering his age and his very unfortunate predicament. Of late I had begun to get a much clearer light on my own character and idiosyncrasies as well as those of many others and to see also quite plainly how few there were who could really afford to cast the stone of righteousness or superior worth. Nearly all, as I saw, were either cursed or blessed, as you will, with some fault or other—either of bigotry, ignorance, or a driving vice of some kind—and most of them secretly doing one thing or another, which publicly they would denounce and which, if exposed, would cause them to be shunned or punished. Sex vagaries, as I was beginning to see, were not as uncommon as the majority supposed and were perhaps not to be visited with too sharp a punishment if strict justice were to be done to all. Yet here was I, however, at this moment, yelping at the heels of this latest errant, largely—quite entirely, I suppose—because he had been found out or exposed in rather a public way. No doubt there were others, many of them, just as bad as himself, who if they were caught should fare even worse, but who were merely more fortunate in keeping it concealed. At the same time, I cannot say that I was very much moved by the personality of this individual or that he appealed to me in any way intellectually or otherwise. He looked to be narrow and closefisted. Nevertheless, as I looked at him, I wondered how a businessman of any acumen could be connected with so shabby an affair or, once being caught, could be so dull as to offer any newspaper man so small a sum as ten dollars to suppress a story like this, or as not to know that, being numerous and watchful, practically all the papers would have to be seen and adjusted. How about the other papers, I thought—the other reporters who might hear of it? Did he expect to buy all of them off for ten dollars each? The fact that he had admitted the truth of the charges, however, left nothing to say. I could not even talk to him about it. I found myself as nervous and incoherent as he himself, and finally left, rather discomfited and puzzled as to what I should do. When I returned to the office and told Wandell, he seemed to be rather dubious also, and more or less disgusted.

"You can't make much out of a case of that kind," he commented. "We couldn't print it if you did. The public wouldn't stand for it. You can't tell what really happened, and if you attack the police for concealing it, then they'll be down on us. He ought to be exposed, I suppose—but—well—write it out and I'll see."

I therefore wrote it up in a weary and somewhat guarded way, telling in a roundabout way just what had happened and how the police had not entered the charge, but it never appeared. And somehow I for one was rather glad of it, although, as I thought at the time, he should have been punished or some harm come to him. Still, I was not so sure either. Would any real advantage have flowed therefrom? I was inclined to doubt it,—to doubt even whether sex perversions as such were the heinous crimes which nearly all seemed to deem them. Was not the child with its instinct to accept almost as much to blame as the man? I pondered over this, wondered long and never did reach an acceptable conclusion. As for the story I wrote—well, it is entirely possible that it was killed because of the indifferent manner in which I wrote it.

CHAPTER XLVIII

Story number two has an entirely different quality and revealed something about myself to myself which I had never deemed possible before. Indeed it shook my faith in the theory of self-control and raised the question of whether one is really always master of one's own mind—I of mine, for instance—and whether the rise to eminence of certain individuals is not as much a matter of hypnotism as anything else.

It came about in this way. While I was on the *Globe-Democrat* there was a sort of racetrack tout, gambler, amateur detective, and political and police hanger-on generally, who was, incidentally, a purveyor of news not only to our police and political man but to the sporting and some other editors—a sort of jack-of-all-news, or "tipster," as a sobriquet of the time had it. To me, from the first he was both somewhat ridiculous and disgusting—loud, bold, uncouth—the kind of creature who begins as bootblack or newsboy or both and winds up as the president of a racing association or a baseball team. Ostensibly he was Irish and so claimed to be—"Red" Galvin by name—having a taciturn, freckled Irish face, red hair, gray-blue eyes, and rather large hands and feet. In reality he was not Irish at all, but one of those South Russian Jews who, looking so much like the Irish as to be frequently mistaken for them, had the wit to see that it would probably be of more advantage to him to be thought Irish than Jewish, and in consequence had changed his name of Shapirowitz, or something like that, to that of Galvin. One of the most offensive things about him to me when I first encountered him was that his clothes were truly loud, just such clothes as touts and gamblers affect who wish to appear au fait in their world— hard bright-checked suits of a more or less reddish-brown color, bright yellow shoes, ties of the most radiant hues, hats of a clashing sonorousness, and rings and pins and cuff links glistening with diamonds or rubies—clothes worn by the kind of people who are absolutely convinced that clothes and a little money make the man, as they quite do in many such instances.

But this same Galvin, or Shapirowitz, was even worse than this in some respects, having the social and moral point of view of at once the hawk and the buzzard, or so I thought at the time. According to Wood, who early made friends with him (quite as he did with the Chinese and others for purposes of study, I presume), he was constantly identified with some houses of prostitution in which he had a small financial interest—as well as various political schemes then being locally fostered by one and another group of those low politicians known locally as assemblymen (the equivalent of aldermen in other cities) who were constantly getting up one scheme and another to mulct the city in some underhanded way. He was really a species of political and social grafter, having all the high ideals of a bagnio detective. And soon after I came there he began to interest Mr. Tobias Mitchell, who was really a creature of an allied if slightly higher type, and the pair soon became reasonably good friends. Mitchell began to use him as an assistant to Hazard, Bellairs, Bennett, Hartung and myself, that is, as a man who would supply us or the paper with stories which we should rewrite. And I for one used to laugh at him more or less to his face as being a freak, which generated only the kindliest feelings, of course, between us. I think, however, as a matter of fact, we took a violent dislike to each other on sight (mere incompatibility of temper), and, so doing, I despised him and all his works, laughing into his teeth in consequence. He always suggested to me the type of detective or plainclothesman who would take money from street girls—prey on them, as indeed I constantly suspected him of doing.

I wondered how it was that along with his other profitable tasks or grafts he could make anything profitable out of this newspaper connection, seeing, as Hartung and others told me, that he could not write, or only so badly as made it necessary to rewrite his stuff almost entirely. His great recommendation to Mitchell and others was that he could apparently glean news of things where other reporters couldn't, among the police, the detective politicians, and the like, with whom obviously he was hand in hand. By reason of his underworld connections, apparently, many amazing details as to one form of political and social jobbery came to light, making him invaluable no doubt to a city editor who could use others like myself, for instance, to rewrite his stuff. Just the same, I used to wonder where he secured all his material, bustling in as he did with news of horses, prizefights, political schemes, and the like, and at the same time apparently keeping in with all his various underworld associates.

When some of his stories were given to me, we were brought into immediate and almost clashing contact. And because of his cool cynical leers and unabashed bravado even when he knew he could not write two good sentences in order, I frequently wanted to brain him, but took it out in smiles and dry cynical comments. His most frequent expressions, as I often noted, were "See?" and "I sez tuh him" or "He sez tuh me," always more or less accompanied by a contemptuous wave of the be-rubied hand or a chin that was pugnaciously protruded and a lip that was curled. One of the principal reasons why I hated him, I think, was that not long after I had known him Dick Wood told me that he had once cynically remarked that newspaper work was a beggar's game at best, and that *writers grew on trees*, meaning that they were so numerous as to be negligible and not worth considering. How a Hebrew ever came to achieve so much of Kerry bravado and American tough sang-froid was a mystery to me.

Just the same, as a duty, of course, I made the best of these trying situations when I had to do over a story of his, extracted all the information I could and then wrote it out as well as I could, which resulted in some of his stories getting excellent space and position in the day's news. And, as I saw it at the time, this merely set him up in his own estimation and made him all the more pugnacious and sure of himself, while at the same time actually making him of more value to the paper. This was not as it should be, of course, as I argued at the time. He should constantly prove of less value. However, as I have previously shown, in due time I left the paper. And then somewhat to my astonishment and irritation he appeared one day at the North 7th Street police station, which I was then regularly covering. He was now a fully fledged reporter, if you please, having been given a regular position by Mitchell and set to doing police work, out of which task at the Four Courts, if I remember rightly, he finally ousted Mr. Jock Bellairs, who was given to too much drinking.

More or less to my surprise and chagrin, I noticed at once that he was—and as if by reason of past intimacies of which I had never had the slightest idea—far more en rapport with the various sergeants and the captain than I had ever dreamed of being. It was "Charlie" here and "Cap" there whenever he was addressing the lieutenant or the captain! In addition he gave himself all the airs of a newspaper man proper, swaggering about and talking of this, that and the other story that he had written—I having done some of them myself. And what was more, in so far as this particular station was concerned, it being a real news centre, he was soon closeted intimately with the captain in his room, strolling in and out of that sanctum as if it were his private demesne and somehow giving me the impression of being in touch with realms and deeds of which I was never to have the slightest knowledge. This made me doubly apprehensive lest, in these secret intimacies, tales and mysteries should be unfolded which should have their first light in the pages of the *Globe-Democrat* and so leave me to be laughed at as one who could not get the news. In consequence, I watched the *Globe-Democrat* more closely than I ever had before for any evidence of such treachery on the part of the police here as would result in a scoop for him and at the same time redoubled my interest in such items as might appear. In consequence, on more than one occasion I made good stories out of things which evidently Mr. Galvin had dismissed as worthless; and, au contraire, now and then a case into which I had inquired at the station house appeared in the *Globe-Democrat* with details which I had not been able to obtain and concerning which the police insisted that they had known nothing. At such times Mr. Galvin would usually be at the station house during the day with a satisfied or contemptuous smirk on his face, which showed me only too plainly that he was seeking by some such sub-surface intimacies as I could not achieve to "scoop me," as the phrase went. It was galling.

However, for a long time, by dint of energy and a rather plain indication to all concerned that I would not tolerate any false dealing on the part of anyone, I managed not only to hold my own but occasionally to give my confrere a good beating, and that with considerable flare. For one instance, one late August night, a negro girl, in one of those crowded alleys I have previously described, was cut nearly to shreds by an ex-lover armed with a razor, and for reasons which, as my personal investigation proved, were highly romantic. In this case it appeared (but only after the greatest industry on my part) that some seven or eight months before, this same girl and the negro who cut her had been living together as man and wife in Cairo, Illinois, where they had first met. The lover was a coal passer or stevedore working now on one boat and now on another plying the Mississippi between New Orleans and St. Louis. He was plainly wildly fond of her and became suspicious and, finally satisfying himself that his mistress (who was a real beauty after her kind) was faithless to him, set a trap to catch her. On one occasion, when she imagined him to be away on a river steamer for a week or two of labor, he returned suddenly and bursting in upon her found her with another man. Death would have been her portion as well as that of her lover on this occasion if it had not been for the interference of friends or a timely warning, which permitted the pair to escape.

Subsequently, however, he had set out to follow her wherever she might be, for she had left him for good and this apparently was a case of true and driving romance or passion. Lacerated by the double offenses of betrayal and desertion, he had decided to hunt her and her lover out wherever they might be, and to this end he first returned to his task as stevedore, working his way thus from one river city to another. Arriving then in any particular city such as Memphis, Natchez, New Orleans, Vicksburg, or St. Louis, he made it a point to disguise himself when on shore as a peddler selling trinkets and charms, and in this capacity walked the crowded negro sections of all these cities calling his wares. One of these trips brought him finally to St. Louis, and here on this late afternoon in August, ambling up this stifling little alley where so many negroes lived, he finally encountered her, for when he called out his charms and trinkets, his false love, apparently not recognizing his voice, put her head out of the doorway where she was now dwelling with her other lover. On the instant the damage was done. He had recognized her. Dropping his tray he was upon her in a flash with his razor, crisscrossing and slashing his false beauty until she was cut out of all semblance to her former self. With quite fiendish cruelty he cut her cheeks and lips, arms, legs, back and sides, so much so that when I arrived at the City Hospital where she had been taken she was unconscious and her life despaired of. Great cuts all of a foot in length and as much as an inch deep had been made in her thighs, back and arms. I am not sure now that subsequently she did not die. On the other hand, the lover, abandoning his tray of cheap jewelry which was later brought to the station house and exhibited, made good his escape and was not captured—at least not during my stay in St. Louis. Her present paramour had also gone his way, leaving her alone to suffer.

Curiously, this story in the *Globe-Democrat*, owing possibly to Galvin's underestimate of its romance, received only a scant stick as a low-dive cutting affray. In the *Republic*, on the contrary—and I am not seeking to overestimate my own skill in the matter—I had turned it into a black romance which received all of a column or more. Into it I had tried to put the hot river waterfronts of the different cities which the lover had visited, the crowded negro quarters of Memphis, New Orleans, Cairo—the low, bold negro life which two such truants as the false mistress and her lover might enjoy. I had tried to suggest the singsong sleepiness of the levee fronts and the boat landings, the stevedores at their lazy labors, the idle, dreamy character of the slow-moving boats. Even an old negro refrain appropriate to a trinket peddler had been introduced:

"Eyah—rings, pins, buckles, ribbons!"

Somehow the barbaric character of the alley in which it occurred, lined with rickety curtain-hung shacks and swarming with the idle, crooning, shuffling negro life of the South, appealed to me intensely. An old black mammy with a yellow-dotted kerchief over her head, who kept talking of "disha Gawge" and "disha Sam" and "disha Magnolia" (the girl), moved me almost to a poetic frenzy. From a long-enduring crowd of blacks who hung about the vacated shack of the lovers for hours after the girl had been taken away, I picked up the main thread of the story—the varying characteristics of the girl and her lover. And then having visited the hospital and seen the victim lying there, I hurried to the office and endeavored to convince Wandell that I had an important story. He was not inclined to think so at first, negro life being almost a little too low for local consumption, but, after I had entered upon some of the details, he exclaimed, "Well, do it your way. We'll see." I wrote it out just as I felt about it and as I have described it, with a result that it went in on the second page. The next day, meeting Galvin, and having first examined the *Globe* and seen what had been done, I beamed on him cheerfully, if not contemptuously, with the result that I was met with a snarl of rage.

"You think you're a hell of a feller, dontcha, because you can sling a little ink?" he exclaimed. "You think you've pulled off sompin' swell. Well, say, you're not near so much as you think you are. Wait and see. I've been up against you wordy boys before, and I can work all around yuh. All you guys can do is to get a few facts and then pad 'em up. You never get the real stuff—never," and his lip curled and he even snapped his fingers under my nose. "Wait'll we get a real case sometime—you an' me," he went on. "I'll show you sompin'."

He glared at me with hard, cold, revengeful eyes, and, to tell the truth, he then and there put a lusty fear of him into me from which I never really recovered, although at the time I merely smiled and replied,

"Is that so? You think so, do you? That's easy enough to say now that you're trimmed, but I guess I'll be right there when the time comes."

"Aw, go to hell," he snarled, and I walked off smiling, at the same time beginning to wonder nervously just what it was he was going to do to me and how soon, if at all.

CHAPTER XLIX

The sequel to this story about Galvin, however, is what I have been desiring to narrate from the first. Sometime before this, say four or five months, when I was still working for the *Globe-Democrat*, there had occurred on the Missouri Pacific, about one hundred and fifty miles west of St. Louis and between there and Kansas City, another story or news item which interested me quite as much at the time, although I had nothing to do with it in any way. According to the reports telegraphed from the scene of the crime at the time, seven lusty and daring bandits, all heavily armed and desperate as any bandits might well be, had held up a seven- or eight-car Pullman and baggage express train between one and two of the morning at a lonely spot on the road's route. After overawing the passengers in each of the several cars and compelling the engineer and fireman to dismount, uncouple the engine and run it a hundred paces ahead, the two latter had been ordered to return and help break open the door of the express car, which they did, using a stick of dynamite or giant powder handed them by one of the bandits. Subsequently both were compelled to enter the express car, and, under the eye of one of the bandits who entered with them—so the story went—and despite the presence of the express messenger who was armed but overawed, they blew open the safe, carried forth between twenty and thirty thousand dollars in bills and coin and, depositing them on the ground in sacks and packages for the dear bandits, reentered their engine under duress, backed it up, and after coupling it to the train proceeded upon their journey, leaving the bandits to gather up their booty in peace and to depart. Naturally, such a story was of considerable interest to St. Louis and all the other great cities so near at hand. It smacked of the lawlessness of the forties and later, when packtrain and stagecoach robberies were the rule and not the exception. All banks, express companies, railroads and financial institutions generally were intensely interested. The whole front page was given to this particular deed then, and it was worth it. During my short career in journalism in this region, no less than seven, and I think as many as a dozen, amazing train robberies took place in as many months in the region bounded by the Mississippi and the Rockies, the Canadian line and the Gulf. Four or five of them occurred within, say, a hundred miles of St. Louis. When one thinks of it, this has quite an oriental sound, something like those caravan robberies in Asia and Africa, but so it was.

But to return to this particular robbery. As it really happened, and astounding as it may seem, there had not been any seven bandits at all (all heavily armed, or otherwise) but just one, and he an ex-railroad man and before that a farm hand turned robber for this occasion only and armed, as subsequent developments proved, with but a brace of revolvers, each containing six shots, and a few sticks of fuse-prepared giant powder! Despite the glowing preliminary newspaper accounts which made of this a most desperate and murderous occasion, there had been no prowling up and down the sides of the cars by various bandits, all armed to the teeth, as a number of the passengers insisted (among whom by the way was the governor of the state, his lieutenant-governor—who by virtue of his office was also head of the state militia—as well as several officers of his staff, all returning from a military banquet or feast somewhere). Nor was there any shooting at any passenger who ventured to peer out in the dark, although the papers said so, but just one lone bandit as aforesaid, who was very busy at the time up in front attending to the robbing. What made this story all the more ridiculous in the light of subsequent developments was that at the time that the train stopped in the dark and these various imaginary bandits began to shout and fire their numerous shots and even, as it was claimed, to rob the passengers of their watches, pins, purses and the like, these worthies of the state—the governor, lieutenant-governor and all his military attendants—crawled under their seats or into their berths and did not again emerge from the same until the train was well on its way once more—or so at least it was claimed in guffawing newspaper circles. In addition, the single bandit was not so much to contend with physically, as time also proved, but that may rest for the present. What is really important at this point is that long before the true story of the lone bandit came out, this other of the governor and his staff was well known and lent considerable lustre to the deed and strengthened the interest which subsequently attached to the story of the true bandit.

Be that as it may (and the St. Louis newspaper files for 1893 will show whether I am correct or not), this same lone bandit had—owing to an interesting strain of love and poverty into which his life at just about this time had drifted—plotted this astounding coup which, once all its peculiar details were revealed, seemed, for an hour at least, to fascinate the entire American public from coast to coast. The psychology which had caused a lone individual to undertake such an astounding task was uppermost in everybody's mind at the time, including those of our local city editors, and to the task of unraveling it, once the identity of the robber became known, they now bent their every effort.

At the time the robbery occurred, as I say, I was still working for the *Globe-Democrat*. Later when it was discovered by detectives working for the railroad and the express company just who the star robber was, I was connected with the *Republic*. Returning very early one afternoon from some unimportant assignment which had proved a failure, I was shown a telegram from some backwoods town in Missouri—Lebanon—that one Sam Wilson, an ex-employe of the Missouri Pacific, had on that day or the day before been arrested by detectives for the road and the express company, who had then and there discovered most of the stolen money in his room; that because of various other facts with which he had been confronted, he had already confessed that he and he alone had been guilty of the express robbery; that he had already shown the detectives where the remainder of the money lay hidden; that this very afternoon he would be en route to St. Louis, scheduled to arrive over the St. Louis and San Francisco, a road leading in from that region; and that here he would be confined in the county jail until sentenced. Imagine the excitement. The story was immense. The burglar had not yet told anyone how he had accomplished this great feat, and here he was now en route to St. Louis and might even be met and interviewed on the train coming in, providing the right connection could be made.

"I'll tell you what you do, Dreiser," exclaimed Wandell when he saw me. "George! I thought you wouldn't get back in time. Here's a St. Louis and San Francisco timetable. According to this you can take a local that leaves here at 2:15 and get as far as this place, Valley Park, where this incoming express stops. You can get on there, and that will give you a good hour and a half in which to interview him. It's just possible that the *Globe* and the other papers haven't got hold of this story yet, and then again maybe they have. But anyhow, whatever happens, we won't get licked, and that's the main thing." He cautioned me to hurry and, intensely interested in the tale myself and anxious that the paper should do at least as well as the others, I bustled down to the Union Station. But on inquiring for a ticket for Valley Park, the slightly disturbing response of "Which road?" was made.

"Are there two?" I asked.

"Yes. Missouri Pacific, and St. Louis and San Francisco."

"Which train leaves first?" I inquired.

"St. Louis and San Francisco. It's waiting now."

I hurried out and got aboard, but the thought of this other road in from Valley Park troubled me. Supposing, by any chance, the bandit should not be on this train, but the other. I consulted with the conductor when he came for my ticket, and I was informed by him, after due consultation of timetables, that Valley Park was the only place really at which these two roads met, the one going west, the other southwest from there. "Good," I thought. "He is certain to be on this St. Louis and San Francisco train then."

But now another thought occurred to me. Supposing that other reporters from other papers were aboard, especially the *Globe-Democrat*. I had not seen any, but still—. If there were not, I would have this fine task all to myself and could work it out in my own way, but if there were—then the usual squabbles and bickerings and pushing for place. I rose up and walked forward to the smoker, which was the next car in front, and there, to my intense disgust and nervous dissatisfaction, I spied this same Galvin, redheaded, serene, a cigar between his teeth, crouched low in his seat, smoking and reading a paper, as calm as though he were bent upon the most unimportant task in the world.

"What now?" I thought. "The *Globe* sent that swine! Here he is now, and these country detectives and railroad men, whoever they are or wherever they come from, will be sure on the instant to make friends with him and do their best to serve him. They like that sort of man. They may even give him details and character bits which they will refuse to give me. I shall have to interview my man in front of him, and he will get all the benefit of all my questions. The devil! They may even refuse to let me interview him. Such situations are not uncommon. Horrors!"

I returned to my seat nervous and much troubled, all the more so because I now recalled Galvin's venomous threat. At the same time I was at once determined to give him the tussle of his life. Let him think now what he would really do. Now we would see whether he could beat me or not—not if any fair play were exercised, of that I felt confident. Why, he could not even write a decent sentence. Why should I be afraid of him? But just the same, I was.

The dreary local speeding on and drawing nearer and nearer Valley Park, I became more and more nervous. For me the whole charm of this beautiful June landscape through which we were speeding was spoiled. It was a really lovely June day, warm and bright, but, oh, the misery of it. As we neared Valley Park in something over an hour and a half out, I began to get more and more restless, and as we drew up to the platform I jumped down, all alive with the determination not to be outdone in any way. As I did so, I saw Galvin leaping out, who on the instant spied me, and at once I saw his countenance cloud over. I never saw a man change more quickly from an expression of ease and assurance to one of bristling opposition and distrust. How he hated me. He fairly bristled like a savage dog and glared at me as he looked around to see who else might dismount. Then, seeing no one, he bustled up to the station agent, who was out on the platform, to see when the train from the west was due. At once I decided not to trail but instead sought information from the conductor who, stepping down beside me, assured me that the eastbound express would probably be on time, five minutes later.

"We take the siding here. You'll hear the whistle in a few minutes."

"It always stops here, does it?" I asked anxiously.

"It always stops."

As we talked Galvin came back to the platform's edge and stood looking up the track. At the same time this train pulled out, and a few moments later the whistle of the express was heard. Now for a real contest, I thought. Somewhere in one of these cars would be this bandit surrounded by detectives, and my duty was to get there first, explain who I was, ingratiate myself and begin my questioning, overawing Galvin perhaps with the ease with which I would take charge. It would probably be a hard interview. The bandit might not want to talk. I would probably have to do the interviewing, but this wretch would make notes or make a deal with the detectives. In a few moments the train was rolling into the station, the local on which we had arrived having sidetracked, and then I saw my friend Galvin leap aboard and with that iron effrontery and savageness of his which I always hated in him, so animal-like was it, begin to race through the cars. I was about to follow him when I noticed the conductor, a portly genial-looking soul, stepping down beside me.

"Is Sam Wilson, that train robber they are bringing in from Lebanon, on here? I'm from the *Republic,* and I've been sent out to interview him."

"You're on the wrong road, brother," he smiled. "He's not on here. Those detective fellows have fooled you newspaper men, I suppose. They're bringing him in over the Missouri Pacific. But I'll tell you," and here he took out a large open-face silver watch and consulted it, "you might be able to catch that yet, if you run for it. It's only across the field here. You see that little yellow station over there? Well, that's the Missouri Pacific depot," he added, as he saw my brightening face, I suppose. "I don't know that it stops here, but it may. It's due now, but sometimes it's a little late. You'll have to run for it, though, if you make it. You haven't a minute to spare."

"You wouldn't fool me about a thing like this," I pleaded. "It's most important to me."

"Not for anything," he replied. "I know how you feel. If you can get on that train I think you'll find him on it, unless they've taken him off somewhere."

I don't know whether I even stopped to thank him. His whole appearance and manner had really convinced me that he was telling the truth. Instead of following Galvin into the cars, I now leaped to the little path which cut diagonally across this long field and which was evidently well worn by human feet. As I ran I looked back once or twice to see whether my enemy was following me or had seen me, but apparently he had not. I now looked forward eagerly toward the other station, only, as I ran, to see the semaphore arm, which stood at right angles opposite the station, lower itself for a clear track for some train. At the same time I spied a mailbag hanging out on an express arm, indicating that whatever this train was, it was not going to stop here. The mail would be picked up at full speed. I turned, still uncertain whether I had made a mistake in not searching the other train after all. Supposing that conductor had fooled me. Railroad men were sometimes purposely malicious, as I knew. Supposing the burglar was on there, and Galvin was already beginning to interview him! Oh, Lord, what a beat! And what would happen to me? I actually slowed up in my running, chill beads of sweat bursting out on my face, but as I did so I saw the St. Louis and San Francisco train begin to move, and from it leap down, as if shot out of it, the significant form of Galvin. "Ha," I thought, "then the robber is not on there! The conductor told me the truth, and Galvin has just discovered it! He knows now that he is coming in on this line." For I could see him running along the path. "Oh, kind heaven, if I can beat him to it," I thought, "get on and leave him behind. He has all of a thousand feet still to run, and I am here." And as I thought this I was right close to the station—a good three minutes ahead of him.

Desperately I ran into it—a tiny thing—sticking my eager head in at the open office window and calling to the short, stout, truculent little occupant of it, "When is this St. Louis express due here?"

"Now," replied he surlily.

"Does it stop?"

"No, it doesn't stop!"

"Can it be stopped?"

"It can*not!*"

"You mean to say you have no right to stop it?"

"I mean I won't stop it." (There came the ominous shriek of its whistle in the distance as he said this.)

"Oh, Lord," I thought. "Here it comes now, and he won't let me on, and Galvin will be here any minute." For the moment I was even willing that Galvin should catch it too, if only he would stop it and let me on. Think of what Wandell would think if I missed it.

"Will five dollars stop it?" I asked desperately diving into my pocket for my purse. I opened it quickly.

"No."

"Will ten?"

"It might," he replied crustily.

"Stop it," I urged him doggedly and handed over the bill with an eager urgent motion. The agent took it, and grabbing a tablet of yellow order blanks which lay before him, scribbled something on the face of one, and going outside, held it out toward the track where the engineer could see it, I presume. At the same time he called to me, "Run on down the track. Run after it. She won't stop here. She can't. She'll go a thousand feet before she can slow up. Get on down there, and after you're on I'll let 'em go ahead."

Without further instructions I began to run while he stood there holding up this thin sheet of yellow paper between his thumb and forefinger. At the same time as I ran I heard the express rushing up behind me. On the instant it was alongside and past, its wheels grinding and emitting sparks. True enough, it was stopping! I was going to be able to get on. Oh, glory be! It was far ahead of me now but almost stock-still, and as I was running I would make it in a moment or two more. If only Galvin could not reach it too. Lord, what a beat! I would do him beautifully. As I thought and ran I could hear the final gritty screech of the wheels against the brakes as the train came to a full stop, and then coming up to it breathless, I climbed aboard. Only, looking back, I saw to my horror that my rival, who had taken a diagonal course across the common in the direction I was running, had caught up, or nearly so, and was close at hand, not a hundred feet behind. He had seen me and divined my scheme. He would almost make the train as quick as myself.

"Oh, Lord," I sighed, "and I've just given up ten good dollars to do this, and now he'll get the benefit of it."

I tried to signal the agent behind to let the train go on, but he had already done so. The conductor coming out on the rear platform, I appealed to him. "Let her go," I said. "It's all right. Go on."

"Don't that other fellow want to get on too?" he asked curiously.

"No, no, no!" I exclaimed. "Don't let him on. I arranged to stop this train. I'm from the *Republic*. He hasn't any right on here. Go ahead." But even as I spoke, he came up breathless and perspiring and crawled eagerly on, a leer of mingled triumph and joy over my discomfiture written all over his face. Plainly, he knew what I had been up to. It gave him immense satisfaction to frustrate me.

"Is that so?" he sneered. "You think you'll leave me behind, do you? Well, I fooled you this trip, didn't I?" and, his lip curled, he dashed into the car.

Plainly, I was beaten so far. It was an immensely painful moment for me—to lose this way just when I had everything in my own hands, as it were. My spirits fell so for the moment that I did not even trouble to inquire whether the robber was on the train, but, content to follow my rival, who had proceeded his eager way, I ambled after him, satisfied that I should have to beat him in the quality of the interview but not by its complete monopoly. Alas, alas! for all my bright dreams.

CHAPTER L

E ven here I was destined for another drubbing, as I shall now proceed to show, illustrating once more how man proposes but fate disposes. Following Galvin forward through the train, I soon discovered the detectives and their prisoner in one of the forward cars. To my surprise I found the prisoner a most unpromising specimen for so unique a deed: short, broad-shouldered, heavy-limbed, with a squarish, inexpressive, even dull-looking face, blue-gray eyes, dark brown hair, big, lumpy, rough hands—just the hands you would expect to find on a railroad hand or baggage-smasher—a tanned and seamed skin. He had on the cheap nondescript clothes of a laborer—a blue "hickory" shirt for instance, blackish-grey trousers, brownish-maroon coat and a red bandana handkerchief tied around his neck in lieu of a collar. On his head was a small round brown hat, pulled down over his eyes after the manner of a cap. He had the still, indifferent expression of a captive bird, and when I came up after Galvin and sat down, he scarcely looked at me or at Galvin or, if so, with eyes that told nothing. I have often wondered since what he really thought.

Between him and the car window, to foil any attempt at escape in that direction, and fastened to him by a pair of handcuffs, was the sheriff of the county in which he had been taken, a big bland, inexperienced creature whose sense of his own importance was plainly enhanced by his task. He was really bursting with pride. Facing him was one of the detectives of the road or the express company, I forget which, a short, canny, vulturish-looking person, and opposite again, across the aisle in another seat, was still another "detective." There may have been still others, but I failed to inquire. I was so incensed in the first place at the mere presence of Galvin, considering him an interloper, and secondly by what I considered his coarse and cheap methods of ingratiating himself into any company, and especially one like this, that I could scarcely speak or endure the sight of him. "What," I thought to myself, "when the utmost finesse would be required to get the true inwardness of all this, send a cheap pig like this to thrust himself forward and muddle what might otherwise prove a fine story! Why, if it hadn't been for me and my luck, he wouldn't be here at all. And he was now posing as a reporter—the best man of the *Globe*! Pah!"

He had the average detective-politician-gambler's habit of simu-
lating an intense interest and an enthusiasm which he did not feel—his
face, for instance, wreathing itself in a cheery smile, the while his eyes
followed you like those of a basilisk, attempting all the while to
discover whether his assumed enthusiasm or friendship was being accepted at the value he wished it to have.

"Gee, sport," he began familiarly in my presence, patting the
burglar on the knee and fixing him with that basilisk gaze of his, "that
was a great trick you pulled off. The papers'll be crazy to find out how
you did it. My paper, the *Globe-Democrat*, wants a whole page on it if it
can get it. It wants your picture, too. Did you really do it all alone?
Well, that's what I call swell work, eh, Cap?" And now he turned his
ingratiating leer on the country sheriff and the other detectives. In a
moment or two more he was telling the latter and the sheriff what an
intimate friend he was of "Billy" Desmond, the chief of detectives of St.
Louis, and Mr. Harrigan, the chief of police, as well as various other
detectives and policemen.

"The dull stuff!" I thought. "And this is what he considers place in
this world. And he write a whole page for the *Globe*. My word! He'd do
well if he wrote a half-column alone."

Still, to my intense chagrin, I could see that he was making
headway after a time, not only with the country sheriff and the detectives, but the burglar himself. The latter smiled a raw, wry smile and
looked at him as if he might possibly understand such a person. Galvin's
good clothes, always looking like new—his bright yellow shoes, sparkling rings and pins, and gaudy tie—seemed to impress not only the
burglar but the detectives. So this was the sort of thing these people
liked, and they took him for a real newspaper man from a great
newspaper. Inwardly I boiled.

Indeed, the only time when I seemed to obtain the least grip on
this situation, or to impress myself on the minds of the detectives and
the prisoner, was when it came to those finer shades of questioning
which concerned just why—for what ulterior reasons—he had attempted this deed alone, and then I noticed that my confrere was all
ears and making copious notes. He knew enough to take from others
what he could not work out for himself. In the main, in regard to all the
principal or general points, I found that my Irish-Jewish friend was as
swift at searching out facts as anyone and as eager to know how and

why. And always, to my astonishment and chagrin, the prisoner as well as the detectives paid more attention to him than they did to me. They turned to him as to a lamp and seemed to be really immensely more impressed with him than with me, although the principal lines of questioning fell to me. All at once I found him whispering to one or other of the detectives while I proceeded to develop some thought which he had dropped, only, as I say, whenever I turned up anything the least new, or asked a question which he perchance had not thought of, he was all ears again and back to resume the questioning on his own account. He irritated me frightfully and at the same time appeared to be intensely happy at the thought of doing so. My contemptuous looks and remarks did not disturb him in the least. He was as iron or leather. By now I was so dour and enraged that I could think of but one thing that would really have satisfied me and that was to attack him physically and give him a good beating—although I seriously questioned whether I could do that even, he was so contentious, cynical and savage.

However, by degrees and between us, the story was finally extracted, and a fine tale it made. It appeared that up to seven or eight months preceding the robbery, possibly a year, this same train robber had been first a freight brakeman or yard hand on this same road at one of its division points, and that latterly he had been promoted to be a sort of superior switchman and assistant freight handler at some station where there was considerable work of this kind. Previous to this he had been a livery stable helper in the town where he was eventually apprehended and before that a farm hand somewhere near the same place. About a year before the crime, owing to the approach of hard times, this road, along with many others, had laid off a large number of men, including himself, and reduced the wages of all others by as much as ten percent. Naturally, a great deal of labor discontent ensued, and strikes, riots and the like were the order of the day. Curiously, a certain number of train robberies which were charged and traced to discharged and dissatisfied ex-employes now followed. The methods of successful train robbing were so clearly set forth by the average newspaper that nearly any burglar so inclined could follow them. In addition, while working as a freight handler at the particular station in question, Sam Wilson had heard, among other things, of the many money shipments made by express companies in their express cars, their large amount, the manner in which they were guarded and the like.

The particular road for which he worked at this time, the Missouri Pacific, was, as he now learned, a very popular route both west and east for money shipments of bullion, bills and the like in transit between St. Louis and the East and Kansas City and the West. Although express messengers (as those in charge of the car and its safe were called) were even at this time well and invariably armed, owing to numerous train robberies which had been occurring in the West of late, still these assaults had not been without success. In addition, the deaths of various messengers, engineers, firemen, conductors, and even passengers who had no occasion for risking their lives in defense of the roads but who occasionally ventured to give these bands battle, as well as the fact that much money had recently been stolen and never recovered, had encouraged the growth of banditry everywhere. These events had put such an unreasoning fear into most employes connected with the roads that but few—even of those especially picked guards occasionally put on the trains by the roads or express companies to guard their property—ventured to give these marauders battle. I myself, during the short time I had been in St. Louis, had helped report three such robberies in its immediate vicinity, in all of which cases the bandits had escaped unharmed.

But just the same, the motive which eventually resulted in the amazing single-handed attempt and success of this particular individual was not so much that he was a discharged and poor railroad hand unable to find any other form of employment, although that was a part of it, but that in his idleness, having wandered back to his native region where he had first started out as a livery hand, he had fallen in love with a young girl there. And then finding that he was rather hard pressed for cash and unable to make her such presents as he desired, he had first begun to think seriously of some method of raising money. Latterly, when another ex-railroad hand who had been laid off by this same company showed up and proposed, in connection with a third man whom he knew, to rob a train, he had at first quietly rejected it as not feasible—not wishing to tie himself up in any crime, let alone with others. But later, after the man had been gone for some time, and his own condition had become more pressing, he had eventually begun to think of robbing a train on his own account.

Why alone?

That was the point we were all most anxious to find out—why single-handed with all the odds against him.

For the life of us, neither Galvin nor myself could make him make this point quite clear, although once I raised it, we were both most eager to solve it. Didn't he know that he could scarcely expect to overcome engineer and fireman, baggageman and mailman—for there was a mail car on the train—to say nothing of the express messenger, the conductor and the passengers?

Yes, he knew, only he thought he could do it! Other bandits—so few as three in one case of which he had read—had held up large trains. Why not one? Revolver shots fired about a train easily overawed all passengers as well as the trainmen apparently. Anyhow, it was a life or death job either way, and it would be better for him if he worked it out alone instead of with others, or so he thought. Often, he said, other men "squealed" or they had girls who told on them. He knew that. I looked at him, intensely interested and moved to admiration by the sheer courage of it all—or "gall" or grit or what you will—imbedded somewhere in this stocky frame. Why he should have imagined that he could do this was beyond me, and yet he had, and here he was alive and ready to tell the tale.

How he had come to fix on the particular train he did was this. Every Thursday and Friday a limited which ran west at midnight carried larger shipments of money than on other days—or so he heard while he was assistant freight handler at the station where he worked. This was due to exchanges being made between eastern and western banks, although he did not know that. Having decided on this particular train, although not on this day, he proceeded by degrees. And really weeks before the crime was eventually committed, he secured first a small handbag from which he had scraped all evidence of the maker's name; then later, from other distant places, so as to avoid all chance of detection, six or seven fused sticks of giant powder such as farmers use to blow up stumps; and still later, two revolvers holding six cartridges each, some cartridges, and cord and cloth out of which he proposed to make bundles of the money if necessary. Placing all of these in his bag, he eventually visited a small town nearest the spot which previously, because of its loneliness, he had fixed on in his mind as the ideal place for his crime. And then reconnoitering it and its possibilities, he finally arranged all of his plans to a nicety.

Here, as he now told us, just at the outskirts of this hamlet, which was selected because of its proximity to a still loner woods and marsh, stood a large water tank at which this express as well as nearly all other trains stopped for water. Beyond it, just about five miles, was the woods with a marsh somewhere in its depths, an ideal place to quickly, if temporarily, bury one's gold. The express, as he learned, was regularly due at this tank at about one in the morning. The nearest town beyond the woods was all of five miles—a mere hamlet, like this one. His plan, as he now explained, was to have concealed himself near this tank when the train stopped, and just before it started again, to slip in between the engine tender and the front baggage car, which was "blind" at both ends. Another arrangement, which he carefully executed beforehand, was to take his handbag, minus its revolvers and sticks of giant powder, which were now on his person, and carry it out along the railroad track five miles to a spot near the track exactly opposite that point in the woods where he wished the train to stop. Once he had concealed himself between the engine tender and the baggage car as planned, and the train had resumed its journey, he would keep watch until the headlight of the engine revealed this bag lying alongside the track, when he would rise up, revolver in hand, and, climbing over the coal box, compel the engineer to stop the train. So far, so good.

As it turned out, however, two slight errors—one of forgetfulness and one of eyesight—caused him to finally lose the fruit of his plan. On the night in question, between eight and nine, he arrived on the scene of action and did as planned. The bag was put in place, the train boarded. However, on reaching the spot where he felt sure the bag should be, he could not make it out. Realizing that he was at about the spot where he wished to work, he rose up and, covering the two men in the cab, compelled them to dismount as planned. Then—compelling them to precede him to the rear of the engine, where under duress they uncoupled it—he drove them from behind to opposite the express car door, where he presented them with a fused stick of giant powder and ordered them to blow it open fast. This they did, the messenger within having first refused to open the door. Later they entered the car for him and blew open the safe, throwing out the packages of bills and coin as he commanded. But during this time, realizing the danger of either trainmen or passengers climbing down from the cars at the rear and coming forward, he had fired a few shots backward toward the passenger coaches, calling to purely imaginary burglars to keep watch there. At the same time, to put the fear of death into the minds of both engineer and fireman, as well as those inside the express car, he called to purely imaginary confreres on the other side of the train, pretending that they watched too.

"Don't kill anybody unless you have to, boys," is what he said he said, or, "That's all right, Frank. Stay over there. Watch that side. I'll take care of these two." Then he would fire a few more shots, and so all were deluded.

Once the express car door and the express car safe had been blown open and the money handed out, he had compelled the engineer and fireman to come down, recouple the engine, and pull away. Only after the train had safely disappeared did he venture to gather up the various packages, making a bag for them of his coat since he had lost his grip, and with this over his shoulder he staggered off into the night, eventually succeeding in concealing the bag in the swamp, and then making off for safety himself.

The two errors which finally caused his discovery, and one of which gave him great uneasiness at the time, were first the loss of bag, which, after concealing the money he returned and attempted to find but without any success; and second (and this he did not even know at the time) that in the bag which he had lost he had placed sometime before, and then forgotten apparently, a small handkerchief containing the initials of his love embroidered in one corner. Why he might have wished to carry the latter about with him was understandable enough, but why he came to put it in his bag and then forget it was not clear even to himself. He had merely forgotten that he had placed it there. From the detectives we now learned, in addition, that the next day at noon the bag which he could not find was found by a posse of detectives and citizens just where he had placed it, and that the handkerchief extracted had given them their first clue. With this as a beginning they decided to hunt for the woman, but first the woods were searched, without any success, however, save that footprints were discovered in various places and measured. Again, experts meditating on the crime decided that owing to the hard times and the laying-off and discharging of employes, some of these latter might have had a hand in it. And so, in due time, the whereabouts and particular movements of each and every one of those who had worked for the road were gone into, resulting in the discovery finally that this particular ex-helper had returned rather recently to his semi-native town and had there been going with a certain girl and was even now about to be married to her. Next, it was discovered that her initials corresponded to those on the handkerchief. Presto, Mr. Wilson was arrested, a search of his room made, and nearly all of the money recovered. Then, being caught "with the goods," he confessed, and here on this day was he, being hurried into St. Louis to be jailed and sentenced, while we harpies of the press and the law were now gathered about him to make capital of his error.

The only thing that consoled me, however, as I rode St. Louis-ward and attempted to piece the details of this crime together, was that if I had failed to make it impossible for Galvin to get the story at all, still, when it came to the narration of it, I could unquestionably write a better story—a more connected and continuous narrative. He would have to tell his story to someone else, as I argued, while I should be able to write mine myself, putting in such touches as I chose. Only one additional detail remained to be arranged for, and that was the matter of a picture. Why neither Wandell nor myself, nor the editor of the *Globe,* had thought to include an artist in this expedition was more a fault of the time than anything else, illustrations for news stories being by no means as numerous as they are today and the peripatetic news-paper photographer having not yet been invented. However, neither we nor the *Globe* apparently had thought to attend to this, and here we were, therefore, with this amazingly interesting figure before us and no power of making a picture. As we neared St. Louis, Galvin evidently began to see the import of this very clearly and suddenly began to comment on it—saying he guessed we would have to send to the Four Courts afterward and have one made. Suddenly, however, his eyes filled with a shrewd cunning, and he turned to me and said: "How would it be, old man, if we took him up to the *Globe* office and let the boys make a picture of him—your friends, Wood and McCord? Then both of us could get one right away. I'd say take him to the *Republic,* only the *Globe* is so much nearer" (which was true), "and we have that new flashlight machine, as you know" (which was also true, the *Republic* being very poorly equipped in this respect). He added a friendly aside to the effect that, of course, this depended on whether the prisoner and the officers in charge were willing.

"Not on your life," I replied suspiciously and resentfully—"not to the *Globe* anyhow. If you want to bring him down to the *Republic,* all right. We'll have them make pictures, and you can have one."

"But why not the *Globe*?" he went on. "Wood and McCord are your friends more'n they are mine. Think of the difference in the distance. We want to save time, don't we? Here it is nearly six-thirty, and by the time we get down there and have a picture taken and I get back to the office it'll be half past seven or eight. It's all right for you, I suppose, because you can write faster, but look at me. I'd just as leave go down there as not, but what's the difference? Besides, the *Globe*'s got a much better plant, and you know it. Either Wood or McCord'll make a fine picture, and when we explain to 'em how it is you'll be sure to get one, the same as me, just the same picture. Ain't that all right?"

"No, it's not," I replied truculently, "and I won't do it, that's all. It's all right about Dick and Peter. I know what they'll do for me if the paper'll let 'em, but I know the paper won't let 'em, and besides you're not going to be able to claim in the morning that this man was brought to the *Globe* first. I know you, and if I say that he wasn't, what good'll it do me, huh? Don't begin now to try to put anything over on me, because I won't stand for it, see, and if these people do it anyhow, I'll make a kick to headquarters, that's all."

For a moment he appeared to be quieted by this and to decide to abandon his project, but later he took it up again, seemingly in the most conciliatory spirit in the world. At the same time, and from now on, he kept boring me with his eyes—a thing which I had never known him to do before. He was always too hangdog in looking at me, but now of a sudden there was something bold and friendly as well as tolerant and cynical in his glance. "Aw, come on," he argued. He was amazingly aggressive. "What's the use being small about it? The *Globe*'s nearer. We've got the new flashlight plant up there. Think what a fine picture it'll make. If you don't, then we'll have to go clear to the office and send an artist down to the jail. You can't take any good pictures down there tonight."

"Cut it," I replied, "I won't do it, that's all." But even as he talked, a strange feeling of uncertainty or confusion began to creep over me. For the first time since knowing him, and in spite of all my opposition of this afternoon and before, I found myself not exactly hating this man—but feeling as though he weren't such an utterly bad sort after all. What was so wrong about this *Globe* idea anyhow, I began to suddenly ask myself, even while inwardly or downwardly, or somewhere within me, something was telling me that it was all wrong and that I was making a big mistake. I felt half asleep or surrounded by a cloud of something which made everything he cared to say seem all right. Still, I wasn't asleep and knew I didn't believe a word he said, but—. "To the Globe—sure," I found myself saying to myself in spite of myself in a dumb, half-numb or sensuously warm way. "That wouldn't be so bad. It's nearer. What's wrong with that? Dick or Peter will make a good picture seven or eight inches long, and then I can take it along." Only at the same time I was also thinking to myself—"I shouldn't really do that. He'll claim the credit of having brought this man to the Globe office. I'll be making a big mistake. The Republic or nothing. Let him come down to the Republic."

In the meantime we were entering St. Louis and the station. By then, somehow, he had not only convinced the sheriff and the other officers but the prisoner. They liked him and were willing to do what he said. I could even see the rural love of show and parade gleaming in the sheriff's and the two detectives' eyes. Plainly, the office of the Globe was truly the great place in their estimation for such an exhibition. Was it not the leading paper? At the same time, between looking at me and the prisoner and the officers, he had knitted a fine mental net from which I seemed unable to escape. It was very curious. Even as I arose with these others to leave the train, I said, "No, I won't come in on this. It's all right if you want to bring him down to the Republic, or you can take him to the Four Courts. But I'm not going to let you get away with this. You hear now, don't you?" But then it was too late, or nearly so.

Outside Galvin laid hold of my arm in an amazingly genial fashion and hung on to it. In spite of me, he seemed to be master of the situation and to realize it. Once more he began to plead and, getting in front of me, seemed to do this best to keep my optical attention. From that point on and from that day to this, I have never been able to explain to myself clearly what it was that did happen. All at once, and much more clearly than before, I seemed to see that his plan in regard to the Globe was the best. Why not? It would save a little time. And besides, he kept repeating in almost a singsong way that we would go first to the Globe and then to the Republic. "You come up with me into the Globe, and then I'll go down with you to the Republic," he kept saying. "We'll just let Wood or McCord take one picture, and then we'll all go down to your place—you see?"

Although I didn't see, I went. For the time, actually nothing really seemed important. If he had stayed by me I think he could have prevented my writing any story at all. As it was, he was so eager to achieve this splendid triumph of introducing this celebrated bandit into the editorial rooms of the *Globe* first—and to my old chief, the redoubtable McCullagh—and there having him photographed, that he hailed a carriage. The six of us crowding in it, we were bustled off in a trice to the door of the *Globe*. Once I reached it and saw him and the detectives and the bandit hurrying across the sidewalk, I suddenly awoke to the asininity of it all. "Wait!" I called. "Say, hold on! Cut this! I won't do it! I don't agree to this!" but by now it was too late. In a trice the prisoner and the sheriff and the two detectives and himself were up the two or three low steps of the main entrance and into the hall, and I was left outside to meditate on the insanity of the thing that I had done.

"Great God," I suddenly exclaimed to myself, "what have I let that fellow do to me? I've been hypnotized, that's what it is! Allowed him to take a prisoner whom I had really had in my own hands at one time into the office of our great rival to be photographed—and that first. He's put it all over me on this job, and I had him beaten. I had him where I could have shoved him off the train—and now I let him do this to me. Tomorrow there'll be a long editorial in the *Globe* telling how this fellow was brought first to the *Globe* and photographed—and his picture to prove it. Oh, Lord, what shall I do? How am I to get out of this?" I swore and groaned for blocks as I walked toward the *Republic*, wondering what I should do, but to no purpose.

Distinct as my failure was, it was so easy, even when practically admitting the whole truth, to make it seem as though the police had deliberately worked against the *Republic*, and that in spite of anything I could do. I did not even have to do that but merely recited my protests, without admitting or insisting on hypnotism, which Wandell would not have believed anyhow. On the instant he burst into a great rage against the police department, seeing apparently no fault in anything I had done and vowing vengeance. They were always doing this—these police. They did it to the *Republic* when he was on the *Globe*. Wait, he would get even with them yet—and rushing a photographer to the jail he had various pictures made, all of which appeared with my story, but to no purpose. The *Globe* had us beaten. Although I had slaved over the text, given it the finest turns I could, still, there on the front page of the *Globe* was a large picture of the bandit, seated in the sanctum sanctorum of the great G-D, a portion of the figure, although not the head, of its great chief standing in the background. Over it all, in extra-large type, was the caption

"Lone Train Robber Visits Office of *Globe* to Pay His Respects" and underneath in italics a full account of how he had willingly and gladly come there.

Was I beaten?

Well, rather.

And did I feel it?

I suffered tortures, not only for days—for weeks and months. Absolute tortures. Whenever I thought of Galvin I wanted to kill him. To think, I always said to myself, that I had thought of the two trains and then run across the meadow and paid the agent for stopping the train, which finally permitted Galvin to see the burglar at all, and then to be "done" in this way. And what was worse, he was so gaily and cynically conscious of having "done" me. Meeting me on the street one day, his lip curled with the old undying hatred and contempt, he exclaimed, "These swell reporters! These high-priced ink-slingers. Say, who got the best of the train robber story, eh?"

And I replied—

But never mind what I replied. It wasn't fit to print anyhow, and no publisher would have printed it.

And as for Galvin, he wouldn't fight me, or anything of that sort. He wasn't that kind. But he could smile leeringly, and that under the circumstances was as good a drubbing as anyone would care to receive at any time.

CHAPTER LI

Things like these taught me not to depend too utterly on my own skill. I might propose and believe, but there were things above my own planning or powers. Apparently creatures I might choose to despise were not so helpless after all. It fixed my thoughts permanently on the weakness of the human mind as a directing organ. You might think and think till doomsday in terms of human ideas, but apparently over and above ideas there were forces which superseded or controlled them. That was one thing that was driven home to me, and it was important. My own fine, contemptuous ideas might be superseded or set at naught by the raw animal or psychic force of a man like Galvin. Wasn't that an amazing thing? It was to me, certainly.

During the next few months a number of other things happened which seemed to broaden my horizon considerably. For one thing, my trip to Chicago having revived knowledge of me in the minds of a number of newspaper men there and having seemingly convinced them of my success here, I was bombarded with letters from one and another wanting knowledge of positions and my aid in obtaining the same. At the close of the Fair in October hard times were expected in newspaper circles, so many men being released from work in that field. I had letters from at least four, one of whom was a hanger-on by the name of Hutchinson, who had attached himself to me largely because I was the stronger and he expected aid of me. I have often meditated since on how frequently in my life exactly this has happened—one of my typical experiences, as it is of everyone, I presume, who begins to get along. And again, it is so much easier for the strong to tolerate the weak than the strong. Strength, I have always been sorry to note, craves sycophancy. We want only those who will swing the censer and fan the little flame of our ambitions and desires. This individual, Hutchinson, or "Hutch" as I always called him, was one such. He was really a poor hack who had been connected with a commercial agency where daily written reports had to be written out as to the financial and social condition of John Smith, the butcher, or George Jones, the baker. This led this individual, who was a farm boy to begin with, to imagine that he could write and that he would like to run a country paper, only he thought he might succeed in the city first, or get experience. By some process of which I forget the steps, he fixed on me—even while I was on the *Globe*—and through me and McEnnis, who was then so friendly to me, secured a tryout. Apparently, after I left McEnnis quickly tired of him, and later I heard from him as working for the City Press, an organization which served all newspapers—and paid next to nothing. Then I heard that he was married (having succeeded so well), and still later he began to bombard me with pleas for aid in connection with a place in St. Louis. Also there were letters from much better men: H. L. Dunlap, who subsequently became the chief press adviser of President Taft; an excellent reporter by the name of Brady, whom I have previously mentioned; and a little later and via Dunlap, a letter or word from John Maxwell, with which I will deal later.

At the same time, and in spite of my great failure in connection with Galvin, my standing with Wandell seemed to rise, rather than sink. Believe it or no, I became more or less of a privileged character about this institution or its city room, a singular thing in the newspaper profession at least. Because of specials I was constantly writing for the Sunday paper, I was taken up by the sporting editor, who wanted my occasional help in his work; the dramatic editor, who asked for my help on his dramatic page, asking me to see various plays from time to time; and the managing editor himself, a small, polite, soft-spoken, red-headed person from Kansas City, who began to invite me to lunch or dinner and talk to me as though I knew much—or ought to—about the world he represented. I was so unfitted for all this, intellectually and otherwise, my hour of stability and feeling for organization and control having not yet arrived, that I scarcely knew how to take it. I was nervous, shy, retiring, poorly spoken and inexpressive verbally, at least in their presence, while at the same time, inwardly, I was blazing with ambition, vanity and self-confidence. I really wanted nothing so much as to be alone with my own desires and labors, while at the same time I believed that I did not—and that I was lonely and neglected!

In regard to Wandell, I began to see him as but a minor figure in this journalistic world—or only one of many, likely to be here today and gone tomorrow—and I swaggered about taking liberties which I never would have dreamed of taking four months before. I think he talked to me too freely and showed me that he relied on my advice and judgement and admired my work. All of the out-of-town assignments of any importance were given to me; and besides, he himself began to say—at seven, for instance—that if I'd wait a minute he'd buy me a drink, a not very wise thing in connection with me, it seems, at the time. Later, because I would stroll out of the office at, say, eight-thirty or nine p.m. after completing one big assignment or another, he wrote me several monitory letters, couched in the most diplomatic language, but insisting that I abide by the rules which governed other reporters. If you will believe it, by now I had grown so in my own estimation that I smiled happily, knowing very well that he would not fire me. His writing me this way instead of dropping me forthwith was such a testimony.

In addition I would reform for a time. Only occasionally I could plead that the managing editor or the dramatic editor had asked me to do thus and so. "To hell with the managing editor!" he one day exclaimed in a rage. "This is my department. If he wants you to sit around with him, let him come to me, or you first see that you have my consent."

At the same time, as I say, he was most friendly himself, would sit and chat over proposed stories and how to do them, and as one man after another left him, or he needed to enlarge his staff, would confidentially inquire of me if I knew anyone who would make a good addition. Having these appeals from Dunlap, Brady and several others here in St. Louis, I named first Dunlap, because I felt so sure of his merit, and then these others whom I believed would give him good service. To my surprise he asked me to first write Dunlap to come to work, and then, Dunlap having "made good," he asked me to invite the others to come and see him. By degrees, five men who had appealed to me as excellent, both in Chicago and here, were transferred to the staff of the *Republic,* and that with full knowledge of the fact that I was the one to whom they owed their opportunity. You may imagine the air with which I took myself.

At the same time still another thing occurred which raised me in my own estimation almost more than anything which had happened so far in my career. Strolling into the Southern Hotel one evening, just after the listing of assignments for the night, I chanced to note my old chief, Joseph B. McCullagh, sitting near one of the pillars of this beautifully decorated lobby reading his evening paper. It had always been such a pleasing and homelike thing in my days on the *Globe* to be able to walk into this lobby around dinner time and see this great chief in his low shoes and white socks sitting and reading here as though he were in his own home. It took away a bit of the original loneliness of the city for me. And now, for the first time since I had so ignominiously retired from the *Globe,* I saw him as before, smoking and reading. I had hitherto carefully avoided this and every other place at such hours as I was likely to encounter him. But now I had grown so in my own estimation and away from the feeling of being a complete failure that I was now not quite so much afraid of him. He was still wonderful, but I was beginning to feel that I had a future of my own and that I could achieve it, regardless of the error that had so pained me then—and by another route, perhaps. Nearing the newsstand, which was not far from where he was sitting, and hoping that he would not see me (as I would then have to bow and endure his gaze), I suddenly saw him get up and come forward, apparently to secure a cigar or another paper. Nearing me he saw me, and in spite of all my bravado, I flushed guiltily.

"Good evening, Mr. McCullagh," I said politely.

"How de do," he returned gutturally but with such an air of sociability as I had never noticed in him before, certainly not in regard to myself at least. "How are you? You are still about, I see. You are on the *Republic*, I believe."

"Yes, sir."

I was immensely charmed and flattered to think that he should trouble to know where I was.

"You like it over there?"

"Yes, sir. Fairly well, sir."

I was as humble in his presence as a jackie in the presence of an officer. I could not help it. He seemed always so forceful and commanding.

He paused a moment then, as if meditating just what to say.

"That little matter of those theatres," he said after a moment, turning and walking back to his chair where I followed him. "Um! Um! I don't think you understood quite how I felt about that. I was sorry to see you go. Um! Um!" (and he cleared his throat gutturally). "It was an unfortunate mistake all around. I wanted you to know that I really did not blame you so much. Um! You might have been relieved of other work. I do not want to take you away from any other paper, but—um!—if you ever find yourself free and you want to come back, I want you to know that you can. Um! There is no prejudice in my mind against you." He had a way of coughing or clearing his throat between sentences which was highly individual, in the least.

I don't know when anything moved me so much. It was wonderful—positively thrilling to have him say this to me. I was so happy and touched that I could scarcely speak, and I would not have known what to say if I had. I stood there, finally blurting out, "I am very sorry, Mr. McCullagh, I did not mean to do what I did. It was a mistake. I had that extra assignment and—"

"O-oh, that's all right, that's all right," he insisted gruffly and as if he wished to be done with it once and for all. "No harm done. I didn't mind that so much. But you needn't have left. That's what I want you to understand. You could have stayed if you had wanted to."

As I viewed it afterwards, my best opportunity for secure position in St. Louis was there and then. If I had only known it, or knowing, had been at all quick to take advantage of it, I might have profited considerably by this, I suppose. My ex-editor's mood was plainly warm toward me. He probably looked on me as a foolish and excitable but fairly capable boy whom it would have been his pleasure to assist in the world. He had brought me from Chicago. Perhaps he wished me to remain under his eye. At any rate, a word and I could have returned, I am sure of it, never to have left the paper save for excellent reasons. As it was, I was so nervous and excited I took no particular advantage of it—none at all, as I see it now.

I flushed again, unable to think what else to say. I would have liked to have gone back, I think, but I was so nervous and embarrassed in this great man's presence that I could scarcely think. Possibly he noticed it and was pleased. At any rate, as I mumbled my thanks and how grateful I was for all he had done for me, and said that if I were doing things over I would try and do differently, and then turned to walk away, he interrupted me with:

"Just a moment. It may be that you have some young friend whom you want to help to a position here in St. Louis. If so, send him to me. I'll do anything I can for him. I'm always glad to do anything I can for serious young men."

I bowed and smiled and flushed and said, "Thank you," but for the life of me I could not think of anything more. It seemed so strange—so tremendous, if you will—that this man should want to do anything for me after all the ridiculous things I had done under him, that all I could do was to hurry away, out of his sight. Once in the shielding dark outside I felt better but sad. It seemed as if I had made a mistake, as if I should have asked him to take me back, but I hadn't.

"Why, he as much as offered to take me back," I said to myself. "I can go back there if I want to any time. Or he'll give me a place for someone else. Think of it. Then he must think much better of me than I thought he did. He doesn't consider me the fool that I thought he did. Oh, this is wonderful, splendid!"

For days thereafter I went about my work trying to decide whether I should resign from the *Republic* and return to him and ask for a place, only I seemed now so much better placed that it hardly seemed wise. I had no real excuse for leaving the *Republic* and going back to the *Globe*, and as always in other moments of crisis or uncertainty, there was this feeling that I should be moving on elsewhere. I should work on and eventually leave for some other city. McEnnis had cautioned me to do so, and somehow his words had become as tablets of the law. For days I debated and did nothing, until still another newspaper man wrote me from Chicago and asked for a place—a friend of Dunlap's, by the way. I eventually gave him a letter, and he was put to work on the *Globe-Democrat*. So my reputation for influence in connection with local newspaper affairs became suddenly very large—out of all proportion to my true power or import in either office.

And in the meantime still other things had been happening to me which seemed to complicate my life here considerably and make me almost a fixture in so far as St. Louis was concerned. For one thing, worrying over the well-being of my two brothers, Ed and Al, who were still in Chicago, and wishing to do something which might possibly improve their condition, it occurred to me—why, I don't know, I am sure—that St. Louis would be as good a place as any for them to try their hand. They had seemed unhappy in Chicago, or so I imagined, and I had gotten along here. As I then saw it, my station, in spite of my salary, was considerable. At any rate, I had a comfortable floor with ample room, in case I chose to invite them as guests, to entertain them comfortably, and meanwhile my advice or my enthusiasm might inspire them to do better. In addition there was in me, and has remained (in a fading form, I am sorry to say), a sort of home-longing—the German *Heimweh,* no doubt—which made me look back on everything in connection with our troubled lives with a sadness, an ache to remedy or repair, if I might, some of the ills and pains which all of us, like all the rest of the creatures of this erroneous and haphazard world, had endured. We had not been happy together all of the time—what family ever has been? But what of it? I thought. We had quarreled and even fought over trivial things—Ed, Al and myself among others. But quarreling and fighting betimes, as we had, was nothing—and there had been happy hours also. How many! With just these two brothers of mine, if no more—laughing, singing, walking the streets together looking for work, wishing, wishing, planning, dreaming in childish or youthful ways. And now we were separated. And they were not doing as well as I was.

I say it in faint extenuation of all the many hard, unkind things I have done in my time, that at the thought of the possible misery some of my brothers and sisters might be enduring at one time or another—the lacks from which they might be hopelessly suffering—my throat ·has swelled and my heart hurt. What, Ed wishing something dreadfully and not being able to afford it—shoes or clothes or a good meal, for instance—or Al, the same! Truly it hurt me, far more than any lack of my own ever could. It never occurred to me that they might possibly be wishing to extend me aid or, if they were, that they should. It was always I, hard up or otherwise, wishing that I might do something for them. And this longing in the face of no particular complaint on their part and no means on mine to translate it into anything much better than wishes and dreams.

But, however that may be, my present idea was that if I should bring them here and afford them out of my own purse, as it were, a little leisure to look about, they would better themselves, of course, and then—well, and then I would not need to worry about them so much. They might even thus, through me, get on the main road to better days. Thinking so, and with no plans beyond this, I first wrote Ed and then Al; and the former, being younger and more restless, I suppose, and always more attached to me than any of the others, soon replied in the affirmative and came, whereas Al, more conscious of the import of a bird in the hand, I presume, required a little more time to think. At any rate, in the course of time the two of them, by what processes I can now scarcely recall, appeared and were installed in that front room, for which I now paid my landlady an additional five dollars. We now kept a kind of bachelor's hall, gay enough while it lasted, but more or less clouded over all the while by the necessity the two of them had to look for work and their non-success in finding any.

How did I expect to support them on twenty-one dollars a week? I don't know. I don't suppose I did, really. But their presence, for the time being, satisfied an emotional or psychic longing in me to have them near me, and beyond that I did not think. Before they came and after, I painted the city of St. Louis—its large size and opportunities—in glowing colors, I suppose, and once they were there, like a leader of a small flock, put myself to the task of showing them its charms. We went to as many places as we could together—restaurants, parks, outlying places. As long as it was new and they felt that there was some hope of getting something to do, they were gay and interested, and we had some delightful hours together, visiting the parks and curious summer gardens where beer and music were to be had à la Berlin, and the theatres too. But as time wore on and fading summer days proved that their dreams and mine were hopeless and that in all likelihood they could do no better—if as well as—here than in Chicago, their moods changed, as did mine. The burden of expense, particularly on me, as you may well imagine, was considerable. While paying gaily enough for food and rent and even washing for the three, I began to wonder whether I should be able to endure the strain much longer. Love them as I might in their absence, and happy as I was with them, still it was not possible to keep up this pace. I was depriving myself of bare necessities, and they saw it, I suppose. I said nothing myself—of that I am positive—but after a month or six weeks of trial and failure, they themselves began to see the point and to be unhappy over it. Our morning and evening hours—whenever I could see them in the evening, which was not often—became less and less gay. Finally Al, with his usual eye for the practical and the sensible, announced one evening that for his part he was tired of searching here and was about to return to Chicago. He did not like St. Louis anyhow. It was a "hell of a place"—much worse than Chicago—a third-rate city. He was going back where he could get something, and Ed, recalling past joys of which perhaps I had no knowledge, said he was going too. I cannot recall now how things were eventually arranged, but I know that they left and that once more I was alone. In the meantime we had visited one or two country places—lakes, for instance—to fish, had seen various outlying portions of St. Louis and planned all sorts of re-encounters in the future under better circumstances. But to no particular purpose. I saw Al but once after that and then under most unsatisfactory circumstances. As for Ed, I later persuaded him to join me in New York, where I kept him by me until he grew practically self-supporting. But as for these six weeks: They taught me how foolish sentimental dreams are without some underlying practical scheme of self-support.

CHAPTER LII

During this same period it was that I took to calling upon at least two of the girls whom I had met in Chicago (entirely aside from Miss White) and whose homes were here in St. Louis. My affair with Mrs. X, which was in about the same state when I returned as when I left it, or so I thought, soon, and during the stay of my brothers, underwent a great change. I don't know whether it was due to the fact that, having previously had me all to herself, she now resented this introduction of an alien atmosphere or that my brother Al took an almost instant and abiding dislike to her (dubbing her, according to some amazing patois which he had picked up in that brash underworld with which he was familiar, a "tart" and a "blister"—words which I had not previously heard and which disgusted me greatly—words which meant, at their mildest, a nonconformist in the matter of sex). But just the same a coolness sprang up between us which I have always blamed more or less on Al. He was just at that intermediate stage in his mental development where you could say of him that he was neither fish, flesh nor good red herring—a youth who had got wind of the classics and the boundless seas of intellectuality and yet who was by no means free of the endless scaffolding of uncertainty and illusion which characterizes, or has to date, all our American intellectual adventures. Small, wiry, irritable, with some nervous complaint due to earlier sexual indiscretions, he was all for freedom of the mind and a higher intellectual life, only, not having got very far, he was pausing to snap and bark at every social failure en route. He did not realize that intellectuality like wealth and power is always personal, not general. Perhaps because she did not take to him, Mrs. X was a horrible creature—a vile, low temptress, et cetera. He seemed to conclude, from what evidence I knew not, that she was first and foremost one of these creatures named, and whom he disliked, of course, or said he did; second, that being intimate with me (which I stoutly denied, deeming it my duty), she was not faithful to me, being especially free with all the male roomers, which he took as sufficient evidence of her infidelity; and third, that she was too "cocky" and self-assured, presuming, as he thought, on her obvious ability to make her own way in the world—a thing which many males cannot possibly endure. But I liked him just the same, and was exceedingly sad over him at times because I was beginning to realize that in all the matters of individual development we fare alone. No one really accompanies us all the way if we are going far, or even for a lengthy part, save some chance wayfarer on the same road with whom we may for a time keep company. Branch roads are forever coming into view and luring this one and the other. Our own pace slackens or speeds, or we ourselves choose a bypath, imagining it the ultimate highway. So be it. But is there one?

"Say," he observed to me one day in one of his most sarcastic tones, "do you think a tart like that can be faithful to anyone? You're crazy. She's in with four or five of these gazabos around here right now."

"Well, what do I care?" I demanded, irritated by the thought but also irritated by what I deemed his officiousness, I never having confessed that I was intimate with her. "It doesn't make any difference to me. Supposing she is intimate with them? What of it?"

"Well, a lot. Don't you think I'm on? Don't be a mark. All this 'honey' and 'dearie' stuff" (terms she occasionally used to me in the presence of both Al and Ed—much to my confusion at times). "Don't you think I can see? And at the same time she's around all the time when you're not here, dearie-ing up these other nuts." (This last charge first lit the flame of jealousy.) "I see her, and that's why she don't like me. Look out she don't hand you a disease."

"Oh, the devil," I replied irritably, slightly sickened by his rough words. "Don't be so rough. What's the use talking like that? I tell you I'm not in with her. Let me alone."

"Oh, all right," he replied. "Don't get sore. I'm just telling you for your own good. You ought to know it if you don't. I'm your brother, you know."

"Yes, I know," I replied, "but what's the use picking on her? She's not so bad." He merely smiled tolerantly.

The result of this was that in spite of myself I became suspicious and less sure of my charm or my import to her. This had held me up quite a little at certain times in my own estimation. What a blow it is, indeed, always, to realize that you are not quite as important as you think you are, and yet how swiftly and weed-like this belief grows in the poorest of soils.

In spite of myself I began to think and watch. And now, in

addition, there was another thing on which I had not quite counted when I invited them down, and that was that I would not be able to see her quite so much alone in my room, a thing which must have irritated her. Previous to this I was all alone and she came and went as she chose. Now they were always here, day or night, or nearly so. Our rooms were one. In addition, the younger girls I had met at Chicago having diverted my mind, and she never having represented the ideal of youth and innocence or, rather, inexperience which I desired, my thoughts were for straying elsewhere. I was never really enthusiastic about her, and so, these various things combining—. Once or twice now when I returned late—not having been able to see her during the day—and tapped at her door downstairs, as had been my custom before leaving, she did not choose to let me in, or, rather, pretended that she was asleep, a fact that I was too sensitive to comment on. A little later, however, Al and Ed having returned to Chicago, I expected the status quo ante to be restored. I chanced to return home late one warm September evening, when, pausing outside the street door where a low iron fence separated a very small space of grass from the windows of her room, and speculating as to whether I should tap at her door again or not, I thought I heard voices—hers and a man's—and in this room. This shocked me no little at this hour, and with no light, it was significant, to say the least. One of the voices was assuredly hers, as I now made out—she had a gay, penetrating, shrilly giggle—while the other was that of a man (a young man like myself, I instantly imagined), one of her other roomers, no doubt. I listened intently—all alive to the desperate import of it. What! With another man, and unfaithful to me, as Al had said. The lack of worth or charm in myself which this implied was most painful. It dropped me to the lowest depths. And there was no mistaking the import of what was going on. It was all too plain, I am sorry to report—the smothered laughter, the giggles, the whispering.

"Well, this is a hell of a note," I thought to myself angrily. "This is certainly a fine way to treat me—and pretending all the while to be so fond of me. What does she think I am—a sucker? Well, I guess not. What does she take me for, anyhow?" And forthwith I laid plans to leave the place at once—to quit her life forever. Somehow she had got the best of me and made it unimportant whether I staid or left, save to my own peace of mind.

But, oh, how infuriated I was really, and how pulled down in my own esteem and made sad and unhappy. And in this state of mingled rage and depression I ambled off up the street, meditating on how lightly my charms were held, and how unimportant I was to her and so probably to all women, and how cruel life was. I had placed my faith in her and she had broken it! No thought, you see, of my own faith. And so—. It was the first good kick my growing bump of self-confidence in the direction of women and sex had received, and it left me considerably reduced and gloomy. Indeed, I actually felt sad for some time—the perfidy of women! After a while, however, my natural bump of hopefulness and self-esteem was restored, and I began to see things in a better light. After all, she was but one woman, and there were many. Had I not two or three interested in me at this very time, and was it fair to complain if one turned away from me? And, besides, had it not been plain from the first that she had not cared for me very much or I for her? I had not been faithful in any way, nor did I expect to be. Why should she be? Still, in spite of all this, I now disliked her intensely, for she had injured my vanity—made a fool of me to my teeth. That was the great crime.

As soon thereafter as possible—the next day, I think—I secured a most uninteresting room over in Morgan Avenue, and having packed up my things in my one trunk and a box or two, I suddenly announced that I was leaving, and left her to think what she would. My manner must have told her something, for she did not even trouble to ask why, but looking me over in her pert way, said "Very well." I made no comment on that but paid my bill, and the expressman calling while I was there, my trunk and box, or boxes, were bundled out, and that was the end of that.

But, oh, the charm of it during those June or July days when I was working on the ball game, and when she was my keenest diversion during hours of seemingly profound luxury.

The other interests which I had been attempting to establish at this time were no more successful—if as much so. Miss Ginity, as time proved, was much, much too Catholic for me—in the sectarian or religious sense, I mean. Seeking her out a week or two after my return, I found her in a typically Irish-Catholic neighborhood in the north end of St. Louis, full of small cottages and open lots and ambling goats, and somehow redolent of a workaday world. To my dissatisfaction, in spite of all her personal charm, which I had felt so keenly in Chicago, here she seemed narrow and much too poorly placed. Gone, you see, were the blue lake and the blue skies of Chicago and the white fairy buildings of the Fair and that atmosphere of romance and hope which surrounded us all like a spell. In commonplace St. Louis, always less artistic to me for some reason than Chicago—less imaginative and dreamful—and because, perhaps, of this poor or rather tasteless neighborhood, she seemed much less interesting. Perhaps it was not that so much either, for certainly the neighborhood in which Lois had once dwelt had not been so very much better, but the atmosphere of Catholicism, or, as I felt it to be, religious bigotry, which seemed to surround her here, was too much for me. I could not stand the thought of it. Ever since leaving my home and the church, and even before, the barest suggestion of anyone's accepting the Romanistic belief, let alone of adhering to all of its forms and dogmas, was enough to evoke in me a sense of chains and slavery. "Kind heaven!" I exclaimed to myself on meeting her parents—stout, workaday peasant types both—"can these be her parents?" And then seeing Catholic pictures on the wall—a blue Virgin with an exposed red heart pierced by a dagger, and a Christ in the same condition, to say nothing of an image of St. Joseph and a crucifix—I was ready to leap from my chair in horror. "What? Take up with another Irish-Catholic maid, after I had hitherto fled all that I had known?" Why, hitherto I had not even been able to think of a Catholic priest or nun or any of the Catholic formalities even, without thinking of the dullness and effrontery of it all—so emancipated was I. And now to return to it. Never. Our own home had been too much driven and harried by it—and to what end? A horrible revolting satiety in me, for one. To think, as I well enough knew, that the church (its dogmas) could slip in between a man and his girl, a husband and his wife, fathers and children, and drive them into bickering and disquiet, or dictate the exact rules of their lives. Never! Be happy with anyone who deemed it a sin not to go to church on Sunday or to confession and communion at least once a month—and that, even though the pleasures of sex were involved and waiting. Never. And besides, now that I saw her here, involved in her own environment, I was not so sure whether the latter would be as easy of accomplishment as I had imagined. Anyhow, the religious part was offensive to me. Without giving her affection much of a test as to whether it would carry her outside the rules of her faith, I began to think I had best drop the whole matter—and with this end in view began at once to make derogatory or at least questionable remarks in regard to the religion she professed.

I recall one very disillusioning conversation I had with her, walking out to a park somewhere the second or third week I was back. By then she had returned to the city and was probably brushing up on her fall school work, for this conversation, as I recall it, seemed to start with some reference to that. But soon it was off into the realms of what should or should not be taught in the schools—religious dogma, for instance—and whether any religion, and most particularly the Catholic, ever got the facts of history or science straight. I contended not, of course. To my disgust and dissatisfaction I found her adamant, apparently—an uncompromising dogmatist.

"You don't really mean to say you believe all that stuff, do you?" I demanded, thinking no doubt of the dreamy acolyte of Venus and romance—Lois—and all the other pleasant pagan girls I had known.

"I certainly do," she replied, "and I think you ought to be ashamed of yourself to talk like that. It's just as good as any other religion, and I think I have a right to believe as I choose."

"Oh, Lord," I said or thought, and then and there a distinct coolness arose, more I really think on my side than on hers, for on this subject I was distinctly intolerant. We did not exactly fight, but I said to myself, "What's the use?" And my time being limited anyhow, and these formal evening calls stolen from other work and at considerable risk to myself or my position, I was not so anxious to follow her up and argue. It was so easy to prove to myself that her physical beauty was not so great after all, or at least that I could do without her. I think I called as much as twice thereafter, because somehow, in spite of our argument, I felt the pull of affection there. But the old subject being in the air, if not mentioned, I soon gave it up and saw her no more. The intense pleasures I had promised myself with her had vanished into thin air.

CHAPTER LIII

There was another girl, never mentioned before, I believe, in this narrative, who also faded in this same way—one of the Chicago party to whom I paid some attention there, with the hope, of course, of interesting her in me. She was not quite as attractive physically as either Miss Ginity or Miss White, although she proved far more agreeable and less squeamish as to her religion, which was also Catholic. She lived somewhere in this same vicinity, as I found when I returned, and was a warm friend apparently of Miss Ginity, although not close enough to prevent her from taking the latter's "beau" away (as she well enough understood me to be) in case I desired to come. When I first made friends with her in Chicago in between my other interests, she too, like Miss Ginity, had charged me with being the property of another—only in this case it was Miss Ginity who was my keeper, whereas Miss Ginity had charged me with being Miss White's—which charge, like the other, I denied, as becomes a romanticist and a life-lover. I was not doing her any real injury, I think, since her chief ambition appeared to be to prove a love victor over the others.

Once here in St. Louis, and more or less dissatisfied with Miss Ginity, I looked her up, only to find that she was not quite as compelling to me as the other. I liked her, and she had looks, only the fact that I had proved unsatisfactory to Miss Ginity, or she to me, made this other a second choice, as it were. I liked her, as I found, but not enough to grow enthusiastic over her, and after calling four or five times, taking her to Forest Park, and getting so far as to embrace her and tell her that I really liked her, I decided that I didn't—or not enough—and merely neglected to call. I never heard from her. She did not trouble to follow me up in the matter, but afterward I felt a little puzzled about myself and my interest in women. What was this that made me so squeamish about them, or easily dissatisfied when, on the other hand, I was so eager to find some one—or many, as you will—who could satisfy my sex admiration and passion? I might be blazing with an unsatisfied sex interest all the time, but when it came to fulfillment in any but a, to me, ideal way, it wasn't just that either. Plainly, many things had to enter into it, as I now saw. I was decidedly finicky, as time was to prove. I was always demanding, as I considerably later began to realize, a daring and a wisdom as well as a passion which the ordinary woman did not have at all. And as soon as I found this lacking or difficult to come at (the obstacles many), I was inclined to desist, for plainly I was not as interested in a mild flirtation or just a conventional love affair as I thought I was. These two girls were interesting enough. I'm sure they both found many men subsequently, or could have, who were intensely interested in them, and to whom no doubt they responded with more passion and seeming freedom. But as for me—

The third of my Chicago affairs, however, proved dramatic and forceful enough. Once I had returned, and because I knew Miss White lived some distance from the city and would remain there until her school season opened, I neglected to write to her at first, postponing my attentions until these other affairs had been adjusted, or, rather, until they had proved abortive, and until such time as she should be nearer. But, once I had followed these blind leads to their futile conclusion, I returned in thought and somehow with redoubled interest to her; and thinking of her seeming simplicity and charm, I one day sat down and indited a brief epistle to her which recalled our days in Chicago, wondering, in words, how long it would be before she would be returning to my vicinity. I was rather nervous now lest she should not answer, and busied myself building her up as a paragon.

In due time, however, but after I was beginning to think that I had mortally offended her in not writing, a note came. While it merely thanked me for writing and stated how very pleasant her memories of Chicago were, it still made clear that she expected to be at Florissant, about twenty or twenty-five miles out of St. Louis, by September fifteenth, when her school work would begin; and while she could not see me there, conditions not permitting, she would be glad to see me in St. Louis shortly thereafter in case she visited an aunt who lived there. There was something so seemingly simple, direct and yet artful about the letter that it touched me deeply. It was so brief, direct and with such a nice choice of words. Her handwriting was clear and clean, the paper good and faintly scented. As I have said, I really knew nothing of the conditions which surrounded her, and yet from the time I received this letter, as before in Chicago, I sensed something which appealed to me—a rurality and simplicity plus a certain artful daintiness (flying hair and lifted knee)—the power, I suppose, to pose under my glance and yet evade, which held me as in a vise. There was something about her physical make-up, a delicacy plus a sensuality, represented in part to me by her high color, plus a lymphatic paleness at times. And the immense quantity of red hair which she possessed and which I had seen and admired, falling almost to her knees at the beach at St. Joseph, placed me quite beside myself at times when I thought of her. Such innocence! I thought. Such innate worth, such sweetness, not at all like the others, who somehow by contrast seemed harder, bolder, of coarser fibre.

It does not matter now, but as I look back on it, there appears to have been more of pure, exalted or frenetic romance in this mating experience at first (and even for a year or so afterwards) than in any of which I have any recollection, with the possible exception of that with Lois. For the life of me, for a little while anyhow, I could not even connect her with physical passion, although it was plainly present, but saw in her something above that, as I imagined! She was too good! too pure! Unlike most of my other affairs, this, in the beginning at least, seemed more a matter of pure romance or poetry—a desire to see and be near her under circumstances more or less devoid of the sex atmosphere. I thought only of walking with her in the woods, of riding with her along some leafy country lane, of rowing in a little boat on some stream, of sitting with her under trees in a hammock, of watching her play tennis somewhere on pleasant days, which she had said she did, of being with her where were grass, flowers and a blue sky overhead and some lovely landscape in the distance. Quite without reason I persistently placed her in a social station far above that which she was then able to occupy. Always, when I would think of her at first, thoughts like these would flash up—thoughts so simple that they surprised and delighted me. This was the perfect love, I began to think. Here was your truly sweet, pure girl who inspired a man with a nobler passion than mere lust. I began to picture myself with her in a home somewhere, possibly here in St. Louis, of going with her to church even— and regularly, for I fancied she was of a strict religious bent—of pushing a baby carriage, and, indeed, leading a thoroughly domesticated life, and being happy in it! Even when I thought of her as being with me here in St. Louis at some future time, it was seldom connected with anything more than going to a theatre or a restaurant, buying her flowers and candy, accompanying her possibly on a shopping tour, and the like. The utmost to which my fancy strayed in connection with her was a kiss or the winning of an affectionate smile.

This much came of these first notes. Later we fell into a desultory correspondence which swiftly took on a regular form and resulted after a time in a most extended correspondence on my part, letters so lengthy from me that they surprised even myself. Without quite realizing it, I suddenly found myself in the grip of a letter-writing fever such as had hitherto never possessed me. As a matter of fact, I never would have imagined that I could have written such letters as I now found myself pouring forth without difficulty—long, personal, intimate accounts of my own affairs, my work, dreams, what not, and, in addition, of what I thought of her, of the beauty of life as it appealed to me at Chicago and elsewhere—my theories and imaginings in regard to everything. As I see it now, this was perhaps my first and easiest attempt at literary expression, the form being negligible and yet sufficient to encompass and embody without much difficulty all the surging and seething emotions and ideas which had hitherto been locked up in me, bubbling and steaming to the explosion point. Indeed, the newspaper forms to which I was daily compelled to confine myself offered no outlet; and in addition, in Miss White I had found a seemingly sympathetic and understanding soul, one which required and inspired all of the best that was in me. In the most asinine spirit, also, I now told myself that I had seen so much more than she, most likely—and knew so much more—that there must be many phases of life with which I was now familiar which must forever remain a sealed book to her! I was, as I now told myself, on the verge of something wonderful, a new life, no less. I must work, save, advance myself and better my condition generally so as to be worthy of her. At the very same time, if you please, I was still able to see beauty in other women and the cloying delights of those who would never be able to be as good as she! They might be good enough for me, forsooth, but far beneath her whose eyes were "too pure to behold evil." By what legerdemain of so-called "mind" and emotion do such folderol absurdities come about, anyhow?

In the meantime—and I think this was about October first or the latter days of September—she put in her first appearance in St. Louis and gave me my first delighted sight of her since we had left Chicago. I think by now I was absolutely at the topmost toss of my adventures in St. Louis. I was, as I now assumed, to myself at least, somebody—as little as that was. By now also, in so far as my room was concerned, I had made one more move—this time to the very heart of the city, having tired of my desultory meanderings farther out—and was leading a bachelor existence under, as I thought, much more truly metropolitan circumstances. This new room was on Broadway near the Southern Hotel and the Olympic Theatre, two institutions which at that time constituted almost the sole art and pleasure centre of St. Louis—

certainly the midnight supper centre, if St. Louis could be said to have had one. One block south were the Southern Hotel, Faust's Restaurant and the Olympic Theatre, three of the principal metropolitan features of the city. In the block the other way was the courthouse and Dick's old room, which by now, I might remark in passing, he had abandoned, having, in spite of all his fine dreams as to a resplendent heiress, married that girl whom he and I had met in the church some months before—a circus rider. Thereafter he had removed to a highly prosaic flat on the south side, an institution which seemed to me but a crude and rather pathetic attempt at worthless domesticity—far less interesting than his hitherto bachelor solitude on Broadway. But let that go.

My own room, which was in the rear of the building I occupied, and on the third floor, looked out over some nondescript music hall, whose glass roof was just below me, and from whence nightly and frequently in the afternoons, especially on Sunday, issued all sorts of garish music hall clatter, including music and singing and voices in mono- or dialogue until far into the night. Here, therefore, because my place was now more of a centre than that of either Dick or Peter, I had managed to set up a kind of garret salon which was patronized by these two, as well as Rodenberger, Hazard, Dunlap, Brady, and a number of those newer acquaintances whom I had recently made, too numerous to mention here. Indeed, no sooner was I settled here than that hanger-on Hutchinson, whom I had caused to be transferred from Chicago and to the staff of the *Republic*, took a room here, as well as a third person of whom you may be surprised to hear—John Maxwell, no less. Because of untoward conditions in Chicago, he had come to better his fortunes in St. Louis as best he might, and with my aid, if you please! But more of that later.

In spite of my various labors and attempts at helping others, it was this latest affair, however, which was now engrossing me completely. So seriously had I taken this new adventure to heart, and such a keen interest had I developed by now, that I was scarcely able to eat or sleep. Once I knew definitely that she was inclined to like me, as her letters proved, and the exact day of her arrival had been fixed, I walked on air. Since I had been on the *Republic*, I had not been able to save so much money—about a hundred dollars all told I think, or one hundred and fifty—but of this I took twenty or twenty-five and indulged in a new fall suit of a most pronounced if not exactly startling pattern, the coat being extra long and of no known relation to any current style—an idea of my own, you see—to say nothing of extra money spent for patent leather shoes, ties, collars, a new bright grey hat—all especially purchased for her. Although beyond this I had little cash for what I considered the essentials of courtship—boxes at the theatre, dinners and suppers at the best restaurants, flowers, candy and the like, still I hoped to make an impression. Why shouldn't I? Being a newspaperman and an ex-dramatic editor, to say nothing of my rather close friendship with the present critic of the *Republic*, I could easily obtain theatre tickets, although the exigencies of my work might prevent my accompanying her for more than an hour at a time, if so much. And I could see that she received some flowers and attentions in other ways.

CHAPTER LIV

The day of her arrival was really a red-letter one for me. She had informed me a number of days before, possibly a week or ten days, that on this particular Saturday—morning or afternoon—I would find her at her aunt's in one of those simpler home streets of the west end; and here, true enough, after arraying myself in my utmost and arming myself with flowers, candy and two seats for one of the reigning successes then playing in St. Louis, I found her. I had been so fearful lest my afternoon assignment for that day prove a barrier to my seeing her at all that I made my way to her place as early as ten-thirty, intending to offer her these tickets and arrange for my stopping by for her afterwards at the theatre, if I might—or failing that, seeing her for a little while in the evening if my assignments would permit—or failing that, the next morning. I was so vain of my standing in her eyes—so anxious to make a good impression—that I was ashamed to confess that my reportorial duties made it difficult for me to see her at all. After all my free days at Chicago, I wanted to make it appear as though I were considerably more than a mere reporter—a sort of traveling correspondent and feature man. Which in a way I was, I suppose, only my superiors were determined to keep me for some reason in the ordinary reportorial class taking daily assignments as usual. Instead of frankly confessing my difficulties, as many another would have, no doubt, I made a great show of freedom—with what effect, however, I haven't the slightest idea. It all seems so odd now—somewhat like an illusion or a dream, and with an element of the ridiculous in it.

However, as I say, on this morning I made my way to this quiet street as early as ten-thirty or eleven and found her in a small, tree-shaded, cool-looking brick house, with a brick sidewalk before it and a space of grass to one side. Never did place seem more charming. I stared at it as one might a shrine. Here at last was at least the temporary home of my beloved, and she was within.

I knocked.

A slip of a girl, as attractive as any, replied—her niece, as I discovered later—and by her I was shown into a long, dustless, darkened parlor, as clean and pleasing as a Dutch interior. Presently, after I had weighed the taste and affluence of her relatives according to my then standards, she arrived—the beloved, the beautiful. In view of many later sadder things, it seems now that I should at least attempt to do her full justice. She seemed exquisite to me then in the true sense of the word—a slim, agreeable sylph of a girl with a lovely oval face; stark red hair braided and coiled after the fashion of a Greek coin; a clear pink skin; long, narrow (almond-shaped) grey-blue eyes; delicate, graceful hands; a perfect figure; small, well-formed feet. There was something of the wood or water nymph about her, as I felt then, a seeking in her eyes, a breath of wild winds in her hair, a scarlet glory to her mouth. And yet she was obviously such a simple and inexperienced country girl, caught firm and fast in American religious and puritanic tradition, and with no least hint in her own mind of all the wild, mad ways of the world. Sometimes I have grieved that she ever met me,—or that I so little understood myself as to have sought out her.

I first saw her, after this long time, framed in a white doorway, and to me she made a fascinating picture—greeting me with shyness and affection, or so I thought. There was something richly sensuous in her nature, as I came to know, a sensuality so vigorous that even then it tortured her stern puritan soul, but—. Here, as in Chicago, she seemed shy, innocent, questioning, like one who might fly at the first sound. I gazed in admiration. Despite a certain something in her letters which had, seemingly, indirectly assured me of her affection or her desire for mine, still she held aloof, extending a cool, pale hand, and asked me to sit down, smiling tenderly and graciously. I felt odd, out of place, and yet wonderfully drawn to her—passionately interested, no less—now more so than ever.

What followed by way of conversation I can scarcely remember— talk of the Fair, I suppose, some of those we had known, her summer, mine. I had brought roses. She pinned some of them on, putting the rest in a jar. There was a piano here. She played, as I understood. I was eager to hear her. She consented after a time, and played a Mexican thing—"Manzanillo"—then the "Fifth Nocturne." The leaves were turning. I remember mentioning that. In a moment it seemed it was twelve-thirty and then I had to go—regardless.

I walked on air because she had been gracious. It seemed to me that I had never seen anyone more beautiful—and I doubt now that I had. There was no reason to be applied to the thing. It was plain infatuation—a burning, consuming desire for her. I think if I had lost her then and there, or any time within a year thereafter, I would have deemed it the most amazing affair of my life—herself the irreplaceable. As it was, I took some assignment and followed it without interest, thinking of her. By three-thirty I cut it short, whatever it was, to get back to the Grand Opera House in order to sit beside her, for a little while at least. The play was an Irish love drama—one of those Mid-western trivialities of the time—with Chauncey Olcott, "the singing comedian," in the title role. With her beside me, I thought it perfect. Love! Ah, love! Could anything be more wonderful? When the performance ended I was ready to weep over the torturing beauty of life. Outside were the matinee crowds, the carriages, the sense of fall gayety and show in the air. A nearby ice-cream and candy store of some social prominence was crowded to suffocation. Young "flappers" of the better families hummed like bees. Because of my poverty and uncertain station I felt depressed, and yet at the same time pretended to a station which I felt to be most unreal. I, if you please, was as great as any—only I was not. The mixture of ambition and uncertainty, pride and the inability to flaunt it at its true measure, a gay coaxing in the air, plus a need to return to conventional toil—how these tortured me! Nothing surprises me more, now, than my own driving emotions all through this period. I was as one possessed.

We parted at a street car—when I wanted a carriage. We met at her relatives' home at eight-thirty because I saw an opportunity of deliberately evading an assignment and reporting at midnight or there-about. In this simple parlor I dreamed in her presence, the wildest, the most fantastic dreams. She was, plainly, the be-all and the end-all of my existence. Now I must work for her, wait for her, succeed for her! Her unquestionably mediocre piano technique seemed perfect. Her voice, for she sang, ideal! Never was such beauty, such color. St. Louis, quite like Chicago, now took on a glamour which it had never previously possessed, only it was still not Chicago but a darker, grosser, more material thing. Still, it was beautiful now. If only this love affair could have gone on to a swift fruition, it would have been perfect, blinding.

As it was, all the formalities, traditions, beliefs, nuances of a conventional and even puritanic region were in the way. Love, as it is in most places, and despite its consuming blaze, was a slow process. Here there must be many such visits, as she understood it—and as I grimly accepted—a slow process of love-making. I was to be permitted to take her to church, to concerts, the theatre, a restaurant occasionally, but nothing more. The next morning, for instance, I went to church with her—some solemn specimen of the M. E. Church South. The next afternoon unavoidable work kept me from her—a startling poisoning case which was just beginning—but that night, just the same, I shirked a phase of it and stayed with her until eleven, finding that I had missed nothing of importance—fortunately. The next morning, since she had to catch an early train for Florissant, I slept late, but during the next two weeks—for it appeared she could not come oftener, having to spend one Sunday with her "folks," as she referred to them—I poured forth my amaze and delight on reams of thin paper, for which I searched in order to make the letters seem less bulky. I wonder now where they are. Once there was a trunk full—or nearly so.

But those letters! Perhaps the most interesting effect of this sudden fierce passion was the heightened color it lent to everything—my work, my ambitions, my dreams. Never before had I realized quite so clearly, I think, the charm of life as life—its wondrous, singing, intense appeal. I remember witnessing a hanging—standing beside the murderer when the trap was sprung and seeing him die—but when I returned to the office there was a letter there from her, and the world was once more perfect. I followed up the horrors of a political catastrophe in which a city treasurer shot himself to escape the law—but a letter from her, and the world was beautiful. A negro in an outlying county assaulted a girl, and I arrived in time to see him lynched. But walking in the woods afterward, away from the swinging body, I thought of her—

and life contained not a single ill! Of such is infatuation. If I had been alive before, now I was much more so, within my own blood and nerves. I fairly tingled all over with longing and aspiration in various forms—to be an editor possibly, a publisher, a playwright, a—I know not what. The simple homes I had dreamed over before as representing all that was charming and soothing and shielding were now twice as attractive. Love—all its possibilities—paraded before my eyes a gorgeous fantastic and sensual procession. Love! Love! The beauty of a woman's body. The charm of a home in which it would find its most appropriate setting. The brooding tenderness of it. Its healing force against the blows of ordinary life. To be married, to have your beloved with you, to have a charming home to return to of an evening or at any hour, sick or well!

At the same time my thoughts were now probing like a keen ray into the mystery of life itself. Where did we come from? To where were we going? What was this keen disrupting attraction of sex anyhow—of form, color, thought, temperament? Often it occurred to me that now I was at the topmost toss of things. I was young, in good health and spirits. In a few years I would be neither so young nor so vital. Age would descend, cold, gray, thin, passionless. This glorious, glorious period of love—desire—would be gone. And then what! Ah, and then what? If I did not achieve now and soon all that I desired in the way of tenderness, fortune, beauty—now when I was young and could enjoy it—my chance, once and for all, would be over. I would be helpless. The tread of immeasurable law would be behind me, driving me on, on. Youth would come no more. Love no more! I might not have a soul. Never might I in all endless time appear spiritually anywhere. But now, now—. Life was sounding, singing, urging, teasing, but also—also—it was running away fast, fast, and what was I doing about it? What could I do? What could I do?

CHAPTER LV

There followed approximately five months of this activity, during which I did much of the newspaper work previously described and more like it. It was for me a period of high color and high moods—the richest, the most exotic period of rank romanticism I have ever endured. At times I could laugh, at other times sigh over the incidents of this period, for there is as little happiness in love, or passion apparently, as there is out of it, at least in my case. If I had only known myself (whoever does?) I might have seen, and that plainly, that it was not any of the charming conventional things which this girl represented—the "spiritual," as they say—but her charming physical self, her innate responding passion, which I craved. The world, as I see it now, has trussed itself up too helplessly with too many strings of convention, religion, dogma and the like. It has accepted too many rules, all calculated for the guidance of individuals in connection with the propagation and rearing of children, the conquest or development, presumably, of this planet. This is all very well for those who are intensely interested in that, but supposing you are not? Supposing your aim is to picture or decipher life as you find it, or to follow up a purely private aim? Is it everybody's business to get married and accept all the dictates of conventional society—that is, bear and raise children according to a given social or religious theory? Cannot the world have too much of mere breeding? Are two billion wage slaves, for instance, more advantageous than one billion—or one billion more than five hundred million? Or an unconquered planet less interesting than a conquered one? I would like to know. Isn't mere contact via sex and love, if it produce ideas, experiences, tragedies even, as important as raising a few hundred thousand more or less of coal miners, railroad hands or "heroes" destined to be eventually ground or shot in some contest between autocratic or capitalistic classes? I for one think so. And furthermore, I am inclined to suspect that the monogamous standard to which the world has been tethered much too harshly for a thousand years or so now is entirely wrong. I do not believe that it is nature's only or ultimate way of continuing or preserving itself. Nor am I inclined to accept that it produces the highest type of citizen. The ancient world knew little of strict monogamy. And some countries today are still void of it. Even in our religious or moralistic day we are beginning to see less and less of its strict enforcement. Fifty thousand divorces in one state in one year is but a straw. It is a product, I suspect, of intellectual dullness—a mental incapacity for individuality. What we have achieved, if anything, is a vast ruthless machine for the propagation of people far beyond the world's need—even its capacity to support decently. On the other hand, in special cases where the strong find themselves, we see more of secret polygamy and polyandry than is at all suspected by the dull and the ignorant. The shrewd, avid woman, keener than her mate, has more than one man. Ditto the man. Economic opportunity plus love, or attraction, arranges all this—all the churches, codes, laws, disasters to the contrary notwithstanding. Love or desire, where economic conditions permit, will and does find a way. The world can, and I think will, get too much of mere commonplace monogamous propagation. After a while it may achieve brains sufficient to ask itself why another system may not be as good. It if does—by the board go all current marriage law and religious theories and sacraments relating to this condition. Imagine a world dull enough to make a sacrament of marriage!

However, to return to myself in this situation. Here I was dreaming (or imagining that I was) of all the excellencies of which the conventionalists prate in connection with home, peace, stability and the like, anxious to put my neck under that yoke, when in reality what I really wanted, and the only thing which my peculiarly erratic and individual disposition would permit, was mental and personal freedom. I did not really want any such conventional girl at all and, if I had clearly understood what it all meant, might have been only too glad to give her up. What I did want was for her, with her beauty and passion, to give herself to me—the joy of possessing her without any of the hindrances or binding chains of convention and monogamy. Was I to have them? No, not with her consent—at least as she saw matters then. She was very anxious for love and its fruits, but on her terms only. On the other hand, I was so much of the conventionalist myself—a mere nosing cub—that I applauded her for this even though it debarred me, while at the same time seeking, quite without reasoning about it, to push my advances as far as her judgement would permit. I hadn't the faintest dream at first of being permitted to do more than put my arms about her waist and kiss her. Later I pleaded with her to sit on my lap, which she never would do, insisting that this was for marriage only! I contented myself, as I have indicated, by taking her to theatres, a restaurant or two, to church on some Sundays when she was in the city and to the few concerts of any importance which were given during the time when I knew her here. Betimes, I wrote her more and more of those amazing letters—letters which must have been all of five thousand words in length, some of them anyhow—and betimes dreamed of her and the happy days to come when she should be wholly mine.

Positively, this period stands out in my mind as one of the most intense and disturbing in this way that I have ever experienced. I think part of the intense ache and urge I endured nearly all of the time— quite all of it, indeed—was due to an unsatisfied sex desire plus a huge world sorrow over life itself—the richness and promise of the visible scene, the sting and urge of its beauty, the briefness of our days, the uncertainty of our hopes, the smallness of our capacity to achieve or consume where so much is. Imagine being an ant, where Caesar's armies may tramp the earth—a fly, and Napoleon rides triumphant after Austerlitz! The beginnings of aches and thoughts and visions that subsequently all but paralyzed my energies were here. I was so staggered by the promise and the possibilities of the visible scene, while at the same time growing more and more doubtful of my capacity to achieve anything before it would be too late physically and mentally so to do, that I was falling into a profound sadness, or on the verge of it. Yet I was only twenty-two, and between these thoughts would come intense waves of do and dare. I was to be all I fancied, achieve all I dreamed. As a contrast to all these world thoughts and fancies as well as depressions, I indulged in a heavy military coat or cape of the most disturbing length and numerous folds, a Southwestern soft-brimmed Stetson hat, gloves, a cane, soft pleated shirts—a most outré equipment for any but these few occasions on which I could call on her or take her to any theatre or restaurant. I remember one Saturday morning, when I was on my way to see my lady love and had stopped in at the Olympic to secure two seats for some show, gratis, meeting a dapper, rather flashy ex-newspaperman who had connected himself with the local stage as a ticket seller.

"Well, for Christ's sake, old man, what's up?" he called, seizing me by the arm in passing. I had on the aforesaid coat of rich folds and the hat—most amazing institutions both—a pair of bright yellow gloves, narrow-toed patent leather shoes, a ring, a pin, a suit brighter than his own, a cane, and, if my memory does not fail me, I was carrying in addition a bouquet of roses which I had purchased for my lady love, done up in paper, of course. I was about to take a street car, if you please, out to the region in which she dwelt, not being prosperous enough in my own estimation to hire a carriage. Cabs were almost non est in St. Louis as it was. And besides, I had put nearly all my spare cash in these fineries.

"What's the idea?" he went on. "You're not getting married, are you?"

"Aw, cut the comedy," I replied, or words to that effect. "What's eating you? Can't a fellow put on any decent clothes in this town without exciting the natives? What's wrong?" I demanded.

"Nothing, nothing," he replied cheerfully and apologetically. "You look swell. You got on more dog than ever I see a newspaperman around here pull. You must be gettin' along great. How are things down at the *Republic*, anyway?"

We conversed now more affably. He touched the coat gingerly and with interest, felt of the quality of the cloth, looked me up and down, seemingly with admiration—more likely with amazement—shook his head approvingly and said, "Some class, I must say. You're right there, sport, with the raiment," and walked off. I have never been able to decipher from that day to this whether he was wholly jesting with me or no, but I am strongly inclined to suspect that he was, as flashy and gay as he was himself.

Be that as it may, it was in this style that I prosecuted my quest. For my ordinary day's labor I wore entirely different clothes. Only sometimes, when stealing a march on my city editor Saturday afternoons or Sundays or evenings, I was compelled to do a lightning change act in order to get into my finery, pay my visit and still get back to the office between eleven and twelve, or before six-thirty, in my ordinary clothes—those in which I had left. Sometimes I changed as many as four times in one afternoon and evening—once between one and two in the afternoon after I left the office and wanted to put them on, again between five and six when returning to the office, again between seven and eight when leaving ostensibly on another assignment, and again between eleven and twelve before I entered the office. My room being right here, on my path and in the heart of things, as it were, facilitated this. Again, most of the assignments, as it so chanced and by very great luck, were of no great import. Sometimes they caused me trouble, but not always. A little later, when I was more experienced, I aided myself to this speed by wearing all but the coat and hat, an array in which I never presumed to enter the office. Even my ultra-impressive suit— very heavy and of startling pattern—and my shoes, shirts and ties attracted attention.

"Gee whiz, Mr. Dreiser!" my pet office boy at the *Republic* once remarked to me as I entered at noon in this array, "You certainly do look as though you ought to own the paper. The boss don't look like you."

Wandell, Williams, the sporting editor, the religious editor, the dramatic editor, all eyed me—I will not say askance, but with evident curiosity. "You certainly are laying it on thick these days," Williams once genially remarked, beaming on me with his one eye. And the dramatic editor began most urgently to take me about with him to some curious souls: a banker, who had an amazing studio in the red-light district, the walls covered with signed photos of actresses; a clairvoyant and mind reader, who was a patron of the stage, also living in this region; a lawyer and a railroad man, both bon vivants in the local sense, and both having rooms away from their wives—if even in their own homes—where wines, liquors, cigars, books and the like were to be found, and presumably a wider knowledge of the world than the rest of the city provided.

I am not sure, but, as I recall it, I don't think I was very much impressed. One heard here gossip of high life—risqué gossip. Once I took too many hot Scotches at one place, between two and five a.m.— the first I had ever had, by the way—and lay gloriously sick the next day. Having a severely congested appendix, which I did not know at the time, I had no stomach for such matters. As for my lady love— well, I reached the place where I could hold her hands, put my arms about her, kiss her, but never induce her to sit upon my lap. Never. That was reserved, as I was to learn, for a much later date.

CHAPTER LVI

Love transports are given to all of us, and to each, I presume, they are the ultimate of sensation. I will pass over mine with what I have already said, save this, that each little variation in her costume, however slight, or her manner of doing her hair, or the way she looked or walked amid new surroundings—at church, for instance, or a restaurant or a theatre—all seemed to re-emphasize the perfection of that which I had discovered and was so fortunate as to possess. I secured from her a picture, framed it in silver and hung it in my room. I begged for a clipping of her hair and, finding a bit of blue ribbon that I knew belonged to her, purloined that. She would not allow me to visit her at Florissant where she taught, being bashful possibly about confessing this new relationship, but just the same on several Sundays when she was not there but at her home "up the state," I visited this glorious region, hallowed by her presence, and tried to decide for myself just where it was she lived and taught—her sacred rooms! There was, a little later, an exposition or state fair, given then in the enormous exposition building at 14th and Olive, and here, when the Sousa concerts were on, and later when the gay Veiled Prophet's festivities began—a sort of Roman Harvest rejoicing, winding up with a great parade and ball—I saw more of her than ever before. It was during this time, by the way, that she confessed in a letter that she truly loved me—a letter that was followed by more intimate though still reserved personal relations. Before this, however, seeing that I made no progress in any other way, being allowed no least intimacy beyond an occasional stolen kiss, I had proposed to her and been accepted with a kind of morbid formalism, which impressed me greatly. I had to ask her in the most definite way and be formally accepted as her affianced husband. Thereafter I squandered my last cent purchasing a diamond ring at wholesale, secured through a friend on the *Globe,* and then I felt myself very set up in the world—as one who was destined to tread the conventional and peaceful ways of the majority.

I have little to say of the days that followed save this—that in spite of my profound infatuation, and apparently it was such, I was still able to see beauty in other women and be moved by it. The idiosyncrasy of our nature which permits this needs no explanation here, perhaps, but it might have taught me to look with suspicion on my own emotions. I think I did imagine that I was a scoundrel in harboring admirations of and lusts after other women, when I was so deeply involved with this one, but I said to myself that I must be peculiarly afflicted in this way, that all men were not so, that I myself should and probably would hold myself in check eventually, et cetera. All of which merely proves how disjointed and non-self-understanding are the average processes of the average human mind. We not only do not see ourselves as others see us, but we haven't the faintest conception of ourselves as we really are.

One of the current incidents which might have proved to me how shallow was the depth of my supposed feeling, or how purely identical it was with a strong sex-desire, was this. One night—about eleven-thirty or twelve—a telephone message to the *Republic* stated that on a branch extension of one of the local car lines about seven or eight miles from the city a murder had just been committed. Three negroes, entering a lone "owl" car which ran on this line from the city terminus to the small village it served some four miles beyond, had shot and killed the conductor and fired on the motorman. A young girl who had been on board—the only other passenger, by the way—had escaped via the front door and had not since been heard of, or so the one who telephoned the message stated. Being in the office at the time, I was assigned the story.

By good luck I managed to catch a twelve o'clock theatre car and arrived at the end of the line at twelve-thirty-five or forty. There I learned that the body of the dead man had been transferred to his home at some point farther out on the line and that a posse of male residents of the region had already been organized and were now helping the police search this country round for the negroes. When I asked about the girl who had been on board, whether she had been found or not, one of the men at the barn exclaimed, "Sure. She's a wonder. You want to tell about her. She hunted up a house, borrowed a horse, and notified everybody along the route from here to Winstead. She's the one that first telephoned us the news."

Here was a story indeed. A girl hero, no less. Midnight, a murder, dark woods, lonely country. A girl flees from three murderous, drunken negroes, borrows a horse and notifies all the countryside. What more could a newspaper want? I was all ears, and alive to the import of the story. Now if she were only good looking. Actually, I saw myself falling in love with her, if such were the case.

And now I realized that my first duty was not so much to see the body of the dead man and interview his wife, although that was an item not to be neglected, or the excellent motorman who had escaped with his life, although he was here and told me all that had happened quite accurately, but to see this girl, who, being not more than seventeen or eighteen, so they said, must, of course, be a most fascinating specimen of womanhood.

The car in which the murder had been committed was here in the barn now—in service still—for it was the only car on the route, just traveling to and fro shuttlewise. The bloodstains of the victim were still to be seen on the floor. I learned from the motorman as much as he could remember of the appearance of the negroes, and then took this same car, which was now carrying a group of detectives, a doctor and some other officials to the dead man's house or to the house of this girl, I forget which. When I arrived there, however, I discovered that a larger, comfortable residence some little distance beyond that of the dead man was the present scene of all news and activity. For here it was that the girl had first applied for aid, here the body of the conductor had been carried, and from here she had taken a horse and ridden far and wide, presumably calling others to her aid. When I arrived and hurried up to the door, where by the lights and the crowd one could easily tell that excitement of some kind was abroad, she had returned and was holding a sort of levee, being feted and praised, as it were. The large living room of this house was fairly crowded with people—residents of the vicinity, I presume—and in the centre, under the flare of a hanging lamp, was this same maiden, still white-faced from her exertions, I presume—rather pretty (beautiful, I thought at first), with her hair brushed straight back from her forehead, and her face alight with the import and intensity of her recent experiences and actions. I drew near and surveyed her over the shoulders of others as she talked, finally getting closer and engaging her in direct conversation, as was my duty. She was exceedingly simple in her manner and speech—not quite the dashing heroine I had imagined—and still with much of a lure and flare about her, at that. For my benefit, and possibly for the dozenth time, she re-narrated all that had befallen her from the time she boarded the car and the negroes entered it until she had leaped from the front step after the shot and hid in the woods. She had found her way to this house shortly afterwards and borrowed a horse to notify others, be-cause, for one thing, there was no telephone here, and secondly, there was no man at home at the time who could have gone for her—only an old mother and a rather anaemic daughter. With a kind of naive enthusiasm she explained to me that once the shot had been fired and the conductor had fallen face down in the car (he had come in to rebuke the boisterousness of these blacks who were addressing rather bold remarks to her), she was cold with fright; but that after she had leaped through the front door and into the dark, past the motorman who had turned to discover what the trouble was, she felt calmer and determined to do something to aid in the capture of the murderers. Hiding behind bushes, she had seen the negroes dash out of the rear door of the car and run back along the track into the dark. She then hurried in the other direction, coming to this house and summoning aid. It was a fine story—her ride in the dark and how people rose to come out and help her. I made copious notes in my mind, took down her name and address as well as those of others, visited the motorman's wife who was a little distance away and then hurried to the nearest phone to communicate my intelligence while I made my way back as best I could.

But during this conversation with this girl I had made an impression—or so I thought—in spite of my fear that I would not, and the very peculiar and disturbing nature of the scene in which I was cross-examining her. As we talked I had drawn quite close, and my enthusiasm for her deed had drawn forth various approving smiles. When I took her address I exclaimed, "I should like to know more of you," and she smiled as she said, "Well, you can see me anytime tomorrow." This was Saturday night.

It so chanced that the *Republic*, among its various circulation-building ventures at this time (and it had a number, and very clever ones, I must say) had instituted what it called "a reward for heroism" medal to be given to whosoever should perform during the current year a truly heroic deed within the confines of the city or its immediate suburbs. A gift of one to someone else previous to this had called it to my attention—a silly award, I had thought at the time. Thinking over this girl's deed as I went along, and wondering how I should proceed in the matter of retaining her interest, I thought of this medal and asked myself why it should not be given to her. Why not, indeed? She was certainly worthy of it. Plainly she was a hero, riding thus in the dark for help and in the face of such a crime—and good looking, too!—and eighteen! After I had proceeded to the office and written a most glowing account of all this for the late edition—the death of the conductor was a mere bagatelle by now—I decided to speak to Wandell the next day, and did. He fell in with the idea at once, and most enthusiastically. "A fine idea," he squeaked shrilly. "Bully. We'll do that. You'll have to go back, though, and see whether she'll accept it. She may not, you know. Sometimes these people won't stand for all this notoriety stuff. They don't want it. But if she does—. By the way," he paused quickly, "is she good looking?"

"Sure," I replied vigorously, thinking of all I had seen. "She's very good looking, a beauty, I think."

"Well, if that's the case, all the better," he went on. "She might not have been, you know. Be sure and get a good picture. Don't let her crawl out of that, if you have to bring her down here or take her to a photographer. If she accepts I'll order the medal tomorrow, and you can write the whole thing up. It'll make a fine Sunday feature, eh?" he smirked. "Dreiser's girl hero! What!"

I pretended to be greatly embarrassed and misjudged by all this, when as a matter of fact I was getting momentarily more and more interested. This medal idea was just the thing to take me back to her with great savoire faire—the excuse that I needed, and one that ought to bring her close to me, if anything could. By now, for the time being, I had forgotten—or nearly so—all about Miss White and her charms. She came into my mind, but it was so all-important for me to follow up this new interest—and one that I could manage as well as not, along with Miss White. I put on my very best clothes the next morning, excluding the amazing coat since I was going to the country, and sallied forth to find my new maiden wherever she might be. After considerable difficulty I finally managed to place her in a very simple home on what plainly was once a farm, but now a mingled truck garden and plot property. Her father, as I discovered on reaching the place—for he first came to the door—was a German of the most rigid and austere mien— a Lutheran, I think. Her mother was a simple and pleasant-looking fat house-frau. In this garish noon light my heroine was neither as melo-dramatic or as poignant as she had seemed the night before. There was something less alive and less delicate in her total composition, mental and physical, and yet she was by no means dull. Perhaps she lacked the dash and the crowd. She had a peculiar mouth, a little wide but sweet, and a most engaging smile. Incidentally, as it now developed, she had a younger sister, darker, more graceful, almost more attractive than herself.

The two of them, as I soon found upon entering into conversation and explaining my errand, offered that same curious problem in American life that so many children of foreign-born parents do. In this case, although by no means poor—quite the contrary—they were restless, if not unhappy, in their state. This old German and his wife, as I soon learned, owned much of this vacant property hereabout, destined to be overtaken and made valuable by the city. At the same time, he was one of those stern religionists and moralists who plainly all his day had held, or tried to hold, his two children in severest check. At the same time, as was obvious on the face of it, this keen, strident American life was calling to them as never had his fatherland to him. They were intensely alive and eager for adventure—both of them. You could see it in their eyes. Never before, apparently, had they seen a reporter—the younger one, at least—never been so close to a really truly, thrilling tragedy. And Lizzie (that was my heroine's name) had actually been a part of it—how, she could scarcely think. Her parents, apparently, were not at all stirred by her triumph or the publicity that attached to it. In spite of the fact that her father owned this property and was sufficiently comfortably placed to maintain her in school or idleness—American style—she was already a clerk in one of the great dry goods companies of the city, holding a small cashiership. Also her sister was preparing to go to work. She had just left school. On this particular evening Lizzie had stayed in town to join a house party of store girls, I presume, and had left in time to make this twelve o'clock suburban for her home, expecting, as she said, to find a crowd of homecoming theatregoers aboard. Only these negroes came aboard, however.

I cannot tell you how, but in a few moments we three had struck up a most ardent conversation. There was an old fireplace in this house with some blazing wood in it, and before this we three sat and laughed and chattered while I explained just what was wanted. Their mother and father did not even remain in the room. Both sisters were most eager to see it done, especially the younger. I could see that the latter was for urging her sister on to any gayety or flirtation and was eager to share in one such herself. She came very close to me and gazed into my eyes while I talked. It ended by my suggesting that they both come down to dinner with me some evening—a suggestion which they welcomed with enthusiasm, but explained that it would have to be done under the rose. Their parents must not know. Their father was so old fashioned that he would not let them take up with anyone so quickly. He would not even let them have any beaus come to the house—and besides, it was so far out. But they could meet me—or Lizzie could—and stay in town all night with friends. Occasionally she did this. She laughed, and the younger sister clapped her hands for joy.

I made a most solemn statement of what was wanted after a time to the parents, secured two photos of the charming Lizzie and departed, having arranged to see them the following Wednesday at seven at one of the prominent corners of the city—6th and Olive, I believe.

CHAPTER LVII

Concerning these two girls and their odd, unsophisticated, daring point of view and love of life, I have always had the most confused feelings. What should be done with two such giddy life-lovers, pray? They were, as I soon discovered, literally crazy and starving for something different to what they knew, gayety and interest of some kind. What, in this queer American atmosphere, had become of all the staid and dull sobriety of their parents? These latter had no interest in or patience with any such gayety or restlessness. In regard to their two girls, it would have been as easy to seduce one or both of them in the happy, seeking mood in which they met me as to step off a car, or nearly so. Plainly they liked me—both of them, apparently. If they had ever seen a newspaper man before, it was not apparent in their actions. My conquest was so easy that it detracted from the charm. I was puzzled and not a little curious. Plainly the weaker sex, in youth at least, has to be sought to be worthwhile. I began to question whether I should proceed in this matter as fast as they seemed to wish. What would be the consequence if anything should happen to one or both of them?

But now that they had made friends with me, I liked them both just the same. We were to meet, as appointed, in the business heart, and did, at a commonplace restaurant. Only, after a commonplace meal, I was a little puzzled to know what to do with them, rarely having a whole evening to myself to do anything with. Finally I invited them to my room, wondering if they would come. It seemed a great adventure to me, most daring, only I doubted whether I should be able to make much out of it, even if they came. I couldn't make up my mind quite which one of the two I preferred, and I had not yet reached the place where I could trifle with two at once in their joint presence. It seemed abnormal. Just the same they came with me, looking on it, apparently, as a great and delicious adventure. As we came along Broadway in the dark after dinner, they hung on my arms, laughing and jesting over what their parents would think, and when we went up the dimly lighted stair—an old, wide, squeaky flight, by the way—they chortled over the fun and mystery of it. Then they invaded my private sanctum with a gayety and an assurance of well-being that was charming. The room was nothing much—the same old books, hangings and other trifles—but it seemed to please them greatly. The advantage of a place like this in St. Louis was that it was half office building and half furnished rooms—kept, in so far as my particular room was concerned, by a middle-aged German couple who were among the most indifferent of the indifferent. I never saw either of them save when I went to say that my room was now open to be cleaned or to pay my rent—and as for what I might do in it or whom I might bring there, they never gave it a thought, I am sure. As for these two girls, they saw the point at once and commented on it. Think of living like this, by yourself, in the heart of the city, where you could come and go as you pleased! And at home they couldn't stir without their father or their mother wanting to know where they were going. They browsed about at first, laughing and jesting, but because there were two of them, I was somewhat at a loss how to proceed. Never having been confronted by just this situation before, and being still backward—very much so—I did little or nothing except discuss generalities. The one I had most favored, the heroine, was, as I now found, more retiring than the younger, less feverish but still gay. On the other hand, the latter had a way that suggested the wildest escapades. For instance, at their suggestion, or because of their interest, I began to describe certain phases of underworld life not so far from this region. They were all ears and suggested what a lark it would be if they could see some of it at once or soon.

"But you couldn't," I assured them. "You couldn't get into most of these places. The only way you would be able to see any of it would be to dress up in men's clothes, and then you couldn't very well. The police would detect you."

"Oh, wouldn't that be fun," declared the younger. "I bet they wouldn't make me out." She began to look at my clothespress in the most inquiring way and finally suggested that I might get them both boys' clothes. I was actually startled by the daring of it, but I had no intention of laying myself open to any such adventure. I hadn't the courage really, and I didn't believe it could be done. Instead I contented myself with promising them that I would sometime, and at the same time playing with them here in a bashful sort of way, both of them clinging to me like two young puppies, or collies, almost pushing each other out of the way in their effort to get nearest. What surprised me though was that neither exhibited the least feeling of rivalry or an ambition to be the only one, although I rather felt that my loyalty should be to the elder, whom I had met first, and this made me feel queer about the whole adventure. What was I to do? Which take? My sexual education, I am sorry to report, was by no means so complete as to permit me to think that I could have them both at once, although I am convinced now that I might have. It was something of this thought, perhaps, that took the romance out of it; and in addition I would not have known how to go about an adventure of this kind, not possessing the courage, for one thing. I was still too doubtful whether I was sufficient for one, let alone two. Here in this room I put my arms around the two of them at once, and kissed them irrespectively, finding a curious satisfaction in the situation, as though they had been one. And they on their part, perhaps, found a courage and an abandon due to their being together which they might not otherwise have felt.

What came of this particular evening? Nothing much, beyond this. (Of how many related contacts in my life would I have to say the same thing!) As I have before pointed out, the novelty or strangeness of the situation for me was sufficient to make me shy. After all, on this occasion I had but from seven to ten-thirty in which I could be with them. They had to be at the house of a friend by eleven-thirty, although they indicated that on another occasion they could arrange to stay later. They were willing to run away for days apparently, or to come back at any time! I was so overwhelmed by the completeness of the situation—my conquest, or what you will—that I began to doubt my fitness as a Lothario and to commiserate myself on the lack of this, that, and the other quality for engaging in such an adventure—the method of the weak, always. A little more iron in my blood, I suppose, and I would have done with these two as I wished—and as they wished also. Instead I made some acceptable excuse about work after a time and took them to a car going nearest their friend's. Afterward, a few days later, I secured the medal and took it to the store to Lizzie, who received it and me with the greatest pleasure, wanting to know where I had been and when I was to see her again. I made an arrangement then and there to see her later—to call for her at the store—which, if I remember rightly, I never did. It meant, as I reasoned it out, that I would have to go farther with her and her sister at once—and that, much farther than I had before. Not being sufficiently impelled or courageous, I dropped the whole matter, if you please. Instead I wrote up the article about her and sent her that. Then, because Miss White (and now especially by contrast) seemed more significant than ever, I returned to her with, I presume, a fuller devotion than ever before.

There set in now a period of mental dissatisfaction and unrest which finally took me out of St. Louis and the West and resulted in such a period of distress as seemed all but destined to do for me at the time. Sometimes, I sincerely believe, certain lives are predestined to undergo a certain given group of experiences, else why the unconscionable urge to move and be away which drives some people like the cuts of a lash? Aside from the salary question there was little reason for the fierce and gnawing pains that assailed me—and toward the last even this was not a factor, for when it became very definite that, money or no, I was about to leave, my whilom employers were quick enough to offer me more, and definite advancement into the bargain. By then, however, my self-dissatisfaction, to say nothing of my contempt for my earning power as a newspaper man, was so great that little short of a larger salary and a higher position than they could have afforded to have given me at my years would have detained me, and scarcely that. Toward the last I seemed fairly to be possessed by the idea of going East—why, I could scarcely have said. New York—New York—and the great cities of the East and Europe seemed to call me far more definitely than anything the West had to offer, although many here were always discussing the great advantage of going West and making money, a thing which I never saw myself doing very clearly. I might long for money and dream of making it in some weird way—largely by accident, I presume—but I never had any sensible or practical plan for so doing.

And now, curiously, various things seemed to combine to drive or lure me forth, things as clear in retrospect—and in their force—as they were indistinguishable and meaningless then. One of these forces, aside from that of being worthy of my new love and lifting her to some high estate, which was then one of my great ideas, was that same John Maxwell, no less, who had done me such inestimable service in Chicago when I was first trying to get into the newspaper business and who, as I have indicated before, had now arrived on the scene and was trying to connect locally. Fat, cynical, cyclopian John. Was there ever a more Nietzschean mind in a more amiable body? His doctrine of ruthless progress, as I now rather clearly saw, was so tall and strident, whereas his personal modus operandi so compellingly genial, human, sympathetic. He was always talking about slaying, burning, shoving people out of your path, doing the best thing by yourself and the like, while at the same time actually extending nearly every one a helping hand and doing as little to advantage himself personally as any man I ever knew. All, or nearly all, was theory, plus a certain inherent desire to expound. All, or nearly all, of his literary admirations, in so far as I could make out, were of a turgidly sentimental or romantic character. As, for instance, Jean Valjean of *Les Misérables* and the good bishop; also Père Goriot, Camille, poor Smike in *Nicholas Nickleby,* and of all things, and yet really quite like him in judgement, the various novels of a then reigning celebrity—Hall Caine (*The Bondman, The Christian, The Deemster,* et cetera). "My boy!" he used to say to me with a fat and yet entirely impressive vehemence, which I could not help admiring whether I agreed with him or no, "That character of Jean Valjean is one of the greatest in the world—a masterpiece—and I'll tell you why," and then he would begin to enlarge on the moral beauty of the latter's carrying the wounded Marius through and out of the sewer, his taking up and caring for the poor degraded mother, abandoned by the students of Paris, his gentle and forgiving attitude toward all poverty and crime. Actually, he seemed obsessed by the beauty of this character. Similarly in regard to old Goriot, he understood and approved of his self-beggaring love for his daughters, while as for the humble Smike, and the lady of the camellias—he confessed they made him want to cry. In re Hall Caine—well—

The amusing thing about this, of course, was that in the next breath he would reiterate that all men were dogs and thieves and that in all cases you had to press your advantage to the limit and trust no one— that you must burn, cut, slay, if you wished to succeed! Imagine! Once I said to him, thinking still at the time that the world might well be full of tenderness, charity, honesty and the like,

"John, you don't really believe all that. You're not as hard as you say."

"The hell I ain't," he replied. "The trouble with you is you don't know me. You're just a cub yet, Theodore,"—and his face had that adorable, fat, cynical smirk—"full of college notions of virtue and charity and all that guff. You think because I helped you a little in Chicago that all men are honest, kind and true. You'll have to stow that pretty soon. You're getting along yourself now, and whatever you think other people ought to do, you'll find it won't be very convenient to do it yourself, see." And he smirked angelically once more. To me, in spite of what he said, he seemed anything but hard or mean. Although at this time John was beginning to think that I was a swelled-headed little ingrate, and that, because of my power in St. Louis (entirely on his part assumed), I was exercising some malign influence which was keeping him from making a proper connection here, the truth is that I was actually in a most adoring mood toward him and doing the little that I could to assist him. I wonder, in case he is alive and should read this, if he would understand. To me he was just as wonderful as ever—as able and as generous. Being in hard lines, he had come to St. Louis, not at my suggestion but at that of Dunlap and Brady, both of whom no doubt assured him that I could secure him a position instanter. On the other hand, neither they nor he, as I now take it, had felt it incumbent on him to speak or write to me in person. One day Dunlap had come to me and said that John wasn't getting along very well in Chicago and that he was coming to St. Louis "to try to connect." I thought immediately what, if anything, I could do to help him, but so overawed was I still by his personality that I felt that the least that was his due was to get him a place as copyreader or an assistant city editorship—and that was a very difficult matter, indeed—really beyond my local influence, as I understood it. I was myself too young and too inexperienced to recommend anybody for any such place, although my Chicago friends had come to imagine, I suppose, that I could really do anything here. Besides, I had the foolish notion that John would speak to me before or after he came—but so sensitive was he on the subject of what was due from me to him that he thought (I am guessing merely) that I should bestir myself without any direct word. However, he came and for days, owing to some misunderstanding, I presume, never came near me, and I did not even know he was here. He had gone to a hotel and only later sent word by Dunlap, with whom by now he was on the most intimate terms, that he was in town and looking for a place. I assume now that it was but the part of decency and the like for me to have hurried to call on him or to have asked him to come and see me—a thing which I never would have thought of doing, still feeling him to be my superior in every way. But still so different was my position and so hurried was I with a number of things that I never even thought of doing it at once. I fancied somehow that he would come to the office with Dunlap, or that a day or two would make no least difference. At the end of the second day after Dunlap spoke to me of his being here, he said, "Don't you want to come along with me and see John?"

"I certainly do," I replied, delighted at the invitation, and explaining why I had not gone before, and that same evening followed Dunlap to John's hotel room. It was a curious meeting, full of an odd diffidence on my part and I know not what on his. By now, as I have said, he had gathered the idea that I was unduly successful here and therefore, according to his logic, in a position to be uppish and, of course, would be—whereas I was really in a most humble and affectionate frame of mind. At once he surveyed me with a most cynical, leering expression which did not put me anything at ease, by any means. I felt strange and out of place. John seemed at once reproachful, antagonistic and contemptuous,—unnecessarily so.

"Well," he began at once, "I hear you're making a big hit down here, Theodore. Everything's coming your way, for a while anyhow."

"Oh, not as good as that, John," I said. "I don't think I've done so wonderfully well. I hear you want to stay here. Have you found anything yet?"

"Not a thing yet," he smiled. "I haven't been trying very hard, I guess."

I told him what I knew of St. Louis and how things went generally. I offered to give him letters or personal introductions to McCullagh, a managing editor on the *Chronicle*, Wandell and several others. He thanked me, and then I invited him to come and live in my room, but he declined, winding up by taking one next door to mine on the same floor—largely because it was inexpensive and central, and not particularly, I am sure, because it was near me. Here he took up a stay which endured for nearly three or four weeks, during which time, no doubt, he made various efforts to find something, and I also for him. Suddenly he was gone, and then a little later, and much to my astonishment, Dunlap informed me that John had concluded, before he left, that I, of all people, had been instrumental in keeping him from obtaining work here! This he had deduced not so much from anything he knew or had even heard, but by some amazing, almost Freudian, theory of contraries—i.e., that being much beholden to him and in a position to assist him, I, by some amazing and yet customary (in his mind) perversion of nature, would resent his coming and do everything in my power to keep him out!

Imagine!!!

CHAPTER LVIII

Nothing in my life ever gave me a queerer sense of being misunderstood and defeated in regard to my very best intentions. It was so ridiculous—so sadly not true. Of all the people I knew, I would rather have aided Maxwell than anyone. Still, such was his feeling, or so Dunlap had explained it; and in the diffidence I felt in regard to Maxwell, it was quite impossible to have it out with him. I felt that if I said, "Here, John, this is not at all true. I want to do anything I can for you and will," I would be thrusting myself forward to a man who felt that I should do every possible thing for him, yet without presuming to indicate that I was now grown so that I could. Besides, I felt so sure that I could not recommend him into anything good enough for him that I. felt ashamed to try. I might get him a job as a reporter, say, but that would be beneath him. I am sure that if I had, he would not have taken it. And what local paper would have taken him for a higher place on my recommendation? As I say, I did the little that I could, but nothing happened, and after a while he left without bidding me goodbye, and with the opinion, I presume, of which I have spoken.

In the meantime, however, as I have said, he had taken a room in the same building in which I had mine, and here on a number of occasions, mornings before going to work and late at night, I found him, sometimes alone, sometimes in company with Dunlap, Brady and others whom he had met here and whose names I have forgotten. Always, on these occasions, he assumed the same condescending and bantering tone he had toward me in Chicago, and which I did not resent in him, but which made me feel as though he thought my present standing a little too much for me. To me it was the same as if he had said, in so many words, "The idea, Theodore, of your being anything yet—or trying to be—of being in a place where you can presume to help me." And yet at times, in his more cheerful moods, he seemed the same old John—tender, ranting, filled with a sincere desire for the welfare of any untutored beginner—and only because he was meshed in financial difficulties, I am sure, so restless and irritable.

At that, he attempted to do me one more service which, although I did not resent it very much, I completely misunderstood. This was in regard to Miss White, whose picture he saw and whose relation to me he now gathered to be serious, although, also, what he said related more to my whole future than to her. One noontime it was, while living in Broadway in the same building, he walked into my room, suspenders down, as he was wont to do while we were both still dressing, and chancing upon the photo of my new love, which was hanging on the wall, he paused first to examine it—then to enter into a discussion in regard to it.

"Who's this?" he inquired curiously.

I can see him yet, coat- and waistcoatless, his fat stomach pulled in tight by the waistband of his trousers, his fat face pink with health, his hair tousled loosely on his fine, round head.

"That's the girl I'm engaged to," I announced proudly. "I'm going to marry her one of these days, when I get on my feet."

He examined her without comment, although cynically, I thought, then put the picture back.

"Where'd you meet her?" he asked. "Here?"

"Yes." Then, lover-like, I began to expatiate on her charms.

He still continued to study the picture.

"Have you any idea how old she is?" he queried, looking up with that queer, cynical, unbelieving look of his.

"Oh, about my age."

"Oh, hell," he said roughly. "She's older than that. That girl is thirty if she's a day. She's eight or ten years older than you are, at the least. What do you want to get married for anyhow? You're just a kid yet. Everything's before you. You're only now getting a start. Now you want to go and tie yourself up so you can't move."

He ambled over to one of the windows, which commanded the tumbledown music hall below, and stared out. Then he sank comfortably into one of my chairs, while I uttered some fine, romantic bosh about love, a home, not wanting to wander around the world all my days alone. As I talked he contemplated me with one of those audacious smirky leers of his, as irritating and disconcerting an expression as I have seen on any face. It was so full of ribald laughter and tolerant contempt.

"Oh, hell, Theodore!" he remarked finally, as if to sweep all I had said away. Then after a time he added, as if addressing the world in general, "If there's a bigger damn fool than a young newspaper man in or out of love, let me know. I've seen a lot, but young newspaper men are the worst of all. Here you are, just twenty-two. Why, damn it, you're only starting out. You've got everything before you. You come down here to St. Louis from Chicago, and by the aid of friends get a little start so that you might possibly do something, and the first thing you want to do is to load yourself up with a wife and two or three kids in a year or so. Then you'll fuss around afterward trying to make a half-assed living and wonder why you don't get along faster." He added something about his own career and that of Dunlap's as being cases in point. He had even met Hutchinson, who was now in the city, jobless and worrying about his young wife, how to support her, and he referred to him.

I don't know what I said in reply, although I was impressed and flattered by his interest in me, of course, but I do know that by now I had achieved a smart bantering tone of my own, intended to fend all attempts on the part of anyone to get too close to my sacred personality, particularly those who wished to give me advice. And I am sorry to say this applied as much to John as to anyone. At the same time, while I personally was feeling that I was in no position to marry, and did not feel that I would unless I should be able to better my condition radically, still I felt that my part in this situation was to defend marriage, especially as I was convinced that if I had money I would marry Miss White, even though I should break away from her later. Also it looked good and kept up John's passing interest in me. And especially was I convinced that he was all wrong as to her age and what he seemed to think was a marked difference in temperament between us, which he now commented on.

"Now, I know damned well," he said, noting the look of easy toleration on my part, no doubt, "that what I am going to say won't make you like me any better, but I'm going to say it just the same. You're like all these young newspaper scouts. The moment you get a start, you think you know it all. Well, Theodore, you've got a long time to live yet, and you'll find a few things to learn. I had something to do with getting you in this game, and that's the only reason I'm talking to you now—because I'd like to see you go on and not make a mistake. In the first place, you're too young to get married, and in the second, as I said before, that girl is ten years older than you are, if she's a day. I think she's older—" and he got up, walked over and re-examined the picture, while I spluttered, insisting that he was crazy, that she was no more than two years older, if so much. "In addition," he went on, ignoring me almost as much as if I were not present, "she's one of these Middle West girls, all right for life out here, but she won't understand the newspaper game or you. I've been through all that, and I know. Just remember, my boy, that I'm ten years older than you are. She belongs to some church, doesn't she?" he interrogated.

"Methodist," I replied ruefully.

"I knew it. You can see something of that in this. Mind you, I'm not knocking her. I'm not saying that she isn't still pretty or virtuous or anything like that. She's older than you are, and she's narrow—or you'll find her so in a little while. Why, man, you don't know your own mind yet. You can't. You don't know where you'll want to go, or what you'll want to see. In ten years from now when you'll be thirty-two, then she'll be forty-three. She knows more about practical things than you do, and that's probably why you're interested, but she's feeling and believing things which in a few years will make you tired. You'll never agree with her, or if you do, so much the worse for you. It's always the way with these early marriages. What she wants is a home and children and a steady provider, and what you really want is freedom to go and do as you please, only you don't know it. After you marry her you'll have to settle down and work, or break it up, and that isn't so easy, particularly if you have children. It's easier to do before than after.

"Now I've watched you, Theodore, and I hear what people say about you down here, and I think you have something ahead of you, possibly, if you don't make a fool of yourself. But if you marry now— and a conventional and narrow woman at that, one older than you are—you're gone. She'll cause you endless trouble. In three or four years you'll have children, and you'll get a worried, irritated point of view. Take my advice. Don't do it. Run with girls if you want to, but don't marry. Now I've said my say, and you can do as you damn please."

He smirked genially and condescendingly once more, and to tell the truth, I felt very much impressed and put down. After all, I knew very well that what he said was true, and in addition that it would be best for me if I devoted myself solely to work and study, and let women alone—or I thought so. But also I knew that I couldn't. My sweetheart did not seem as old to me as he said. Therefore she wasn't. In addition, I wanted her intensely. That is the crux of most of these situations, I believe. After he went out a little while later, I re-examined the features of my beloved to see if what he said were true, and for the life of me I couldn't see it. Knowing her in the flesh, perhaps, whereas Maxwell didn't, made the difference. In real life she looked so young. At the same time, I brooded over this, and decided that perhaps I ought to go slow. What he said was hard but probably true. Maybe I ought never to get married. But what sort of a life would that be? The next time my beloved came to the city, I decided to talk with her about this very thing—not to question her as to her age, but the likelihood of my changing, differing.

We were walking along a leaf-strewn street—I remember it so well—the red, brown, yellow and green leaves, thick on the brick walk, of a grey November afternoon. It was after a matinee for which I had provided the seats, but which I had not been able to attend.

"And what would you do then?" I asked, referring to my fear of changing—not caring for her any longer. She meditated for a while, kicking the leaves with her boot and staring at the ground without looking up. Finally she surveyed me with clear appealing blue-gray eyes.

"But you won't," she said. "I'm sure. Let's not think of anything like that any more. We won't, will we?"

Her tone was so tender and appealing it moved me tremendously. I never felt more sad about anything in my life. She had this power over me—and retained it for years—of appealing to my deepest emotions. I felt so sorry for her—for life—even then. It was as if all that Maxwell had said was really true, and close at hand. She was different, older, she might never really understand me. But this craving for her, and her real charm for me! What to do about that? All love, the fiercest passions, might cool and die out, but how did that help me now? In the long future before me, would I not regret having given her up—never to have carried to fruition this delicious fever? It seemed so. Where would I be in ten years—where she? We went on to her parlor, embracing and kissing there in a kind of fever of sadness, but still, in spite of it, all that

John had said haunted me. I could not get it out of my mind, and, years after, it came to me with even greater force. I ought never to marry. I ought to leave St. Louis. I ought to go on. My life oughtn't to end out here. It couldn't. I must leave—and as for children, that was impossible. And I assumed, of course, that she would want these. What religionist would contend against them?

For weeks thereafter my thoughts were colored by the truth of all John had said. She would never give herself to me without marriage, and here I was, lonely and financially unable to take her, and spiritually unable to justify my marriage to her even if I were. The tangle of life, its unfairness and indifference to the moods and longings of any individual, swept over me once more, weighing me down far beyond the power of expression. I felt like one condemned to carry a cross and so unwilling and unhappy in doing it. (I do not think we ever overestimate the miseries of difficult love and passion.) I wanted really, I suppose, to have her yield herself to me without price or exaction, but that was not to be. The delirious, painful meetings went on and on. I suffered untold tortures via my desires and my dreams.

Those dreams! Those dreams!

And they were destined never to be fulfilled. Glorious fruit that hangs upon the vine too long, and then decays.

Another thing happened at this time that made a great impression on me, tending more firmly, if anything, than even Maxwell's remarks to alter my point of view and make me feel that I must leave St. Louis and go on. Also that, after all, marriage was not for me, or at least not yet, or at best only temporarily so. This was the arrival of my brother Paul, who, as the star of an amazingly claptrap melodrama entitled *The Danger Signal,* now put in an appearance. He was one of four brothers of mine who were out in the world making their own way. The last time I had seen him was just two years before at about this time in Chicago, shortly after I had entered upon my newspaper career there. He was then in another play, entitled *The Tin Soldier,* by the then reigning farceur, Hoyt. His had not been the leading role at that time, as I understood it, but somehow his skill as a comedian had pushed him into that role. Previously he had had leading parts in such middle-class plays as *A Midnight Bell, The Two Johns* and other things of that sort. He was also an "end man"—one of two principal parts in several famous minstrel aggregations.

It seems curious to thus abruptly introduce this particular brother here, seeing that since about my tenth year a most delightful and fascinating relationship had existed between us, but so it must be, in so far as this volume is concerned. Imagine, if you can, a most riant Falstaff—not nearly as worldly and subtle as Shakespeare's ponderous humorist—but young, handsome, an absolute lady-killer of sorts, one for whom beautiful women of various stations apparently had a fatal fondness, a composer of a certain type of melodramatic and tearful yet land-sweeping songs ("The Letter That Never Came," "The Pardon Came Too Late," "The Convict and the Bird," "I Believe It for My Mother Told Me So," "The Bowery"), and at the same time a comedian of relatively acknowledged standing who could earn as much, say, as one hundred and twenty-five to two hundred dollars a week in the roles that he essayed. Already he had led a most varied career: as a village sport in Terre Haute, where he was born; and later on as a student for the Catholic priesthood, from the institute for which he ran away; then as a strolling singer with so humble a current traveling medicine company as Hamlin's "Wizard Oil" Company, Number Six (let us say); then as a genuine end man in various famous minstrel companies; and finally as a comedian and composer of sentimental songs, which were giving him quite a vogue among those who are fond of that sort of thing, and which gave him a connection with a popular music house in New York (Willis Woodward and Company) and a standing with acting tours throughout America. In the two or three years preceding my entering the newspaper profession in Chicago, I had been becoming a little envious of him and irritated by my own low state to the point of ignoring him. But now that I appeared to be rising in the world, my mood had changed or was changing, and he was my own dear brother once more to me—one of whom I was really and more or less unselfishly fond. I was so eager to have him get along and be a great success (some selfishness in that, I suppose) and only recently had been wondering what had become of him—where he was.

Now walking along South 6th Street here in St. Louis once in this same late November, in the region of the old Havlin Theatre where all the standard melodramas of the time played, I was startled to see his face and name staring at me from a billboard, and beneath it the lines, "The Danger Signal, with Paul Dresser."

"Ah," I thought at once, "my famous brother. Now these people will know whether our family amounts to anything or not! Here he is at last, right here in St. Louis, and I can point to him with pride. At least he can act and write successful songs. Wait'll they hear he is my brother." The *they* referred to not only all those whom I knew personally or who might know of me, but incidentally the world at large. We could show them, every one of us, if we would! (This referred to the remainder of our interesting, restless family.) Always the idea was with me that I was to do something, too, although just what or how or when or where, I could never make out. It was all a nebulous nothing as yet. Only as I realized now—at least in so far as I was concerned—newspaper work as a profession was a farce. It contained no hope of real advancement for me. At the same time, Paul's picture on this billboard recalled so many pleasant memories of him, his visits home, his kindness to and intense love for my mother, how in my tenth year he had talked of my being a writer, heaven only knows why. Once in Warsaw in my fourteenth year, when he was home on a visit for the summer, he had set me to the task of composing a humorous essay of some kind— which for some insoluble reason, considering my ultrameditative character, he felt sure I could write! Willingly and singly I essayed it, but when I chose the ancient topic of the mule and its tendency to kick, his face fell, and he tried to show me in the gentlest way possible how hackneyed that was and to put me on the track of doing something original. Dear, genial, kindly soul, how little he ever understood me at any time, as interested as he was so to do. Now, after all this time, and scarcely knowing whether he knew that I was here or not, I was to have the pleasure of seeing him once more, and to make clear to him my worldly improvement, and to greet him as a brother should. I do not say it to boast, but I honestly think that there was as much if not more joy in the mere thought of seeing him again and knowing that he was doing well and feeling happy, as there was in showing him off and garnering a little personal credit for his being a success. Possibly not, but I think so.

CHAPTER LIX

As I look back on my life now, I realize clearly that subsequent to my mother's death, the only one of all the members of my family who truly understood me—or better yet, sympathized with my intellectual and artistic point of view—was Paul. (Paul Dresser was his stage name, and under that slight variation also he wrote all his rather successful and well-known—in his world—songs.) Not that he was in any way fitted intellectually or otherwise to enjoy the higher forms of art and learning and so guide me. He was not. (All of my other brothers were much better able intellectually to appreciate the better writers and thinkers.) Or that he understood even in later years (long after I had written *Sister Carrie*, for instance) what it was that I was driving at intellectually or otherwise. He never did. His world was that of the popular song, the middle-class actor or comedian, the middle-class comedy and such humorous esthetes of the writing world as Bill Nye, Petroleum V. Nasby, and the authors of the *Spoopendyke Papers* and *Samantha at Saratoga*. As far as I could make out—and I say this in no lofty, condescending spirit by any means—he was entirely full of simple, middle-class romance, middle-class humor, middle-class tenderness and middle-class grossness—all of which I am very free to say I admire very much, indeed. After all, we can't all be artists, statesmen, generals, thieves, or financiers in the accepted or classical sense. Some of us, the large majority, have to be just plain everyday middle-class, and a very comfortable state it is indeed under any decent form of government. But so much said, there was so very much more to be said of him, things which persistently raise him in my memory to a height far more appealing and important, humanly and artistically speaking, than that of hundreds of greater and possibly surer fame. For after all, my brother was a humanist of so tender and delicate a mold that to speak of him as a mere artist of sorts or a middle-class thinker and composer of a successful kind would be to do him a gross injustice and miss the entire significance and flavor of his being. For some people (ignoramuses, if you will), errant religionists, actors, songwriters, playwrights of an humble turn, are artists in the truest sense (spiritually speaking), whether you will or no. Vide Bunyan, John Howard Payne (the author of "Home, Sweet Home"). This tenderness or sympathy of his—a very human appreciation of the weaknesses and errors as well as the toils and tribulations of most of us—was by far his most outstanding and engaging quality, and gave him a very definite (beautiful indeed) force and charm. Admitting, as I am glad to, that he was very sensuous (gross, some people might have called him), that he had an intense, possibly an undue fondness for women (I am free to say that I have never been able to discover where the dividing line in such matters is to be drawn—certainly, for most temperaments at least, not at one life, one love), a frivolous, childish, horse-play sense of humor at times. Still he had other qualities which were positively adorable. That sunny temperament, that vigorous—if stout—body and nimble mind, those smiling sweet blue eyes, the air of gayety and well-being that was with him nearly all the time, even at his most trying times. Life seemed positively to bubble in him. Hope sprang upward like a fountain. He always seemed immensely successful even when he was not—for the time being, say. You felt in him a capacity to do, in his possibly limited field—an ability to achieve, whether he was so doing at the moment or no. Some people are so successful even when to themselves they seem least so. You know that they eventually *will do*, whether they are doing now or not. Of such was my brother. Never having the least power to interpret anything in a high musical way, still he was always full of music of a tender (sometimes sad, sometimes gay) kind—the ballad-maker of a nation. Personally, I was always fascinated by this latter skill of his—the lovable art that attempts to interpret sorrow and pleasure in terms of song, however humble. And on the stage, how in a crude way, by mere smile and gesture, he could make an audience laugh. I have seen houses crowded to the ceiling with middle- or lower-class souls, shopgirls and -boys perhaps, factory hands and the like, who tittered continuously over his every move so long as he was on the stage. He seemed to radiate a kind of comforting sunshine and humor without a sharp edge or sting (satire was entirely beyond him)—a kind of wilding asininity—your true clown in cap and bells, which caused even my morbid soul to chortle by the hour. Was there ever another such, so gay, so genial, so kind! Shakespeare has set forth Jack Falstaff as an amusing and enduring type. Beside him (and safely) might be placed my brother Paul, a modern theatrical Jack—tender, wistful, adventurous, child-like. What a darling, really. No wonder women, those eager seekers after tenderness and understanding even when fickle, were so fond of him. I can understand it thoroughly.

And all of his songs, however commonplace to the cognoscenti, musically speaking—most asinine sighings over home and mother and lost sweethearts and dead heroes such as never were in real life, perhaps—were still full of a sweet and moving significance to me, quite touching at times, the music especially. They bespoke, as I always felt, a wistful, seeking, uncertain temperament, tender and illusioned—

with no practical knowledge of life in any line, but full of a true poetic feeling for the mystery and pathos of life and death, the wonder of the waters, the stars, the flowers, accidents of life, death, success, failure and the like. (After all, is there anything more engaging than that in either man or woman?)

In real life, in addition, he was not unlike his songs, given to the most compelling bursts of emotion over poor widows, orphans, the halt, the blind, the maimed, the bereft, the unfortunates in every walk of life.

What are you to say of such a temperament? Laugh as one will, or misdoubt, or call it idiotic or asinine, still there it is, and it answers to one of the most vital impulses in us, that of appeal for mercy or aid to powers greater than ourselves. We pretend so often to scorn the sympathetic or the emotional as fools, failures, those unable to protect themselves. But do we really? Is not the wish to be realistic in this respect always destructive to our own hearts and our inner understanding?

My good brother not only felt with his heart or emotions and interpreted them in his songs, such as they were, but he carried his feelings into material practise, reaching on occasion the lorn widow with a ton of coal, or a sack of flour; the reckless, headstrong boy whose parents might be too poor to save him from a term in jail or the reformatory with fine-money or an appeal to higher powers for clemency; the wastrel actor or actress "down and out" and unable "to get home to New York" with his or her railroad fare wired prepaid; and often, often, the wastrel dead with a coffin and a decent form of burial—some creature he had known years before, possibly, in some obscure way somewhere. Have I not myself often seen him take a train or a car to visit a sick person somewhere in some remote forsaken region, far from the central portion of New York, which he loved so much, in order to carry some form of solace—sympathy, money, his mere gladdening presence—and always on the theory that however worthless and forgotten they might be now, still it was only human not to forget them entirely!

"You know how it is, Thee" (as he sometimes called me), "when you're old and sick. As long as you are up and around and have money, everyone's your friend. Once you're down and out, no one wants to see you any more."

Almost amusingly, he was always sad over those who had once

been prosperous and pleasure-loving, perhaps, but now were old and forgotten. Some of his silliest tender songs conveyed as much. (If I could, I would ask him to take this as my humble tribute to his truly wide and almost perfect humanity.)

"But," I once complained, apropos of some particularly flagrant case of incompetence ending in want and sickness, "why didn't he save a little money when he had it? He made as much as you'll ever make or more." (The man had been a successful vaudeville performer.) "He had plenty of it, didn't he?"

"Well, you know how it is, Thee," he explained in the kindliest and most forgiving way. "When you're young and healthy like that you don't think—you wouldn't right now if you had it—and anyhow, that's the time to spend your money if you're going to get any good of it at all, isn't it? Of course, when you're old you can't expect much, but still I always feel as though I'd like to help some of these old people."

His eyes at such times always seemed to melt and transfuse in some mystic way—a most warm and tender look.

"But, Paul," I insisted on another occasion when he had just wired twenty-five dollars somewhere to bury someone. (My spirit was not so much niggardly as fearsome. I was constantly terrified in those days by the thought of a poverty-stricken and lonely old age myself—why, I don't know. I was by no means incompetent.) "Why don't you save your money? Why should you give it to every Tom, Dick and Harry who asks you? You're not a charity organization, and you're not called upon to feed and clothe and bury all the wasters who happen to cross your path. If you were down and out, how many do you suppose would help you?"

"My boy," he replied—and his voice and his manner were largely those of my mother, the same wonder, the same wistfulness and sweetness, the same bubbling charity and tenderness of heart—"what's the use being so hard on people? We're all likely to get that way. You don't know what pulls people down sometimes—not wastefulness always. It's ignorance or trying to be happy. Remember how poor we were and how mama and papa used to worry." (So often in reference to my mother or father or their difficulties, tears would rise to his eyes.) "I can't stand to see people suffer, that's all—not if I have anything," and his eyes glowed sweetly. "And after all," he added apologetically, "the little I give isn't much. They don't get so much out of me. They don't come to me every day."

No, not every day, to be sure, but how often they did come, and how generous was his response! As he was lying dead years later, at least a hundred men and women, whom I had never seen or heard of before, ventured into the chamber, knelt down and prayed—and many of them cried as they did so.

Why? From what glorious realms of force is it that issue the hosts of mercy, their hands extended, their hearts bleeding for the misery of the world?

Well, this was my brother Paul—the same whom I have described as stout, gross, sensual—and all of these qualities went hand in hand. I have no time here for more than the briefest glimpse, the faintest echo, although I should thrill to write a book concerning him alone—the wonderful—the tender. But now he was coming to St. Louis, and in my youthful vainglorious way I was determined to show him what I was now—to entertain him. He should be introduced to Peter, Dick and Rodenberger, my cronies. I would have a feast in my room in his honor after the theatre. I would give another—a supper at Faust's, then the leading restaurant of St. Louis, of a gay bohemian character—and invite Wandell, Dunlap, my managing editor (I can never think of his name), Bassford the dramatic editor, Peter, Dick and Rodenberger. They should all see how wonderful my big, successful brother was. At the same time, I proposed to bring my new love to his theatre, some afternoon or evening performance, perhaps, and introduce her, for how often had I casually hinted to one and all of those with whom I was most intimate that the well-known songwriter and actor, Paul Dresser, was my brother. How, next to shedding radiance ourselves, we all crave the warming beams of another's light!

I hurried to the office of the *Globe*, where in the art department I found Dick and Peter, and communicated my news and plans. They were very much for whatever it was I wanted to do, and so to meet Paul, of course. "Gee, sure!" exclaimed the excitable Dick. "It'll be fine. Where's he going to play?" I told him. Also within the next twenty-four hours, I am sure, I had not only written to Miss White, but told Wandell, Bassford, the managing editor and nearly everyone else. I dropped in at Faust's and secured an estimate on the kind of meal I thought he would like, having the headwaiter plan it for me, and then eagerly awaited his arrival. I had been informed by the man at the box office of Havlin's that the company would very likely reach the city

Sunday morning or noon, as this theatre opened all its new shows on Sunday night. I must say I was quite beside myself with satisfaction, eager to see the man once more by whom my youth had been so influenced and by whom my immediate future, however little I might guess, was to be influenced, for a while anyhow.

Sunday morning came, and, anxious to see him once more, I called at about eleven, and, sure enough, there he was on the stage of this old theatre, entirely surrounded by trunks and scenery of various kinds, looking for some one trunk, apparently, from which he wished to get something. There was with him at the moment a very petite actress—one Rosabel Morrison—the female star of the company, who, as I subsequently discovered, was one of his passing flames. He was as stout as ever, a little more so, if anything, and dressed in the most engaging Broadway fashion: a suit of good cloth and smart cut, a fur coat, a high hat, and a gold-headed cane—all the earmarks, in short, of passing prosperity and comfort. What a wonderful thing he and the stage, even this world of claptrap melodrama, seemed to me at the time—this old smelly theatre, the juggernaut scenery of the play, this rather attractive young actress by his side, smiling on him in the affectionate but condescending manner of the average pretty mistress of the stage. I felt on the instant, somehow, as though I were being treated to the unusual in the matter of passing earthly spectacles and also as though I were better established in the world than I thought, to be thus connected with one who traveled over the country in this way. The whole world seemed to come much closer because of him. "Hello," he called, plainly astonished. "Where'd you come from?" And then seeing perhaps that I was better dressed and poised mentally than he had ever known me before (I must always have appeared the mere stripling to him, up to the time he had last seen me), he looked me over in an odd, slightly doubtful way, like a stranger might, and then introduced me to his friend. Seeing him apparently pleased by my arrival and eager to talk to me, she quickly excused herself, saying she had to go on to her hotel, while he fell to asking me questions about how I came to be here, how I was getting along, et cetera. I am sure he was slightly puzzled and possibly disturbed by my sharp change from a shy, retiring boy to one who, if he did not push himself forward much, still examined him with the chill and weighing eye of the newspaper man. (What a tribe they are for cold, fishy, examining eyes!) To me, all of a sudden, he was not so much merely one whom I had to like or admire because he was my brother, my oldest living brother, or one who knew more about life than I. Rather less, I now thought, looking at him and gathering his intellectual import (at least his faculty for understanding life was not as good as mine, I took it). But, as I soon found, he had a certain soft, generous, "too-easy" character, or so I imagined at the time, which would tend rather to hold him back financially than advance him. Instantly this appealed to me, as against one who might have turned out much more dull or shrewder in certain ways—one like myself, for instance. He soon seemed to realize that I found him appealing, and his own manner softened, became more natural. He reminded me a great deal of my mother, looked like her, and I could not help recalling how loving and generous he had always been with her in all his relations, contributing regularly to her support, sending home all his cast-off clothing for the younger ones (bless her tired hands), crying with her at times over her troubles and his. I liked always to think of him in this way. I thought of him so then and do now—the simple, home-loving mother-boy. It brought him so close to us all. Even then, I doubt very much whether he liked me at first, finding me so brash and self-sufficient. Still, he accepted me once more as a part of the family and so of himself, a brother, another of mother's boys, so simple and communistic were the laws by which his charming mind worked. And so whether he felt inclined to or not, he must love me a little, or like me anyhow. How often have I heard him say of one or another of us (or to some other person, not a member of our family, in regard to some immediate relation) concerning whom some acrimonious debate might be going forward—"After all, he's your brother, isn't he?" or "She's your sister," as though mere consanguinity should dissolve all our honest (or otherwise) dissatisfactions and rages. Isn't there something humanly sweet about that in the face of all the cold, decisive conclusions of this world?

CHAPTER LX

Well, such was my brother Paul, in part at least (may he fare well), and now here he was. After a moment or two of fixed contemplation I made up my mind to like him intensely—a mood that never varied thereafter in me. Never before was he so much my dear brother as now, never so appealing (although I always had and have been able to waive blood ties as being of no great import, to me at least). So generally delightful and admirable was he in so many ways that I would have liked him quite as much, I am sure, had he been no relative of mine at all—the veriest stranger—had chance, say, provided the necessary contacts. After a few moments of explanation as to my present state, I offered to share my room with him for the period of his stay, but he declined. Then I offered to take him to lunch, but he was too hurried or engaged. He agreed to come to my room with me after the show, however, and offered me a box for myself and my new friends. So much faith did I have in Peter's and Dick's and Rodenberger's good sense—their certainty of appreciating the charm of a man like Paul— that I ventured to go and get them that same night and bring them here, although I knew the show itself must be a mess. There were, among other things, a scenic engine used in it somewhere, a heroine lying across the rails. My dear brother was a comic switchman or engineer or something in this act—evoking roars of lowbrow laughter by his antics and jokes, of course.

I shall never forget how these three friends took all this. On hearing that he was actually here and playing that night, they were close enough to me to take him into their affectional consideration on my account, almost as though he belonged to them. He was "Dreiser's brother Paul"—even "dear old Paul" afterwards. (That was Dick's name for him.) Because working conditions favored us that night, we all descended on the Havlin together, a most bumptious and raucous crew, sitting in the box while the show was in progress—or a part of the time, anyhow—but spending all the intermissions and periods before and after the play in Paul's dressing room or on the stage with him. Having overcome his first surprise and possibly dislike of my brash newspaper manner, he was all smiles now and plainly delighted with my new friends. Rodenberger and Peter, the latter especially, appealed to him immensely as being characters like himself—individuals he could understand—and in later years, after I was in New York, he was always asking after them, and especially after McCord, and singing their praises. Indeed, I myself rose in his estimation, I am sure, because of them. They were so interesting to him. Dick also came in for a share of his warm affection, only in a slower way. He thought Dick was amusing, but queer, like some strange animal of some kind. On subse-

quent tours which took him to St. Louis, he was always in touch with
these three and would even report to me what they were doing. Above
all things, the waggish grotesqueries of McCord's mind moved him immensely. His incisive personality and daring unconventionality seemed
to him positively fascinating. "Wonderful boy, that," he used to say to
me, almost as though he were confiding a deep secret. "You'll hear from
him yet—mark my word. You can't lose a kid like that." And time
proved quite plainly that he was right.

Rodenberger also touched him, but in a different way. He couldn't
quite make him out, and yet he seemed to sense something important.
"Wonderful fellow, that. He's got such queer eyes. He seems to be
laughing at you all the time, and yet he isn't, I suppose. He hardly ever
smiles."

"Well, he's laughing just the same," I replied, "and don't you think
he isn't. Rodenberger is a devil, that's all. He's like a gargoyle smirking
at you, unable, quite, to make up his mind whether he'll eat you or
not."

Dick took to the newcomer like a younger brother. It was "dear old
Paul" here and "dear old Paul" there, in Dick's effusive, almost feminine manner. At once he decided to attempt a sketch of him in his
engineer costume, an amazing suit of overalls, with the tufts of his red
wig sticking out over his ears, but it was a failure. Dick had no skill at
character drawing. Essentially he was a writer, not an artist at all. In the
play Paul sang one of his own compositions, "The Bowery," which
appealed to all three as a splendid example of current song skill and
humor, and I really think they were right. It was an exceptional comic
song, quite destructive of the good name of the Bowery forever—so
much so that ten years later the merchants and property owners of
that famous thoroughfare petitioned to have the name of the street
changed, on the ground that the jibes involved in the song had destroyed its character as an honest business street forever. So much for
the import of a silly ballad and the passing songwriter. What are the
really powerful things in this world, anyhow? Who knows?

And I really think we were all quite beside ourselves with the
pleasure of mussing around freely behind the stage, seeing the scenery
struck, the actors and actresses bustling about, the curtain go up from
behind and Paul actually walking out and doing a part. Afterward we all
adjourned to some scowsy music hall in the vicinity of this old theatre,

which Dick insisted would amuse Paul, by reason of its very wretchedness, although I'm sure it didn't (he was not, as I say, a satirist). And then to my room, where I had the man who provided the midnight lunch for the workers of the *Globe* spread a small feast—a large can of coffee, beer, sandwiches and pie. I had no piano unfortunately, but Paul sang just the same, and Peter gave an imitation of a street player who could manipulate at one and the same time a drum, a mouth organ and an accordion. We had to beat my good brother on the back to keep him from choking.

But it was during a week of breakfasts which now followed and which Paul and I regularly ate together that the first and really impressive conversations in regard to New York occurred, conversations that finally imbued me with the feeling that I should never be quite satisfied until I had reached there. I do not know whether this was due to the fact that I now first told him about myself—my present state and ambitions or dreams and my somewhat remarkable success here—or that he himself was now getting to the place where, because of his success on the stage and with his songs, he was able to suggest ways and means and at the same time indulge a somewhat paternalistic streak in himself. But just the same, during this week he persisted in the most florid descriptions of the city on the Hudson and my duty to go there— its import to me intellectually and otherwise. And finally he had me fairly convinced that I should never really reach my true intellectual status unless I did—that I must eventually leave St. Louis, at no far distant date really, and venture into this great metropolis of the East. Other places might be very good, he kept insisting—they all had their value—but there was only one place where one might live in a different way, more keenly and vigorously than anywhere else in America, and that was New York. It was *the* great city—the only cosmopolitan city— a wonder-world in itself. Say what you would, go where you pleased, you would never find anything like it, never. It was great, wonderful, marvelous—the size, the color, the tang, the beauty.

"My boy," he exclaimed at one point one morning, "you will never get it straight unless you come there and see for yourself. All these Western places are all right in their way, but there is only one New York, just one."

Then he went on to explain in less glowing strophes that the West was narrow, slow, not really alive like New York. There one might always do, think and act more freely than anywhere else. The air itself was tonic. You touched life at more points. All really ambitious people, people who were destined to do or be anything in any line, eventually drifted there—editors, newspaper men, actors, playwrights, songwriters, musicians, money-makers—the town was full of them, and the best of it was that the best ones succeeded there. You couldn't keep the able down in New York. Somehow those needing you eventually found you out. He pointed to himself as a case in point—how he had ventured there, a gawky stripling doing a monologue, and how one Harry Minor, of now antique Bowery Theatre fame, had seized on him, carried him along and forwarded him in every way. Some one was certain to do as much for me, for everyone who had any ability. He would, if necessary. In passing, he now confided in me that only recently, from having been the star song-writer of a well-known New York music publisher (Willis Woodward), he had succeeded, along with two music publishing clerks of that same city, in organizing a music publishing company of his own—or rather one in which he had a third interest. It was to publish his songs, as well as those of others, and was pledged to pay him for once an honest royalty (a thing which he insisted so far had not been done) as well as his full share as partner. Naturally, he was in a more comfortable and hopeful spirit in regard to himself than he had ever been before and eager to go further. In addition, under the friendly urging of some ambitious stage manager who wished to star him, he was now writing a play to be known as *The Green Goods Man*, in which in another year or two at the least he would appear as the star. Also he reminded me that our sister Emma, who had long since moved to New York (as early as 1886), was now living in comfort, or so I understood, in West 15th Street, where she would be only too glad to receive me if I would come. He was always in New York in the summertime, living with this same sister. "Why not come down there next summer when I am there off the road and look it over?" he added on several occasions. "Then you can decide for yourself." There he could entertain me and show me about.

As he talked, New York came nearer than ever it had before, and I could see the light of conviction and enthusiasm in his eyes. It was plain, now that he had seen me again, that he wanted me to succeed. My friends, I think, had already sung my praises to him, and in addition it must have been rather plain that I was fast emerging from my too shy youth. St. Louis might be well enough—I did not doubt it—and Chicago—but New York, New York! Ah, me! Ah, me! One who had never seen it, as I had not, but who was eager to see the world could not help but sniff and prick up his ears. It must be fascinating indeed.

I confess that this invitation, more than anything else that had happened so far, fixed New York in my mind as an objective and something rather easily achieved—now. I had a sister there. My brother was in the publishing business there! Ha! Think of that, ye who would attempt to write us down as unimportant—a publishing business, no less! It was a place to go. I had had it in my mind's eye all this time, only I had never been sure that I would really go. It was so large—so distant from my Middle West. But now, somehow, my general plan of life seemed to be changing in spite of myself. Only recently that before-mentioned Hutchinson—the scribe who had come to St. Louis to obtain my aid in securing a place—had been harping on the supreme advantage of being a country editor, the ease of the life, its security. He was out of work now and anxious to leave, and he had about convinced me of the merit of his claims. On his part he was convinced, I think, that I was financially in a position to buy a half interest in some fairly successful country paper (which I was not), while he took the other half interest on time. At any rate I had been thinking of that as a way of getting out of the horrible, pointless grind of newspaperdom, and did think much more of it later. Only this mood of my brother's seemed to reach down to the very depths of my being, depths hitherto not plumbed by anything, and put New York into me as a kind of ultimate certainty. I must go there at some time or other whatever I did between whiles—edited a country paper or what. Indeed, it might be a good thing to go and run a country paper for awhile, if I could. It might make me some money—give me station and confidence. But ah, the great city with its multimillionaires, its tremendous newspapers and magazines, its great hotels and theatres, its Wall Street, Broadway and Fifth Avenue. When would it be that I would actually arrive there? Already he had described the two latter—Broadway aglow of a night from 14th to 34th Streets, with its theatres, restaurants, hotels and seeking crowds; Fifth Avenue jingling with its carriages and wealth, flaunting its security and expensive toys! I had not yet read Balzac— that master interpreter of the lure of success and material display, of the social dreams of the comfortable, as well as the despairs of the failures,—but

Balzac or no, the significance of it all, as exemplified by New York, was with me at last, and unfortunately to stay for many a torturing year.

Ha! The misery of desire—those hooks of the flesh that pull as definitely to failure and despair as to success and security. Must not the Maker of this scene be indeed an artist to have invented the two things most useful in whipping slaves to a purpose—hunger and hope?

CHAPTER LXI

It was during this week also that I gave the supper previously mentioned and took Miss White to meet my brother—the latter event a thing most important to me though not, I fear, to him. I am satisfied that she liked him, or was rather amused by him, not understanding the least thing in connection with his life or the character of the stage. Whereas the sole comment of any import that I could get out of him was that she was charming, but that if he were me he would not think of getting married yet—a statement which had more light thrown on it years later by his persistent indifference to and private dislike of her, although he was always too courteous and mindful of the privacies of others to express himself openly to me. It came to me in other ways. All of which also is really neither here nor there, now. At the time, however, I pondered over this as a somewhat mild confirmation of Maxwell, but said nothing. Both in a way were wrong, I was sure. Marriage was not so bad as they thought—nor is it, for those who crave it. Think of the intense delight involved—the comfort.

In addition, the later public supper was somewhat of a failure also, for while I had all my listed friends present, no one failing me, and the food was all that it should be—appetizing—still the whole thing went off with a curious sense of error, or inappropriateness in the combination, which disappointed me greatly. I had counted on it as being such a certain pleasure to all—or that they would succeed in making it so. But, alas, for the best of our plans—or hopes. Without knowing it, I was trying to harmonize elements which somehow at this time would not mix—at least not on such short notice. The true bohemianism and at the same time exclusive camaraderie of such youths as Peter, Dick and Rodenberger, and the rather stilted intellectual sufficiency of my editorial friends and superiors of the *Republic*, plus the utter innocence and naiveté of Paul himself proved too much. There was no fun in the dinner at all. It was stilted, formal, inconceivably boring. It is entirely possible that if I had confined it to Dick, Peter, Rodenberger and Paul—or to Wandell and the editorial group—all would have gone well. As it was, we seemed not to be able to find any common topics for discussion. My dear brother was as barren of intellectual grip as a child. No least current problem of any import such as might have interested these editorial men—the art of the stage, for instance, or current political or social topics—had apparently the least interest for him or had ever been weighed by him. He could not discuss them. Although I fancy if we had turned to prizefighters or baseball heroes or comic characters in general, he would have done well enough. All his life he seemed absolutely fearsome in regard to anything truly intellectual— never venturing to express an opinion in my presence but always referring the matter to me. Indeed, his and their thoughts were so far apart, I am sure, that they all but found him dull, and me with him. For, struck all at once by the ridiculousness of my attempt, I couldn't talk gaily or naturally, and the more I tried to bring things round the worse it became. I had no skill in managing such a thing at that time. Instead, I was on pins and needles, and finally the whole thing was saved from utterly ridiculous boredom by Wandell remembering rather early that he had something to do and returning to the office. Seizing their opportunity, the managing editor and the dramatic editor went with him. The others and myself now attempted to rally—but it was too late. A half hour later we also broke up, and I accompanied my brother to his hotel door. He made none but pleasant and complimentary comments, but the whole thing was such a fizzle that I could have wept. Always my grandest efforts seemed to end in some such way.

By Sunday morning he was gone again, however, and then my life settled into its old routine apparently—only it didn't. Now, once and for all, or much more than ever, I felt myself a flitting figure in this interesting but plainly humdrum local world, prosperous enough perhaps but with no significant future for me connected with it. The idea of New York as a great and glowing centre—better perhaps, as my brother had said, than any other place—had taken root. His publishing house, my sister's home, the fact (as he had also confided to me during this week) that he was writing a play—a comedy or farce—in which he was to be the star the next year or the year after, all caused me to think that there might be some opening for me. It wasn't like venturing into a strange and distant land without anyone to guide you.

At the same time, in the face of my growing estimate of myself, backed by the plaudits of such men as Peter and Dick who were receiving twice my salary if not more, to say nothing of the assurances of my brother that I was bound to succeed in some line, that I had that mysterious thing personality et cetera, I was still always cramped for cash and without the slightest sign on the part of my employers at the *Republic* that I would ever be worth any more to them. Apparently I might write and write (as I did) page specials every week, assignments of all and sundry forms, one or two a day at the least—theatrical and sport reviews at times—and still, after all the evidence that I could be of exceptional service to them, twenty-two or -three dollars was all I could get. They were always pleasant and even intimate with me and seemed to admire me or what I did and to have great hopes for me in their service, but nothing happened. Some two or three months later——

But let that rest for the present.

Dogging my heels also at this time was that same Hutchinson,—a cheerful, comforting soul in the main—one who believed in me entirely, or pretended to, but who was an absolute burden on my hands. It has always been a matter of the greatest interest to me to observe how (particularly in my life) there are certain types throughout nature—parasites, barnacles—who fix on others willy-nilly, decide in their own minds that they are to be aided or strengthened by another and fix on that other quite as their rightful due. They are at home with that other, whoever he or she may be. Without a "by your leave" or any other form of courtesy they seem to "edge in," as someone used to say, bring their trunk or bag and make themselves at home. Ants, I believe, have scores of parasites of different kinds living upon them.

In my case, Hutchinson was such an one. Although I can sincerely say that I never really liked the man very much or that he even amused me in any marked way, still here he was, idling about, worrying about a job or his future, living in my room toward the last, eating his meals (or at least his breakfast) with me, and talking about the country and the charm, ease and profit of editing a country newspaper!

Now, of all people in this dusty world, it seems to me that I can imagine no one *less* fitted than myself, temperamentally or in any other way, to edit a country paper. Imagine—Theodore Dreiser, editor of the Credulia (Spartensburg County) *Star*, circulation three thousand. The mental limitations of such a world! My own errant disposition and ideas—my contempt for and revolt against the average, standardized and clockwork motions and notions of the average man and woman! And at that time—with my seething mood. In six months I would have been arrested or drummed out by the preacher, the elders and all the other worthies for miles around. Let sleeping dogs lie. The louder all conventionalists snore the better—for me anyhow.

Well, in spite of these few minor objections—as some one used to say, these mere bags of shells—here I was listening to this silly drivel and wondering whether it might not offer an avenue of escape from the humdrum and clam-like siphoning into which I seemed to have fallen. And beside me constantly from November on, or after my brother left, was this very cheerful mediocrity, someone of about the warmth and intelligence of a bright collie, telling me daily how wonderful I was and that I "ought to get out of here" and into something which would really profit me and get me somewhere—into the editorship of a country weekly, for instance!

At any rate, here was one such, the poorest of specimens it may be, but still one, and mingling with his admiration and confidence this desire to get on personally. What jocular fates trifled with my sense of the reasonable or the ridiculous at this time I may not know, but suffice it to say that I was interested—largely, I presume, because I was too wandering and nebulous in my mood to think of anything else to do. This cheerful soul, who had begun by telling me of the import and ease of editing such a sheet, finally ended by indicating one in particular— the Weekly Something of Grand Rapids, Ohio (not Michigan)—near his father's farm (see pp. 247–255, A *Hoosier Holiday*), which according to him was just the thing and should offer a complete solution for all his and my material and social aspirations in this world. Via this particular paper or some other of its kind, one might rise to any heights—political or social, for instance, state or national. I might become a state assemblyman from my county, or senator—a congressman, or United States senator! Some country editors made as much as three or four thousand a year out of their papers (the noble sum of sixty or eighty dollars a week!). When you owned a country paper you were an independent person. (Imagine the editor of a country paper being independent of the conventions of his community!) Not like a poor harried scribe on a city paper, unable to say from week to week whether he was to be retained any longer. There were the delights of a country life—the sweet simplicity of a country town, away from the noise and stress and gaudy, shabby nothingness of a great city. Heigh Ho! I listened to the picture of his native town, his father's farm, how we could go there and live for awhile, months no less. (Imagine the consideration involved in imposing ourselves and his wife on these amiable people for the benefit of our future careers—and no thanks to them particularly.) My imagination mounted up, and once more I was off, Bellerophon style, to the highest heaven of unadulterated success, peace, joy, et cetera. Already I had rented or bought and paid for a small vine-clad cottage in Grand Rapids, Ohio, where, according to Hutchinson, was a wonderful sparkling rapids to be seen glimmering in the moonlight at times, a railroad which took you into Toledo, a city of one hundred thousand, within an hour, fertile farmland all about, where both gas and oil had recently been struck, making the farmers fairly prosperous and ergo in the mood for a first-class country newspaper such as we would edit. We were sure to be a great hit. There was no doubt of it. It would be possible to get nearly all the storekeepers and merchants of this happy village to agree to take so much space in our paper, per year, in advance, for the purpose of advertising one thing and another,—hay, grain, feed, groceries, et cetera—thus guaranteeing our livelihood, or a portion of it, anyhow. Rooms and board would be a mere nothing. People could live cheaply and well in Grand Rapids. Once he and his wife were properly settled, I could live with them.

Et cetera, et cetera, et cetera.

CHAPTER LXII

All my life I have been more or less surrounded and forwarded by people who have insisted that I was this, that, and the other— that I should press forward and do thus and so. (And I say this in no ungrateful or captious spirit—far from it.) That this was always done in an unselfish spirit I cannot say—not always. Occasionally, definite personal ambitions were obviously involved. On the other hand, there have been such glistering examples of individuals who, having an ideal of their own and not being able to forward it as fast as they would like, have turned to others, myself among them, as a possible means of realizing something. (The thought of them with their seeking faces—their spiritual dreams—is sobering.) What these ideals were may not, in all cases, have been clear, even to themselves. I have an idea that with many it was little more than a nebulous dream of beauty to be realized in any such way as might be possible, the implement or servant by whom the ideal was to be realized being of small import. I know that many have taken up with me on this basis—and to what end? (The faces of those who have sought it through me! The nothingness of their reward! What is form that we should seek so eagerly to achieve it? Beauty that we should strive with such vehemence—such huge despairs—to behold its perfect lines?)

My thoughts were now turned, more definitely than I myself realized at the time, I think, not to the idea of rural life and editing a country newspaper (although I vaguely imagined that was what I might do for a time), but to New York, or at least the East. And the things which were turning them and driving me were, on the one hand, the indifference of the *Republic* to my merits as I saw them, and on the other, the necessity of discovering some field of endeavor—other than newspaper reporting, which I was coming to despise—which would open up an avenue of genuine advancement and provide the means for marrying and supporting my prospective bride in comfort. Yet I can truly say of myself at the time, as of myself in later scenes and situations, that I felt myself to be a little unreal,—not an actual spiritual participant but one who was doing little more than playing a part. There were moments when I appear to have believed that I was to settle down as a country editor. There were other moments in which I appeared to sense that I should do no such thing—that it was all a joke or an excuse for moving and so escaping the rut into which I had fallen. Again, there was the idea that the apparently intense interest I was taking in Miss White was not genuine after all, that as much as I appeared to love her, I did not—or in a much less significant way than I thought—and that I could do without her if need be, and easily. It was not her, but life, love—as expressed by her in this instance—in which I was interested. Again, there was the feeling that whatever I thought as to any temporary destination, my real abode was New York and that I would soon come there, although in reality I did not at that time believe that I was going to New York. These were the opposing moods: (1) that I would spend the remainder of my days doing "hack reporting," a restless, underpaid, dissatisfied failure, unmarried and worthless, and (2) the very definite feeling that never, never would I allow such a fate to overtake me. I talked and talked to Hutchinson, to my future wife, to Dick and Peter in a roundabout hinting way, and developed all sorts of theories as to the future which awaited me—or myself and Hutchinson, or myself and Mrs. Dreiser. More to buoy up my faith in myself, I tried to make her feel that I was a personage and would do great things. How nature would ever get on without total blindness, or at least immense credulity, on the part of its creatures at the mating and other times, I cannot guess. Certainly if women in their youth and love period had any more sense than the men, they would not be impressed with the balderdash dreams of such swains as myself at least. They must want to believe. Or they cannot help themselves. Nature must want them to believe. How the woman who married me could have been impressed by me at this period is beyond my reasoning. Yet apparently she was—or saw nothing better in store for her than myself, and in consequence was willing to abide by the insane outcome.

But that she was impressed and that I, moved by her affection for me or my own desire to possess her, was impelled to do something to better my condition, is obvious. Hints thrown out at the *Republic* office, to my sponsor Wandell in particular, producing nothing, I decided quite casually sometime during January or February 1894 to take up Hutchinson's proposition, although I did not see how, other than via gross luck, it could come to anything. Neither of us had any money to speak of, and yet we were thinking of starting a country newspaper. For a few days in the late fall I had debated this with him and then sent him north to his home town to look over the field there and report, which he immediately did, writing most glowing reports concerning an absolutely worthless country paper at Grand Rapids, Ohio, which he was positive we could secure for a song and turn into a paying proposition at once. I did not believe it, yet I felt called upon to believe it even in spite of myself, and so to leave St. Louis. I reasoned that should it come to nothing I could go on to some nearby city and get work as a newspaper reporter. At the same time, I felt the tug of an immense physical desire toward my sweetheart, which, were there any such thing as sanity in life, might have been satisfied without any great blow to society. As it was, the rigid, churchly conventions of her world, if not mine, kept her safe as bait and not as fulfillment. In the meantime, I had the pain of separating from her in this mood—realizing that youth, and therefore tensity, was slipping away; that in the uncertainty of all things there might never be a happy fruition to this (as there was not); that I might never even see her again.

For a long time then and later, the end of this particular chapter of my life—and it was an end of one—wore none but a tragic aspect to me. There were several weeks there which quite shook me, during which I was reaching a final decision, severing my connection with the *Republic*, saying good-bye to my friends and my girl. The circumstances, however trivial they may seem to another, seemed to induce in me a deep psychic depression. I had been happy in St. Louis, relatively successful, had developed some remarkable friendships and this love affair. Now I was once more confronted by a deeply etched illustration of the evanescence of all things. To have such a brisk, vital, and even charming, period such as this come to a definite close and never to be any more—ever—well, I was oppressed and made intensely sad.

I recall going on the Sunday night previous to my departure the next day to see my girl and bid her a final farewell. I would not mention it here save for the immense impression it made on me at the time. It was all so intense and so sad. (In Chapter XIV of Book I of The "*Genius*" I have indicated something of it—not all.) All that I have previously described was in my mind. I think I promised all sorts of glorious things and hinted at all possible forms of failure. I know that I was tremendously impressed with the sterling worth and connections of this girl from a purely homey, conventional and prosaically constructive point of view—also with my unfitness for fulfilling her dreams in this respect. She was for life as it had always been lived by billions—by those who interpret it as a matter of duty, simplicity, care and thrift. At best, I think she saw before her at some time a modest little home in which would be children, after the Middle Western fashion, enough money to clothe them decently, enough money to entertain a few friends, and eventually to die and be buried respectably. That dream! On the other hand, I, if anything, was little more than a pulsing force, no convictions, no definite theories or plans. In my sky, the latest cloud of thought or plan was the great thing. Not myself but destiny, over which I had no control, had me in hand. I felt, or thought I felt, the greatest love. I would do thus and so—while within me at the very time was a voice which said, "What a liar, what a pretender! You will satisfy yourself, make your own way as best you can. Each new day will be a clean slate for you—no least picture of the past thereon, none at least that might not be quickly wiped away. It is entirely possible that as much as you desire the girl now, you will not so desire her soon. Any beautiful woman would satisfy you." Still I suffered torture for her and myself, and left the next day—or the day after—absolutely lacerated by this postponed or defeated desire for happiness or satiation in love.

In closing, I may say that my attitude on leaving the *Republic* was one of complete indifference, coupled with a kind of satisfaction at the last moment that, after having seemed previously totally indifferent to my worth, the city editor, managing editor, and even the publisher, seemed to come to a realization that I might be of greater value to them supposing I should choose to stay, and so made rather hearty, if belated, efforts to detain me. On my very sudden announcement—the Monday or Wednesday before the Saturday on which I did leave—that I was going, Wandell expressed the greatest regret. Was I sure of what I was going to do? Wasn't I making a mistake? Hadn't I better stay here? He had always had the idea that with a little more time he could do something for me. I said I thought not. He interrupted our conversation to visit the managing editor's room, from which he soon returned but said nothing. That afternoon my friend the managing editor caught me as I was leaving the building on an assignment. He wanted to know of my plans, said if I chose to stay he believed that soon a better place in the editorial department could be made for me. Having by now made up my mind to leave, and having previously notified Hutchinson that I was coming to join him, I felt it impossible not to leave. Besides, there was a satisfaction in refusing, rather indifferently, these belated courtesies. I now wished to go, and I was going. He then said, very graciously, if such was the case, the publisher would be glad to give me a general letter of introduction which might stand me in good stead in other cities. I thanked him. True enough, on the Monday on which I left, having gone to the office to say farewell, I was met by the publisher, who came into the office of the managing editor while I was there. I was by the publisher requested to wait for a letter of introduction which he soon handed me. It was of the "To whom it might concern" variety and related my labors and capacities in no vague words. I have since often thought that in many a strait I might have used this letter to advantage, but I never did. Rather, by some queer inversion of thought, I concluded that it was somewhat above my true capacity—said more for me than I deserved—and might secure for me some place that I could not fill. For over a year I carried it about in my coat pocket, often when I was without a job and with only a few dollars in my pocket and worrying sharply as to my fate, and still I did not use it. Why, I have often wondered since. It seems a little dull to me now, from a purely practical point of view, and yet so it was. More than three years went by without my ever having presented it anywhere, although I do believe it would have done me great good. Then, the paper being soiled and worn, I decided that so sad looking a document would seem outworn as to its spirit and import, and so I then put it by in a trunk, where it remained for years until finally I lost the trunk. But the ridiculous part of it is that in the very next city into which I ventured after my pointless adventure looking for a country paper—and in several cities subsequent to that one where I might have used it to great advantage—I contented myself with applying to the reigning city editor or Sunday editor, whoever he might be, with a formal request that he employ me on my looks and my word.

As little as I would understand such a thing in another, so little do I now understand this in myself.

CHAPTER LXIII

One of the things which made this departure so impressive to me was the fact that never but once before in my life, and that when my home was still open to me to return to at any time, had I ventured of my own accord to leave one position, even in the same city, without having first secured another one. And as for venturing forth in the world alone—with no definite place to return to—I had scarcely ever thought of it before. When, for instance, I had left Chicago to come to St. Louis, it was to a position previously arranged for. In addition I was leaving the one person who was truly—even violently—fond of me, and many things are to be set aside easily, but scarcely (at least with the sensitive person that I was) affection. I craved it too intensely. It was, in a way, as the breath of life to me—a compound of all beautiful and delicious things. I thought this maid of mine beautiful, the joy she offered as glorious as any life might boast, and so to be compelled to surrender her in this fashion grieved me frightfully. I was literally the substance of morbid reflections, and carrying my "grips" down to the great Union Station on the particular evening I had fixed upon— having previously said good-bye to Dick and Peter—I felt that my life represented the substance of failure.

Other men had money. They need not thus go jerking about the world seeking the beginnings of a career. So many youths and maids had all their ease and comfort arranged for from the beginning. They did not need to fret as I was doing about the makings of a bare living. The ugly favoritism of life which piles comforts and place in the laps of some while snatching the minutest crumb of satisfaction from the lips of others was never more apparent to me. I was in a black despair and made short work of the business of getting into my berth once the same was made up. For a long time I stared at dark fields outside, punctuated betimes by lamps in scattered cottages, the dreadfully gloomy and lonely-looking little towns, their darkness and poverty of life emphasized by small oil lamps, and began to speculate as to whether this really could be the form of life to which I was condemning myself and whether, by any possibility, I could endure it. Finally I slept and was not aroused until, a ray of sunshine being thrust into my eye by a fortuitous curve, I lifted one of my "blinds" and saw the regulation cornfields of the Middle West, this time of northern Ohio,—the brown stumps of last year's crop protruding through the snow. Commonplace little towns such as I had known all my life, the minute brown or red railway stations with the adjoining cattle runs for cattle shippers, and some bony gas well derricks protruding out of dirty, snowless soil, made me realize that I was approaching the end of my journey. Normally I should have been put down at eight-thirty, just one hour this side of Toledo, but as was no doubt customary with trains on this line—an undistinguished system beginning at St. Louis and ending at Toledo—I was one hour late. Therefore I had ample time to dress, shave and breakfast in the buffet adjoining the car, a thing I proposed to do if it proved the last pretentious, liberal, courageous or heroic deed of my life.

For was I not leaving civilization? And though I had but a hundred dollars, having never developed anywhere the least tendency to save, might my state not soon be made worse? I have often smiled since over the awe in which I then held the regulation Pullman car, its porter, conductor, and indeed all that went with it. To my inexperienced soul it seemed to me to be the acme not only of elegance but of grandeur. Could life offer anyone really anything more than the privilege of riding about the world in these mobile palaces? To sit "on the plush," as one slangy newspaper friend used to describe it, and gaze forth loftily over passing towns and fields or down upon poor, untraveled, moneyless and inexperienced denizens of minor hamlets and "burghs," creatures who had never even seen St. Louis or Chicago. God! What superiority! What grandeur! And here was I this sunny winter morning so blessed, if you please, and with money enough in my pocket to indulge in a breakfast if I chose. Though—spendthrift that I was, or at least if I kept up this thoughtless, reckless pace—I might never again have sufficient money so to do. Was I not jobless now, and all but hopeless in my mood?

Nevertheless I did so rise and finally breakfast, seating myself at a table adjoining one at which sat two drummers who talked of journeys far and wide, of large sales of binders and reapers and the condition of trade here and there. Truly I must have been much of a child yet at heart, for I was greatly impressed. They seemed to me to be very fortunate men indeed—high up in this world as positions go, able to steer straight and profitable courses for themselves, which I evidently was not. Because they had the half of a broiled spring chicken each, I had one such half—and coffee and rolls and French fried potatoes, as did they, feeling all the while that I was indulging in limitless grandeur. The meal cost me, with a ten cent tip, in the neighborhood of one dollar and twenty-five cents for breakfast, a for me quite fantastic expenditure. Think of it. To sit alone thus in a Pullman breakfast car, cruising forth quite alone and into an unknown world, with only one hundred dollars to my name and paying one dollar and twenty-five cents for a single breakfast. At one station at which the train stopped, some poorish-looking farm boys in jeans and "galluses" and wrinkled hats gazed up at me with interest as I ate, and I, unduly sensitive as to the wonder of my temporary and yet false grandeur, stared down at them, hoping the while that I would be taken for some touring millionaire or rising young magnate to whom this was little more than a wearisome commonplace. Indeed I felt fully capable of playing and even overplaying the part, so much so that I gave everyone a cold and repressing glance, satisfied that the way to establish my own true worth was to make everyone feel small by comparison. And at times I actually believed that I was succeeding in so doing!

The town of Grand Rapids, as I now shortly learned, lay in the extreme northwestern portion of Ohio, on the Maumee River, a little stream I came greatly to admire afterwards and which begins somewhere west of Fort Wayne, Indiana, and runs northeast to Toledo, emptying into Lake Erie at that place. The town itself was traversed by but this one railroad, which, as I have said, began at St. Louis and ended at Toledo. It consisted, as I now shortly saw, of a number of small frame houses and stores, with a few brick structures of one and two stories by way of variety. In spite of my pride and my breakfast, I reached it fairly dusty and tired. I had not arranged with Hutchinson that he should meet me at any given time, having been uncertain as to the time of my own departure from St. Louis, and so it was now my duty to look him up. He lived a mile or two from town. As I stepped down at the little depot, crisp with the freshness of a cold February morning, I could not help noting, and with admiration after the city, the small houses with their snow-covered yards, the bare trees and the glimpse of rolling country roundabout which I caught through the open spaces between. There was this river too, as I now shortly saw, a wide and shallow affair, flowing directly through the heart of the town and tumbling rapidly over grey stones, a spectacle which had suggested the name of the town and impressed me more than anything else—far more, for instance, than the well-being of the citizens here or anything which was more intimately connected with the prospects of the paper I proposed to edit. So little was I interested in my own personal welfare from the point of trade that I was far more concerned as to whether I should at some time or other be able to write a poem or story about the river than I was to know whether a local weekly could possibly subsist here. And yet the town did not over-impress me either, despite its rural charm, for the few people I saw walking about or crossing desolately from one store to another or passing in and out from their own yards were not very interesting looking. I had been "raised on" small-town people in the past. After the hurry and bustle of St. Louis, the crowded condition of the stores and the streets there, and the energy and bustle of the life of cities in general, this struck me as being a poor exchange. I felt now, almost for the first time, that I had made a dreadful mistake and wondered why I had been so foolish as to give up the opportunities suggested by the *Republic*, or my sweetheart, when I might have remained there and married her under the new conditions.

"And yet what else could I have done?" I asked myself. "I did not wish to stay there indefinitely either. About all that St. Louis could have swiftly taught me I had already acquired." Despite my backward yearnings I realized that I should have left there sometime, and that being on my way, though penniless here, I was better off. "At least if I cannot do anything here, I can go on east. Toledo is not very far away. And neither is Cleveland or Pittsburgh. I shall go to those places if worst comes to worst." And I fingered apprehensively the roll of somewhat over a hundred dollars which I had in my pocket.

I walked on to the main corner and inquired where my friend lived and, having placed him, walked out the country road indicated to me as leading toward his home or, rather, that of his parents.

The latter was an old rambling frame house, with a lean-to and walk-connected kitchen and springhouse, to say nothing of corncribs, a barn twice the size of the house and various smaller buildings. All rested comfortably on a rise of ground which concealed the river which the house faced and from which the tops of its old-fashioned chimneys could be seen a mile away. Apple and pear trees surrounded it, now leafless in the wind. A curl of smoke rose significantly upward from the small lean-to, which indicated very plainly where the cookstove was. As I entered the front gate I felt the joy that I always did when I traversed the precincts of a country home. It told of simple and plain things, food, warmth, comfort, minds content with routine and even slight things.

As I came through the gate, Hutchinson appeared at the door and greeted me most enthusiastically as I knew he would, thereafter introducing me to the remainder of his family with the exuberant youthfulness of a boy out of school.

"This is Dreiser," he told his father, a little old dried-up quizzical person, who looked at me over his glasses in a wondering way and rubbed his mouth with the back of his hand. I shook hands with him cordially.

"Maw, this is my friend that I have been telling you so much about," Hutchinson exclaimed to his mother. "Here he is. Now you see him."

I colored slightly and gave my hand to the wrinkled little old mother who looked as though she had gone through a thousand worries.

"I'm glad to meet you, Mr. Dreiser," she said simply. "Winfield has been talking about you so much lately."

"And this is my wife," he added, presenting a dark, chubby, brown-skinned girl, who looked for all the world like a hundred other farmer maidens I had seen, stocky and not over-intelligent. I smiled at her. "I never did get to see you in St. Louis," I said, "though at one time I thought I would. Winfield was speaking of having you come down before he left."

"Yes, I thought I was coming," she replied.

The family invited me to sit down and make myself at home. Hutchinson inquired where my luggage was and promised to go and get it in the afternoon. They listened to my account of my experiences in getting here, and then Winfield volunteered to show me about the place.

Though the family was very considerate of me, it was a homesick day I spent there, for the reason that my thoughts were all the time back in St. Louis in the little parlor out in Kay Street, and Miss White was in my arms as I had last held her. That little earthling haunted me as a spirit, and I could only think of her form and face, the prettiness of her hair and the beauty of her eyes. The long miles that intervened, the plains that I had traversed, only accentuated my misery. I looked at the snow-clad fields about the house, stretching drearily westward, and wondered when I would traverse them again—when I would have money enough to return.

The members of the family that I was now among were not very well suited to my nature, though I could see that they were all rather kind and well meaning. My aspiring mind revolted at the thought of such a humdrum life as this for myself, though I was constantly touched by its charm—for others. I followed the elder Mrs. Hutchinson into the lean-to and watched her cook, went with Winfield to the barn to look over the livestock, and returned to talk with Hutchinson senior about the prospects of the Republican party in Ohio. The latter was much interested in a man named McKinley, a politician in Ohio, who had been a congressman for years and who was being talked of as probably the next candidate of the Republican party for the Presidency. I had scarcely heard of him up to that time, and still he wanted to know how I thought he stood in the West.

I gave him my opinion, such as it was,—mere newspaper hearsay. We sat about the big "drum" sheet-iron stove, heated by natural gas, then but newly discovered and piped in that region. After dinner I proposed that Winfield and I go into the village and inspect the printing plant which he had informed me was for sale. We walked along the road discussing the possibilities, and it seemed to me as we talked that my companion was not as enthusiastic as he had been in St. Louis. Although his letters had glowed with the possibilities of this venture, now that I was here his thoughts seemed rather tame. Perhaps my own doubtful attitude had already affected him.

"I've been looking into that fellow's plant down here," he said vaguely, "and I don't know whether I want to give him two hundred dollars down for it. He hasn't got anything. That old press he had there is in pretty bad shape, and his type is all worn down. We might be able to get the paper out on it for a little while, but it wouldn't last long. It wouldn't do us any good to print the paper that way anyhow."

"Why wouldn't it?" I inquired interested.

"Well, a clean-looking sheet is what's needed to begin with," he began, and I noted that he was doubtful himself.

We went to the office of the *Herald,* a long dark loft in a brick building, over a feedstore, where a press and some stands of type were indifferently arranged, and a table, apparently for editorial purposes, stood before the two front windows, which looked west. It was un-lighted save by these windows and two in the back, and contained no provision for artificial illumination beyond two or three tin kerosene lamps.

The editor, a youth named Slazey, was not in. The man in the feedstore said he had gone "up the street" somewhere. We walked about and examined at leisure the contents of the room, which were in a run-down condition. The town was small and slow, and even an idealist could see that there was small room here for a career. The county seat, some eighteen miles away, was much more important. Presently the proprietor returned, and I was presented with a somewhat sad specimen of the genus "country editor" of those days.

I recall him very well, a sleepy or sickly-looking lad with a spare, gaunt face and a head which had the appearance of an egg with the point reversed, that is, turned to the back. His hair was long and straight, and peculiarly thin, with the back part of it growing down over his dusty coat-collar. He had on a pair of baggy trousers of no shape or distinguishable color, and his coat and vest looked greasy. His hands were rough and thin, and he had a general air of lassitude and indifference. Upon introduction, he extended a damp, indifferent hand to me.

"I hear you want to sell out," I said, with the air of a possible buyer.

"Yes, I'm willing to sell," he replied sadly.

"Do you mind showing us again what you have here?"

"No, I'll show you."

He went about mechanically, like a galvanized corpse or metal automaton, and pointed out the press and the type and some paper he had in stock.

"Don't you think this type is in pretty bad condition?" Hutchinson commented.

"Well, it's not so good as it might be. Still, you can get the paper out on it."

"Let me see that list of subscribers you showed me the other day," added Hutchinson, who was now, I thought, somewhat more interested in convincing himself that there might be something in all this.

Slazey brought it out from an old drawer, and together we examined it, spreading it out on the dusty table and looking at the names which had been checked off as having been paid. There were not more than a thousand of these all told. Some of the them had another mark, a cross, beside the check, which excited my curiosity.

"What's this cross here for?"

"That's the person that's paid this year already."

"Isn't this this year's list?"

"No, it's last year's. I just thought I'd check up the new payments on the old list. I haven't had time to make out a new one."

Hutchinson's and my countenance fell. The names checked with a cross did not aggregate five hundred. The other subscribers had evidently failed to renew their subscriptions.

"I'll tell you what we'd better do," observed Hutchinson heavily, and feeling that I had become suddenly depressed. "Suppose we go around and see some of the merchants here and see if they'll support us with their advertising."

I agreed, feeling all the while that the whole venture was taking on a ridiculous aspect, and together we went about among the comparatively silent stores, talking with strange conservative men, who to my mind represented all that was most discouraging and wearisome in life. Their stores were all but empty, their visitors few. Here they stood all day long calculating in pennies and dimes, whereas the city merchant counted in hundreds and thousands. It was disconcerting and dispiriting to me. Ambitious as I was and yearning for more life, not less, the thing took on a kind of horror. Think of living in a place like this, I thought—among such people.

"I might give a good paper my support," said one man, a long, lean, sanctimonious person who looked as though he were possessed of narrow notions and firm determination to rule in his small world. "But it's mighty hard to make a paper that would suit this community. The young fellow who runs the one we have here ain't the person to run it. 'Pears to me he ain't no interest in it nor the people. He'd rather go down to Toledo s'far as I kin see and see a show than he would to collect the news here where it is. We're a religious and hardworking community here, and we like the things that interest religious and hardworking people. 'Course if it were run right by a bright young chap it might pay pretty well, but I dunno as 'twould neither. Ye never can tell."

I saw at once that here was one hard customer to deal with anyhow, regardless of the others. If there were many like him! The poor, thin-blooded, calculating world which he represented, with its narrow passion and narrow interests, frightened me.

"How much advertising do you think you could give to a paper that was 'run' right?"

"Well, that depends," he said gloomily and disinterestedly, feeling a grizzly saw. "I'd have to see how it was run first. Some weeks I might give more than others. It all depends on how you run it."

Even Hutchinson nudged me slightly, for he was not immune to the dullness and wretchedness of this atmosphere. Out of sheer love of argument, I fear, he temporized over such general propositions as whether, for instance, a community like this could support a paper at all. I looked at them in weariness and amazement and then, going outside, studied the character of the village once more—its surrounding landscape.

"I forgot to tell you," said Hutchinson, joining me after a little time, "that he's a Baptist and a Republican. He'd expect you to run it in favor of those institutions if you got his full support. Some of the men around town won't feel that way, of course."

"Exactly," I replied, and wondered how much longer I would be willing to trifle with this impossible idea.

In the dusty back room of a drugstore we found a country chemist who did not know whether a weekly newspaper was of any value to him or not, and could not contribute more than fifty cents a week in advertising, supposing it was. The proprietor of the village hotel, a thickset, red-faced man who had the air of a country evildoer of sorts, said that he did not see that a local newspaper was particularly valuable to him. He might advertise. It would be more as a favor than anything else.

I began to sum up the difficulties of our position. We would be handicapped, to begin with, by a wretched printing outfit. We would be beholden to a company of small, lean-living, narrow men who might, and no doubt would, take offense at the least show of individuality and so cut us off entirely from aid or support. We would need to busy ourselves gathering trivial items of news, dunning hardworking, indifferent farmers for small amounts of money, and reduce all our thoughts and all our ambitions to the measure of this narrow world. I saw myself dying by inches. The thing gave me the creeps. Youth and hope were calling. Life. God, suppose one were perforce compelled to lead such a life against his will.

"I don't see this," I said to myself almost frantically, in the slang of the day. "It's horrible. I should die here."

"Suppose we give up our canvassing for today anyhow," I said to Hutchinson.

"I think we might as well," he replied, for he could see well enough by now that I was dissatisfied and discouraged. "There's a paper over at Bowling Green that is much better, and I believe it's for sale. We might go over and look at that in a day or two. We might as well go home now. We can't do much more here this afternoon."

I agreed. We turned down one of the streets that led out to the country road and followed it. I recall so well even now the character of that afternoon, the snow on the ground, the bright sun veering toward the western line, the gaunt vignetted trees. I knew nothing of my destiny, but I knew that it had little to do with this. I understood the land well enough—the import of the farmer and his small-town tradesman, but they were not for me. The great wide fields, many of them already thriftily sown to wheat under the snow, these hundreds of oil or gas well derricks stalking across and promising a new source of profit to many, the cleanly farm houses and neatly divided farms all appealed to me, but, alas, this world was not for me. I was thinking of something different, richer, more poignant, less worthy possibly—although I doubt it—more terrible, more fruitful for the moods and the emotions. What could these bleak fields offer me of those? I thought of St. Louis, the crowded streets, the vital offices of the great papers, their thrashing presses, the hotels, the crowds, the trains. What, bury myself here? I thought of the East—New York possibly, at least Cleveland, Buffalo, Pittsburgh, Philadelphia. Actually, there came into my mind the absence of red lusts here, of resorts of pleasure, saloons, theatres, all the brutal, shabby life of the city. Even that was worth much—here.

"I like the country, but it's a hard place to make a living, isn't it?" I said.

"That's right," assented Hutchinson gloomily, "I've never been able to get anything out of it, but I haven't done very well in any city either."

I sensed the mood of an easily defeated man.

"I'm so used to the noise and bustle of the streets that these fields seem lonely," I replied.

"Yes, but you might get over that in time, don't you think?"

Never, I thought, never, but I did not say so.

Instead, respecting his mood, I added: "That's a pretty sky, isn't it?", and Hutchinson, pausing in his thoughts, perhaps, looked blankly to where a touch of purple was creeping into the cold background of red and gold.

"Yes," he replied indifferently.

We reached the house at dusk, and the lamps inside were casting a golden radiance on the snow outside.

"I don't see how I can go in this with you, Hutchinson," I said gloomily. "There isn't enough in it."

"Well, don't worry about it any more tonight. I'd rather not have the girl see you worrying. We'll talk it over in the morning."

"All right," I replied, and assuming an air of good fellowship and good feeling, as if we had had a fairly prosperous day, the two of us entered the house.

CHAPTER LXIV

Disheartening as this village and country life might seem as a permanent field of endeavor, it was pleasing enough as a spectacle or the temporary scene of a vacation. In fact, few places I have ever been pleased me more, and a return visit paid twenty-one years later (*A Hoosier Holiday*, pp. 247–259; 265–266) confirmed these earlier impressions completely. Although it was still wintertime—late February—when I came and there was snow on the ground still, a day or two later a warm wind and sun drove most of it away and left it dry and bare, if cold, and very refreshing. As I recall, there was a full moon, or nearly so, rising in the east every night, and a sense of approaching spring even at that early date, or I thought so. And before this charming old farm house flowed this quite wonderful little Maumee River, dimpling over a wealth of stones and spreading out quite wide as though it desired to appear much more than it was. There is madness in moonlight ever, and there is madness in that chemical compound which is youth. The investigations of men like Crile and Loeb cause one to feel that there is some huge madness in nature itself, which, blind and yearning, dashes itself into inconceivable forms and marvellous accidental harmonies. There is insanity in that thought alone. Here in this simple farming region, and once free of the thought that by any chance or hocus-pocus I might be compelled to remain here, I felt strangely renewed and as free as a bird. Although as always I was also sad or morbid—not so much for myself, I think (although I identified this feeling with my own lacks and needs), as for life itself, the lapse and decay of things, the impossibility of anyone tasting or knowing even a fraction of the glories and pleasures that are everywhere outspread. Although I had not had a vacation in years, not since I had left my home in Warsaw six years before (unless college work and worries and my trip to the Fair be considered vacations), I was as eager to be on and at work as any caged bird. The greatness of life, its possibilities, the astounding dreams of supremacy which might come true, were calling to me, and my blood was responding. I wanted to be on, to find what life had in store for me, and yet I wanted to stay here too, for awhile. This home was so simple, so purely and typically American farmer.

Hutchinson's father, as well as his mother and wife, interested me

intensely, for they were of that simple, industrious, believing and idealistic turn which causes me to wonder whether the childhood of Greece
was not here once more re-enacted on our commonplace American
soil. Depend on it, they were good Baptists or Methodists or Presbyte-
rians, though I cannot recall now whether they professed a faith or no.
The grizzled little old farmer who had built up this place, or inherited a
part of it and added the rest, was exactly like all the other farmers I have
ever known,—genial, apparently kindly, fairly tolerant, curious as to
the wonders of the world outside, full of a great faith in America, its
destiny, sure that it was the greatest country in the world and that there
had never been one other like it any time, anywhere. There was
something the matter with all the others, I am sure, for they were not
like us. That first night at dinner and the next morning at breakfast and
the next day and the next—at every meal and in between—this old
man questioned me as to life, its ways, my beliefs or theories, ignorant
and fumbling as they were. And I am positive he was delighted to have
me there, for it was wintertime and he had little to do other than
feeding his cattle and reading his newspaper.

The chief newspaper, or that of largest circulation in this region,
was the *Blade* of Toledo, the nearest large city, which same he read
assiduously, as did his wife when she was not working. The thing that
interested me about the household was that in these winter days she
and the daughter-in-law (but principally the mother) did most of the
work. She was forever busy—at times with the help of her son's wife—
getting breakfast or dinner, cleaning the rooms, milking, making butter and cheese, gathering eggs from a nearby hennery. She had a large
cellar stocked with jellies, preserved fruits, apples, potatoes, turnips
and some other vegetables. They had also, as I discovered, an ample
store of bacon, salted pork and beef left over from previous years and
falls when the killing was done. I noted that no fresh meat other than
fried chicken was served, but the meals were delightful and plentiful—
delicious American biscuit and jelly, fresh butter, eggs, ham, bacon,
salted pork or beef and the rarely absent fried chicken. While I was
there the redoubtable Hutchinson shot several rabbits which were also
served. During my stay he appeared to do nothing but idle about the
barn practising on a cornet, which, he said, had saved his lungs at a
time when he had been threatened with consumption, and had given
him the impressive chest development he certainly possessed. But his

playing! I wonder the cure did not prove fatal. The father, as I have said, did little beyond read the papers and magazines, of which there were a number. There was no wood to saw or split, as natural gas in that region was exceedingly cheap, a well having been opened on an adjoining farm, and the same gas burned in every stove. I was interested by his intense interest in what the discovery of this gas in this region would do for it. He was more or less certain that all the small towns hereabout would now become prosperous manufacturing centres. There would be work for all. Wages would go up. Many, many people would soon come here and be rich. While all this talk had some value for me, it was most alien to my thoughts. I could in no wise fix my interest on trade and what it held in store for anybody. I knew that it must be so and that America was destined to grow materially, but somehow the thing did not interest me from that angle. Rather, my thoughts leaped to the artistic spectacle such material prosperity might subsequently present, not to the material yield of factories. I could never think of the work done in any of these places without passing from the work itself to the lives behind it, the crowds of commonplace workers, the great streets which they filled, the minute and bare homes, the spectacles or dramas of their individual lives. I was also tremendously fascinated by the rise of the various captains of industry then already bestriding America, their opportunities and pleasures, the ease and skill with which they organized "trusts" and combinations, their manipulations of the great railroads, their oil and coal fields, their control of the telegraph and the telephone, their sharp and watchful domination of American politics. At that time Grover Cleveland was president, nominated for the second time at the time I was introduced into the newspaper world, and his every deed was paining the Republicans quite as much as it was gratifying the Democrats. But I could already see or feel that the lot of the underdog varied little with the much heralded changes of administration,—and the underdog always interested me, his needs, his woes, his simplicities. I saw men get vastly excited or parade and all but weep over the results, pro or con, of one election or another—city, state or national—the while the rival newspapers seethed with bitter denunciations, the one of the other, or of the rival parties which they represented. But when all was said and done, and America had been "saved" or the Constitution "defended" or "wrecked," I noted that the condition of the average man, myself included, was about as it was before. My father, who had passed through all of ten national elections in his time and had regularly, every two or four years, been intensely moved by the end of "liberty" when the opposition won, was not nearly as well off at the end as at the beginning. His seething interest in America had served to amuse him and pass the time, but little more. So I was beginning to doubt the import of all this.

But this man, Hutchinson's father, was a Republican and grieved over the deeds of Cleveland and the menace his administration spelled to America. At the same time, he was curious as to the results of women's suffrage, then freshly inaugurated in Colorado, and appeared to feel that it might work out well enough. At least he was not opposed to it. He seemed to think there was something impossible about Dr. Mary Walker, then parading Washington in men's clothes and a high silk hat. At one meal I recall Hutchinson's mother, as well as his wife, clucking with their tongues over the "disgrace" the deeds of such a woman spelled to their sex. As for myself I cannot recall what I thought. I imagine, however, judging by my general mind, that I approved of their aspiration in some general, semi-indifferent, semi-tolerant way.

The few days that I spent there have ever since remained fresh in my memory because somehow they represented an interlude between an old and a new life. I have always felt that in leaving St. Louis I put my youth more or less behind me; that which followed was both sobering and broadening. But here on this farm, beside this charming river, I paused for a few days and took stock of my life thus far, as it were. And it certainly seemed rather pointless and unpromising thus far. I recall thinking desperately as to my future, the huge uncertainty of it—as though at that age and with my very special and already proved ability anything seriously destructive could have happened to me, in so far as the mere making a living was concerned. At the same time, my eye was always fixed upon the pleasures or luxuries of life as enjoyed by others—the fine houses, the fine clothes, the possession of beautiful women, the privilege of traveling, of sharing in the social functions and amusements of the rich and the clever. And here I was, as I argued, put at the very foot of the ladder of success, with not the least skill for making that first requisite of pleasure, money,—and, so, compelled to make my way upward as best I might. However much I might earn in a newspaper or journalistic way, I had sense enough to know that as mere scribe it would yield me little or nothing. And besides I was haunted by the feeling that however much money I might make I would never be successful in the one—I might almost say the only, or at least the principal—way in which I preferred to be successful. I hereby confess that always and ever, up to my middle forties at any rate, I longed to be attractive to and preferred by not all but a given type of beautiful woman—that type, for instance, which is between the sixteenth and twenty-second or twenty-fourth years, at the topmost of its appeal and charm. As Lincoln once said of his school days and gingerbread, no one could have craved it more or secured less, or at least so I thought. I have long been convinced that with the slightest self-confidence on my part—the ability to rid myself of an ingrowing sense of deficiency in this respect—I might have done well enough, even better than many. For so often the very type of girl I craved seemed to be drawn to me almost in a hypnotic way, whereas I myself was being terrorized by the thought that it could not be true—that if I evinced the least sign I would merely lay myself open to slight and laughter, that the glances and gestures which I fancied I perceived were an illusion, a notion born of my own intense longing. And so, no doubt, occasion after occasion passed without the least power or skill on my part to take advantage—and in truth I know this to be so, as I will show in time. Even to this day the looks and gestures of a certain type of maiden—beautiful and placed within the period mentioned— are more than likely to prove disconcerting to me. At the same time, certain other types of women, equally attractive physically and probably far more interesting mentally, have literally thrust themselves into my life and made love to me, and yet this has never really comforted me nor proved very profitable to them. Even at the period of which I write, and when I had not as yet reached the stage where women, owing to my books and my repute, were likely to become aware of me, it flattered me not at all that a certain type of young married woman or widow, or experienced girl of the streets, sought me out either with her eyes or her gestures. As I have said, my mind as well as my eye when occasion offered was fixed on this other type—the stinging richness and thrill of girlhood; the limpidness of eye, the animation of gesture; that gayety and shyness which go with a certain innocence of mood and thought and which cannot be retained after understanding settles upon and destroys the soul. Robert Burns seems to have sensed and even caught it in such a poem as "Green Grow the Rashes, O."

And in our lush and green American world, how often I was

encountering them, the rarest types of springtime beauty anywhere, I think. Other nations boast beauty, I know, but we of America in our little towns and cities, our country homes and city mansions, churches, social gatherings, picnics and pleasure resorts of all kinds, can boast as sweet, if not the sweetest and seemingly most carefully guarded, flowers in the world. I stand in awe before them even now when the time has passed that I might interest them, or they me, perhaps.

CHAPTER LXV

During the few days that I was here Hutchinson and I wandered over the country some on foot, seeing what there was to see. During this time he told me something of the history of this region—more especially that of some Indians, presumably the Wyandottes, so little did he know about it; and also of a battle which later I learned was called Fallen Timbers, fought very near the site of this farm, at which General "Mad Anthony" Wayne had defeated the remnants of what must formerly have been a portion of the Iroquois, who for this occasion had concealed themselves behind the trunks of trees which had been felled by a storm. Since my mother had been reared in this region and had always appeared familiar with the Indian life that had formerly held here, I was more than interested. Again, I discovered another thing which interested me greatly: the rapid slope of the land in this northern section toward Lake Erie. At one point near Bowling Green, the county seat (to which place we paid a visit to look at a second country paper priced to us finally at eight thousand dollars), we encountered a gully over seventy feet wide and all of forty or fifty feet deep which paralleled the road along which we were driving. It had been washed out in recent years by rains. The water following the gully to one side of the road had done this. Later at Cleveland I saw the Cuyahoga River which in three miles below Cuyahoga Falls, near the city of that name, falls more than two hundred feet, a fascinating picture and an opportunity for water power which impressed me even then.

But more than anything, as I have said, I was profoundly interested in the simplicity and rural charm of this region. It seemed so wild and bovine. The land yielded great crops, I was told. Cattle flourished mightily. It was no great struggle to make a living. Most farmers hereabout owned farms of from one hundred to one hundred and fifty acres and valued them at from fifty to seventy-five dollars an acre. Every farm nearly was dotted with those skeleton wood towers wherewith oil wells are wont to be driven—all the farmers expecting to be made rich by gas or oil. Hutchinson could have staid here and farmed and succeeded to the property since he was an only son, only he did not want to. He was determined to shine as a journalist, if in no more than a rural way. At last, seeing that he was utterly futile in so far as my life was concerned, I left him and his family, not without several preliminary visits into Toledo, the character of which, as well as my prospects there, interested me. After a second or third visit into town on which occasion I discovered that I could get work there, I said farewell to him and his parents and never saw them after. Indeed I never saw Hutchinson again but once. In 1919—twenty-six years later—he called me up one evening at dinner time. To my astonishment, his voice sounded as natural and as hollow and unimportant as ever. Curious as to the changes time might have made in him, I invited him to accompany me and a friend with whom I was dining. Time, as I found, had done practically nothing for him. He was as aimless and shallow and insignificant as ever—a kind of American clown, working for an automobile company and trying to write short stories "on the side." I questioned him closely. His father and mother were dead. He had succeeded to the farm and sold it, using the money to aid him in his literary labors. He had worked on many small-town papers, finally drifting into trade as a necessity. His wife was still alive. He was here to attend a trade convention. I bade him farewell and never expected to see him after. To me he seemed as hollow as a drum.

But my first visit to Toledo. It was my first free and unaided flight into the unknown. I recall choosing a Monday morning, as bright and comforting for sunshine as any day might well be. The railroad in from Grand Rapids ran beside a canal—the old Miami and Erie, I presume—which in its turn paralleled the Maumee. That stream, visible at times, rippled and sparkled in the light. At odd moments, between forebodings as to my future, I studied the springtime charm of this realm—the amazing newness of America—and felt that life was as much before it as before me. The land indeed was only partially cultivated, the towns mere hamlets. Near Toledo were long stretches of woodland—second growth, the original timber having been cut away—in no wise being farmed. And the houses of farmers were comparatively few. The people were all comfortable, or could have been, had they had any skill. And yet even then, here and there you would see as poor specimens of humanity and as wretched farms as you would see anywhere—bony horses, tumbledown barns, unpainted sheds of houses and barns where some one lacking the skill to fence with life was eking out a miserable existence. I myself was as much worried about my future and the mere wherewithal to live as though the land were filled with famine sufferers. And yet, as I have shown, I was fairly well equipped to make my way.

And Toledo, when I reached there, made a most satisfactory impression on me, far more agreeable than St. Louis, which being much greater (nearly 500,000) had districts which were positively appalling for their poverty and vice. Whereas here was a city of not quite 100,000 which was as clean and fresh and comfortable looking as any human city could well be, I fancy.

For I recall in getting off at the Union Station (still in existence as I write this) and walking into the city some little distance westward, being struck with clean asphalt streets, a cleanly canal or waterway in which many lake vessels were riding, and houses and stores, the houses mostly frame, which seemed if not exactly new yet clean. The town had a young atmosphere and—as I now know to be a fact, knowing American cities and towns as well as I do—one of romance and illusion. Ambling into the then principal hotel, the Boody House, to secure them, the first papers that I bought, the *Blade* and the *Bee*, were full of the usual American small-city bluster as to Toledo's own growth, together with columns and columns anent American politics and business and who was likely to be the next governor and mayor. This hotel, as I saw, was a fair specimen of the best type of American hotel then extant: a grand sky-lit lobby, parquetry stone floors, noble clerks' desk, newsstand, bar, barbershop and dining room. The typical American salesman, business man, politician, and negro servants were everywhere in evidence.

Before seeking any position, I decided to examine the town, for I felt, as was a customary mood of mine, as though I were traveling, might not stay long and might never see it again. I was intensely interested in America—its cities—and wondered, in spite of my interest in New York, in which one, if any, I was likely to take up my permanent resting-place. For in spite of my wandering and restless disposition—far more interested in moving on and in seeing everything than in staying anywhere—I was constantly speculating as to this, my probable permanent abode. When, if ever, was I to have a home of my own? Would it be as pleasing and agreeable as one of these many which here and elsewhere I saw in quiescent rows shaded by trees, many of them blessed with spacious lawns and suggestive of that comfort and security and well-being so dear to the mollusk-like human heart? For nothing appears so important or so desirable to the human organism, after security, as rest or at least ease. The one thing which the life force appears to desire to escape is work—or at any rate the least suggestion of striving. One would think that man had been invented against his will by some malign power and was being harried along ways and to tasks against which his soul revolted and to which his strength was not equal. At any rate, like the squirrels, he hides away his little hoard of financial nuts and, as opportunity affords, builds himself one of these minute kraals or pockets wherein, safe, or presumably so, against earthly disaster, he may sit himself down to rest and enjoy his hard-earned or dearly bought immunity against work and danger.

Some such thought was certainly at the bottom of my dreams, and as I walked about the streets of this particular city, as about those of many another after, my soul panted after the seeming comfort and even luxury of so many of them. Their well-kept lawns, their shuttered and laced and light-tinted windows—especially at night! The wonder of evening fires over snow and through a biting wind in winter! Of open, cool and shadowy doors in summer! Swings and hammocks on their lawns and porches! Flowers radiant in their windows and the formal beds on their lawns! The carriage house at the back with its visible vehicle! The tennis court! The croquet ground! Children or young people like myself playing or idling about! The luxury of the rocker and the book! Somehow in the stress of my own disturbed youth I had missed most of this—had not been permitted to taste of the seemingly perfect dish. That it might have its drawbacks—and probably did, as I was by no means so dull as not to know—made no least difference. There it was, seemingly perfect. Or at least the one I could have, were I so fortunate as ever to possess one, would be perfect—and so——. At any rate my youth was slipping away in a struggle to attain that which others were endowed with, out of hand as it were and by virtue of fortunate parentage, without so much as an effort on their part—and so——.

And yet who has most—he who yearns and craves, building the gorgeous castles of the mind, or he who, sitting down to the dull dish reality can prepare, realizes at last the futility of human hands in their efforts to rear that which the soul has imagined? Who?

Regardless of these cogitations, I was greatly taken with Toledo, only the thought occurred to me at once that in so small a city one could scarcely hope to find either stirring or profitable work, so very little was there in all likelihood in the way of interesting local news. The large cities were paying little enough for the burden of work they offered; and as for such reportorial work here as I would be compelled to accept, at first at least, the return would no doubt be small. Nevertheless, after a day spent in investigating the city and a return to the farm of my friends, I decided to make a second visit, this time either to stay or make my way farther east.

So a week later, after securing a room in one of those old residence-turned-boardinghouse regions, I applied to the city editor of the leading morning paper, and, as I have narrated elsewhere, encountered one of the big intellectual experiences of my life. For at the city editorial desk in a small and not too comfortable city editorial room sat a small and decidedly cherubic individual with a complexion of milk and cream, soft light brown hair and a serene blue eye, who contemplated me quizzically, as much as to say, "Look what the latest breeze has wafted in." His attitude was not antagonistic, but neither was it welcoming.

He was so very assured and contented that I half-detected, even on sight, the speculative thinker or dreamer. Yet in the role of city editor of a western manufacturing-town paper, one must have an air, if not the substance, of commercial understanding and ability (executive control and all that), and so in this instance, my young city editor seemed to breathe a determination to be very executive and forceful.

"You're a St. Louis newspaper man, eh?" he said, estimating me casually and in a glance. "Never worked in a town of this size though? Well, the conditions are very different. We pay much more attention to small items—make a good deal out of nothing," he smiled. "But there isn't a thing that I can see anyhow. Nothing much beyond a three- or four-day job, which you wouldn't want, I'm sure."

"How do you know I wouldn't?" I questioned.

"Well, maybe. I'll tell you about it. There's a street car strike on—you may have noticed it—and I could use a man who would have nerve enough to ride around on the cars which the company is attempting to run, and report how things are. But I'll tell you frankly, it's dangerous. You may be shot or hit with a brick."

"Yes," I said, smiling and thinking of my need of experience and cash. "Just how many days' work would you guarantee me, if any?"

"Well, four. I could guarantee you that many."

He looked at me in a mock serious and yet approving way. I could see that he was attracted to me—fate only knows why. Something about me (as he told me later) affected him vigorously. He could not, he admitted, get me out of his mind. He was slightly ashamed of offering me so wretched a task, and yet urged by the necessity of making a showing in the face of crisis. He, too, was comparatively new to his task.

I accepted and went about the city on one car line and another, studying the strange streets, expecting and fearing that any moment a brick might be shied at me or the conductor or the motorman through the window, or that a gang of irate workingmen would board the car and beat me up. As it was, nothing happened, not a single threatening workingman anywhere, and I so reported and was told to write it up and make as much of the story as possible. Frankly, without knowing anything of the merits of the case, my sympathies were all with the workingmen. For I had seen enough of strikes elsewhere—and of poverty and the quarrels between the money-lords and the poor—to be all on one side. I had been told that the quarrel arose over a demand for a ten per cent increase and that the workingmen would probably lose the strike. As was the custom in all newspaper offices with which I was ever connected, and where labor and capital were concerned, I was told to be neutral and not antagonize either side. Already in those days the unions were becoming powerful. I wrote my story, and it was published in the first edition—out in the streets by two o'clock. Then, at the order of this same youth, I visited some charity bazaar, at which were being exhibited all the important paintings owned in the city—a pointless lot—and wrote an account which was headed, if I recall aright, "As in Old Toledo," with all the silly chaff about "gallants and ladies gay." After which I spread my feet under a desk, being interested, if I might, to talk more with the smiling if indifferent youth who had employed me. I had not failed to note that without any regard for my personal welfare he had seen fit, I being a stranger, to send me over the presumably dangerous strike route. But what would you? It was characteristic of the profession and of life, and I really thought nothing more about it.

The opportunity to talk with him soon came. Apparently he was as much interested in me as I in him, for he came over after I had submitted my second bit of text and announced that it was entirely satisfactory—complimenting me on some phraseology which I had idly employed. A member of the composing room entering and commenting on the fact that James Whitcomb Riley and Eugene Field were billed to lecture in the city that day—or soon—I remarked that I had once seen Field in the office of the News in Chicago. This brought out the fact that my city editor had once worked in Chicago, had been a member of the Whitechapel Club, knew Field, Finley Peter Dunne, Brand Whitlock (then secretary to Governor Altgeld of Illinois), Ben King, and others. At the mention of the magic name of Ben King—the author of "If I Should Die To-night" and "Jane Jones"—the intoxicating atmosphere of Chicago of the time of the Whitechapel Club and Eugene Field and Ben King returned—a glistering dreamworld to me—and I was raised to the zenith of delight. For the Chicago of that period had somehow been the same as fairyland to me. During that very period—the latter end of it—I had achieved my first real rise. I had learned to write, had been helped upward on my course, been made to dream wonderful things and see visions of the future. And here was one who had been of it, who sympathized with it all, seemed to understand it even better than myself.

At once we fell into a varied and gay exchange of intimacies.

I will not go into this further than to say that, during the course of years, it resulted in an enduring and yet a stormy and disillusioning friendship. If he had been a girl I would have married him, of course. It would have been inevitable, even though he was already married, as he was. That other marriage would have been broken up. We were intellectual affinities at the time at least, or thought we were. Our dreams were practically identical, approaching them though we were at different angles. He was more the sentimentalist in thought, though the realist in action; I the realist in thought and sentimentalist in action. He kept looking at me, and that same afternoon, after I had ridden about over all the short lines unharmed and made up the dramatic trash concerning the elder Toledo in Spain, he was ready to hear the tale of my wanderings. It was the same as though Damon had met Pythias— Gawain, Ivaine. We talked and talked and talked. We went out to lunch, and stayed nearly three hours. He took me out to dinner. Though he was newly married and his delightful young wife was awaiting him in their home a few miles out of the city, duty compelled him to stay in town. He had worked in Detroit, had been to New York and knew various newspaper geniuses there. He had dreams of becoming a poet and novelist—I of becoming a playwright. Before the second day had gone, a book of fairytales and some poems he had completed and was publishing locally had been shown me. Under the action of our joint chemistries I was magically impressed. I became enamored of him and the victim of a delightful illusion, one of the most perfect I have ever entertained.

Because he was so fond of me, so strikingly adoring, he wanted me to stay on. There was no immediate place, he said, but one might open at any time. Having very little money I could not see my way to that, though I did try to obtain a place on the rival paper. That failing, he suggested that although I wander on toward Cleveland and Buffalo, working at what I chose, still, if a place opened, I could return. He would telegraph me (as he subsequently did at Pittsburgh). Meanwhile we reveled in that wonderful possession—intellectual affection, a passionate intellectual rapprochement in youth. I thought he was wonderful, perfect, great. He thought—well, I have heard him tell in after years what he thought. Even now, at times, he fixes me with hungry, welcoming eyes.

Alas, alas, for the dreams and the perfections that never stay!

CHAPTER LXVI

But whether I should go east or west for some reason suddenly became a question with me. I think I had the feeling that I might do better in Detroit or some point west of Chicago; only the nearness of such cities as Cleveland, Buffalo, Pittsburgh and those farther east deterred me. The cost of reaching them was small, and all the time I was moving toward that brother who had the most interest for me and who was now fairly well established in New York. In consequence, after dallying with the westward idea, making inquiry at the office of the *Bee* (a local daily) for a possible opening and finding none, and learning from several newspaper men there that Detroit was not considered a live journalistic realm, I decided to travel eastward, but only after lingering here a few more days.

There was just a touch of spring in the air, and the town had for me a homey and romantic texture. There was a river, the same that was passing my friend's farm, and this provided me with several rambles and with many dreamy hours viewing the steep banks between which it ran, its curves, and a number of graceful islands in its course. Lake Erie, into which this river emptied, also attracted me but was difficult of access. The house in which I had my room was comfortable, and a day or two after my arrival came two girls, milliners from smaller nearby towns, who were interested to study the local imports of fashion. With these I made friends, and we took several walks of an evening, but I made no progress with either, owing to a kind of rivalry which sprang up between them. With a gay assumption of a cavalier spirit, I put an arm about either and walked beneath the leafless trees and under a full, cool moon. Despite my protests of affection for Miss White and with the vague feeling that I was devoted to her, I still found no difficulty in doing this. If I had not been a romantic dunce of the worst kind, a mooning, melancholy Tom Jones, I might have realized that what was torturing me was not a grand and exclusive passion for her, but for life itself—all youth, all beauty, all the mirages of pleasure and comfort which make up this somewhat nebulous world. Even while wishing to come into intimate (if passing) union with one of these girls—either one would have done—I spent much time in my room composing long melancholy letters to Miss White, which, should they ever be discovered, would permanently do for me as anything save a romantic and impossible silly.

There was in me a kind of uncontrolled, untrained (and by me even unsuspected) romanticism which led me into all sorts of extravagant assertions, dreams, plaints, enthusiasms. I think I rose and fell in my moods and ambitions and fervors generally about as does a wind harp touched by and responding to every vagrom zephyr. I wrote and wrote and wrote—volumes—letters seventy, eighty, a hundred pages long. They must have been the equivalent of short stories or novelettes, and yet what they were about I have not the slightest idea—love, beauty, loneliness, sex, animal desire, of which I did not dare speak too plainly, or so I thought. Another reason why I wrote so fully was not that I loved her passionately, though I may have, but that my bubbling and untrained literary nature needed expression, and this was the only available medium. I knew nothing of the short story, novel or poem or essay as a medium for me. Like some voiceless and tormented animal or physical mechanism of some kind, turbid with internal fires or chemic responses, I could only make disjointed and perhaps inharmonious sounds.

The reason I give so much space to these bubbling and inchoate effusions here is that, as I see it now, they were but the troubled and uncontrolled forerunners, preliminary spoutings or gushings, of a repressed and hitherto unopened well of mood and material which later on—and not so very much later—were to take a very definite literary form. I was at the high watermark of imaginative feeling, though the fulness of my powers had not burst through in any literary form which would be of service to me or the world, supposing my writings were to be of any worth to the world. I could write neither verse nor prose of any condensed artistic merit for the very good reason that my ideas were too confused for this and my passion too great. I was merely a chaotic volume, large, inchoate, and dreadfully wearisome to myself, and to others no doubt. I was constantly looking into the face of the world, cognizant of much of its beauty, and finding no words wherewith to express myself, groaning immensely. It might have been truly said that later I might write more significant matter than letters, but never again perhaps would I write anything with equal fervor. That is the great asset of youth—its fervor. Age brings many things but not that. The penalty of growth and change is a steadily lessening fire.

Finally finding my money dwindling, I decided that I had better move on. I then purchased a ticket over the Lake Shore and Michigan Southern to Cleveland, and, bidding my friend Henry a brief farewell, entered on a somewhat similar career there.

Of all the cities that I encountered on my rather slow progress eastward, uncertain as I was as to where I would eventually establish myself, I think I liked Cleveland as well as any. It was raw, dark, dirty, smoky, only partially built in any interesting way, and yet possessed of one thing: force—raucous, clattering, only semi-intelligent force, which same appealed to me. I remember finding it one bleak March afternoon, after a rather quick run along the banks of the tumbling Lake Erie, a rough wind whipping the waves, gulls flying, an occasional vessel to be seen in the distance. And then once in it, and my humble bag left at a parcel-room in the depot, I wandered about its principal streets staring at the large office buildings, department stores and what not and wondering what, if any, nook or cranny it would provide for me. America was then so new industrially—in the furnace stage of its existence, as I see it now. Everything was in the making—fortunes, art, its social and commercial life, everything. The most impressive things in it perhaps were its rich men, their houses, factories, clubs, office buildings, and institutions of commerce and pleasure generally; and this was as true of this city as of any other. Nothing else had occurred. There was nothing to see but business and a few hotels—one superior one, really—in every average city, and a few great homes, all closely stuffed with impossible furniture mostly. Add a few theatres and a number of commonplace churches, and the tale is told.

All American cities, and all of the inhabitants of each, were busy with one thing—commerce. They ate, drank, slept trade and trade only. The air was odourous of it. And to all this Cleveland was no exception. I remember looking at the great soldiers' monument (it is still there in the principal square) and wondering why so large a monument. I did not recall that any man of Cleveland had particularly distinguished himself in the Civil War, though I was not sure. And then the long, wide, commonplace streets running in parallel lines and at right angles to each other and lined with commonplace little wooden homes—too uninteresting as to design and too grey with smoke and dirt to be pleasing. In one place in my wanderings this very first afternoon I found a huge steel works, the first I had seen East—and a world of low, smoky, pathetic little hovels about it. Although I was not given much as yet to reasoning about the profound illusion of equality under democracy, this evidence of the little brain toiling animalwise for the big one struck me with great force and produced a good deal of speculative thought later on. The houses were so small and mean, the streets so narrow and dirty and treeless and grassless. Dirty, ill-dressed children were about; slatterns in lieu of women also. The filthy, greasy saloon and the brothel also, and then this huge mill, or series of them, diminishing it all. Personally I was trying to adjust this contrast with liberty, opportunity, brotherhood, and making a mess of it because I left out the natural tendency toward inequality and favoritism and unfairness as to preliminary endowment in nature itself.

But the one thing that impressed me most, after I had been there a day or two or three and had established myself in a sombre room in a sombre neighborhood once occupied by the very rich, was the import of those still greater and newer residences in Euclid Avenue, where huge lawns and iron or stone statues of stags and dogs and deer abounded, an emanation of the artistic taste of the time. Its rich men—and famous, of course—were John D. Rockefeller and Tom Johnson, then already discussed, and Henry M. Flagler. Rockefeller had just given millions and millions to revivify the almost defunct University of Chicago— previously a small Baptist college—to say nothing of having been hailed (newly then) as the richest man in America. All of these people were living here in Euclid Avenue, and I was interested to look up their houses and all the other places of interest, envying the rich and wishing that I was famous or a member of a wealthy family, and that I might meet some one of the beautiful girls I imagined I saw there and have her fall in love with me and make me rich.

Tra, la! and heigh ho! There's nothing like being a passionate, romantic dunce if you want to taste this wine of wizardry which is life.

But perhaps almost as much as this huge and exclusive region with its great houses and lawns, the older one in which I dwelt impressed me with its faded and now dirty and decrepit mansions of a generation that had already gone long before I appeared on the scene. They were nearly all of frame, square, with a square cupola on top, and painted what colors I know not, but faded now to a rusty, dirty black-brown. The "yards" or "lawns," where once were flowers and trees and no doubt iron statues of deer and dogs, were now unkempt and grassless and treeless, the same having been killed by the smoke and cinders of the nearby railroad yard which now paralleled the lake. The once handsome wooden fences with huge squarish wooden posts at intervals were all but rotted to the ground. Gates hung on squeaky hinges. The room which I had, and two of whose windows commanded the stormy lake in the distance with its gulls and ships, had once boasted a chandelier of some beauty but was now lit by an oil lamp. The handsome furniture which no doubt once had filled the great space had given way to an imitation walnut dresser, washstand and table. A threadbare red carpet graced the floor—nothing more. From here, after paying two dollars and fifty cents for one week in advance, I sallied forth the next morning to discover what the city might hold for me.

I think, of all the melancholy periods of my life, and there have been a number, this one which covered a period of several weeks, during which I searched for an opening to a future livelihood, was as dark as any. Being of a peculiarly sensitive and brooding nature, doomed by what stars to an irritatingly painful response to all that went on about me, I was constantly examining my own heart, or my character and my assumed past misdeeds and follies. I judged myself already as one of the outcasts of the world who, by the unfortunate surroundings of my birth, my mental inequalities and inconsistencies, and the mistakes which my own false judgment had given rise to, was already being led down to a wretched end—failure and distress. Although only twenty-three, I was already troubled over the long road I had traveled, the time I had already consumed without getting anywhere! It seemed to me, as I looked the world over, that most young men of my age were already exceedingly well placed—that so many of them were richer, better, wiser—and this mayhap by reason of their own efforts, so little was I ready to believe that man is almost a helpless creature of circumstance, foredoomed before his birth to the luxuries or the vicissitudes he is to encounter. Each one made his own career in spite of all obstacles, or so I thought, because, forsooth, so I had been taught. The fault was not in our stars but in ourselves—and yet about me were all the huge thrashing forces delaying or furthering the individual's frail craft. The fault was in myself and nowhere else, as I saw it—and yet as I studied and speculated upon all that went on about me, I was prone to question this. Was I as weak as I thought, as erring, as this, as that? If I had studied some of the hapless children about the steel mills, I might have decided in favor of unfavorable stars.

The trouble with me, as I see it now, was that I was possessed of too great an imaginative power for my immediate use. If I had been able to write then, as I dimly felt I might later, much of this pitiful aching would have given place perhaps to a more charitable consideration of myself and others. As it was, I could only look and long—the brilliant, glorious, at times sad spectacle of life haunting me on every side, and with every one of its phases.

The paper with which I eventually connected myself for a very little time, and with no particular profit to myself, was the *Cleveland Leader*, a paper which, as I discovered afterward, represented much that was conservative in the local life. Wandering into its office on the second or third day, having previously made the rounds of the others and been uniformly rebuffed, I was met at the desk of the city editor by a small boyish-looking person of a ferret-like countenance who wanted to know what I wanted. I told him, and he replied that there was nothing, but on hearing of the papers I had been connected with in the past and the nature of the work I had done, he suggested that possibly I might be able to do something for the Sunday paper. There was, he said, a slight boom in Sunday material, owing to the rivalry of an afternoon paper which had recently put a Sunday edition in the field, and this was why I might be taken on.

The editor of the Sunday edition proved to be a tall, melancholy person, with sad eyes, a sallow face, sunken cheeks, narrow shoulders, and a general air of weariness and depression which somewhat shocked me. I considered myself a gloomy spectacle, but this man preyed on my mind.

"What is it, now, you want?" he asked slowly, looking up from his old, rather musty-looking rolltop desk in some out-of-the-way room in the building—as bare and unprepossessing as a barn.

"Your city editor suggested that I might do some Sunday work. I've had experience in this line in Chicago and St. Louis."

"Yes," said the tall man, without asking me to sit down. "What did you say your name was?"

I told him.

"Yes. Well, now, what do you think you could write about?"

This was a poser to me. I had not thought of anything and could not, on the spur of the moment, being so new to the city.

"Well, that's pretty hard for me to say on the moment," I replied with a smile. "I haven't been here very long. If you would give me a few hours, I think I might prepare a subject."

"There's one thing," said the gloomy Sunday man slowly, and utterly ignoring my suggestion, "that you might write about if you could. Did you ever hear of a new-style grain boat they're putting on the Lakes called—"

"Turtleback," I put in.

"Turtleback," went on the editor indifferently. "Well, there's one here now in the harbor. Do you suppose you could get me up something on that?"

"I'm sure I could," I replied. "I'd like to try. Do you use pictures?"

"You might get a photo or two. We could have drawings made from them."

I stirred and started for the door, eager to be about this when he said: "We don't pay very much. Three dollars a column."

Realizing that the reward was almost negligible, even for me, still I went out filled with the joy of doing something. It seemed like a wonderful opportunity to me, for the reason that it was not reporting and that it was connected with the Sunday issue, which same, anywhere, had always seemed the quintessence of literary opportunity to me. I stopped on my way out at the business office and purchased a copy of the last Sunday issue, after which I immediately proceeded to the waterfront, scanning the paper closely.

The Sunday issue, as I found, although I did not feel so at the time, was a poor sort of makeshift, composed of a half-dozen articles on local enterprises and places of picturesque or curious interest, written prosily and illustrated with a few crude drawings which were supposed to represent the persons and places in question. I read one or two of them eagerly, wondering if I could do as well, and then looked up my waterfront boat, finding it eventually tied up at a dock, adjoining an immense railroad yard and an imposing grain elevator. For some time I was not able to find any one connected with it, but later nosed out the bookkeeper of a grain elevator nearby, who informed me that the captain of the boat had gone to the company's local office, situated in a nearby street. I hastened to the latter place, where I found a bluff old Lake captain in blue, a short, stout, ruddy, coarse person, who volunteered almost with a "heigh!" and a "ho!" to tell me something about turtlebacks.

"I think I ought to know a little something about 'em. I sailed the first one that was ever sailed out of the port of Chicago."

I listened with distended ears—it was so important to me, this assignment. Thereupon I caught a disjointed story of plans and specifications, Sault Ste. Marie, the pine woods of Northern Michigan, the vast grain business of Chicago, and the Lake ports, early navigation on the Lakes, the theory of a bilge keel and a turtleback top, all strung together with numerous "y'sees" and "so nows" which fairly distracted me. I made notes, however, copious notes, on backs of envelopes, scraps of paper and finally a pad furnished me by the generous book-keeper. This, with a permit to photograph the boat, I carried back to the paper.

The Sunday editor was out. I waited patiently until half-past four of that day, and then, finding the light fading, gave up the idea of going with a photographer to the boat. Instead I went to a faded green baize-covered table and began to write my story. I had no sooner composed a paragraph or two than the Sunday editor returned, bringing with him an atmosphere of lassitude and indifference.

"Well, I see you're back," he said. "Did you get it?"

I arose and went over to him. I began eagerly to explain what I had done.

"Well, write it up. Write it up. We'll see," and he turned away to his papers. Later he looked up long enough to say that he might send a photographer down the next afternoon if it proved bright.

I labored hard over my story. By seven or eight o'clock I had ground out two thousand words of colorful description which had almost more of the bluff old captain in it than it did of the boat. The Sunday editor took it when I was through and shoved it in one of his pigeonholes, telling me to call in a day or so and he'd let me know. I thought this was strange, but said nothing. It seemed to me that if I were working for a Sunday paper I should work every day.

Such, however, as I discovered in this instance was not the case. He had but few assignments to give out. I called the next day, but Mr. Loomis, as I had learned his name to be, had not read it, though he volunteered to send a photographer then and there, which he did. The next day when I called he said that the story was well enough written, though rather long.

"You don't want to write so loosely. Stick to your facts closer."

This same day I suggested a subject of my own, "The beauty of some of the new suburbs," but the Sunday editor frowned at this as offering a lot of free advertising to a lot of real estate men who ought to be made to pay. Then I proposed an article on the magnificence of

Euclid Avenue, which was "turned down" as old. I then spoke of a great steel works which I had learned was but then coming to the city and which must already be planning the nature of its plant, but as this offered a great opportunity to all the papers, the editor judged poorly of it. He compromised a day or two later by allowing me to write up a chicken farm which lay outside the city, but not until a full week of my time had gone trying to get things into the paper.

Naturally this made a poor showing for me at the cashier's desk. At the end of the second week, my article having appeared, I was allowed to put in a bill of seven dollars and a half, which fairly staggered me. I did not realize that I had wasted so much time for so little. When I figured out what was coming to me for what I had since written, I began to have qualms in my financial conscience and decided to appeal to all the editors again for a regular staff position, but without avail. There was no opening. It began to look as if I would have to leave Cleveland soon, and I wondered where I would go next—Buffalo or Pittsburgh, both equally near.

CHAPTER LXVII

During this time I spent such numerous gloomy hours as would try the soul of any Hamlet. Outside of waiting for other assignments and visiting other newspaper offices, there was so little I could do. On one gray day I followed the bleak lakeshore for miles, meditating on the beauty of nature, examining the whipped and distorted trees that graced portions of its bank, watching the wheeling gulls, building a fire of driftwood at the end of a spit of sand from which in the distance I could see the city, covered by a pall of smoke. On another day I hunted out the Cuyahoga and followed it—as picturesque and tortuous a stream as one will find anywhere, most impressive. After the flat, even landscape of the Middle West it was wondrous. The public library acquainted me for the first time with Laurence Sterne in A Sentimental Journey—a book recommended to me by my friend Henry of Toledo, and which I now hastened to read. Also a brief history of Russia, which fell somehow into my hands. When not thus employed I wrote more of those amazing letters or, being hungry, sought out small, out-of-the-way beaneries, where for a dime or twenty cents I could satisfy my appetite.

Always and always the clang of an iron and constructive life was in my ears. Huge street cars crowded each other in the principal thoroughfares, their varying colors providing the one artistic, picturesque note. Heavy trucks and polished carriages swarmed the streets about the great stores. The huge railroad yards were crowded with cars loaded with steel and iron and coal. I saw youth, beauty, hope, ambition, daring, courage, to say nothing of failure, written in a hundred thousand faces perhaps. One of my chief resources was the principal hotel of its day there—the Hollenden—which, commanding one of the main thoroughfares and having huge glass windows backed internally by rows of comfortable chairs, offered a lounging place at such hours as I was not otherwise employed or able to spiritually bear up alone. Here seated during such hours as I could think of nothing better to do, no friend or place of amusement to turn to, I could still extract comfort and satisfaction beholding the assumed prosperity and pleasure of others.

It was so well conducted, this institution; its crowd of guests and visitors so obviously prosperous—or so they seemed. Walking the streets in a kind of glum despair or tiring of the stillness of my room or the meagre comfort of the library, I would eventually turn here, to find myself speedily lifted to the plane of hope and so of effort once more. What is there, I have so often asked myself, about a bustling, prosperous scene of the most successful type that it should be so comforting to the lorn and the dispirited, the mere beholding of it with the eyes? Surely, where so many were prosperous, so much doing in commercial and financial ways, there must be room for me somewhere. And yet the great question with me was not so much how it was that people come to be successful as how it was that they came to be at all in the first place. What were the underlying laws of our being? How did it happen that human beings had thus been able to separate themselves from cosmic solidarity and navigate alone? How was it that we all happened to have much the same tastes, appetites, desires? Why should two billion people on earth have two feet, two eyes, two hands? The fact that Darwin had already set forward his facts as to evolution did not clear things up for me at all. I wanted to know who started the thing evolving, and why. And so I loved to sit about in places like this where I could see people and think about it.

Incidentally, I wanted to think about government and what it might do for one if it chose; also of the growth of cities and the value and charm of different professions, and whether my own somewhat enforced profession (since I had no cunning, apparently, for anything else) was to be of any value to me. I was just at the age when the enjoyment of my life and strength seemed the most important thing in the world. I wanted to live, to have money, to be somebody, to meet and enjoy the companionship of interesting and well-placed people, to seem to be better than I was. While I by no means condemned those above or beneath, nor ignored the claims of any individual or element to fair and courteous treatment, still, materialist that I was, I wanted to share on equal terms with the best, in all the more and most exclusive doings and beings. The fact that the world (in part) was busy about feasts and pleasures, that there were drawingrooms lighted for receptions, diningrooms for dinner, ballrooms for dancing, and that I was nowhere included, was an aching thorn. Having sated myself optically at this hotel, I used to stroll to where the theatres were just receiving their influx of evening patrons, or where some function of note was being held, and stare with avid eyes at the preparations. I felt lone and lorn. A rather weak and profitless tendency, say you? Quite so; I admit it. It interests me now quite as much as it possibly could you. I am now writing of myself as I was, not as I am.

An interesting thing about the newspaper men of the time and since, as I had then and since noted, was the assurance with which they, myself included, could make themselves at home anywhere. Their kaleidoscopic contact with the rough facts of life and their commercial compulsion to go, do, see, under all circumstances and at all hours, soon rob them of that nervous fear or awe which possesses less sophisticated souls. When you are sent in the morning to attend a wedding or a fire, at noon to interview a celebrity or describe a trial, and at night to report an explosion, a political meeting or a murder, you soon lose all that sense of unwelcomed intrusion which restrains the average citizen. Celebrities become mere people. Gorgeous functions melt into commonplace affairs, no better than any other function that has been or will be again; and an hotel like this becomes little more than a lounging place to the itinerant scribe, to the comforts of which as a representative of the press he is entitled.

If not awe or mystery, then certainly nervous anticipation attaches to the movements and personality of nearly all reporters for me. To this day, although I myself have been one in my time, I stand in fear of the average reporter. I never know what to expect, what scarifying question he is going to hurtle at me, or what cold, examining eyes are going to strip me to the bone—eyes that represent brains so shrewd and merciless at times that one wonders why they do not startle the world long before they usually do.

Lingering there and working as I have described, I finally decided that I had no additional hours to devote to this city and so finally moved on, concluding that I might as well visit Buffalo since it was but a few hours' run and from there go to Pittsburgh if need be—why, I could not say. Pittsburgh drew me. I had the feeling that I would like to go there. But the Falls at Buffalo and its repute as a mart interested me,—and so I wanted to go there too.

And so after Cleveland came Buffalo, another mercantile city clattering over its task of making a living or a fortune and building as scattered a collection of commonplace homes as a part of the process as one would ever care to have seen. It was really not as interesting a city—not nearly so much so—as Pittsburgh proved to be. Yet being young and rather new to travel, I was impressed, but not so much so since by now the novelty of traveling through cities all very much alike was beginning to wear off. I had already seen Chicago, St. Louis, Toledo and Cleveland and found them not vastly different. At Buffalo, of course, were the Falls, and aside from looking for work I was determined to see these—the much advertised, the very much self-advertising.

When I reached there, the end of March was already come, and the possibility of some such better days as had already been was strong. But aside from the Falls, as I have said, I found Buffalo a little tame, no especial snap to it—not so much as I had noted in Cleveland, at any rate. For the brutal picturesqueness of smoke and cold and soot and snow characteristic of that city at that time was somehow wanting here, to the same degree at least. There was snow still, but it was thinner and cleaner. What interest there was for me I really provided myself, wandering about in odd, drear neighborhoods, about grain elevators and soap factories and railroad yards and manufacturing districts generally, studying the cots and the deprivations of the many. Here, as in Cleveland, I could not but see that in spite of our boasted democracy and "equality of opportunity" (what a mockery this nation has made of that phrase) there was as much misery and squalor and as little decent balancing of opportunity against energy as anywhere else in the world. The little homes! The little homes! The poor, shabby, colorless, drear, drab little homes with their grassless "yards," their treeless "yards," their unpaved streets, their uncollected garbage, their fluttering, thin-flamed gas lamps, the crowds of ragged, dirty, ill-cared-for children! Near at hand was always—and in number—the inevitable and wretched and gross saloon (what a perversion of the word *salon*). It was not satisfying, as it well might have been, a legitimate need and pleasure in a decent way, but pandering instead and always to the lowest and most conniving and most destroying instincts—not only of the lowest politicians and heelers and grafters and crooks and rapers that the community could produce, but the huge battening financial and manufacturing magnates at top with their lust for power and authority and the very flesh of the weaker elements of life. I used to listen on occasion, as a part of my reportorial duties, to the bletherings of thin-minded, thin-blooded, thin-experienced religionists, pulpiteering of a Sabbath, as well as daily to kept editorial writers, as to the merits and blessings and opportunities and this, that and the other of our noble and bounteous land. But whenever I encountered such regions as this I knew well enough that there was something radically wrong with their noble maunderings. For plainly their words did not apply save within the suave halls of their comfortable auditoriums. America was not like that. Life was not like that either. Shout as they might, or oilily argufy, there was here displayed before my very gaze ample evidence that somewhere there was a screw loose in the "Fatherhood of God—Brotherhood of Man" machinery. Things like these neighborhoods in Buffalo and elsewhere simply proved one of two things: that the machinery of life needed much looking after or that it could not be made to work as those noble-spirited religionists who spouted so gaily on Sunday believed. And I, for one, was inclined to believe that it could never be made to work as neatly as my mentors would have me believe.

Some men and women were too strong and able, too gifted, to begin with. At the dicing which created them, the dice were loaded in their favor. Others were too meagrely equipped for the quick and heartless adventure before them. Else why sons of rich men, turning no hand, doing no useful labor, yet freighted with money and respect and smooth greetings; and women given the *open sesame* of beauty, or a great voice, or a commanding artistic gift of some kind. And on the other hand these poor drabs and drudges, the offspring of as poor or poorer drabs or drudges, slanting about the world without a thought or gift to aid them—every probability, and hope even, arrayed against them? The Fatherhood of God, indeed! And above them, seeking like sharks to prey upon their weakness and lack of wit and opportunity, the huge, ignorant, blazing, strident, avaricious, uncharitable, ambitious captains of hundreds and thousands and millions all bent upon their own glory and comfort, and nothing more and nothing less. Religion— what a mockery! Why pray? Justice—what a joke! Of whom to ask it? The one who loaded the dice at the start? If any justice or equality were ever established anywhere, as I saw then and see now, man not God will have to establish it, for, plainly, God will not. He has not intended justice or any exact equation. It is not His way. He has not even furnished the means wherewith man may establish these things him- self, giving him neither the brains nor the impulse nor the power so to do. Life merely moves on in a huge, blundering semi-adequate, semi- inadequate way, now and then achieving a period of peace and comfort for some, and now again not. The upwellings of Alaric and Attila, a Christ and a Mahomet, the Crusades, the horrors of the Inquisition, the follies and impositions of kings, the endless wars, slavery, caste, plagues, depressions, drouths, insanities. Can life be made to show more than a very low percentage of comfort for some? I doubt it.

The thing which interested me first, of course, after I had placed myself in a decidedly commonplace neighborhood near the business heart, where I had a room for two dollars a week, was the newspaper offices and their editors. Although I had in my pocket at the time a letter from the publisher of the St. Louis *Republic,* extolling my virtues as a reporter and correspondent, so truly vagrom were my mood and practical judgement that I never presented it to anyone. And looking back afterward—years afterward—I have always wondered why. A more brisk and self-interested youth no doubt would have made it pay him well, securing passes, jobs and what not, but not I. Instead, I merely mooned in, feeling that I should be able to secure a place without it, or that they might not value it even though I presented it, or that they might resent it for some reason in one so young, yet at the same time very doubtful as to whether I could secure a place! Why in the first instance should I not have assumed that people—editors—would like me and give me work? Why assume, always, that they would not, and so, very likely, generating via mental telepathy the very indifference or opposition which I most feared? I cannot say, but so it was. Entering one office after another (there were only four papers all told), I was fairly well convinced before entering that I would not get anything, and I did not. One young city editor, who seemed to take at least an interest in me, assured me that if I would remain in Buffalo as long as six weeks he could place me, some changes being scheduled after that period—but since I had not sufficient means to sustain me so long I decided not to wait for that. Ten days spent in reconnoitering these offices daily and I was finally convinced that it was useless to remain longer. I would soon be without any money and with no one to whom to turn. In the meantime I had visited the Falls, the Lake, and Suspension Bridge, another of the advertised wonders of the region.

I traveled by trolley to Niagara, nearly forty miles away, and looked at that tumbling flood, which was then not chained or drained by turbines and their sluices. I was impressed, but somehow not quite so much as I thought I would be. Standing out on a rock near the greatest volume of water, under a grey sky, I was awed by the downpour and then finally became dizzy and felt as though I were being carried along, whether I wanted to or not. Farther up stream I stared at the water as it gathered force and speed, and wondered how I should feel if I were in a small canoe and were fighting it for my life. Below the Falls I gazed up at the splendid spray and wanted to shout, so vigorously did the water come down and smash the rocks below. There were still, owing to the fag end of winter, huge stalagmites and stalactites of ice and snow. I recalled then that one Blondel, a famous French swimmer of his day, had, some ten years before, swum these fierce and angry waters below the Falls. And looking at them I wondered how he managed, so wildly did they leap, huge wheels of water going round and round and white-caps leaping and spitting and striking at each other. When I returned to Buffalo and my room, I congratulated myself that if so far I had got nothing else out of Buffalo, at least I had gained this.

CHAPTER LXVIII

And so finally, after various such slim adventures, I decided that perhaps Pittsburgh would be as good a seeking-field as any. And seeing one morning a sign outside a cut-rate ticket broker's window— they were as thick as mushrooms in all railroad centers in those days— reading "Pittsburgh, $5.75," or something like that, I then and there decided to leave and forthwith returned to my small room, packed my bag and departed. I had not seen the sign before nine-thirty, shortly after my meagre breakfast, and by ten-thirty I was on the train, and that without a word to my landlady, arriving at Pittsburgh at dusk—about six-thirty or seven.

Of all my memories of American cities in which I ever worked or lived—and I have worked and lived in quite a number—I think those of Pittsburgh are the most agreeable, and I worked and lived there somewhat over six months. Perhaps it was due to the fact that my stay included only spring, summer and fall, or that there I found a, to me, peculiarly agreeable and easy newspaper atmosphere, or that the city was radically different physically to any I had thus far seen. But whether owing to one thing or another or all, certainly no newspaper work I ever did seemed so pleasant or agreeable, or any city any more interesting physically, artistically or spiritually. What a city for a realist to work and dream in. The wonder to me is that it has not produced a score of writers, poets, painters and sculptors instead of—well—how many? And who are they? I came down to it through the brown-blue mountains of western Pennsylvania, and all day long we were winding at the base of one or another of them, following the bed of a stream or turning out into a broad, smooth valley between hills and crossing directly at the centre of it, or climbing some low ridge with a puff, puff, puff and then clattering rapidly and almost recklessly down the other slope. I should take into consideration, perhaps, the fact that I had never seen any mountains before, having come east along the shore of Lake Erie, or that I had never seen any little semi-isolated mountain towns with their low brown cottages and unpainted stores. Certainly the sight of sooty-faced miners at certain places—walking along country roads in groups, their little oil and tow tin lamps fastened to their hats, their tin dinner pails on their arms—impressed me as something new and fairly strange and reminiscent of the one or two small coal mines about Sullivan, Indiana, where I lived when I was a boy of seven. And then here too—somewhere midway between Buffalo and Pittsburgh—was an interesting brand of mountaineer such as I had not seen before in our peaceful Midwestern realm: tall, angular, osseous, in long frock coats and wide-brimmed black hats, riding on horses and with guns slung over their shoulders—part of the then already inaugurated Pennsylvania State Mounted Police, I presume, or perhaps they were merely rurals of the region. At other places, usually at the ends of "runs" or gaps or long narrow gullies in the mountains, were the barest and most pathetic collections of unpainted miners' cabins or shacks— the most unprepossessing group of human habitations I have ever seen—ranged along either side of walkless, grassless, treeless, roadless streets, merely winding yellow mud lanes, faced by sooty yellow houses, sometimes slightly weathered.

It being a warmish spring day, clear and bright, I saw for the first time really a peculiarly heavy-faced and heavy-bodied type of foreign peasant woman with a black or brown or green or blue skirt and a contrasting bodice of one or other of these colors and a neckerchief or headcloth of still another color, trailed by one, two or three children of equally solid proportions—all out of doors, hanging clothes or washing or doing something else about their miserable places. These were, only I did not then know it, those much maligned and abused "foreigners" just then being imported by the large manufacturing and mining and steel-making industries of the country to take the place of the restless and less docile American working man and woman. I marveled slightly at their appearance and their number, and assumed—American fashion—that in their far-off and unhappy lands they had heard of the wonderful American Constitution, its guaranty of life, liberty and the pursuit of happiness, as well as the bounteous opportunities afforded to each and all by this great land; and that, being duly impressed, they had arisen and, forsaking their miseries, had come all this way to enjoy these greater blessings, such as I here and now saw. I did not then know of the manufacturers' foreign labor agent, with his lying propaganda among ignorant and often fairly well-contented peasants, painting America as a country fairly rolling in wealth and opportunity, while really bringing them to take the places of more restless and greatly underpaid foreigners who, having been brought over by the same gay pictures, were becoming irritated and demanding more pay. I did not then know of the padrone, the labor spy, the company store, five cents an hour for breaker children, the company stockade, all in very full operation at this time. All I knew was that there had been a very great steel strike in Pittsburgh recently; that one Andrew Carnegie as well as other steel manufacturers—the Olivers, for one, and Frick—had built fences and strung them with electrified barbed wire in order to protect themselves against the "lawless" attacks of "lawless" workingmen; that large numbers of state or county or city-paid deputy sheriffs and mounted police and city policemen had been "sworn in" and set to guarding the company's very honorable property; and that one H. C. Frick, a leading steel manager for Mr. Carnegie, had been slightly wounded by a desperado named Alexander Berkman, who was about the ignoble task of inflaming these same workingmen—all foreigners of course, and lawless and unappreciative of the great and prosperous steel company, which was paying them reasonable wages and against which they had no honest complaint, or so I had frequently read.

Indeed, our Midwestern papers, up to the day of Cleveland's election in 1892 and for some time after, had been full of the merits of this labor dispute, with long and didactic editorials intended in the main to prove (1) that the workingman was not really so greatly underpaid, considering the type of labor he performed and the intelligence he brought to his task; and (2) that the public was not, in the main, vastly interested in labor disputes, both parties to the dispute being usually unduly selfish; and (3) that it would nevertheless be a severe blow to the prosperity of the country if the labor disputes were too long continued; and (4) that, unless labor was really reasonable in its demands, capital would become disheartened and leave the country— arguments which somehow always struck me as a little confusing and as smacking of a jesuitical desire to befog the issue. However, I had not at that time made up my mind that the argument was all on one side, although I did know and could see on every hand that the average man in America (despite its great and even boundless opportunities) was about as much put upon and kicked about and underpaid as anywhere. Indeed, at this time there was a vast growing labor problem. It crystallized two years later in the Free Silver campaign and the "gold parades" in New York and elsewhere. The "full dinner pail" was then invented as a slogan to counteract the vast economic unrest, and the threat to "close down" and so bring misery to the entire country unless William McKinley was elected was also freely posted. Henry George, Father McGlynn, Herr Most, Emma Goldman and a score of others were abroad and voicing the woes of hundreds of thousands and millions who were supposed to have no woes.

Indeed, the spirit of America at that time, as I see it now, was remarkable. It was just entering then upon the most lurid phase of that vast, splendid, most lawless and most savage period in which the great financiers, now nearly all dead, were plotting and conniving the enslavement of the people and belaboring each other for power. Those crude and parvenu dynasties which now sit enthroned in our democracy, threatening its very life with their pretensions and assumptions, were then at the beginning. John D. Rockefeller was still in Cleveland. Flagler, William Rockefeller, H. H. Rogers, were still comparatively young and secret agents. Carnegie was still in Pittsburgh—an iron master—and of all his brood of powerful children only Frick had appeared. William H. Vanderbilt and Jay Gould had only recently died. Cleveland was president, and Mark Hanna was an unknown business man in Cleveland. The great struggles of the railroads, the coal companies, the gas companies, to overawe and tax the people to their hearts' content were still in abeyance, or just beginning. The multi-millionaire had arrived, it is true, but not the billionaire. On every hand, apparently, giants were plotting, fighting, dreaming. And yet in Pittsburgh, as in every other American city that I then visited, there was still a singing, illusioned spirit. Actually, the average American then, outside of such hours as he was on strike or complaining, believed that America was still an ideal land for him or, if not that, at least that the possession of money would certainly solve his every earthly ill. Money, money, money. It was the greatest lure of all. You could see it in the faces of the people, in their step and manner. Power, power, power—everyone was seeking power in the land of the free and the home of the brave. They were wildly desirous to place themselves above their fellows—to push them down into a kind of abject, cringing wage slavery, and this in the face of their constant yelping about equality, fraternity and the like. There was almost an angry dissatisfaction with inefficiency of any degree, or slowness, or age, or anything indeed which did not tend directly to the accumulation of riches. The

American of that day wanted you to eat, sleep and dream money and power.

And I, to whom my future was still a mystery (would that it were so still!), was not dreaming so much of power as of love and happiness, poor dunce, but with no least theory as to how I was to come by either and with no deep hope that I would ever really achieve them. The truth was that I scarcely knew what I wanted, and knowing this, I was naturally unhappy. All day, after a fifteen-cent breakfast in some cheap restaurant, or some twenty-five cent dinner in another, I would wander about, staring at these great streets and their crowds, the high build-ings, the great hotels, uncertain whether to go or stay anywhere. Ah, I thought, if I could just be a great newspaper man, like McCullagh of St. Louis or Dana of New York! In my pocket was my letter from the proprietor of the St. Louis *Republic*, telling all and sundry what a remarkable youth he had found me to be, but somehow I never felt courageous enough to present it. It seemed so vainglorious. Instead, I hung over the rails of bridges and the walls of waterfronts, either of rivers or lakes, watching boats or gulls, or stopping before the windows of shops and stores and outside great factories, and staring, always staring. At night I would return to my gloomy room and sit and read, or, having eaten somewhere, walk the streets. I was heart-hungry—soul-hungry—but for what? Life—and ever more life, I presume, until I should weary of all life. If it was not really this I cannot now say what it was.

CHAPTER LXIX

Nevertheless Pittsburgh, in spite of its labor troubles, proved for me one of the most fascinating places in which ever I worked. It was, for me, so new and so very different. Coming out of a railway station, which was directly across the Monongahela River from the business heart and at the end of Smithfield Street, I was immensely impressed with the huge walls of hills which arose on every hand: a great black and almost sheer ridge rising to a height of five or six hundred feet to my right and enclosing this river, on the bosom of which below lay side- and rear-wheel steamboats of good size. Before this very station, indeed, ended a pleasingly designed bridge of good size which led to the city beyond, and across it trundled in unbroken lines street cars and wagons and buggies of all sizes and descriptions. The city itself was already smartly outlined by lights, a veritable galaxy climbing the hills in every direction, and below me as I walked out upon this bridge, after leaving my bag, was an agate stream reflecting the lights from either shore. Below this one was another bridge, and upstream another. And then as I walked, an interesting clangor of life about me, the whole river for a mile or more was suddenly lit to a rosy glow, a glow which, as I saw upon turning, emanated from the tops of some forty or fifty stacks all at once belching a deep orange-red flame. These tongues rose to a height of ten or twelve feet above the tops of the stacks and waved and licked about in a slight breeze. At the same time an enormous pounding and crackling came from somewhere—as though titans might be at work upon subterranean anvils. I stared and admired.

> For to admire an' for to see,
> For to be'old this world so wide—

Kipling had not written that as yet, perhaps, but the sentiment was then and there mine. I felt I was truly adventuring into a new and strange world. I was almost glad now that I had not found work in Toledo or Cleveland or Buffalo. Perhaps, if I had, I now told myself, I never would have seen a thing like this.

And for me, the city beyond the river proved as interesting this night as had the river cliffs and forges beyond. As I walked along I discovered the name of the street on which I was and which began at the bridge's end—Smithfield—one of the principal streets of the business heart, yet lined with buildings of not more than three or four stories in height. Quite at the bridgehead on the city side stood a large smoke-colored stone building, which later I discovered to be the principal hotel—the Monongahela—and beyond that again a most attractive and unusual post-office building. Into the hotel often later I adventured for the free use of its lavatory and towels. The post office, holding no prospect of mail, was merely surveyed as an architectural charm. A cross street which I came to finally (Fifth Avenue), brightly lighted and carrying unusual traffic, caused me to turn into it, which same soon led me to a somewhat—though not much—more vivid region of restaurants, theatres, a hotel or two. I found this central region, on this first evening, to be most puzzlingly laid out, and so did not long attempt to solve its mysteries, but instead entered a modest restaurant in some side street and ate. Later I hunted up a small hotel, because I was dusty and tired, and for a dollar secured a room for the night. Then, retired and resting, I speculated as to how I should make out here. Something about the city drew me intensely. I wished I might remain for a time anyhow.

And the next morning, because my funds were low, I was up bright and early, walking about, picking up the morning papers and finding out the names of the afternoon ones. I discovered to my satisfaction that there were four at least—the *Dispatch* and *Times* (morning papers) and the *Gazette-Telegraph* and *Leader* (afternoon ones). To me, on reading them in a small restaurant which I entered, they appeared to be most interesting and different from those of Buffalo, Cleveland and other places in which I had worked. Such items as these arrested and held my attention at once:

Andy Pastor had his right hand lacerated while at work in the 23-inch mill yesterday.

John Kristoff had his right wrist sprained while at work in the 140-inch mill yesterday.

Joseph Novic is suffering from contused wounds of the left wrist received while at work in the 23-inch mill yesterday.

A train of hot metal being hauled from a mixing house to open hearth No. 2 was sideswiped by a yard engine near the 48-in. mill. The impact tilted the ladles of some of the cars and the hot metal spilled in a pool of water along the track. Antony Brosak, Constantine Czernik and Kafros Maskar were seriously wounded by the exploding metal.

And then such names as Squirrel Hill, Sawmill Run, Moon Run, Hazelwood, Wind Gap Road, Braddock, McKeesport, Homestead, Swissvale, somehow fixed my attention and held it. "What interesting names," I thought. "This is the centre of the great coal and iron region of America. I must find out something more about it before I leave"— and I was determined so to do.

The *Dispatch* and *Times*, as I saw at a glance, represented the two rival political camps of the state and the nation, the first being obviously Republican—the dominant political party of the state, if not the city or nation—the other, Democratic. Both were evidently edited with much conservatism as to local news, for there was little of it. In the main, the items were telegraphic and commercial or political. Here, I said to myself at once, is a region with interests somewhat different from any of those in which I have ever been; and again I marveled at such names as Allegheny, Youghiogheny, Kittanning, Sewickley, Squaw Run and the like. I also noted articles relative to the probable resumption of work in one of the great steel plants which had been closed for months; another reference to Carnegie's comfortable life at Skibo Castle in Scotland, where apparently he was at the time; as well as the names of men and women obviously prominent in society here of whom I had never heard.

I forthwith made haste to visit the several afternoon newspaper offices, only to discover that they were fully equipped with writers. I then proceeded in search of a room and finally found one near Wylie Avenue, a, to me, curious street which slowly and steadily climbed a hill to its top and then stopped, and up which ran a cable car. Most of the car service of the city, as I had occasion to note, was cable, the overhead and underground conduit trolley having as yet achieved no such prominence here as elsewhere. Here, almost at the top of this hill and in an old yellow stone-front house, the rear rooms of which commanded a view of a long and deep and, to me, strange canyon or "run," I took a room for a week, and for the same sum as elsewhere I had been compelled to pay. The canyon held my almost undivided attention for an hour before I decided to stop looking at it and go once more in search of work. The family of this house, as I later discovered, rented rooms to several others—clerks—who looked and proved to be a genial and pleasant sort, holding a kind of court on the front steps of an evening as did the other residents of the vicinity, and jesting and singing in an idle, cheerful way to their hearts' content.

But so having placed myself in this way as to reduce my living cost, I now made haste to visit the offices of the two morning papers, going first to the *Times,* which had handsome rooms in its own building, a truly handsome one for the time—and one of the two or three high office buildings of the city, as I soon discovered. The city editor, a well-built cordial man of about forty, received me most graciously but could

promise nothing. He seemed very easy and restful and courteous—
qualities characteristic of the entire journalistic life of Pittsburgh at this
time, as I soon found. He said his staff was full, and would be, and made
no inquiry as to where I came from, my experience or anything else. At
the *Dispatch*, on the contrary, which was published in a low three-story
building at the corner of Smithfield and Diamond Streets, I found an
individual who, for some reason, expressed much more interest. He was
a slender, soft-spoken, one-handed man, as I immediately noticed, the
other hand having been cut off and replaced with a gloved dummy.
This man seemed, for the moment at least, interested in what I wanted
and where I came from. In shirt sleeves and with a cloth cap such as
engineers and firemen wear pulled down over his head, he looked to me
more like an engineer than anything else. Unfortunately his one good
hand was his left, and with this he wrote, holding the paper down with
his right. I found him on very short acquaintance to be a shrewd and
canny person, gracious always, suave, exceedingly reticent and uncommunicative and yet an excellent judge of news, such as there was here,
and plainly holding his job not so much by reason of what he put into
this paper as by what he kept out of it. I sensed at once on this occasion
from a very few things that he said, as well as the general atmosphere of
the office, that there was a necessity for conservatism here which was
not common to at least some papers in most other cities. He wanted
to know where I had worked previous to my coming to Pittsburgh,
whether I had ever been connected with any paper here, whether I had
ever done feature stuff. I described my experience as nearly as I could,
and finally he said that there was nothing now but that he was rather
expecting a vacancy to occur soon. If I could come around in the course
of a week or ten days—. I drooped sadly, and I think he noticed it—
well, then, in three or four days or a week at most, he thought he might
do something for me, but he couldn't be sure. I must take the risk. The
salary would not be more than eighteen the week. My spirits fell at
that, but I said nothing.

His manner was so agreeable, however, and his hope for me so
keen that I felt greatly encouraged and told him that I would wait a few
days anyhow. My new friend in Toledo had promised me that he would
wire me at the first possible opening, and having already wired him my
new address I was expecting some word from Toledo. This I told this
new city editor, and he seemed interested. "Well," he observed rather

dryly, "you might wait until you hear from him anyhow." A thought of my possibly lean purse did not seem to occur to him, and I marveled at the casual manner in which he assumed that I could wait. But in spite of myself I felt encouraged.

Thereafter, pending developments here or elsewhere, I roamed the city and its environs, and to my actual delight and perpetual interest found it to be one of the most curious and fascinating places I had ever seen. From a nearby stationery store I first secured a map and figured out the lay of the town. At a glance I saw that the greater part of it stretched eastward along a tongue of land that lay between the Allegheny and the Monongahela Rivers, and that that was Pittsburgh proper. Across the Allegheny on the north side was the city of Allegheny—a separate municipality but so completely connected with Pittsburgh as to be identical with it, and connected with it by many bridges. Across the Monongahela again, on the south side, were various towns—Mt. Washington, Duquesne, Homestead—all really a part of the populated region but probably having separate governments. I was interested especially in Homestead because of the long and bitter contest between the steelworkers and the Carnegie Company, which for six months and more in 1892 had occupied space on the front page of every newspaper in America.

Having studied my map and having nothing else to do, I explored, going first across the river into Allegheny and finding there what was to me a most interesting municipality, a city built for the main part about the base of high granite hills or between ridges in hollows called "gaps" or "runs," with now and then a street or car line clambering with many turns and twists directly over them. The oldest and best streets followed the levels of the Ohio and Allegheny rivers and were as flat as cornfields until they reached these hills. A charming park and boulevard system had been laid out, with the city hall, a public market and a Carnegie public library as a centre. The place had large drỹ goods and business houses of its own. It appealed to me as restful, comfortable and home-like. Again, on another day I crossed to the south side and ascended the hill called Mt. Washington via an inclined plane on a trolley, such as later I discovered to be one of the commonest transportation features of Pittsburgh. From the top of Mt. Washington, walking along an avenue called Grand View Boulevard which skirted the brow of the hill, I had the finest view of a city I have ever seen. In subsequent years I looked down upon New York from the heights of the Palisades and the hills of Staten Island, also on Rome from the Pincian gardens, and on Florence from the region of San Miniato, as well as on Pasadena and Los Angeles from the slopes of Mt. Lowe. But never, anywhere, I can honestly say, have I ever seen a scene which impressed me more, not only for the rugged beauty of the mountains which encircle the city on every hand, but for the three rivers which run as threads of bright metal, dividing it into three parts, and for the several cities which here joined together as one, their clambering streets presenting a checkered pattern empha- sized here and there by the soot-darkened spires of churches and the walls of the taller and newer and therefore cleaner office buildings.

As elsewhere in most American cities of large size of the time, the skyscraper, that pest of every present-day municipal outline, was just being introduced and being welcomed as full proof of the growth and wealth and force of the city itself. No city was complete without at least one—and the more, of course, the grander. I was one, of course, to share this lockstep illusion, and many a time and oft since, I have repented of it. After twenty years of the standardized American dry- goods-box hotel, the American dry-goods-box hotel lobby, the tall building done into streets and alleys, I would bestow a crown of bay upon any American municipality which had either the courage or taste to ignore the skyscraper office building as a necessity and could go about the business of making a building or a street beautiful first—and tall, if necessary only, afterwards. Why every American dunklet of ten thou- sand or more should have a skyscraper is more than I can understand. It passes the bounds of reason completely.

Yet, speaking of Pittsburgh in this connection, I can honestly say that it has a better claim to the skyscraper as a sheer commercial necessity than almost any other American city that I know. The tongue of land which lies between the Allegheny and the Monongahela, very likely not more than two or three square miles in extent, is still the natural heart and centre for the commercial life of fifty, perhaps even a hundred square miles around. Here meet, in the first instance, three large rivers, all navigable and all—much more so than most American rivers I have seen—used. Here, again, the natural runs and gaps of the various hills about, as well as the levels which pursue the banks of the streams on the one side and the other and which are the natural vents or routes for railroad lines, street cars and streets themselves, come to a common centre. All meet somewhere in this level tongue of land, whether by bridges from Allegheny, or the south bank of the Ohio or Monongahela, or along the shores of the Allegheny and Monongahela within the city of Pittsburgh itself; and here, then, of a sheer necessity, is the natural corporation heart. So without the tall building as a solution, I cannot see how one-tenth of the business which would and should be normally transacted here would ever come to pass. The space is too small. To Pittsburgh, then, the high building was certainly a godsend, though that it has added any to its natural beauty I am by no means willing to admit. Really, I think the reverse is true.

CHAPTER LXX

But I was talking of this marvellous view which commanded so wide a scene. The city of Pittsburgh proper, barring two or three tall buildings, was of a simple and homelike aspect. Only a few blackened church spires, a small dark city hall in Smithfield Street and an old market house which interrupted Diamond Street near Wood gave it point. Little white steamboats on the river and, below me, a long stretch of huge blast furnaces, black as night, and the various and lightly constructed bridges over the rivers gave the whole thing an airy grace and charm which I have never been able to forget. From where I walked I could see a large flock of pigeons wheeling and turning over the river boats and the city hall beyond.

Since the houses up here were very simple, mostly working men's cottages, and the streets—back from the sheer slope—of a twisting and winding character, with most startling and effective views of green hills and even mountains beyond, I decided then and there that should I be so fortunate as to secure a place I would move over here. It would be like living in a mountain resort, and most inexpensively. Descending I took a car which followed the Monongahela upstream to Homestead, and here for the first time had a view of that enormous steel plant which only recently (June to December 1892) had played such a great part in the capitalistic-industrial drama of America. At that time the details of the quarrel were fairly fresh in my mind—how the Carnegie Steel Company had planned, with the technicalities of a wage-scale readjust-

ment as an excuse, to break the power of the Amalgamated Steel
Workers, who were becoming too forceful and who were best organized
in their plant; and how the latter, resenting the introduction of three
hundred Pinkerton guards to "protect" the plant, had attacked them,
killing several and injuring others, and so permitting the introduction
of the state militia, which speedily and permanently broke the power of
the strikers. They could only wait then and starve, and they had so
waited and starved for six months, when they finally quit and returned
to work, such of them as would be received. When I reached there in
April 1894, the battle was already fifteen months past, but the feeling
was by no means so. I did not know then what it was about this town
(Homestead) that was so depressing, but I learned afterward, in the six
months in which I staid here, that it was a compound of a sense of
defeat and sullen despair which was over all. The men had not forgotten. Even then the company was busy, and had been for many months,
importing Poles, Slovaks, Hungarians, Lithuanians and what not to
take the place of the ousted strikers. Whole colonies were already here,
housed under most unsatisfactory conditions, and more were coming.
Hence the despair of those who had been so signally defeated.

But at this time only the general aspect of the town was open to
me for understanding. Yet with only that as a guide I could gather
the stark implication of the domination of money in a democracy.
Along the river itself, where once were green, fertile fields, no doubt,
sprawled for all of a quarter of a mile—perhaps a half or more—the
huge low length of the company's furnaces. These were huge black
bottle-like affairs with rows of stacks interplaced and long low sheds
or buildings paralleling them—sheds from which came a continuous
hammering and sputtering and the occasional glow of red fire. The
whole was strikingly shrouded by a pall of grey smoke, even in the
bright sunshine which this particular day provided. Above the plant,
on a slope which rose steeply behind it, were a few moderately attractive dwellings grouped about two small parks, the trees of which
seemed to languish for want of nourishing air. Behind and to the sides
of these again were the spires of several churches, those soporifics
against failure and despair. Turning up the side streets, which some of
these were, you found—invariably—uniform frame houses, closely
built and dulled by smoke and grime. And below, on the flats behind
the mill, were cluttered alleys so unsightly and unsanitary as to shock

me into the belief that I was once more witnessing the lowest phases of Chicago slum life—the worst I had ever seen.

There were many, many Slavic laborers and their children already here. The streets were mere mud tracks and unpaved. Where there were trees (and there were few here) they were dwarfed and their foliage withered by a metallic fume which was over all. And though the sun was bright in heaven at the top of the hill, down here it was grey— almost cloudy—at best a filtered dull gold haze. "Good heavens," I thought, "is it such people as these that this great and powerful corporation has been fighting? And can they be satisfied—whatever their earnings are—to pay them so little as to make them live like this?" I knew no one to ask. I had no accurate statistical details and so I could only wonder and guess, but I suspected from the rapid and unprecedented growth of multimillionaires and huge fortunes in America that it was the usual case of greed, without care or mercy, exploiting the ignorant and therefore helpless. A pretty spectacle for a so-called democracy, to say the least, and one hardly more than a hundred years old. Yet I was destined for more interesting revelations still, only I did not expect them then.

The place held me until night. I browsed around its saloons of which there were a large number, most of them somewhat idle during the drift of the afternoon, yet with a number of men loafing and playing cards in some of them. The open gates of the company held my interest for a while; for through them I could see open furnaces, huge cranes, switching engines, cars of molten iron being hauled to and fro and veritable mountains of powdered iron ore and scrap iron piled in hills here and there, waiting the hour of new birth in the smelting vats. When the sun had gone down and I had watched a shift of men, hundreds, coming out with their buckets and coats over their arms and other hundreds entering in a busy bee-like rush, I returned to the city with a sense of the weight and breadth and depth of this huge effort which was here—really everywhere in this mountain metropolis. Here bridge and rail and plate steel was made for all the world. And of all these small units who dwelt and labored here, scarce a fraction sensed even a fraction of the import of all they did. I knew that Carnegie had become a multimillionaire out of his profits as had Phipps and others, and that he was beginning to give libraries as Phipps had already given several floral conservatories, and that their "lobbies" in Congress were even then bartering for the patronage of the government on their terms. But the poor units in those hovels at Homestead—what did they know?

On still a third day while I was waiting, going each morning to the other newspaper offices, I explored the east end of Pittsburgh, which was, as I could easily see, the exclusive residence section of the city and an appropriate contrast to such hovels and deprivation as I had witnessed at Homestead and among some shacks across the Monongahela and below Mt. Washington. Truly, never in my life, I think, neither before nor since, either in New York, Chicago or elsewhere, was the vast gap which divides the rich from the poor in America so vividly and forcefully and impressively brought home to me. I had noted on my map that there was a park called Schenley, and thinking that it might be interesting I made my way out a main thoroughfare called (quite appropriately, I think) Fifth Avenue, the one really great thoroughfare of the city at that time, and one lined farther out with some of the finest residences of the city. Never, I think, owing perhaps to Homestead and a world of low small yellow shacks which lay to the right of this thoroughfare as I walked east, did the mere possession of wealth—a great house and grounds, a carriage and the like—impress me so keenly. Here, once the Schenley Park region was reached, were homes of (to me at that time) the most imposing character—huge, verandahed, tree-shaded affairs, with immense lawns, great stone or iron or hedge fences and formal gardens and walks of a most ornate character. It was a region of well-curbed, well-drained and well-paved thoroughfares. Even the streetlamps were of a better design than one might see elsewhere, so eager was a young and democratic municipality to see that superior living conditions were provided for the rich, since all shared in the expense. There were avenues lined with handsome well-cropped trees. At every turn one encountered—sometimes counter-streams of them—most carefully and expensively made carriages, their horses jingling silver or gold-gilt harness, their front seats occupied by one or two footmen in livery, while reclining aft sat Madame or Sir, or both, gazing most condescendingly upon an all too comfortable and agreeable world about them.

Perhaps if it had not been that only the day before I had visited Homestead and that its degradation as well as my own lean purse was in my mind, I would not have been so keenly impressed, but because of these I was. The houses here were so very, very noble—vast, roomy, restful, graceful affairs, with shaded walks and portly entresols—and across the river, beyond these shielding hills, was that other thing. In Schenley Park, as I found, was a huge and most interesting aroboretum or botanical garden under glass—a most oriental and Aladdin-like affair given by that same Phipps of the Carnegie Company, one, as I later learned, of the chief financial beneficiaries of the plant at Homestead. And here again was a huge and graceful library of white limestone—only then still in process of construction, and not to be seen as more than a plan—perhaps four or five times the size of the one in Allegheny, and given by the same man, Andrew Carnegie. And he was another of the chief beneficiaries of Homestead, the possessor of a great house in this very region, as of another in New York and another in Scotland, a man for whom the unwitting "Pinkertons" and contending strikers had been killed.

Like huge ribbons of fire these and other names of powerful steel men—the Olivers, Thaws, Fricks, Thomsons—seemed to rise and band the sky. How curious, as it seemed to me, was it that some men could thus rise and soar about the heavens like eagles, while others, drab sparrows all, could only pick among the offal of the hot ways below. What were these things called Democracy and Equality about which men prated—in America especially? Had they any basis in fact? There was constant palaver about the equality of opportunity which gave such men as these their chance, but I could not help speculating as to the lack of opportunity which they themselves created for others beneath them, as at Homestead. If equality of opportunity had been so excellent for them, why not for others—especially those in their immediate care, for instance? True, all men had not the brains to seize upon and make use of that which was put before them, but again, as I thought at the time, all men of brains had not the blessing of opportunity as had had these few men. The strong, as I felt, should not be too arrogant or too forgetful of the accident or chance by which they had arrived here at all. They might do something for the poor—pay them decent living wages, for instance. Why so masterful in manner, so intolerant, so uncharitable? And were they planning to subject their sons and daughters to the same equality of opportunity which they were so eager to recommend to the attention of others? Not at all. In my walk, in this very neighborhood, I passed an exclusive private school for girls, with great grounds and a handsome wall—another sample of the equality of opportunity.

However, I was a mere ambling penniless youth at the time, with no certainty as to my own judgement in these matters and no weight attaching to anything I might think or say. And since in democratic America it was already becoming dangerous, if it had not always been so, for the penniless upstart to voice his views, I was content to think and wonder and to question whether the guiding powers of life were as kind or just or merciful as I was told and as the church pulpits mouthed so fulsomely from Sabbath to Sabbath.

CHAPTER LXXI

Exploring the city so to pass the time and finally calling again at the *Dispatch* office on the fourth day of my stay, I was given a position—but only after the arrival of a telegram from Toledo, which played a vital part in this transaction. My friend Henry had assured me that if as I moved I would wire him my latest address, he would certainly come to my rescue with the first opening that offered. I had notified him of my address here and was the recipient this fourth or fifth morning of a telegram saying, "Position open at eighteen per week. Wire if you will accept."

Now in St. Louis I had long since passed out of the eighteen-dollar stage of reporting, so this was by no means a comforting message. Neither would it stand me in any service here since, if I showed it, I was confident the *Dispatch* city editor would look upon it as a rate of pay very likely acceptable to me and in consequence refuse to offer me more. Yet if the telegram could be shown it would probably hasten his decision to accept me, assuming that he was interested. In consequence, after some hesitation, I decided not to use it then but to go first to the *Dispatch* and see what if anything had come about in my favor. Therefore, at one o'clock—the hour at which most morning city editors have finished handing out assignments to their regular staff and know if there is anything left over for a newcomer—I invaded my friend's sanctum and was greeted by a friendly smile.

"Nothing yet," he called. "Drop 'round tomorrow or Saturday. I'm sure to know then, one way or the other."

I went out and, in the doorway below in Diamond Street, stood and meditated. How was I to do? If I delayed too long my friend in

Toledo would not be able to do anything for me, and if I showed this message, while it might expedite matters a little, it would surely fix my salary at a level below that which I felt I deserved. Thinking about it, I finally hit upon the idea of changing the eighteen to twenty-five, but fearing that the change, if I made it, would be noticeable, I decided to take it to a telegraph office and get some girl to rewrite it for me. Not finding, after some effort, the particular girl whom I would be willing to approach, I finally took the message and worked over it myself, carefully erasing and changing until the twenty-five, while a little forced and scraggly, looked reasonably natural. With this in my pocket, at five in the afternoon I once more returned to this city editor's office and, finding him alone, as I expected, said with as great an air of certainty and satisfaction as I could achieve that I had just received this message and was a little uncertain what to do about it. "The fact is," I said, "I have started from the West to go East. New York, I suppose, is my eventual goal, unless I find a good place somewhere this side of it. Still, I'm up against it now and unless I can do something here, I think I'll go back there for the present anyhow. I wouldn't show you this now except that I can't wait any longer, and I must answer it tonight."

He read it, then looked at me quizzically and uncertainly. He seemed troubled as to what to do. Finally he got up. "Wait a minute," he said and went through a nearby door. After a minute or two he returned, saying, "Well, that's all right. We can do as well as that, anyhow, if you want to stay at that rate."

I had great difficulty in concealing my satisfaction. "That's all right," I replied as nonchalantly as I could. "When do I start?"

"Drop 'round tomorrow at twelve," he said. "I may not have anything for you, but I'll carry you for a day or two until I have."

I trotted down the nearby steps as fast as my feet would carry me, anxious to get out of his sight so that I might congratulate myself freely and unobserved. At the same time I made for the nearest telegraph office in order to reject my friend's offer. To celebrate my cleverness and success I decided to indulge in a good meal and, because I was all alone, sought out the best and liveliest-looking restaurant I could find—a place which subsequently I preferred to patronize when I was in funds, it was so good. Here I sat, and to prepare myself for my work examined that day's *Dispatch,* as well as the *Times* and all the other daily papers, with a view to unraveling their method of treating a feature or a striking piece of news, and also to discover what they considered a feature. By nine or ten I had solved that mystery as near as it was possible for me to solve it, and then to quiet my excited nerves I walked about the business heart. Finally I crossed to Mt. Washington and ascended it on the inclined plane in order that I might view the lighted city by night from this great height.

Because it was radiantly clear up there, although always smoky in the valley below, and because a young moon was shining, I had the advantage of looking down upon as wonderful a night panorama as I have ever seen anywhere—a winking and fluttering field of diamonds that outrivalled the sky itself. As far as the eye could see and in every direction were these lamps blinking and winking in the pleasant spring air. And overhead was another glistering field of stars. Below me was that enormous group of stacks with their red tongues waving in the wind. Far up the Monongahela, where lay Homestead and McKeesport and Braddock and Swissvale, other glows of red fire indicated where other huge furnaces were blazing and boiling in the night, and this was also true of that region which lay upstream along the Allegheny. There was ever and anon that enormous pounding as of Titans. To me it now showed itself most clearly as a world of capital and industry, a true hive of labor that night and day hummed over its great task of forging the rails and bridges and battle plates of the world.

Then I thought of that nest of slums I had just seen out at Homestead, and of those fine houses in the east end, and of Carnegie with his libraries, and Phipps with his glass-housed conservatories. Their station and power in the world seemed so much; that of their hirelings so low. How to get up in the world—how to be somebody—was my own thought now, and yet as I thought of my own peculiar bent and tastes I knew I should never achieve anything that way. Wealth was not for me—neither fine houses nor lands nor corporations. The best I should ever do, as I knew, was to think and dream, standing aloof as a spectator; and the thought of all I should miss in a material and constructive way perhaps made me sad. Still there was but one thing to do, and that was to go on in my field and with the equipment which was mine.

The next day I returned and began work on this interesting paper, and for six months thereafter I was a part of it, beginning first with ordinary news reporting, but gradually and by chance, as it were, taking up the task of preparing original column features, first for the daily and latterly for the Sunday issue, the editor of which was drawn to me, I assume, by my daily work. Still later, and not long before I left, I was by way of being an unpaid assistant to the dramatic editor, and a traveling correspondent, going on several occasions into the coal regions to report threatening strike conditions that had arisen.

But the thing which impressed me about my work here was not its strenuousness, for it proved by far the easiest and most agreeable reporting and writing that I had ever done. Rather it was the peculiar character of the city and the newspaper world, the more or less somnolent nature of its population (apart from the steel companies and their employes) and the genial and sociable character of the newspaper men themselves. Never in any city that I ever worked in did I encounter more intelligent or helpful or companionable, albeit cynical, men than I did here. Newspaper men everywhere are in the main a nobly dour and cynical or skeptical company—they know too much about life—and these, although sociable to a degree, were no exception. Invariably they seemed all of them to have been permanently cured of a romantic or sentimental point of view by the stern realities with which they are constantly meeting up. They knew the world, and their opportunities for studying public as well as private impulses and desires and contrasting them with public and private performances were so great as to make them puzzled if not always accurate judges of affairs and probable events of any kind anywhere.

You can always talk to a newspaper man—especially an alert reporter, city editor or Sunday editor in active contact with the life of his day and city—with full confidence that at least you are talking to one who is free of moralic mush and rose-colored illusions so nauseatingly common to the average man. As a rule, if anything they are a little too cynical. If they have been for any length of time in the business, nearly everything in connection with those trashy romances of justice, truth, mercy, patriotism and indeed public professions of all sorts has already and forever gone. They are not always hard or unkind, quite the reverse in many instances, but they are, or were in my day, far from hopeful. And yet of all people in public or private life that I ever met they are usually nearer than most to a sound concept of what is toward in every field. The religionist of every sect is seen by them for what he is, a swallower of romance or a masquerader looking to profit and preferment via the illusions of others. Of the politician, they know or believe but one thing—that he is out for himself, a trickster, artfully juggling with the moods and passions as well as the ignorance of the public. This is equally true of the average lawyer. Judges are men who have by some chance or other secured good positions and are careful to trim their sails according to the moods and passions of the strongest element in any community or nation in which they chance to be. The arts in the main are to be respected, only in many instances they frankly confess that they do not understand them. A dullard or a romanticist in any office is laughed at. One has to be most careful as to how one expresses oneself in regard to any mooted question or any fact for fear of being most cruelly and unmercifully taken to task by someone who in all likelihood has a better if not a most amazing grasp of the subject in hand. As a rule in my own case, as I have elsewhere indicated, they kept me very wary as to what I said, regardless of what I thought. And yet at any moment, once I had attained to their respect or confidence I could enter upon the most delightful and illuminating conversations with them, apropos of fields and aspects of life with which they were most familiar.

In a very little while I came to be on friendly terms with the political, police, labor, religious and other department or feature men of this and some of the other papers—men who, because of their intimate contact with local political and social conditions, were well fitted to enlighten me as to the exact economic and political conditions prevailing here, and who did not hesitate to do so. Two men in particular, the political and labor men of this paper, being especially drawn to me, were most helpful in this respect. The former, a large, genial, commercial-drummer type—who might also have been a most excellent theatrical manager or promoter—provided me with as clear an insight into the general cleavage of local and state politics and political personalities as personally I could have attained had I been working here in direct touch with these matters for a year or two. He was, as I was told afterwards by others, very close to the mayor, the chief of police and the director of public works of this and the adjacent city of Allegheny—almost more so than his paper approved of. It gave him too strong a hold over his own affairs and interests and permitted him at times, so I heard, to conceal what he did not wish to reveal. He knew the aldermen, the state and national representatives, the judges and petty officials of this and the adjacent city and the state's two senators. At the same time and on account of this, he was most helpful in aiding the paper to come at a true sense of things on one and another occasion, and so was retained and was close to those in power. He was hand in glove, as I noticed, with the city and managing editors and even the publisher himself, who was constantly in the front office.

The other individual was a slow, silent, medium-built, very dark, square-shouldered and almost square-headed person, who drifted in and out of the office at different and uncertain times without my even noticing him at first—so remote and peculiar were his duties. He it was who attended—when permitted by the working people themselves— all coal and steel labor meetings in the city or elsewhere, as far east at times as the hard coal regions about Wilkes-Barre and Scranton. And as he himself told me, he was the paper's sole authority for such comments or assertions as it dared to make in connection with either the mining of coal or the manufacture of steel. He was an intense sympathizer with labor, as I learned later, but not so much with its organized as its unorganized phases. He believed, and made me believe after a time, that labor here two years before had lost a most important battle, one which would show in its contacts with the money power in the future—which was true. He pretended to know or believe that there was a vast movement on foot among the monied elements generally in America to cripple if not utterly destroy organized labor, and to that end he assured me once that all the great steel and coal and even oil magnates were in a conspiracy to flood America with cheap foreign labor, whom they lured or were luring here by all sorts of dishonest devices. Once here these same were used to break the demand of better-paid and more intelligent labor. He pretended to know that in the coal and steel regions thousands had already been introduced and more were on their way, and that all such devices as showy churches and schools for defectives were used to keep those who were already here ignorant and tame. "But you can't say anything about that in Pittsburgh," he once said to me. "If I should want to talk I would have to get out of here. The papers won't use a thing unfavorable to the magnates in any of these fields. They won't even publish all the news if you give it to them, especially where it's favorable to the miners or workers. I write all sorts of things—or suggest them from time to time—but they never get in." He read the *Congressional Record* daily, as well as various radical papers from various parts of the country, and was constantly calling my attention to statistics and incidents of one kind and another which proved that the workingman was being most unjustly put upon and undermined; but he never did it in any urgent or disturbed manner. Rather, he seemed to me to be profoundly convinced that the cause of the workingman everywhere was hopeless. They hadn't the subtlety and the force and the innate cruelty of those who ruled them. They were given to religious and educational illusions—the parochial school and church paper which left them helpless. They drank and caroused, wasted their money when they had any. In the course of time, and because I expressed interest in and sympathy with these people and because I had the time, he took me into various mill slums in and near the city to see how they lived. I shall touch upon some of those visits a little later.

CHAPTER LXXII

In the meantime I went about my work, and an easy task it proved. My city editor, cool, speculative, diplomatic soul that he was, soon instructed me as to the nature of news and its limitations here. "We don't touch on labor conditions here except through our labor man," he told me, "and he knows what to say. Anything of that kind has to be submitted to him. There's nothing to be said about the rich or religion, except in a favorable sense. They're all all right in so far as we know. We don't touch on scandals in high life. The big steel men here just about own this place, so we can't. If a story of that kind comes up we have to handle it with gloves. We never want more than the bare facts anyhow. Some papers out West and down in New York, I know, go in for sensationalism, but we don't. I'd rather have some simple little feature if I could, a story about some old fellow with eccentric habits of some kind, rather than any of these scandals or tragedies any time. Of course we do cover them when we have to, but we have to be mighty careful what we say."

So much for a free press in Pittsburgh A.D. 1894.

Similarly I found that the city itself, possibly by reason of the recent great defeat administered to organized labor and the soft-pedal character of the newspapers generally, presented, superficially at least, a most quiescent and even somnolent aspect. There was little local news of any kind, if one could judge by the papers: a fire now and then, a shooting or a brawl in some saloon, the proposed construction of a new office building or hotel or theatre, or the resumption of work after a shutdown, or the enlargement of some steel plant. Suicides, occasional drownings, a wedding or death in high society, the visit of some celebrity or the remarks of some local pastor combined to provide the pabulum on which the local readers were fed. Occasionally there was coverage of an outside event, such as the organization by General Coxey of Canton, Ohio, of his "hobo" army which at that time was moving eastward from Los Angeles to Washington, there to petition Congress against the doings of the trusts; or the dictatorial and impossible doings of one Grover Cleveland, opposition President to the dominant party of the state, as well as the manner in which the moribund Democratic party of this region was attempting to steal an office or share in the spoils. These and the grand comments of various gentlemen in high financial positions here and elsewhere as to the outlook for prosperity in the nation or the steel mills or the coal fields seemed to occupy the best places in the newspapers persistently. I never knew a great commercial metropolis, as daring and forceful and economically and socially as restless as this, to be, from a newspaper point of view, so quiescent or to say as little about the huge emotions and ambitions which were animating the men at the top and their schemes, pleasures and vices or the like. When it came, however, to labor or the unions— their restlessness or unholy or anarchistic demands—or the trashy views of some third-rate preacher complaining of looseness in dress or morals, or some actor voicing his views on art, or some politician or statesman, so-called, commenting on some unimportant phase of our life, it was a very different matter. These papers here were then free enough to say their say.

I recall very clearly that Thomas B. Reed, then Speaker of the House, came to town once. He was passing through the city and had stopped off, probably to visit with some friendly steel magnate. I was sent to interview him and obtain his views as to the menace implied or contained in the organization by that same "General" Coxey previously mentioned of his "army," so-called—a band of poor mistaken theorists who imagined that by marching to Washington and protesting to Congress they could compel a trust-dictated American Senate and

House to take cognizance of their woes. This same able statesman—and he was no fool by any means, being at that time in the councils and favor of the money power and looked upon as the probable Republican presidential nominee—pretended to me to believe that a vast national menace lay in such a movement and protest. "Why, it's the same as revolution," he protested, washing his face and hair with soap and water in his suite in the Monongahela, the while his suspenders swayed loosely about his fat thighs. "It's an unheard-of proceeding. For a hundred years the American people have had a fixed and constitutional and democratic method of procedure. They have their county and state and national conventions and their power of instructing delegates to the same. They can write any plank they wish into any party platform and compel its enforcement by their votes. Now comes along a man who finds something that doesn't suit his views, and instead of waiting and appealing to the regular party councils, he organizes an army and proceeds to march on Washington."

"Still, he has been able to muster only three or four hundred men all told," I suggested mildly. "As I understand it, he isn't attracting very many followers."

"The number of his followers isn't the point," he insisted. "If one man can gather an army of five hundred, another at some time or other can gather an army of ten or a hundred or five hundred thousand. It all depends. That means revolution."

"Yes," I ventured, "I should think it might." I was thinking of the possible size of their grievance and their innate courage. "But what about the thing of which they are complaining?"

"It doesn't matter what their grievance is," he replied somewhat testily. "This is a government of law and prescribed political procedure. Our people must abide by that."

I was ready to agree, only I was thinking of the easy manner in which delegated and elected representatives everywhere were proceeding to ignore the interests if not the mandates of the body politic at large and listening to the advice and "needs" of self-interested financiers and trust builders generally. Already the air was full of complaints against monopoly. Trusts or combinations of every kind were being organized and the people being taxed accordingly. And Congress—this same Congress he was so anxious to protect—was then willing more. Then as now, however, newspapers and politicians and "representatives" (that misapplied word) were most sensitive as to the feelings and moods and interests of the latter. Once you had it, all property, however come by, was so sacred in America. The least protest of the mass anywhere was most revolutionary, or if not that, the upwellings of worthless and never-to-be-countenanced malcontents. I was not one who could believe this. I firmly believed then, as I do now, that the chains wherewith a rapidly developing financial oligarchy—or autocracy—meant to bind a liberty-deluded mass were then and there being forged. I felt then, as I do now, that the people of that day should have been more alive to their interests,—that they should have compelled at Washington or elsewhere, by peaceable political means if possible, by dire and threatening uprisings if necessary, a more careful concern for their interests than any congressman or senator or governor or president, at that time or since, was giving them. Laws and methods of political procedures are made by and for the people, not the people for the laws and the methods. And as I talked to this noble chairman of the House my heart was full of exactly these sentiments, only I did not deem it of any avail to argue these matters with him. He would not have listened to me. I was a mere cub reporter and he was the Speaker of the House of Representatives—but I had a keen contempt for the enthusiasm which he managed to manifest for law when it came to the people's desires. When it came to what the money barons desired—the manufacturers and trust organizers hiding behind a huge and extortionate tariff wall—he was, as I then well knew, one of their chief guards and political and congressional advocates. If you doubt it look up his record. However, I reported the substance of his views as carefully as possible and without obtruding anything of all I thought, of course, and was told to make as much of it as possible and that a scarehead would be put on it.

But it was owing to this very careful interpretation of what was news and what was not, locally, that I owe I think some of the most delightful newspaper hours of my life. Large and time-consuming features being scarce, I was assigned in their absence to do "city hall and police, Allegheny," as the city editor's assignment book used to read. And with this mild task ahead of me, I was in the habit almost daily of crossing the Allegheny River into the city of Allegheny, and there of ensconcing myself in a chair in the reporters' room of the combined city hall and central police station or in the cool, central, shaded court of the Allegheny General Hospital, with the head interne of which I soon made friends, and of waiting for something to turn up. And so little ever did turn up—nothing of any real import in all the time I was there. As is usual with all city and police and hospital officials everywhere, the hope of favorable and often manufactured publicity animating them, I was received most cordially, not only by the sergeant of police but by the mayor and such other officials as chanced to be in evidence. All I had to do was to announce that I was from the *Dispatch* and assigned to this bailiwick, and I was informed—or was promised that I would be informed—as to anything of import (a fire, suicide, street fight or what not) which had come to the surface and so to the notice of the police during the last ten or twelve hours. These, if important or far distant— too far for me to undertake without leaving this centre for the after- noon or evening—I telephoned to the office, asking usually the assis- tant city editor, who took the desk from one-thirty to five, for further advice. If there was nothing, and usually there was not—not a thing worth mentioning—I either sat about with several other reporters who came here at the same time I did or with the head interne of the hospital, a most delightful soul. Or having no especial inquiry of any kind to make, I crossed the street to one Squire Daniels, whose office was in the tree-shaded square facing this civic centre, and here inquired if anything had come to his notice. (A squire was the equivalent of a very petty police magistrate of the old aldermanic, police magistracy character in Pittsburgh, a man who judged in the first instance between street fighters, renters and their landlords, drunkards and the law, and who occasionally held inquests in morgues and elsewhere, or married enthusiastic and non-religious couples.)

This man, a large, bald, pink-faced individual of perhaps three hundredweight or slightly less, used of a sunny afternoon, these warm spring days, to sit out in front of his office, his chair tilted against his office wall or a tree, and, with three or four or more neighborhood or political or police cronies, retail the most delicious stories of old-time political characters and incidents in Pittsburgh that I ever heard. He was, as I almost immediately discovered, a veritable mine of this sort of thing, and an immense favorite in consequence with all the newspaper men and politicians who frequented or could manage to linger in his vicinity. Either on the second or third or fourth day I was taken to meet him by a little, nervous, wiry reporter who worked for the *Leader* and who chose to take a kindly interest in me and my work, as did all Pittsburgh newspapermen, as I noticed. There was none of that bitter rivalry and even antagonism, where not frosty indifference, which existed in Chicago and St. Louis. "Oh, you want to know Squire Daniels if you don't know anyone else over here. He's a great fellow for stories, and sometimes he can give you a tip. You'll find his place a pleasant place to loaf, when you haven't anything else to do." And he led the way across the plaza which faced this particular building to the Squire's low, white, one-story office. There he was, out in front, his coat off, his chair tilted back, one or two cronies with him, and as I was introduced, he surveyed me pleasantly.

"From the *Dispatch*, eh. Well, take a chair if you can find one. Sit on the curb if you can't, or in the door there. Many's the man I seen from the *Dispatch* in my time. Your boss, Harry Gaither, used to come around here a lot before he became city editor. So did your Sunday man, Funger. I know 'em all, nearly, or used to. There ain't much news that I can give you, but whatever there is you're welcome to. I always treat all the boys alike." And he smiled, and then, I having leaned against a tree, he proceeded with his tale, something about an old alderman or politician who, in order to bring a pig up to certain prize specifications and so win a prize, had painted it once, to be found out later because the "specification" wore off. He had such a zestful and appetizing way of telling his stories as to literally compel amusement. One laughed, somehow, because he laughed.

And then directly across the street, to the east from the city hall, was the Allegheny Carnegie Library, a very handsome affair architecturally, and one containing, in addition to the library, an auditorium in which had been placed as usual "one of the largest if not the largest" pipe organs in the world. Why is it that the principal organ in every city is usually the largest and most expensive of all organs anywhere? At any rate, this one had one advantage. It was equipped or supplied with a paid city organist who on Sundays, Wednesdays and Saturdays, of an afternoon, here entertained the public with a free recital. And so capable was he that seats were at a premium and "standing room only" the rule, unless one arrived far ahead of time. This particular manifestation of interest on the part of the public pleased me greatly and somehow qualified, if it did not atone for, in part at least, Mr. Carnegie's indifference to the living welfare of his employes elsewhere.

What pleased and impressed me most about this institution was its forty or fifty thousand volumes so conveniently arranged that one could walk from stack to stack, looking at the labels above and satisfying one's interest by looking into and nibbling at the various subjects undertaken by so many. I was intensely curious as to literature of all sorts at this time, having only recently taken up with Smollet, Fielding, Sterne and Dryden, and being curious as to the existence of other masters of whom I might not have heard. The place had most comfortable window nooks and chairs between stacks and in alcoves, and in one of these, behind a leaded window which looked out upon the street and the park, I frequently established myself, browsing over one book and another in the hope of finding something which would interest me intensely. And so one afternoon, having nothing else to do, or at least nothing immediately pressing, I came here and by the merest chance picked up a volume entitled *The Wild Ass' Skin*, by one Honoré de Balzac, no less. I examined it curiously, reading incidentally a preface which fairly shimmered with his praise. He was the great master of France. His *Comédie Humaine* covered and even exhausted every aspect of the human welter. His character interpretations were exhaustive and exact. His backgrounds, abundant, picturesque, gorgeous even. In Paris his quondam home had been turned into a museum and at the time of the writing of this book contains his effects as they were at the time of his death.

I turned to the first page and began, and from then on until dusk I was sitting in this charming alcove, beside this window, reading. And it was as if a new and inviting door to life had been suddenly thrown open to me. Here was one who, as I saw it then, thought, felt and understood and could interpret all that I was interested in. Through him I saw at a glance a prospect so wide that it fairly left me breathless—all Paris, all France, all life through French eyes, and those of a genius. Here was one apparently with a tremendous and sensitive grasp of life, yet one highly philosophic, tolerant, patient, amused. At once I was personally identified with his Raphael, his Rastignac, his Bixiou, his Bianchon and with their supposedly cataclysmic miseries, especially Raphael's astounding and mystical discovery of the magic skin. With him then I entered the gaming house in the Palais-Royal, looked despairingly into the waters of the Seine from the Pont Royal, turned from it to the shop of the dealer in antiquities, was ignored by the perfect young lady before the shop of the print seller, attended the Taillefer banquet, suffered horrors over the shrinking skin. The lady without a heart was all too real—a flame of my own, indeed. I doubt if any book subsequent to my reading of *Dr. Jekyll and Mr. Hyde*, some five years before, had impressed me so much. It was for me a literary revolution, and this not only for the brilliant and incisive manner in which this man grasped life and invented themes or vehicles whereby to present it. In my own estimation at least, the type of individual he handled with most enthusiasm and skill, the brooding, seeking, ambitious beginner in life's affairs—social, political, artistic, commercial (Rastignac, Raphael, de Rubempré, Bianchon)—was, as I thought, so much like myself, their exact counterpart.

Indeed, subsequently taking up and consuming almost at a sitting such books as *The Great Man from the Provinces, Père Goriot, Cousin Pons, Cousin Betty*, it was so easy to—almost impossible for me not to—identify myself with the young and seeking aspirants to be found in each volume, sometimes three or four in each volume. The brilliant and intimate pictures of Parisian life, the exact flavor of its politics, arts, sciences, religions, social goings to and fro, to say nothing of their locale, impressed me so to accomplish for me what his imaginary magic skin had done for his Raphael, namely, transfer me bodily and without defect or lack to the centre as well as the circumference of the world which he was describing. I knew it and all of his characters as well as he did, or seemed to, so magical was his skill or so sensitive was I to what he had to relate and to that in which he was interested. His grand and somewhat pompous philosophical deductions, his easy and offhand disposition of all manner of critical, social, political, historical, religious and other problems, the manner in which he assumed as by right of genius intimate and irrefutable knowledge of all subjects (doctrines, mysteries, sciences, arts), fascinated and captivated me as the true method of the seer and the genius. Oh, to possess an insight such as this; to know and be a part of such a cosmos as Paris; to be able to go there—work, study, suffer, rise and even end in defeat, if need be, so fascinatingly alive and interesting were all the earth journeys of his puppets. What was Pittsburgh, what St. Louis, what Chicago? And yet somehow and in spite of myself, while I found myself adoring his Paris, still quite unconsciously I was obtaining a new and more dramatic light upon the world in which I found myself here. Pittsburgh was not Paris,

America was not France, but in truth they were something, and Pittsburgh at least had aspects which somehow suggested Paris. These
charming rivers, these many little bridges, the sharp contrasts presented between the east end and the mill regions, the huge nature of
the industries here and their import to the world at large, now impressed me, if anything, more vividly than before. I was in a workaday,
begrimed, and yet vivid Paris of sorts. Taillefer, Nucingen, Valentin
were no different to some of the immense money magnates here. Their
ease, luxury, power,—or at least the possibilities of the same which
they possessed—were duplicated here, and theirs were scarcely superior. Great books might be written here—and of these men. Coming
out of this library this day, and day after day thereafter, the while I
rendered as little reportorial service as was consistent with even a show
of effort, I marveled at the physical similarity of the two cities as I
conceived it, at the chance for pictures here as well as there. American
pictures here as opposed to French pictures there. And all the while I
was riding with Lucien to Paris, with his mistress, courting Madame
Nucingen with Rastignac, brooding over the horror of the automati-
cally contracting skin with Raphael, poring over his miseries with
Goriot, practising the horrible art of prostitution with Madame Marneffe. If ever one writer impressed another, and that violently, it was
Balzac—and yet, as it turned out, for a time only, for another god arose
not so very long after. For a period of three or four or five months at
least, I think I ate, slept, dreamed, lived him and his characters and his
views and his city. Thinking of reading as a pleasure as well as a
development, I can neither imagine nor wish any reader any greater joy
and inspiration than I had of Balzac these spring and summer days in
Pittsburgh. Idyllic days—dreamy days—poetic days—wonderful days,
the while ostensibly I did police and city hall in Allegheny. The like for
pleasure I scarcely ever saw again.

CHAPTER LXXIII

It would be decidedly unfair to myself, and to the *Dispatch* in one
sense, to indicate, as the foregoing would seem to, that I rendered no
adequate return for the stipend paid me. It was not much, and I would

not have suffered in my conscience if I had rendered much less than I did. But as a matter of fact, owing to the peculiar character of the local news conditions here, as well as my own creative if somewhat poorly equipped literary instincts at the time, I was able to render them just such service as they most craved, and that with scarcely a wrench to my mental ease. For what they craved more than news of a dramatic or disturbing character was some sort of idle feature stuff which they could use in the place of news at times and still interest their readers, and this I was able to supply, as were several other reporters who were attempting the same thing at their behest. The spring and summer time, Balzac, the very picturesque nature of the city itself, my own idling and yet reflective disposition, caused me finally to attempt and, as they viewed it at least, achieve a series of mood or word pictures anent the most trivial of news matters—a summer storm, a spring day, a visit to a hospital, the death of an old switchman's dog, the arrival of fly time and the first mosquito—all of which I apostrophized in paragraphs and sentences to the length of a column or more each, and which gave me the realest taste of what it means to be a creative writer of any that I had yet had.

My city editor asking me one day if I could not invent some kind of a feature—there being no assignment for me—I sat down in the office and meditated on one theme and another. Finally, and because I was being pestered by several, I began to think on the fly as the possible subject of an idle skit. He was arriving about now; being young and ambitious and having freshly crawled out of some breeding-pit somewhere, he alighted on the nearest fence or windowsill, brushed his head and wings reflectively and meditated on the possibility of a livelihood or a career of sorts. What now, pray, could be open to a young and ambitious fly in a world all too crowded with flies? There were barns, of course, and kitchens and horses and cows and pigs of different degrees and stations, but these fields, being plebeian to a degree, were very much overrun. And this was a sensitive and somewhat cleanly and, to a degree, meditative fly. Looking about him and, indeed, flying about here and there to inspect the world, he encountered within a modest and respectable home somewhere a shiny pate which seemed to offer a rather polished field of effort. Why not apply one's efforts to the matter of extracting comfort as well as sustenance from so agreeable and handsome a thing as a bald pate? Here, as he thought, was at once a mirror, a dancing-floor and a reasonable vantage point from which the matter of obtaining sustenance might well be conducted. However, so energetic was the protest of the individual to whom the pate belonged that after a short and somewhat energetic contest it had to be abandoned.

Then came, in due course, the discovery of a handsome baby's crib and its occupant. Why not settle here and, while resting upon the pleasant texture of the child, explore a neighboring milk bottle, the child's ears, its open mouth, and what not? As in the first instance, a disturbance as well as some seeming opposition ensuing, the fly enters finally upon a three-cornered contest with the child and in addition the mistress of the house, who now appears and upon whom the fly looks as an unwarranted interloper. With commendable pluck and courage, it essays to defend itself and drive off the latter. To no result. A broom is finally introduced, and it seeks cover in a dark corner behind a fragment of loose wallpaper. The opposition withdrawing, it once more, after due meditation and with commendable grit, makes its appearance, and finding a dinner table in process of arrangement and food being carried in, it now begins wildly to rejoice in the discovery of butter, bread, jam, a container of sugar and what not, congratulating itself that at last and easily it has solved the matter of a happy sustenance.

Alas for the energy and ambition of all ambitious flies. The mistress returning with a fly-flipper, chase is given. By now the appetite and even the lust of the fly for such obvious delicacies having been aroused, it gives determined battle, proposing not to be ousted save at the end of the broom itself. To satisfy itself and escape the enemy at one and the same time, it essays quick descents upon the butter, the bread, the sugar, the jam, and even a bowl of soup which has been carried in. Finding itself pursued and defeated in many instances, it makes one desperate descent upon the jam, only to be mired—a new danger—and from which it succeeds in extricating itself by a fraction of an inch before a scooping spoon essays its capture. Then from the top of a windowsill, sadly loosening its feet and wings, it decides upon a second desperate attempt and so dives into the butter, all but losing its life in the process. The enemy now aroused and harrying it from wall to wall, it still keeps up its courage, but being struck and injured and left defeated, as it were, upon the edge of a moulding, it finally decides upon an heroic and unforgettable death. It will dive into the jam, then the butter, then the soup, and at last sink with a despairing sigh and a "Farewell, cruel world" to the bottom of the mistress's steaming coffee cup, which same it does.

This idle fancy, a thing which took me not more than three-quarters of an hour to pen once I thought of it, and which I deemed quite worthless and was almost afraid to submit, produced, once I handed it in, so remarkable a change in the attitude of the office as well as in my life and career here that I hesitate to say how much. I had several times before noted in connection with newspaper work that some trivial thing like this had advantaged me greatly—and here was the same thing repeated, only more so. I have not before mentioned, I think, a small, retiring, sentimental soul, one Jim Israel by name, who was assistant city editor at the time and one of the most gracious and approachable and lovable individuals I have ever known. He it was to whom I turned over my skit, and who took it with an air of kindly consideration, and hopefulness even, which would have softened the blow of its rejection had it been returned. Wherever he is, I wish him godspeed.

"Trying to help us out, are you?" he said with a smile, and then added when I predicated its worthlessness, "Well, it's not such an easy thing to turn out that stuff. I hope it is something the chief will like."

He took it and, as I noticed, read it the first thing, for I hung about to see, and then I saw him begin to smile and finally chuckle. "This thing's all right," he called. "You needn't worry. Gaither'll be pleased with this, I know," and he began to edit it. His manner was very hearty.

I went out to walk and think, for I hadn't a thing to do except to wander over to Allegheny and see if anything had turned up. Since nothing had, I went into the library there, but feeling too pleased with myself to work, wandered about, following the queer, narrow, rather winding streets of this place and thinking on what more if anything of this kind I could do. Finally I hit upon a probably acceptable theme, but before doing so visited a new park which was being proposed or laid out somewhere—some worthless tract to be called Riverwood, I believe—and in idleness I went out there to see what if anything the politicians were planning to "hand" the city. I found it, to my astonishment and delight, one of the most picturesque and wonderful sites I had ever seen for a park: high beetling cliffs, wonderful gulches and valleys, most far-reaching and splendid views in every direction. And this I proposed to describe some day. "Here is one instance," I recall thinking to myself, "where a city, being handed otherwise worthless land by the usual political jobbery method, cannot be swindled. It will eventually get its money's worth out of this, whatever it pays." And I am sure it has since. It was all so beautiful, so very impressive.

But to return to my composition. Returning at six I was greeted by my city editor with a smile and told that if I would I could do that sort of thing as much as I liked. "Try and get up something for tomorrow, will you?"

Delighted and scarcely believing in my luck, I agreed that I would. The next day, a spring rain descending with wonderful clouds and a magnificent electrical display, I put off the theme I had thought of—a matter of a complaining grocery horse commenting on his owner. I described instead how the city, dry and smoky and dirty, lay panting in the deadening heat, and how out of the west came, like an answer to a prayer or a wish, this sudden and soothing storm—battalion upon battalion of huge woolly clouds riven with great silvery flashes of light and yet darkening the sun as they came. And how, suddenly and despite the fact that shutters clapped and papers flew and office windows and doors had to be closed and signs squeaked and swung and people everywhere ran to cover still weary and oppressed by the heat, the thousands upon thousands who had been patiently enduring it vented a sigh of gratitude.

Continuing in this vein I described how the steel mill hovels, the homes of the rich, the office buildings, the factories, the hospitals, and jails changed under these conditions, and then ventured upon specific incidents and pictures of animals and men. As on the preceding day, this was received with congratulations almost as hearty, especially by the assistant editor, who, as I afterwards learned, was more partial to anything sentimental than his chief, the other preferring humor and farce. Now, feeling that I had hit upon a vein of my own, I was not inclined to favor the moods of either but to write such things as appealed to me most. And this I did from day to day—or time to time—as a fancy struck me, wandering out into the country or in strange neighborhoods, or indeed new fields of thought (for me) for ideas, and so varying my studies as my mood dictated. I noticed, however, that all my more serious or sentimental attempts, while popular with the assistant and some others about the office, were not so popular with my chief as the lighter and sillier things. He liked humor and badinage. And this might have been a guide to me, had I been so inclined, leading to an easy and popular success—so obvious was my success here and so obvious had been my success in St. Louis with the same type of thing. But by instinct and observation, as I even then noted, I was inclined to be interested in the larger and more tragic phases of life. Mere humor, such as I could achieve when I chose, appeared always to require for its foundation the most trivial of incidents, whereas huge and almost massive conditions underlay tragedy and, indeed, all the more forceful aspects of life. Temperamentally, always, I was for those.

But what pleased and surprised me was the manner in which these lighter as well as the more serious things were received—the change which they made in my standing. Hitherto I had been merely a newcomer, being tested as yet and by no means secure in my hold on this particular position. They had been short a man for general work and, fearing that the staff might be permanently reduced by one unless a man was employed, I had been put on. So until this request came, I had had no least opportunity to show whether I could write or not. But now, of a sudden, my status was entirely different. I was a feature man, one who had succeeded where others apparently had failed at this work, and so I was made more than welcome. My city editor, to my surprise, asked me one day, after suggesting that I get up another feature if I could, whether I had had my lunch. I gladly availed myself of a chance to talk to him, and he told me a little something of local journalistic life, but not much—who the publisher was, his politics, his views. Another time, the assistant city editor invited me to dinner, and this on the ground that his wife was intensely interested in the man who was doing these things! She came to meet us and made me blush with her praise. The Sunday editor, the chief political reporter, the chief city hall and police man drew near, and I found myself not only going to lunch with one or the other, but being taken to the press club after midnight, and occasionally to a theatre by the dramatic man. Finally— this was after several months, however—I was invited to contribute something to the Sunday pages and, later still, asked to help out the dramatic man with occasional criticisms.

If you will believe it, I was a little puzzled and made quite nervous, though not vain, by this sudden rise. Since I did not look on myself as a writer of anything more than news, and this thing that I was doing was really too trivial for words, I scarcely knew how to take it. The managing editor, for instance, came to shake hands with me, and after him the son of the publisher himself, fresh from some European trip or about to sail. I was more taken aback than set up, for I deemed myself unworthy of it all and believed that it couldn't really last—all this flattery. Yet when the son, Florence O'Neill I believe his name was, a stocky florid creature of about twenty-eight or thirty, told me how interested he was in the kind of things I was doing and that he wished he "could write like that," I remember feeling a little envious of the latter, with his fine clothes and his easy, if flattering, manner, and wishing that I like him had been born to wealth. An invitation extended by him to dine at his home soothed me in no way. I felt that life had been unduly unfair in my case and was inclined to resent it. I never went.

Similarly some talk of sending me to report a proposed commercial conference somewhere—at Buffalo, I believe—looking to the construction of a ship canal from Erie or Buffalo to Pittsburgh, interested me not much. I was not interested in those things—really not in newspaper work—and yet scarcely knew what I wanted to do if not that. One thing sure, I had no underlying commercial sense whereby I might have profited by all this. I do not wish to give the impression by any means that I was being feted or dined and wined, or that my future was secured by this, but certainly I could have made it mean more than I did.

After the second or third sketch had been published, there was, as I have said, a decided list in my direction, and this I might have utilized in more ways than one. But I did not. Instead, I merely mooned and dreamed as before, taking a small room in a private home on Mt. Washington, where I began to be interested in a most colorless and unimportant girl, reading at the Carnegie Library, arriving at the office at times at twelve or one, at other times not until six, and, being excused, writing and delivering the next day one of these sketches, and then going home again or to the press club or the library. Occasionally I ate with the dramatic editor or the political or police man. Betimes I gathered all sorts of data as to the steel magnates—Carnegie, Phipps and Frick especially—their homes, their clubs, their local condescensions and superiorities. The people of Pittsburgh were, as I began to understand, fairly looked upon as vassals by some of these. Their interviews on returning from the seashore or the mountains or on setting out for the same at different seasons of the year partook of the nature of a royal farewell or return and an occasional address from the throne. The poor here were so very poor, the rich so rich, and their self-importance was beyond measure.

I remember once about this time being sent to the Duquesne Club to interview Andrew Carnegie, fresh from his travels abroad or from Skibo, in Scotland, and being received by a secretary who allowed me to stand in the back of a room in which Mr. Carnegie, short, stocky, bandy-legged, a grand air of authority investing him, was addressing presumably the elite of the city on the subject of America and its political needs. No note-taking was permitted, but afterwards I was handed a typewritten address to the people of Pittsburgh and told that the *Dispatch* would be allowed to publish that. And it did. I smiled then, and I do now, at the attitude of press, pulpit, officials and what not of this amazing city of steel and iron. All of them seemed so genuflective and bootlicking, and yet they seemed not to profit to any great degree by the presence of these magnates, who were constantly hinting at removing elsewhere unless they were treated thus and so—as though the life of a great and forceful metropolis depended on them and them alone. The effrontery! The nerve!

CHAPTER LXXIV

At this time I began to establish most cordial relations with the short, broad-shouldered, dark and rather sad-faced labor reporter whom I have previously mentioned and who was concerned with all the labor news of this region for this paper. At first he appeared to be a little shy of me or, if not that, then not interested, but, as time passed and I seemed to have established myself in the favor of the paper, this individual appeared to grow more friendly. I have often thought that it was not so much that he did not wish to know me at first as that he was suspicious of all facile friendships. His own position was too delicate. This was not a pro-labor paper by any means, and he was decidedly a pro-labor individual. He had to be most careful of all he said and did, as he afterwards told me, in order not to offend the chiefs above him.

But as time went on, in my case at least he became more and more friendly and communicative in regard to his work and finally took me rather completely into his confidence. He was really a radical at heart, only he did not dare let it be known here. Often of a morning, after we became better acquainted, he would spend as much as an hour or two in the office, before any of the other reporters appeared on the scene, discussing the nature of coal mining and steel making, the difficulty of arranging wage conditions which would appeal to all the men and not cause friction. But in the main, as I noted, he commented on the shrewd and cunning way in which the bosses and owners were more and more overreaching their employes, preying upon their prejudices via religious and political dodges, and at the same time misusing them shamefully via the company store, the short ton, the cost of mining materials, rent and the like. At first, being wholly inexperienced in these matters, I was inclined to doubt whether he was as sound as he seemed to think. Later as I grew in personal knowledge, I began to think that he might really be too conservative, so painful did many of the things I observed with my own eyes and his aid appear.

For one thing, owing to his kindness and interest I was allowed to visit some of the "homes" of the foreign workers in the steel and other mill and factory districts here—the tobacco district for one, which latter merely interested him as an allied labor field. Viewing these of a night and at other times, I was inclined to think his asseverations in regard to all of this were all too mild.

For, while he sympathized with workers here, there, and every- where, as I noticed, still he was convinced that there was another side to the story, however small it might be, and that industrial leadership with its rather large rewards could never be done away with. I have always been inclined to agree with him as to that. The only problem with me has been as to the size of the rewards of the leaders. As an employee of the *Dispatch,* and because he was married and had a child, he insisted that he could do little or nothing about it, which was true, I suppose—could not even talk very much to anyone—least of all to the superiors of this paper. They did not want pro-labor news or sympathies even, and since his first duty appeared to be to his wife and child he did not appear to be willing to express himself. And yet, perhaps because he was so helpless, his interest and sympathy appeared to be all the more intense. He reminded me at times of bottled dynamite, or some retained and yet dangerous chemical, not likely ever to explode, however, because of the care with which it was packed and handled. And yet it might have at that. All he ever did, in so far as I could see, was to feed his irritated soul on facts and the reported injustices and cruelties and brutalities of employers here and there which he could never use. He always had his labor papers and congressional or state reports anent this, that, and the other, which he would analyze and grumble over, but no more.

One morning I remember we were talking of steel and iron and the methods of making the same. (I was always speaking to someone of the marvellous picture the great mills just below Mt. Washington made and how I liked to look in their doors and how on first coming here I had visited the mill tenement streets at Homestead.) He interrupted me to say, "You haven't seen anything yet. Ever been in any of the mills?"

"No," I replied.

"You ought to go sometime."

"But I don't believe they welcome visitors very much, do they?"

"No, they don't. The stranger is under suspicion, but I could take you through sometime, if you wanted to go. I know the foremen of some of the mills out there and other places around town."

I jumped at the chance. So one night when I had nothing better to do I went with him, to Homestead first, then to some tenements there and in some other mill district nearer Pittsburgh, the name of which I have forgotten. What astonished me in so far as the steel mills themselves were concerned was the large number of furnaces going at once, the piles, almost mountains, of powdered iron ore ready to be smelted, the long lines of cars in the vicinity—flat, box, and coal cars—and the nature and size and force of the machinery used to roll steel. The work, as he or his friends the bosses showed me, was, in so far as blast furnaces were concerned, divided between the "front" and the "back." Those working at the front of the furnace took care of the molten iron and slag which was being "puddled." (I will explain that later.) The men at the "back," the stock and yard men, filled huge steel buckets, suspended from traveling cranes, with ore, fuel and limestone, all of which were piled near at hand, and, trundling them to a point over the mouth of the melting vats or "skips" as they were called, "released" them via a movable bottom. At this particular plant I was told the machinery for handling all this was better than elsewhere, the company being richer and more progressive. In some of the less progressive concerns the men filled carts with raw material and then trundled them around to the front of a hoist, which was at the back of the furnace, where they were lifted and emptied into the "skip." In this particular mill all a man had to do to fill a steel bucket with raw material was to push one of them, suspended from its trolley, under a chute and pull a rod. Then the "stock" tumbled into it. From there it was trundled, via machinery, to a point over the "skip." These furnaces were charged or fed constantly by feeders working in twelve-hour shifts, twenty-four hours every day, so that there was little opportunity to rest from the beginning to the end of each man's twelve hours. Their pay, as I learned, was not more than half of that paid to the men at the "front" because the work was neither so hard nor so skillful, although it looked quite hard enough to me, and tedious.

But the men at the front, the puddlers, were almost the labor princes of this realm and yet among the hardest worked. A puddling or boiling furnace, as I learned here, was a brick structure like an oven, about seven feet high and six feet square, with two compartments, one a receptacle into which pig iron was thrown, the other a fuel chamber beside it where the melting heat was generated. The drafts were so arranged that the flame swept from the fuel chamber directly upon the surface of the iron. From five hundred to six hundred pounds of pig iron were put into each furnace at one time, after which it was closed and sufficient heat applied to melt down the iron. Then the puddler began to "work" it with an iron rod passed through a hole in the furnace door, so as to stir up the liquid and bring as much as possible in contact with the air. As the impurities became separated from the iron and rose to the top as slag, they were tipped out through a center notch. As it became freer from impurities, a constantly higher temperature was required to keep the iron in a liquid condition. Gradually it began to solidify in granules, much as butter is formed after churning. Later, as I was shown, it took on the form of, or was worked into large malleable balls or lumps or rolls like butter—three to any given "charge" or furnace. Then, while still in a comparatively soft but not molten condition, these were taken out and thrown across a steel floor or "hearth" to a "taker" to be "worked" by other machinery and other processes.

As I saw here and really marvelled, puddling was so hot and trying that it was a full-sized man's job—none more so. There were always two men and sometimes three to a single furnace, and they took turns about at working the metal, as a rule ten minutes to a turn. No man could stand before a furnace and perform that backbreaking toil continually. Even when working by "spells," as I then saw, a man was often nearly exhausted at the end of his "spell." He had, as a rule, to go outside in the air and sit on a bench, or stand and sweat, the perspiration running from his face, neck, arms and hands. When at work, these men stood in front of the furnace in the full glare of its flames and worked the metal via a rod through a hole in the door. The intensity of the heat in those days (1894) was not as yet relieved by the device of shielding the furnace with water-cooled plates. The wages these men earned were in the neighborhood of three dollars a day, the highest then paid. The great strike had served to compel them to take less than they had previously received—which had been, for these particular men at least, much more.

But perhaps the men who most fascinated me and commanded my respect were those who—once the "puddler" had done his work and thrown his lump of red-hot iron out upon an open hearth, as it was called—took the lump and threw it to a "rougher," who in turn fed it into a second machine which rolled or beat it into a more easily handled and workable form. The exact details of the process escape me now, but the picture these men presented in these hot, fire-lighted, noisy and sputtering rooms which were here in rows is by no means invalidated thereby.

Here, as I then saw, agility and even youth were at a premium, and a false step meant, possibly, death. There was no room for a man with stiff joints or one whose eye was not keen. I remember one man whom I watched later in the mill below Mt. Washington, who, picking up billet after billet from furnace after furnace, threw them along the steel floor to the "rougher." Dressed only in trousers and a flannel shirt with his sleeves cut off at the shoulder, the sweat pouring from his body and his muscles standing out in knots, this man handled billet after billet of red-hot metal with the skill and agility of a tightrope performer. At the same time, during his spell of ten or fifteen minutes or more, the "rougher" to whom these billets were tossed was constantly leaping about, thrusting the red billets almost in a stream through the first pair of rolls for which they were intended, and yet, before he could turn back, there was always another billet on the floor behind him. The rolls into which he was feeding these billets were built in a train, side by side in line; the billets went through one pair, only to be seized by a "catcher" and shoved back through the next. Back and forth, back and forth they went at an ever increasing speed, until the catcher at the next to the last pair of rolls, seizing the end of the rod as it came through still red-hot, described with it a fiery circle high in the air, the snake-like thing leaping and straining against the restraining force which yet bent it back again to enter the last roll. It was wonderful.

And yet these men were not looked upon in this region as anything extraordinary. While the places in which they were were metal infernos of sorts and their toil of the most intense and exacting character, they were not allowed to organize to better their condition any. The recent great victory of the steel magnates had settled that. And yet at that very time in that very city and elsewhere these same magnates were positively rolling in wealth. Their profits were tumbling in so fast that they scarcely knew what to do with them. Vast libraries and universities were being built with their gifts. Immense and stuffy mansions crowded with art and "historic" furniture were being erected here and elsewhere. Their children were being sent to special schools to be taught how to be ladies and gentlemen in a democracy which they contemned; and on the other hand these sweating men here were being denied an additional five or ten cents on the hour and the right to organize. If they protested or attempted to drive out imported strike-breakers they were fired and state or federal troops called in to protect the mills. They could not organize then, and never since have they been allowed so to do.

Martyn, who was intensely sympathetic toward them at that time, was still more sympathetic toward the individuals who were not so skillful—mere day laborers who received from as low as one dollar to as high as one-sixty-five at a time when two a day was all too little to support anyone, and this for hard backbreaking labor.

He grew positively melodramatic as he told me of one region and another where these men lived and how they lived, and finally took me in order that I might see for myself. Afterwards, in the ordinary course of reportorial work, I came upon some of these neighborhoods and interiors and individuals. And since they were all a part of the great fortune-building era and illustrate in the first instance how democracy works—or did—in America, and how some great fortunes were built, I propose to put down here a few pictures of things that I saw. Let me first preface this by saying that wages varied from one to one-sixty-five a day for the common laborer to three and even four per day—never more than that then—paid to the skilled worker. In consequence, rents averaged from two-fifteen per week, or eight-sixty per month, paid by the laborer who worked for one-sixty-five a day—or less—to four-seventy-two per week, or some twenty per month, paid by the skilled steelworker.

And the type of living places they could secure for this! One afternoon, on some reportorial mission—taking a census of opinion in Allegheny, I believe, as to whether it wished to unite with Pittsburgh in one greater city—I recall entering a two-room tenement in a court, the character of which first opened my eyes as to the type of home these workers endured or enjoyed, as you will. This court in itself was interesting, for it consisted of four sides with an open space in the centre. Three of these sides were smoke-grimed wooden houses, three stories in height. The fourth was an ancient and odourous wooden stable, where the horses of some contractor were kept. In the centre of this court—about 25x25, if I remember rightly—stood a circular wooden building or lavatory or privy, or what you will, with ten triangular compartments, each opening into one vault or cesspool. Near this again was one hydrant—the only hydrant or water supply for all these houses or rooms. These two conveniences served twenty families (Polish, Hungarian, Slavonic, Jewish and Negro) of from three to five people each, living in the sixty-three rooms which made up the three grimy sides above mentioned. There were twenty-seven children in these rooms, for whom this court was their only playground. For twenty housewives this was the only place where they could string their wash-lines. For twenty tired, sweaty, unwashed husbands this was the only near and neighborly recreation and companionship centre. Here of a sweltering summer night, if you please, after playing cards and drinking beer—"rushing the duck" as the phrase went—they would frequently stretch themselves to sleep.

But this was not all.

As waste pipes were wanting in the house, heavy tubs of water had to be carried out and in, and this in a smoky town where a double amount of washing and cleaning was necessary. When the weather permitted, the heavy washes were done in the yard. Then, of course, the pavement of this populous court, covered with tubs, wringers, clothes baskets and pools of soapy water, made a poor playground for children. But in addition these privies must be used, and in consequence a situation was created which may be better imagined than explained. Many of the "front" windows of these "apartments" looked down on this centre. In these instances, this handsome centre was only a few yards from the kitchen windows, creating a neat sanitary as well as uplifting condition. In addition, while usually only two families used one of these compartments, in some other courts like this three or four families were compelled to use one, giving rise to indifference and a sense of irresponsibility for their condition. In consequence, they were filthy. Again, while all the streets had sewers, and by borough ordinance these outside vaults must be connected with them, still, ordinarily, they were flushed only by the waste water—emptied tubs, et cetera. When conditions became unbearable the tenants washed the vault out with a hose attached to the hydrant, but in winter time, when there was danger of freezing, this was not always possible, and warm thawing days brought sweet conditions. There was not one indoor closet in any of these courts.

But to return to the "apartment" in question.

The kitchen, perhaps 15x12 feet, was steaming with vapor from a big washtub set on a chair in the middle of the room. The mother, who had carried this water in for some reason was trying to wash and at the same time to keep the older of her two babies from tumbling into the tub full of scalding water that was standing on the floor. On one side of the room was a huge puffy bed, with one feather tick to sleep on and another for covering. Near the window stood a sewing machine, in the corner an organ—all these besides the inevitable cookstove upon which, in the place of honor, was simmering the evening soup. To the left, in the second room, were one boarder and the "man of the house" asleep. Two boarders, so I learned, were at work, but at night would be home to sleep in the bed now occupied by one boarder and the "man of the house," and from which these would soon get up. And this was a court and a home of the better sort—or at least as good as any. This little family and these boarders, taken in to help out on the rent, worked and lived so in order that Mr. Carnegie might give the world one or two extra libraries with his name plastered on the front, and Mr. Frick a mansion which will unquestionably be torn down some day to make room for an apartment house on his magnificent Fifth Avenue site.

Question: Did they ever see or hear of or care about these tenements? I doubt it.

CHAPTER LXXV

But it was to Martyn and his interest that I owed still other views, all equally entrancing. There was a boardinghouse to which he took me—one of perhaps fifty or a hundred, but of which this one was a "sample"—in which lived twenty-four people, all in two rooms. And yet to my unutterable astonishment and confusion it was not so bad at that, so great is the value apparently of intimate and somehow cheerful human contact, and these people were cheerful. As Martyn explained to me at the time, few of the very poor day laborers who were young and unmarried cared how they lived so long as they lived cheaply and could save a little. I myself was an illustration of that. This particular institution—in Homestead it was—was in one of those courts such as I have described, and still it was not so bad. It consisted of two rooms, one above the other, each measuring perhaps 12x20. In the kitchen at the time was the wife of the "boarding boss," getting dinner—some sort of hot apple cake and a stew of the cheapest cut of meat. Along one side of the room was an oilcloth-covered table with a plank bench on each side; above it were a rack holding a long row of handleless white cups, and a shelf with tin knives and forks. Near the up-to-date range, the only real piece of furniture in the room, hung the "buckets" in which all mill men carried their noon or midnight meals. These made a picture somehow—bright and pleasing. A crowd of men were lounging cheerfully about, talking, smoking and enjoying life, one of them playing a concertina. They were all of the nationalities previously indicated—Hungarians, Lithuanians, et cetera. With commendable zest and animation they were making the most of a brief spell before their meal and departure for work. In the room above, as the landlord—the landlord of two rooms—cheerfully showed us, were double iron bedsteads set close together and on them comfortables neatly laid. In these two rooms, besides the "boarding boss" and his wife—both stalwart Bulgarians—and their two babies, lived twenty men. They were of those who handled steel billets and bars, unloaded and loaded trains, worked in cinder pits, filled steel buckets with stock, and what not. They all worked twelve hours a day, and their reward was this and what they could save over and above it out of nine-sixty per week. Martyn said a good thing about this at this time: "I don't know how it is. I know these people are exploited and misused. The mill owners offer them the lowest wages, the landlords exploit these boardinghouse keepers as well as their boarders, and the community which they help and make by their work don't give a darn for them, and yet here they are, happy in their way, and I'll be hanged if they don't make me happy. It must be that just work is happiness and makes people that way—." And after hearing that, I thought and thought and have never been able to get it out of my mind. Plenty of work, something to do, the ability to avoid the ennui of idleness and useless, pensive, futile thought—what a treasure.

But I could go on with these pictures registered at this time, indefinitely. An incident which made an impression on me at this time or a little later here was that of a woman, the mother of a family and the wife of a steelworker of the poorer sort, who said, when I asked her how she made out for amusement: "My boys are so musical, and the other fellows come in and we all have such a good sing together. Then Mamie dances the Highland Fling. They offered to pay her to do it down at the vaudeville, but the boys won't let her do it away from home. My old man don't care for nothing but his pipe and a newspaper." (There were no theatres, and the movie and the phonograph had not as yet arrived.)

Well, so much for that side of it. There was another which I always thought was, in part at least, connected with this, and that was the vice situation in this particular city, which struck me as decidedly plethoric. There were so many girls who walked the streets here; and back of the *Dispatch* and post office buildings, as well as in the streets ranged along the Monongahela below Smithfield—Water, First and Second—were a large number of "houses of disrepute," as large and flourishing an area as I had seen in any American city up to that time. As I learned by talking with the political man and the police man (a very charming and intelligent character, the latter), the police here as elsewhere "protected" vice—or, in other words, preyed on it. The captains had their wardmen; the chief "got his" from the captains; the politicians and ward leaders got theirs in being let down easy on taxes, licenses and whatever institutions they were interested in; and big business got let alone to do about as it pleased. In other words, whenever big business squawked or protested, the police and the politicians moved, and that very civilly and genuflectively. They never attempted to fight big business, which could stir up the churches and the "Christian dubs," as this particular police reporter was wont to refer to them. Hence this large and comfortable vice area which the authorities at the top, here as elsewhere, would never admit existed.

But I was speaking of the problem in general, and in this particular city as elsewhere, I think, quite definitely it was connected with poverty. There is always among both the rich and the poor the "girl who goes wrong," primarily in the sense that she yields herself for love outside marriage, but that is by no means the same as saying that in consequence she goes upon the streets or into a house of prostitution. Lust might conceivably drive her in some such instances, but I doubt it. With the girl who walks the streets, poverty, the need of a little finery which she sees others possess and she herself cannot afford are the impelling forces. No girl, I am sure, could look upon promiscuity as a means of pleasure, although the *seemingly* easy cash acquired might in her estimation contribute to her subsequent pleasure in some form or other—possibly with some man even, whom she could admire. In consequence, where a home is colorless and drear—and where in any city more than Pittsburgh at this time there could have been more of such, I cannot think—she might and probably does take to the streets, especially after some such first step as I have indicated. The solution is not new, I am sure. But when I think of the homes I saw there, and the mill and wage conditions which went with them, the high and mighties at the top preying upon the poor fish at the bottom, the wonder to me is that the pavements were not even fuller of the so-called "fallen."

And then in Pittsburgh at this time there was another phase of this same situation which might have contributed to so large a vice district, and that was the presence in great numbers of girls who worked in the garment, paper, millinery, confectionary, cigar and other trades here— from ten to forty per cent of each, as Martyn guessed—who boarded away from home. At that time the Y.W.C.A. and those other phases of the uplift or social service movement, which even then was tending to bring about some slight amelioration of the living condition which surrounded such girls, had not yet come into full swing. Poverty was sending the seeker for room and board into districts of a grade as low as, sometimes lower than, the usual slum. Several unsightly shacks in one unpaved alley near the very building in which I worked, as Martyn explained to me, offered room and board to such girls at three dollars a week. In others, by sleeping in the kitchen and helping with the housework, a girl could get board for the same sum. Most of these girls, in this vicinity at least, were makers of the famous "Pittsburgh Stogie" in the dozens of factories which abounded in this very region. She could scarcely find a room for rent in the thickly settled parts of the city for less than ten dollars a month. Even at that price she could not be sure that the character of the house was above reproach. It gave me a fresh appreciation of the problem faced by the homeless girl to hear, as I once did in this very region, of a weekday morning when I was idling in one of those streets studying the city, a conversation between two would-be lodgers and a slim Jewess whose house and its furnished-room sign were probably a blind for a place of another character. They had evidently asked her if she had a room, and she stood in the door, arms akimbo, looking them over, the while they shrunk back more like prisoners or evildoers than wage-earning girls, which they plainly were, earning their living. Their untidy dresses, stocky figures and cheap hats and shoes did not promise much for Madame's line of business, so she was very short.

"Well, I'll tell you," she said after a time and after inquiring where they worked, "my rooms is two-fifty a week, and I might as well tell you I don't allow no companies, no gentlemen friends and no lady friends. I can't be having no noise and talking in my house. Now if youse want to see the rooms youse can."

"My lady," I wanted to chip in, "you don't want working girls at all. It's another type entirely you're after."

But what I have been trying to reach in connection with all this was my own attitude—my own personal and private response to it all—and it will puzzle me even now quite as much as it did then to say what I thought, but I will do the best I can. Vice as such has never been an unmitigated evil to me by any means. The world needs it, and it is either a part of the scheme of the Creator or it is an accidental evolution which He cannot avoid, and therefore its presence puts Him in as helpless a condition in regard to it and us as the rest of us. Vice districts or vice manifestations in any form are, I am sure, merely equational or reciprocal manifestations of something which is not vice—an antithesis, for instance, to too much virtue, too much repression of or indifference to a force or impulse, the possibly proper expression of which is something less than rampant brutal sexuality. But since in nature the norm, while apparently sought, is never attained, vice as well as its antithesis, militant virtue, will always remain. The twain are probably necessary in order that any sense or realization of life at all may be had. Nature, not reason or any super wisdom the import of which as yet we have not been able to apprehend, seemingly carries all impulses of whatsoever character too far—or not far enough. If ever the dead level or desired norm were reached by all at one and the same time, there would be no life in any form. Of this I am sure. It is by some tic or obstruction or over-impulse of some kind that the norm is always avoided or swung past or never reached, and it is due to this selfsame miss or seeming failure that all so-called expression or a sense of life is attained. Otherwise there would be a vast sea of inert force which would mean just nothing at all.

In so far as sex is concerned—denuded as it must be for me of all elements of chicane and trickery and graft and cruelty and profit such as characterize vice in its lower forms—I have only the greatest admiration. The whole matter of the sexes, their contacts, the sense of beauty and color and romance that surrounds the physical lure each has for the other, is to me more beautiful than I can say, the quintessence of beauty. I balk only when these same come to be identified—as they nearly always do in large cities, where ignorance and poverty and predatory force and religious and social fear make pariahs of so many— with barter and sale and craft and cunning in a hundred horrible commercial and even criminal forms. These latter variations and horrors have nothing to do with sex proper but only with finance and commerce and robbery—the same as that which produces crooked gambling houses and races—and these same should be harried by every device which law, representing nature and society's sense of fair play or balance, can devise. The cold-blooded trafficking in sex, not for any reason of necessity but because of the possibility of gain—and easy gain for some who are only interested in it from a money and criminal point of view—is too despicable for words. And it is always an interesting thing to note that the protectors and defenders and even creators, I might say, of vice in this form are not always by any means the women whose bodies and charms are the substance of it, but the police and the owners of commercially defunct property in wretched regions, and the grafters and panderers who make an easy living by the adulteries of others and whose only interest in the same is money—very hard cash—not beauty or passion or lust, all commendable or pathetic enough. Such swine should be harried down any available hill into any available sea.

Returning to my particular views at that time, I should like to say that I was young, romantic, lonely and passionate. While women of various types and charms were forever manifesting an interest in me (I never lived in a house or home anywhere where some woman or girl did not begin a flirtation), still I was of that peculiar turn of mind which was scarcely willing to accept the evidence of its own eyes. The approaches and inviting glances of a thousand women were not sufficient to convince me that I was interesting to women, so convinced was I that I was not—why, I don't know. At the same time, while I desired to interest and, had I tried, might have interested a most exclusive type of girl perhaps, my mood and the conditions under which I worked made it difficult. My evenings were always employed, and mornings and afternoons seemed somehow inauspicious for philandering. In consequence, while I was parleying with myself as to what I ought to do about feminine contact of one sort or another, I became unutterably lonely. Occasionally driven by desire, I would turn to one or other of those "nymphs du pave," as one of the reporters on our paper called them, going into the region back of the post office or along Smithfield or Fifth Avenue, where they walked, to look for them. And in spite of the fact that a great to-do is made by many who feign to look upon such as utterly worthless and even loathsome, I found them not so bad by any means. There is a type of girl between fifteen and twenty-three or -four, who for reasons of poverty or the hope of finery takes to the streets, and a few of these I made friends with. Two or three in particular, in the course of this summer, made a passing impression on me: a large olive-complected, black-haired girl of perhaps twenty-three or -four, who came to general delivery for mail and who met me afterwards in a rooming house in this immediate vicinity, with the mistress of which she appeared to have an arrangement. It is a little curious, when one comes to think of it now, that all I can recall of her, or nearly all, relates to her body—that it was large and soft and white, with big hips and small feet and hands. Of her mind, if she had one, I scarcely remember anything save that she told a few lewd and yet amusing stories and shocked me by her references to various parts of the body and its needs and impulses in terms to which I was not accustomed. I thought her *low* and yet nice, and my relations with her as low, but, so long as no one knew, it was all right and quite wonderful. But as for her, she was still low for doing for cash, or indeed for any other reason, what I wished her to do. Can human asininity and folderol go further!

The second one was smaller and more dapper, a red-headed girl of not more than eighteen or twenty, whom I first saw at city hall talking to a reporter and later encountered walking the pavement (or I thought she was) about the post office, which was one of the principal centres for this. She recognized me and, agreeing to my overtures, took me to another house in this same region with which she had a working arrangement, as she admitted. She was, as she finally told me after several visits, a "hand" in a tobacco factory near here, or had been when she chose to work, which was not often, as she admitted, because she could make more in this other way. She too was experienced and, so, *low* in my eyes, although I have no doubt she thought me a fool of sorts, and she was quite right. For the very worst things she did or said—words and expressions she used when rutting, or comments she made, or positions she was willing to take—while delighting me most, still shocked me and permanently established her reputation in my mind as *low*. She was irretrievably lost, of course—but not I, who shared this sensual traffic with her. Can you beat it?

There was still another girl, a most impressive and dour beauty for one on the street in this fashion, who has lived most distinctly and sharply in my memory ever since for reason of what I am about to narrate. She was still young—not more than twenty-four or -five, if so much—and amazingly smooth and gracefully formed for one in her walk of life, a most appealing and graceful, light chestnut type, which in America at least has always appealed to me as of the best physically. She was so trim and light of figure and yet well rounded. When we met it was after eleven at night and raining. I think she had come out to a drugstore for a drug. What her station or condition or her past experiences were I have not the slightest notion. When I accosted her, noting her charms, she surveyed me with still, indifferent and yet haunting blue eyes, eyes that seemed not to see me at all, and when I asked her if she would go with me, she replied very simply and indifferently, "All right." I walked with her up the street, and finally she turned in a large and once handsome residence which had fallen upon hard times and been turned into a lodging house of sorts. There were wide stone steps, a handsome fanlight over the door, and a handsomely carved staircase within, but all lit by a feeble gas jet only. When we reached her room, it proved an immense old-fashioned bed- or living room with deep windows and a parqueted floor, but most shabbily furnished now. The cheap lace curtains were dusty—the furniture mere imitation nothings. She turned up a low-burning gas jet, and when I began to fondle her (the pathos of these illicit, necessitous desires!) she said nothing about pay, but merely began to unbutton her dress and remove her clothing. She had worn, as I recall, a dark blue cape in the street.

But what astonished me most was the beauty of her body and face—a face so delicate and intelligent and a body so gracefully and delicately formed that I was almost breathless with delight. There was only one flaw, in so far as I could see—her left arm from her hand fully halfway to the elbow was dotted with a thousand, as it seemed, needle pricks. She was a dope fiend—a consumer of cocaine or heroin or what not, via the needle.

With silly, boyish ignorance and bravado and innocence I began some hortatory and moralic discourse anent the error and pity of all this. Why should she, a beautiful, et cetera girl, do this, that and the other?—although only a few minutes before I had been attempting to persuade her so to do. Why she ever listened to me at all I can never guess, unless it was that she was partially drugged at the time and everything was all right—even I. At any rate she looked at me dully, the while I examined the punctured skin most curiously, and she did not even resent that. Finally, when my chidings or asinine pleas for virtue and self-preservation grew too dull perhaps, she withdrew the arm and, sighing, said contemptuously, "Oh, great God! Why do you talk? What do you know about life anyhow?"

I was not such a fool but that this rang centre. What did I really know, I asked myself at once. What, and especially about her? This old

house, this bare room, this street, her pretty body marred in this way—
why should I venture to guess what it all spelled or to suggest that there
was some quick easy remedy, via reform, for instance? What could it all
mean, if not some misery or pressure too complicated and wearisome
perhaps for me to guess—something not easily solved or disposed of by
trashy, asinine, moralic comments and advice or kind words?

My primary lust vanished on the instant. I sensed a kind of misery
and hopelessness here and, for once in my life anyhow, did a decent
thing. I had not much myself, but I took out three dollars—about all I
had—and laid it on the nearby mantle. "That's all right," I said, when
she looked at me oddly. "I'm glad to give you this. You don't want me
tonight anyhow," and I went out in the rain and so on home, thinking
of her and the old house and the bare room and the punctured arm—
and I have so thought of her since, if once then a thousand times. And
I never saw her after.

CHAPTER LXXVI

An interesting commentary on the import of all moods and emotions, in my case at least, was this: that although engaged and so
presumably fixed in my choice of a woman and so emotionally and
sexually and matrimonially done for save in that one direction, I was
nevertheless indulging, and that almost without thinking about it, in
these rather innocent side affairs. Yet at the same time I was dreaming
of an ideal in the shape of one woman which had nothing to do with
the woman to whom I was engaged or really to any one woman in
particular, but concerned women in general, or some archetype which
was to be richer and more perfect in any way than any one woman
could ever be. And yet, at the same time, I was imagining constantly
that I was still in love with my fiancée. Let whoever can explain this. I
wrote still more of those long, impossible letters, not so many now that
I was working again but reasseverating many things which I had said
before. Only in the back of my mind at some moments was the thought
that I really did not believe or feel all that I said and that a brief period
of pleasuring with her might be sufficient after all—only I really did not
let myself think this in any open, direct and forceful way by any means.

Rather, I had disapproving thoughts about myself as an evil fellow and the like, not worthy really to enjoy the love of a really worthy woman. The thoughts of anyone who thinks at all deeply are as a rule so complicated that it is impossible to trace them out. They make almost a blur, as of colored glass, to which there is no pattern. The human act— or the event—is really the great thing. One's act and the events which follow thereon due to whatsoever causes external or internal may not show one his true soul or mood, but they are almost the only guide he has to go by.

One of the things which were serving to deflect my mood at this time was New York—the great metropolis, now only a night's ride away—and this as much as anything because my brother Paul was there.

But in addition there were other things which constantly colored my mood and caused me to wish to go there. One of these was the fact that this particular paper, as well as the others here, gave great space to New York events and affairs—much more so than had most of the other Midwestern papers with which I had been connected. Also there was a millionaire steel colony here which either had already connected itself with the so-called "Four Hundred" of New York, as well as the royal social atmosphere of England and France—or was most anxious so to do. Their comings and goings as well as their doings at New York, Bar Harbor, Newport and elsewhere were chronicled so fully as to leave a poor seeking pensioner such as I was a little agape. I had, I am sorry to report, a natural thirst for luxury and travel and social pleasuring of all sorts, yet very little capacity for fulfilling the same. I was little more than a pair of eyes and ears and an eager craving or thirst. About me, as I imagined, was moving a world of feasting and entertainment and socializing, a part of which at least I was compelled to report, and yet no least share of which was mine. Occasionally I was sent to ask after the details of certain marriages or engagements or trips that were proposed and would find the individuals in the midst of the most luxurious preparations for marriage, say, or travel. One night, I recall, I was sent to ask a certain rich steel man concerning the rumored resumption or extension of work in one of the mills. His house was but a dot on a great estate, the reaching of which was very difficult, and I encountered him at about ten at night at a moment when he was stepping into a carriage to be driven to the local station, which was placed at the foot of his grounds. A through train for Philadelphia and New York, as I saw afterwards, had been ordered by some one to stop for him.

Although I was going to the same station in order to catch a local back to the city, he did not ask me to accompany him. Instead, he paused on the step of his carriage to say, as it were, that he could not say definitely whether what I wanted to know would be done or not. He was entirely surrounded by bags, a gun, a fishing basket and other paraphernalia, after which a servant was looking. When he was gone I walked along the same road to the same station and saw him standing there. Another individual, a neighbor apparently and one of a wealthy group housed in this vicinity, I presume, came up and greeted him. "Going down to New York, George?" he inquired.

"No, just for a few days to the Chesapeake. My lodge man tells me ducks are plentiful there now, and I thought I'd run down and get a few."

The other said something about being too busy to get away for a little while yet, and then the through train rolled in and stopped—a train that barely stopped at Pittsburgh. I waited for my smoky local, marvelling at the comfort and ease which had been already attained by a man not much more than forty-five years of age.

But in addition there were other things about this region and this summer which seemed always, to me at least, to talk of New York. One of these was a new weekly which I picked up one evening for the first time in a beanery to which I resorted after my work was done. It was called the *Standard,* a theatre and chorus girl paper of the most photographic and alluring, or I might say lurid, character—somewhat like the motion picture papers of today. It pretended to report with accuracy the gayeties of the stage, the clubs, the tenderloin or white-light districts and those of society of the racier and more spendthrift character. I have often thought since of the influence of papers generally, especially on the young and restless and ambitious or playful, since this paper, however valueless save from an entertainment point of view, moved me greatly. It was solidly composed of page after page of photographs of the type of maiden then known as chorus girl, with only a few lines of text below each picture. This type probably corresponded to the ancient Greek Bacchae and was beginning to supply a Dionysian note to American life and journalism hitherto entirely wanting or absent. She was gay, showy, sexy, youthful, of course—the type that had led the world to dancing and madness since the beginning of time. And since this paper talked of and pictured only pleasure—yacht parties, midnight suppers, dances, scenes behind the stage—and of seemingly blissful young stars of the theatrical, social and money worlds, it interested me immensely. If one could have judged by its pages, a fairyland revel of young millionaires, clever and pleasuring geniuses of all walks, and beautiful girls of the stage and society seemed to be being held in New York. Here was ease. Here was luxury. In New York, plainly, was all this, and I might go there and by some fluke of chance perhaps taste of it. The spirit as well as matter of the paper was most meretricious, as I knew, idle and wasting, but at my age and under the conditions under which I then found myself, it had a most definite lure. I studied this paper by the hour whenever I could secure a fresh copy— dreaming of all it suggested.

And then there were two other papers, both of which exercised a related influence and turned my thoughts once and for all from the West, and neither of which I had ever seen before. They may not, for all I know, have even been in existence before that time. The first of these was *Munsey's*, which at that time was making its first great stir— the first and as I learned afterwards the most successful of all the ten-cent magazines then coming into existence and being fed to the public by the ton. I saw it first, piled up in huge stacks in front of one of the news and book stores in Pittsburgh—perhaps as many as eight hundred or a thousand in several stacks—above which a great yellow sign stretched entirely across the storefront announcing the latest *Munsey's*, only ten cents. The size of the pile of magazines and the price induced a cursory examination, and then, having examined it, I bought it and read the captions under the pictures. That was enough. Poor as it was intellectually—and it was poor—it contained, if I remember rightly, an entire section of highly coated paper devoted to actresses, the stage and scenes from plays, and still another carrying pictures of beauties in society in different cities, and still another devoted to successful men in Wall Street and to European and American personalities generally. It breathed mostly of New York—its social doings, its art and literary colonies and what not. Like an elixir or a hormone dropped into the blood, it seemed to fire me with an ambition to see New York, although looking back on it now I can scarcely see why. The zest must have been in myself—not the magazine.

The third paper, *Town Topics,* while really the best at that time, being most brilliantly edited by a man of exceptional literary skill, C. M. S. McLellan, was to me the most inflaming of all. It related (or purported so to do) to exclusive society in New York, London and Paris, the homes, palaces, yachts, restaurants and hotels, and goings and comings of the owners of these same generally. Although it really poked fun, or purported so to do, at all this and other forms of existence elsewhere, still there was an element of envy and delight in it too which fitted my mood to a T. Stuffed as it was to the covers with these same comings and goings and doings of society in its most elusive and exclusive forms, it gave one the impression that there existed in New York, Newport and elsewhere (London principally) a kind of Elysian realm in which forever there basked these elect of fortune and where was neither want nor care, but only ease and peace, plenty and beauty and the wanderings and splendorings of these earthly angels of fortune—these multi-millionaire gods or goddesses.

How I brooded over all this—the marriages and rumors of marriages, the travels, engagements, feasts and all those other doings such as a score of facile novelists subsequently succeeded in picturizing to the enthrallment and disturbance of nearly all rural America. For me in this realm all was flowers, sunshine, smart restaurants, glistering ballrooms—ease, comfort, beauty arrayed as only enchantment or a modern newspaper Sunday supplement could devise. And while I knew that in the main it must be romance and that back of it must be the hard contentions and realities and disappointments and despairs such as everywhere hold and characterize life, still I preferred to believe that the romance was true. In reading these several papers, which I did regularly for a little while—stuffing myself with them—I refused to allow myself to cut through to the reality. Life must hold some such realm as this, and here it was. Spiritually I belonged to it, or should, and sometime, somehow, somewhere I would achieve something like this, I was sure. Only would I?

Here I was already twenty-three years of age—and what had I accomplished? Meditating on my sad state I would forthwith compose amazing letters to my fiancée or most sentimental and unimportant features for this paper—then recovering my courage via praise from some source would go on dreaming more furiously than ever. I wished most of all now to go to New York and enter upon this atmosphere as pictured by one or other of these papers. Why not? I might bag an heiress or capture fortune in some other way. And although I could not see how, clearly, still the splendor and possibility were there—and anything might happen. Yet the remoteness of it, however near, plus the cost and the difficulties involved combined to inject a kind of terror into me also. I must make some money first, I told myself—save something. Then, financially fortified against starvation at least, I might reconnoiter this great city afterwards—and, who knows, might succeed in conquering a dozen fascinating phases of it. Balzac's heroes had seemed so to do. Why not I? It is written of the Dragon God of China that in the beginning it swallowed the world.

And then to cap it all, I had a letter one day here from my good brother, who, as I have said, had at that time an interest in a music publishing house there. In it he inquired how I was getting along and how long I would be "piking" about the West when I ought to be in New York. The letter was so optimistic and cheerful—full of gay quips and some improvised verse, and all laughing at my rurality—that I was half inclined to leave at once. He asked me to come and see him this summer and said that I could stay with him if I would. Why didn't I take a week or two off now in the summer time and so do? New York was at its best. He would show me Broadway, Manhattan Beach—a dozen worlds. He could introduce me to some New York newspaper men who would introduce me to the managers of the *World* and the *Sun*. (The mere mention of the papers, so overawed was I by the fames of Dana and Pulitzer, frightened me.) I ought to be on a paper like the *Sun*, he said, since to his mind Dana was the greatest editor in New York, and I might be someday. I meditated over all this, but still I was not prepared to go. I was really afraid. In consequence I put this venture off until another time, deciding that when I had more cash I would go, but that I would begin now saving to this end, which same I did. I then and there started a bank account, putting in as much as ten or twelve dollars each week, and in a month or two began to feel that sense of security which a little money stored away gives one.

There was another thing which had a strange psychologic effect on me at the time, as, indeed, it appeared to have on most of the intelligentsia of America. That was the publication in *Harper's* magazine this spring and summer of George Du Maurier's *Trilby*, a romance the effect of which was, in my case at least, electric—one of profound emotional perturbation, leaving me as sadly craving and seeking in my spirit as any other event ever in my life. I have often doubted the import of novel writing in general, but viewing the effect of that particular work on me as well as on others, one might as well doubt the import of power or fame or an emotion of any kind. There was, as I recall, a young newspaperman working on the *Times,* who had induced me to eat at the same boardinghouse he did, which was near the office and was supposed to save me several dollars per week. He was a small, pudgy, romantic soul, who, as I had discovered before this, was always reading novels. And one day, meeting me at the noonday table, he said to me: "Have you been reading this new novel that's running in *Harper's*—'Trilby'?"

I shook my head.

"Say," he said, "you don't want to miss that. Oh, it's wonderful." And he began to tell me of the pictured studio life in Paris, the mystic power of Svengali the Jew, the pathos of Trilby, the devotion of Little Billee, the Laird and several others. I doubt if even then I should have paid so much attention to it if at that moment I had not been so deep in the Paris of Balzac and these other things which I have mentioned and which somehow seemed to confirm the atmosphere he indicated. He had all the back numbers of the magazine so far. So enthused was he that he had torn out and kept together the pages which contained the story, and one day, later, enthusing over it again, he offered to loan them to me. In consequence I took them, he having brought them the next noon, and stuffed them in my pocket. Sitting in the reporters' room in the Allegheny City Hall afterwards I began the tale.

As long as I live I shall never forget the effect. It was not so much one of great reality and insight such as Balzac at times managed to convey—and majestically, according to my taste then—but rather of an exotic mood or perfume of memory and romance conveyed by some one who is in love with that memory and improvising upon it as musicians do upon a theme. Instanter and with a superimposed yearning, I saw Paris and Trilby and the Jew with his marvellous eyes. Trilby's being hypnotized and controlled and carried away from Little Billee seemed to me then of the essence of great tragedy. I fairly suffered myself, walking about and dreaming the while I awaited the one or two final portions. Indeed, I was lost for the time being in the beauty of Paris and the delight of studio life, and resented more than ever, as one might a great deprivation, the need of living in a land where there was nothing but work.

And yet America and this city were fascinating enough to me at this time, only, owing to the preponderant influence of foreign letters on American life, it seemed that Paris and London must be so much better, since everyone wrote of them. Like Balzac's *The Great Man from the Provinces,* this book seemed to connect itself with my own life and the tragedy of my not having the means to marry at this time or earlier when I wanted to and of being compelled to wander around in this way, unable to support a wife. At last I became so wrought up that I was quite beside myself. I pictured myself, I think, a kind of Little Billee, to the extent at least that I would eventually lose via poverty, as he via trickery, the thing I most craved—my Western sweetheart. Meditating on this, as on some phases of New York, I vented some of my misery, I think, in the form of sentimental vaporizings in my feature articles, but that again seemed merely to heighten my misery.

Finally, some sentimental letters being exchanged between myself and my love, I felt an uncontrollable impulse to return and see her once more—and St. Louis, the scene of my few fascinating but now forever departed experiences. I decided that before I went farther away, possibly never to return, I should retrace my steps and see her. The sense of an irrecoverable past which had pervaded *Trilby* had, I think, something to do with this—so interfused and interfusing are all thoughts and moods. At any rate, having by now considerable influence with this paper, I proposed a short vacation, and the city editor, wishing no doubt to propitiate me, suggested that the paper would be glad to provide me with transportation both ways. If nothing else would have decided me, this would have, and so I made haste to announce a grand return, not only to my intended but also to McCord, Wood and several others who were still in St. Louis.

CHAPTER LXXVII

As one looks back on youth—at least as I look back on my youth—so much of it appears ridiculous and maundering and without an essential impulse or direction. Yet as I look at life itself I am not sure but that indirection or unimportant idlings are as much a part of life's method and of that of the creative impulse as anything else. For whereto is it going save within itself, changing its face to itself, if one can conceive of such a thing? And aside from this where can it get, if not to new phases of pleasure in contemplating itself? From everlasting to everlasting such apparently is its fate. It cannot escape itself. And as for man, a representation of one of its moods at least, so much is accomplished by him accidentally or by indirection. We oftentimes think we are doing some vast or important thing, whereas in reality we are merely marking time. At other times when we appear to be marking time we are growing or achieving at a great rate, and so it may have been with me. As it was, instead of pushing on directly to New York, as I might have, and taking advantage of conditions that were favorable to me or at least finding out about them, I chose to return to St. Louis and grasp one more hour of that exquisite pleasure which had so exalted me then—drink one more cup of the nepenthe that love is. And whether it profited me any other than as pleasure is profit I cannot tell. Only,—may not pleasure be the ultimate profit? I see no other. And is there any other? One thing is sure: only by a second letter from my brother, forwarded to me to St. Louis from Pittsburgh, in which he urged me to come and stay with him for a while and *see* New York, was I induced finally to go there—and only after I had exhausted nearly all my spare cash in this other enterprise.

But our passions control us, not our interests, save only where our interests coincide with our passions—and that is not always, by any means.

However, this trip, judging by the after-results in later years, was for me a most pivotal and deranging thing, possibly a great mistake. It led to so many subsequent pains. At that time, of course, I could in no wise see that. Instead, for the time being and via an enthusiasm induced by I cannot tell what—youth, unrest, too much reading—I was completely lost in the grip of a passion which was as unreasonable and ill-adjusted as subsequently it proved detrimental or devastating. It concerned lust—a special and graceful lust—but aside from that what? Indeed, as I have pointed out before, it had more to do with youth and beauty as ideals than with this, its immediate object. In reality I was seeking to establish a temporary contact only, no more. Any really beautiful girl of a temperament similar to that of this one—and temperaments like other things are duplicated in life, I am sure—any idyllic scene, could have done for me all the things which this particular girl with her charming temperament and the scene in which she was embedded were doing or could do then. Only thus far I had chanced to meet her and none other who could displace her. And by this, I am by no means disparaging or underestimating her worth or charms. She was delightful. And in a way I knew that, too—only I somehow realized in a deep and even psychic way that one beautiful specimen was as good a key to the lock of earthly delights as another. Only there were so many locks or chambers to which one key would fit, and how sad, in youth at least, not to have all the locks—or at least a giant illusion as to one! All this may sound more of the laboratory than of love, but such is the nature of the seeking, inquiring humanologist. One might as well turn youth and beauty over to a laboratory for dissection and examination.

This return began, then, with a long hot trip in July via the B. & O.–S. W. to St. Louis, and then a quick change in the Union Station at St. Louis at evening, which took me by midnight to the small town in the backwoods of Missouri, near which she lived. It was hot—the very soul of summer. I recall the wide hot fields and small wooden towns of southern Ohio and Indiana and this Missouri landscape in the night. The frogs! The katydids! The summer stars! Such days come not any more. Youth, intensity, chemic lust and zest, make the fire by which life is heated to a flame in the soul. I ached and yearned—not so much over her, as I seemed to think, but over youth and love and the evanescence of all material fires. Perhaps my deepmost psyche, in its material cell, was weeping over that—the evanescence of all things. Only the body of youth cried, and sang, at the same time.

The little cottages with their single yellow lamps in the fields through which the hot dusty train ran!

The perfumed winds!

At last the train stopped somewhere and left me standing at midnight on a rattly wooden platform with no one to greet me. The train was late. A liveryman who was supposed to have looked after me did not. At a lone window sat the telegraph operator, stationmaster, baggage agent and what not else, all in one. A green shield shaded his eyes. Otherwise the station was bare and silent except for the katydids in some weeds near at hand and some chirping tree toads. And yet, as I soon learned, a hotel was a part of this station. The aforesaid agent in due time told me so. The railroad ran it, I think—or he ran it for the railroad. Upstairs over the baggage and other rooms were a few large, barn-like sleeping chambers, carpetless, dusty, cindery, the windows broken in places and curtainless and—save for some all but slatless shutters—unshielding from the world and the night. The door was keyless, and anyone might wander in or out as he chose. I put a chair against mine to protect me—or at least to wake me up so that I might try to protect myself. A greasy tin lamp, hot and dusty, provided the only light. Despite all this and knowing not what else to do, I took a room and slept—my purse with my money under my pillow, my bag near at hand. During the night several long freights thundered by, their headlights lighting the room. Yet lying on a mattress of straw and listening to the frogs and katydids outside, I slept just the same—a part of the time anyhow. The next morning I tied a handkerchief over my eyes and slept some more, arising about ten to continue my journey. There was, as I learned here, no telephone by which I could communicate with this family seven or eight miles away. A long and hot road lay in between, and there was nothing to do but charter a vehicle and proceed, which I did, arriving about noon. En route I viewed lovely wheat and corn lands, distant windmills and red barns, a winding stream through which the horses waded at different times.

Never in my life, I think, up to this time was I more impressed with a region and a home. It was all so simple. This one to which I was going chanced to be part of an old and very thoroughly decayed village, once a point on a trail or stagecoach route, once the prospective capital of the state but now nothing—a courthouse and some quaint tree-shaded homes gathered near it, all lost or islanded in a sea of corn. Reaching it we rode up a long tree-shaded lane to its very end, where, stopped by a wide, enclosed lawn, aisled with trees and a walk and a road, we passed through a gate and at the far end came upon a worn, faded, and almost rain-rotted house facing a row of trees.

But though old and decayed, how exquisite! The old French windows—copied from where and by whom?—reaching to the grass; the long, graceful rooms, the cool hall, the verandah before it, so very Southern in quality, the flowers about every window and door. I found a home in which a distingué but poverty-stricken and yet spiritually impressive patriarch ruled, a mother who might serve as an American tradition—so civil, simple and gracious in her way—sisters and brothers who were reared in an atmosphere which somehow induced a gracious, sympathetic idealism and considerateness such as I was never after able to efface or detract from. Poor as they were, they were of the best, perhaps the best family here. The father had been an officeholder and one of the district leaders in his day, and one of his sons still held an office here. A son-in-law was the district master of all the congressional district, which included seven counties, and could nearly make or break a congressman or a senator. All but three daughters were married, and one of the three remaining was engaged to me. Another, too beautiful and too hoyden to think of anyone in particular, was teaching school—or playing at it. A farm of forty acres to the south of the house was tilled by the father and two sons.

Elsewhere (in The "Genius") I have indicated this atmosphere, but here I would like to touch on it again, and less imaginatively if possible. As I see it now, it was impressive and so idyllic that it intrigued me completely. We Americans have home traditions or ideals, created as much by song and romance as anything else—"My Old Kentucky Home," "Swanee River" and the like. I can only say that despite any willing on my part, this home seemed to me to fulfill the spirit of those songs. There was something sadly romantic about it. The shade of the great trees moved across the lawn in stately and lengthening curves. A stream at the foot of a slope leading down from the west side of the house dimpled and whimpered in the sun. Birds sang in the branches. There were golden bees about the flowers and glistering wasps under the eaves of the house. Improvised hammocks of barrel staves, and others of better texture, were strung between the trees. In a nearby barn of quaint design were several good horses; in the field adjoining, several cows were maintained for milk and butter. Chickens, ducks and geese were maintained, the latter flocks solemnly padding to and fro between the house and the stream a score of times daily.

The air was redolent of corn, wheat, clover, timothy, flowers—a score of grateful odours. In the blue sky above hung buzzards, sailing speculatively over wide, wide fields. It seemed to me as I idled here for a few days, possibly a week or more, that all the spirit of rural America was here—its idealism, its dreams, the passion of a Brown, the courage and patience and sadness of a Lincoln, the dreams and courage of a Lee or a Jackson. The very soil smacked of American idealism and faith, a fixedness in sentiment and purely imaginative American tradition, in which, alas, I could no wise share. I marvelled. I was enraptured. Out of its charms and its sentiments I might have composed an elegy or an epic, but I could not believe that it was more than a frail flower of romance. I had seen Pittsburgh. I had seen Lithuanians and Hungarians in their "courts" or hovels. I had seen the girls of the same city walking the streets at night to get a little money to help out. This profound faith in God, in goodness, in virtue and duty that I saw here in no wise squared with the craft, the cruelty, the brutality and the envy that everywhere else I saw holding. These parents were gracious, kind and God-fearing but, to me, asleep or adream. They did not know life and would not—could not. These boys and girls, as I soon saw, respected love and marriage and duty and a score of things which the idealistic American still clings to, and perhaps finds enough value in. This home in which they all were was not narrowly religionistic, but religionistically ideal. The Golden Rule was here at least an attempted thing.

But then outside was all this other life that I had seen and was seeing, and of which these people apparently knew nothing. They were as if suspended in dreams—lotus-eaters. My fiancée—the girl whom I had fixed on as so worthwhile—I saw now, at a glance, was lost in this same romance. She no more comprehended me or my true thoughts than a fly understands trigonometry. I was thinking, if anything, of her beauty, for she had it—the wealth of her sensual hair, the color of her cheeks and eyes, the sensual beauty of her figure—and the pleasure she could give me. She might have been, and no doubt was, thinking of the same thing—possibly more indirectly—but also of the dignity and duty and sanctity of marriage, however much the opportunity for pleasure may have moved or appealed to her. For her, marriage and one love were for life. For myself—whether I admitted it to myself or not, or even knew it or not—they were things much less stable. Indeed I was not thinking of marriage at all—or whether I even wanted to marry now or not—but rather whether I could be happy here and now, and how much I could extract out of love. Or perhaps, to be just to myself, I had better say I was as much a victim of passion and romance as she was—possibly more so—only to the two of us they did not mean the same thing.

At any rate I found her distressed as to my failure to arrive the night before, filled with some wild fear that having seen the meanness of the town in which was the station, I had repented of my interest in her and gone back—a thought which astonished me as much as it seemed to have appealed to her. For a little while she was distant and resentful until I had fully explained. Yet recalling that, I have sometimes wondered whether it might not have been better spiritually for me if I had gone back. Instead now this delightful atmosphere, as I have said, intrigued me completely. Unconsciously I now identified her with the beauty of all I saw, and yet I felt that it was all so different to anything I knew or believed that I wondered how if ever she would fit in with the type of life toward which I was moving. How overcome this rigidity in duty and truth? Her sister Rose, whom I now saw again, appealed to me as far better suited to the facts of life as I understood them. She was gayer, less unsophisticated, more cognizant of how the world was going. She was reading a book, *The Heavenly Twins*, and with me laughing over the romanticism of it. After a day or two I found myself thinking as before that I would like her better, only, because of her sister, she would none of me, of course, giving no least sign.

And so in this atmosphere I lingered ten days, wishing, as I had before, that love was not a matter of poky marriage vows and incomes and houses and children, a whole life long of duty and drudgery, but rather one of pagan, Dionysian contact. Why not instead the green fields and hills of Greece—the fauns, satyrs, nymphs, in merry rout and chase, old Triton's horn sounding from the sea and Pan's delicate flutings in the hills and thickets? Why not Bacchus with his merry company—and Venus and Eros with their garlanded servitors? Perhaps (who knows?) it is better that the world should carry its heavy constructive load, with its factories, rents, armies, slaves. But the slaughter of romance itself—the drag on pleasure. Verily, love is the bait and marriage the trap that lead to procreative slavery. We carry a burden for something which uses man as a tool—who knows?—the victim mayhap of the lust of a larger power or powers.

CHAPTER LXXVIII

It was while I was here that an incident occurred which showed me how thin is the veneer of training and custom and religious theory and acceptance as against the innate paganism and Dionysian texture of the human soul. Social necessity first, no doubt, and religious theory afterward repress and twist people into various moods and beliefs, but in reality the sources from which life itself is derived are not so. Nature is by no means accurately moral any more than it is accurately immoral. It is neither, but of apparent necessity strikes a balance between various contending forces and extremes, and the rough and wobbly equation thus struck at times between one thing and another has come to have to some, who have as yet had nothing happen to them, the look of accurate justice and virtue. It is the wish for some happy and non-disturbing mean which makes these things look real—not their reality.

Both of us being inflamed by this chemic lust for each other, it was the most difficult thing for me to look upon Sara and not crave her physically, and there was in her, as she subsequently admitted, the same physical or lustful yearning toward me. At the time, however, she was all but horrified by the thought which ran counter to all the principles impressed upon her since early youth. Sex itself in all its manifestations this side of wedlock—the ring and the book—was wrong, low. Yet in consequence of the fierce chemic impulse to mate even though it was wrong, there was set up here between us in this delightful atmosphere a conflict between tradition and desire, the religious training of her youth and such lure as I possessed for her, as caused the very atmosphere of this old house to vibrate when she was near me. The hot faint breezes about the house and in the trees seemed to whisper of secret and for-bidden and sensual yet delicious contact. The perfumes of the thickly grown beds of flowers by day and by night, the languorous sultry heat of the afternoon and the night, the ripening and blooming and pollen-making fields beyond—the drowsy, still, starry character of the nights themselves with their hum of insects and croak of frogs and the purrs and whimpers and barks of animals—seemed to call for but one thing. All nature was fecund. And I could never look at her, tripping about this cool house, in the pleasant shadows beyond the garish sun, without the intense character of my admiration and desire all but overcoming me and my passion seeming to affect her likewise.

Her mood and color were gay. There was about her an intense zest for and delight in living. She could dance and skip and sing—and did. No doubt she longed as much to be seized as I to seize her, and yet there was a careful, moral elusiveness which added even more to the chase. I was not willing to wait any longer, but was anxious to take her then—

and she unconsciously agreed with this, as I knew, only the prejudices of a most careful rearing frightened and deterred her. And yet I shall always feel that this impulse was better than the forces which confuted and subsequently defeated it. For then was the time to unite, not years later when—however much all the economic and social and religious conditions which are first supposed to surround and safeguard such unions had been fulfilled—my zest for her and, no doubt in part, hers for me had worn away.

These economic and religious safeguards may, and no doubt do, become too smothering. Too often they delay and destroy. The pagan Dionysian way is romantically if not economically better. Ideally, no doubt, love, whether sane or no, is best in heat—not when its bank account is heavy. The chemic formula which works to reproduce the species, and the most vital examples at that, may but does not appear to be concerned with all the petty local and social and economic restraints which govern all this so much. Life, if it wants anything, appears to want children, and healthy ones, but the weighing and binding rules which govern their coming and training and sustenance may easily become too restrictive, I am sure. Perhaps they are so now. At any rate, the moralic fervor of some Americans in the face of a huge and irritated revolt against the rules of love and marriage is a little ridiculous. We are not now the thin-blooded moralic souls that we were thirty or forty years ago—or at least I hope not. More life and freedom have come into some of our lives, and, if they have not, they should. But at that time the air was even thicker than it is today with religiously and morally constructed theories and rules as to love and marriage—theories and rules of a most dwarfing character. Indeed, people, especially in that region, scarcely dared call their names their own. A sense of sin in connection with all manifestations of sex was much too rife, and in consequence all sorts of shabby and lying subterfuges were resorted to. There was immorality and joy in sex, of course, the longing for and hope of and indulgence in it, but it was all very secret and via the back stairs or window. The region was full of old maids and respectable and recessive youths, and by the same token there were many and healthy and vigorous men, most respectable and God-fearing at home, who had most important and frequent business calls to distant cities also. I am inclined to believe that except for the narrow and even stifling moralic atmosphere which then prevailed, the population of a goodly number of houses of prostitution would have been reduced. Many otherwise normal women, I am sure, and men also, unable to otherwise satisfy their normal carnal appetites legitimately, turned perforce to those places where as a matter of trade—and without exposure—their appetites could be satisfied.

Let that be as it will. The atmosphere of this old house, sacred apparently to every respectable and moral instinct, was charged, for me anyhow, and for her too as I will show, with this same elusive and yet seeking desire. The old chase was on. Whenever we met, which was often, it was to clasp either hands or bodies and kiss. There was an intense desire on the part of both, of course, to be alone, yet since I was a guest we had to give much attention to others, and this in itself was not disagreeable—only, this other was so much more important. At our most intense moments, of course, we feared to be surprised and kept an eye for doors and an ear for sounds. Only at night apparently, when owing to the pressure of farm work the others had retired, were we left alone.

And then one afternoon, I having begun to make more than the usual advances, squeezing her arms and waist significantly, and finally her breasts—at which she protested and fled, only to return—she seemed to break under the strain and yield. Later the same afternoon and after dinner, the heat being all but intolerable, we sat in a hammock in the dusk and under the stars. But only for a while. It would look better, she said, if by nine at least, we went in. But before that once more I had repeated those fondlings which seemed to cause her to all but swoon. Later I suggested that she was too warmly dressed and that she should put on something lighter. To my surprise she agreed, and at nine, when it seemed advisable that we should go in, she did change her clothes and returned to me, draped in a flouncy dress which left her nevertheless as relaxed and yielding to the touch as though she were naked. There was a tenseness of anticipation about it all—and a dread—which was suffocating. An old metal lamp turned low to reduce the heat irradiated the room but dimly. The high French shutters had been closed, or left closed from the heat of the day. We sat on a couch with our backs to them, out of view of anyone who might choose to look, although she protested the uselessness of fear. No one would misjudge her.

It was interesting,—her faith in the exact order of this place. She knew by then that her father and mother and her two brothers were in bed. They retired so early always in summer to arise at dawn. Her sister, the only other one present at this time, was sewing in a room at the other extreme of this charmingly arranged old home. My room was the one to the right of us, at this extreme of the house, a room from which two doors opened upon the smooth grass of the lawn and the fields beyond. In the silence and heat we burned, those inner flames of each titillating each other, I venturing a little, more and more—she resisting and yet yielding, an internal conflict between prejudice and desire flickering its shadows of mingled ecstasy and agony upon her face.

And as we sat so, and without our being conscious of it, a summer storm came up. Quite before we were aware of its approach, there were rumbles of thunder and glittering flashes of diamond light without— then a thrashing wind and rain. But until the rain itself beat against the shutters we were all but unconscious of it. Like two animals in the heat of a jungle, we faced each other; or like two birds that flutter in a spiral, now high, now low; or like butterflies that spin in an ecstasy of life above a sunlit field. We were facing each other at last.

And having gone so far it was impossible seemingly for us to retreat. Whatever my thoughts of her and hers, I cared no longer but for one thing. My hand opening her dress and forcing its way to her naked breasts caused her to sink in a kind of swoon. I lifted her lengthwise across my knees, feeling her limbs, then, feeling her yielding and willing, picked her up and carried her toward the silent room beyond.

And even then, and in the face of the great storm without, there was no earnest resistance, no fierce protest. Passion had at last mastered training, prejudice, every aspect of narrow, conventional training. Here in this very home, the sanctity of which was almost as impressive to me as to her, the thing might have been done. Only at the very last, a moan of distress and failure emanating from her, a half-whispered plea, I paused because it was out of the uttermost depths of conventional fears and prejudices. "My father, my mother," I heard her say, "this house. Oh, not here, not here. You are so strong. I cannot help myself, but you save me."

I put her down, meditating. I was not really so daring then as I thought, so ruthless. The desire was there and the will, but not the courage or the indifference to offend this prejudice, which affected me almost as much as it did her. My Western home training was working too. Instead I stood there, thinking. Should I? Was it right or fair? A more ruthless youth would have gone his way unthinking, I am sure. I took these other things into consideration, impressed by them. Sorrow—a kind of romantic reverence for morality and the feelings of these others—detained me. As I see it now, however, the other way would have been better. Nature's way is correct. Her impulses are sound. The delight then would have repaid her for her fears and me for my ruthlessness. A clearer and better grasp of life would have been hers and mine. There is little in conservative sympathy, much more in obedience to great impulses. The coward sips little of life—the strong man drinks deep. Old prejudices must always fall, and life must always change. It is the law.

CHAPTER LXXIX

Not strangely, this was the end of this romance for me. At the time, of course, it did not immediately appear that it had ended. On leaving her a few days later I was under the impression that I was more than ever attached to her. She seemed if anything more desirable, more wonderful. Life, however, in the face of this postponement, took on a grayer and more disappointing aspect. Because we had waited at that moment when, if ever, was the time to act, life's brevity and evanescence, the fact that nothing ever repeated itself, came home to me with crushing weight. No doubt the antique wisdom of all the force that is life, or that minute spark of it which each of us represents and which was in me, understood or remembered with a kind of tragic sadness that nothing stays or comes again. Youth, at its topmost pinnacle of vigor and illusion, may well regret or resent or fear that its prime may not be appropriately employed. Some such elegiac mood was holding me then.

And yet I tried to tell myself that better days were surely in store. I would return East and in some way place myself so that we soon might be reunited. It was a figment of hope. At the time when by reason of experience and self-training I was finally capable of maintaining her economically, my earlier mood had also changed. That Elysian hour which we had then known—or might have—had gone forever. By then I had seen more of life, more of other women, and although even then she was by no means wholly unattractive, the original yearning had vanished. She was now but one of many, and there were those who were younger and more sophisticated, even more attractive, who appealed to me more. I had already begun to see that this earlier mood was but one of many, or might be. Life, rather than any enduring phase of it, was the thing.

And yet before I left here, what days. The sunshine! The lounging under the trees! The drowsy summer heat! The wishing for what might not be! Yet having decided that her wish was genuine and my impulse to comply with it wise, I stood by it, wishing that it might be otherwise. I consoled myself thinly, as I have said, with the thought that the future must bring us together, and then left, journeying first to St. Louis and then afterwards to New York. For while I was with her that second letter from my brother to which I have referred came, urging me once more to visit him. Just before leaving Pittsburgh I had sent him a collection of those silly "features" I had been writing, and now more than ever apparently, he was impressed. I must come to New York. Some metropolitan paper was the place for me and my material. I could surely connect with some one of the great papers there if I tried. Anyhow, I would enjoy visiting there in the summertime more than later.

In consequence, because I had asked for several weeks' leave, and also because in looking over my funds I realized that I had enough left to make this trip if I chose, I decided to go. He was living with my sister Emma at that time, and she with her husband and two children occupied an apartment in West 15th Street. And his letter had included a cordial invitation from her. She would be delighted to have me stay. So since all I required was the fare and the time, I decided that I might as well go. I wired him that I would arrive within a certain time, and then after a day or two set out for St. Louis and a visit among my old newspaper friends there.

I do not know how most people take return visits, but I have often noted that it has only been as I have grown older and emotionally less mobile that they have become less and less significant. In my earlier years nothing, it seemed, could have been more poignant or more melancholy than my thoughts on any of these occasions. Wherever I had once lived, if I returned and things had changed, as they always had, of course, I was fairly transfixed by an oppressive sense of the evanescence of everything—a mood so hurtful and dark and yet with so rich if sullen a lustre that I was left wordless with pain. I have no idea why this change should be. It is one of the great mysteries of being—a characteristic of the all-force perhaps, which never is again as it was before. At any rate, I was always all but crucified at realizing how unimportant I was and everything was, how nothing staid but all changed. Scenes passed, never to be recaptured. Moods came—and friendships and loves—and were gone forever. Life was perpetually moving on. One might protest, but so it was. The beautiful pattern of which each one of us, but most especially myself, was a part was changing from day to day, changing so that things that were an anchor and a comfort and delight yesterday or today were tomorrow no more. And though perhaps innately I desired change, or at least appropriate and agreeable changes for myself, I did not wish this other—this exterior world—to shift, and that under my very eyes. The beauty that had been or of which I was a part I was by no means willing to relinquish.

The most haunting and disturbing thought always was that hourly I was getting older. Life was so brief. It was a very little cup at best, this living, that was offered one, and so soon, whatever its miserable amount or character, it would be gone. One would have lived it out, and that—in so far as I was concerned, or so I felt—with no least part in all the accidental wonders which might so easily befall one. Some had strength or capacity or looks or fortune or all at their command. Perchance they were born with a gold spoon in their mouths. Then all the world was theirs to travel over and explore. Beauty and ease were at their command, and love perhaps, and the companionship of interesting and capable people; but I, poor waif, with no definite or arresting skill of any character—not even that of commerce—must go fumbling about, looking in upon life from the outside, as it were. I was wanting in any worthy talent—or so I thought—or any compulsive charm or skill. Beautiful women, or so I argued, were drawn to any but me. The great opportunities of the day in trade and commerce were for any but me. I should never have a fraction of the means to do as I wished or to share in the life that I most craved. I was an Ishmael, a wanderer.

And so here in St. Louis, finding a few changes already, I was oppressed beyond words. Of the newspaper men who had been living on the same floor with me on Broadway, there was not one. They had all moved. At the *Globe-Democrat* already a new city editor reigned. My two friends, McCord and Wood, while delighted to see me, told me of those who had already gone. They seemed immersed in many things which had arisen since I had departed and were curious as to why I should have returned at all. I hung about for a day or two, wondering why I did so, then took the train and traveled east.

Of all my journeys thus far this to New York was the most impressive and important for me. It took on at once, the moment I had left St. Louis, the character of a great adventure, for New York was all unknown and enticing. For years my mind had in a way been centred upon it. True to the law of gravitation, its pull was in proportion to its ever-increasing size. As a boy in Indiana, and later in Chicago, I had read daily papers sent on from New York by that sister, Emma, who lived there. In Chicago, owing to a rivalry which existed on Chicago's part (not on New York's, I am sure), the papers were studded with invidious comments, which, like all poorly based criticism, only served to emphasize the salient and impressive features of the greater city. It had an elevated road, which then I had thought of with wonder, that ran through its long streets on stilts of steel and carried hundreds of thousands, if not millions, in the miniature trains drawn by small engines. It was a long, heavily populated island surrounded by great rivers, America's ocean door to Europe. It had the great Brooklyn Bridge, until then unparalleled anywhere, Wall Street, Jay Gould, Cornelius Vanderbilt—a huge company of millionaires. It had Tammany Hall, the execrable; the Statue of Liberty, unveiled not so many years before when I was a boy in Sullivan, Indiana; Madison Square Garden, the Metropolitan Opera House, the Horse Show. It was the centre and even home of fashionable society, the Four Hundred so-called; and of all fixed and itinerant actors and actresses. The "Rialto" was there. All great theatrical successes began there. Of papers of largest circulation and greatest fame, it had nearly all—the *Sun*, the *World*, the *Herald*, the *Tribune*. In Chicago, St. Louis, Pittsburgh and elsewhere I had seen how day-to-day doings of New York were chronicled as often of more import than those of local occurrence. As an ignorant understrapper, unwitting of my ignorance, I had often contended, and that noisily, with various passing atoms of New York, as condescending as I was ignorant and stubborn, as to the relative merits of New York and Chicago, of New York and—eke St. Louis! There could not be so much difference! There were many great things in these minor places. Someday, certainly, Chicago would outstrip New York! Well, I have lived to see many changes and things, but not that. Instead I have seen the great city grow and grow until it stood un-rivaled, for size and force and wealth at least, anywhere.

And now after these few tentative adventurings I was at last to enter it. Although I had a position of sorts and was not coming as a homeless, penniless seeker, still even now I was dreadfully afraid of it—why, I cannot say. Perhaps it was because it was so immense and mentally so much more commanding. Still I consoled myself with the thought that this was only a summer visit and I was to have a chance to explore it without feeling that I had to make my way then and there.

And so I can always recall clearly the hot late afternoon in July, when, after stopping off at Pittsburgh to refresh myself and secure a change of clothes, I took the train for New York. The Pullman which I entered was so hot and stuffy, the long run through the mountains before dusk not very comfortable. Only at dusk and after was the ride endurable. There was, as I noted, with eager travel-hungry eyes a succession of dreary forge and mining towns; miles of blazing coke ovens, paralleling the track and lighting these regions with a lurid glow after dusk; huge, dark hills occasionally twinkling a feeble light or two. After dinner in the diner, where I sat moodily reflecting on all this and life, there followed a half-wakeful night in the berth in which I dreamed and meditated in a most nervous, chemic way, ending at seven in the morning at Jersey City. At dawn I was awake, watching our passage through Philadelphia, and then Trenton, New Brunswick, Metuchen, Menlo Park, Rahway, Elizabeth and Newark. Of all of these save only Menlo Park—the home of Edison, who was then invariably referred to by journalists and paragraphers as "the Wizard of Menlo Park"—I knew nothing. But that place had fixed itself in my mind.

Although the day had broken fair, as we neared New York the sky was overcast, and at Newark it began to drizzle. At seven, when I stepped down, it was pouring, and there at the end of the long train shed—the immense steel and glass affair that once stood in Jersey City opposite Cortlandt Street of New York—awaited me my fat and smiling brother, as sweet-faced and gay and hopeful as a child. He was most obviously pleased to see me, and began at once, as was his way, a patter of jests and inquiries. How had I liked my trip west? St. Louis and Pittsburgh were well enough, but now that I was here, I would see New York was the only place. He led me to a ferry entrance, one of a half dozen in a row, through one of which, as through the proscenium arch of a stage and for the first time, I caught a glimpse of the great Hudson and the bay below it. It was gray and raining. A heavy mist of rain seemed suspended over it through which might be seen dimly the walls of the great city beyond. Various puffing and squatty tugs, as graceful as fat ducks but no more so, attended by overhanging and impressive plumes of smoke, chugged noisily in the foreground of water. The latter was a deep and salty gray-green, oily in its quality, and heaving and tumbling before a rough wind. At the foot of the outline of the city beyond, only a few "skyscrapers" having as yet appeared, lay a fringe of ships and docks and ferry-houses. No ferryboat being present, we needs must wait for one labeled "Desbrosses," as I saw the slip in which we stood was labeled. And eventually it came.

But betimes I was talking to my brother and learning of his life here and of that of my sister Emma, with whom he was living. She was well, as were her husband and children. They would be delighted to see me. He himself had various pleasant trips in store for me. The ferry eventually nosing into the slip and discharging a large crowd, we in turn, along with a vast company of commuters and travellers, bags in hand, entered into it. Its centre, as I noted, was stuffed with vehicles of all sizes and descriptions—those carrying light merchandise as well as others carrying coal and stone and lumber and beer.

I can recall to this hour the odour of ammonia and saltpetre so characteristic of the ferryboats and ferry-houses, where huge companies of horses were practically stalled each day and night, waiting for the arrival and departure of these boats; the crowd in the ferry-house on the New York side, waiting to cross over once we arrived there; as well as the miserable little horsecars, then still trundling along West Street and to and fro between 14th and Broadway and the ferries and Gansevoort Market. They were drawn by one horse, and you deposited your fare yourself.

And this in the city of the elevated roads.

The car which we boarded, however, had two horses and traveled up West Street from Desbrosses to Christopher Street, and thence along that shabby, antique thoroughfare to Sixth Avenue and 14th Street, where we changed. At first, aside from the sea and the boats and the sense of hugeness which goes with immense populations everywhere, I was disappointed by the seeming meanness of the streets—all that I saw on this occasion. Many of them were still paved with cobblestones à la the worst and oldest parts of St. Louis and Pittsburgh. The buildings—houses and stores alike—were for the most part of a shabby red in color and varying in height from one to six stories, not more, and most of them of an aged and contemptible appearance. This was, as I soon learned from my serene and confident brother, an old and shabby portion of the city. I was not seeing *it* yet. These horsecars, in truth, were one of the jokes of the city. They added to its variety. "Don't think because they have these that they haven't anything else. This is just the New York way. It has the new and the old mixed. Wait'll you're here a little while, sport. You'll be like every one else. There'll be just one place—New York."

And so it proved after a time, only I would not have believed it then.

The truth was that the city then, for the first time in all of a half century if not longer, was but beginning to emerge from as frightful a period of misrule at the hands of as evil a band of mercenaries as ever garroted a body politic. It had been and was still being looted and preyed upon in a most shameful and seemingly impossible manner. Graft and vice still stalked hand in hand. Although Tammany Hall, the head and centre of all the graft and robbery and vice and crime protection of every character and quality, had been delivered a stunning blow by a reform wave which had temporarily ousted it and placed reform officials over the city, still the grip of that organization had not relaxed. The police and all minor officials as well as the workmen of all departments, such as those of docks, ferries, water, gas, streets and what not, were still its tools, and, as I subsequently learned, collected graft and tribute from nearly all, even under the very noses of the elected officials—perhaps with their aid. The Reverend Doctor Parkhurst, a most militant local minister and but newly arisen, was preaching à la Savonarola the destruction of these corruptionists of the city. To accomplish his end he had personally entered upon all sorts of vice himself, bribing the police for protection and playing at leapfrog with inmates of the protected houses of ill fame in order to bring home the horror of police graft and misrule. But still when I arrived the streets were not cleaned or well lighted, their ways not adequately protected or regulated as to traffic. All vehicles rattled loudly over the ill-paved ways. Uncollected garbage lay in piles, the while the city was paying enormous sums for their collection; small and feeble gas jets fluttered, where in other cities the arc light had for fifteen years already been a commonplace. As we dragged on, on this slow-moving car, the bells on the necks of the horses tinkling rhythmically, I stared and commented.

"Well, you can't say this is very much."

"My boy," cautioned my good and cheerful brother, "you haven't seen anything yet. This is just an old part of New York. At that, there's more money down here than you think. This isn't a slum. But wait'll you see Broadway and Fifth Avenue. We're just coming this way because it's the quickest way home."

I subsided, but the great city, in so far as this section was concerned, seemed a mess.

Yet when we reached 14th Street and Sixth Avenue I was very differently impressed. We had traveled for a little way under an elevated road over which trains thundered, and when we stepped down I beheld an impressively wide thoroughfare, surging with people even at this hour in the morning, on the south side of it at least. The north side, curiously, was all but bare, no stores of any importance fronting on it. Here was Macy's—a famous emporium. And northward stretched an area which I was told was the shopping heart of the vast metropolis— Altman's, Ehrich's, O'Neill's, Adams', Simpson-Crawford's—all huge stores and all in a row lining the west side of the street. A swarm of clerks and shopgirls was already hurrying toward the entrances of the same. We made our way across 15th Street to the entrance of a narrow brownstone apartment house and ascended two flights, waiting in a rather poorly lighted hall for a reply to our ring. The door was eventually opened by my sister, whom I had not seen since my mother's death four years before. She had, as I saw, become disturbingly stout. The trim beauty for which a very few years before she had been notable had entirely disappeared. I was disappointed and yet very shortly reassured and comforted by an inherently kindly and genial disposition, which expressed itself in much talking and laughter—a slightly bizarre sense of humor.

"Why, Theodore, I'm so glad to see you. Come in and take off your things. Did you have a pleasant trip? George, here's Theodore. This is my husband, Theodore. Come on back, you and Paul. George, show Theodore where to put his things. Well, I am glad to see you,"—so she rattled on.

"And I'm glad to see you, Emma," I returned, studying the rooms, which were not unattractive by any means. "Bad weather, isn't it?"

"Awful. Come on back."

I studied her husband, whom I had never seen before, a dark and hawk-like person who seemed always following me with his eyes. He was an American of Middlewestern extraction but with a Latin complexion and Latin eyes.

"We've been looking forward to your coming for nearly a year now," he said to me. "Paul's been saying he'd get you to come on."

Emma's two children were introduced, a boy and girl, four and two years of age, respectively. A breakfast table was waiting, the food ready to be served.

"Now, my boy," began my brother, heartily, "this is where you eat real food once more. No jerkwater hotels and restaurants about this. No Pittsburgh newspaper restaurants about this. Ah, look at those biscuits—look at those biscuits!"—this as a maid produced a creamy plateful—"and here's a steak, my boy, that I bought yesterday myself. Steak and brown gravy and biscuit! See, in your honor—steak and brown gravy and biscuit!"—he rubbed his hands in admiration. "I'll bet you haven't seen anything like that since you left home—ah, good old steak and gravy."

My brother's interest in food was always intense.

"It's been many a day since I've had such biscuit and gravy as these, Em," I observed.

" 'It's been many a day since I've had biscuit and gravy such as these, Em,' " echoed my brother cheerfully.

"Get out, you. Ho! Ho! Just listen to him now, the old snooks. I can't get him out of the kitchen, can I, George? He's always eating. 'It's been many a day'—Ho! Ho!"

"I thought you said you were dieting," I inquired.

"So I am. You don't expect me not to eat this morning? I'm doing this to welcome you."

"Some welcome!" I scoffed.

"That's pretty good, Paul," added Hopkins amusedly, his shrewd dark eyes wandering over him. I wondered casually whether my good and cheerful sister really loved this man.

However, we fell to chattering, which same grew more serious as the first glow of welcome wore off.

During it all I was never free of a sense of the hugeness and strangeness of the city and the fact that at last I was here. And in this immense and far-flung thing my sister had this minute nook. From where I sat I could hear strange moanings and blowings which sounded like the foghorns of boats.

"What is that I hear?" I finally asked, for to me it was eerie.

"Boats. Tugs and vessels in the harbor. There's a fog on," explained Emma's husband.

"Boats!" I stopped and listened to the variety of sounds—some far, some near, some mellow, some hoarse. "How far are they away?"

"Anywhere from one to ten miles."

"You don't say!"

I stopped and listened again. Suddenly as I did so the full majesty of the sea sweeping about this island at this point caught me. This entire city was surrounded by water. Its great buildings and streets were all washed about by that same sea-green salty flood which I had seen on my entrance and which I had just crossed, and beyond were the miles and miles of dank salt meadows, traversed by railroads, sown with lush green marsh grass. There were gulls flying about these waters. Huge liners from abroad even now were making their way thither. At its shore were ranged in rows great vessels from Europe and all other parts of the world, all floating quietly upon the bosom of this great river. There were tugs and small boats and four-masted sailing vessels, and beyond all these, eastward, the silence, the majesty, the deadly earnestness of the sea.

"Do you ever think how wonderful it is to have the sea so close?" I suddenly asked.

"No, I can't say that I do," replied Hopkins, putting his coffee cup to his lips.

"Nor I either," said my sister. "You get used to all those things here, you know."

"It's wonderful, my boy," replied my brother, as usual helpfully interested. He invariably seemed to approve of all my moods and approaches to sentiment and, like a mother who admires and spoils a child, anxious to encourage and indulge me. "I often think of it. Great subject, that, the sea."

I would have smiled but I could not. He was so naïf and simple and intellectually innocent and sweet. Instead I lifted my cup and listened to the ships. There they were, crying in the fog and rain.

"It's a great city," I said suddenly, a measure of the import of it all sweeping over me. "It's a great city. I think I'd like to come and live here sometime."

"Didn't I tell you! Didn't I tell you!" exclaimed my brother most gaily and chuckling. "They all fall for it. They can't help it. Now it's the ocean vessels that get him. You take my advice, my boy, and move down here. The quicker the better for you."

I replied hopefully that I might, and then tried to forget the vessels and their sirens, but I could not. The sea! The sea! It called and called. And this great city. I was never so anxious before to explore a great city, and never before so much in awe of one either. It seemed so huge and powerful and terrible even. There was something about it that, unlike any other city into which thus far I had adventured, made me seem useless and trivial and helpless. It was so immense, so powerful, so glorious really with youth and force and illusions as to life. Whatever else one might have been elsewhere, what could one be here? What?

CHAPTER LXXX

The character of my sister's husband having something to do with this narrative, I will avail myself of this occasion to touch upon his history as well as that of my sister. In her youth Emma in the matter of looks and a certain pleasing geniality of temperament was one of the most attractive of all the girls of our family. From a physical point of view she was beautiful, but always, as I heard my father say, inordinately vain and light headed. In so far as I knew, she never had any intellectual or artistic interests of any kind. If she ever read a book, I never heard of it. On the other hand, from the point of view of geniality, sympathy, industry, fair-mindedness and an unchanging and self-sacrificing devotion to her children, I have never known anyone who could outrival her. In that respect I have always looked upon her as a paragon. Without any adequate intellectual training, save such as is provided via the impossible theories and teachings of the Catholic Church, she was but thinly capacitated to make her own way in the world.

At eighteen, however, or nineteen, things at home not being to her liking, she had run away and gone to Chicago, where, working at what and doing what I can only guess, she had eventually encountered this same Hopkins, who had apparently fallen violently in love with her. He was a man somewhere near fifteen years older than herself and moderately well versed in the affairs of this world. At the time she met him (I am only reporting family rumor, for I never really knew) he was the rather successful manager of a wholesale drug company, reasonably well placed socially, married and the father of two or three children— the latter all but grown to maturity. Subsequent to his meeting with Emma, he was apparently taken with this violent passion for her, and together they eloped, going direct to New York. At the time this was a great shock to my mother, who managed to conceal it from my father although it was a three-days' wonder in the journalistic or scandal world of Chicago of that day. After that, nothing more was heard of her, by me at least, save that she had gone to New York, until several years later, a dangerous illness having overtaken my mother in Warsaw, she came hurrying back, but for a few days' visit only. Subsequent to this again there was another silence—ended by the last illness and death of my mother in Chicago, when, but a day or two before her death, she once again appeared, a distrait and hysteric soul. I never knew any one to yield more completely to her emotions than she did on this occasion. She was weird and almost fantastic in her grief, pathetic.

But during all this time she had been reported to me as married and living in New York and, with the passing of time, as the mother of two children. She and her husband were supposed, by me at least, to be quite well placed. A little later, talking to Paul in St. Louis, I gathered that Hopkins, while not so very successful since he had gone East, was not a bad sort, pleasant and all that, and that he had managed to connect himself with politics in some way, and that he and my sister were living comfortably in 15th Street. This I believed. The truth was that at the time I arrived there he was by no means comfortable. The Tammany administration, under which a year or two before he had held an unimportant inspectorship of some kind, had been ended the previous year by the investigations of the once-famous Lexow Committee, with its astounding exposures of metropolitan political practices and graft and vice; and he was without work of any kind. In addition, instead of having proved a continuously faithful and loving husband, the opposite was true. A little success having come to him at first, he had long since wearied of his wife and proved unfaithful with other women, occasionally going to the length of striking her. Having later fallen from his success, he was now tractable.

At one time preceding my coming, there had been some connection between him and some form of disreputable graft—a small coal or trucking company which was a blind for a politician or politicians who were bleeding the city. This was now ended, however. He had induced Emma to rent rooms until the arrival of my brother Paul, who for reasons of sympathy, I presume, had agreed to share the expenses here; but for the summer during which I arrived this had been given up. With the aid of my brother and some occasional political work he still did— what, I have often wondered—they were living not uncomfortably. As I saw at once, however, my sister, if not quite happy, was still the devoted slave of her children and a most pathetically dependent housewife. This was her world. Whatever fires or vanities of her youth had originally compelled her to her meteoric career, she had now quieted into one who was content to live for her children. She was in no wise interested in vanities or gayeties of any kind. Her youth was over, love gone. And yet she managed to convey an atmosphere of cheer and hopefulness even now, which was greatly sustaining to me.

On the other hand, as I could see, my brother Paul was in the best of spirits. His health was excellent. He held a fair position as an actor, being the star in a road comedy and planning to go out the ensuing fall in a new one which he had written for himself and which subsequently enjoyed many successful seasons on the road. In addition, he was by way of becoming nationally known as a songwriter. Also he had, as I have previously noted, connected himself as a third partner in a song-publishing venture, the business of which was to publish his own and others' songs, and this also, despite its smallness, was beginning to show unmistakable signs of a future success.

One of the first things he did this morning was to invite me to come and see this place, and about noon, the rain having ceased and the sun appearing, we walked across 15th Street and up Sixth Avenue, the heart of the then shopping district, to 20th Street and thence east to between Fifth Avenue and Broadway. On the third floor his own concern was housed here in a one-time fashionable but now somewhat decayed dwelling given over to small wholesale ventures—later a part of the old Lord and Taylor store at 20th. This location, as I afterwards discovered, was nearly in the centre of a world of smart shops (later removed to upper Fifth Avenue) and near several great hotels—the Continental, Bartholdi and Fifth Avenue. Directly next door, east, and on the same side of the street, was Lord and Taylor's, one of the great dry goods concerns of the city. Just below this again, on the next corner, south, at 19th and Broadway, was the Gorham Company, silversmiths, and below that the Ditson Company, a great music house, and Arnold, Constable and Company, and others. There were excellent restaurants and office buildings, all newly introduced and all crowding an older world of fashion that was rapidly giving away. I remember being impressed with the great number of severe and fashionable-looking brownstone houses still extant here, with their wide flights of stone steps, their entresols, conservatories and porte cocheres. Fifth Avenue, to the west, and 20th Street were still full of handsome and attractive victorias and coaches. I also remember noting a sign on the door which led via a flight of stairs to the third floor, on which was my brother's place. It was a small oblong black and gold affair reading *Howley Haviland & Co.*, and underneath "Wing & Sons, Pianos."

"Are you the agent for a piano?" I inquired.

"Huh-uh," he replied. "They let us have a practice piano in return for our putting up that sign."

The ways of trade.

However, it was via this short walk up Sixth and across 20th to Broadway that I gained my first distinct impression of the greatness of New York's shopping centre. This was, as I could see, the crowded centre of nearly all the great stores—at least five, each a block in length, standing in one immense line on one side of the street. And the later much-famed Siegel-Cooper with its enormous building had not even arrived. And the carriages! And the well-dressed people! Showing me the windows of Altman's on the west side of the street at 18th, Paul declared that it was the most exclusive store in America, that Marshall Field and Company of Chicago was as nothing, and I had the feeling, I must confess, from merely looking at it that this might be true. It was so very well arranged and spacious and well looked after. Its windows, in which carefully selected materials were most gracefully arranged and contrasted, bore out this impression. There were so many vehicles of the better sort constantly pausing at its doors and putting down most carefully dressed women and girls. I marveled at the size and wealth of a city which could support so many huge stores all in a row.

But on the way over, what a pleasant chat. My brother was so stout that he was in consequence a slow walker—yet a gayer, more Falstaffian and more youthful and spirited soul could not be imagined. En route from a street vendor he paused to purchase a small glucose or rubber-composition face such as then apparently was being sold for the first time. As we walked along, he amused himself and me by squeezing and so contorting this that it took on the most amazing and astounding aspects, so startling and at times so ridiculous as to cause us both to fall to laughing and finally, in order to recover ourselves, to go to the curb and lean against a lamppost to stay our convulsive mirth. As a part of this my first initiation into the wonders of the city he led me into what he insisted was one of the wealthiest and most ornate of the Roman Churches then in New York, that of St. Francis Xavier in 16th Street (from which place subsequently he was buried). Standing near or in this, he told me of some Jesuit priest, a friend of his, who was here most comfortably berthed and "a good sport in the bargain, Thee, a bird." However, having had my fill of Catholicism and its ways in earlier years, I was not very much impressed, either by his friend or his character.

But Sixth Avenue in this sunshine and newly washed by the rain (from 14th to 20th Streets)—how it did impress me. Yet if anything, once entering my brother's small publishing office, I was even more impressed with that and his partners and the probability of success which they seemed to suggest and which came true—so important is the individual as against the world and the alien mass. The senior member of this—one P. J. Howley—was a young, small, gargoylish hunchback with a mouthful of large, protruding, yellow teeth, and hair and eyes as black as those of a crow—the eyes as piercing. He had longish, thin arms and legs which, because of his back, made him into a kind of a spider of a man, who went bustling about spiderwise, laughing and talking, yet always with a heavy "Scutch" burr that would have done credit to any "Heelander" anywhere.

"We're just aboot gettin' un our feet here nu," he said to me with his thick accent, his queer twisted face screwed up into a grimace of satisfaction and pride, "end we heven't ez yet s'mutch to show ye. But wuth a leetle time I'm a theenkin' ye'll be seein' theengs a lookin' a leetle bether." He actually pronounced *better* "bether," and that always. I laughed.

"Say," I said to Paul a little later, once Howley had gone about some other work, "how could you fail with him around? He's as smart as a whip, and they're all good luck anyhow." I was referring to the superstition which counts all hunchbacks as lucky—at least to others.

"That's right," said my brother. "I know they're lucky, sport. And he's as straight and honest as they make 'em. I'll always get a square deal here." And then he began to tell me how his old publisher, by whom this youth had been employed, had "trimmed" him, as he phrased it, and how this youth had "put him wise" and so began and built up this friendship which had resulted in this partnership. The chemistry of trade!

The space which their firm occupied consisted merely of one square room, twenty by twenty, in one corner of which was placed the free "tryout" piano of Wing and Sons. In another, between two windows, two tables stood back to back, as it were, and piled with correspondence. In a third a somewhat longer table paralleled the rear wall, and it was piled in part with published music which was there being wrapped and shipped. On the walls were some wooden racks or bins containing the "stock" of the few songs thus far published. As I learned this day, the firm, while only a year old, had already several songs which were but now beginning to sell a few copies daily each—one of them but then newly published, entitled "On the Sidewalks of New York." By the following summer, by which time I had arrived and was working here, this song was being sung and played all over the country and in England, an international "hit." Yet this office, as I now learned, in this very busy centre, was then costing them twenty dollars a month, a bargain as I saw it, and their "overheed expeenses," as Howley persisted in pronouncing it, were "juist nexta nothing." I could see that my good brother was in competent hands for once.

And the second partner, who arrived just as we were sitting down at a small table in a restaurant near at hand for lunch, was an equally interesting youth and one whose personality seemed to me to spell success. At this time he was still connected as "head of stock," whatever that may mean, with a large wholesale and retail music house in Broadway—just around the corner from this place at 18th Street—the celebrated Ditson Company, of New York and Boston. Although a third partner in this new concern, he had not as yet resigned his connection with the other and was using it, secretly of course, to aid him, or his firm rather, in disposing of some of their published wares. He was quite young—not more than twenty-seven—very quick and alert in manner, very short of speech, avid and handsome as to face and figure, a most attractive and clean-looking young person. He talked so rapidly as to give one the impression of words tumbling over each other or coming out abreast, and he shot out questions and replies as one might bullets out of a gun.

"DidyaseeDrake? Whaddesay? AnynewsfromBaker? Thedevilyasay! Yadon'tmeanit."

I was moved to study him with the greatest care. Out of many anywhere, I told myself, I would have selected him as a rather pushing and promising and very self-centered person, but by no means disagreeable. The impression he made on me was entirely pleasing. Speaking of him later, and Howley, my brother once said: "Y'see, Thee, New York's the only place you can do a thing like this. You could only get fellows with their experience here. Young Howley used to be with my old publisher, Woodward. He was the one that put me wise to the fact that Woodward was trimming me, and then I made the suggestion to him about starting a new place. And Haviland was a friend of his working for Ditson, and used to come around and buy of him." Yet from the first I had the feeling that this firm of which my brother was now a part would certainly be a success. There was a certain something about it— a spirit of victory and health and joy in life—which convinced me that beyond any doubt these three would make a go of this as yet very petty affair. I could see them ending in wealth—as they did, before disasters of their own invention overtook them. But that was still years away and after they had at least eaten of the fruits of victory.

Seeing that I was eager to see all that I might before I should be compelled to return West, my brother, as we left here, and because of the heat of the day, insisted on calling a hansom cab, of which the streets in this vicinity seemed full, for "just a short ride. I want to show you something. I want to show you Broadway, my boy." What he really wanted to show me was not the full length of Broadway from the Battery to Harlem but rather that section that lay between Union Square and 42nd Street, the gay "Rialto" of that day and the haunt of all the summering thespians from Maine to California. Its uppermost limit was 42nd Street at Seventh Avenue. Beyond this were nothing but dreary, dirty boarding houses, sombre and colorless and undifferentiated.

And so in this cab, rolling first down Fifth Avenue from 20th to 14th in order that I might see where Delmonico's once was, and then across that thoroughfare to Broadway, we began our northern journey from there—and I can recall even now the somewhat impressario and yet "barker-like" manner in which he delivered his comments. Just south of Union Square, at 13th Street, was the old Star Theatre, subsequently removed to make way for a great retail clothing establishment, of which he said: "There you have it. That used to be Lester Wallack's Theatre twenty years ago. The great Lester Wallack. There was an actor, my boy, an actor, a great actor! They talk about Mansfield and Barrett and Irving and Willard and all these other people today. All good, my boy, all good, but not in it with him, not in it. Mansfield's a great actor—and so is this fellow Barrett—but this man here was a genius. And he packed 'em, too. That's the place. Many a time I've passed there when you couldn't get by the door for the crowd." And then he proceeded to relate that in the "old days" when he came to New York, all of the best part of the theatrical district was still about and below Union Square—Niblo's, the old London on the Bowery, and what not.

I listened but slightly impressed. What had been had been. It might all have been very wonderful but it was not so any more—all done and gone in so far as I was concerned, and I was new and strange and wished only to see what was new and wonderful now. The sun was bright on Union Square *now*. This was a newer world in which we were living, he and I, this day. What was it to me, new seeking soul, coming to see New York as it was now, what it had been in the past or where? It only concerned me a little that this once great theatre had fallen to be a home of cheap melodrama. I wanted to see the home of newer and grander things, and so after a minute here, pausing on the west side of Broadway to look at it and listening to this tale of older things, we turned north. So the newest wave of the sea invariably obliterates the one that has gone before. And that was only twenty years ago, and it has all changed again.

But from here on, jogging north in this comfortable cab, it was all so bright and enchanting, the fresh, smart, gay, vigorous world of Broadway, pruned of almost every trace of poverty or care and spread interestingly before us. My brother would not allow the driver to do more than walk his horse, so interested was he to show me all. At that time Tiffany's was still at 15th and Broadway, its windows glittering with jewels; Brentano's, the famous booksellers, at 16th on the west side of Union Square; and Sarony, the famous photographer, between 15th and 16th, a great gold replica of his signature indicating his abode. The Century Company, to which my brother called my attention as an institution in my line and something that I would some day be connected with, so great was his optimism and faith in me, stood on the north side of Union Square at 17th. At 19th and Broadway, as I have said, were the Gorham Company and Arnold, Constable Company. At 20th, Lord and Taylor, their great store adjoining the old building in which was housed my brother's firm. At 20th Street also stood the old Continental Hotel, alive with patrons, a most popular and excellent restaurant occupying a large portion of its lower floor, and where I was often to eat later. At 21st Street was then standing one of the three great stores of Park and Tilford, the others being at 59th and Fifth Avenue on the east side and at 72nd and Sixth Avenue on the west. At 23rd on the east side of the street, facing Madison Square, was another till then successful hotel, the Bartholdi, and opposite it on the west side, the future site of the Flatiron Building.

Across Madison Square to the northeast, at 26th and Madison Avenue—its delicate golden-brown tower soaring aloft and alone, no huge buildings then to dwarf it, the park as a green carpet at its feet—stood Madison Square Garden, its delicate arches and columns suggesting old Spain, the Cabildo; high in the blue air above, Diana, her arrow pointed to the wind, giving naked chase to a mythic stag, her mythic dogs no doubt at her heels. The west side of Broadway, between 23rd and 24th, was then occupied by the famous Fifth Avenue Hotel, the home, as my brother was quick to inform me, of the then famous or infamous Senator Platt, the Republican boss of the state, who, with "Dick" Croker, divided the political control of the state. In the lobby of this hotel was the famous "Amen Corner" where, or so the tale ran, Platt held open court at times, his pathetic political henchmen being supposititiously allowed to ratify with an amen all his suggestions. It was still a great hostelry, the centre of much gayety and public sociability.

Between 24th and 25th on the same side of the street were two more hotels, the Albemarle and the Hoffman House—the latter a centre for more smart political and social life. Just north of this, at 26th and Broadway, on the east side of the street, and running through to Fifth Avenue, was Delmonico's, not so long since removed there from 14th Street and Fifth Avenue. And into this, in order that I might see, of course, we now ventured, my good brother hailing, chipperly and genially, some acquaintance who happened to be in charge of the floor at the moment. Here as elsewhere he was known. The waiter who served us greeted him familiarly and I was much impressed, for this, to me, had been advertised as the sanctum sanctorum of the smart social life of the city, and my brother had risen this much anyhow! I stared in awe of its pretentious and ornate furniture, its noble waiters and the something about it which seemed to speak of wealth and power. How easily five cents crooks to five million.

And a block or two north of this there appeared the old Fifth Avenue Theatre, most ornate as to design and then a theatre of the first class, but later changed and devoted to vaudeville; and at 29th the Gilsey House, one of the earliest homes of this my Rialto-loving relative. At 30th and Broadway, on the east side, stood Palmer's Theatre (formerly named Wallack's in honor of the actor whom my brother so much admired), famous for its musical or beauty shows. Between and above that again, at 30th and Broadway, on the west side of the street, stood Augustin Daly's famous playhouse, its facade suggestive of older homes remodeled to this new use. And already it was coming to be passé. Weber and Fields', which subsequently was placed in the block south of this, had not even appeared. And in my short span it appeared and disappeared and became a memory. Between 28th and 34th Streets were several more important and for years successful hotels—the Grand, the Imperial (note these very democratic American names). And between 33rd and 34th in Sixth Avenue, which there becomes a part of Broadway, and facing the 33rd Street L station (now a part of the

Gimbel Department Store site), the old Manhattan Theatre, still at that time the home of many successes, yet also, like Daly's, drawing to the end of a successful career.

In 23rd, west of Broadway, a part of the Macy store's present site, was the then renowned Koster and Bial's Music Hall, managed by a man who subsequently was to become most widely known but who then was really only beginning to rise, Oscar Hammerstein, the builder of so many opera houses, the real innovator of American opera. And around the corner, in Broadway again, at 35th, a very successful theatre, the Herald Square, facing the unique and beautiful Herald Building directly opposite. And beyond that again, in 35th not many feet east of Sixth Avenue—which at that point is still a part of Broadway—the Garrick, or, as it was then known, the Lyceum, managed by Daniel, the brother of the famous Charles Frohman. And above these again, at 36th on the west side, the famous Marlborough, at which, subsequently, in his heydey my brother chose to live. At 38th, on the southeast corner, stood the then popular and exclusive Normandie, one of the newer hotels, and at the northeast corner of this same intersection, the then new and imposing Knickerbocker Theatre, with a drugstore so terrorizingly exclusive as to all but repel such plebians as might choose to enter and lay their coins upon its altars. At 39th was the far-famed Casino, with its famous choruses of girls, the mecca of all night-loving Johnnies and rowdies; and between 39th and 40th, on the west side, the world-famed Metropolitan Opera House, still unchanged save for a restaurant in its northern corner. At 40th over the way here stood the exclusive Empire Theatre, with its stock company of the same name, a company which included the Drews, Favershams and what not; and in this same block, between 40th and 41st, was the famous Browne's Chop House, a resort for thespians and night-lovers generally, or so I was informed. At 42nd and Broadway, the end of all Rialtodom for my brother—and from which on reaching it he turned and sadly exclaimed, "Well, here's the end,"—stood that mecca of meccas, the then newly opened Hotel Metropole, with its restaurant opening on three streets, its leathern seats backed to its walls, its high open windows looking out on a summery thespian scene. About this, of course, there was an air of super theatrical and sport wisdom, as all might see. Here gathered daily, of all those sportively *au fait*, the exquisites of the pugilistic, racetrack, gambling, theatrical and other worlds; and here we paused once and for all, as it were, for a drink and to see and be seen.

How well I remember it all, the sense of ease and well-being that seemed to pervade this particular place, and all Broadway for that matter in the summer time—the loud clothes, the bright straw hats, the canes, the diamonds, the "hot" socks, the air of security and well-being assumed (if not real) by those who had won at last an all-too-brief hour in that pretty, petty world of make-believe and pleasure and fame of sorts. And here, as I now truly saw, my very good brother was at his best. It was "Paul" here and "Paul" there. Already known for several songs of great fame ("The Pardon Came Too Late"; "The Letter That Never Came") as well as his stage work and his genial story-telling personality, he was welcomed everywhere, as I could see. "Why, hello, Dresser. You're just in time. Have a drink. Have a drink. What'll it be? No, this is on me—this one, anyhow. Say, Paul, here you are—let me tell you a new one—a good one, Paul, this—a peach—wait and see." Then drinks, cigars, my brother telling and paying and har-har-ing as freely as any. I felt as though I were in the heart of fairyland itself.

And then, ambling down the street in the comforting shade of its west wall, what amazing personalities, male and female, and so very many of them pausing to take him by the hand, slap him on the back, pluck familiarly at his coat lapel and then pour into his ear or his capacious bosom magnificent tales of successes made, of great shows traveled with on the road, of fights and deaths and love affairs and tricks and scandals—a most picturesque and colorful selection of narratives. And all the time my good brother smiled and laughed or sympathized, as you would. There were moments with prizefighters, reigning or ex-, and with long-haired thespians down on their luck and anxious for a dime or a dollar, and bright, petty upstarts of the vaudeville and stage world, resplendent as the sun itself. I was amazed. Retired miners and ranchmen out of the West, here to live and recount their tales of hardships endured, battles won, or of marvellous winnings at cards, trickeries in racing, prizefighting and what not, now ambled by or stopped and exchanged news or petty stories. There was news of what "dogs" or "swine" some people were, what liars, scoundrels, ingrates, and eke the magnificent, magnanimous, "God's-own-salt" sort of creatures others were. The oaths! The stories of women: what low, vice-besmeared, crime-soaked ghoulas certain reigning beauties of the town were; and what hard, cold, kind or greedy this, that and the other certain other female citizens of the stage were! My good brother seemed to know them all. He had been here, there and the other place, with this, that and the other company or individual. Cordially he asked after this one's wife or mother, that one's friend or manager. I was amazed. What a genial, happy, well-thought-of, successful man. What a wonderful thing it was to be so.

I may add that I have rattled off the names and positions most glibly, as if, at that time, they were all familiar to me and well fixed in my mind. The reverse was true. They were a jumble, a colorful, brilliant, pyrotechnic and even confusing manifestation of life in the form of names, buildings, fames, atmospheres, romances of life and happiness. Only years of residence afterwards succeeded in clearing it up in part for me. Broadway, with its wealth of hansoms and carriages and cars and vehicles of all descriptions, was under my eyes and my feet, but a jumble, and I could scarcely take it all in or sense it. It was so rich and colorful to me. The shops, the grills, the bars, the theatres, the hotels were all open and passing in an unbroken and seemingly endless procession, and they made a maze for me. The walls of the buildings to the west broke the rays of the afternoon sun and produced an agreeable shade in which ambled a smart and seemingly happy company of idlers in straw hats, white trousers, blue coats. Canes and cigarettes and cigars were merely incidentals emphasizing the sense of leisure and pleasure. These people were in the main comfortable and spiritually at ease, or so I thought. Life was surely good to them if not to others. They seemed happy. So many windows were open and revealed leisurely diners and winers idling over their luncheons or afternoon drinks. This succession of thirty blocks seemed picked out and beflowered with beautiful and therefore (to youth at least) delight-ful women and girls in the softest and most clinging and most carefully harmonized and graceful of summer frocks and the smartest and most colorful and harmonizing of hats. These were beauties of the stage world, as my brother told me, seeking new engagements or merely ar-ranging for engagements already secured. To me it seemed as though I had never seen smarter women, prettier shops and equipages, brighter stores and restaurants and hotels, or more numerously gathered the-atres. There was about it all an airy sense of leisure and pleasure and well-being such as I had not elsewhere encountered in America. "Oh,"

I fairly gasped to myself, "how delicious! How refreshing! How I would like to live here!"

It was all true then—the beauty, the power, the interest, the charm of New York. I felt at once as though I would like to write a poem about it, that never again would I like to live anywhere but here—never.

CHAPTER LXXXI

During all this, of course, there had been much talk as to the character of those we met, the wealth and fashion that purchased at Tiffany's or at Brentano's, those who loafed at the Fifth Avenue, the Hoffman House, the Gilsey, the Normandie. My brother had friends in many of these hotels and bars. A friend of his, as he now told me, riding up this sonsie street, was the editor of that very *Standard* which I had so much pored over—one Roland Burke Hennessy—and, did I choose, he would take me up and introduce me to him. Another was the political or sporting man of the *Sun* or *World* or *Herald.* Here came one who was the very manager of the Casino or the Gilsey! Here was one who was a writer, a playwright, a songwriter or a poet. A man of facile and cheerful friendships, my brother, as you see. As we passed 23rd Street he made it perfectly plain that here was a street which recently had begun to replace the older and more colossal Sixth Avenue, some of the newer and much smarter stores—Best's, Le Boutillier's, McCreery's, Stern Brothers'—having built in here.

"This is really coming to be the smart street now, if you want to know, Thee, this and a part of Fifth Avenue above 23rd. The really exclusive stores are coming in here. If you ever work in New York, as you will, you'll want to know about these things. You'll see more really smart women in here than in any other shopping street"—and he called my attention to the lines of lacquered and befurred and beplushed carriages, the harness of the horses aglitter with nickle and gilt, the toy dogs detained by obsequious footmen, the double satellites of this ilk on the boxes, milady in the smartest of smart frocks idling and waiting for some one within the store to return. I felt very poor and very small and very unimportant indeed, as I was.

Passing Daly's he said: "Now here, my boy, is a manager. He makes actors—he don't hire them. He takes 'em and trains 'em. All these young fellows and girls that are now making a stir"—and he named a dozen, among whom I noted such names as those of Maude Adams, Willie Collier, Drew, and Faversham—"worked for him. And he don't allow any nonsense. There's none of that upstage stuff with him, you bet. When you work for him you're just an ordinary employe like any one else and you do what he tells you, not the way you think you ought to do. I've watched him rehearse, and I know, and all these fellows tell the same story about him. But he's a gentleman, my boy, and a manager, a manager, see? Everybody knows that when he finishes with a man or woman they can act."

I accepted this verdict. As a critic in the West I had heard it all before.

And at 33rd Street he waved his hand in the direction of the Waldorf, which then was but the half of its later size.

"Down there's the Waldorf," he said. "See it? There's the place. That's the last word for the rich. That's where they give the biggest balls and dinners, there and at Delmonico's and up at the Netherland." And after a pause he added—"Sometime you ought to write about these things, Thee. They're the limit for extravagance and show. The people out West don't know yet what's going on, but the rich are getting control. They'll own the country after a while. A writer like you could make 'em see that. You ought to show up some of these things, so they would know."

Youthful, inexperienced, unlettered—the whole scroll of this earthly wallow a mere guess, as it is to this day—I accepted that as an important challenge. Maybe it ought to be shown up. Perhaps it ought! As though picturing life—or indicting it—has yet ever changed it! But he fancied, dear heart, always, that it might be so—and I too.

Parting from me this day at three or four, his interest ended because the wonders of Broadway had been exhausted, he left me to my own devices, leaving all the great, strange city still to be explored, and merely arranging for us to meet for dinner at my sister's. And I, making inquiry as to directions and distances, soon found myself in Fifth Avenue at 42nd Street, most eager to see, as I had just seen Broadway. For here, represented by mansions at least, was the agglomeration of wealth which, as I then imagined, solved all earthly ills for so many.

Here, for those who had so much wealth, must be, of course, an end of care, the perpetual enjoyment of pleasure. Beauty was here, of course, and ease and dignity and security, that most wonderful and elusive thing in life. Seeing, I admired and resented in part, being poor and seeking myself. But having only recently seen the great showplaces, in so far as mansions were concerned, of Pittsburgh, St. Louis, Chicago and Cleveland, and so many wondrous streets in all of those places, I was by no means as much overawed and impressed at first as I had thought I would be.

For Fifth Avenue, then, was lacking at least a few of the buildings which since have added somewhat to its impressiveness, not much— the Public Library, for one, the present Metropolitan Museum facade at 82nd Street, as well as most of the great houses which now face Central Park north of 59th Street. But in their places was something which has since been lost and will never be again, I am sure,—a line of quiet and in the main unpretentious brownstone residences, which, often crowded together on spaces of land no wider than twenty-five feet, still had about them an air of exclusiveness which caused one to hesitate and take note. For between 42nd and 59th, as I found this afternoon walking northward, there was scarcely a suggestion of that coming invasion of trade which subsequently, in a period of less than twenty years, changed its character entirely. Instead there were some clubs, a few huge but rather sombre-looking residences, such as Russell Sage's, for instance, and these huge, quiet and graceful hotels such as the old Plaza and the Windsor, long since destroyed, and the very graceful Cathedral of St. Patrick. All the cross streets in this area between 42nd and 59th from Park to Sixth Avenue were lined uniformly with brownstone or red brick houses, principally brownstone, of the same height and general appearance: a high flight of steps leading to the front door, a side gate and door for servants under the steps; but other than these houses, nothing. The one thing that struck me most forcefully in the dry heat which reigned was that nearly all of these homes were most carefully and closely boarded up for the summer. There was scarcely a trace of life anywhere, save here and there where a servant or maid lounged idly at a side gate or talked to a policeman or a cabman sitting on the front steps.

And yet for all that, this region had that air of security and ease and wealth to which I have referred. There was no traffic to speak of, the street burning lonesomely under a summer sun. At 50th Street the great church on its platform was as empty as a drum. At 59th Street where stood the Savoy, the Plaza and the Netherland, as well as the great home of the late Cornelius Vanderbilt, all was as bare as a desert. Lonely hansom cabs plupped dismally to and fro, seeking a fare perhaps; and the father or mother of the present Fifth Avenue bus, an overgrown closed carriage, little more, rolled lonesomely to and fro between Washington Square and 110th Street. Central Park had most of the lovely walks and lakes which grace it today, but no distant skyline. Central Park West as such had not even appeared. That huge wall that breaks the western sky, looking west from Fifth Avenue, was wanting. Along that then dismal thoroughfare there trundled occasionally and slowly an equally dismal yellow horsecar line along a track laid between cobblestones and through a region bare of anything save a hotel or two and some squatter shanties on rocks, with their attendant goats.

But for all that, keeping on as far north as the Museum, I was steadily more and more impressed. For one thing, an atmosphere of fame hung over it which held me completely. It was not beautiful, but perhaps, as I thought, it did not need to be. The congestion of the great city and the power of a number of great names were sufficient to excuse it. Somehow it smacked of travel, the sea, European capitals, yachts, great financial institutions and industries, Newport, Lenox, Bar Harbor. And ever and anon would come a something, the Gould home at 61st, the Havemeyer and Astor residences at 66th and 68th, the impressive Lenox Library between 70th and 71st, which redeemed it. Even the old red brick and white stone Museum—now but the central core of the much larger building—with its attendant obelisk, had a charm and a dignity not to be gainsaid. So far I wandered—then took the bus and returned to my sister's apartment in 15th Street.

If, however, I have presented all this mildly, or seemingly so, it was by no means a mild experience for me. Sensitive to the brevity of life and what one may do in a given span, vastly interested in the city itself, I was swiftly being hypnotized by a charm which was more elusive than real, a thing more of the mind than the eye perhaps, but which seized upon and held one so tensely that soon I was quite unable to judge sanely of all this I saw and could only view its commonplace and even mean face in a most roseate light. The beauty, the hope, the possibilities that were here! God! It was not in any sense, as I see it now, a handsome city, and today is not in parts. Indeed, as I look back on it now, there was much that was gross and soggy and even repulsive about many of its phases. It had indeed too many hard, treeless avenues and cross streets, bare of anything save stone walls and stone or cobble pavements and wretched iron lampposts. The tenement and slum characters of so many of its areas were even more disgusting. There were sections which, as I could see, were painfully crowded with poverty, dirt, despair even; or perhaps its buildings, too often and in the main, were too uniformly low and compact, squeezed almost. Outside of the more exclusive residence and commercial areas there was no sense of breadth or space, and much of it was unswept and unlighted.

Yet by now having seen Broadway and this peculiarly barren section of Fifth Avenue, I could no longer think of it in any save a biased and favoring way—the magnetism of large bodies over small ones holding me, I presume. Its barrenness, curiously, did not now appal me as it had at first nor did its lack of beauty irritate. There was something else here which, as I was now beginning to feel, made up for all this, a quality of life and zest and security and ease for some, cheek by jowl with poverty and longing and sacrifice, which is what gives to life everywhere its keenest albeit its most pathetic edge. Great and even unbelievable masses of people were housed here. Their ideals were not the same apparently as those of our bustling, idealistic Western towns. Here was none of that clattering, eager snap so characteristic of so many of our Western cities, which, while it arrests at first, eventually palls. No. No city that I had ever seen had exactly what this had. As a boy, of course, I had invested Chicago with immense color and force, and they were there—illusioned, ignorant, American, semi-conscious, seeking, inspiring. But this was something different again. If I were to try to characterize it in a line I would say that it had the feel of gross and blissful and contented and parading self-indulgence. It was as if here—and as nowhere else—self-indulgence whispered to you that here was its true home. You could feel it, even perceive it. The look of so many!—their walk! their mood! The life was harder perhaps, more aware, more cynical and ruthless and brazen and shameless, and yet for these very reasons perhaps more alluring.

Wherever one turned one felt a consciousness of ease and even gluttony, indifference in the main as to ideals however low or high, and coupled on the part of many with a sense of power that had found itself and was not easily to be dislodged, or of virtue that has little idealism and is willing to yield for a price. There were huge dreams and lusts and vanities which here hourly and daily were being gratified. And being one who sighed for pleasure, I sensed this.

Yet all truths need by no means be proclaimed by word of mouth or shown to the eye or blazoned in print in order to be known of and understood by the mind and the heart. Chemically, ionically, possibly, certain facts reach us all—especially when we're appropriately sensitized or attuned. And at its best life is unquestionably material and sensual—the idealists to the contrary notwithstanding. So these streets and this very air said something to me. They were attainted with lust and materiality, perhaps, but also with a color and an appeal that was, for me at least, thrilling. They had a definite if as yet semi-conscious message for me, being eager and appropriately attuned. I wanted to know the worst and the best of it—or, as a sensualist might say, the two in one.

And during the few days that I was permitted to remain here, I certainly obtained an excellent sip. This brother of mine, while associated with these other two as a partner, was still, in so far as the internal economy of the firm was concerned, so small a factor as yet that he was not needed other than as a handshaker on Broadway, one who went about among vaudeville and stage singers and actors, and song-composers generally, and advertised by his very agreeable personality the existence of the firm and its value to them as well as his connection with it. And this was not done in any open, obvious way but rather as one loafs and dreams and amuses oneself generally. There was about him a geniality and gift of facile affiliation with all and sundry, which speedily caused the firm to grow and prosper. Indeed he was its very breath and life, there being about him a kind of lure and promise which seemed to cause most to be drawn to him and so his firm. So I always think of him now as idling along Broadway in the summertime, seeing singers who could sing songs and writers who could write them, and inducing both, largely by the compelling charm of his personality, to resort to his firm. He had a way with people, affectionate, reassuring, intimate, which drew them—quite all—to him. So it was that by reason of his acquaintanceship and his genial personality he or his firm had already secured one song which the following season was destined to be a huge success ("On the Sidewalks of New York"). Two vaude-villians whom he knew having written it, they were induced because of him to bring it to his firm. It was due to him that others, equally suc-cessful, were brought to the firm: the works of one Gussie L. Davis—a negro—for one, and those of one Charles Miller for another. He was a veritable magnet and lure which drew the young and the old, the sophisticated and the unsophisticated, to his house. And then he wrote successful songs himself which swept the land—"Just Tell Them That You Saw Me," "On the Banks of the Wabash." Gradually, and because of him and his fame, his house prospered mightily, and yet I doubt if even his two associates understood how much he really meant to them as businessmen. Not a businessman himself, he still contributed to his firm an atmosphere of pleasure and charm—just that, a something which no businessman could provide and without which the firm would have failed of its greatest successes. His house was young and unimpor-tant, yet within a year or two after, it had forged its way to the very front of its field, and this was due to him and none other. The rest was merely sound commercial management of what he provided in great abundance. And I am not flattering him in the least.

And for this very reason then, the while he waited for his regular theatrical season to resume, he was most excellently prepared to enter-tain one who might be interested in Broadway. There were so many individuals of all sorts and descriptions ambling up and down Broad-way, or connected with the various institutions which lined it, whom he seemed to know and to be on the best of terms with—hotel clerks, hotel managers, saloon managers, barkeepers, policemen, street sweep-ers, actors, songwriters, publishers, theatrical managers, prizefighters, priests and ministers who had parishes near the street, druggists, cigar dealers, editors of small theatrical and sporting papers, and who not else—a vast company, and of great interest to an outlander like myself. I never saw anything to equal it, this facility of his. If anyone was ever destined to succeed in the song-publishing world it was he. And he was so genial and idle and happy at it all.

This first night then, after dinner at my sister's, he said, "Come on, sport," and together, after promising faithfully to be back by midnight since my sister wished to visit with me, we ambled forth, strolling across 15th Street to Sixth Avenue and then taking a car,—a horsecar, but under an elevated road, mind you—to 33rd and 34th

Streets, the real true centre of all things theatrical at the time. Here, at Broadway and 35th, opposite the *Herald* Building and the Herald Square Theatre, stood the Hotel Aulic, a most popular rendezvous for vaudeville and road actors and singers, with whom at this time my brother was most concerned. And this was because he needed to make friends with them—these second leads and light comedians and minstrel and vaudeville singers and dancers. And here they were in number, the sidewalks on two sides of the building alive with them, a world of glistering, spinning flies. I recall even now the agreeable summer evening air, the bright comforting lights, the open doors and windows, the showy clothes of all of these, their gusto, the laughter, the jesting, expectorating, back-slapping geniality generally of each and all, each conveying to the other with great vehemence and earnestness how he "knocked 'em" here, there or somewhere else. It was wonderful, the spirit and the sense of happiness, and delight even, which seemed to pervade all this. Men do at times attain to happiness, paradise even, in this shabby, noisome, worthless, evanescent, make-believe world. I have seen it with mine own eyes.

And here, as in that more pretentious institution at 42nd Street, the Metropole, my brother was at ease. And his way (as I learned later, for at the time I did not know what it was he was about) was by no means the trade way of a drummer or salesman but rather that of one who, like these others, was merely up and down the street seeing what people he might and how he might spend a pleasant evening. He drank, told idle tales, jested unwearyingly. But, as he told me afterwards or then, he was really looking for certain individuals who could sing or play and whom in this very roundabout and casual way he might lure to be interested in the particular song or instrumental composition he was then interested in furthering. "And you never can tell," he said, "you might run into some fellow who would be just the one to write a song, or sing one for you."

I was being rapidly illuminated as to the business methods of publishers.

Apropos of this entertainment side, he was not without ample provision, only his methods were his own. Stopping here and there, after leaving the Aulic, he joined small groups at different points along the streets, actors and celebrities who were merely idling or out at gaze, under the stars and the lights. He surveyed the passing throng, nodding to friends like himself, commenting on the scattered company of attractive women and girls, who were here always walking up and down and flirting and jesting, as were the men, either for hire or as an adventure. It seemed a little odd to me and rather hard, at times a little shabby (although I myself had done as much and later would do the same thing over again) that so many grown men of profession and position should thus employ themselves, but so it was. Aside from the joy of seeing and being seen and nodding to those who were of repute or force or prosperity and being nodded to in turn, most of these were eagerly employed at the task of flirting. As each new and especially attractive girl or pair of girls came into view—decked out in all that smart yet shabby finery that the flirt or the street prostitute employs when out for hire—these plump, comfortable, well-fed souls would nudge each other and smile or make some comment coarse or humorous as to her "shape" or face or dress. They seemed a bit cynical, and yet, as one with more insight than myself might have known, they were as much victims, if not more, of the fierce and unrelenting sex urge which drives the race as those at whom they pretended to level their jests. Beauty, a desire for life, was as much their master as it was that of those at whom they scoffed. They were all sex-hungry, the allured and the alluring, the man and the woman, sex-hungry and soul-hungry, if so we may speak of the chemic urge and stuff which is life. And all of their banter and jest was more to conceal their own eagerness before the faces of their companions and friends than to really cast obloquy upon those at whom they pretended to sneer. They were desirous, pathetically, movingly so; and had any of these girls or women at whom they laughed, or pretended to, vouchsafed any the least courtesy in their direction they would have, I am sure, most eagerly welcomed it. But for their own evasive secretive peace of mind they had to pretend that they would not, hence the great show of superiority and indifference, and contempt even.

CHAPTER LXXXII

But the "sinks" of so-called "iniquity" into which a very little while afterward on this walk I was quite casually introduced! And the sense of intense pleasure and revelation that went with it all despite the said iniquity! How comes it that force, which is indestructible and therefore of timeless cosmic experience, can be so intensely gratified by this passing contact with itself in the guise of "others"? The male and the female, both compounded of this force and therefore of endless duration in some form, delight in these mutual admirations and con-tacts in this form. Several girls passing, and we being of a group which was watching them from a corner or curbside, one of the men of this group said to another: "There they are. That's the pair. They look French, all right. Whaddye say?"

"I'll go you," replied the other, and then two of the group went bustling up the street after this pair that had all but disappeared in the throng. I stood there listening to the conversation of those who re-mained, but observing this not unfamiliar development.

"They're French all right," said one. "They belong in this joint around the corner. I know. But they're new, this team." Being rather unsophisticated in these matters I did not quite understand what was meant by *French*. I assumed that it meant that they were French girls.

"Are they French?" I asked of my brother idly, not understanding why the mere fact of their being French counted for so much. "They look pretty much like Americans to me. What difference does it make?"

My brother gave way to a gale of laughter. "Listen," he said, in a laugh-broken voice to some one else. "He says 'what difference does it make?' They look like Americans to him."

They all burst out laughing. I felt a little queer, but began laughing myself, a little sheepishly perhaps. My brother pulled me affectionately to one side by the arm and said: "Don't you know, sport, what people mean when they say *French*?"

"No," I said, "I don't." The vocabulary of sex is so varied and so changeable that I did not feel myself much to blame.

"It's not just that they're French girls," he went on. "It's the different way of doing it. They don't do it the ordinary way. They go down on you—blow the pipe—play the flute. Aren't you on?"

"Oh," I said dumbly, "that's it." Actually I was considerably shocked by this open group discussion of this thing. I knew of it under another name, but had always thought of it as some dreadful thing, terrible really, not to be talked about except among extreme intimates and then only as a fearsome moral adventure, and would not have dreamed of suggesting to a woman that she do so to me. "Is that what they went after those two girls for?" I asked.

"Sure," he said genially. "Haven't you ever had that done to you?" "Never in my life," I replied. "Well say, sport, you've missed something. It's great. Do you really mean to say—" he turned as if to reveal this great discovery to those others, but I pulled his coat.

"Now cut that," I said. "Don't talk about it."

There was something as childlike as there was experienced about my brother. He was as easily repressed as a child, and as easily hurt.

"All right," he said. "I won't. But you're foolish to think there's anything wrong about it."

The two men who had gone after the girls repassed, each conducting one grandiloquently by the arm. Something about their walk, their smiles, the hoyden quality of it all, thrilled me like an electric current. Perhaps I was a fool. These men knew more about life than I did. They were living in a gayer, quicker way. Their authority with women was more. I felt as though in a way I were a damper and a drag and so de trop. I really did not belong in this world. It made me feel a little sad.

The conversation changed and the group adjourned to a nearby bar for a drink. After a time the two who had left returned. They were making a joyous to-do of their adventure. It was fine. The place around the corner, they said, had a lot of girls, some peaches. Two of those who were still of the group seemed to think that this adventure was delicious and to look and talk as though they might pay it a visit. My brother seemed of a sudden a little interested and amused. He was one too well provided with women, as I knew, to bother with casual commercial ventures, and yet because of me I think he was interested. The fact that I had confessed that I had never indulged in this phase of sex amused or piqued him. He was, I believe, really concerned lest I take some ascetic point of view which would leave me lacking at some time in breadth or tolerance. I probably seemed a little undernourished sexually and socially and in some other ways.

"How about you, sport?" he said, looking at me significantly. "Are you game?"

I confidently believe that he expected me to reject the suggestion.

"Sure," I said bravely, and yet with a sense of undertaking a dreadful and perilous and shameful adventure. To think of going round to one of these dreadful red-light houses and there, for cash—. The group was already moving. We turned into a side street and, not a dozen doors from Broadway, into what appeared to be the side door of a

restaurant—then up a flight of stairs. Madame, the French propri-
etress, was there, of course, at the head of the stairs, plump and
businesslike and genial, and Monsieur, bustling most helpfully about!
They were seemingly doing a fairly lucrative business.

"We wished—? Of course. Right this way." And we were ushered
into a large, shabby, poorly-lit "parlor," round the walls of which were
chairs and some tables. Would we have a little something to drink?

Even as we talked there bustled or, rather, fluttered or romped in
as many as eight or nine girls, all reasonably young and of different
types, stocky, slender, dark, light, French, American, possibly some
other nationalities, or at least derivations of the same. Rather dubiously and troubled by the superfluity I chose one, dark and French, as
I judged, and rather attractive, not because I had carefully selected her
out of all the others but because, rather, she had chosen me. She came
pirouetting and posing before me, saying: "You will come wiz me, yes?"
Seeing that the others had apparently no difficulty in selecting those
whom they preferred, I agreed that I would follow her and at once she
led the way rather gaily and chirriply to the floor above, a hall bedroom, the latticed shutters of which gave glimpses of the street below. I
was nervous and shy, as on all such occasions then. She seemed
attractive enough—very—with dark curly hair and, as a subsequently
removed shirtwaist proved, graceful round arms. I was by no means
dissatisfied with her but rather with the thought of being in the same
room with one who made her living doing this very different thing for
money. She came forward, wishing to introduce the proceeding apparently with some little byplay or make-believe of affection, or at least
good-fellowship, but I—I recoiled as though I were about to be stung or
bitten by a snake. The idea of fondling her, or letting her place a cheek
to mine, as rather plainly she would have! I drew back—and then
seeing that with a light toss of her head she made nothing of all this, but
was for accepting it all in good part, and was proceeding to unloose and
remove her shirtwaist, which revealed the pretty arms and neck, I was a
little softened. Plainly she would not harm me unless I wanted her to.
Gingerly and ridiculously, as I see it now, because of the combination of
shamefaced curiosity, lust and what not else in myself, I approached
and began to smooth her arms and breasts. What fools and hypocrites
and utter dubs and perhaps swine, I now think, some of these experienced women of the street and the tenderloin must take the average

man to be! They meet the raw, chaffering, operating forces of life face to face and stripped of all the thin make-believe of romance and character.

"Ah, you like my arms, anyhow," she smiled like some competent tradesman selling something. "And my breasts too." She turned up rather soulful liquid black eyes.

I resented and yet still enjoyed the coarseness and coolness and bravado which would permit her to say this, and that in the face, as I thought, of what she was about to do. The lowness of life! Its great evils! Nevertheless there was something of chic audacity about all her ways which pleased me. She was bright, amusing, laughing. Noting that I made no further advances, she loosened and kicked off a skirt, revealing herself in lace pantalettes of some sort. I thought then she was proposing to hold the customary and normal relation with me and at once prepared to defend myself if need be. Never—never that, with such as she. So ran my thought, make of it what you will. She ran, however, to the bed, and sitting down, or rather kneeling on it, signalled me to come to her. I approached, and as I once more felt her arms and neck and hair, she fell to playing with me, waiting until my desire was very obvious and then, jumping to the floor, causing me to sit down and dropping to her knees between mine.

I felt as though I were witnessing one of the great horrors and crimes of the soul and the world, a thing, or sin, which once one passed out of life, might certainly cause one to be grilled in hell, and that rightly, as the church had taught. And yet, in spite of my great shame and horror, or perhaps all the more because of it, it was all too delicious, a wild, blood-racking, brain-scarifying experience, blissful beyond words. I was fairly beside myself, writhing and groaning, until after a few seconds it all too swiftly ended and I felt myself shaking and as though my muscles had been torn. Then began the sad thought, drilled in by many past advices and preachments, that I had really done a dreadful and shameful thing, that my brother knew it, that it was such deeds as these that produced softening of the brain, that I might have, and very likely had, from such a low and shameful person, contracted a low and shameful disease. Life or God might punish me for this! Maybe there was something to the dread Catholic doctrine that this was mortal sin, punishable by eternal fire! Certainly such places were low. They ought to be suppressed by the police, or at least some of them ought; it was only right—although I was in one. And in addition, and because of an intense ache, due very likely to the novelty of the experience, and which now set up and lasted for perhaps an hour, I even fancied that I might have seriously injured myself.

As for my paramour, as gay and unconcerned as before, she had rinsed her mouth with a glass of water, readjusted her skirt, and was now fixing her hair. And then coming toward me and bending forward, her lips pouted, and holding her skirt back with her hands, she said mockingly: "You like to keez me, maybe?"

As before I recoiled. Think of kissing such a creature—I, the sacred Theodore. My face must have showed rather plainly what was in my mind, for she turned sidewise and with the airiest grace, and throwing her head far to one side, said: "Well, zen, zhust a leetle waan, on my neck—so—see—," and as she said "so—see" she touched her fingers ever so lightly on the proposed spot. I shook my head dourly. Impossible. It couldn't be done. Not I. Instead, I took out my purse and laid down five dollars, which she as lightly took and tucked into her stocking. Then I went out, meeting my laughing, jesting brother in the room below.

"Well, sport," he called, and then began to tease me as to how I had enjoyed it. I felt too shamefaced to talk even to him, saying with a grand and condescending air that "it was all right; nothing wrong with it."

But I wish now, whenever I think of the rather charming creature who served me so gracefully, that I could have just one good kick as the snooping, fearsome, moralistic ass that I then was.

CHAPTER LXXXIII

There was another place, seen this same night, which made almost as great an impression on me, though it included nothing more than mere observation, no additional sex adventures of any kind. I was too greatly concerned about the possible results of the one preceding. This was a visit, paid after midnight, and as we two were ambling southward toward our home, to an institution known, so my brother was telling me as we walked along, as *The House of All Nations*. It

appeared that up to the preceding year and under the patronage of
Tammany Hall it had flourished as a most expensive and still democratic affair, where one might go and, naming the type of female and
nationality or color, procure her. This was one of the institutions, so he
said, which had been most loudly denounced by the Reverend Dr.
Parkhurst, then still fulminating, and which, under his ascetic fire as
well as that of various anti-vice societies and quarters, had been compelled to close—but for a time only. The police, in spite of these good
government officials and storms and elections, had still managed to
continue their protection and their graft, and so this place had reopened, only now on a somewhat modified scale. Before, as I understood, there had been a great room in which, to the sounds of a small
orchestra (imagine—the helpful ragtime or jazz orchestra had not as yet
appeared—not even ragtime being known) and with the comfort of
many liquors dispensed, there were to be found parading, as at a fashion
show or ball, examples—the youngest and freshest, of course—of all
the various nationalities and races, even Indian, Chinese, Japanese
and Negro. One selected his type and paid the price, something like
twenty-five dollars.

Now, however, he explained, it was by no means so easy to come
and go as before. The same madam was in charge, but one had to be
known. One could still sit in the great room, but the old forward parade
had been abolished. One could still obtain any type or color, but they
came in, if present, after one had asked. Or they could be sent for. I
sighed for the absence of those grander days.

However, in spite of this defect, he proposed that we should stop
and look at the place. He knew the lady, of course, an old friend of his,
an ex-actress or madam from some other city. The house and rooms
were finer than any he had seen elsewhere, he said. "They have mirrors
in the ceilings over the beds, sport," he informed me, "and on the side
walls too." My erotic youthful imagination fell on this fact as an hungry
animal upon meat. It needed no amplification by him. It was entirely
possible that we could see this, he added, and with this information I
was piloted to a rather imposing residence, east of Broadway, somewhere in the upper Thirties, but where I cannot recall. A ring at a
gracefully grilled double door which opened level with the street, and,
after a certain amount of delay in which a little panel about even with
one's eyes was opened, the door itself opened. We were let into a

ground or lower hall which, once the servant had disappeared and returned and opened another door, gave into a room which looked like a small reception room, only the back part of it appeared to have been shut off and devoted very likely to culinary purposes. (There had been some exchange of names between my brother and this servant.) However, this room was gracefully panelled throughout and gave, via a wide winding stair, to the floor above. The whole house could not have been less than fifty feet wide. At the head of this stair, which debouched into a room fifty feet wide by twenty or thirty feet in depth, not untastefully if somewhat showily furnished—a solid gilt piano, for one thing, many gilt chairs and divans, pictures, rugs, some white marble busts on black stone pedestals, and the like—we were met by a stocky and rather passé woman of fifty, florid and peroxided and most richly and not unbecomingly dressed, who was all geniality and smiles. She seemed very well acquainted with my brother and began, "Why, hello, Paul. Who's your friend?" and then being assured that I was his brother and a newspaper man out of the West, smiled on me condescendingly, but with no great regard for my import, as I guessed. I was not the type which flourished in a realm such as this. At one end of this room several men and girls, the latter quite attractive for their world, were seated, drinking and talking. They had a summery, pleasure-loving look. At once, my brother began to explain in a rather low tone that he was just passing—that I was a stranger to New York and on my first visit, and since I was so new he was piloting me about and was anxious for me to see a few things. "I was telling him how it used to be," he concluded.

She laughed and looked over the room as though she were seeing it as it formerly was. "Yes, those days are gone, though, for a little while anyhow. We have to be very careful now. Would you like a little something to drink?"

Drinks of some kind were brought, and then we three sat down. It appeared that this fair madam had known him elsewhere, of course. It appeared also that she knew many men and women with whom my brother was familiar. Such remarks as "Oh, yes. No, I haven't seen George in over a year now," or "Oh, Frank? Sure. He was in here last week"—or "last month"—were common. My brother cautiously inquired if all types and colors were still available, and she nodded. "Only it isn't like it was, you know. We can't keep them here like we did then because we can't do the business. There isn't enough liquor sold. Why, as you know, in the old days this room was crowded every night. We can't do that now. There's too much talk, but we can get them."

I wondered at the "we"—and afterwards learned that politicians shared in the profits and that our madam was really little more than a high-priced manager. After a time she very graciously condescended to say, "Would you like him to see some of the rooms?" and being assured that we would, she led us back and afterwards up through or past a series of chambers, many of which were closed, but others of which conveyed the desired effect. They were comfortable after the fashion of a semi-luxurious home of the time, the only distinguishing feature being that in some of the smaller rooms, of which there were a number, the ceilings were of mirror. The others, much larger, were such as any superior residence might boast, with canopies for the beds and pier mirrors at the ends or sides of the room. I was impressed, but not overly so, by these. They were common enough. It was the smaller rooms that interested me and the fact that here one could procure all types. The thought of all that might have and probably had gone on here in days past, as well as what the future (and these rooms) held in store for some, quite weakened me. I pretended to a passivity and an easy familiarity which I by no means felt. I had never even heard of the idea before, and it made a deep impression. As was the character of all my moral meditations of the time, I oscillated between an intense desire to share in the pleasures which all this suggested and a kind of Christian horror of the evil involved. As the moralists had long insisted, so I half believed, in spite of my proclivities, that in that direction lay disease, deterioration and death even—if not, as I had once feared, eternal damnation.

Yet the adventure of this night merely served to whet my interest in the great city. It was not now quite the great mystery that it had been before, but if I felt illuminated in part, I also felt that I had not even begun to sense its possibilities. It was, as I could see, different, more fully human and resourceful and daring. The next day, then, because of other matters which took up my brother's time, I was left to my own devices and visited City Hall and Brooklyn Bridge, the only one of the five great bridges which now span the East River which was then extant, as well as Wall Street and the financial and commercial sections generally. As stale as the topic of Wall Street has since become (and the topic of big business generally), I still venture to comment on it for reason of the steady but sure decline of the street from the once colorful and compelling height to which it had then attained, but which, since, it has never equalled, not even during the trying days of the panic of 1907 and even before. For then, more than ever since, I believe, the national consciousness was keyed to the idea of great wealth and what it meant in the matter not of mere comfort and fame but of actual spiritual bliss, and to Wall Street as the source of that wealth. Here then was the centre of all that was essential and important to the average American bent upon dollar-making—and nowhere else. To have attained control of a million dollars or so was the young and old Americans' one idea of heaven, I am sure. At that time—and it is scarcely more so today—there was no other avenue of any special importance open to any American. He was of the firm conviction, I am sure, that once a man obtained a million or so, every other avenue of delight and distinction was his by right of wealth. He could then later do, be anything he wanted to. If you had pointed to Jay Gould the elder, wandering around the world in search of health, his nerves gone, his stomach awry, the whip of physical misery driving him, he still would not have believed it. What?—a man with a hundred million or nearly so, such as Jay Gould then possessed, not happy! It could not be true. There must be some mistake, some money way around or out of all human ills. Though sick and spiritually miserable, he must still be ideally happy, having so much money. Any good American would have told you that; he would even have offered to change places with Gould, so sure was he of that. Ditto the crusty and disgruntled Sage. Ditto the ill-tempered Vanderbilt the elder.

Personally having no least skill for making money myself and being intensely hungry, or so I thought, for all the things that money would buy, this street—which represented the apex of money success for a few at that time, a kind of cloudy Olympus in which foregathered all the gods of finance—I stared at it with the eyes of one who hopes to extract something by mere observation. It was by no means then as it is today, the centre of a sky-crowding area of tall buildings. On the contrary, there were few if any really high buildings below City Hall, few higher than ten stories at most. Wall Street was simply a curved, low-fronted affair—more like Oxford Street, London, than anything else—and beginning, as some one had already appropriately pointed out, at a graveyard and ending at a river. The house of J. P. Morgan, just then being assailed for its connection with a government gold-bond-milking scheme, was quite as much, if not more, in the public eye then than later. The offices of Russell Sage and George Gould (the son), as well as those of the Standard Oil Company below Wall in Broadway, as well as of a whole company of now forgotten magnates, were very much in evidence. Any messenger boy, postman or police-man of the area could have led you to them. But the thing that impressed me more than anything else really was this, that the street was vibrant with something which, though far from pleasant—craft, greed, cunning, niggardliness, ruthlessness, plus a smart or swaggery ease on the part of some, and a hopeless, bedraggled or beaten aspect on the part of others—was still impressive, terribly so, as might be a tiger or a snake. In truth I had never seen such a world and have not since encountered anything like it. It was so busy, paper-bestrewn, messenger-and-broker-bestridden, as to make one who had nothing to do there feel utterly dull and commonplace and out of place. One thought only of millions made in stocks overnight, of yachts, orgies, travels, fame and what not else. Since that time Wall Street has become much tamer—less significant—but then one had a feeling that if only one had a tip or a little skill one might become rich overnight; or as though, easily, on the other hand, one might be torn to bits, and that here was no mercy. At the hour I arrived, a little before noon, the ways were alive with messenger boys and young clerks and assistants gener-ally. On the ground was a mess of papers, torn telegrams and letters, read and then cast aside by hurrying speculators perhaps. Near Broad and Wall the air was filled with a hum of voices and typewriter clicks issuing from open windows. Just then, as with the theatrical business later, and still later with the motion picture industry, you were an important "somewhat" if you were in the Street, however thin your connection. To say "I am in Wall Street" suggested a world of prospects and possibilities. The fact that at this time, and for all of twenty years after, the news columns were all but shut to suicides and failures in Wall Street, so common were they, illustrates how vagrant and unfounded were the dreams of so many, how intense and gruelling the lure.

But the end of Wall Street as the unchallenged seat of American money domination might even then have been foretold. The cities of the nation were growing. New and by degrees more or less independent centres of finance were being developed. In the course of fifteen years it had become the boast of some cities that they could do without New York in the matter of loans, and it was true. They could, and today more than ever they are so doing. Many enterprises go west, not east, for their cash. In the main, Wall Street has degenerated into a second-rate gamblers' paradise. What if any significant Wall Street figures are there today?

CHAPTER LXXXIV

At Broadway and 22nd Street, where subsequently on this and some additional ground extending to 23rd Street the quondam-famed Flatiron Building was placed, there stood at that time a smaller building, not more than six stories in height. Its north blank wall (that which commanded upper Broadway) was completely covered with a huge electric sign—so rapidly had the electric sign idea developed in New York—which read, one great line below another:

SWEPT BY OCEAN BREEZES

THE GREAT HOTELS

PAIN'S FIREWORKS

SOUSA'S BAND

SEIDL'S GREAT ORCHESTRA

THE RACES

NOW—MANHATTAN BEACH—NOW

Each line was done in a different color of lights—light green for the "Ocean Breezes" line, white for "Manhattan Beach" and "The Great Hotels," red for "Pain's Fireworks" and "The Races," blue and yellow for "Seidl's Orchestra" and "Sousa's Band." As one line was illuminated the others were dark until all had been flashed separately, when they would be flashed simultaneously and held for a time. When I walked up or down Broadway during the next several years, and especially of a hot summer night, this sign was an inspiration and an invitation to me, an urge, as it must have been to thousands. It made one long to go to Manhattan Beach.

But on this, my first visit to New York, it was especially so. To begin with, I had never seen so large a fire sign. In the next place, I had, if anything, heard as much or more of Atlantic City and Coney Island, but this sign blazing over Broadway lifted Manhattan Beach into rivalry with fairyland. It captivated my imagination completely. Riding up Broadway on my second or third night, I saw it and it seemed to make the great city even more wonderful. "Where is that?" I asked of my brother. "Very far from New York?"

"Not more than fifteen miles," he replied. "That's the place you ought to see. I'll take you out there Sunday if you'll stay that long."

Since I had only been in the city a day or two and Sunday was close at hand, I agreed, and on that day toward noon we made our way, via horsecars, first to the East 34th Street ferry from where, by ferry and train, we could eventually reach the beach.

And never before, anywhere, unless by chance it was at the World's Fair in Chicago, had I seen anything to equal this seaward-moving throng. The day fortunately was hot and bright, and all New York seemed anxious to get away. The streets and ferries and trains were crowded. Indeed, 34th Street near the ferry was packed with people carrying bags and parasols and all but fighting each other to obtain access to the dozen or more ticket windows. The ferry on which we crossed was packed to suffocation, as were all such ferries leading to Manhattan Beach of summer weekends for years afterward—or until the automobile arrived and destroyed the nearer beaches entirely. The clerk and his prettiest girl, the actress and her admirer, the actor and his playmate, brokers, small and exclusive tradesmen, men of obvious political or commercial position, their wives, daughters, relatives and friends, all appeared outbound toward this much above the average resort. It was some such place, as I found on arriving, as Atlantic City and Asbury Park are today, only considerably more restricted. There was but one way to get there unless one chose to travel by yacht or sailboat, and that was via this train service across Long Island. You could not get there by carriage, and, as I have said, the automobile had not as yet arrived. Indeed, much of the intervening distance was still occupied by marsh grass and water.

Only via these long, hot, red trains, leaving Long Island City and threading a devious way past many pretty Long Island villages, pleasant with awnings and hammocks and grassy dooryards, could one reach there. The trains presented such pleasant views until at last, leaving possible homesites behind, they took, via double tracks on trestles, to the great meadows, traversing miles of bending marsh grass astir in the wind and crossing a half-hundred winding and mucky lagoons where lay agate water in green frames and where white cranes, their long legs looking like reeds, might be seen standing in the water or the grass, and the occasional boat of a fisherman hugged some lucky bank. It was delightful. White sails of small yachts, the property of those who used some of these lagoons as a safe harbor, might be seen over the distant grass, their sails full-spread as they made a winding course to the sea. It was the very stuff of beauty, romance, poetry,—fairyland.

And the beach with its great hotels, its crowds, amusements, music, bathing, dining. All summer long all that was best and most leisurely and pleasure-loving in New York's great middle class sought this resort for pleasure or comfort. There were, as I knew at the time, other and more exclusive or worse beaches, such as those of Newport and Coney, but this was one which served a world which was plainly between the two—a world of politicians and merchants and of dramatic and theatrical and commercial life generally. I never saw so many reasonably prosperous-looking people in one place, nor more with better or smarter clothes, albeit a little showy. The straw hat with its blue or striped ribbon, the flannel suit with its accompanying white shoes, light cane and saw-toothed straw, the pearl-gray derby, the check suit, the diamond and pearl pin in necktie, the silk shirt. What a cool summery, airy-fairy realm. And the women. I have lived long and seen much since, but my heart leaped up as I stepped out of the train at the beach that day and, with my brother as guide, walked the long board-walks which paralleled the sea, looking now at the blue waters and their distant white sails; now at the great sward of green before the hotels with their formal beds of flowers and their fountains; and now at the two enormous hotels—the Manhattan and the Oriental—each with its wide veranda packed with a great company, easy at tables or in rockers, eating, drinking or smoking and looking outward over the formal grass and the gardens to the blue sea beyond. Or I stood by the sea wall itself, the spray flying; or watched the airy summery throng on the beach itself—the white and striped and pink costumes, the gay, ribbony, flowery straw hats, the brilliant parasols, the beach swings and chairs and shades and the floating diving-platforms and the tumbling, laughing, splashing swimmers.

"Oh," I thought to myself, as any rural youth of the time might have, "I have never lived at all until now. I haven't seen anything. This is wonderful, sure enough. Look at all the beautiful women here—the comfortable well-dressed men. Everyone is really much better dressed than I am. And these marvellous gardens and flowers here by the sea—this great, wide, clean walk—the cool winds, the bright sunshine, and then these splendid verandas with their diners and idlers." I felt as though I might be looking at all New York and as though, if I should after this be compelled to return to the West and remain there, I should die. And the ache grew worse as my brother explained to me that here in these two enormous hotels were crowded thousands who came here and lived the summer through. The wealth that permitted this—the ease! Some few Western senators and millionaires brought their yachts and private cars, so he told me. The state boss, Senator Platt, and one of the other two important politicians of the state made the Oriental, which was the larger and more exclusive of the two hotels, their home for the summer. Along the verandas of both the Manhattan and the Oriental, as I was shown during the course of an afternoon, the entire company of Brooklyn and New York politicians and bosses with their wives and daughters and female relatives, dressed to the limit and so making the scene all the more striking, were to be seen basking in the shade and enjoying the breezes and the supreme view. On the walks without and those between the tables on the verandas, my good brother seemed to encounter a moderate proportion of all the more popular actors and actresses of whom I had ever heard. He was by nature a raconteur and humorist and idler, and here was his field. By dusk or late night it seemed to me as though he had nodded or spoken to a thousand.

And the delicious and invigorating nature of the amusements here offered! Out over the sea, at one end of the huge Manhattan Hotel, had been built a circular pavilion of great size in which by turns were housed Anton Seidl's great symphony orchestra and Sousa's band. I can hear the music carried by the wind of the sea and see the dancers in one of the great ballrooms of the Oriental dancing even now. As we came out of the train shed and strolled along the walk, I heard for the hundredth time that summer the strains out over the water of the ever popular "Washington Post March," being played by Sousa's band, which he himself was conducting. Beyond the hotels in a great field surrounded by an immense board fence, began at dusk, at which time the distant lighthouses over the way began blinking, a brilliant display of fire-works, an entertainment to which admission was charged, but which was almost as visible to the public as to those who paid to enter the grounds. Earlier in the afternoon there were many whose only desire appeared to be to reach the racetrack in time for the afternoon races. There were hundreds and even thousands of others to whom the enclosed beach appeared to be all. The hundreds of dining tables along the veranda of the Manhattan facing the sea seemed to call most vitally to still other hundreds. And yet, again, the walks among the parked flowers, the wide walk along the sea, and the more exclusive verandas of the Oriental, which provided no restaurant but merely rocking chairs, seemed to draw and entertain still other hundreds, possibly thousands.

But the beauty of it all, the wonder, the airy, insubstantial, almost translucent quality of it all, a bright-colored bubble, or many of them. Never before had I seen the sea, and now here it was, a huge blue rocking floor, its distant horizon dotted by white sails, and the smoke of but faintly visible steamers dissolving in the clear air above them. Wide-winged gulls were flying by. Hardy rowers in red and yellow and green canoes paddled an uncertain course beyond the breaker line. Flowers most artfully arranged decorated the parapet of the porch, and about us rose a babel of laughing and joking voices, while from some-where came the strains of a great orchestra, this time within one of the hotels, mingling betimes with the smash of the waves beyond the seawall. And as dusk came on over the darkening water, the lights of a dozen lighthouses blinked warningly and a little sadly, I thought (so treacherous is life), and, still later, the glimmer of the stars over the water added an impressive and to me melancholy quality to it all.

It seemed all too beautiful. I was so wrought up by it all that I could scarcely eat. It was all so wonderful that I was quite beside myself. Beauty, beauty, beauty. That was the message and the import of it all—the will to and the search for beauty. By the hard processes of trade—profit and loss, and the driving forces of ambition and necessity, and the failures and despairs of some and the successes of others, and the love of and search for pleasure—this to me very wonderful and en-trancing thing had been accomplished. Unimportant to me now how hard some of these people looked or were or had been—or how selfish or vain or indifferent. They had sought and bought and paid for this thing, and it was beautiful. How sweet the sea here, how beautiful the flowers and the music and these parading men and women. I saw women and girls for the favor of any one of whom, in the first flush of my youthful ebullience, I imagined I would do anything. And at the very same time, in the face of my brother's courtesy and geniality and generosity, I was still being seized with a tremendous depression and dissatisfaction with myself, so much so that I could have sweated tears. Who was I? What did I amount to? How little of all this had I ever known—or would! How little of true beauty or fortune or love! It mattered not that life for me had only begun and that I was seeing much and might still see much more. My heart was miserable. (Greedy? Very likely.) I could have invested and beleaguered the world with my desires and my capacity. How dare life with its brutal nonperception of values withhold so much from me and give so much to others? How dare so many live and be gay and comfortable whereas I was not or could not be so? Who had loaded the dice in their favor and not in mine, and why? All doors—and at once, as I saw it then, and that by right of desire and capacity—should have been opened to me. But they had not been or were not being opened. I think I made a rather doleful, if not sour, companion for my very good brother.

And he was so genial and optimistic through it all, a person who by reason of temperament and a certain limited vision saw much of life in terms of his capacity and understanding. Men who looked to me to be selfish and savage looked to him to be cheerful and kindly, the doers of many delightful and charming things, and so they behaved to him. Women, selfish and indifferent enough, however physically attractive, but drawn to him by his charm, looked to him to be angelic, the doers and livers of delightful lives. And so they behaved to him. To one less genial and optimistic, as it seemed to me that I was, the world showed a very different face.

And yet, whenever I ventured to intrude some such darkly critical thoughts as these, he was all for brushing them aside and not thinking so blackly of life and of people. "They're not so bad—once you know them," he invariably insisted and genially enough—and truthfully also, I presume. The truth was that my brother was a good swimmer and I was not, or I thought I was not. He was blessed with that all-essential thing in so far as life is concerned, a certain shortness of vision, plus a length of geniality and humor. Life made him laugh, or at least smile—

although at times it made him cry over all-but-imaginary ills. He was one of those remarkably fortunate and interesting beings who by chance had been properly outfitted for the great adventure. And to a degree I was also, only at that time, I could by no means believe it. Life then looked dark, or at least sombre, as though I subconsciously knew beforehand some of the very dark days that were in store for me—the horrible hours, the veritable Golgotha sweats.

And yet what is it that the heart seeks? Where is its true haven? What is it that will truly satisfy it? Has anyone ever found it? Since that time I have had at least some of the things which my soul at that time most eagerly craved, the possession of which as I then imagined would satisfy me: a measure of repute, the satisfaction of accomplishing certain tasks and achieving certain ideals or dreams, the admiration of some, the love of others, beauty in most definite and enticing forms, a little leisure—along with many lacks and needs. And is my or any other heart really satisfied?

Each day the sun rises, and with it how few with whom a sense of contentment dwells. For each how many old dreams unfulfilled, old and new needs unsatisfied? Onward, onward is the lure—what life may still do, not what it has done—and to ask of anyone that he count his blessings is but an ungrateful bit of meddling at best. He will none of it. At twenty, at thirty, at sixty and at eighty the lure is still the same, however feeble. More and ever more. Only the wearing of the body, the snapping of the string, the weakening of the inherent urge, ends the search. And with its end the sad by-thought that what is not realized here may never be realized anywhere. For if not here, where is that which could satisfy one, since it is of life here that we know—and only of life as it is here? Of all the pathetic dreams, that which pictures a spiritual salvation elsewhere for one who has failed in his dreams here is the thinnest and palest, a beggar's dole indeed.

Twenty-five years later I chanced to visit a home on the very site of one of these hotels, facing the sea, a home which was a part of a new real estate division but newly exploited. And of the old great life, not a trace. In twenty-five years the beautiful circular pavilion had fallen into the sea. A part of the grounds of the immense Manhattan had been eaten away by winter storms; and, new resorts developing and Coney Island drawing too near, the grand patronage had departed, and the hotels themselves had been removed, leaving no trace. The Jersey

Coast, Connecticut, Atlantic City had superseded and effaced all this. Also the introduction of the automobile had sounded its knell. Even the great Oriental, hanging on for but a few years at most and struggling to accommodate itself to new conditions, had at last been torn down. Only the beach remained, and even that had radically changed to meet new conditions. It had become a Jewish beach. The land about and beyond the hotels had been filled in, planted to trees, divided by streets, and sold to those who craved the freshness of this seaside isle.

But of this older place not one of those with whom I visited knew aught. They had never seen it, had only dimly heard of it. So clouds in the sky gather, are perchance illuminated by the sun, dissolve and are gone. And youth, viewing old realms of grandeur or terror, sees the world as new, untainted, virgin—a realm to be newly and freshly exploited, as, in truth, it ever is.

But we who were—!

CHAPTER LXXXV

Having seen so much and sensing so much more, I was eager to stay and seek a place here, but magnifying the value of a position here and the leanness of my purse, as well as the difficulty of securing a place, I finally brought myself to the dour and very unsatisfactory task of returning. Never, as I can tell you, did one city dwarf another more, at least in my imagination, than did New York Pittsburgh. On one of my mornings in the former city I had wandered up Broadway to the *Herald* Building and looked in its windows, where were visible a number of great presses in full operation—much larger than any I had seen in the West. And my brother, on my telling him of my having done so, had recalled the fact that James Gordon Bennett, the then owner and editor of the *Herald,* had once commissioned Henry M. Stanley, the great explorer but at that time a reporter on the paper, to go and find Livingstone in Africa, furnishing all the means and equipment therefor. And my good brother, who romanticized all things,—my supposed abilities and possibilities included—was inclined to think that once I came to New York some such great thing might happen to me. And he had made me feel the possibility of it.

Again, on another day I had gone to Printing House Square and, gazing at the *Sun* and *World* and *Times* and *Tribune*, all facing City Hall Park, had sighed for the opportunities which they represented. But I did not act. Something about them as yet overawed me, especially the *World*, the owner and editor of which had begun his meteoric career in St. Louis years before, and which since had become the foremost paper in New York, in point of circulation at least. It had become the "biggest" and most daring in point of news and action, and this tempted me. At this time I had some hope of connecting myself with it later, although that seemed a little bold on my part. Compared with the Western papers with which I had been connected, all New York papers seemed huge, the tasks which editorially and reportorially they represented so much more difficult.

The fact was that, in the language of a subsequent decade, "they had me bluffed." They were so ponderous, as to structure at least, veritable Goliaths, and this seemed something, as contrasted with the *Dispatch*, for instance, which had only a very small building, merely an old-time house remodeled. Again, the editorial pages of all of these papers, as I had noticed even in the West, fairly bristled with cynical and condescending remarks anent that region—as well as many other things in life—and their voices, representing, as they did, greater circulation and wealth and the vantage point of a position in New York, gave them amazing weight in my eyes. Although I knew what I knew about the subservience of newspapers to financial interests, their ratlike fear of religionists and moralists generally, their shameful betrayal of the ordinary man at every point at which he can possibly be betrayed, yet still I knew the power they have by reason of lies and pretence and make-believe to stir him up to his own detriment and destruction. I was frightened by this very power which in subsequent years I came to look upon as the most deadly and forceful of all in nature: the power to masquerade and betray.

For plainly nature is dual. There are the exact facts of the mechanical laws of the universe, knowledge of which may be acquired via mathematics, chemistry, physics and those allied interpretations of fact which they permit: astronomy, geology, botany, physiology, et cetera—supposing life permits the development of a mind so to reason. But in addition to these facts, there is something,—an impulse and a power to betray them—which manifests itself in all forms of organized intelligence and which works apparently to undo or delay that which exact fact would achieve. I refer to the desire for subsistence and self-protection and self-advantage in all living forms which, when these facts interfere with this desire, will proceed to betray them. And although the light of fact may eventually burst through, as does the sun on occasion through miasmatic mists, still these mists do occur and appear to be an intimate and working part of this very scheme which is so exact. That is one thing which the mechanists who are inclined to boast of the reliability of eternal law as proofs of a moral order in nature (Haeckel for one—Spencer for another) have yet to explain. (The religionists do not need to explain anything since they ignore facts.)

Returning to these New York newspapers, however, there was about them that air of assurance and righteousness and authority and superiority as well as general condescension toward all, which over-awed and frightened me. True, a brother of a famous playwright with whom I had worked in St. Louis had come East and connected himself with the *World* and was now there, and I might have called on him and spied out the land, but I was not satisfied to take his success as a favorable augury of mine. For some reason he seemed more advan-tageously equipped for the task than was I—why, I cannot say. He had fortified himself with a most favorable record in the West, as had I, only I did not look upon mine as being as favorable to me as his had proved to him. Again, a city editor once of St. Louis was now here, had become city editor of one of the city's great papers, the *Recorder;* and another, a Sunday editor of Pittsburgh, had become the Sunday editor of the *Press* here. Still, to me these appeared to be exceptional cases. Really, I reconnoitered these larger and in the main rather dull institu-tions with the eye of one who seeks to take a fortress.

To work on the *Sun!* the *Herald!* the *World!* How many cubs, from how many angles of our national life, were not constantly and hope-fully eying these same, from the very same sidewalks or benches in City Hall Park, as the ultimate solution of all their literary, commercial, so-cial, political problems and ambitions. The thousands of pipe-smoking collegians who had even up to that time essayed the quondam *Sun* alone, scullion Danas, embryo Greeleys, office-boy Bennetts! In conse-quence, I thought best to return to Pittsburgh and save a little money, say three hundred dollars, after which I might return and take one of these very frowning editorial offices by storm. And in consequence, I did so return to Pittsburgh, but in what a reduced mood. Pittsburgh, after New York, and all that I had seen! Yet, in a darkly brooding and indifferent spirit, I did resume work there. A sum of money sufficient to sustain me for a period in New York was all that I really desired now.

And in the course of the next four months or thereabouts I did so save and set aside the sustaining sum of two hundred and forty dollars, with which (and some clothing and books) I returned to that city. So to do, I endured, however, deprivations which I marvel at even now— breakfasts, for instance, consisting of a cruller and a coffee; dinners that cost me no more than a quarter, sometimes no more than fifteen cents. I bought no clothes. I economized in every way, in a vain attempt to save the whole of my salary. Indeed, I lived on so little that I think I must have done myself some physical injury which told against me later in the subsequent struggle for existence in New York, for I had a very bad spell of nerves later.

In the meantime I worked as before, only to greater advantage if anything, because I was by now more sure of myself. My study of Balzac and these recent adventures in the great city had so fired my ambition that nothing could have kept me in Pittsburgh. Again, at this time I had the fortune or misfortune to discover not only Huxley and Tyndall but Herbert Spencer, whose *First Principles*, the remarkable introductory volume to his *Synthetic Philosophy*, quite blew me to bits intellectually. Hitherto, until I had read Huxley at least, I had had some lingering filaments of Catholicism trailing about me—faith at least in the existence of Christ, the soundness of His moral and sociologic deductions, the brotherhood of man, for instance. But reading Huxley's *Science and Hebrew Tradition* and *Science and Christian Tradition*, I found both the Old and New Testaments to be not compendiums of revealed truth but mere records of religious experiences, and very erroneous ones at that. And then taking up *First Principles* I discovered that all that I had deemed substantial—man's place in nature, his importance in the universe and on this too too solid earth, his very identity save as an infinitesimal speck of energy or a "suspended equation" drawn or blown here and there by larger forces in which he moved quite unconsciously as an atom—was questioned and dissolved into other and less understandable things. I was completely thrown down in my conceptions or non-conceptions of life and made very gloomy.

Naturally inclined to seek to solve the riddle of existence if I could—always digging at the whyness of everything—*First Principles* proved to me that there could be no answer. Ordinarily more or less detached intellectually from family, home, nation and race even, and without a binding anchor anywhere, I was still staggered now to find myself, as it were, an unaccountable wisp of energy or mist or nothing, moving via inexplicable laws and for inexplicable reasons, or none, from nowhere to nowhere. Indeed I was really months in getting over it (I never did wholly)—getting to a place where I could believe in the importance of anything. Up to this time there had been a blazing and unchecked desire to get on and the feeling that in doing so we did get somewhere. Now in its place there was the definite conviction that spiritually one got nowhere, that there was no hereafter, that one lived and had his being because he had to, and that it was of no import, no more so than that of any bug or rat. Of his ideals, his struggles, deprivations, sorrows as well as joys, it could only be said that they were chemic compulsions—something which for some inexplicable but un-important reason responded to and resulted from the hope of pleasure and the fear of pain. He was a mechanism, undevised and uncreated—and a badly and carelessly driven one at that. He was governed by creature desire, and when the means of subsistence failed he was without life. And nature was by no means mindful of that.

I cannot make you feel now, I am sure, how all of a sudden, or in the course of a few weeks' reading, these things came upon me and left me numb, my gravest fears as to the unsolvable disorder and brutality of life entirely verified. At times now I felt as low and hopeless as a beggar. My self-importance was gone—for the time being anyhow. There was of course this other matter of necessity—internal chemical compul-sions—remaining, and to these I had to respond whether I would or no. I was daily facing a round of duties which now more than ever verified all that I had suspected and that these books showed. With a gloomy eye I began to watch how the mechanical forces operated through man and outside him, but especially through man, and this under my very eyes. Suicides seemed sadder since there was no care for them—failures the same. One of those periodic scandals breaking out in connection with the care of prisoners in some local or state jail in Pittsburgh while I was still there, I saw how self-interest—the hope of pleasure or the fear of pain (which for some might follow on lack of means)—caused jailers or wardens or a sheriff to graft on prisoners, feed them rotten meat, torture them via a black cell into silence and submission. And then, politics interfering (the hope of pleasure again and the fear of pain on the part of some) and the whole thing being hushed up, no least measure of the sickening truth broke out in the subservient papers, of which the *Dispatch* was one. Life could or would do nothing for those whom it so shamefully abused. Only chance might have, and it had not operated in this case.

Again, there was a local poor section—one street in the East Pittsburgh district—which was shut off by a railroad at one end (the latter having built a high fence to protect itself from trespass) and by an arrogant property owner at another, one of the great land holders of the city (he had built a high fence to protect his property from trespass). Those within were actually left without means of ingress and egress; yet instead of denouncing either or both, the railroads being so powerful and the citizen well-known and prosperous and within his "rights," I was told to write a humorous article, but not to "hurt anybody's feelings"—an assignment which caused me to want to spit. There were also always before my eyes here those selfsame regions of indescribable poverty and indescribable wealth previously mentioned, which were always carefully distinguished between by the local papers, all the favors and compliments and commercial and social aids going to those who had, all the sniffs and indifferences going to those who had not; and yet when I read my Spencer I could only sigh. Martyn's despair as to the cause of the ordinary numbskull workingman seemed trebly well-based. His case was indeed hopeless. All I could think of was that since nature would not or could not do anything for man, he must, if he could, do something for himself. But of this I saw no prospect, he being a product of these selfsame accidental and so indifferent and hence bitterly cruel forces.

And so I went on from day to day, reading, thinking, doing apparently fairly acceptable work since I was constantly called upon to do more, but always withdrawing spiritually more and more into myself. As I began to see it now, the world could not understand me, nor I it, nor men each other very well. We met and exchanged pleasant comments and thoughts, but I could find few if any who were thinking as I was. Then a little later I turned and said that since the whole thing was hopeless I might as well forget it and join the narrow, heartless indifferent scramble, but I could not do that either, lacking the temperament and the skill. All I could do was think, and since about all this I was voiceless, no paper such as I knew being interested in any of the things about which I was thinking, I felt hopeless indeed. Finally, in late November, having as much as two hundred and forty dollars saved, I finally decided to depart this dismal scene, seeking the charm of the great city beyond and holding the thought that possibly, in spite of my mood, I might succeed at something, be eased and rested by some important work of some kind. At any rate, I was willing to try.

"Too much thinking hath made him mad."

CHAPTER LXXXVI

My departure was accelerated by a conversation I had one day with that same political reporter of whom I have previously spoken but whose name I have forgotten. By now I had come to be on agreeable social terms with quite all the men connected with the local staff, so much so that most of my meals, previous to this period of saving, had been eaten in company with one or another of these associates. And at midnight or thereabouts it was my custom to drift around to the Press Club, where might be found a goodly company of men who worked on the different papers. Whenever a celebrity chanced to be in the city he was more than likely to be brought here, and no dues were asked or money expected, apparently, from any of the working reporters. The older newspaper men—those in better positions—apparently carried whatever burdens there were.

But this one man, being of a solid practical turn and very secure in his work and liberal in his ideas and knowledge of affairs, had attracted me, and one night as I entered the Press Club I found him there drinking beer and eating sandwiches, and forthwith he asked me to join him. The conversation turned to many things, among them the huge hubbub being made about General William Booth, the head of the Salvation Army, then touring America. He had addressed five thousand people in some great opera building the day before, and I had been called upon to report the sermon and write an introduction. We debated the value of the Salvation Army and the General's sincerity. He had appealed to me as a very remarkable man. Then we fell to discussing local conditions in general and the importance of newspaper work, and finally he said: "I cannot understand why you stay here. Now I wouldn't say that to anyone else in the game for fear he'd think I was plotting to get him out of his job, but with you it's different. You can stay or go as you choose, but they're not likely to drop you. But I don't see why you stay. There's no great chance here, and you have too much ability to waste your time on this town. There's no chance here. They won't let you do anything. The steel people have this town sewed up tight. The papers are muzzled. All you can do is to write what the people at the top want you to write, and that's very little. With your talent you could go down to New York and make a place for yourself, I'm sure. I wouldn't say that to anyone else right now because I've been there and came back on account of my family. The conditions were too uncertain for me. I have to have a regular income. But with you it's different. You're young, and apparently you haven't anyone dependent on you. If you do strike it down there, you'll make a lot of money and what's more, you might make a name for yourself. Don't you think it's foolish for you to stay here? Don't think it's anything to me whether you go or not. I haven't any axe to grind, but I really wonder why you do stay."

I explained that I had been drifting, that I was really on my way to New York but taking my time about it, and so the discussion ended. But in addition, only a few days before, I had been reading of a certain Indo-English newspaper man—fresh out of India with his books and short stories—who was making a great stir. His name was Rudyard Kipling, and the enthusiasm with which he was being accepted and received made me not jealous but wishful for a career for myself. He was coming to America, or was even then on his way, and the wonder of such a sudden success was filling my mind. The tributes to his brilliance were so unanimous, the article said, and he was a mere youth as yet, not more than twenty-seven or -eight. I half decided then and there that I would go—must go—and accordingly, before the following Saturday when my next pay envelope was due, gave notice of my intention. My city editor merely looked at me, as much as to say, "Well, I thought so"—then said, "Well, I think you will do better there myself, but I'm not glad to have you go. You can refer to us anytime you want to."

On Saturday—or whenever it was—I drew my pay at noon, and by four o'clock had once more entered that express which deposited me in New York the following morning at seven. My brother had long since left New York, as I knew, and would not be back until the following spring. We had kept up a genial correspondence. Similarly I had exchanged a word or two with my sister and found that she was not prospering. Since Paul had gone on the road, she had been compelled to let rooms, her husband not having as yet found anything to do. I judged by the tone of her letter that she would be glad to have me stay with her, and I had notified her that in case I came I would live with her. In consequence, I now wired and next morning walked in on her.

But if anyone imagines that I did all this cheerfully or that I was thrilled by the thought of an early fulfillment of my wish for recognition or success, he is greatly mistaken. I never made a more trying or depressed journey in my life. Having seen so much of New York, and having been so overawed and impressed by it, I was by no means sure that I should succeed, and this despite various kind words said to me and my determination to go. Indeed, I was haunted by the thought that I was sure to fail; and in addition that very remarkable book of Balzac's, *The Great Man from the Provinces,* so recently read, in which was recorded the poignant failure of such a youth as myself, was weighing upon me to a degree. Again, there was this fixed belief in the nothingness of everything as shown by Spencer, which held and grilled me. All night I lay in my berth and thought, wondering how if at all I should make out. The city was so vast. Its successes when achieved were so thrilling, but its failures—or so I imagined—were bitter. Would I succeed or would I be compelled to return? The click of the trucks over the rails, the puff of the engine on grades, the rather regular whistles before crossings—long and sad in the dark—seemed to emphasize and punctuate this very disturbing question.

I often think of the mental operations of many people under such circumstances as having a rather close resemblance to the fulgurous, bubbling and changeful, crater-like character of a volcano, or the lurid flickering aftermath of a midnight storm. The mind in stress seems ever to alternate between a cloudy, uncertain quiescence in which thought sinks to dusk, and night even—or no thought—and then bubbles and flares afresh to a smoky redness, or less often an electric vividness, in which, as by a lightning stroke and clearly, one may discern the most distant things of fancy. Vast outlines of mountains and valleys of thought appear—distant fields and houses—occasionally only a lone horse of thought in a cloudy field of mentation. So on this night, and on many another. Lying in this berth and thinking, now darkly, now clearly and sadly, I was whisked Eastward across bridges and through gorges into that vaster sea of life, where, for the better part of my days at least, I was now to reside.

And my sister on seeing me again was so delighted. I did not know then, or perhaps I would not have been so pleased, that I was looked upon by her as the possible exit from a very difficult and trying crisis which she and her two children were then facing. For, as I have said, love, as well as prosperity, had certainly died here. And Hopkins, from being a onetime fairly resourceful and successful and aggressive man, had slipped into a most disconcerting attitude of weakness and all but indifference before the onslaughts of the great city. Like so many of the other millions about him and before him, he had already failed spiritually and was now living a hand-to-mouth existence, as it were, waiting for something to turn up. I had not liked him on my first visit, and this return but confirmed my impression, but I did not know until some little time later the definite and to me unsatisfactory share I was to play in all this.

My brother, as I have said, had left for the season, and while apparently perfectly willing to live here and pay a reasonable rate for accommodations while in the city during the summertime, there was apparently no reason, seeing that Hopkins was as physically able as himself, why he should be called upon to do anything while away. And aside from renting their rooms to him and others, there was apparently no other source of income here—at least none which Hopkins troubled to provide. He appeared, as I saw it afterwards, to be spiritually done for—played out. Like so many men who have fought a fair battle in youth and then lost, he was weary of the game. He saw no interesting position for him anywhere in the future, and so he was drifting. And my sister, like so many of the children of ordinary families the world over, had received no practical education of any kind and knew nothing other than housework—that useless trade. In consequence, within a very short time after my arrival, I was faced by one of two alternatives, namely: that of retiring and leaving her to shift as best she might—a step which, in view of what followed, would have been wiser but which my unreasoning sympathy would not permit me to do—or of assisting her with what means I then had. But this latter alternative, had I had sufficient practical brains so to reason at the time, would be merely postponing the day of reckoning for all of them and bringing a great deal of trouble upon myself. For finding me willing to pay for my room and board there and, in addition, as it proved, to advance certain sums against necessities which had nothing to do with my obligations, Hopkins felt that he could now drift a little while longer and so did. Through his wife he accepted such doles as I was willing to make and even urged her to seek them, looking no harder than he had before for work. And my sister, fumbling, impractical soul, flowing like water into any crevice of opportunity, accepted the sacrifice on my part to an end which, had she reasoned, she must have seen could only postpone the day of reckoning. What I had with me, or could be legitimately made to pay, was not sufficient to assist them but a very little way anyhow, at the end of which time a separation or effort of some kind must necessarily have followed.

I sometimes think, looking back on this and other phases of my life, that if anyone desires full confirmation of the mechanistic view of the universe, all he needs to do is to contemplate people—organized or so-called organic life, as opposed to inorganic life—the manner in which all of us rest or drift, inert, until compelled by forces outside ourselves to move or waste our substance; the certainty with which all of us follow the line of least resistance; the way hunger or its equivalent, necessity, drives us to action, while luxury or a sufficiency causes all to rest and drift or cease all effort—the great lethargy where pressure is removed. Nothing is accomplished save where need compels or one force moves or diverts another. And, curiously, one force or another is always moving. Why? And not thought but unreasoned impulse or accident or chemical flames not lit by man bring about all the crises of life, such as earthquakes, drouths, excellent or poor crops, wars, rivalries and what not. And these without reason, in so far as man can see. And only by reason of an urge to escape pain or achieve pleasure is man moved to avoid danger or to take advantage of opportunity such as these accidents and conditions present, to seek out and use all the accidentally stored resources of nature.

A growth in population permitted by the presence of non-man-manufactured resources results eventually in pressure upon resources once more and the driving of all sorts of human atoms into all sorts of seeking relationships, purely mechanical in their import and without meaning to the future any more than to the past. Not thought but

chemical, and hence mechanical, fires, plus shortages as well as sur-
plusages here and there, bring about those necessitous movements of
defence or attack and exchange. The vessels which sail to Brazil for
coffee or to China for tea or silk but predicate a mechanical want of
these elsewhere, and these very movements are mechanical. The great
thing, life, appears to be an accidental clocklike device which may not
have within it the power to stop or rest. It may be conditioned by a tor-
turous and inescapable perpetual motion. Its greatest security against
itself may then be amnesia. By that it could and perhaps does achieve
the marvel of illusion, newness, strangeness, hope, ambition; for having existed so long how could it have these things if it could not forget
and seemingly begin all over again? No wonder there is such a thing as
laughing gas and the sad tendency to cynicism as life approaches even
so little a thing as a brief memory of what it has been in the past. Not
love of the task, but necessity—and an unreasoned one at that—may
cause life to dig the earth for coal or to sail the deep for remote cargoes.
Even the desire to fly might never have troubled man but for the
illusion of necessity for life and fame in this form. The pathos, one
might almost say the horror, of it all.

But just now, this first morning and for days after, I was very much
alive to, if frightened by, the possibilities which the city held for me. To
be sure, I had, as I saw, a comfortable place to stay and from this
vantage point could sally forth and reconnoitre the city at my leisure,
but still, as I felt, I had so little to go on. As in every instance in which I
had previously entered a new city, I now devoted a day or two to
rambling about, surveying the world which I was seeking to manipulate
to my advantage, and then on the second or third afternoon began to
investigate those newspaper offices with which I was most anxious to
connect myself.

I can never forget the severe shock I received when, on my first
entering the *World*, then the *Sun* and subsequently the *Herald*, I discovered that, whatever the modus operandi in the West, here one
could not even so much as get in to see a city editor, or indeed any
editor; for that worthy was guarded via a minute lobby or anteroom in
which were posted as lookouts and buffers or men-at-arms as well as
errand boys as goodly and gallant and erratic and cynical and contentious a company of youths and hallboys as it has ever been my lot to
meet up with. These same were so self-sufficient, supercilious, scoffing
and ribald that from the first they did for me completely. Whenever I

entered one of these places, there were as many as two or three on guard (sometimes four or five in the *World*), wrestling, as a rule, for the possession of an inkwell or a pencil or an apple, or slapping each other on the back, throwing paper wads and kidding each other. And although there were usually four or five people patiently waiting for something, whenever a new visitor arrived with an inquiry or a name of some kind, these young banditti would cease their personal brawling only long enough to place themselves as a barricade between the newcomer and the door giving into the editorial sanctum, whereupon they would go through a routine formula the while they vigorously masticated gum or an apple before the astonished physiognomy of the newcomer.

"Whoja wanta see?"

"Who?"

"The city editor (or managing or society editor as the case might be)."

"Whatja wanta see him about?"

"What?"

"A job?"

"No vacancies. No, no vacancies today. He says to say 'no vacancies' today, see. You can't go in there. He says 'no vacancies.'"

"But can't I even see him?"

"No, he don't want to see anybody. No vacancies."

"Well, how about taking my name in to him?"

"Not if you're lookin' fer a job. He says 'no vacancies.'"

The tone and the manner, especially if there were present a group of waiters and you chanced to be slightly sensitive, were most disconcerting. To me, decidedly new to the city and rather overawed by the size of these buildings, to say nothing of the reputation of these editors and the publications themselves, this was all but final. For a little while after each rebuff, I did not quite see how I was to overcome this difficulty. Plainly, they were overrun with applicants, and in so great a city why would they not be? After going into each one on this revelatory first trip, I emerged completely nonplussed and not a little discouraged. How was one to do? I thought. One must get in or write or call up on a telephone, but would any city editor worthy the name discuss a man's fitness or attempt to judge him over a telephone or via a letter?

And besides, the tempo of these realms into which I had ventured seemed so opposed to any so pale a method as that suggested by a letter. They were hard and raucous and inconsiderate. I had never seen newspaper offices which seemed so tense and permeated with urge and troubled effort and unrest. These little exterior offices fairly hummed with a kind of life which suggested the vast and complex interests of a metropolitan daily. All sorts of queer-looking people were hanging about with all sorts of requests, no doubt, and ever and anon there passed through them, going into or coming out from the great central office, individuals who seemed of a decidedly different world, so self-complacent, assured and superior. I knew the type well enough. It was that of the successful and assured young newspaper man or critic or editor or department chief of some kind—one such as I myself wished to be.

Rather dourly and speculatively, then, after I had visited these three offices and some others with exactly the same result in each instance, I went finally into City Hall Park, which fronted the majority of them—the *Sun, Tribune, Times, World, Press*—and stared at them, their great buildings. About me was swirling that old-time throng which has always made that region so interesting—the vast mass that bubbles upward from the financial district and regions south of it and crosses the plaza to Brooklyn Bridge and the elevated roads. The subways had not come yet, but you would not have sensed a difference. Along Broadway and Park Row as well as up Chatham Place was tramping as impressive a throng as has ever been. About me on the benches of the Park was—even in this grey, chill December weather— that same large company of "benchers" so frequently described as bums, loafers, tramps, idlers—the flotsam and jetsam of the great city's whirl and strife. I looked at them and then considered myself and these great offices, and it was then, if ever, that the idea of Hurstwood was born. The city just then seemed so huge and cruel. I recalled gay Broadway of the preceding summer, and Manhattan Beach, and the baking, iso- lated, exclusive atmosphere of Fifth Avenue, all boarded up because of the wealth that had executed its summer flight to the sea. And now here was I in the wintertime, with this great newspaper world before me—and most unfriendly, apparently—and I did not see quite how I was to get on. Dubiously, at four in the afternoon, I turned my steps northward along the great and bustling and, even then, solidly com- mercial Broadway to 15th Street, walking all the way and staring into the shops and stores. Those who recall Sister Carrie's wanderings may find a taste of it here. In Union Square, before Tiffany's, I stared at an immense Christmas throng already beginning to buy. Then in the dark I wandered across to my sister's apartment, and in the warmth and light there sat me down, thinking how to do. At once she recognized my mood and after a little while said: "You're worrying, aren't you?"

"Oh, no, I'm not," I said rather pretentiously.

"Oh, yes, you are too. You're wondering how you're going to get along. I know how you are. We're all that way. But you mustn't worry. Paul says you can write wonderfully. You've only been here a day or two. Why do you worry so soon? You must wait until you've tried a little while and then see. You're sure to get along. New York isn't as bad as you think, only you have to get started."

I thought after a time that this was true enough and, deciding that I had made no effort at all as yet, proposed to give myself time to think up something which would compel their reception of me.

Then after my dinner and an hour or two's reading and talking, I went to sleep.

CHAPTER LXXXVII

But the next day and the next and the next, as I discovered, brought me no solution to the problem. The weather had turned cold, and for a time there was a slushy snow on the ground, which certainly made the matter of job hunting all the worse. Those fierce youths in the anterooms were no more kindly on the second and fifth days than they were on the first. In fact, the moment they came to know me, they seemed to take a kind of delight in turning me away, in shunting me out with their contemptful "no vacancies."

But by now, in addition to becoming decidedly dour, I was becoming a little angry. These boys were such impossible creatures. And in addition, as it seemed to me, it was, to say the least, the height of inconsiderateness and discourtesy (not to say rank brutality) for newspapers to thus give evidence of their own lack of courtesy by placing such unsophisticated and blatant and ill-trained upstarts, as these youngsters certainly were, between themselves and the general public.

Especially newspapers which boasted a social and humanitarian leadership of their fellows in American life—indeed, an absolutely omniscient and sacrosanct wisdom in regard to everything relating to progress, intelligence and what not. Men and women of all shades and degrees of intelligence, by chance and without knowing the character or routine of a newspaper office, were compelled to communicate directly with them in some such informal manner. My distinguished contemporary, Henry L. Mencken, has written: "The average American newspaper, especially the so-called better sort, has the intelligence of a Baptist evangelist, the courage of a rat, the fairness of a prohibitionist boob-bumper, the information of a high-school janitor, the taste of a designer of celluloid valentines, and the honor of a police-station lawyer." Judging by some of my experiences and observations, I would be willing to subscribe to this. The unwarranted and unnecessary airs! The grand assumption of wisdom! The heartless and often brutal nature of their internal economies, their pandering to the cheapest of all public instincts and tendencies in search of circulation!

But I digress. The thought I wish to emphasize here is that even then, fresh from the so-called untutored West, I was oppressed and disgusted by this evidence of inconsiderateness on the part of these assumed leaders of public thought. They preach so freely, and practise not at all. These wretched boys, with their wrestling matches, their gum chewing and their delight in exhibiting a little authority, seemed typical not only of these newspapers but of New York and America itself, its hard, assured, contemptuous attitude, and, in a larger sense, of the successful and ignorant, and hence the indifferent, everywhere. Were not America a land of greedy and boastful and vainglorious beginners and new-rich, one might look upon the whole process as despicable, but it is really the natural consequence of ignorance. It has not, as yet, learned better. The sickeningly brash anteroom boy is still on every hand,—especially in the newspaper and theatrical and movie worlds. He seems a part of newly achieved prosperity in America everywhere. But why not courteous old men or women, pray, if no young ones can any longer be secured, individuals carefully instructed in the matter of common politeness? Why the ignorance and hostility and pugnacity of youth invariably put forth as a buffer? A matter of a few cents more to the corporation? I should think that any public office or corporation worthy the name would be ashamed to give such an exhibition of cheap economy and non-understanding of public life and courtesy as to tolerate such a show. And I should think especially that the *World* and the *Herald* and the *Sun* might have been ashamed of themselves.

But once more I digress. What I wish to say is that after several days of such receptions, and being satisfied after two attempts that at least the idea of telephoning was worthless, I made up my mind to see the city editors of all these papers, regardless of hallboys, and so going up one afternoon (about one o'clock) to the *World*—the paper with which I most desired to connect myself—I started to walk right in, but, being intercepted as usual, lost my courage and retreated. However, as I have sometimes since thought, perhaps this was fortunate, for going downstairs I meditated most grievously as to my failure, my lack of skill and courage in carrying out an intention once firmly arrived at. So thoroughly did I castigate myself that, like a kicked dog, I recovered my nerve, and returning I re-entered the small office and, finding two of the several youths usually there still on hand and waiting to intercept me, I brushed both of them aside as one might flies—actually threw them against the wall—and opening the much guarded door, walked in.

To my satisfaction and astonishment, the while they followed me and by threats and force attempted to persuade me to retreat—to shoo me out, as it were—I gazed upon one of the most interesting city reportorial and general editorial rooms that I have ever seen. It was a huge affair—apparently forty or fifty feet wide by a hundred or more deep, and lighted, even by day in this gray weather, by a blaze of lights upon desks and enclosed in light-bowls set in the ceiling. And the entire space from front to back was literally crowded with desks—a larger number than I had ever seen in any newspaper office. These same—flat- and rolltop desks—stood side by side and back to back and along the side walls, their backs to the wall, with aisles in between. A varied company of newspaper men, most of them in shirt sleeves, a number of them operating typewriters or writing by hand, and in many instances smoking, were hard at work, bending over their desks and lost in their duties. In the forward or western part of the room, near the door by which I had entered and upon a platform, were several desks at which three or four men were seated—the throne, as I quickly learned, of the city editor and his several assistants. Two of these, as I could see, were engaged in reading and marking papers. A third, who looked to me as though he might be the city editor, was consulting with several men at his desk. Office- and copyboys were ambling to and fro, their usual lackadaisical and casual manners singling them out as patrons and favorites of the entire staff. From somewhere came the constant click-click-click of telegraph receivers and the occasional bawl of "Coppee!" I think, at that, that I might have been forced to retire had it not been for the fact that as I was standing there, threatened and pleaded with by my two adversaries, a young man—since most distinguished in the journalistic world, one Arthur Brisbane by name—chanced to be passing, and, seeing me thus beleaguered, stopped and, looking at me curiously, inquired most courteously: "What is it you want?"

"I want," I said, half-angered by the spectacle I was making and that was being made of me, "a job."

"Where do you come from?" he inquired, looking me over.

"The West," I replied.

"Wait a moment," he said, and the youths, seeing that I had attracted his attention, immediately withdrew. He did not need to command them. Instead he went toward the man at the desk whom I had singled out in my mind as the city editor and, getting his attention for a moment, turned and pointed to me. "This young man here," he said, "wants a job. I wish you would give him one."

The man nodded, and my very remarkable interrogator, turning to me, said: "Just wait here, please," and disappeared.

I did not know quite what to think, so astonished was I by this sudden turn, but with each succeeding moment my spirits rose, and by the time the city editor chose to motion me to him, I was in a very exalted state indeed. So much for courage, I told myself. Surely I of all people was fortunate, for had I not been dreaming for months—years even—of coming to New York and, after great deprivation and difficulty perhaps, securing a position. And now of a sudden, and in the face of all my doubts and despairs, here I was, thus suddenly remarkably vaulted into the very position which of all others I had most craved. Surely this must be the influence of a star of fortune. Surely now, and soon, if I had the least trace of fortune or ability, I would be in a better position than ever I had been in my life before. This way indeed lay success.

I looked about the great room, as I waited patiently and even delightedly, and saw pasted on the walls at intervals printed cards which read: *Accuracy, Accuracy, Accuracy!*; *Who? What? Where? When? How?*; *The facts—the color—the facts!* I knew what those signs referred to, especially the second. It epitomized the proper order for beginning a newspaper story. A fourth—and all of these were pasted in triplicate or more—insisted upon *Promptness, Courtesy, Geniality*. Most excellent traits, I thought, and excellent to achieve, but not as easy as comfortable publishers and managing editors might suppose under some circumstances. But with my newfound fortune in my teeth I felt myself the equivalent of any news-gathering condition or necessity.

And then in a little while as I stood there, I was called over and told to take a seat—"I'll have an assignment for you after a while." That statement meant work, an opportunity, a salary, as I thought, and it thrilled me almost as much as the command to put me on had. I felt myself growing apace. Only the eye and the glance of this my immediate superior was by no means as cheering and genial as had been that of the other. It was harder—as he was—or seemingly so, a trait which I am sure invariably springs from a sense of strain, which springs from a sense or fear or knowledge of a lack of sufficiency for the task in hand. Really strong and bubbling and vital men who have much to give are not hard. They cannot be. They have too much to be grateful for. But lesser men are likely to be so, those whom fortune has buffeted, or who find themselves by reason of the unkindness of nature or fate not sufficiently equipped for the tasks thrust upon them or ones they would like to shoulder or retain. And this man was like that. He was holding a difficult position, one of the most difficult of any in newspaperdom in America at the time, and under one of the most eccentric and difficult of publishers the country contained.

The latter, Joseph Pulitzer, no less, was a brilliant and eccentric Magyar Jew, whom another writer, one Alleyne Ireland, subsequently characterized in so brilliant a fashion as to make this brief sketch trivial and unimportant save for its service here as a link in this tale. At that time this man was already sixty or thereabout years of age, semi-dyspeptic and half-blind, having wrecked himself physically almost, or so I understood, in his long and grueling struggle to ascend to pre-eminence in the American newspaper world. He was the chief owner, as I understood it, of not only the New York *World* but the St. Louis *Post-Dispatch*, the afternoon paper of largest circulation and influence in that city. While I was in St. Louis, the air of that newspaper world was surcharged or still rife with this remarkable publisher's past exploits—how once, when he was first starting in the newspaper world as a publisher, for instance, he had been horsewhipped by some irate citizen for having published some derogatory item of some kind. And then having first tamely submitted to the castigation, he had rushed into his sanctum and given orders that an extra should be issued detailing the attack, in order that the news value might not be lost to the counting room. Similarly, one of his St. Louis city or managing editors—one Colonel Cockerill by name, who at this very time or a very little later was still one of the managing editors of the New York *World*—after conducting some campaign of exposure against a local citizen by order of his chief, and being confronted in his office by the same citizen, evidently come to punish him, had drawn a revolver and killed him. That was a part of what might have been called the makings of this great newspaper figure.

Here in New York, as I already knew, after his arrival on the scene in 1884, at which time he had taken over a moribund journal called the *World*, he had succeeded literally in turning things upside down, much as did William Randolph Hearst after him, and as had Charles A. Dana and others before him. Like all aggressive newspapermen worthy of the name, he had seized upon every possible vital issue and attacked, attacked, attacked, Tammany Hall, Wall Street (then defended by the *Sun* and the *Herald*), the house of Morgan, some phases of society and many other features and conditions of the great city. For one thing, he had cut the price of his paper to one cent, a move which was reported to have infuriated his conservative and quiescent rivals, who were getting two, three and five cents, and who disliked to be disturbed in their peaceful pursuits. The New York *Sun* in particular, which had been *made* by the brilliant and daring eccentricity of Dana and his earlier radicalism, and the *Herald*, which originally owed its growth and fame to the monopoly-fighting skill of Bennett, were now both grown conservative. They jointly attacked him as low, vulgar, indecent and the like—an upstart Jew whose nose was in every putrescent dunghill, ratting out filth for the consumption of the dregs of society. But is not this always the experience of any one who seeks to break through from submersion or nothingness into the white light of power and influence? Do not the resultant quakes always infuriate those who have been becoming or are at last comfortably quiescent and who do not wish to be disturbed? And are not all such newcomers invariably described as of the dregs? Witness Dana in his day, Bennett in his, Pulitzer and Hearst in theirs, and, simultaneously, the Harmsworths of London.

Allons.

Just the same, at this time this man, because of his vital, aggressive, restless working mood and his vaulting ambition to be all that there was to be of journalistic force in America, was making a veritable hell of his paper and the lives of those who worked for him. And although he himself was not present at the time but was sailing around the world on a yacht, or living in a villa on the Riviera, or at Bar Harbor, or in his town house in New York or London, you could feel the feverish and disturbing and distressing ionic tang of his presence in this room as definitely as though he were then and there present in the flesh. The oxygen fairly sizzled with the ionic rays of this black star. Of secretaries to this editor-publisher, and traveling with him at the time but coming back betimes to nose about the paper and cause woe to others, there were five. Of sons, by no means in active charge but still present, two. Of managing editors, all slipping about and, as the attendant newspaper men seemed to think, spying on each other, at one time as many as seven. He had so little faith in his fellowman, and especially such of his fellowmen as were so unfortunate as to be compelled to work for him, that he played off one against another as might have the council of the Secret Ten in Venice, or as did the devils who ruled in the Vatican in the Middle Ages. Every man's hand, as I came to know in the course of time, was against that of every other. All were thoroughly distrustful of each other and feared the incessant spying that was going on. Each one, as I was told and as to a certain extent one could feel, was made to believe that he was the important one, or might be, presuming that he could prove that the others were failures or in error.

Proposed editorials, suggestions for news features, directions as to policy and what not were coming in every hour via cable or telegraph from him. Nearly every issue of any great importance was being submitted to him by the same means. He was, as described by the writer whose name I have mentioned, undoubtedly semi-neurasthenic, a disease-demonized soul who could scarcely control himself any more in anything—a man who was fighting an almost insane battle with life itself, trying to be omnipotent and what not else and being most unwilling to die. Indeed, the very air of this building and this room was full of corruscating and fulminating ions which issued from him. There was an immense sense of strain—I never felt it more keenly anywhere. It was as if all of these men were working with a kind of sword of disaster suspended above them by a thread—the sword of discharge or of bitter reprimand or contempt. Nearly all of them hurried to and fro in a nervous, jerky, irritable way. They had a kind of nervous, resentful terror in their eyes as have animals when they are tortured. All were either scribbling busily or hurrying in or out. Every man was for himself. If you asked a man a question or two, as I ventured to do while sitting here, not knowing anything at all about how things were done here, he looked at you as though you were a fool, or as though you were trying to take something away from him or cause him trouble of some kind. In the main, they bustled by or went on with their work without troubling to pay the slightest attention to you. I had never encountered anything like it before, and only twice afterwards in my life did I encounter anything which even partially approximated it, and both times in New York. After the peace and ease of Pittsburgh—God! But it was immense just the same. It was terrible.

CHAPTER LXXXVIII

And let me tell you I rose very swiftly to the import of it all as I sat here, but that did not help me very much either. I saw, or thought I did, that this was unlike anything I had ever known, and one must work—or so I imagined—in a new and more efficient way. All at once, and because of stage fright, of course, I was inclined to credit these men with brighter intellects and more subtlety, courage, skill in divining news and executing assignments than I had. If I lasted so much as an hour in so brilliant and desperate a realm as this, I must think quickly and act in the same fashion. All bosh. They were not a whit the more able than a hundred newspapermen whom I had encountered and known in the West. But because they were centered in this greatest of American cities, housed in this, to me, most imposing of newspaper offices, connected with the paper of largest circulation anywhere and, more especially, most vigorously *harried into undue activity*, they seemed more wonderful—and I assumed the seeming to be true. Any well-shaken or rattled substance, as I might have known, always seems more important and effective than that which is quiescent. The illusion is in the activity—which merely seems more interesting and therefore more important. The threescore or more of them who worked there then and who were hourly being tossed out and into or against most difficult and impossible or unprofitable assignments (not unlike the soldiers of but average capacity whom a general throws into the most hell-like craters of opposition and cannon fire, and often with no more chances of success) were but little different to the better sort of men such as I had known everywhere in the West. Many of them were not even their equals. But here—.

I sat and studied them, wondering if by any chance I could ever possibly do as well, and then after an hour or so of waiting—and that without lunch—I was faced by a boy who said, "The city editor wants to see you." I hurried forward to the desk of that pooh-bah of this maelstrom, who merely handed me a small clipping from another paper giving an account of some extraterrestrial manifestations which had been taking place in a graveyard near Elizabeth, and was told to "see what there is in that." Unsophisticated as I was as to the ways of the metropolis, and assuming Western fashion that I might ask a question or two of my new chief, and being considerably flustered into the bargain, I ventured a feeble "Where is that?" For my pains I received as contemptuous and almost, I might say, as black a look as it is possible for one human being to give another.

"Back of the directory! Back of the directory!" came the semi-savage reply, and, not quite realizing what was meant by that, I retired precipitately, trying to think it out.

"Well," I said to myself, "a reporter is certainly of small consequence on this paper. It doesn't much matter, apparently, what you have done elsewhere."

Almost mechanically I went to look up a directory, but fumbling through that part of the book which relates to streets and their numbers, I began to realize that Elizabeth was a town and not a street as the clipping showed, and that presumably the import of the short advice was that I was to find out for myself. Did my chief dislike me then? Had I made a most ridiculous mistake?

At a desk near the directory in the front part of the office I noticed a stout man of perhaps forty, rotund and agreeable, who seemed to me less fierce and self-centered than some of the others. He had evidently only recently entered and had kicked off a pair of overshoes and laid a greatcoat over a chair beside him and was scribbling something.

"Can you tell me how I get to Elizabeth?" I inquired.

"Sure," he said, looking up and beginning to chuckle. "I haven't been in the city very long myself, but I know where that is. It's on the Jersey Central, about twelve miles out. You'll catch a local by going down to the Liberty Street Ferry. I heard him tell you 'Back of the directory,'" he added genially and chuckling. "You mustn't mind that— that's what they always tell you here, these smart alecks," and he chuckled again, very much like my friend McCord. "They're the most inconsiderate lot I ever went up against, but you have to get used to it. Out where I came from they'll give you a civil answer once in a while, but here it's 'Back of the directory'"—and he chuckled again.

"And where do you come from?" I asked.

"Oh, Pittsburgh originally," he said—which same gave me a spiritual lift at least—"but I haven't been in the game for several years. I've been doing press-agent work for a road show—one of my own," and he chuckled again. "I'm not a stranger to New York exactly, but I am to this paper and this game down here." He chuckled again.

The fact that I had found someone who had even been in Pittsburgh soothed me, and I desired much to stay and talk with him, but I had no time.

"Is this your desk?" I asked.

"No, they haven't deigned to give me one yet," and he chuckled again. "But I suppose I will get one eventually, if they don't throw me out." Once more that chuckle. He was like sunshine.

"I hope I'll see you when I get back."

"Oh, I'll be around here, if I'm not out in the snow. It's tough, isn't it?" And he turned to his work again. I bustled out through that same anteroom where I had been so cavalierly restrained and, seeing one of my pestiferous youthful opponents, I observed, "Now just take notice, Eddie. I belong here, see? I work here. And I'll be back after a while."

"Oh, dat's all right," he replied with a grin. "We gotta do dat. I seedje git de job. We gotta keep mosta dese hams outa here, dough. Dat's de orders we got."

"Hams," I thought. "God! They let these little snips speak of strangers and inquirers as hams. That's New York for you."

Without eating I sought out the ferry and, finding by the timetable that I had a half hour to wait, sought a nearby beanery and partook of "ham and" and coffee. Then I made that short, dreary commuter's trip, staring at the little homes of Bayonne and beyond, white with snow. Once I reached the modest city, I sought the particular graveyard and the caretaker referred to. There was not a scintilla of truth to the story. No man by the name of the dead man mentioned had ever been buried there. No noises or appearances of any kind had been recorded. "They're always publishing things like that about New Jersey," said the caretaker. "There's not a thing to it. I wish they'd quit it. Some newspaper fellow out here just wanted to earn a little money; that's all."

I tramped back, caught a train around seven, and put in an appearance at the office at eight. Already most of the evening assignments had been given out. My city editor was not around—gone to dinner. The office was comparatively bare, a shaded, green-lamped realm. At a desk at a side wall was a long, lean, dyspeptic-looking soul, his eyes shaded by a green shield, who seemed to me to be the night editor, so large was the pile of "copy" beside him. But when I ventured to approach him, he merely glared sourly. "The city desk's not closed yet," he growled. "Wait'll they come back."

I retired, rebuffed again.

Presently one of the assistants whom I had seen clipping or marking papers during the afternoon reappeared, and I ventured to report to him. "Nothing to it, eh?" he observed, and then added, "There ought to be some kind of a josh to that, though." But I did not "get" him. Instead, since he told me to "wait around," I sought out another empty desk and sat down. The thing which was interesting me was how much if anything I would be paid per week and what he meant by "There ought to be a josh to it." Not being quite able to solve that, I contented myself with counting all the desks and wondering about the men who occupied them—who they were, what they were like, and what they were doing now.

And as I sat I proceeded further to analyze the office. To my right against the north wall were two rolltop desks, at one of which was already seated a very dapper, actor-like man writing and posting. He was arrayed in a very close-fitting and so English-looking gray suit with a bright-colored vest and an exceedingly high collar, and was working at the time with his coat off and his shirt sleeves held up by dainty rubber bands. Finally, because of some theatrical programs which I saw him examining, I concluded that he must be connected with the dramatic department, presumably *the* dramatic critic. Having done this work myself on occasion in the West, I was naturally interested and a little envious. The dramatic department of a great daily paper in New York seemed a wonderful thing to me.

Again, after a time, as I sat there, there entered another individual who opened the desk next to the dramatic critic. He was medium tall and stocky, with a mass of loose wavy hair hanging impressively over his collar, not unlike the advance agent of a cure-all or a quack Messiah, and his body was encased in a huge cape-coat which reached to his knees after the best manner of a tragedian. He wore a large, soft-brimmed felt hat, which he now doffed rather grandiosely, and stood a big cane in a corner. Altogether he had the attitude and look of a famous musician—the stage-type—and evidently took himself very seriously. I was impressed by this character also, and in my mental notebook, which was rapidly being filled, I put him down as the musical critic at least—some great authority on the paper of whom I should hear later.

Time went by, and still I sat there. The city editor had not returned although his assistants had, reading and clipping as before. And at his desk against the south wall scratched my cadaverous friend, editing copy. Now and then he would bawl: "Boy! Boy! Where the hell are you, anyhow?" This as some gum-chewing, paper-wad-throwing office fixture came ambling up. A more waspish and savage man I never saw at that desk before, a veritable tarantula.

I looked at the windows. Through them, from where I was sitting (I was on the eleventh floor), I could now see the tops of one or two other buildings, their pinnacles as it were, one holding a clockface lighted with a green light. After a time, being weary of sitting, I ventured to leave my seat and look out. Then for the first time I saw that great night panorama of the East River and the bay with its ships and docks, so visible from the *World* Building at that time, and the dark mass of buildings in between, many of them still lighted with occasional lights. It was beautiful, a great scene, and, looking at it, a sense of awe came over me. New York was so vast, so varied, so rich, so hard.

How was one to make one's way here, anyhow? I had so little to offer, or so I thought, a little gift of scribbling, no more; and money, as I could see, was not to be made that way. Yet here were pleasures and allurements beyond the gift even of fame. How was one to seize upon a modicum of it and not go hungry, be sent away empty-handed? Now, of course, I was nothing. Might I some day hope to be anything, or might I never succeed? But, oh, the color, the beauty, the possibility of it all!

Presently the city editor returned and, seeing me along with a few others present, he began to take us in hand. Signalling me at last, he said: "Nothing came of that other item, eh?"

"No, sir."

"Well, here's another little thing. I think you will still have time to get it." He handed me a clipping relating to some proposed meeting of some committee somewhere on the west side which looked to the better lighting and cleaning of a certain district. It was all but too late, I knew, and if reported would be given an inch or two of space—not more. I took it nevertheless and turned to go, and then fell the worst blow of all. "Wait a minute," he said, as I moved to depart. "I wanted to tell you. I can't make you a reporter yet. There is no vacancy on our regular staff. I'll put you on space, though, and you can charge up whatever you get in at seven-and-a-half a column. It's nearly as good. We allow fifty cents an hour for time here. Just show up tomorrow at eleven, and I'll see if anything turns up."

My heart sank to my shoes. Then I was not to have a regular place after all—only space—and I was not sure that this meant anything. No reportorial staff with which I had ever been connected had been paid by space. I went out trying to assure myself that there might be something to it, but I could not believe it. It seemed an easy way of getting rid of one. I went to the meeting in question and found it nothing of importance. The data, when cut by the amazing figure who posed as night editor, made one inch, as I discovered the next morning by a most careful examination of the paper. And a column of the paper measured exactly twenty-one inches. So my efforts this particular day, allowing for time charged for my first trip—three hours at fifty cents an hour, aside from my expenses—had resulted in a total of one dollar and eighty-six cents, or a little less than street sweepers and snow shovelers were receiving outside.

But this was not all. Returning at about eleven o'clock with this item and turning it in, I ventured to say to the night editor now in charge, "When does a man leave here?"

"You're a new space man, aren't you?"

"Yes, sir."

"You have the late watch tonight."

"And how late is that?"

"Until after the first edition is on the press," he growled.

Not knowing when that was, I still did not venture to question him but returned to another reporter working near at hand. "You're supposed to stick around until three, anyhow," he informed me.

I hung about, consoling myself with the thought that perhaps on certain days I would get better assignments. Maybe, with my talent for devising or striking something, I might become a staff favorite. Who knows? Once more my spirits soared. At any rate I was on the paper and receiving assignments. At three a.m. my green-shaded mentor called, "You might as well go now"—and at that hour, having been in or around this building since one p.m. of the preceding day, I made my way to the Sixth Avenue L and so home. The cheerful face of my sister sleepily admitting me to her home was quite the best thing that this brisk day in the great city had provided.

CHAPTER LXXXIX

The next morning, coming down at eleven as suggested and sitting about and checking up my own miserable item as suggested, I encountered my friend of the day before, who was here even before me, looking through the newspaper and checking up such results as he had been able to achieve. I had not realized it at the time but he was in exactly the same position as myself, a space man who had secured this chance via friendship, but who was plainly not thinking very well of it.

"Tst! Tst!" he clicked to himself as he went over the pages, looking high and low, and here and there checking a minute squib which he had managed to get in. "This is dreadful. Why, a man wouldn't pay himself out for shoe leather at this rate. It's terrible," and then looking around and seeing me near at hand, began to address me. "Positively, this is the worst paper in New York. I've always heard it was, and now I know it. This damn crowd here has a method of playing favorites. They have an inside ring, a few pets who get all the cream, and fellows like you and myself, who are as good as any of them, get the short ends. Take me yesterday. I was sent out on four lousy different little stories, not one of which amounted to anything. I tramped and rode all over town in the snow and listened to a lot of fools I wouldn't give a minute to, and this morning I have just three little items. Look at that—and that—and that—" and he pointed to check marks on different papers where he had marked a total of, say, seven or eight inches, the equivalent in cash of less than three dollars. "And I'm supposed to live on that," he went on, "—and I have a boy and a girl in school. How do they figure that a man like you or myself is to get along? What they do is to get men like you and me who are strangers here, or any of these down-and-out newspapermen who are always walking up and down Park Row looking for a job—the town is full of them—and get them to work on *space* because it sounds bigger to a greenhorn. Sure, they have space men here who amount to something, fellows who get big money—four or five of them, but they're not like us. They make as much as seventy-five and a hundred dollars a week, but they're rewrite men—old reporters who have too big a pull and who are too sure of themselves to stand for the low salaries they pay here. They have kicked and threatened to leave unless they are paid more, and so then they put 'em on space and throw 'em enough of such things as we dig up to keep 'em satisfied, and give us time instead.

"But they're at the top. We little fellows are told that stuff about space, but all we get is legwork. If you or I really did get hold of a good story by any chance, don't you ever think they'd let us write it, because they wouldn't. I know that much now. They'd take it away and give it to one of those rewrite fellows. There's one now," and he pointed to a large, comfortable person in a light brown overcoat and brown hat, who was but now ambling in. "He rewrote one of my stories the other day. If they really wanted you at all for regular work, they'd make you take the regular salary for fear you'd make too much out of space. I know. But even then they wouldn't pay you more than between twenty and thirty. They just keep us little fellows as extras to follow up such things as they hate to waste a good man on. Don't it beat the devil? I've heard it all now from a dozen boys around here, and besides they're always firing a big crowd of men every three or four months in order to keep up the zip of the staff, to keep 'em worried and working hard. So if you've worked hard to get a salaried place, and you get one, you'd go out anyhow in a few months unless you had a pull. But not the favorites at the top, not at all. I hate the damn business though, and I wish that I could get out of it. I told myself in Pittsburgh that I never would get back in it again, but here I am. Still I won't be here long. I'm not this kind of a man."

The revelation made me a little sick. I merely gazed at him. So this was my grand job, and this was how I would be served. A long period of drudgery for little or nothing, my hard-earned money exhausted—and then what?

"Just now," he went on, "there's nothing doing around the town, or I wouldn't be here. I'm staying on here until I can get something better, but you bet not any longer. It's a dog's life, though, I tell you. There's nothing in it. I worked here all last week, and what do you think I made? Twelve dollars and seventy-five cents for the whole week—time included. Twelve dollars and seventy-five cents! It's an outrage." He began to chuckle, though, as if it were a joke.

I agreed with this. I could see the force of it. "What is this 'time' they allow you?" I asked. "How do you figure—expenses and all?"

"Sure, they allow you expenses," he said, "and I'm going to figure mine more liberally from now on. It's only a little bonus they allow you for the time you work, and you don't get anything anyhow. I'll double any railroad fare I pay. If they don't like it, let them get somebody else. A part of that twelve dollars I made last week was made that way," and he chuckled again. "But they won't let you do too much of it, though. If you can't make a little salary on small stuff, they won't even keep you." He grinned.

I looked at him solemnly. "Your items didn't pan out very well, though, did they?"

"No; they never do. They don't give me enough to keep me alive. Anything big goes to the boys on a salary, and if it's real big, the space men who are on salary and space also get the cream. Did you see that big, heavy, lumbering fellow around here who wears the long light Newmarket coat and carries the gold-headed cane?"

"No, I only came here yesterday, as I told you."

"Well, you will. He's the star man. He gets the best of all the stories. He's supposed to be a word-slinger. I went out on a story the other afternoon and tramped around in the rain and got all the facts, and just as I was going to sit down and write it—well, I hadn't really got started—one of the managing editors (there are about fifteen of 'em around here) came up and took it away from me and gave it to him. All I got was my 'time.' Gee, but I was sore. Still, I don't mind," he added heavily. "I'll be getting out of here one of these days," and he chuckled his good-natured chuckle.

Having been handed this dose of fairly inspiring information, I was in no particular mood for what followed. But I decided that since he was an older man than myself and possibly not very efficient—I couldn't tell, of course—these series of ills which were now befalling him might be due to that, whereas in my case, being young, efficient, et cetera, the usual mental bonus youth hands itself, I should do better. At least I hoped so. But when it came to my assignments this day and the next and the next—and each night I was "handed" the late watch in addition—I went through experiences almost identically the same. Each day I was handed most unimportant or, if not that, improbable things—rumors and verification tales, which came to nothing. So keen was the competition between the papers—especially the *World,* the *Sun* and the *Herald*—that most everything suggested by one or the other was looked into and criticised if possible by the others. Thus the items assigned to me this second day were (1) to visit the city morgue and there look up the body of a supposedly young and especially beautiful girl who was supposed to have drowned herself or been drowned, and see if this was true, as another paper had said (and of course she was not beautiful at all); (2) to visit a certain hotel to see about a hotel beat who had contracted a bill of one hundred dollars which he could not pay and for which he had been arrested (this item, although written, was never used); (3) to visit a Unitarian conference somewhere, called to debate some supposed changes in faith or method of church development, the date for the assembling of which however had been changed without notice to the papers, and for which, as for the others, I was allowed "time" and carfare. My "time," setting aside as worthless the long and wearisome hours in which I sat in the office awaiting my turn to be assigned, netted me the wonderful sum of two dollars and fifty cents. I began to see wherein I had been wise in equipping myself with some cash before I came to New York. And all the time in this very paper, as I noticed one night, I could read the noblest and most elevating discourses anent duty, character, the need of a higher sense of citizenship, and what not. Thinking of these particular things in connection with this particular paper, I used to frown at the shabby pecksniffery of it—the cheap buncombe that would allow a great publisher to bleed and drive his employes at one end of his house and deliver exordiums as to virtue, duty, industry, thrift, honesty and what not at the other.

The sweet picture which life, and especially the enormously suc-cessful man or institution, so often presents!

However, despite these little setbacks and insights, I was not to be discouraged, at first anyhow. The fact that I had succeeded elsewhere and had been praised for my work made me feel sure that somehow, in some way, I would succeed here. Nevertheless, in spite of this sense of efficiency in so far as my particular line of work was concerned, I was most strangely and psychologically, as I subsequently saw, overawed and made more than ordinarily incompetent by the hugeness and force and seeming heartlessness of the great city, its startling contrasts of wealth and poverty. An air or feel of ruthlessness and indifference and disillusion was, for me at least, over it all. For only recently, as I should have pointed out (and full details of which had been published in our Midwestern papers), there had been a most amazing and disgusting exposure of the putrescence and heartlessness and brutality which underlay so much of the social structure of the city and which seemed all along to have been taken as a matter of course. There had been, for one thing, already, the Lexow Investigation with its sickening revela-tions of graft and corruption and the protection and encouragement of vice and crime in every walk of political and police life. The most horrible type of brothels had been proved to be not only winked at but preyed upon by the police and the politicians via a fixed and graded monthly tax, in which the patrolman, the "roundsman," the captain and the inspector—to say nothing of the district leader—shared. There was undeniable proof of the police and the politicians and even the officials of the city being closely connected with all sorts of gam-bling, wiretapping, bunko steering, and even the subornation of mur-der. To the door of every house of prostitution and transient rooming house the "station police captain's man" came as regularly as the rent or gas man, and took more. A book I read about this time, called *The Confessions of a Thief*, proved it. "Squealers" had been murdered in cold blood for their "squealing." A famous chief of police, one Byrnes by name, reputed at that time far and wide for his supposed skill in unraveling mysteries, was faced by a saturnalia of crime which he could not solve. Finally, in self-defense, he had caused to be arrested, tried, convicted and electrocuted—all upon suborned testimony, not a trace even of honest evidence—an old and helpless and half-witted bum known as Old Shakespeare, whose only crime was that he was worthless and defenceless. But the chief had thereby saved his "reputation." Not far from the region in which my sister lived, although it was respectable enough in its way, tramped countless girls by night and day, looking for men—the great business in New York—and all preyed upon by the police. On several occasions, coming home from my work on the *World* after midnight, I personally found a man lying hatless, coatless, his trousers pockets pulled out, his watch and money gone, possibly his skull fractured—I could not tell—so inadequate or indifferent or conniving was the so-called police protection. Broadway, from 14th to 39th as well as all its adjacent streets, as I had personally seen, was heavily and visibly sprinkled with streetwalkers who plied their trade. Nowhere before, as I now began to realize, had I seen such lavish show of wealth or, by way of contrast, such bitter poverty. In my reporting rounds I came swiftly upon the East Side; the Bowery, with its endless line of degraded and impossible lodging houses, a perfect whorl of bums and failures; the Brooklyn waterfront, parts of it terrible in its degradation; and then by way of contrast again the great hotels, the mansions along Fifth Avenue, the smart shops and clubs and churches. In this office, as I soon learned, were a number of newspaper men whom I had known in the West, but who, now having succeeded, or being by way of succeeding, met me with a very different air. New York seemed to have made them harder and colder. When I went on errands into Wall Street, the Tenderloin, the Fifth Avenue district, the East and West Sides, I seemed everywhere to sense either a terrifying desire for lust or pleasure or wealth, accompanied by a heartlessness which was freezing to the soul, or a dogged resignation to deprivation and misery which was discouraging to a degree. I never, anywhere, for instance, saw so many down-and-out men—in the parks, along the Bowery and in the lodging houses which lined that pathetic street—as I did this first winter, thousands of them. They slept over gratings anywhere from which came a little warm air, or in door- and cellarways free from the biting winds. In a half-dozen places in different parts of the city I soon discovered those strange charities which function to supply a man a free meal, a loaf of bread, or a lodging for the night, assuming that he will come at a given hour and wait long enough. In later years I "wrote a number of them up." At the same time, I had never seen anywhere so much show and downright luxury. It was astounding. Nearly all of the houses along upper Fifth Avenue and its side streets boasted their liveried footman in colored knee trousers, coats and stockings à la England. The carriages and coaches along Fifth Avenue and elsewhere (in the shopping district, for example) boasted their two and even three men on the box—two in front always, and occasionally one behind to run and open the door for milady, while the twain sat bolt upright, dignified and statuesque. Wall Street, as I began to sense very clearly, was a seething sea of financial trickery and legerdemain—a realm so crowded with shark-like geniuses of finance that one's poor little arithmetic intelligence was entirely discounted and made ridiculous. The average man could by no means confront these wizards or contend with them. They were like Bluebeards who could master and slay a thousand wives, or ogres who ate the labor and stores of little men. How was a snivelling scribbler such as myself to make his way in a world such as this? Nothing but chance and luck, as I saw it, could further the average man—or lift him out of his pathetic rut—and since when had it been proved, and where, that I was a favorite of fortune? A crushing sense of incompetence and general inefficiency seemed to settle upon me, and I could not shake it off. Whenever I went out on an assignment anywhere—and I was always being sent upon those trivial, shoe-wearing affairs—I carried with me this sense of my immense unimportance, fortified by what I had read in Spencer and what I saw here.

In addition to the swarms of people who seemed to be moving like huge streams of water in every direction by night and by day, one of the things which rather terrified me was this: the columns of this very paper on which I was daily working reeked daily with the most painful and revolting disclosures as to how the inmates of local insane asylums, hospitals and poor farms were even then not only being neglected but tortured and abused, beaten to death in some instances, and that by the kindly ministrations of paid employes of the city—or the henchmen of the reigning political organization rather—employed to care for them. Politicians of the grossest and most revolting types physically, as I myself by personal contact now saw—the worst of any I have ever seen anywhere—ruled in every precinct and district. The vilest of vile types—human hogs really, whose huge faces and gross mustaches invariably sickened me—ruled in police stations and nearly every public office. And the smug organs of the successful and comfortable ruling classes of the city defended them at every turn. One could read the most fulsome and flattering comments on their merits in the *Sun,* the *Tribune,* the *Herald* and the *Times.* The voters of the city, or their votes, in so far as I could make out, were either bought and paid for like so many cattle and delivered in blocks, or they were miscounted or thrown out, the ballot boxes being stuffed and the tally sheets destroyed. The Reverend Doctor Parkhurst, one of the fiercest of the passing Elijahs, who had helped to bring about a most ghastly exposure in connection with financed prostitution, had actually proved how women and girls were sold into vice, their clothes removed, themselves restrained and made to serve men at so much per visit or per minute— and although I was no boob-hunting reformer nor one inclined to sniff about the terrors of vice, these evidences of graft and brutality and vice run mad sickened me. Daily long reports from one committee and another taking testimony under oath and against the wills of those testifying, caused me to feel that Sodom and Gomorrah were pikers in the vice business—that the city in which I now was was a kind of hell or slough, or, better yet, a jungle in which the lowest forces of lust and cunning and greed and hate were allowed to work their will, and that almost without let or hindrance.

CHAPTER XC

Now it is entirely possible that due to some physical or mental defect of my own, I was in no way fitted to contemplate so huge and ruthless a spectacle as New York then presented. And aside from what I saw and the verified testimony of the various committees, I am willing to accept this possibility as true. The crystal sphere looks different to each one. Yet in line with my work as a newspaper man I saw much, and, by way of verification from those with whom I worked, I heard much more.

After a few days of the kind of work I have described, I was already in touch with several newspaper men from the West—a youth by the name of Graves, another by the name of Elliott, both formerly of Chicago, and a third individual who had once been in St. Louis, Wynne Thomas, the brother of the famous playwright, Augustus Thomas. All were working on this paper, two of them in the same capacity as myself, the third a staff man. At night we used to sit about together between eleven-thirty or twelve and three in the morning, doing the late watch and spinning all sorts of newspaper tales.

Like myself, all of these men had wandered here and there. They had seen—heavens, what had they not seen! They were completely disillusioned. Here then, as in all newspaper offices everywhere and from such men as these, one could hear the most disconcerting tales about human cruelty, depravity and what not else. I think that in the several hours I spent with these each night (although I did not always have the late watch), I learned as much about New York and its difficulties and opportunities, as well as its different social strata, its most outstanding figures, socially, politically and otherwise, as I might have in months of reporting and reading. They seemed to know nearly everyone likely to figure in the public eye—the mayor and the city's principal officeholders, the police captains and chiefs, the big men in Wall Street, society, the sporting, the theatrical and religious worlds. From time to time nearly all of these seemed to figure in the talk of stories done—old difficulties and assignments overcome and written up. By degrees they introduced me to others, and all confirmed the conclusions which by degrees I was reaching. New York was a difficult and at present revolting realm. The police and politicians were really a menace. Vice was at the topmost toss of its career. Wealth was shamelessly showy, cold, and brutal in its coldness. In New York the outsider or beginner had scarcely any chance at all, save as a servant. The city was overrun with hungry, loafing men of all descriptions, newspaper writers included. Here on the *World*, as well as on the *Sun* and elsewhere, men such as myself, with no particular pull, were used to do the fag work on the big papers for the benefit of those who had to be permitted to earn large salaries.

After a few weeks of experimenting, however, I had no need of confirmation from any source. An assignment or two having developed well under my handling, and I having reported my success to the city editor, I was only allowed to begin to write my story, after which, once I had gotten part of the introduction done or the first fourth or third of it done, I was called off, given another assignment and told to turn my story over to the large gentleman with the gold-headed cane. This not only infuriated me but it discouraged me, yet I said nothing for I wished to retain my place. I thought it might be due to the city editor's conviction—so far not disturbed by any opportunity that I had had— that I could not write.

However, one night, not so long after that, a small item about a fight in a tenement house having been given me to investigate, I went to the place in question and found nothing beyond the fact that it was a cheap beer-drinking brawl on the upper East Side which had its origin in the objection of one wretched neighbor to the noise made by another. I constructed a ridiculous story of my own to the effect that the first irritated neighbor was a musician who had been attempting at the midnight hour to construct a waltz, into which the snores, gurgles, moans and gasps of his slumberous next-door neighbor would not fit. Becoming irritated and being unable by calls and hammering and knocking to arouse his slumberous friend (or so I described him), or to bring him to silence, I had him finally resort to piano-banging and glass-breaking of such a terrible character as to arouse the entire neighborhood and cause the sending in of a riot call by a policeman, who thought that a tenement war had broken out. Result (so the story ran): broken heads and an interesting midnight parade to the nearest police station.

Somewhere in the text I used the phrase "sawing somnolent wood." Finding no one in charge of the city editor's desk when I returned, I handed the item to the night city editor. The next morning, lo and behold, and to my great astonishment and satisfaction, there it was on the first page and consuming at least a fourth of a column. I was delighted and measured it most carefully, and although the whole item was worth only two dollars or thereabouts, still I was on the first page at last. And then, to my further surprise and gratification, once the city editor appeared, I noticed a change of attitude in him as regards myself. Betimes, between twelve and one, waiting for an assignment, I caught his eye examining me, and finally he came over, paper in hand, and pointing to the item said, "You wrote this, didn't you?" I began to think that I might have made a mistake in creating this bit of news and that it had been investigated and found to be a fiction. "Yes," I replied. Instead of berating me, as I half feared he might, he smiled most agreeably, a repressed, nervous, jerky smile, and said, "Well, it's rather well done. I may be able to make a place for you after all, after a while. I'll see if I can't find an interesting story for you somewhere."

And true to his word, that very day or the next, he selected a type of story that was on this order. In the Hoffman House bar (as I saw by the next item he handed me), one of the garish showplaces of the city, then at Broadway and 25th Street, there had been staged the day before quite a brawl, a fight between a well-known society youth of great wealth who owed the hotel money and would not pay as speedily as it wished, and a manager or an assistant manager who had sent him some form of disturbing letter. All the details, as I discovered on reading the item, which had been clipped from the *Herald*, had been fully covered by that paper. And what was more, all that remained for me, twenty-four hours later, was to visit these same principals already discussed and extract some humorous side comments or additions to the tale, which plainly I was expected to revamp in some humorous fashion.

Now as I have said, humor has never been specifically in my line. I have achieved it largely in passing, as it were, and without paying it the close attention which no doubt it deserves. In addition I had by no means overcome my awe of the city and its imposing and much advertised "Four Hundred." As a matter of fact, now that I was really here and working, my awe was hourly growing instead of lessening. In connection with the city as a whole, its wealth and power and indifference, I saw myself as the most trivial and most unimportant of beings. And now to be called upon to invade one of its principal hostelries, one of the gayest and most exclusive of them all, and beard the irate and lofty manager in his den, to say nothing of the sprig or species Vanderbilt or Goelet—well——. In addition, viewing my present work as a reporter and noting the wretched type of items I was once more being called upon to investigate—and this after I had only recently concluded that I was now above this sort of thing and called upon by genius to do semiliterary or feature stuff or better—well, I suffered a great revulsion of feeling.

How was it, I now asked myself, after nearly three years of work in which I had been a reporter, a travelling correspondent, a dramatic editor, and a staff feature man doing Sunday and daily features, I should now once more be called upon to do this wretched reportorial stuff?

Why couldn't I be singled out for what I was and given a chance. This wretched grind of following up these trivial facts seemed too demeaning and cheap. I was as good as any of the hotel managers and society men, only my day had not come. Even so, there must be a better way for me somewhere. No doubt when I reached this particular hotel, the manager would take a very lofty tone and refuse to discuss the matter—which was exactly what happened. He was infuriated to think he had already been reported as fighting. Similarly, should I succeed in coming in touch with the society youth, I would probably be snubbed or shunted off in some cavalier fashion—which was exactly what happened. I was not able to come in touch with the latter.

Besides, it was raw and grey and sloppy underfoot. I visited the hotel and a bachelor suite in 58th Street, only to be told that my Mr. X was not there. Then, as a conscientious newspaper man, I knew I should return to the hotel and, via cajolery or bribery, see if I could not induce some barkeeper or waiter who perchance had witnessed it all to describe some angle of it which I might use, or to create some new phases of it out of whole cloth. That Accuracy, Accuracy, Accuracy stuff did not apply, I was sure. In fact I had been told so by others and shown how and where. But on the other hand, I was now in no mood for this kind of fakery, and besides I was afraid of these New York waiters and managers and society people generally. Suppose they complained of my tale and denounced me as a faker—then what? To get something really worthwhile, if I could, I returned to the hotel, only its onyx lobby and bar and its heavy rococo decorations and furniture overawed me and took my courage away. I lingered about but could not begin my inquiries and finally walked out. Then I went back to the apartment house in which my youth lived, but still he was not in and I could extract no news from the noble footman who kept the door, and I did not see how I could conjure up humor from the facts in hand, not knowing the principals. Finally, after turning it over in many ways in my mind, I dropped it as unworthy of me and returned to the office. In doing so I had the feeling that I was turning down or aside an item by which, had I chosen to fake, I could have furthered myself greatly. By now I was really sure that what my city editor wanted was not merely drab "accuracy" but a kind of flair for the ridiculous or the remarkable, even though it might have to be invented, in order that the pages of the paper—and life itself—might not seem so dull. Also I realized that a more experienced man, one used to the ways of the city and acquainted with its interesting and eccentric personalities, might make something out of this and not come to grief. But not I. And so I let it go, realizing as I did so that I was losing an excellent opportunity.

And I think my city editor thought so too. For on my returning and saying that I could not connect with anything interestingly new in connection with this, he looked at me as much as to say, "Well, I'll be damned!" and threw the clipping upon his desk. I am satisfied that if any reporter that day had succeeded in uncovering any least aspect of this case not previously used, I would have forthwith been deprived of even this minute connection to the paper which I now had.

As it turned out, however, nothing new was developed, and for a little while anyhow I was permitted to drag on as before, but with no further favors, rather the contrary.

Yet one day, being given a part of a "badger" case to unravel—a man and woman working together to divest a hotel man of a check for five thousand dollars, and which same they had succeeded in doing—and I having succeeded in persuading the lady in the case, then under arrest, to make some interesting remarks upon her part in the affair and badgering in general, I was not allowed to write this but had to content myself with seeing my very excellent yarn incorporated in another man's story while I took "time," fifty cents an hour—a thing which I blamed upon my previous failure in the hotel case. And another day, having developed another excellent tale of a runaway marriage in connection with the daughter of a family of some standing, I was not allowed to write that. I was beginning to see that I was a hopeless failure as a reporter here.

And then in regard to my sister's affairs, things were developing in so untoward a way that I could not see how I was to endure for long without a sensible increase in my income. Having been here now a number of weeks and during that time having "drawn down," as the newspaper phrase had it, such remarkable sums as eleven, fifteen, thirteen dollars and the like for a week's work, I was inducted by her into the true state of her affairs. She was, as she now told me, without cash or resources of any kind, her only income being the rent from two roomers—a total yield of eight dollars a week. Christmas had come and gone, and there had been, as I knew, little or nothing for herself or the children. In addition, and worst of all, her husband having by now by his connection with the old Tammany regime and its vile political methods thoroughly degenerated himself, he was now suggesting to her not only to borrow anything that I might have but also that she, or they rather, let rooms to "transients," a word which at that time spelled but one thing: those who desired a room for an hour or two for immoral purposes. His excuse was, aside from their wretched situation and need, that vice was still most flourishing and highly protected for cash, and that he knew the captain of this particular district or police station—a friend of his—and so could arrange with him for protection; that is, by paying fifty dollars a month they would be let alone. Also that the city was then thick with such institutions, all profitable, and all of them paying tribute to the police or otherwise being raided, and that hence it was no disgrace. Also that times were hard and would not soon be better. Also that the police, via cabmen and patrolmen, would be willing to direct inquiring customers to their apartment—as they were now doing to others. I do not quite recall now how wretched all this may have seemed to my sister, but I know that she cried.

As for my part, the thing that most shocked me about this at the time was not that other people should indulge in adultery and conveniences of this character—that seemed well enough, a part of the natural drift and freedom and joy of life—or that other people should pander to or make use of such conveniences (I had rented such rooms myself). What shocked me was that this man (who, although married to my sister and the father of her children, seemed somehow alien to me, an interloper really, and one who did not care for her) should still look upon her and his children, and by inference myself as a relative, with so little respect as to be willing that she should do this. I cannot quite straighten out the logic of it for you. I am merely stating the facts. Unaware of or indifferent to the incongruity inherent in my attitude toward morals in general and morals in so particular a case as this (the element of self-preservation, which really is the basis of self-respect, having entered into this), I now, as usual, pushed all finespun theories as to right and wrong to one side and denounced him roundly. He was a this, a that and the other thing. He should be forthwith pitched out in the snow and made to go to work for himself if not for her. How could she tolerate him? How did he dare make a suggestion like that to her, with his own children here in their rooms with him? The thing had a most sickening look to me.

And yet my sister, as troubled as she was, was by no means as rampant as I was. After all, he was her husband and these were his children as much as they were hers. Besides, as she now repeatedly told me, she had been crazy about him once—absolutely insane, as she phrased it—so much so that, as she now recalled it and thought of what I proposed, she cried. So one may see how difficult it is to unravel these pathetic entanglements.

And in addition there was the matter of these children of whom he was the father and from whom he might not be utterly separated, as bad as he was. They were a pretty pair, and at times he appeared to be fond of them, taking them for walks and disporting himself in a most fatherly manner. And again, and regardless of whatever wretched things he had done in the past—she would never confess as to this—he seemed to deserve some consideration if not sympathy on this score. "You know," she once said to me with wet eyes, having only previously berated him most fiercely, "little George looks like him, and I love him so." In the face of such a chemic entanglement as this, what would you? And there was the fact that they had been together the usual ten years—association and time being such a cementing if not ultimately binding thing.

In the next place also, I think she half blamed herself for the original flirtation which had brought all this about—that chemic, thoughtless and uncalculated thing, on both sides perhaps, which had caused him to desert his wife and children. Those other children had been full-grown when she came into his life, to be sure, and as usual he had complained that he was wrongly mated and that his wife was this, that and the other, but still she had done that—and now the whole thing had come to this wretched end. She was wretchedly unhappy— terribly so; and because of this and the futility and ugliness of his point of view, it was now absolutely necessary for her to devise some way to get rid of him and yet, in addition, to give him just a little time at least in which perhaps he might be able to find at least a place for himself and she a place for herself since she could not keep this place, it being too large. In consequence there was nothing for me to do save to shoulder the current expenses, temporarily at least. There was then the rent, forty dollars, reasonably high at that time, and food and some incidentals, by the shouldering of which I saw much over one hundred of my hard-earned savings going in a lump.

And then, once this matter was adjusted and in spite of her attempt to conceal it, which could not be done, Hopkins, seeing that an immediate crisis had been tided over, seemed to think that all that was needed now was for my sister to undertake his wretched scheme. At any rate he did nothing, and my sister, meditating on I scarcely know what, took her time, or at least she seemed to look upon the whole thing as a very difficult thing to undertake. She was actually afraid of the man—what he might do to her or the children—and delayed on this account, until finally in desperation I proposed that she lie to him about it. According to my proposition, it was best to say that I had decided that I could not succeed in New York and was going back to Pittsburgh, which was somewhat nearer a truth than falsehood at that, and that I had no more money to contribute, which was reasonably true. Secondly, since he could not make a living for her here—and I could there—that she was going with me as soon as I could arrange for her to come, which was to be immediately. And, thirdly, supposing he would permit, she was to take the furniture because she was assuming the care of the children. Fourthly, we were then to secure an apartment somewhere, near or far (there were some in the immediate vicinity, as I saw), and instead of our leaving the city we were to move all into this new place—a deal with the moving van company which was to move the things being considered all that was necessary to succeed with this lie.

The only thing, however, as both of us saw, which would persuade him to this was for her to refuse to accept his transient scheme, threatening by way of defense to tell me; and secondly for me to move out, cut off all means of support, leaving her only enough cash to feed herself and the children until such time as he would see that there was nothing more to do. Then, the rent falling due and the furniture being in danger of being set in the street, Hopkins would no doubt accept her terms. She was the more sure of this because, as she said, she knew he was infinitely weary of her and the burden, and this was an easy way out. Besides, supposing he wished to dispute the matter of furniture or the children, he would either have to arrange for storage or take a new place, and she felt sure he would not wish to do either. Which was as it was. He still, as she insisted, had some slight regard for his children, and since I was offering a refuge to them, he would certainly permit her to keep the furniture—that being the only condition, she was going to say, on which I would aid her as I had no money to buy more. Once rid of him she was going to forget him entirely, rent rooms to support herself, and so hide away and never communicate with him in any fashion.

As a matter of fact, aside from the loss of time and money to me and the assumption of an almost impossible financial load and worry, which subsequently I was unable to continue but which Paul assumed for a time, the thing worked out well enough. In order to give the whole thing a great air of similitude, immediately after the first of February I began to pull a very sad face, as easily I might, and to say that since things were going so badly with me I had decided that I must soon cease my efforts here and return whence I had come. At once I noticed that this had a very depressing effect on him. Again, when next he urged my sister to borrow of me, she returned to him with the tale that I had refused—that I could not do it since I did not see my way clear myself. Next I actually secured a room in East 4th Street, east of the Bowery, on the East Side (about which more anon), and, having made her and him a most stagey and formal farewell, departed, having agreed with her beforehand on certain meetings by which we were to adjust our difficulties. Then via a friend in Pittsburgh—one of the reporters on the *Dispatch*—I had a letter mailed to her in which I said that I had reinstated myself and that, if she wished to come and bring the children and the furniture, et cetera—especially the *furniture*—I would be glad, et cetera, but that I could only agree to assist her and the children for a time. Following this there was nothing to do save wait and meet occasionally, as we did in a restaurant in 14th Street, to hear how things were working out.

Finding her unwilling to enter on his scheme, as he now did, and he being weary of her anyhow and the great load under which he felt himself to be, he must have decided that, after all, my proposition was the best, for he first decided that he would seek work. Then finding his search unavailing and the first of the month with its rent bill drawing near, he decided that it was best for her to depart. Fortunately, since it avoided complications in connection with packing and shipping, he secured a temporary job in connection with a hotel in Brooklyn, which left him no time to aid. She told him that per my advice she was turning over the furniture to a moving and storage company for packing and shipping, which was true. One afternoon when he was at work the goods were then transferred to a small apartment in 17th Street, west of Seventh Avenue, and there for several years my sister lived. Because he was working and could not conveniently get away, on the day that she left she made a stage appearance at his hotel, taking the children to say farewell. What transpired at that meeting I have often wondered. On more than one occasion, explaining his sudden elimination from her life, she declared that he really did not care for her or the children. Whether she ever saw him afterwards I do not know. I know I never saw him but once after, a most washed-out and deteriorated-looking person, and then he did not see me. A few years later, as she learned, he died—still working for the same hotel. Without her communicating to him he could not have found her, for we were at great pains with the van company to arrange for secrecy, and I do not believe he ever did. At any rate, there I was then with my sister and her two children on my hands and a most unprofitable newspaper job. And so I continued my by now rather dubious newspaper career. My only consolation was that I had rescued her from a most wretched and impossible existence, and I think I did.

CHAPTER XCI

The things which principally contributed to my want of newspaper success in New York and so eventually drove me, though much against my will and understanding, into an easier and more agreeable phase of life were, first, that awe of those grinding and almost disgusting forces of life itself discovered in Spencer and Huxley and Balzac, which now persistently haunted me and, possibly due to a depressed physical condition at this time, made it impossible for me, for the time being at least, to work with much of the zest that had characterized my work in the West. Next, there was that astonishing contrast between wealth and poverty, here more sharply emphasized than anywhere else in America and now most persistently noted, which gave the great city, at least to me at this time, a gross and cruel and mechanical look; and this same was emphasized not only by the papers themselves, with their various summaries of investigations and exposures, but also by my own hourly contact with it—a look so harsh and indifferent at times that it left me a little numb. Next, there was something so disgusting and disillusioning in the sharp contrast (daily noted by me) between the professed ideals and preachments of such a constantly moralizing journal as the *World* and the heartless and savage aspect of its internal economy. There one might live or die on a meagre salary or none—it was nothing to the management so long as its editorial and journalistic or financial ends or aims were served or accomplished. Men such as myself were mere machines or privates in an ill-paid army to be thrown into any breach. The hours of service exacted were appalling. There was no time off for the space men, unless it was for all time. You were plainly expected to achieve the results requested or get out; and if you did achieve them the reward was nothing anyhow, at least in my case. There was that atmosphere of stress and peril previously noted, and never for a moment relaxed. One day, meeting an acquaintance on another newspaper and asking after an ex-city editor out of St. Louis who had come to New York but whom previously I had worked for, he said: "Oh, Cliff? Didn't you hear? Why, he committed suicide, killed himself down here in a West Street hotel."

"What was the trouble?" I asked, rather depressed by the bad news, for I had known of him as a brisk and rather determined fellow.

"Tired of the game, I guess," he replied rather airily. "Cliff always was a little pessimistic, you know. He didn't get along as well down here as he had out there. I guess he felt he was going downhill."

I walked away, meditating on that, for I had known the man well. He was an excellent newspaper man, as good as any, and as brisk and self-centered as one need be to prosper. The last time I had seen him he was in good physical condition, or so he seemed to me, yet here, after something like a year in New York, he had blown out his brains. And there was that other newspaper man of Pittsburgh, the there-successful political reporter who had confessed to me that New York was too much for him and had gone back there because he could be sure of a living wage there, whereas here he could not.

However, my mood was not that of one who runs away from a gruelling contest. I had no least notion of so doing or of leaving New York, whatever happened, although I constantly speculated as to what would be the nature of my state and my movements once all my money should be gone. I have already outlined my thoughts concerning myself as a writer, and I had no trade, or profession, other than this. Still, looking at this work and at life in general, I was convinced that there must be something else that I could do—only what was it? Come what may, I was determined that I would ask no least favor of my brother; and as for my sister, who was now a burden on my hands (but not wholly so, since, having moved, she had been successful in subletting a portion of her apartment), I was determined that as soon as the burden became too great I would take up her case with Paul, outline all that had been done and ask him to shoulder the difference until such time as I could find myself in whatever work I was destined to do.

But what was it?

One of the things which oppressed me as much as anything at this time was the fact that on this very paper (as well as upon some of the others, as by now certain chance contacts with them had illustrated to me) was a group of men as young as myself who were apparently of a very different texture, mentally if not physically. Life and this fierce contest which I was taking so much to heart seemed in nowise to disturb them. By reason of temperament and insight apparently, or possibly the lack of it (to me they represented as much a lack of insight as anything else), or, what was more likely, certain fortunate circumstances which attended their youth and upbringing, they were part and parcel of that already oncoming host of professional optimists and yea-sayers, chorus-like in character, which for thirty years or more thereafter, in American life at least, was constantly engaged in the pleasing task of joyfully emphasizing the possibilities of success, progress, strength and what not for all in America and elsewhere. At the same time they were humbly and rather sycophantically genuflecting before the strong and the lucky, or at least the prosperous in every field. You perhaps know the type I mean.

There is a species of mind which is apparently sealed to the misery of others and fixed solely and narcissistically upon itself. Such brains or temperaments can only view and grasp their own or similar merits and perfections, and, in consequence, what life is likely to do for them. They can no more visualize the circumstances and conditions which delay and betray and beleaguer another than they can interpret time or space. Little if anything of the grilling forces of nature—its harrying storms, inequalities, traps, lures, deprivations and congenital defects, which delay or destroy the millions via whose defects such brains or temperaments prosper—is ever or even vaguely comprehended by them. To the eyes and the minds of such mannikins the fate of every individual is in his own hands. All one need do to be successful, attractive, powerful and so admired, is to try, to bestir oneself, to gallop here and there, willing that this, that and the other thing shall be, in order that it shall be. The unbelievable handicaps and weights which delay and finally mire the many in the slough of despond or worse are to these unknown. Coming into the world reasonably well-equipped mentally and physically, via the fortune of chemistry and birth, blessed, say, with a healthy and so non-troubling body, some little gift of face or form or skill, these same never see themselves as startling exceptions to the unfortunate whose lacks betray them at every step and turn, but rather as excellent illustrations of all that the mass might do and be and achieve if but it wills. To them the less successful individual is never so by reason of conditions over which he has not and never can have control, but rather by reason of defects which he himself wilfully incurs—ignorance, weakness, dirt, a shabby mind and a cowardly heart—and by reason of which, and the non-willingness on his part to overcome these same, he fails. All men are victims of their own idleness, sins and the like. They court failure and eschew success, while the strong and the handsome and the debonair and the magnetic themselves make all the virtues and qualities which further them so rapidly. The asininity of it is of course enough to make an observer of even ordinary intelligence smile, but so it is. Such people are most happily insulated against the depressing effect of the woes of others. Your bark may be sinking, but your cries will never disturb their moonlight ditties as they drift before a favoring wind past the scene of your despair. All is well with life and all men, though you may die before them. There is a merciful God, and He is love of course; He tempers the wind to every shorn lamb—or, if He does not, it does not make so very much difference after all: the lamb was not worthy of the wind perhaps. At the same time, the poor are disgraceful, reprehensible, worthless, et cetera. This catalogue of impossible paradoxes might be extended indefinitely.

And of this type, in the newspaper profession of all places, and in New York at this time, I perceived not a few—healthy, ruddy, swaggering souls of the James K. Hackett–Richard Harding Davis–Mrs. Humphry Ward school of literature and art. On the *World* alone at this time, to say nothing of the other papers about which now I knew a great deal, were at least a dozen, swaggering about in the best of clothes, their manners those of the graduate of Yale or Harvard or Princeton, their minds stuffed with all the noble maxims of the uplifters. There was nothing wrong with the world which could not be easily and quickly righted, once the honest, just, true, kind, industrious, et cetera, turned their giant and selected brains to the task. This newest type of young newspaper man was to have no traffic with evil in any form. He was to concern himself with the good, the true and the beautiful. Coming in most instances from families of means, and themselves equipped with a modicum of cash, they were by no means compelled to counter the rudest facts of life. But seeing them about and hearing them talk and at the same time draw, even here, an exclusive social line made me a little weary. They but served to emphasize what I was already compelled to think of the rest of life.

Again, nationally, as I later perceived, we were already launched upon an era of Anglo-idolatry, which had resulted in creased pants carefully turned up at the bottom, light tan coats with pearl buttons in winter, the brown or pearl-gray spat, the carefully selected cane, the light tan derby set back high on the forehead—and you would have seen as much of it here among these place-seeking youths as anywhere. And so many of them boasted such an intimate working knowledge of so many things—society, politics, finance and what not else. There were several men here who had evidently made themselves indispens- able as ship reporters—interviewers of arriving and departing celebri- ties on the outgoing and incoming liners, as well as trains—and these were now pointed out to me as men worthy of envy and no doubt emulation. One of these who was most enviously called to my attention by someone had, at the behest of the *World*, crossed the ocean more than once between New York and England, seeking to expose the principals in a growing ship-gambling and bunko scandal. He was of the type described. Then there were those who were in the confidence of the mayor, of the governor and some of the lights in Wall Street. One of these, a scion of one of the best families, was the paper's best adviser as to social events and scandals of all kinds. The grand air with which at times they swung in and out of the office quite set me beside myself with envy.

But aside from observing these and the various personalities of all sorts who seemed to come and go here—actors, prizefighters, wrestlers,

656 • NEWSPAPER DAYS

writers of plays and songs—I was permitted to hear the most startling tales in connection with the so-called "bloods" of society, the young heirs to fortunes of incalculable size, and their mistresses and playthings of the stage and the less well-financed walks of life generally. It was all very well to read in your morning paper of the fruits of industry and sobriety and the rewards of virtue, et cetera, but when one sat in the reportorial section of the same journal and listened daily (or, rather, nightly), as I did, to tales of gay suppers and affairs at Sherry's, Delmonico's, the Hoffman House and elsewhere, to say nothing of cruises and wild trips to Europe and the like, the weight of said moral advice, to say nothing of the papers' and the world's entire example, grew a little light. In addition, the condition of my personal affairs tended to make me anything but optimistic. I saw a very serious financial difficulty slowly but surely stalking toward me. I sometimes think that I was entirely too new to the city—too green to its psychology and subtlety to be of any use to a great metropolitan daily. And yet, seeing all that I had seen and then knew, I should not have been. I was only five years distant from the composition of *Sister Carrie*, to say nothing of many short stories and magazine articles before that.

CHAPTER XCII

Yet, drudging along as I was at the most inconsequential of tasks, and unable since my first fluke to cause my city editor or any other to take the slightest interest in me, I was haunted by the thought that in reality I was a misfit, that like the lie put forward by myself and my sister I might really have to give up and return to the West, where in some pathetic humdrum task I would eke out a barren and pointless life. And, in view of this probable end or result, I now began to think that I must not do that but must instead turn to letters, the art of short-story writing, only just how I was to do this I could not see. I had never written one in my life and did not really believe that I could learn how. Yet one of the things that prompted me to this was the fact that on this very paper at this time, or so I understood, were several who had succeeded in that or in allied fields—David Graham Phillips, for one, and James Creelman, then a correspondent for the paper at the war which had broken out between China and Japan, to say nothing of George Cary Eggleston and Reginald De Koven, the latter on the staff as chief musical critic. There was another young man, whose name I have forgotten, who was pointed out to me by my stout friend from Pittsburgh and who was said to be a rapidly growing favorite in the office of the *Century*. Then there were those new arrivals in the world of letters: Kipling, Richard Harding Davis, Stephen Crane and some others, whose success if not work always fascinated me.

All this was but an irritant to a bubbling chemistry which as yet had found no solution and was not likely to find one for some time to come. My reading of Spencer and Huxley, to say nothing of Balzac, in nowise tended to clarify and impel my mind in the direction of fiction, or even philosophy; quite the contrary. The result, if anything, was to confuse rather than clarify. And now, as in a kind of ferment or fever, due to my necessities and my desperation, I set to examining the various current magazines and the fiction and articles to be found therein (*Century, Scribner's, Harper's*). I was more than ever confounded by the wide discrepancy existing between my own observations and those displayed here, the beauty and peace and charm and delight found in everything written about by every one else, the almost complete absence of any reference to the coarse and the vulgar and the cruel and the terrible, which somehow seemed as much if not more a part of the visible scene to me than the other. How did it come that these most remarkable persons, geniuses of course one and all, as I took them to be (and this is not written in any mocking or cynical vein), saw life in this happy and even roseate way? Was it so, and was I all wrong? Love was almost invariably rewarded in these tales, as any one could read. Almost invariably one's dreams came true—in the magazines. Most of these bits of fiction, delicately phrased and colorfully spun, flowed so easily, with such an air of assurance, omniscience and super-condescension, that I was quite put out by my own lacks and defects. How could one as dumb as myself ever hope to write? In the main they seemed to deal with phases of sweetness and beauty and success and goodness such as I rarely if ever encountered anywhere. There were so many tales of the old South, as I had already seen, reeking with a poetry which was poetry and little more (George W. Cable; Thomas Nelson Page). In *Harper's* I found such assured writers as William Dean Howells, Charles Dudley Warner, Frank R. Stockton, Mrs. Humphry Ward and a score of others, all of whom wrote of nobility of character and sacrifice and greatness of ideals and joy in simple things.

But personally, as I viewed the strenuous world about me, all of this that I read seemed not to have so very much to do with it. Perhaps, as I now thought, life such as I saw, these darker current phases, was never to be written about by any one. Maybe such things were not the true province of fiction anyhow. Certainly life as portrayed in these tales was in nowise like that about me. I had only to recount my daily newspaper experiences to myself to know this. I read and read these tales, all of which seemed of a firmament far above the world of which I was a part, but all I could gather was that I had no such tales to tell and, however much I tried, could not even think of any. Indeed, I began to picture these writers to myself, one and all, as creatures of the greatest luxury and refinement, gentlemen and ladies all, most carefully nurtured, most artistically and comfortably housed, masters of servants, possessing estates, or bachelor quarters at least, having horses and carriages, entree to the best homes, and being received here, there and everywhere with nods of recognition and smiles of approval. They were gentlemen and ladies of ease and leisure, and this in the face of the gruelling contests which everywhere I saw life presenting under my very eyes. The tales which they recited were of an artistry which I, as I felt, was scarcely able to comprehend, let alone imitate. And I had read Balzac and Spencer!

And so, nonplussed by all this, and quite unable to take myself in hand, I drifted, by no means knowing where I was to wind up. Once I had my sister on my hands, the difficulties of my situation had increased, of course, and to ease matters (but only after a considerable time had elapsed and I was confronting a crisis in my own affairs) I wrote my brother a full account of all that had happened and asked his advice and support. To this he replied by saying that as soon as he returned to New York he would be glad to live with us and contribute his share, meanwhile sending the rent for a month or two. Before this I had all but worn out my welcome at the *World,* not being able to adjust myself apparently to the needs by which they were confronted. The East Side, for instance, once furnishing me a most excellent opportunity which I might have improved had I been in a different mental state, I allowed it to slip through my fingers. It was like this: returning one evening to the office I was handed a clipping relative to a proposed East Side janitors' meeting, called by some one who wished to improve the condition of East Side janitors. Now, I submit that, from any point of view, the idea was novel and capable of a semi-serious, semi-ridiculous treatment which would have fixed me in the esteem of my superiors. And I was capable of so treating it. But although I attended the meeting and noted all its peculiarities (as astounding a group of creatures as I have ever seen, one which haunts me even to this day), instead of being able to take hold of it with any degree of lightness I could only see it as an illustration of the crass and accidental creative power of life which thrusts into the social organism willy-nilly so large a number of the botched and the ignorant and savage to struggle and fight and do horrible things as best they might, undisturbed or un-moved by the niceties or pains which would flavor or deter a more delicately adjusted organism. I might have written this, I presume, only, under the circumstances, the paper would not have printed it. But it might have served to call attention to me, anyhow. Yet all that I did or could do was to gather the bare details as to the meaning of this meeting and report them. Fortunately once more, no other paper chanced to light upon the find or treat it cleverly, and so I was safe.

And then after a little while, being assigned to do routine work in connection with the East 27th Street police station, Bellevue Hospital, and the New York Charities Department, which included branches which looked after the poor farm, the morgue, an insane asylum or two, a workhouse and what not else, I was called upon daily to face as disagreeable and depressing a series of scenes as it is possible for a single human being to witness. Instead of it now being possible for me to come across interesting and possibly amusing things of a lighter character which would have served to fix me in the minds of my superiors as a clever gatherer of news, I was compelled, say, to inquire of a fat, red-faced sergeant who reigned in the police station in East 27th Street what if anything was new, and, by being as genial and agreeable as possible and so earning his favor, to obtain an occasional tip as to the most unimportant of brawls. Yet even so, had I been in a different state mentally, the thickness and incommunicability of this individual would not have been proof against my arts. I could have devised or manufactured something.

As it was, there was one scene with which he was connected which, had I been able to write it up as it occurred, would have reestablished me in favor, I am sure. It was like this:

There was a little, drunken, roystering Irish genius by the name of Mickey Finn, red-headed, witty, cynical, contemptuous, who never appeared to have a dollar or any gift for writing or any particular interest in or loyalty to any paper, or anything else indeed. Yet he was still about every day, afternoons and evenings, working for one and another newspaper, as I heard, and being fired and re-hired as regularly as, say, once in four or five or six weeks by any one of the dozen metropolitan papers. He knew all of the metropolitan papers and their editors and city editors, by name apparently, and cared not a snap of his fingers for any of them. His chief idea, of course, was to make a living of sorts from day to day and without much regard for the future; and to this end he seemed to curry favor with all and sundry, busying himself with meetings and card games and arguments in saloons and restaurants, especially such of the latter as were of a bohemian character and where clever people gathered and before whom he might shine with his wit and geniality and lies. He seemed to know, by name at least, and greet as familiarly as possible, as many notables or persons in various political and trade walks as one individual could possibly remember.

"Ah, there ye are, Garge,"—this perhaps to some whiskerando of the police or fire or corrections department, as solemn and self-important as an owl, who might chance to pass him anywhere and whom, if Finn saw, he immediately hailed, rushing forward and grabbing him by the hand as though he had not seen him for years and was most eager to renew this long-deprived privilege. "Where are ye bound to now? I was just comin' over to your place. What's news? Anything doin' at aal? News is very slack with us now. We have to be lookin' into everything. Ye haven't a cigar about ye, I suppose?"

Whereupon the whiskerando would pause and stare, dubious as to whether or not he was in the presence of some reporter of real significance or some one he knew well but had forgotten, and anxious not to make a mistake lest he offend the emissary of some great paper who might be of service to or injure him in some way at some time in the future. And so, willing to make the sacrifice of a moment's time and a cigar, I suppose, would pause and, pretending an interest he did not feel and a memory for Finn which he did not have, would ask cautiously what paper he was now representing and how long it had been since he had left the last one, and then would convey as gracefully as possible the mulcted cigar and such information or lack of it as he was willing to acknowledge. But that he was ever glad to see this audacious rogue again I doubt. Finn, I am satisfied, invariably counted upon the element of surprise which his sudden descent in this manner provided, the poorness of the memories of most of them whom he so assailed; for although he looked anything but serious or important (he was all of thirty-four or -five, though looking younger), or anything but one who would be likely to be sent by a great paper upon any really serious errand, still he managed to be taken seriously and even with a kind of deference wherever he went.

Hospital internes and executives generally, police captains and sergeants, bureaucrats in every conceivable type of department, received him with a geniality and a courtesy which was a matter of surprise to me. And wherever he went he invariably entered with an air of proprietorship, as much as to say, "See who comes now!"—a little brown frieze hat pulled rakishly over his eyes, his sandy complexion and blue eyes showing snappily above a somewhat wrinkled and faded and almost frayed brown suit, occasionally a thin and worn overcoat tossed over his arm, the better to conceal its threads, I fancy. His shoes were never good, his shirts and ties mussy and of the unstarched variety, but he looked self-possessed and contained and well able to look after himself. Invariably he smelled of tobacco and occasionally of liquor, when he could get enough free, and he invariably served comments and criticisms and news of sorts about all and sundry, as though he were a bureau of some sort in himself, so much so that at first I thought he was one of the most important of all the working newspaper men of the city.

Yet I doubt if he ever had a job which paid more than twenty or twenty-five a week or that lasted so long as three months. In the main, I think he grafted "loans," cigars, meals and whatever else he could, from all and sundry. His side pockets were always stuffed with copy paper. His thumb and forefinger could invariably dig out a stub of pencil. If anything of real news value had occurred anywhere—a fire, a death, a queer tale of some kind—he was capable of asking as many commonplace questions as any living being, and yet I doubt if he ever wrote a good story in his life, or could. I think his principal gift and service to his paper, as well as to every party of which he was ever a part, was in telling about whatever he had heard or seen. Then he was at home and could describe anything with gusto and humor and color; and it was because of this, I fancy, that his city or Sunday editors, anxious to glean good tales from wherever they could for others to write, kept him about and moderately employed.

At any rate, when I arrived on this humdrum circuit, there he was, and a more amusing and curious person I never knew. Wherever a group of reporters chanced to be, or some idle bureaucrats in an office, there he was, and I was never tired of watching or listening to him. The soul of contention and leadership, he was forever arguing about something with somebody, usually about the veracity or accuracy of something some one had said or printed.

"What taalk have ye? Ye're wrong, I tell ye. That wasn't the way of it at aal. Man, haven't ye any memory? There were three hurt and the woman was arrested. Wasn't I there? Ye can find it on the docket if ye like. The sergeant himself will tell ye. What is it ye're tryin' to tell me—me, an old experienced newspaper hand!"

If he used that last phrase once, he used it fifty times in my presence.

Or:

"Him a rayporter? The likes of him write? He wouldn't know a bit of news from a lodge meetin'. Haven't I worked with um? As a rayporter he's just no good at aal. That's it, if ye wanta know."

So it went, anent fires, cases, editors, personalities, past events— I cannot begin to suggest what all.

But in regard to this particular police sergeant, let us return.

This last was a huge, beefy, rather hog-like man with rather darkish brown hair and mustache, who presided in this particular station, where we all called afternoons and evenings, and who was as good an example of police station desk sergeant as one would want to find—dull, coarse, rather uncivil by nature, dictatorial, a bit savage at times, and used to laying down the law to drunks and disorderlies and telling policemen that they were wanted somewhere or must do so and so, but no more. According to instructions from above, of course, or enforced upon the various departments of the city by the newspapers themselves, he was compelled to, or at least supposed to, inform any representatives of any papers who chanced to come there and inquire of such news or facts in any case in which they happened to be interested.

And, in so far as I knew, Finn and this sergeant were invariably on the best of terms. He came and went here about as he pleased, going behind the desk to examine the blotter whenever he chose, or into the cells to converse with any of the prisoners in whom he happened to be interested. Yet at one time during my very short stay in this world, chancing to enter the station late one afternoon, I found Finn defiantly posed below the rostrum on which the sergeant sat, one of his arms and hands raised in a most dramatic manner, his short coattails defiantly protruding, the while he laid down the law to this fat superior.

"So ye'll lock me up, will ye? Ye think ye'll lock me up? Ye, a cheap, fat, two-thousand-a-year police sergeant? And who are ye, I'd like to know? Where do ye get that—tellin' the representative of a great paper what ye'll do or whether ye'll hand out news or not? I've as good a right in those cells as ye have, and more, ye big stiff! I'm not known to yer captain, am I, or to yer Inspector McCaffrey aither, I suppose? Or to yer chief, Mr. Byrnes, himself? And the likes of ye'll stop me from goin' in to interview a prisoner, will ye, or ye'll lock me up if I do? Well, we'll see about that. Wait a little while till I can get down to the ahffice with this, and to yer superiors—we'll see then, whether ye'll lock me up or keep me out or not, or whether yer name'll be mentioned from now on in the papers. Wait now and see. And let me tell ye something else," he added, and the while he shook a dictatorial and threatening finger under the very nose of the fat officer. "There's something else I want to tell ye, and that ye think I don't know. Ye dye yer hair, ye fat bluff! Ye dye it, and I may tell yer fellow ahfficers about that!" and he fairly wiggled his finger under the nose so close that it almost touched a part of said dyed hair, the dark brown mustache.

I doubt if I have ever witnessed a more ridiculous or amusing scene. It may be that dyed hair among the police is a most sinful or shameful thing, but just the same this announcement had a most trying effect. For a moment I thought that certainly the fat sergeant would collapse. His face flushed as red as a beet and his voice trembled as he leaned over and, leaning down, yelled: "Get out of here, ye little red-headed bastard, before I murther ye now! Get, now—get!—before I call an officer and lay a charge against ye." And in proof of this he fumbled about under his desk for the button of a bell, I presume, but no one came; and betimes Finn retreated slowly and defiantly toward the door.

"Lock me up!" he insisted. "Lock me up! I'm here now—lock me up! But ye'll get yers from now on if ye do." And then seeing me, he began to pour a long description of his troubles into my ears, the while we ambled outside. It appeared that, having had the run of the station, he had insisted upon nosing into some case about which the police did not wish him to know, I presume, and hence this row. At any rate, for days the air was blue with words describing the effrontery of this man— only, later on, as I noticed, they were on as good terms as ever, the threat to expose his dark crime to his fellows, possibly, having brought him to terms.

But the nature of this dreary world, in spite of occasional incidents such as this! There was the morgue, for instance. That horrible place— God! Daily from the ever-flowing waters about New York there were recaptured or washed up in all stages and degrees of decomposition the flotsam and jetsam of the great city—its offal, its victims, its what? Every day about noontime when I reached there (it stood at the foot of East 26th Street, near Bellevue Hospital), I invariably found the same old brown-denimed caretaker in charge—a creature so thick and so lethargic and so mentally incompetent generally that it was all I could do to extract a grunt of recognition out of him. He knew all the newspaper men, of course, or appeared to, and was friendly enough, but he was about as alive physically as a log of decayed wood or a crocodile. Yet this creature, if handed a cigar occasionally or a bag of tobacco, would trouble to get out of his chair and let you look over a book or ledger containing the roughly jotted down police descriptions (all done in an amazing scrawl) of the height, weight, color of clothes if any, color of hair and eyes where these latter were still distinguishable, probable duration of time in water, contents of pockets, jewelry or money if any, et cetera—all of which were to be noted in connection with any possible mystery as to the absence or disappearance of any particular person at the time. And there was always some one "turning up missing," as this same Mickey Finn was wont to say when speaking of these cases. I noticed, for one thing, and with considerable cynicism, that rarely if ever was there any money or jewelry of any kind reported as found by the police. Being further persuaded via blandishments or tips of one kind and another, this same caretaker would, if it were necessary or important to the paper, lead the way to a shelf of drawers reaching from the floor to the chest-height of a man or higher and running about two sides of the room, and, opening those containing the latest arrivals, supposing you were interested to look, would permit you to gaze on the last of the chemical formulae which once functioned as a man or a woman here on earth. The faces! The despair! The decay! The clothing! I often stared in sad horror and promised myself that I would never look again, although duty to the paper compelled me so to do again and again.

And then there was Bellevue itself, that gray-black collection of stone and iron structures, facing in wintertime the gray, icy waters of the East River. That scene in winter! The hobbling ghouls of caretakers in their baggy brown cotton suits, the large number of half-well charity patients idling about in gray-green gingham, their faces sunken and pinched, their hair poorly combed! And the chipper and yet often coarse and vulgar and always overbearing young doctors and nurses and paid attendants generally! One need but remember that it was the heydey of the most corrupt period of Tammany Hall's political control of New York, Mr. Croker being still in charge. Quite all of those old buildings have since been replaced and surrounded by a tall iron fence and bordered with an attractive lawn. In those days it was a little different. There was the hospital proper, with its various wards— contagious, alcoholic, et cetera—its detention hospital for the criminal or insane or both, the morgue, and a world of smaller pavilions stretching along the riverfront and connected by walks or covered hallways or iron bridges, but lacking the dignity and care of the later structures. There is a psychology to, and an air which attends, any badly or foully managed institution, and Bellevue at that time had that air and that psychology. It smacked more of a jail and a poorhouse combined than of a hospital, and so it was, I think. At that time it was a seething world of medical and political and social graft,—a kind of human hell or sty. Those poor fish who live in comfortable and protected homes and find their little theories and religious beliefs readymade for them in some overawing church or social atmosphere should be permitted to take an occasional peep into a world such as this then was. At this very time, while I was there as a reporter, there was an investigation and an exposure on in connection with this selfsame institution, which had revealed not only the murder of helpless patients but the usual graft in connection with food, drugs, clothing, et cetera, furnished to the patients and called charity. Grafting officials and medics and brutes of nurses and attendants abounded, of course.

The number of "drunks" and obstreperous or complaining or trouble-some patients doped or beaten or thrown out and even killed, and the number and quality of operations conducted by incompetent or indifferent medics, were known and shown to be large. One need only return to the legislative investigation of that date to come upon the truth of this.

Yet the place was so huge and so crowded that it was like a city in itself. It was, for one thing, a dumping-ground for all the offal gathered by the police and the charity department, to say nothing of being a realm of "soft snaps" for political pensioners of all kinds. At the gate, at such hours and on such days as relatives and friends of charity patients or those detained by the police were permitted to call, the permit room fairly swarmed with people who were pushed and shunted here and there like cattle, and always browbeaten like slaves. I personally, visiting as a stranger, have been so treated. "Who? What's his name? What? Whendee come? When? When? Talk a little louder, can't you! Whatsy matter with your tongue? Whaddya think I am? Over there! Over there! Out that door there!" So they came, procured their little cards and passed in or out.

And the wretched creatures who were "cured" or written down well enough to walk, and so, before a serious illness had been properly treated and because they were not able to pay, were then shunted out into the world of the well and the strong with whom they were then supposed to compete once more and make their way. I used to see them coming and going, and have personally talked to scores—men and women who, never having had a dollar above their meagre wages, once illness overtook them had been swept into this limbo, only to be turned out again at the end of a few weeks or months to make their own way as best they might, yet really worse off in one sense than when they came. For now they were weak in addition to being penniless, and sometimes on the day of their going, as I noticed, the weather was most inclement. And the old, wrinkled, washed-out clothing doled out to them, in which once more they were allowed to wander back to the tene-ments—to do what? There was a local charity organization society at the time, as there is today, but if it acted in behalf of any of these I never saw it. They wandered away, west on 26th Street and along First or Second Avenues—those drear, dismal, underdog streets—to where?

But by far the most irritating of all the phases of this institution, to me at least, and as I observed them at this time, were the various officials and the dancing young medics and nurses in their white uniforms, the latter too often engaged in flirting with one another or tennis-playing or reading comfortably in some warm room, their feet comfortably resting on a desk the while they smoked, the while the great institution wagged its indifferent way. When not actually engaged upon the work of visiting their patients, one could nearly always find them so ensconced somewhere, reading or smoking or talking or flirting. And a more chipper and yet indifferent group it has never been my fortune to see. In spite of the world of misery that was thrashing about them, they were as comfortable as may be. They had nothing to do but suggest or order some one else to do something. And to me, when bent upon unraveling the details of some particular case, they always seemed heartless. "Oh, that old nut? What's interesting about him? Surely you can't dig up a tale about him, can you? He's been here three weeks now. No; we don't know anything about him. Don't the records show?"

Or, supposing he had died: "I knew he couldn't live. We couldn't give him the necessary attention here. Too many as it is. Wanta see an interesting case?" And then he might lead you in to some wretch who had had a queer accident or was out of his mind and had an illusion of some kind. "Funny old duck, eh? But there's no hope. He'll be dead in a week or so."

I think the worst thing I ever saw was betting being indulged in— cash gambling—between two young medics and a young nurse in charge of the receiving ward as to whether the next patient to be brought in by the ambulance, which had been sent out on a hurry accident-call, would arrive alive or dead.

"Fifty that he's dead!"

"Fifty that he isn't!"

"I say alive!"

"I say dead!"

"Well, hand me that stethoscope. I'm not going to be fooled by looks this time."

In a few moments the ambulance would come tearing in, its bell clanging, the edges of the driveway barely missed by the wheels, and out would be drawn upon a stretcher, half-dead or unconscious, or possibly dead even, the latest victim of the far-flung streets of the city. In one particular instance, as the stretcher was pulled out and set down upon the stone step under the archway, the three pushed about and hung over, feeling the heart and looking at the eyes and lips, now pale blue as in death, quite as one might crowd about a curious specimen of plant or animal.

"He's alive!"

"He's dead!"

"I say he's alive! Look at his eyes!"— which to illustrate one eye was forced open.

"Aw, what's eatin' you? Listen to his heart! Haven't I got a stetho on it? Listen for yourself!"

The man was dead, but the jangle lasted a laughing minute or more, the while he lay there. Then it having been proved that he was dead, he was forthwith removed to the hospital morgue, and the loser compelled to "come across" or "fork over." One of the internes who occasionally went out on the "wagon," as the ambulance was called, told me that once, having picked up a badly injured patient who had been knocked down by a car, the selfsame ambulance, on racing with this man to the hospital, had knocked down another man and all but killed him.

"And what did you do about him?"

"Stopped the boat and chucked him into it, of course."

"On top of the other one?"

"Side by side—sure. It was a little close, though."

"Well, did he die?"

"Yep. But the other one was all right. We couldn't help it, though. It was a life or death case for the first one."

"A fine deal for the merry bystander," was all I could say.

The very worst of all in connection with this great hospital—and I do not care to dwell on it at any too great length, since it has been exposed before and the records are available—was this: about the hospital in the capacity of orderlies, doormen, gatemen, errand boys, gardeners, lawn mowers and what not, were a number of down-and-out ex-patients or pensioners of politicians, so old, feeble and generally decrepit mentally and physically that they were fit for little more than the scrap heap. Their principal desire, in so far as I could see, was to sit in the sun or safely within the warmth of a room and do nothing at all. If you asked them a question, their first impulse and greatest delight was to say "Don't know" or refer you to someone else. They were accused by the half-dozen reporters, who daily foregathered here upon one quest and another, to be of the lowest of the low—so low indeed that they could be persuaded to do anything for a little money. And in pursuance of this idea or theory, there was one day propounded by that same little red-headed Irish police reporter whom I have mentioned, Mickey Finn, and who represented the *News* at the time (a paper long since dead), that he would bet anyone five dollars that for the sum of fifteen dollars he could hire old Gansmuder, who was one of the shabbiest and vilest-looking of the hospital orderlies, to kill a man. According to Finn, who had his information from one of the policemen stationed in the hospital, Gansmuder was an ex-convict who had done ten years' time for a similar crime. Now old and penniless, he was here finishing up a shameful existence, the pensioner of some politician to whom he had rendered a service perhaps.

At any rate here he was. And, as one of several who heard Finn's boast in the newsroom near the gate and could not believe as yet, I joined in the shout of derision that went up. "Rot! What stuff!" "Well, you're the limit, Mickey!" However, as events proved, it was not so much talk as fact. I was not present at the negotiations, but it appeared afterward, from amazed accounts by other newspapermen who were "in on" the joke, that, being approached by Finn and one other—Finn first, then the two of them together—for the sum of twenty-five dollars, a part of which (five) was to be paid in advance, the old wretch agreed to lie in wait at a certain street corner in Brooklyn for an individual of a given description and there to strike him in some way as to dispose of him. Naturally, the negotiations went no further than this. There was no man to be killed. But somehow, true or no, this one incident has always typified the spirit of that hospital, and indeed of all political New York at that time, to me. It was a period of orgy and crime; and Bellevue and the charities department constituted the back door which gave onto the river, the asylums, the potter's field and all else this side of complete chemic dissolution.

CHAPTER XCIII

Now, whether due to a naturally weak and incompetent physique or a mind which unduly tortures itself with the evidences of a none-too-smooth working of the creative impulse and its machinery, or whether I had merely had my fill of reportorial work as such and could no longer endure more, or whatever else might have been the cause, the darksome atmosphere of this delinquent and defective world with which I was now connected, plus the strain which my sister's condition put upon me, plus the mental nausea which the whole grim darksome city in its grey, snowy, blowy winter dress seemed to evoke, finally determined me to get out of the newspaper profession entirely, come what might, and cost what it might. Although just what I was to do once I was out and how I was to do it, I could not guess. As I have said, I had no trade and no profession other than this, and the thought of editing or writing for anything save a newspaper was as far from me as, say, engineering or painting. I did not think I could write anything beyond newspaper news items, and with this conclusion many will no doubt be glad to agree with me even unto this day. Yet out of this messy and heartless world in which I was now working I did occasionally extract tales which were printable, only so low was my credit that I rarely won the privilege of writing them myself.

And in the main they were all too sombre and sordid to be worth printing. Yet had I imagined at that time that I could write, I might easily have built up an exposé or color story—out of what I saw in those ways and places or learned inside and out the newspaper reportorial rooms—which would have shocked the souls of the dilettante magazine editors and writers then working, but the former would not have published them. My facts would have been too low, gruesome, drab, horrible—and so beyond the view of any current magazine or its clientele. Life at that time, outside of the dark picture of it presented by daily papers, must be all sweetness and gayety and humor. We must apparently discuss only our better selves, and that via a happy ending; or if perchance this realer world must of necessity be referred to, it must be indicated in some cloudy nebulous manner which gave it more the charm of shadow than of fact—something used to enhance the values of the lighter and more perfect and beautiful things with which our lives must perforce concern themselves. Marriage, if I read the current magazines correctly, was a sweet and delicate affair, never marred by the slightest ion of error or erratic conduct of any kind. Love was made in heaven and lasted forever. Ministers, doctors, and, in the main, lawyers and merchants, were all good men, rarely if ever guilty of the shams and subterfuges and trashy aspects of humanity so common to the lay world. If a man did an evil thing it was due to his lower nature, which really had nothing to do with his higher—and it was a great concession for the intelligentsia of that day (mayhap of this) to admit that he had two natures, one of which was not high. Most of us had only one—a high one—our better nature. When I think of the literary and social snobbery of that time—its utter futility and profound faith in its own goodness, as opposed to the facts of its own visible life—I am compelled to smile.

But aside from all this, it never even occurred to me that I could write in the magazine or literary sense—and as for editing, it never occurred to me at all. And yet this last was the very next thing I did, and I succeeded quite well indeed. Yet at this time I wandered about thinking how I was to do, deciding each day that if I had the courage of a rat I would no longer endure this gruelling, time-consuming game of reporting, and especially for the pitiful sum which each week I was allowed to draw. What could it do for me now? I now asked myself over and over. Make me more aware of the brutality, subtlety, force, charm, selfishness and what not else of life? It could not if I worked so an hundred years—or so I reasoned. And, besides, the pay for me was impossible. Essentially, as I even then saw, reporting was a boy's game, and I was slowly but surely passing out of the boy stage. Swiftly and surely, I had seen the amount I had saved up in Pittsburgh disappear until I had as little as fifty dollars left and not one other thing in sight. Still, in a kind of foolish desperation I hung on, uncertain as to what I was to do if I left. Where turn? What take up? I first tried using some of my time to visit other newspaper offices to see if I could not secure, temporarily at least, a better regular salary commensurate with my work. But, no—whenever I could get in to see a city or managing editor, which was rare, no one seemed to want me. At the offices of the *Herald, Times, Tribune, Sun,* and elsewhere, I knocked, but the same outer office system which had restrained me at the *World* worked to keep me out—and I was by now too indifferent to the reportorial game in general and too discouraged to really wish to force myself in or to continue as a reporter at all. Indeed, I went about this matter of inquiry at the offices of the other papers, morning and evening, so perfunctorily that, had I gained admission, I could not have convinced anyone of my worth. Fortunately or unfortunately, as one chooses to look at such things, I did not. But it seemed far from fortunate then to me, as I can tell you. Finally, one Saturday afternoon, having brought in a fairly interesting story which related to a missing girl whose body was found at the morgue, and being told to "give the facts to ———— and let him write it," I summoned up sufficient courage to say to the assistant who ordered me to do this, "I don't see why I should always have to do this. I'm not a beginner in this game. I wrote stories, and big ones, before ever I came to this paper."

"Maybe you did," he replied rather sardonically, "but we have the feeling that you haven't proved of much use to us."

After this there was nothing to say and nothing to do. I could not say that I had not had any opportunities, for of course I had, but just the same I was terribly hurt in my pride. Without knowing what to do or where I should go, I there and then decided that, come what might, this was the end of this line of work for me. Never again, anywhere, if I died in the fight, would I condescend to be a reporter on any paper. Never. I might starve, but if so—even so—I would starve. Either I was going to get something different, something more profitable to my mind, or I was going to starve or get out of New York. Frankly, I may as well say, in this conclusion my good sister and her troubles played but a small part. I was sorry, but I reasoned that if I could not help myself to anything better, I certainly could not help her, and so there was no need of worrying about that, whatever happened.

Going to the individual named, I turned over my data, then secured my hat and went out. I felt then that even though I did not quit, I would subsequently be discharged anyhow for incompetence and insubordination, so dark was my mood in regard to it all, and so out I went. One thing I did do, however, was, on the following Monday, to visit the individual who had first ordered the city editor to put me on and submit to him various clippings of work done in Pittsburgh with the request that he advise me as to where I might turn for work along that line.

"Better try the *Sun*," was his rather sane advice. "It's a great school, and you might do well over there."

But although I tried I could not get on the *Sun*—not, at least, before I had managed to do something else.

Thus, then, ended my newspaper experiences, never resumed, save as a writer of specials for a Sunday paper, and then under entirely different conditions—but that was ten years later. In the meantime I was now perforce turning toward a world which had never seemed to contain any future for me, and I was doing it without really knowing it. "But that," as Kipling has so often remarked anent some side issue of one of his tales, "is another story." It better belongs under the title of *Literary Experiences*.

THE END

Theodore Dreiser probably made the initial decision to write a full-scale autobiography in 1912. Work on his autobiographical novel *The "Genius,"* completed in 1911 although not published until 1915, may have stimulated the desire to produce a more factual memoir. In addition, he was no doubt inspired by the example of a number of his favorite books: Benvenuto Cellini's *Autobiography,* Jean-Jacques Rousseau's *Confessions,* and especially George Moore's *The Confessions of a Young Man.* Whatever the complex of motives, it is not surprising that so self-analytical and confessional a writer, one who habitually drew on personal and family history for the material of his fiction, should undertake to tell his life story.

Although no detailed record of composition exists, a partial log of the evolution of Dreiser's autobiography can be constructed from references in letters and diaries. Originally he conceived of this project as a multivolume effort, to be called *The History of Myself,* with a separately titled book devoted to each twenty-year span of his life. This scheme worked well for *Dawn,* the first volume, which takes him to age twenty-one. But *Newspaper Days,* the second and, as it turned out, the last of Dreiser's autobiographical volumes, covers only three years.

Precisely when Dreiser began his autobiography is unknown, but a diary fragment dated 24 April 1914 reveals that he was then writing chapter 13 of *Dawn.* The manuscript must have proceeded steadily, for on 24 June 1916 in a letter to H. L. Mencken he indicates that he has completed "Vol 1 of The History of Myself." That volume he locked up for safekeeping, for fear that it would give offense to members of his family. A month later the New York Society for the Suppression of Vice decided that *The "Genius"* contained obscene matter and pressured the John Lane Publishing Company to halt all sales of the novel and to recall copies from booksellers. Dreiser knew that his reputation had been threatened by the notoriety of this suppression; he also knew that his autobiography contained passages that were even more sexually explicit than those in his beleaguered novel. He therefore concluded that the time had not yet arrived for the publication of *Dawn.*

The holograph text of *Dawn,* running to 106 chapters, recounts the main events of Dreiser's life from his birth in 1871 through his journalistic apprenticeship in Chicago in 1892. That apprenticeship is described in the final fifteen chapters, and the manuscript ends with Dreiser's departure in late October 1892 for St. Louis to begin working for the *Globe-Democrat*. As initially planned, the first chapter of the second volume (chap. XVI in the Pennsylvania edition) was to begin with his arrival in that city. On 23 July 1917, he announced in a letter to May Calvert that he had completed twelve chapters of the work he had begun to call *Newspaper Days*, and by 20 December 1917 he noted in his diary that he had completed chapter 46 (chap. LXI in the Pennsylvania edition).

In August 1916 Dreiser met Estelle Kubitz. She soon became his mistress and his editor and typist. She copied the manuscript of *Newspaper Days*, transcribing his handwritten chapters into what she called "rough" typescript (TS1). These typescripts Dreiser would revise (TS1R) and return to Kubitz, who would retype them with his revisions (TS2). Dreiser would then review these second copies and occasionally make further revisions (TS2R). Almost all of the holograph and sixty chapters of the rough typescript survive in the Dreiser Collection at the University of Pennsylvania. The entire second typescript (together with a complete carbon copy) is also there.

Dreiser worked on *Newspaper Days* intermittently during 1918 and 1919 while he labored on four other books: *Free and Other Stories* (1918), *Twelve Men* (1919), *The Hand of the Potter* (1919), and *Hey Rub-a-Dub-Dub* (1920). During this period, he was also devoting much effort to *The Bulwark*, a novel he had been wrestling with since 1914 and for which he had received advances totalling four thousand dollars from his publisher, Horace Liveright. With his meeting of Helen Richardson in September 1919 and their abrupt departure from New York to live in Los Angeles for the next three years, the completion of *Newspaper Days* was further delayed.

In the early months of 1920, needing money and finding himself unable to provide the "new big Dreiser novel" that Liveright wanted, he buckled down to *Newspaper Days*. He offered it to Liveright as a substitute for *The Bulwark*, suggesting that it be published as *A Novel about Myself*, but Liveright's response was lukewarm. He wanted a real novel.

The arrival of Helen Richardson had ended Dreiser's liaison with Estelle Kubitz, but he continued to mail chapters of *Newspaper Days* to her for typing. Through March and April he labored at the manuscript, and at last on 11 May 1920 he was able to note in his diary, "Finished Newspaper Days at 11 a.m." At some point, Dreiser had decided to use the final fifteen chapters of the first volume—those covering his early reportorial experiences in Chicago—as the opening section of *Newspaper Days*. A typescript of these chapters was also made by Kubitz. With this additional material, the book in its final form was ninety-three chapters long.

Dreiser's next concern was to get *Newspaper Days* into a publishable form and to find a publisher. For help he turned to two friends: Mencken and William C. Lengel, the managing editor of *Hearst's International*. Dreiser knew, however, that he had written a book so sexually explicit that no American publisher would dare to print it. He therefore had the most obviously unacceptable passages removed from the text even before showing the manuscript to Lengel and Mencken. No diary entries or letters indicate that he himself did any of this cutting; he probably delegated the task to someone else, most likely to Kubitz.

In early September, Kubitz sent revised and toned-down versions of *Newspaper Days* to Lengel and Mencken. Mencken wrote Dreiser on 1 October 1920: "I read the newspaper book. It is full of excellent stuff. Some of the newspaper chapters are gorgeous." He also had some criticisms: "Considering the great space given to the beginning of the S[ara] W[hite] episode, it seems to me that the thing is dismissed too briefly at the end. So with the Alice business. . . . Yet again the affair with the Bohemian woman is a bit wheezy—the sort of thing all of us have at 22."

These remarks demonstrate that Mencken had read a version that omitted the full account of the near-seduction of Sara White found in chapter LXXVIII of the Pennsylvania edition. His reference to the "Alice business" implies that a similar passage relating to Lois Zahn, Dreiser's Chicago sweetheart (in chap. XV), had been cut. His letter also indicates that he was reading a version in which some identities were concealed by false names. Moreover, the fact that Mencken could take exception to Dreiser's innocuous account of his relationship with Mrs. Zernouse in chapters XXVII and XXVIII suggests that virtually all of the truly sensational chapters (for example, chaps. LXXXV and LXXXII) had been removed from the copy he read. Dreiser surely had approved these omissions; knowing how Mencken had warned him against even the thin eroticism of The "Genius," he could assume that his friend would never regard the graphic sexual episodes in the unabridged Newspaper Days as publishable.

Responding to Mencken on 8 October, Dreiser expressed general agreement with his recommendations. Passages about Peter B. McCord could be omitted because they repeated much of what he had already said in Twelve Men, and "the Bohemian woman stuff" could be deleted. Dreiser also asked Mencken to show Kubitz what passages of "dull philosophy" could be cut, and he intimated that he would be pleased if Mencken himself would undertake a thorough overhaul of the text. This is what Mencken apparently did, working through the text at odd intervals during the next two years.

Through 1920 and 1921 Dreiser dickered with Liveright over Newspaper Days. He was slow to let the publisher see the manuscript and did not accept his early offers to issue it. The two carried on an extensive correspondence by letter and telegram. Liveright pointedly reminded Dreiser of the advances he had already received and repeatedly urged him to finish the big novel, arguing that it would sell much better than any autobiography. For lack of the novel, however, he unenthusiastically agreed to issue Newspaper Days to keep Dreiser's name before the public. Dreiser, on the other hand, was looking for a publisher who would undertake to reissue all of his earlier books, together with Dawn and Newspaper Days, in a uniform edition and to market them in a way most profitable to him. To this end, he negotiated with Harper and Brothers, the Century Company, and Dodd, Mead. He even added to Liveright's anxiety by letting it be known that he was approaching these other houses.

In addition, Dreiser had decided to delay the appearance of Newspaper Days in book form until he could sell sections of it to a magazine for serial publication. The task of marketing the manuscript to a magazine was delegated to Lengel, who, after a year of putting out feelers, sold five episodes to the Bookman for five hundred dollars. These were published from November 1921 through April 1922.[1]

Since Dreiser could not find a publisher who would give him the agreement he desired, in late May 1922 he agreed to let Liveright publish his autobiography. On 5 June 1922 he wired Kubitz to deliver the typescript, and on the same day he wired Liveright that he would accept the title A Book about Myself as a substitute for Newspaper Days or A *Novel about Myself,* neither of which Liveright liked. To Liveright's request for permission to edit the text further, Dreiser responded, "Desire to accept & will consider all cuts & changes really helpful to the work. Have confidence in your judgement & will be reasonable."

The typescript Liveright received (TS3) had already been revised by several people—by Kubitz, Mencken, and Lengel, as well as by Dreiser himself—when Liveright received it. The document was already a radically condensed and bowdlerized version of the work that had been brought to closure two years earlier. It was 699 pages in length and was divided into eighty chapters; the original version, by contrast, had run to 946 pages and ninety-three chapters. A few chapters had been rearranged in sequence, and parts of some chapters had been transferred to others. Many passages had been drastically pruned. All matters of an explicitly sexual nature had been omitted or merely hinted at. For example, no mentions of sex organs, copulation, or masturbation were retained.

Among the longer omissions were the following: most of the passage in chapter XII describing Dreiser's erotic roughhousing with the lusty daughter of the De Good family; the passages in chapter XV relating his sexual misadventures with Lois; the graphic narration in chapter XXVII of his night of love with the girl he took to Mrs. Zernouse's rooming house; the account in chapter XL of his affair with Mrs. X, the passionate landlady; the specific details in chapter XLVI of Jules Wallace's relationship with his female client; the erotic implications in chapter LVII of Dreiser's flirtation with Lizzie Schuble and her sister; the sketches in chapter LXXV of several prostitutes he patronized in Pittsburgh; that part of chapter LXXVIII describing his near-seduction of Sara White; the entirety of chapter LXXXII that detailed his experiences in a "French" whorehouse in New York City; and that portion of chapter LXXXIII devoted to the visit he and Paul paid to the notorious House of All Nations. Surprisingly, most of the original account in chapter XXVIII of Dreiser's liaison with Mrs. Zernouse—"the affair with the Bohemian woman"—was retained. (Liveright got rid of it all, however, when he took his turn at editing the book.) In addition, Dreiser's recital in chapter XC of his sister Emma's marital problems and of how he helped her escape from her husband had been shortened significantly, probably because Emma was still living at the time.

On 28 June 1922 Liveright returned the typescript, now bearing his own excisions and revisions, to Dreiser. (This document is now in the Donaldson Collection of the University Research Library at the University of California, Los Angeles; hereafter it is cited as the UCLA typescript.) Liveright assured him that the work had consisted of "mostly cutting because you left very little else to clean up." He had, he continued, reduced the book by about two hundred pages, leaving it as a five-hundred-page book of seventy-seven chapters. With a few minor reservations, Dreiser accepted all of the excisions, and on 22 July Liveright wrote again, "I'm tickled to death that you were satisfied with my editorial work. Very likely you're perfectly right in the exceptions that you have taken and I am glad to accept them all without any quibbling."

What Liveright had performed on the typescript was a thorough job of textual surgery. Scarcely a page was left untouched. In general, he shortened severely or eliminated altogether passages of philosophical or social commentary (often ironic or sarcastic in tone), of rhapsodic musing and impassioned apostrophe, of detailed analysis of circumstances, motives, and feelings. Most of Dreiser's caustic references to the Catholic church were crossed out, and Liveright made hundreds of stylistic revisions.

Despite the sanitizing process *Newspaper Days* had already undergone, Liveright still found passages to be eliminated. He had no wish to arouse the indignation of the censors. Thus from chapter XII he removed the brief remaining reference to the young De Good woman— the merest suggestion that she had found Dreiser sexually attractive. Dreiser's comments in chapter XXI in defense of prostitution and on unreformable human nature were excised. Eight pages that remained of the story about the girl taken to Mrs. Zernouse's rooming house— mostly innuendo—all had to go. The passage in chapter XXXII describing Dreiser's harassment of the policeman who was trying to arrest "Slippery Annie" was omitted entirely, even though Liveright's typescript contained none of the offensive language found in the original. A passage in chapter XXXIX describing how Mrs. Zernouse was succeeded by Mrs. X was eliminated, "not," Liveright asserted, "because I object to the 'moral tone' but because I think it's thin and uninteresting." From chapter LII went the passage describing the negative reaction to Mrs. X of Dreiser's brother Al, even though the strong language of the original version had been considerably weakened; and along with it went the passage explaining how Dreiser dropped Miss Ginity because of her narrow-minded Catholicism. From chapter LXXV was deleted what little remained of Dreiser's discussion of Pittsburgh prostitutes and how he had patronized them, as well as his unconventional reflections on the nature of vice and the social value of prostitution. And finally, chapter LXXXI was stripped of his speculation that the sex urge lay behind the posturings of the Broadway loungers and strollers he had observed in the summer of 1894.

Yet other passages were eliminated, among them the following: from chapter XXII three pages of characterization of McCord drawn from *Twelve Men;* from chapter XXXIV an extended excerpt from the Sermon on the Mount; from chapter LIX most of the characterization of Paul Dresser that also had appeared already in *Twelve Men;* from chapter LXIV much of Dreiser's description of Grand Rapids, Ohio, and of his feckless friend Hutchinson; from chapter LXVII passages giving Dreiser's thoughts on Cleveland and Buffalo, the futility of prayer, the gross unfairness of life, and the savage way in which the strong prey on the weak; from chapter LXXII a detailed summary of the "fly" article he wrote for the *Pittsburg Dispatch;* from chapter XC what still remained of the sad story of Emma; and from chapter XCII the character sketch of the reporter Mickey Finn and the anecdote about his quarrel with the police sergeant. In addition to these cuts, chapter LXXXIV, devoted to Manhattan Beach, was deleted entirely.

With this additional chipping away at a book already drastically pared down, Liveright probably did succeed in making *Newspaper Days* a more marketable book in 1922. But to a reader familiar with the original, his redaction may seem comparable to a fully grown tree that has had a great many of its main branches lopped off. Gone are some of the most revealing and significant of Dreiser's experiences and a great many passages of commentary most characteristic of his philosophy of life. The prose style of the original is radically changed, losing much of its reminiscential, relaxed, conversational tone. What replaces it is a popularized abridgment. Excessive condensation produced a brisk narrative pace that makes for easy reading but is not the characteristically ruminative discourse of Dreiser. What finally emerged from all this editorial processing was *A Book about Myself,* a work quite different from the original *Newspaper Days.* Indeed, given the number of hands that had a part in shaping it, one might argue that it is more nearly a jointly authored work than one produced by a single author.

After Dreiser had reviewed the Liveright typescript and had made a few revisions, the document was sent to the printer. In mid August, he began examining galley proofs and made a few minor revisions; shortly afterward, probably in early October, he reviewed the page proofs and made still further minor revisions. These galley and page proofs are now in the Dreiser Collection at the University of Pennsylvania.

A *Book about Myself* was finally published by Boni & Liveright on 15 December 1922. In 1931 it was reissued by Horace Liveright, Inc., as *Newspaper Days*. Although it was printed from the plates used for the earlier edition, the 1931 reissue had a different style of binding and a redesigned title page to make it a companion volume to *Dawn*, which was published that year. An "Author's Note," dated July 1931, explained that the book now had Dreiser's preferred title, one more appropriately describing the contents, and that the book was intended as part of a four- or five-volume series. Like the title page of *Dawn*, that of *Newspaper Days* bears the collective heading *A History of Myself*.

With the 1931 publication of *Dawn* and *Newspaper Days*, Dreiser's autobiography was as complete as it would be in his lifetime. In his "Author's Note" he promised that "two more books covering the incidents and influences of my later life are—time and chance agreeing—to follow." But time and chance did not permit, and although in ensuing years he occasionally spoke of his plans to finish these volumes, he never did.

NOTES

1. See Donald Pizer, Richard W. Dowell, and Frederic E. Rusch, *Theodore Dreiser: A Primary and Secondary Bibliography* (Boston: G. K. Hall, 1975), p. 24, for a list of the chapters published in the *Bookman*.

HISTORICAL NOTES

The notes include identifications of unfamiliar persons, places, and events as well as definitions and explanations of obscure terms, phrases, or passages. Figures whose names are still generally well known have not been identified. Allusions to and quotations from unfamiliar poems, plays, and old popular songs have been identified whenever possible.

Each note is preceded by a page and line reference, which indicates its location in the text of this edition. In assigning page-line references, chapter titles are counted; running heads and blank lines are not. The words or phrases quoted directly from the text are set in boldface type.

Sources

The principal sources of information about Dreiser's life used in this edition are the following:

Dreiser, Theodore. *The American Diaries, 1902–1926.* Edited by Thomas P. Riggio. Philadelphia: University of Pennsylvania Press, 1982.
———. *Dawn.* New York: Horace Liveright, 1931.
———. *Dreiser-Mencken Letters: The Correspondence of Theodore Dreiser and H. L. Mencken, 1907–1945.* Edited by Thomas P. Riggio. Philadelphia: University of Pennsylvania Press, 1986.
———. *A Hoosier Holiday.* New York: John Lane Company, 1916.
———. *Theodore Dreiser: Journalism. Newspaper Writings, 1892–1895.* Edited by T. D. Nostwich. Philadelphia: University of Pennsylvania Press, 1988 (hereafter cited as *TDJ*).
———. *Theodore Dreiser's "Heard in the Corridors" Articles and Related Writings.* Edited by T. D. Nostwich. Ames: Iowa State University Press, 1988 (hereafter cited as *HC*).
———. *A Traveler at Forty.* New York: Century Company, 1913.
———. *Twelve Men.* New York: Boni & Liveright, 1919.
Lingeman, Richard. *Theodore Dreiser: At the Gates of the City.* New York: G. P. Putnam's, 1986.
Swanberg, W. A. *Dreiser.* New York: Scribner's, 1965.

In addition to the second edition of the *OED*, *Webster's Second* and *Third International* dictionaries (hereafter cited as *W2* and *W3*), and various editions of the *Encyclopaedia Britannica*, information in the notes has been drawn from the following sources:

Baedeker, Karl, ed. *The United States: A Handbook for Travellers 1893.* New York & Leipzig, 1893. Reprint. New York: Da Capo, 1971.

Barnhart, Clarence L., ed. *The New Century Handbook of English Literature.* Rev. ed. New York: Meredith, 1967.

Bartlett, John. *Familiar Quotations.* 14th ed. Boston: Little, Brown, 1968.

Bordman, Gerald. *American Musical Theatre: A Chronicle.* New York: Oxford University Press, 1978.

Bordman, Gerald, ed. *Oxford Companion to American Theatre.* New York: Oxford University Press, 1984.

Burke, W. J., and Will D. Howe. *American Authors and Books 1640 to the Present Day.* Revised by Irving R. Weiss. New York: Crown, 1967.

Dictionary of American Biography. New York: Scribner's, 1928–81.

Drabble, Margaret, ed. *Oxford Companion to English Literature.* 5th ed. Oxford: Oxford University Press, 1985.

Dreiser, Theodore. *Sister Carrie.* Pennsylvania Edition. Historical Editors, John C. Berkey and Alice M. Winters; Textual Editor, James L. W. West III; General Editor, Neda M. Westlake. Philadelphia: University of Pennsylvania Press, 1981.

———. *Sister Carrie.* Norton Critical Edition. 2d ed. Edited by Donald Pizer. New York: W. W. Norton, 1991.

Hart, James, ed. *Oxford Companion to American Literature.* 5th ed. New York: Oxford University Press, 1983.

Hartnoll, Phyllis, ed. *The Oxford Companion to the Theatre.* 3d. ed. London: Oxford University Press, 1967.

Harvey, Sir Paul, ed. *The Oxford Companion to Classical Literature.* Oxford: Clarendon Press, 1955.

Harvey, Sir Paul, and J. E. Heseltine. *The Oxford Companion to French Literature.* Oxford: Clarendon Press, 1959.

Herzberg, Max J., et al. *The Reader's Encyclopedia of American Literature.* New York: Crowell, 1962.

Johnson, Thomas H., ed. *The Oxford Companion to American History.* New York: Oxford University Press, 1966.

Marks, Edward B. *They All Sang: From Tony Pastor to Rudy Vallée.* New York: Viking, 1934.

Mott, Frank Luther. *American Journalism: A History 1690–1960.* 3d. ed. New York: Macmillan, 1962.

———. *A History of American Magazines 1885–1905.* Cambridge: Harvard University Press, 1957.

The National Cyclopaedia of American Biography. New York: James T. White, 1898–1981.

The New York Times Theater Reviews 1886–1895. New York: New York Times & Arno Press, 1975.

Oberholtzer, Ellis Paxson. *A History of the United States since the Civil War: Volume V, 1888–1901.* New York: Macmillan, 1937.

Partridge, Eric. *A Dictionary of Catch Phrases.* New York: Stein and Day, 1977.

———. *A Dictionary of Slang and Unconventional English.* 8th ed. New York: Macmillan, 1984.

Pizer, Donald, Richard W. Dowell, and Frederic E. Rusch. *Theodore Dreiser: A Primary and Secondary Bibliography.* Boston: G. K. Hall, 1975.

Shepard, Leslie A. *Encyclopedia of Occultism and Parapsychology.* Detroit: Gale Research, 1978.

Webster's Biographical Dictionary. Springfield, Mass.: G. & C. Merriam, 1972.

Wentworth, Harold, and Stuart Berg Flexner, eds. *Dictionary of American Slang.* 2d ed. New York: Crowell, 1975.

Who Was Who in America. Chicago: A. N. Marquis, 1943–81.

Young, William C. *Famous Actors and Actresses of the American Stage.* New York: Bowker, 1975.

Microfilms and bound files of the following 1890s newspapers were consulted: from Chicago, the *Globe* and the *Herald*; from St. Louis, the *Chronicle*, the *Globe-Democrat*, the *Republic*, and the *Post-Dispatch*; from Toledo, the *Blade*; from Cleveland, the *Leader*; from Pittsburgh, the *Dispatch*; from New York, the *Times* and the *World*.

Theodore Dreiser in the early 1890s. (Lilly Library, Indiana University)

"Imagine a dreamy cub of twenty, soon to be twenty-one, long, lank, spindling, a pair of gold-framed specs on his nose, his hair combed à la pompadour. . . . I had already attained my full height, six feet one-and-a-half inches, and weighed only 137 pounds. . . . Aside from one eye—the right—which was turned slightly outward . . . and a set of upper teeth which . . . were overcrowded and so stood out much, I had no particular physical blemish except a general homeliness."

Eugene Field in 1893. (Chicago Historical Society, DN79,960)

"For two years and more I had been reading 'Sharps and Flats,' a column which he wrote daily, and through this . . . I was beginning to understand that I wanted to write. Nothing else I had read so far . . . gave me quite the same feeling; . . . for the subject of his daily notes, poems and aphorisms was Chicago and America. . . . these trenchant bits on local street scenes, institutions, characters, functions all moved me as nothing hitherto had."

Joseph B. McCullagh

Joseph B. McCullagh. (The St. Louis Mercantile Library Association)

"He was a real editor—a great one—one who could write, as contrasted with your namby-pamby 'businessman' masquerading as an editor. . . . He had been a great reporter and war correspondent himself in his day."

John Paul Dreiser in the late 1890s. (Special Collections Department, Robert W. Woodruff Library, Emory University)

"I had found him fussy, cranky, dosed with too much religion; although . . . always in my relations with him there had been . . . something so colorful and tender in his views, charmingly poetic and appreciative. . . . he had suddenly become just a broken old man, whose hopes and ambitions were a failure, whose religion, impossible as it was to me, was still a comfort and blessing to him."

NOTES

Chapter I

3.1   *Newspaper Days* begins at the point at which *Dawn* ends, in December 1891, some ten days before Christmas. Dreiser had just been fired from his job as installment-payment collector for the Lovell Manufacturing Company because he had withheld twenty-five dollars from his collections to buy himself a new overcoat.

3.4   **the Daily News**   Founded in 1876 by Melville E. Stone and published by Victor F. Lawson, this was Chicago's leading newspaper in the 1890s. **Eugene Field** (1850–95) joined the staff of the *Daily News* in 1883 and soon became nationally known for his urbane and witty columns.

4.3   **Auditorium**   This combination hotel, office building, and opera house, designed by Chicago architects Dankmar Adler and Louis Sullivan, was built in 1887. It stands on the northwest corner of Madison Avenue and Congress Street.

4.3   **Great Northern**   Built in 1891 as a combination hotel, office building, and theater and designed by the Chicago architects Daniel H. Burnham and John W. Root, the Great Northern stood on the northeast corner of Dearborn Street and Jackson Boulevard until it was razed in 1940.

4.3   **Masonic Temple**   Principally an office building, this structure was designed by Daniel H. Burnham and John W. Root. It was built in 1891 and stood on the northeast corner of State and Randolph Streets until it was razed in 1939.

4.11   **Goose Island**   An island located less than a mile upstream from the confluence of the branches of the Chicago River, lying between North and Chicago Avenues. In 1891 it was the site of tanneries, storage elevators for wheat, and numerous squatters' shacks. It was named for the wandering flocks of geese belonging to its early Irish residents. In Dreiser's youth it had a bad reputation because of the criminal activities of its inhabitants.

4.16   **Board of Trade**   Site of the grain exchange. Designed by Chicago architect William W. Boyington and located on Jackson Street at the end of LaSalle Avenue, it opened in 1885 and was razed in 1926. The **pit**, a depressed area in the building's vast trading room, where board members stood to trade in grain, is the central setting of Frank Norris's novel *The Pit* (1903).

4.30   **Frank W. Gunsaulus**   (1856–1921) Pastor of the Plymouth Congregational Church from 1887 to 1899. In 1893, he and Philip D. Armour established the Armour Institute (later the Illinois Institute of Technology); Gunsaulus served as its president until his death. In 1898 Dreiser published an article on Gunsaulus: "A Leader of Young Mankind," *Success* 2(15 December): 23–24.

6.5 **Midgely**   In the typescript of Chapter 89 of *Dawn*, Dreiser identifies Frank Midgely as branch manager of the Lovell Manufacturing Company. Chapter 91 of the published version gives his name as Frank Nesbit.

6.8 ***Herald***   Founded in 1881 by James W. Scott, the Chicago *Herald* was by 1891 second in circulation to the *Daily News*. At the time Dreiser applied for his job, the *Herald* had just moved into an impressive new building designed by Daniel H. Burnham and John W. Root that was located on Washington Street.

6.11 The advertisement appeared in the *Herald*'s want-ad column on 17 December 1891, p. 11 (see below). Its wording is different from what Dreiser remembered in that it makes no mention of possible promotion.

YOUNG MEN—TWO, OF GOOD ADDRESS; must be good penmen; salary, $1.50 per day. Apply in person to the business manager of this paper before 10 a. m. to-day.

7.9 The *Herald* began its children's Christmas gift program on 8 December with "Santa Claus Is Jolly," p. 5, and ran daily articles and editorials until 26 December. Much of the work of preparing the toys was done by volunteers. For instance, 9,462 dolls were dressed by women who donated their time and material. Food was not among the gifts distributed (except for popcorn balls and candy), nor was it necessary that applicants' requests be "viséd" by doctors or ministers. According to the *Herald*, the toys were not distributed until Christmas Eve, when they were delivered by volunteer livery wagon drivers to children who had written letters to Santa Claus in care of the newspaper. On Christmas day several hundred parents of children who had not received anything were given presents at the old *Herald* building.

7.31 ***Herald* Christmas Annex**   Located in the old *Herald* building at 120 Fifth Avenue.

9.33 **save the mark!**   Short for "God (*or* Heaven) save the mark." A parenthetical exclamatory phrase expressing contempt or impatience (*W2*).

10.1 **Niobe** and **Priam**   Figures in Greek mythology. A mother of seven sons and seven daughters, Niobe taunted Leto for having only two children and was punished by having her children killed by Apollo and Artemis. Niobe wept for them so long that she was turned into a stone column that continued to shed tears. Priam was king of Troy at the time of the Trojan War. In the *Iliad* he is shown lamenting the death of his sons, particularly Hector.

10.14 **Hey, Rub-a-dub! dub!**   A phrase taken from a familiar nursery rhyme that Dreiser used as the title of his book of criticism, satire, and philosophical musings on American culture, published in 1920.

Chapter II

10.18   **Lois Zahn**   Dreiser changed Lois Zahn's name to Alice Kane in the 1922 edition of *A Book about Myself.*

10.19   **Claire**   Clara Clothilde (Claire, Tillie) Dreiser (b. 1868) was the youngest of Dreiser's five sisters.

10.25   **young Scotch girl**   This person is identified as Nellie Anderson in the holograph of *Dawn.* In the 1931 edition, Dreiser's relationship with her is described in chapters 87–89, in which she is called Nellie MacPherson.

11.23   **Ed**   Eduard Minerod Dreiser (1873–1958) was the youngest of Dreiser's siblings.

11.24   **Al**   Alphons Joachim (Albert) Dreiser (b. 1867), one of Dreiser's older brothers.

11.25   **elder members of the family**   Refers to Theodore's father, Johann Paul Dreiser (1822–1900), and two sisters, Maria Franziska (Mame) (1861–1944) and Mary Theresa (Trace) (1864–97). His mother, Sarah (née Schänäb) (b. 1833) had died on 14 November 1890.

13.7   **eat salt New Year's Eve . . . dream of her coming lover**   This belief and variants of it of different ethnic origins are fairly well known in the Middle West. See *Popular Beliefs and Superstitions: A Compendium of American Folklore,* edited by Wayland D. Hand, Anna Casetta, and Sondra B. Thiederman (Boston: G. K. Hall, 1981), p. 519, items 13075–84.

Chapter III

15.26   **the second**   Dreiser means that Lois Zahn was the second woman to fall in love with him, Nellie Anderson being the first. Though he speaks of them as "sex conquests," subsequent chapters make clear that he does not mean that he had sexual intercourse with them. Apparently his first actual experience of sexual intercourse occurred when he was fifteen or sixteen in Warsaw, Indiana. See *Dawn,* pp. 247–50.

17.36   **Munger's Laundry**   For five or six months—from shortly after his mother's death in November 1890 until late April or early May 1891—Dreiser drove a pickup and delivery wagon for this laundry. See chapters 87–90 of *Dawn.*

18.14   **Conklin**   Dreiser worked for Asa Conklin, an unsuccessful Chicago realtor, from June through November of 1890. Dreiser says he was "the living prototype of Asa Griffiths in 'An American Tragedy.'" See *Dawn,* p. 469.

18.21   **Mr. Sypherstit**   Apparently the manager of the Corbin Company.

20.36   **hetaerae**   Prostitutes.

21.3   **Plutonian**   Infernal; harsh and unpleasing.

Chapter IV

23.9 **Circe** A goddess encountered by Odysseus on the island of Aeaea in Book 10 of *The Odyssey*. She turned his crew into swine but could not transform him because he possessed a protective magic herb. She was eventually forced to restore the others to human form.

23.9 **"beauty like a tightened bow"** The source of this quotation has not been identified. Dreiser uses it again in "The Story of Elizabeth" in "This Madness," *Hearst's International-Cosmopolitan* (April 1929), p. 82.

23.22 **Antonian** Dreiser may be thinking of the words *antonine* or *antoninian*, which refer to the luxurious style or manner of a Roman emperor.

24.15 **And again** Dreiser means that Lois's parents lived in a working-class neighborhood, just as Nellie Anderson's family did.

24.28 **Quaint little soul** Dreiser turned his affair with Lois into fiction in his story "The Second Choice," published in *Cosmopolitan*, February 1918, and republished in *Free and Other Stories* later that same year.

25.6 **Herbert Whipple** At 104.7 Dreiser has Lois refer to her fiancé as "Harry" and at 245.32 as "Mr. Williams."

25.35 **the Andersons** Chapter 88 of *Dawn* gives a fuller account of Nellie's family.

Chapter V

28.30 **Theodore Thomas concerts** Theodore Thomas (1835–1905) gave frequent concerts with his own orchestra in Chicago in the 1880s, but he first conducted the newly formed Chicago Symphony Orchestra on 17 October 1891. Dreiser must be referring to this opening series of concerts. He later published an appreciation of Thomas in the 4 February 1899 issue of *Success:* "His Life Given Up to Music"; reprinted in *Selected Magazine Articles of Theodore Dreiser*, ed. Yoshinobu Hakutani. 2 vols. (Rutherford, N.J.: Farleigh Dickinson University Press, 1987), 2: 23–30.

28.32 **Booth . . . Goodwin** All were among the foremost performers in the American theater of the 1880s and early 1890s: Edwin Booth (1833–93), Lawrence Barrett (1838–91), Helena Modjeska (1840–1909), Fanny Davenport (1850–98), Mary Anderson (1859–1940), Joseph Jefferson (1829–1905), and Nat Goodwin (1857–1919).

31.6 **Here at forty** Dreiser turned forty in 1911, which seems too early a date for this writing. He may simply mean that he is in his forties.

32.14 **Paul** Johann Paul Dreiser, Jr. (1857 or 1859–1906), Dreiser's oldest living brother. He adopted the name Paul Dresser when he went to work in the theater as a singer, composer, and comic actor.

37.12 **Tillie** That is, Claire Dreiser, from her middle name Clothilde.

37.17 **Schubert . . . MacDowell** Franz Schubert (1797–1828), Austrian composer of the romantic school; Edward MacDowell (1861–1908), American composer of piano and orchestral composition.

Chapter VI

41.1 **I deliberately . . . resigned** In the holograph, Dreiser says that he left the Corbin Company on being told that his "services would no longer be required,—why I could never find out." Why he altered his explanation so drastically in TS1 is not clear.

42.14 **David B[ennett] Hill** (1843–1910) Governor of New York (1885–91) and U.S. senator (1892–97).

42.15 **Thomas B. Hendricks** No one with this name is on record as having been active in Democratic politics in 1892. Dreiser is perhaps remembering Thomas Andrews Hendricks, governor of Indiana in 1872 and U.S. congressman (1851–55) and senator (1863–69). Hendricks, who was born in 1819, became Grover Cleveland's vice-president in 1885 but died that year.

42.18 **James G[illespie] Blaine** (1830–93) U.S. representative (1863–76) and senator (1876–81) as well as a Republican candidate for president in 1884.

42.19 **William B[oyd] Allison** (1829–1908) U.S. representative (1862–70) and senator (1872–1908).

42.29 **Wallace and Tyndall** Alfred Russel Wallace (1823–1913) was a naturalist who arrived at the theory of natural selection independently of Darwin and wrote many scientific articles; John Tyndall (1820–93) was a physicist and an author of books that popularized science.

Chapter VII

44.3 **Melville E[lijah] Stone** (1848–1929) Founded the Chicago *Daily News* in 1876 and was general manager of the Associated Press (1900–23).

44.4 **Victor F[reemont] Lawson** (1850–1925) In addition to owning the *Daily News,* Lawson was at various times the owner of several other Chicago newspapers and director of the Associated Press (1893–1925).

44.5 **Joseph Medill** (1823–99) Publisher and editor of the *Tribune* from 1874 until his death.

44.6 **Eugene Field** Although Field had served as managing editor of the Kansas City *Times* and Denver *Tribune,* his position on the *Record* (which was the morning edition of the *Daily News*) was as feature writer. See Charles H. Dennis in *Eugene Field's Creative Years* (1924; reprint, St. Clair Shores, Mich.: Scholarly Press, 1971).

44.7 **William Penn Nixon** (1833–1912) Edited and published the *Inter Ocean* from 1875 until 1897, when it became the property of Charles Tyson

Yerkes, the Chicago traction magnate on whom Dreiser modeled Frank Cowperwood, the protagonist of *The Financier, The Titan,* and *The Stoic.*

44.8 **George Ade** (1866–1944) A reporter for the *Record* from 1890 to 1900. He is best known as the author of *Fables in Slang* (1899), humorous books, plays, and musical comedies.

44.8 **Finley Peter Dunne** (1867–1936) Best known for his humorous fictional newspaper sketches centering on Mr. Dooley, an Irish saloonkeeper-philosopher, which were republished in a series of popular books beginning with *Mr. Dooley in Peace and War* (1898). In 1892 Dunne was a reporter and editor for the *Herald* and its evening edition, the *Post.*

44.9 **Brand Whitlock** (1869–1934) A reporter and political correspondent for the *Herald* (1891–93). From 1905 to 1913 he was the liberal reform mayor of Toledo, Ohio, and from 1913 to 1922 he was U.S. minister and ambassador to Belgium. He gained additional fame as the author of realistic novels such as *The 13th District* (1902) as well as autobiographies and political commentaries.

47.19 **John [Milo] Maxwell** (1866–1929) Newspaperman who became Dreiser's lifelong friend.

Chapter VIII

50.26 **reprobate gambler and financier** Michael Cassius McDonald, a rich Democratic political and gambling boss, owner of an extensive gaming establishment at Clark and Monroe streets called The Store. He is discussed at length by Lloyd Wendt and Herman Kogan in *Lords of the Levee* (Indianapolis, Ind.: Bobbs-Merrill, 1943).

Chapter IX

57.22 **Richard [Parks] Bland** (1835–99) U.S. representative (1873–95 and 1897–99) and one of the leading champions of the Free Silver movement.

58.7 **Benjamin Ryan Tillman** (1847–1918) Governor of South Carolina (1890–94) and U.S. senator (1895–1918). He was opposed to the policies of Grover Cleveland.

60.20 **John G[riffin] Carlisle** (1835–1910) At the time of the Democratic convention, Carlisle was U.S. senator from Kentucky (1890–93). He served as secretary of the treasury from 1893 to 1897.

60.38 **Democratic United States Supreme Court justice** Dreiser had most likely encountered Chief Justice Melville Weston Fuller (1833–1910). A Chicago Democrat, Fuller had been named chief justice by Cleveland in 1888. Of the justices on the Supreme Court in 1892, Fuller is the only one who ever had newspaper reporting experience.

Chapter X

63.3   **Senator** ——   In the holograph Dreiser gives "McEntee" as the senator's name, but then at 65.11 and 65.18 and at 68.12 of chapter XI he leaves a blank space, as if he has begun to have doubts about the man's identity. No one so named has ever been a U.S. senator or representative. No evidence has been found to indicate that either senator from South Carolina was considered a dark horse candidate at the 1892 convention.

63.14   **Richard Croker**   (1841–1922) Head of the Tammany organization from 1886 to 1902.

63.14   **[William] Bourke Cockran**   (1854–1923) Famed for his oratorical skills, Cockran was U.S. representative from New York for several terms between 1887 and 1923.

63.16   **John F. Carroll**   (d. 1911) Richard Croker's most important lieutenant, entrusted with the supervision of the party machine when Croker was out of the country. In 1892 his official position was that of New York City Clerk of the Court of General Sessions.

66.26   **William C[ollins] Whitney**   (1841–1904) Grover Cleveland's secretary of the navy (1885–89) as well as one of his close advisers during the 1892 convention.

Chapter XI

68.33   **Adlai [Ewing] Stevenson**   (1835–1914) U.S. representative from Illinois (1875–77 and 1879–81) and Grover Cleveland's vice-president (1893–97).

72.11   **"Charlie" Seymour**   A close friend of Finley Peter Dunne, with whom he and several other Chicago reporters organized the locally well-known Whitechapel Club. He is said by Elmer Ellis to have been "generally recognized as the greatest reporter of his day in Chicago." See *Mr. Dooley's America* (New York: Alfred A. Knopf, 1941), p. 23.

72.11   **Charles D'Almy**   Said by Elmer Ellis (who calls him Charles D. Almy) to have been the "reporter-editor with the least restraint of all" the members of the Whitechapel Club. See *Mr. Dooley's America* (New York: Alfred A. Knopf, 1941), p. 52.

73.20   **Jean Valjean**   The protagonist of Victor Hugo's *Les Misérables* (1862).

Chapter XII

74.31   **[Henry Morton] Stanley**   (1841–1904) The renowned explorer, who as a young reporter was sent to central Africa by the New York *Herald* to rescue the missionary-explorer David Livingstone.

76.29   **one of my heroines**   In chapter 10 of *Sister Carrie*, Drouet takes rooms for Carrie and himself in Odgen Place.

78.14   **Hogarthian**   An allusion to the grimly realistic street scenes in such series as the "Harlot's Progress" and the "Rake's Progress," engraved by the English artist William Hogarth (1697–1764).

79.39   **the first newspaper special I ever wrote**   "Cheyenne, Haunt of Misery and Crime," appeared in the *Globe* on 24 July 1892. See *TDJ*, pp. 4–7.

Chapter XIII

80.31   **Earlier in this self-analysis**   See especially chapter 36 of *Dawn*.

81.22   **hodden-minded**   This coinage, which for Dreiser may have had an association with *hod-carrier* or *hodman*, implies a person of dull, unimaginative, commonplace mental capacities.

84.14   **a few parables of my own . . . signature of "Carl Dreiser"**   The only story in the *Globe* so signed is "The Return of Genius," 23 October 1892. See *TDJ*, pp. 16–17.

85.22   **lymphatic**   For Dreiser, this word means languid, passive, and lacking in mental and physical energy.

85.27   **my Clarissa**   In chapter XVIII Dreiser twice calls this young woman Katharine. In referring to her here as "Clarissa" he is perhaps recalling the heroine of Samuel Richardson's novel *Clarissa Harlowe* (1747–48) and may be seeing himself as someone like her fascinating but unscrupulous seducer, Lovelace.

86.10   **[Francis] Bret Harte**   (1836–1902) American writer known principally for his short stories about the California gold rush. It is to Harte's rough-hewn characters rather than to Harte himself that Dreiser is referring.

87.16   **vice**   In place of.

90.1   **[Arthur] Schopenhauer**   (1788–1860) German philosopher, known in the 1890s and later for his pessimism and misogyny.

Chapter XIV

91.9   **series of assignments**   Dreiser wrote at least seventeen articles for this series. They appeared in the *Globe* between 15 September and 26 October 1892. For a representative selection and a list of the titles see *TDJ*, pp. 7–15, 387.

93.38   **In company with a private detective . . . released on bail**   None of Dreiser's auction-shop articles describes a situation exactly like this. "Arrested," 19 October 1892, tells of the arrest of an auction-shop proprietor by a police department detective who himself served the warrant and took the man to the station, presumably accompanied by Dreiser. See *TDJ*, pp. 7–15, 387.

95.17 **write out this whole story just as it occurred**   None of Dreiser's auction-shop articles describes such a situation.

95.31 **George Kennan**   (1845–1924) American journalist who in 1891 published *Siberia and the Exile System*. His name has been supplied by the editor because Dreiser was unable to recall it and left blank spaces for it in the holograph and TS1 and TS2.

96.21 **Henry C. Millerand**   Probably an invented name because it does not appear in the *Globe-Democrat* during 1892–93. In the galley proof of the 1922 edition of *A Book about Myself*, Dreiser deleted the Millerand name and replaced it with "a man whose name I have forgotten—Leland, I think—." This name also does not appear in the newspaper during the same period. The man Dreiser could not remember is apparently Walter Barlow Stevens (1848–1939), the *Globe-Democrat's* chief Washington correspondent (1884–1903). See Jim Allee Hart, *A History of the St. Louis Globe-Democrat* (Columbia: University of Missouri Press, 1961), p. 139.

97.2 **Joseph B[urbridge] McCullagh**   (1842–96) Editor in chief from 1879 until his death. A full account of his life and times is Charles C. Clayton's *Little Mack: Joseph B. McCullagh of the St. Louis Globe-Democrat* (Carbondale: Southern Illinois University Press, 1969).

97.15 **easy gossip writing . . . three weeks straight**   Four installments of "Gossip of Chicago's Big Show" appeared in the *Globe-Democrat* from 21 through 24 October 1892. Many, if not all, of the paragraphs were written by Dreiser. For a selection see *HC*, pp. 11–21.

Chapter XV

99.32 **[Jean Antoine] Watteau**   (1684–1721) French painter known for his idealized pastoral scenes.

100.22 **The silly belief I have previously mentioned**   In chapter 49 of *Dawn*, Dreiser explains that because of his youthful practice of masturbation, he believed that he had made himself permanently impotent.

103.10 **matrix**   An archaic word meaning *uterus*.

103.27 **might possibly have ended badly for the two of us**   Dreiser means that he and Lois were running a risk of being arrested for fornication.

104.2 **ethical culture lecture**   A lecture on the nonsectarian religious humanism espoused by the Society of Ethical Culture, founded in New York in 1876 by Felix Adler (1851–1933), German-born social welfare leader.

104.13 **although I had . . . side, not the other**   Dreiser added this passage to TS1 in response to a note at the bottom of the page from his typist, Estelle Kubitz: "Tra-la-la—Hast forgotten Miss Winstead?—Tra-la-la!"

105.9 The holograph of chapter XV continues for five more pages to tell of the termination of the affair with Lois and of her marriage to Harry. Dreiser moved this passage to chapter XXIII of TS1 and expanded it.

Chapter XVI

105.28   **November 1892**   Inasmuch as the last article identifiably by Dreiser appeared in the *Globe* on Saturday, 29 October, he probably went to St. Louis the next day. See "About the Hotels," *HC*, pp. 2–8.

106.16   **the Greek boy**   Dreiser refers to the widely known legend, found earliest in Plutarch's life of Lycurgus (xviii, 1), about a Spartan lad who demonstrated his ability to withstand pain by allowing a fox he had stolen and hidden under his cloak to tear out his bowels with its teeth and claws.

106.23   **Edmond O'Neill**   No one with this name has been identified.

107.30   **"Little Mack"**   This poem is found in Field's *Little Book of Western Verse* (New York: Scribner's, 1895), pp. 36–39. It is reprinted in Charles C. Clayton's *Little Mack: Joseph B. McCullagh of the St. Louis Globe-Democrat* (Carbondale: Southern Illinois University Press, 1969), pp. vii–viii.

108.28   *Nicholas Nickleby*   A novel by Charles Dickens, published in 1838–39.

109.29   **a pale, diaphanous creature**   In a letter to Dreiser of 19 December 1927, Thomas A. Wright, a former *Globe-Democrat* reporter, identifies this man as "Denny—a good routine man," who had died at his typewriter a few years earlier (Letter file, Dreiser Collection, Van Pelt-Dietrich Library Center, University of Pennsylvania).

110.30   **Cerberus**   In Greek mythology, a monstrous three-headed dog who guards the gateway of Hades.

110.34   **Neroic**   Dreiser is referring to the face of the Roman emperor Nero, but the term also appropriately suggests Mitchell's tyrannical, even sadistic, behavior.

111.35   **whirling white mice**   A type commonly called *waltzing mice*, characterized by an inability to progress in a straight line and a tendency to whirl in small circles.

112.36   **Preller Trunk Mystery**   An Englishman named W. H. Lenox Maxwell poisoned his countryman C. Arthur Preller and left his body locked in a trunk in the Southern Hotel. Maxwell was hanged in St. Louis 10 August 1888 after a sensational, nationally reported trial. Dreiser alludes to the case in his story "Dey's Mitey Quair Laws," *St. Louis Republic,* 26 May 1893, p. 12.

112.37   **that big Missouri-Pacific train robbery last year**   Hartung may have been referring to a holdup pulled off the preceding 23 January by two bandits on a train nearing Lamar, Missouri. After killing a policeman, they fled on a freight train and were pursued by two detectives. At Pleasanton, Kansas, their boxcar was surrounded by a posse, and after an hour-long exchange of gunfire, one bandit was killed and the other surrendered.

Chapter XVII

113.24   **Tobias Mitchell**   Dreiser's negative evaluation of Mitchell's character is supported by the comments of a former *Globe-Democrat* reporter who wrote to him after reading *A Book about Myself.* Thomas A. Wright calls Mitchell "that damned, fat, ignorant ass" and relates that McCullagh eventually had to get rid of him because his bumptious, despotic manner was always causing good reporters to quit the paper (19 December 1927, Letter file, Dreiser Collection, Van Pelt-Dietrich Library Center, University of Pennsylvania). McCullagh had him placed as clerk of the St. Louis Board of Health, from which job he was eventually fired for graft and extortion.

113.26   **An old drunken railroad reporter**   Albert Johnson a former *Globe-Democrat* reporter, identifies this man as "Thornton, who told me that most of the reporters on the Globe-Democrat acted too cocky, and, said he, 'they smell cocky, too'" (3 October 1924, Letter file, Dreiser Collection, Van Pelt-Dietrich Library Center, University of Pennsylvania).

116.14   *Post-Dispatch*   Founded in 1878 by Joseph Pulitzer and personally managed by him until 1883 when he moved to New York and purchased the *World.*

116.20   **[Charles Anderson] Dana**   (1819–97) Part-owner and editor of the New York *Sun* from 1868 until his death. From 1847 to 1862 he was managing editor of the New York *Tribune* under Horace Greeley.

116.37   **its oldest and best**   The venerable Planters' House was being replaced by the $2 million New Planters' House, which was completed in 1893.

117.3   **a tremendous defalcation**   In the early morning of 19 December 1892, a fire was discovered in the St. Louis city treasurer's office, and a few hours later Edward Foerstal, the assistant city treasurer, killed himself. Immediate investigation revealed that the city treasury was short in excess of $65,000. It was assumed that Edward had set the fire to destroy evidence. Before long, however, his father, Michael Foerstal, the city treasurer, a respected businessman and prominent Republican, was suspended from office and later charged with embezzlement. The case was a heavily reported city sensation and dragged on for the entire period of Dreiser's stay in St. Louis.

117.8   **Forest**   The eleventh edition of the *Encyclopaedia Britannica* gives the exact size of Forest Park as 1,372 acres.

117.29   *Chronicle*   Founded in 1880, this evening paper was owned by E. W. Scripps until it was absorbed by the St. Louis *Star* in 1905.

Chapter XVIII

120.13   **the Mercantile**   This social club had been established in 1881 and was instrumental in initiating many projects designed to improve the civic and business life of the city. It began the construction of its new club building in 1891.

122.2   **[William J.] Lemp [Brewing Company]**   Founded by J. Adam Lemp in 1842, this company was the second largest brewery in St. Louis when Dreiser lived there. Originator of the famous Falstaff trademark, it went out of business with the onset of Prohibition. See William L. Downard, *Dictionary of the History of the American Brewing and Distilling Industries* (Westport, Conn.: Greenwood Press, 1980), p. 108.

122.18 **he committed suicide** McCullagh died 30 December 1896 as the result of a fall from his second-story bedroom window. Many of his friends and colleagues assumed that he had committed suicide, and the *St. Louis Post-Dispatch* declared that he had killed himself as a consequence of depression and the prolonged sufferings of acute asthma. Carefully weighing the evidence, Charles C. Clayton concludes that his death must have been accidental (*Little Mack: Joseph B. McCullagh of the St. Louis Globe-Democrat* [Carbondale: Southern Illinois University Press, 1969], pp. 216–19), but Jim Allee Hart says that it was an act of suicide (see *A History of the St. Louis Globe-Democrat* [Columbia: University of Missouri Press, 1961], p. 157).

122.26 **telegraph editor** Identified as O. R. Lake by Charles C. Clayton in *Little Mack: Joseph B. McCullagh of the St. Louis Globe-Democrat* (Carbondale: Southern Illinois University Press, 1969), p. 229.

123.21 **Katharine** See note for chapter XIII, 85.27.

124.28 **supported** In the galley proof of *A Book about Myself*, Dreiser crossed out this word and replaced it with "starved."

125.14 **she wrote me . . . pangs of longing** See note for chapter XXIII, 158.20.

Chapter XIX

128.6 **a short period of masturbation** See note for chapter XV, 100.22.

128.14 **I had had no physical contact with women** See note for chapter III, 15.26.

129.12 **[Alphonse] Daudet** (1840–97) French novelist, whose *Sapho* was published in 1884. A play based on this novel had a succes de scandale in New York in 1899 while Dreiser was writing *Sister Carrie*. He refers to the central character, Sapho, an immoral Parisian model, in chapter 7 of his novel.

129.33 **a drunken woman . . . injured in an accident** Such incidents were actually reported by Dreiser for the *Globe-Democrat* and *Republic*. For example, see "A Drunken Mother's Disgrace," *St. Louis Globe-Democrat*, 29 November 1892, p. 9; and "Fever's Frenzy," *St. Louis Republic*, 9 August 1893, pp. 1–2; the latter is reprinted in *TDJ*, pp. 138–46.

130.18 **[Eugene] Sandow** (1867–1925) Nationally known German-born professional strongman and exponent of physical culture whose exhibition at the Columbian Exposition may have been seen by Dreiser.

131.5 **shelter** After this word in the UCLA typescript, Dreiser added the following in his own hand: "and yet half knowing that if it had been offered I would have refused it."

131.37 **North 7th Street police station** This station had jurisdiction over the section designated as the Third District, which in the 1890s extended from the Mississippi River west to Grand Avenue and was bounded on the south by Washington Avenue and on the north by Cass Avenue. In *Newspaper Days*, Dreiser speaks only of the "North 7th Street station," but 1890s newspapers in St. Louis always referred to it as the *Third District Station*, a term also used in Dreiser's own news stories. It was customary turn-of-the-century practice to assign a newly hired reporter to cover a police precinct station for about six months, during which he would be responsible for gathering news of accidents, crimes, arrests, fires, and other disturbances in the district. That Dreiser retained the Third District beat throughout his six months at the *Globe-Democrat* is indicated by the *St. Louis Chronicle's* taunting reference to him in April 1893 as a "police reporter."

132.2 **Edward Butler** (1838–1911) Butler was at the height of his political power when Dreiser met him. Never an office seeker himself, he preferred to organize and control politics behind the scenes. Lincoln Steffens later singled him out as the city's chief "boodler" in his exposé of political corruption in St. Louis (*The Shame of the Cities*, 1904). Dreiser's interview with Butler immediately after the Democrats' loss of the spring 1893 mayoral election is reprinted in *TDJ*, pp. 62–65. Butler was the prototype of Edward Malia Butler, one of Dreiser's best-realized characters in *The Financier*.

132.7 **Terence V[incent] Powderly** (1849–1924) American-born labor leader, who characteristically advocated cooperation rather than such combative union tactics as strikes in negotiating with employers. He headed the Knights of Labor (founded in 1869) from 1879 to 1893, the years of its greatest prestige and influence with American workers. The Knights' General Assembly to which Dreiser refers was held in St. Louis, 14–23 November 1892, in Walhalla Hall, located at 10th Street and Franklin Avenue. The *Globe-Democrat* ran eleven articles covering its activities. Of these, the one that seems best to fit Dreiser's description of the meeting he covered is "Reports and Recommendations," 17 November 1892, p. 9.

133.4 **he was an Englishman** Powderly was of Irish ancestry.

134.31 **One of his sons** James Joseph Butler (1862–1917) was somewhat more accomplished than Dreiser's curt dismissal of him indicates. A graduate of St. Louis University, he practiced law in addition to managing his father's playhouse, the Standard Theater, the largest in the city. A controversial figure on whom some of the resentment against his father probably rubbed off, he represented his district in the 57th and 58th U.S. Congresses (1902–5). His biographer claims that he was a scholar by inclination, had a considerable library and the city's largest collection of paintings, and wrote poetry on occasion. He headed several St. Louis corporations and managed his father's estate efficiently after the latter's death (*National Encyclopaedia of American Biography*, 17:251). Dreiser's negative estimate of him may stem from the fact that in 1893 young Butler was involved in a brothel shooting that led to his dismissal from the office of city attorney. The shooting was indirectly connected with the charge that was made in the *Sunday Mirror* by Dreiser's friend William Marion Reedy that an illegal dice game was being run in the basement of the Standard. See "Shot James N. Leary," *St. Louis Republic*, 27 December 1893, p. 1.

134.33   **Frank James**   (1843–1915) William A. Settle, Jr., confirms that from 1894 to 1901 James "was a doorman at Ed Butler's Standard Theatre, a burlesque house in St. Louis." See *Jesse James Was His Name* (Columbia: University of Missouri Press, 1966), p. 163.

Chapter XX

135.34   **John P[eter] Altgeld**   (1847–1902) Governor of Illinois from 1893 to 1897. As a liberal Democrat, he supported William Jennings Bryan and the Free Silver movement. His most controversial act while governor was pardoning the six surviving "anarchists" convicted for their alleged role in the Haymarket Riot (1886). Altgeld is the prototype of Governor Swanson in Dreiser's *The Titan* (1914).

136.3   **William Joel Stone**   (1848–1918) Governor of Missouri (1893–97). He had been a U.S. representative (1885–91) and was to be a U.S. senator (1903–18). He was the most powerful and influential Democrat in Missouri politics for a quarter of a century.

136.4   **Cyrus P[ackard] Walbridge**   (1849–1921) Mayor of St. Louis (1893–97). A lawyer by profession, he was the part-owner and president of a large drug firm that manufactured patent medicines. He was one of the most influential Republicans in St. Louis politics.

136.11   **Edward [A.] Noonan**   (b. 1849) Mayor of St. Louis (1889–93). A lawyer by profession and an independent Democrat, he was elected over the opposition of the Butler machine. Although regularly attacked by the Republican *Globe-Democrat*, he was a competent and apparently an honest mayor whose chief accomplishment was to persuade railroad companies operating in St. Louis to build a magnificent new depot.

136.20   **1893**   Dreiser appears to be remembering the intense partisan campaigning carried on by the St. Louis newspapers before the spring mayoral election of this year, not 1892 as the holograph reads.

137.25   **of his home**   According to Charles C. Clayton, McCullagh was residing in the home of his sister-in-law at the time of his death. See *Little Mack: Joseph B. McCullagh of the St. Louis Globe-Democrat* (Carbondale: Southern Illinois University Press, 1969), pp. 204, 216–17.

137.31   **Captain [Henry] King**   (1842–1915) A Civil War veteran, King joined the *Globe-Democrat* as columnist and editorial writer in 1883 after working for several Kansas newspapers. He succeeded McCullagh as editor in chief and held that position until his death. See Jim Allee Hart, *A History of the St. Louis Globe-Democrat* (Columbia: University of Missouri Press, 1961), pp. 173–89.

137.31 **Casper S[alathiel] Yost** (1864–1941) Joined the *Globe-Democrat* in 1889 and served as assistant and managing editor and Sunday editor from 1890 to 1915. He also wrote books on such subjects as journalism, history, spiritualism, and religion.

139.1 **[Commodore Andrew Hull] Foote** (1806–63) Commander of the Union naval forces on the upper Mississippi (1861–62). He was at the reduction of Forts Henry and Donelson. In TS3 Admiral Farragut is incorrectly named as the officer McCullagh reported on, an error that was retained in *A Book about Myself*. See Charles C. Clayton, *Little Mack: Joseph B. McCullagh of the St. Louis Globe-Democrat* (Carbondale: Southern Illinois University Press, 1969), pp. 12–17.

139.1 **[General William Tecumseh] Sherman** (1820–91) Civil War commander, most renowned for his devastating "March to the Sea" through Georgia and the Carolinas. McCullagh disliked Sherman, thought him a vainglorious and an inaccurate Civil War historian, and regularly ridiculed him in editorials.

139.8 **Daniel M. Houser** (1834–1915) American-born cofounder of the *Globe-Democrat* who was its president and general manager. Dreiser underestimates the significance of his role in the operation of the newspaper. See Jim Allee Hart, *A History of the St. Louis Globe-Democrat* (Columbia: University of Missouri Press, 1961), pp. 161–72.

140.7 **"Four Courts"** Officially known as the Municipal Courts Building, this structure was located at 12th and Clark streets and had been built in 1869–70 after the design of architect Thomas Walsh. An impressive large building of Second Empire design, it housed the police court, criminal court, and courts of criminal correction as well as the departments Dreiser specifies.

140.24 **buzzard lawyers** That is, unscrupulous second-rate lawyers who hung out at the police station and court hoping to snare clients—the 1890's equivalent of "ambulance chasers."

142.8 **Maggie Sanders' place** During Dreiser's stay in St. Louis, the newspapers carried many stories emanating from Chestnut Street brothels but not from one operated by a woman so named.

Chapter XXI

144.24 **"tenderloin"** A district devoted to vice from which corrupt policemen and politicians extort graft. The word is supposed to have been coined by a

New York City policeman, who compared the lucrative vice district that illegally sustained him to a juicy piece of steak. The earliest citation in *OED* (2nd ed.) is from 1887.

144.35 **[William Edward Hartpole] Lecky**   (1838–1903) Irish historian and essayist.

145.23 **I am in a simple farming region**   During June and July of 1917 when he wrote this chapter, Dreiser stayed at Henry Baille Smith's farmhouse at Westminster, Maryland.

146.1 **Rockefeller Commission . . . Europe and here**   A reference to a commission established by the Bureau of Social Hygiene and chaired by John D. Rockefeller, Jr., which sponsored investigations of prostitution in New York City and eleven European countries. Dreiser had presumably read Abraham Flexner's report, *Prostitution in Europe* (New York: Century, 1914), which argues that a majority of prostitutes return to being respectable citizens but which does not give a specific percentage (see pp. 21–24).

146.20 **[Adolphe William] Bouguereau**   (1825–1905) French artist, highly esteemed in the nineteenth century for his decorative and religious paintings.

146.28 **three . . . individuals**   In addition to Peter B. McCord and Richard Wood, *Globe-Democrat* staff artists at this time were Armand Welcker (see note for 147.30) and C. R. Grimm or Grimes as well as someone who signed his drawings "Rogers."

147.30 **double-page spread . . . new depot**   See "Greatest in the World," *TDJ*, pp. 21–31. This story was not illustrated by McCord but by Richard Wood and Armand Welcker. No *Globe-Democrat* story written by Dreiser and illustrated by McCord has been identified.

Chapter XXII

148.34 **H[enry] W[ashington] Thomas**   (1832–1909) Popular pulpit orator who founded the People's Church after being expelled from the Methodist Church for his liberal ideas and association with nondenominational ministers and atheists. He held Sunday services regularly in McVicker's Theatre in Chicago between 1880 and 1901.

149.3 **Arthur Henry**   (1867–1934) Dreiser and Henry first met in 1894 when the latter was editor of the *Toledo Blade* (see chapter LXV).

149.4 **John Cowper Powys**   (1872–1963) English novelist, essayist, and poet. He and Dreiser met in 1915 and remained lifelong friends.

149.7 **wire to carbon**   A reference to the igniting of an electric carbon arc lamp, a once common means of street illumination.

149.28 Most of the characterization of McCord was later incorporated into Dreiser's essay "Peter" in *Twelve Men* (1919). Reviewing the "Newspaper Days" manuscript in 1920, H. L. Mencken strongly urged that the McCord sketch be omitted as repetitious (see *Dreiser-Mencken Letters*, pp. 400, 402). Dreiser followed this recommendation. See the 1922 edition of *A Book about Myself*, p. 121.

150.24   **[Gaston Camille Charles] Maspero**   (1846–1916) French Egyptologist and author of books on archaeology.

150.25   **[James Anthony] Froude**   (1818–94) English historian, close friend and biographer of Thomas Carlyle.

150.25   **Rawlinson**   Dreiser is referring to either Henry Creswick Rawlinson (1810–95), English Assyriologist, or his brother George Rawlinson (1812–1902), Orientalist and Oxford professor of ancient history.

150.25   **[Jean] Froissart**   (1333?–1400?) French historian. His *Chroniques*, covering the period 1325 to 1400, deal with the affairs of Flanders, France, Spain, Portugal, and England.

150.25   **[Henry] Hallam**   (1777–1859) English scholar and author of English and European histories and of *Introduction to the Literature of Europe*.

151.12   **Zoroastrians**   Followers of the Persian prophet Zoroaster (sixth century B.C.).

151.13   **Parsees**   Descendants of Zoroastrians who sought refuge outside Persia, principally in Bombay.

152.20   **Priapus**   God of fertility identified with a symbolic phallus, worshiped in ancient Greece and Italy.

152.20   **the sex trinity**   Perhaps a reference to Cybele, Dionysus, and Pan, whose orgiastic fertility rites were celebrated together in ancient Greece.

152.21   **Astarte**   Ancient Semitic goddess of fertility and reproduction. Known also as Ashtart, Ashtoreth, and Ishtar.

152.25   **Peter is dead now**   McCord died in 1908.

155.1   **Algernon Charles Claude Veer de Veer**   A synthetic name intended to suggest Wood's snootiness and highly mannered aestheticism.

Chapter XXIII

156.33   **funeral of . . . fire picture**   The first and third stories have not been identified. The second is presumably "The Merry Skaters," which appeared in the *Republic*, 27 January 1894, p. 1, and which is the only story about skating at Forest Park to be printed in either of the newspapers for which Dreiser worked while he was in St. Louis.

157.30   **Nana**   (1880) A novel about a Parisian actress who becomes a dissolute courtesan, *Nana* was for American readers in the 1890s the quintessential "dirty" French novel.

158.20   Dreiser uses most of the details and much of the phrasing of this letter in Book 1, chapter 13 of *The "Genius,"* in which he attributes it to Ruby Kenny, a character modeled in part on Lois.

160.22   **"fast-widowing sky"**   The source of this quotation has not been identified. The phrase evokes the atmosphere of dusk when the sky is losing the sun.

162.14 **another newspaperman.** The man whose name Dreiser could not remember (he leaves a blank space in the holograph) was identified as Arthur Grubb in a letter of 3 October 1924 to Dreiser from Albert Johnson, who adds that Grubb "was killed in an opium joint, (his baby died the same night)" (Letter file, Dreiser Collection, Van Pelt-Dietrich Library Center, University of Pennsylvania).

162.17 **Augustus Thomas** (1857–1934) *Alabama* (1891), the first hit of this prolific playwright, had its initial run in St. Louis the week of 26 September 1892. Between 1885 and 1888 Thomas worked as a reporter in St. Louis, not for the *Star* but for the *Missouri Republican* and the *Post-Dispatch*.

162.19 **Henry [Martyn] Blossom** (1866–1919) Novelist, playwright, and, most notably, librettist for Victor Herbert. His novel *The Documents in Evidence* (1893) may be the book to which Dreiser refers.

162.20 **Alfred [George] Robyn** (1860–1935) Composer of songs and musical comedies (one to a libretto by Henry Blossom). The work Dreiser refers to is *Jacinta*, "a romantic Mexican opera in two acts," then in production in St. Louis and performed in May 1893.

162.25 **Eugene Field** Born in St. Louis in 1850, Field worked for the *Journal* (1873–75) and the *Times-Journal* (1876–80) but never for the *Globe-Democrat*.

162.26 **Mark Twain** Worked as a compositor for the *Evening News* in St. Louis, where he lived on and off between 1853 and 1857. His biographers do not mention his being "drunk and hopeless" during this time. Dreiser may be repeating vague newspapermen's gossip he had heard.

Chapter XXIV

163.12 **Zolaesque scene . . . a hairbrush** In the first chapter of his novel *L'Assommoir* (1877), the French novelist Émile Zola (1840–1902) describes a ferocious fight between two laundresses, culminating in one spanking the other.

163.18 **the Romanist in Henry Esmond** Father Holt, a Jacobite spy, in this 1852 novel by William Makepeace Thackeray (1811–63).

164.6 **literature** In TS3 this word is changed to "realism."

166.13 **W[illiam] C[owper] Brann** (1855–98) Worked as a reporter for the *Globe-Democrat* (1875–87) and again briefly in 1892 when he could have contributed to the "Corridors" column, which first began to appear in December 1890.

167.32 **temptings of Mephistopheles** Dreiser means Mephistopheles' temptation of Faust.

167.37 **Ally Sloper** The name is derived from *Ally Sloper's Half Holiday*, a humorous weekly penny paper published in London (1884–1916). See below.

169.10   **a comic opera laid in Algeria**   Perhaps Dreiser is remembering *The Algerian*, by Reginald De Koven and Glen Macdonough, which is set in Algeria and which ran in St. Louis the week beginning 25 February 1894, shortly before he quit the *Republic* and left for the East.

Chapter XXV

171.16   **the Lindell**   Built in 1874, this hotel was located at Washington Avenue and 6th Street.

173.14   **the Catholic Archbishop**   Peter Richard Kenrick (1806–96) was in declining health, and the newspapers in 1892 and 1893 carried numerous stories speculating on his approaching death and his possible successor. In

April 1893 John Joseph Kain (1841–1903) of Wheeling, West Virginia, was named coadjutor archbishop.

174.23   **great public ball . . . The Veiled Prophet's**   Dating from 1878, this annual fall festivity was sponsored by the Mercantile Club, a social organization of leading businessmen, and was the premier event of the St. Louis social season. In the 1890s it was accompanied by a civic exposition and a parade of elaborately decorated floats. Attendance at the ball was by invitation only, and the highlight of the evening was the selection of the Veiled Prophet's queen from among a group of young socialites. The name of the ball derives from "The Veiled Prophet of Khorassan," the first story in Thomas Moore's *Lalla Rookh* (1817). Dreiser covered this event for the *Republic* on 4 October 1893. See "Brilliant Beyond Compare: The Glittering Ballroom," *TDJ*, pp. 184–88.

175.26   **I.O.O.F.**   Independent Order of Odd Fellows.

175.33   **a triple or quadruple murder**   Dreiser covered this story for the *Republic*, not the *Globe-Democrat*, two months before his coverage of the Veiled Prophet's ball. See "Fever's Frenzy," *TDJ*, pp. 138–46. His summary of the crime is not accurate. The murderer killed only one of his sons. Dreiser seems to have mixed in details of an earlier, somewhat similar murder. See "A Shocking Tragedy," *St. Louis Republic*, 12 May 1893, p. 2.

177.30   **I hurried to the Four Courts**   Dreiser's interview of the murderer occurred six weeks after the crime when the murderer had recovered from his illness and been transferred from the hospital to the jail. See "His Own Story," *TDJ*, pp. 174–79.

Chapter XXVI

180.5   **fine piece of chicane**   During the time Dreiser lived in St. Louis, the only stable fire that claimed a human life and destroyed a multitude of horses occurred on 21 May 1893, while he was with the *Republic*. For an example of one of the stories he wrote about this disaster, see "The Boy's Body Found," *TDJ*, pp. 99–102.

182.11   **Annie Besant**   (1847–1933) English devotee of Madame Blavatsky and president of the Theosophical Society from 1907 until her death. See "Theosophy and Spiritualism," *TDJ*, pp. 36–38.

182.14   **spiritualist . . . mind reader**   On p. 149 of the 1922 edition of *A Book about Myself*, Dreiser supplied the specific names "Eva Fay" and "Bishop." Annie Eva Fay (1855–1927) was a famous American spirit medium who baffled generations of experts. Washington Irving Bishop (ca. 1848–89) was a professional telepathist who performed in theaters.

182.15   **Reverend Sam[uel Porter] Jones**   (1847–1906) Widely known Alabama-born evangelist and revivalist.

182.17   **John L[awrence] Sullivan**   (1858–1918) Defeated by **[James J.] Corbett** (1866–1933) in a match held on 7 September 1892, after which both pugilists took up acting and toured the theatrical circuit. Corbett appeared in St. Louis the week of 29 January 1893 in his own play, *Gentleman Jack,* and Sullivan came the week of 26 February 1893 in *The Man from Boston.* Both productions were reviewed for the *Globe-Democrat* by Dreiser.

182.18   **[Thomas Henry] Hall Caine**   (1853–1931) English novelist, author of such popular stories set in the Isle of Man as *The Deemster* (1887), *The Manxman* (1894), and *The Christian* (1897). Caine did not visit St. Louis while Dreiser was there.

182.20   **Henry Watterson**   (1840–1921) American journalist and politician, famed editor of the Louisville *Courier-Journal* (1868–1918). He lectured in St. Louis on 6 January 1893.

182.20   **Henry M. Stanley**   See note 74.31 for chapter XII. Stanley did not visit St. Louis while Dreiser was there.

182.21   **[Ignacy Jan] Paderewski**   (1860–1941) Famed Polish pianist, who first performed in St. Louis on 12 and 13 April 1893 as part of his second American tour. No interview with him was published in the *Globe-Democrat.*

182.21   **Nikola Tesla**   (1857–1943) American electrician and inventor, born in Austria-Hungary of Croatian parents. He lectured in St. Louis to a convention of electricians on 1 March 1893. The *Globe-Democrat* carried no interview with him but enthusiastically reviewed the lecture.

182.37   **Madame [Elena Petrovna] Blavatsky**   (1831–91) Russian traveler and spiritist; cofounder of the Theosophical Society (1875); and author of *Isis Unveiled* (1877), *The Key to Theosophy* (1889), and kindred works.

183.14   **"walk up . . . open grave"**   On 12 June 1892 Watterson had warned that if the Democratic party went to New York for its candidate "we shall walk through a slaughter-house into an open grave." Quoted in Allan Nevins's *Grover Cleveland: A Study in Courage* (New York: Dodd, Mead, 1932), p. 489.

183.17   **go to "the demnition bow-wows"**   In chapter 64 of Charles Dickens's *Nicholas Nickleby* (1839), the once foppish Mr. Martalini says this of himself when he acknowledges that he has wasted his good fortune and bankrupted himself.

183.24   **old clipping**   This clipping was not Dreiser's interview with Watterson that was printed in the *Globe-Democrat.* See "Mr. Watterson on Politics," *TDJ,* pp. 32–35.

183.25   **John L. Sullivan**   Sullivan appeared in a play in St. Louis the week of 26 February 1893, but no interview with him was published in the *Globe-Democrat.* But see "John L. Out for a Lark," *TDJ,* pp. 90–91.

185.24   **"Be ye . . . as doves."**   See Matthew 10.16.

186.6   **"the Beanery"**   Located next to the Planters' House (a hotel) and known formally as the Commercial Restaurant, this establishment was open around the clock and was a favorite resort of politicians, steamboatmen, reporters, and printers. Not to be confused with the Pine Street "beanery" referred to in chapter XXV, p. 178.

186.14   **If a document . . . take it**   Dreiser may be remembering an incident of the 1893 St. Louis mayoral campaign. When Judge Chester H. Krum wrote a personal letter to the Democratic party chairman explaining why he could not support James Bannerman, the party's candidate, a *Globe-Democrat* reporter stole a copy of it when the judge briefly stepped out of his office. The letter was then reprinted on the front page of the newspaper. See "The Local Campaign," *St. Louis Globe-Democrat*, 28 March 1893.

187.8   **A case of this kind**   Dreiser's recollection differs significantly from the real circumstances. He actually interviewed the defeated candidate after the election, not before. In the interview, Bannerman was not severely critical of St. Louis citizens, nor did he single out "local religionists" for ridicule. Instead he surmised that he had lost principally because the *Globe-Democrat* had supported his opponent. Democratic newspapers did not denounce the interview as a lie; they ignored it. Bannerman himself wrote a letter to the *Globe-Democrat*, protesting that he had been misquoted and that he did not hate Republicans (*Globe-Democrat*, 7 April 1893, p. 12). On p. 6 of this same issue, the *Globe-Democrat* printed a response, insisting that "the publication correctly represented the utterances of Mr. Bannerman in a conversation with a reporter from this paper, which Mr. Bannerman knew was intended for our columns."

Chapter XXVII

192.32   **Ben-Hur**   (1880) and **The Fair God** (1873) are romantic historical novels by the American writer Lew Wallace (1827–1905). **Ernest Maltravers** (1837) is a novel by the English writer Edward Bulwer-Lytton (1803–73). **The Sketch Book** (1819–20) and **The Chronicles of Spain** (i.e., A Chronicle of the Conquest of Granada) (1829) are both by Washington Irving (1783–1859). Charles Dickens's novel **Dombey and Son** was published in 1847 and 1848.

194.7   **Sam Jones variety**   See note 182.15 for chapter XXVI.

Chapter XXVIII

201.20   **second time . . . terrific catastrophes**   Probably the first catastrophe of this magnitude that Dreiser witnessed was the damage wrought by a cyclone in Louisville, Kentucky, in late March 1890. See chapter 75 of *Dawn*.

Chapter XXIX

206.17   **"Edward Reeves . . . Richard Shortwood**   These names and addresses are fictional.

208.33 **There it was** Dreiser's story appeared on pp. 1–2 of the *Globe-Democrat*, 22 January 1893. See "Burned to Death," *TDJ*, pp. 38–47.

209.8 **an editorial . . . trying circumstances** No editorial of this kind appeared in the *Globe-Democrat*.

210.1 **my second day's story** See "Sixteen Dead," *TDJ*, pp. 47–55.

Chapter XXX

211.29 **contemporaneously famous poet** Eugene Field, whose poem "Little Mack" was published in his *A Little Book of Western Verse* (1889).

Chapter XXXI

217.19 **well-known cartoonist** George McManus (1884–1954), among whose widely read comic strip serials was *Bringing Up Father*, which featured the marital tribulations of Jiggs and his wife, Maggie.

218.24 **Booth . . . Anderson** All were leading actors and actresses of the American theater from the 1870s through the 1890s: Edwin Booth (1833–93), Lawrence Barrett (1838–91), Edwin Forrest (1806–72), Helena Modjeska (1840–1909), Fanny Davenport (1850–98), and Mary Anderson (1859–1940). Modjeska appeared in St. Louis in Shakespeare's *Henry VIII* the week of 19 February 1893, and Davenport appeared there in Sardou's *Cleopatra* the week of 26 February 1893. Both of these productions were reviewed by Dreiser for the *Globe-Democrat*.

218.34 **Richard Mansfield** (1854–1907) A famous American actor who starred in plays by writers ranging from Shakespeare to Ibsen and Shaw.

218.35 **Felix Morris** (1850–1900) Comic actor who starred regularly in such repertory plays as *The Paper Chase, Kerry,* and *The Game of Cards,* in which vehicles he appeared in St. Louis the week of 22 October 1893 while Dreiser was there.

218.36 **De Wolf Hopper** (1858–1935) Popular American comic actor, who appeared in St. Louis the week beginning 5 March 1893 in the musical comedy *Wang,* which Dreiser reviewed for the *Globe-Democrat*.

219.2 **E[dward] S[mith] Willard** (1853–1915) English actor renowned for his portrayal of villains and comic figures. He appeared in St. Louis the week beginning 26 February 1893 in four repertory plays, which Dreiser reviewed for the *Globe-Democrat*.

219.4 **about a year and a half as dramatic editor** Actually Dreiser served as dramatic editor of the *Globe-Democrat* from mid January until the end of April 1893. In chapter LI, however, he recalls that he occasionally reviewed plays for the dramatic editor of the *Republic*.

219.5 **Joseph Jefferson** (1829–1905) One of the most beloved American actors of the nineteenth century, known principally for his acting in *Rip Van Winkle,* which ran in St. Louis the week beginning 12 December 1892.

219.6 **Sol Smith Russell** (1848–1902) American comedian and monologist, who came to St. Louis the week beginning 20 November 1892 in two of his familiar vehicles, A *Poor Relation* and *Peaceful Valley*, written for him by Edward E. Kidder (1846–1927).

219.6 **Salvini junior** Alessandro Salvini (1860–96) was the son of the great Italian tragedian Tommaso Salvini (1829–1916).

219.6 **Wilson Barrett** (1846–1904) English actor-manager and playwright, most renowned for his acting in *The Silver King*, which he brought with five other plays to St. Louis for two weeks beginning 5 March 1893. Dreiser reviewed his performances for the *Globe-Democrat*.

219.7 **E[dward] H[ugh] Sothern** (1859–1933) American actor who gained early fame in romantic plays such as *The Prisoner of Zenda*. He later won greater fame for his performances in the plays of Shakespeare, in which he acted with his second wife, the renowned English-born actress **Julia Marlowe** (1866–1950). While Dreiser was in St. Louis, Sothern appeared there in a play, the week beginning 10 December 1893, and Marlowe appeared as a monologist the week beginning 12 February 1894.

219.14 **Charles Frohman** (1860–1915) American theatrical producer and manager; founded the Empire Stock Company to which many of the leading turn-of-the-century actors and actresses belonged; later organized and headed the powerful, monopolistic Theatrical Syndicate. His equally famous and influential brother **Daniel** (1851–1940) was president of the Lyceum Theatre Company.

219.20 **John Drew** (1853–1927) Versatile star of Charles Frohman's company, who specialized in comedies and contemporary plays; the uncle of Lionel, Ethel, and John Barrymore. During the week of 19 March 1893, he appeared in St. Louis in *The Masked Ball*. His performance was reviewed by Dreiser for the *Globe-Democrat*.

219.21 **Mr. [William] Faversham** (1868–1940) A member of the Charles Frohman companies in the 1890s, when he frequently played romantic leads. The week of 9 April 1893 he appeared as a supporting actor in Bronson Howard's *Aristocracy*, which Dreiser reviewed for the *Globe-Democrat*. Faversham was married to **Miss [Julia] Opp** (1871–1921).

219.22 **Miss [Hilda] Spong** (1875–1955) English-born actress.

219.22 **Henry E. Dixey** (1859–1943) Played the lead in romantic musical comedies; his greatest success was in the long-running *Adonis* (1884), with which he toured widely, bringing it to St. Louis in October 1892 shortly before Dreiser arrived.

219.24 **I recall . . . Richard Mansfield** Mansfield came to St. Louis twice while Dreiser lived there: the weeks of 31 October 1892 and 26 November 1893. At neither time was Dreiser writing dramatic reviews, and none of the St. Louis newspapers carries any mention of Mansfield's having dressed down his audience. The actor, however, is characterized as being arrogant and short tempered, and it is not impossible that such an episode as Dreiser relates may have occurred sometime. See *Oxford Companion to American Theatre*.

219.27   **"Baron Chevreul"**   Dreiser has in mind *A Parisian Romance* (1883), by Albert Marshall Palmer (1838?–1905), in which Mansfield played Baron Chevrial, a sensual, brutal roué. The play was performed in St. Louis on 2 November 1892 and 30 November 1893.

220.23   **Henry Arthur Jones**   (1851–1929) English dramatist noted for writing thesis plays as vehicles of social criticism.

220.24   **[Arthur Wing] Pinero**   (1855–1934) English dramatist; like Henry Arthur Jones, a writer of well-crafted problem plays; remembered principally for *The Second Mrs. Tanqueray* (1893) and *Trelawny of the Wells* (1898).

221.16   **Dumas junior**   Alexandre Dumas fils.

222.3   **Thomas Q. Seabrooke**   (1860–1913) Best known for starring in the musical *The Isle of Champagne*, by C. A. Byrne, Louis Harris, and W. W. Furst, which played in St. Louis the week of 26 November 1893.

222.3   **Francis Wilson**   (1854–1935) American comedian who appeared in several popular musicals. He starred in the comic opera *The Lion Tamer* when it appeared in St. Louis the week of 2 April 1893. Dreiser reviewed it for the *Globe-Democrat.*

222.4   **Eddie [Edwin Fitzgerald] Foy**   (1854–1928) Durable American comedian, who starred in *Ali Baba* and a long string of highly popular musical comedies.

222.4   **Frank Daniels**   (1860–1935) Star of comedies and musicals, notably several by Victor Herbert; appeared in St. Louis the week of 29 January 1893 in *Dr. Cupid.*

222.11   **The Middleman**   Jones's 1890 play was performed in St. Louis during the week of 26 February 1893. It starred E. S. Willard and was reviewed by Dreiser for the *Globe-Democrat.*

222.12   **Reginald De Koven**   (1859–1920) Composer of numerous operettas, the best known of which is *Robin Hood* (1891).

222.13   **Harry B[ache] Smith**   (1860–1936) Called the "most prolific librettist and lyricist in the history of the American theatre" by the *Oxford Companion to American Theatre.* A frequent collaborator with Reginald De Koven, their musical *The Fencing Master* played in St. Louis during the week of 16 April 1893 and was reviewed by Dreiser.

222.14   **extravaganzas**   All three were productions of the Chicago-based company of David Henderson (1853–1908): *The Crystal Slipper* was first staged in 1888, *Sinbad* in 1891, and *Ali Baba* in 1892. *Sinbad* was performed in St. Louis the week of 19 November 1893 when Dreiser was living there.

222.16   **Della [May] Fox**   (1871–1913) St. Louis-born soubrette, costarred with De Wolf Hopper in *Wang* when it played in St. Louis the week of 5 March 1893.

222.16   **Edna May [Pettie]**   (1878–1948) American-born actress who achieved stardom in the late 1890s and continued her career in England.

222.24   **The Professor's Love Story**   (1892) This play by James M. Barrie (1860–1937) was performed on 3 and 4 March 1893 and was reviewed by Dreiser for the *Globe-Democrat.*

222.31   **the young actress**   Probably Maxine Elliott (1869–1940), a notable beauty of the American stage, who toured with Willard's repertory company in the early 1890s.

225.19   **an account**   See "The Black Diva's Concert," *TDJ*, pp. 91, 356.

225.34   **Sissieretta Jones**   (1869–1933) Dramatic soprano, who was born in Portsmouth, Virginia, reared in Providence, Rhode Island, and studied at the New England Conservatory in Boston. She sang in solo recitals in the United States and abroad and later became the central figure in the Black Patti Troubadours, a touring company of black singers, comedians, and dancers.

226.12   **editors of the various rival papers**   Dreiser's epitome of the taunting editorial carried in the *Post-Dispatch* is wholly imaginary, for that paper took no notice of his review. What he must have been remembering was a mocking squib from the Democratic *Chronicle* of 1 April 1893, last edition, p. 4, entitled "A Great Editor and 'Black Patti.'" The *Chronicle* was the only St. Louis newspaper to refer directly to Dreiser's review, but another Democratic paper, the *Republic*, inspired apparently by the *Chronicle* item, published remarks critical of Sissieretta Jones; see "Music and Musicians," *St. Louis Republic*, 2 April 1893, p. 32.

Chapter XXXII

229.25   **the senator**   Elihu Root (1845–1937) Distinguished statesman and recipient of the Nobel Peace Prize in 1912; U.S. senator from New York (1909–15).

229.33   Dreiser wrote two newspaper stories about St. Louis's Chinese restaurants: "A Chinese Dinner," *St. Louis Globe-Democrat*, 2 April 1893, p. 38, and "The Chinese in St. Louis," *St. Louis Republic*, 14 January 1894, p. 15 (see *TDJ*, p. 239).

230.9   **Six Companies**   An organization of merchants in San Francisco's Chinatown that loaned money at interest to Chinese immigrants and obtained jobs for them. See Herbert Asbury, *The Barbary Coast* (New York: Alfred A. Knopf, 1933), p. 14.

231.23   **[Pierre] Loti**   (1850–1923) French novelist, of whose many works perhaps the best known is *Pêcheur d'Islande* (1886).

231.24   **[Joseph] Percival Pollard**   (1869–1911) American critic who attacked sentimentality and puritanism and introduced readers to the works of contemporary European writers.

Chapter XXXIII

235.36   **sleep o' nights**   See Shakespeare's *Julius Caesar*, act. 1, sc. 2, line 193.

236.25   **Robin Hood . . . a critic**   The Reginald De Koven comic opera that was performed in St. Louis while Dreiser was dramatic critic for the *Globe-Democrat* was *The Fencing Master.*

236.32 **Albert Johnson** (1869–1957) Said in his *New York Times* obituary to have been "police reporter, feature writer, and telegraph editor" of the *Globe-Democrat.* He served as U.S. representative from Washington in the 63rd through 72nd congresses (1913–33).

237.11 **Iconoclast** Brann published his monthly journal mostly in Waco, Texas, from 1894 until his assassination in 1898. See note 166.13, chapter XXIV.

237.16 **William Marion Reedy** (1862–1920) Edited and published his weekly journal from 1893 until his death. In 1896 it became known as *Reedy's Mirror.* He and Dreiser were good friends.

237.19 **Augustus Thomas . . . In Mizzoura** See note 162.17, chapter XXIII. The play was not performed in St. Louis while Dreiser worked there.

237.23 **Jeremiah I** What is known to survive of the script of this comic opera is reprinted in Richard Lingeman, "Dreiser's 'Jeremiah I': Found at Last," *Dreiser Studies* 20 (Fall 1989): 2–8.

240.4 **man in the fable** Alnaschar in "The Barber's Tale of His Fifth Brother" of *The Arabian Nights.* This character is also referred to in *An American Tragedy,* Book 2, chap. 24, 3rd paragraph.

Chapter XXXIV

243.1 **Sermon on the Mount** Dreiser quotes passages from Matthew in the following sequence: 6.19, 6.25–26, 6.28, 5.39–42, 5.44, 7.7–8, 6.5–6, 7.1–2, 7.21.

243.22 **[Maurice] Maeterlinck** (1862–1949) Belgian dramatist, essayist, and poet. Dreiser is probably referring to Maeterlinck's 1906 essay "The Intelligence of Flowers."

244.18 **McCullagh had begun . . . and Louisville** No news stories on these subjects that Dreiser could have written for the *Globe-Democrat* have been identified.

244.35 **Baudelaire's** Charles Pierre Baudelaire (1821–67) was a French decadent poet, whose poem "Spleen" (LXXVII of *Les Fleurs du Mal*) begins "Je suis comme le roi d'un pays pluvieux."

245.24 **letter from Lois . . . old file** No letters from Lois are known to exist.

Chapter XXXV

251.10 **Republic on . . . three shows** "Several Companies Delayed by Washouts" appears on p. 3 of the 1 May 1893 *St. Louis Republic.*

251.15 **a full account** See "The Theaters," *TDJ,* pp. 93–95. Dreiser's recollection of this episode differs in a few details from the actual events: only two, not three, companies were washed out and unable to perform on the evening of 30 April; the Grand was not one of the theaters affected; Sol Smith Russell was not a member of either delayed company and was not scheduled to appear in St. Louis that week; and the *Post-Dispatch* did not taunt McCullagh about his interest in spiritualism.

252.11   **two leading afternoon papers**   See "An Able Dramatic Critic," *St. Louis Chronicle*, 1 May 1893, p. 4, and "Imaginative Journalism," *St. Louis Post-Dispatch*, 1 May 1893, p. 4. On subsequent days, both newspapers made other barbed references to Dreiser's unlucky blunder: *St. Louis Chronicle*, 2 May 1893, p. 4, and *St. Louis Post-Dispatch*, 3 May 1893, p. 4.

Chapter XXXVI

255.34   **H[arry] B[razee] Wandell**   (1853–?) Wandell was outraged by comments about him in *A Book about Myself.* On 29 December 1922 he wrote to Horace B. Liveright, calling Dreiser "vile, licentious, dishonorable and ignorant" and vaguely threatening libel action. In a letter of 27 September 1929 Arch T. Edmonston informed Dreiser that Wandell was still living in St. Louis and writing for newspapers (Letter file, Dreiser Collection, Van Pelt-Dietrich Library Center, University of Pennsylvania).

257.25   **We had an editorial on it**   The *Republic* printed no comment on Dreiser's blunder.

262.33   **And I . . . crime or sensation**   In TS3 Dreiser expanded this statement with "which I was expected to unravel, . . . and to which always I was expected to write 'the lead,' " showing the confidence placed in his writing ability by the *Republic* since leads were usually supplied by copy editors.

Chapter XXXVII

267.2   **one old man**   See "An Iron Firm Goes Under," *TDJ*, pp. 57–58.
270.5   **These streets are no place fer a girl**   The memory of the compassionate sergeant's stern lecture may have been one of the germs of Dreiser's short story "Butcher Rogaum's Door," *Reedy's Mirror*, 12 December 1901, pp. 15–17 (reprinted in revised form as "Old Rogaum and His Theresa" in *Free and Other Stories* [New York: Boni & Liveright, 1918]).

Chapter XXXVIII

271.16   **laughing superman**   An allusion to the superman concept developed in *Thus Spake Zarathustra* (1883), by the German philosopher Friedrich Nietzsche (1844–1900).

271.31   **a smile . . . upon the great**   Perhaps Dreiser means that love with its enchanting smile could make him walk down little streets as well as great ones or those where he might find splendor, i.e., the splendor referred to in a preceding sentence. He is saying, in effect, that love would lure him into many side streets or byways.

275.19   **I sat down to think**   In TS3 this statement is changed to "I took a drink or two myself."

276.4   **[James Clarence] Mangan**   (1803–49) Irish poet who has been called "the Irish Poe"; used opium and suffered from disturbing hallucinations; died in wretched poverty. His best-known poems are "My Dark Rosaleen" and "O'Hussey's Ode to the Maguire."

276.5   **[Thomas] De Quincey**   (1785–1859) English writer of prose works, the most famous of which is *Confessions of an English Opium Eater.*

277.29   **Dr. Heinie Marks**   His name was frequently in the newspapers because as head physician he was responsible for the care of victims of accidents and violent crime and because he liked to use what were then radical and experimental surgical techniques. His first name was really Heine, but Dreiser's spelling may reflect the way it was ordinarily pronounced.

280.3   **[George Sibley] Johns**   (1857–1941) St. Louis journalist who served for most of his career as editor of the *Post-Dispatch.*

281.13   **Ben[jamin Franklin] King**   (1857–94) Chicago newspaperman. His popular posthumous book of verse went into numerous editions between 1894 and 1923.

281.14   **Charles [David] Stewart**   (b. 1868) Reporter for the Chicago *Daily News,* novelist, and essayist.

281.31   **sociology**   In the galley proof Dreiser substituted "palaeontology" here and in line 33.

Chapter XXXIX

282.22   **my mother's death**   Sarah Dreiser died 14 November 1890.

285.25   **fattest men . . . the Elks**   Although Dreiser made fun of some of the heavyset members of both lodges, the baseball game was not a fat-lean contest.

285.36   **"Blood on the Moon"**   *St. Louis Republic,* 18 July 1893, p. 11.

287.25   **this rough horseplay**   See *TDJ,* pp. 117–20, for "The Trouble Still On," a typical example of the kind of article Dreiser wrote for the Elks-Owls series, and pp. 388–89 for the titles of the other articles.

288.9   **a well-known Congressman**   Charles Frederick Joy (1849–1921), U.S. representative from Missouri (1893–1903).

Chapter XL

294.8   **Mr. ———, our business manager**   In a letter of 19 December 1927, Thomas A. Wright identifies him as "Graham, a little red-headed chap"

(Letter file, Dreiser Collection, Van Pelt-Dietrich Library Center, University of Pennsylvania).

294.12 **Sunday** In the holograph, Dreiser wrote *Thursday,* but the first newspaper article in his series covering the teachers' trip to the fair indicates that they left St. Louis the evening of Sunday, 16 July 1893. See "Teachers at the Fair," *St. Louis Republic,* 18 July 1893, p. 7; reprinted in *TDJ,* pp. 121–23.

Chapter XLI

295.15 **Mr. [Charles Welbourne] Knapp** (1848–1916) Editor and publisher of the *St. Louis Republic* (1887–1915).

295.25 **Mr. [Frank Louis] Soldan** (1842–1908) German-born educator and administrator. At the time of the trip to the fair, he was principal of the St. Louis High and Normal Schools. In 1895 he became superintendent of schools.

295.27 **Mr. Dean** More fully identified as "Phil Dean" in the stories Dreiser wrote about the teachers' trip to the fair.

297.24 **a much earlier . . . all this** A reference to the "Yellow Mss. Rough Copy" (see Textual Commentary), a portion of which Dreiser incorporated into the holograph version of this chapter.

298.12 **Miss Wetherill** Twenty-three teachers in all, some accompanied by friends or relatives paying their own way, made the trip. Of the six women Dreiser names in *Newspaper Days*—Miss Cordon, Genevieve, Annie Ginity, Miss McGanahan, Miss Wetherill, and Sara White—only the last is authentic. The teachers' names are listed in "To Leave To-Day," *St. Louis Republic,* 16 July 1893, p. 11.

300.24 **those nymphs . . . *Nibelungen*** The Rhine maidens in *Das Rheingold,* the first opera in Richard Wagner's cycle of four music dramas, *Der Ring des Nibelungen.*

301.10 **a maiden** Sara Osborne White (1869–1942), who became Dreiser's wife 28 December 1898.

301.25 **As she did so I looked down.** This sentence was omitted from TS3 and *A Book about Myself.*

302.4 **tally-ho** A pleasure coach drawn by four horses.

Chapter XLII

305.3 **seventy-two or three** According to Vera Dreiser, John Paul Dreiser was born 9 September 1821 and would therefore have been seventy-one in July 1893. See *My Uncle Theodore* (New York: Nash, 1976), p. 14. A page from the Dreiser family Bible in the collection at the University of Pennsylvania records that he died 25 December 1900 in Rochester, New York.

308.15 **hotel** Hotel Varsity at 61st Street and Ellis Avenue, four blocks from the University of Chicago and three from the fairgrounds. Identified in "To Leave To-Day," *St. Louis Republic*, 16 July 1893, p. 11.

311.2   **a sister**   Rose White, the model for Marietta Blue in *The "Genius."*

Chapter XLIII

315.28   **"ordentlich"**   Orderly.

317.4   **ready to quit . . . done so**   The span of the *Globe* was 1887–93, according to Winifred Gregory's *American Newspapers 1821–1936.*

317.36   **my first article**   Dreiser wrote six articles on the teachers' visit to the fair, which were published in the *Republic* from 18 through 23 July 1893. See *TDJ*, pp. 121–38.

320.12   **"In such . . . old Aeson."**   *Merchant of Venice*, act 5, sc. 1, lines 13–14. "O'er herself" is misquoted for "ere himself."

Chapter XLIV

325.5   **[Eugene] Witla**   The protagonist of Dreiser's autobiographical novel *The "Genius."*

Chapter XLV

331.8   **Argonautic**   Daring, adventurous, and questing for wealth in the manner of the heroes who followed the legendary Jason on the ship *Argo* in search of the Golden Fleece.

332.18   **C[harles] T[yson] Yerkes**   (1837–1905) Chicago traction magnate on whose career Dreiser modeled that of Frank Algernon Cowperwood in *The Financier*, *The Titan*, and *The Stoic.* Yerkes donated this $23,000 electrically lit fountain in an effort to enhance his reputation as a civic-minded Chicagoan. See Wayne Andrews, *Battle for Chicago* (New York: Harcourt, Brace, 1946), p. 180.

333.37   **St. Joe**   St. Joseph, Michigan.

334.35   **aristocratic suburb**   Identified in chapter LIII, p. 392, as Florissant, Missouri. Before teaching here, she had taught in Pattonville, Missouri.

Chapter XLVI

336.25   **murder mystery**   See "Mystery of a Murder," *St. Louis Republic*, 19 November 1893, p. 9; reprinted in *TDJ*, pp. 207–21.

336.28   **great train robbery**   This incident is described in the *St. Louis Republic*, "On the Scene," 6 September 1893, p. 1, and "Bandit Pennock," 7 September 1893, pp. 1–2. The latter article is excerpted in *TDJ*, pp. 165–70.

336.32   **change of train service**   See "Fast Mail Train," *St. Louis Republic,* 19
          June 1893, p. 1.
337.2   **a famous mind reader**   J. Alexander McIvor Tyndall. See the following
          in the *St. Louis Republic:* "Tyndall's Tests," 9 August 1893, p. 12; "Almost a
          Riot," 11 August 1893, pp. 1–2; "They Met and Lunched," 12 August
          1893, p. 5; "Failed to Connect," 14 August 1893, p. 2; "Blindfolded He
          Drove," 18 August 1893, p. 1. The second, third, and fifth articles are
          reprinted in *TDJ,* pp. 147–61.
337.24   **a spiritualist**   Jules Wallace. In the holograph, Dreiser calls him "Mr.
          Mooney," which name is retained in *A Book about Myself.* The correct
          name has been adopted here for historical accuracy. Wallace figures briefly
          in chapter 5 of *Sister Carrie,* p. 48 of the Pennsylvania edition. The *Republic*
          opened its campaign against Wallace on 9 September 1893 with a lengthy,
          front-page exposé written by several hands, probably including Dreiser's:
          "Jules Wallace, Faker, Fraud, Medium, Healer!" This was followed by a
          sequence of articles, presumably by Dreiser himself: "Wallace on Wallace,"
          10 September, p. 6; "A Spiritualist Fraud," 11 September, p. 3; "Going to
          the Spiritualistic Congress," 18 September, p. 5; "Jules Wallace Denies,"
          23 October, p. 2; "A Faker's Victim," 24 October, p. 1; "May Have No
          Visitors," 26 October, p. 4; "Warrants for Wallace," 28 October, p. 5;
          "Wallace Has Skipped," 29 October, p. 13; "Wallace's Work," 30 October,
          pp. 1–2. See items 60 and 64–66 in *TDJ,* pp. 170–74, 188–206.

Chapter XLVII

350.24   **the story**   See "He Got a Ride," *St. Louis Republic,* 26 August 1893, pp.
          1–2; reprinted in *TDJ,* pp. 161–64. In the holograph, Dreiser names "K
          Street" as the site of the incident and "Mr. So-and-so" as the principal.
          The correct names, taken from the *Republic,* have been substituted here for
          historical accuracy.

Chapter XLVIII

356.16   **I wrote . . . the Globe**   The only *Republic* story from this time that even
          remotely resembles the piece Dreiser describes is "I'm Luckin' fer Mer
          Wife," 26 May 1893, p. 12; reprinted in *TDJ,* pp. 102, 371. Galvin's
          version of the story is "In Search of His Wife," *St. Louis Globe-Democrat,*
          26 May 1893, p. 4.

Chapter XLIX

357.3   **Sometime before this**   The robbery actually occurred on 24 May 1893,
          at which time Dreiser was working for the *Republic.* It took place near
          Pacific, Missouri, some thirty miles southwest of St. Louis.

357.17 **giant powder** Blasting powder consisting of a mixture of nitroglycerine and diatomaceous earth (kieselguhr).

358.14 **lieutenant-governor** Actually the governor was accompanied by the state treasurer.

359.14 **Lebanon . . . Sam Wilson** In the holograph, Dreiser uses the fictional names "Bald Knob" and "Lem Rollins." The actual names are supplied here for historical accuracy.

359.32 **Valley Park** In the holograph, Dreiser names the town of Pacific, but his story in the *Republic* shows it to have been Valley Park. "His Own Story," 4 June 1893, pp. 1–2; reprinted in *TDJ*, pp. 103–14.

Chapter L

365.11 **"hickory" shirt** A work shirt made of strong twilled cotton that had vertical stripes.

366.16 **Harrigan** The holograph has "So-and-so." The actual name is supplied for historical accuracy.

368.26 **he had fallen in love with a young girl** At that time, Wilson had a wife and three little children. None of the contemporary newspaper stories mentions a young girl or a romantic motive for his crime.

376.1 **on the front page of the *Globe*** The story of Wilson's robbery and capture was detailed in a full-page spread in the *Globe-Democrat*, 4 June 1893, p. 2. Headlined "Wilson Behind Bars," it bore as its last subheading "A Visit to the Globe-Democrat Office in the Custody of Officers—The Prisoner and His Captors in the Hands of an Artist." The story is illustrated with drawings of the principals in the case and an imaginary picture of Wilson pointing a gun at Governor Stone, but it has no picture of Wilson in the newspaper office with McCullagh in the background. The concluding section of the story, entitled "At the Temple of Truth," does not mention a rival reporter and briefly describes how the *Globe-Democrat* reporter boarded the train in details quite different from those in Dreiser's version.

376.26 **But he . . . any time** Dreiser turned this episode into fiction in "A Story of Stories," published in *Free and Other Stories* (New York: Boni & Liveright, 1918).

Chapter LI

378.35 **monitory letters** One such letter is quoted by Richard Lingeman in *Theodore Dreiser: At the Gates of the City*, p. 123.

Chapter LII

385.3   **two of the girls**   In addition to Miss Ginity, Dreiser called on a teacher
whom he calls "Miss McLean" in the holograph of this chapter. He deleted
the reference to her from the revised typescript.

Chapter LIII

390.33   **another girl**   Presumably Miss McLean. See note 385.3 of chapter LII.
392.12   **a brief epistle**   Although no letters are known to survive from the early
days of this courtship, Dreiser wrote a version of his first letter in chapter
XXV of the "Yellow Mss." version of *Newspaper Days*. Directed to "Anita
Greenough," it may reproduce or closely approximate what he actually
wrote to Sara White:

> It has been some time since I saw you last, but I have not forgotten the
> delightful days I spent with you in Chicago. The last time we were together you told
> me you expected to be in St. Louis from time to time, and that I might hope to see
> you. Have you been? And have you forgotten me so quickly? I had scarcely thought
> you would do that, after the pleasant days we enjoyed together, or were they
> pleasant?
>   Since leaving you that evening I have been following a wearisome round of
> duties. Newspaper work is rather arduous. During all of this time, though, I have
> thought of you many times and wondered how you were getting along. I have not
> been able to forget for one moment how we strolled about the Fair together and how
> delightfully beautiful those days were. Have you forgotten our little trip to Lincoln
> Park?
>   Won't you tell me when you are to be in St. Louis again, and if so, if I may not
> call on you or take you to a theatre? I have access to most of the theatres here, but as
> a rule, no one to keep me company. I would be delighted, if when you are in the city
> again you would let me know. It seems as if a pleasant acquaintanceship such as ours
> should not be allowed to lapse. What do you think? Won't you let me know?

394.24   **"too pure to behold evil"**   The source of this quotation has not been
identified.
395.8   **a circus rider**   Unidentified. In *A Book about Myself*, p. 320, Dreiser
added that Wood's wife died about a year later and that subsequently he
married Sopheronisby Boanerga Watkins, a carpenter's daughter, who in
turn died accidentally several years afterward.

Chapter LIV

398.21   **Chauncey (i.e., Chancellor) [John] Olcott**   (1860–1932) American
tenor and actor in Irish musical dramas. Composer of the popular song "My

Wild Irish Rose" (1899). Olcott's first appearance in St. Louis was during the week beginning 1 January 1894.

399.18 **a startling poisoning case**   No poisoning case was reported in the *Republic* while Dreiser was with the paper.

399.26 **I wonder now where they are**   Some of Dreiser's courtship letters to Sara White are preserved at Indiana University, but none is from the 1893–95 period. Richard Lingeman reports that Gupton Vogt, the great nephew of Sara, told him that his mother "burned a lot" of letters "because they were 'too personal' " (Letter to T. D. Nostwich, 1 May 1986).

399.32 **I remember . . . him die**   See *St. Louis Republic*, "At a Rope's End," 12 January 1894, pp. 1–2, and "The Hanging of Welsor," 13 January 1894, p. 5; reprinted in *TDJ*, pp. 226–39.

399.35 **political catastrophe . . . escape the law**   See note 117.3 of chapter XVII. So many stories about the Foerstal defalcation were printed in the *Republic* that it is impossible to identify Dreiser's from the brief reference here.

399.37 **A negro . . . him lynched**   See *St. Louis Republic*, "This Calls for Hemp," 17 January 1894, p. 1, and "Ten-foot Drop," 18 January 1894, pp. 1–2; reprinted in *TDJ*, pp. 249–58.

Chapter LVI

406.6 **There was . . . parade and ball**   These events took place during the week beginning 1 October 1893. See note 174.23 for chapter XXV.

406.36 **One of the current incidents**   Dreiser's version here differs in several particulars from the event as he reported it for the *Republic*. For example, the newspaper articles mention four robbers, not three; they state that the conductor was operating the car without a motorman; and they report that Miss Schuble found Mr. Cragen at his house, to which she had run for help, but he would not lend her a horse because he was afraid the robbers would steal it from her. Miss Schuble had to wait until one of Mr. Cragen's neighbors agreed to accompany her to the trolley before she could check on the fate of the conductor. See "Unprovoked Murder," 24 September 1893, p. 1; "A Deep Mystery," 25 September 1893, p. 1; "Will Wear the Medal," 1 October 1893, p. 29. The last article is reprinted in *TDJ*, pp. 179–84. Dreiser probably also wrote these follow-up stories: "Murdered Fitzwilliam," 8 December 1893, pp. 1–2; "Murderers Talk," 9 December 1893, pp. 1–2; "Fitzwilliam's Slayers," 10 December 1893, p. 7.

411.6 **Lizzie**   In the holograph the girl is called "Gunda." The correct name is supplied here for historical accuracy.

Chapter LVIII

424.27 **The Danger Signal**   (1891) A comic melodrama by the American playwrights Henry C. De Mille (1853–93) and Charles Barnard (1838–1920), rewritten from their *The Main Line* (1886).

424.29   **last time . . . two years before**   Paul Dresser had appeared in St. Louis in the same play just a year before, during the week beginning 12 February 1893. Dreiser reviewed the performance for the *Globe-Democrat*. See "The Theaters," 12 February 1893, p. 30, and 13 February 1893, p. 9; reprinted in *TDJ*, pp. 85–87.

424.32   **The Tin Soldier**   (1886) Written by the American playwright Charles Hale Hoyt (1860–1900). In his *Annals of the New York Stage* (vol. 14, p. 582), George C. D. Odell indicates that Paul Dresser appeared in this comedy during the 1890–91 season.

424.36   **A Midnight Bell**   (1889) A comic melodrama by Charles Hale Hoyt.

424.36   **The Two Johns**   A farce vehicle of the vaudeville company of J. C. ("Fattie") Stewart, who apparently wrote it himself and staged it annually between 1882 and 1894. George C. D. Odell states that Dresser appeared in it with Stewart during the 1888–89 season (*Annals of the New York Stage*, vol. 14, p. 163).

425.11   **"The Bowery"**   This famous satirical song was written by Charles Hale Hoyt and Percy Gaunt to be sung in Hoyt's popular play *A Trip to Chinatown* (1891).

425.16   **the institute**   St. Meinrad Seminary in southern Indiana.

425.34   **late November**   Actually Dresser performed in St. Louis the week beginning 28 January 1894. See *TDJ*, pp. 258–60. Dreiser either misremembers here, or he may be deliberately rearranging events for dramatic effect.

Chapter LIX

427.11   **Bill [Edgar Wilson] Nye**   (1850–96) Popular American humorist who worked as a newspaper columnist and lecturer.

427.12   **Petroleum V. Nasby**   Pseudonym of David Ross Locke (1833–88), editor and owner of the *Toledo Blade* and author of humorous newspaper letters.

427.12   **Spoopendyke Papers**   Humorous newspaper sketches written for the *Brooklyn Daily Eagle* by Stanley Huntley (1847?–85) and published in book form in several editions beginning in 1881.

427.13   **Samantha at Saratoga**   (1887) One of a series of popular "Samantha" books written by Marietta Holley (1836–1926) under her pseudonym "Josiah Allen's Wife."

427.31   **[John] Bunyan**   (1628–88) Author of *The Pilgrim's Progress* (1678).

427.31   **John Howard Payne**   (1791–1852) American playwright, who wrote the lyrics to "Home, Sweet Home."

431.20   **[Homer] Bassford**   Remained as dramatic editor of the *Republic* until its absorption by the *Globe-Democrat* in 1919. See Harry Rosecrans Burke, *From the Day's Journey* (St. Louis: Miner, 1924), p. 167.

432.11   **Rosabel Morrison**   (1869–1911) Daughter of a well-known actor and producer, Lewis Morrison (1845–1906), in whose productions she sometimes appeared. She had also been with *The Danger Signal* company when it performed in St. Louis in January 1893.

Chapter LX

435.28   **ten years later . . . name of the street changed**   Dreiser apparently is recalling a news story reporting that Bowery merchants wished to rename their street because the song had "cast odium on the thoroughfare" and caused business to go into a decline. See "To Change the Bowery's Name," New York *World*, 11 April 1895, p. 2.

435.38   **scowsy**   Mean. Eric Partridge conjectures that the word was formed from "scabby" and "lousy" (*A Dictionary of Slang and Unconventional English*).

437.10   **Harry Minor**   Perhaps a reference to Henry Clay Miner (1842–1900), theatrical agent and founder of vaudeville houses.

437.10   **Bowery Theatre**   Founded in 1826, it survived through numerous fires and rebuildings until 1878 when it became the Thalia, a house for German and Yiddish productions. It was finally destroyed by fire in 1929.

Chapter LXI

441.10   **to them. Apparently I**   In the galley proof of *A Book about Myself*, Dreiser made the following insertion between these two sentences: "Toward the very last, as I have said, they changed, but then it was too late."

442.12   **mere bags of shells**   A play on the familiar phrase "mere bagatelles."

443.12   **Bellerophon**   The mythical Greek hero who attempted to ride to heaven on Pegasus, the winged horse.

Chapter LXII

447.38   **a letter of introduction**   In the Dreiser letter file at the University of Pennsylvania are two such letters, both signed by C. W. Knapp, the owner of the *Republic*; the first was dated 2 March 1894 and the second 2 April 1894.

Chapter LXIII

453.22   **Kay Street**   St. Louis city maps of the early 1890s do not show this street.

454.24   **the Herald**   The *Wood County Herald* had its office in Weston, Ohio, approximately five miles southeast of Grand Rapids.

Chapter LXIV

459.17   **[George Washington] Crile**   (1864–1943) American surgeon and author. Dreiser is probably thinking of Crile's *Origin and Nature of the Emotions* and *A Mechanistic View of War and Peace*, both published in 1915.

459.17   **[Jacques] Loeb**   (1859–1924) German-born biophysicist. Dreiser was most impressed by his *The Mechanistic Conception of Life* (1912).

462.10   **Colorado**   In 1893 Colorado became the second state (after Wyoming) to provide for women's suffrage in its constitution.

462.12   **Dr. Mary Walker**   (1832–1919) American physician and advocate of women's rights, which cause she propagandized by wearing male clothing. For an anecdote about her probably written by Dreiser, see *HC*, p. 27, no. 19.

463.8   **As Lincoln . . . so I thought**   In his first debate with Stephen F. Douglas (21 August 1858), Lincoln said: "I was not very much accustomed to flattery, and it came the sweeter to me. I was rather like the Hoosier with the ginger bread, when he said he reckoned he loved it better than any other man, and got less of it."

Chapter LXV

464.14   **Fallen Timbers**   The battle was fought 20 August 1794 near Defiance, Ohio, a good twenty-five miles west of Grand Rapids. The main adversaries of General Anthony Wayne (1745–96) were the Shawnee Indians.

464.18   **my mother had been reared in this region**   Sarah Schänäb was born 8 May 1833, six miles west of Dayton, Ohio, where she and her family lived for the next nine years before moving to Kosciusko County, Indiana. See Richard Lingeman, *Theodore Dreiser: At the Gates of the City 1871–1907*, p. 20.

465.33   **Miami and Erie**   Dreiser left the name of the canal blank in the holograph. The identity has been established by reference to a map of Ohio's canal routes in the *Encyclopaedia Britannica*, 11th ed.

468.20   **city editor**   Arthur Henry. See note 149.3, chapter XXI.

468.21   **as I have narrated elsewhere**   See *A Hoosier Holiday*, pp. 253–55.

469.34   **I wrote my story**   For Dreiser's reports on the strike, see items 80–83 in *TDJ*, pp. 269–75.

469.35   **Then, at the . . . and ladies gay."**   In the "Yellow Mss," chapter XXXIV, p. 5, Dreiser says he was also told that he could contribute to a "hotel column" modeled on "one in a Western paper," by which he presumably means the *Globe-Democrat's* "Heard in the Corridors." He says that he immediately wrote several paragraphs that were deemed acceptable, among them one praising the charm of the Maumee River, which particularly delighted Arthur Henry. These paragraphs, printed in five installments under the heading "Men Who Talk," appeared in the *Blade* between

27 March and 2 April 1894. They consist of seventeen paragraph-long comments by people purportedly interviewed by the reporter at various Toledo hotels, and they touch on a diversity of topics. That on the Maumee River is attributed to Hugh Hartung. Among the other supposed interviewees are Paul Dresser, Harry Dunlap, H. B. Wandell, and Dick Wood.

470.1 **"As in Old Toledo"** The actual title was "As If in Old Toledo." See *TDJ*, pp. 275–77.

471.5 **Damon . . . Pythias—Gawain, Ivaine** Exemplars of devoted friends, the first pair is from classic Greek history and the second from a fourteenth-century verse romance, *Ywain and Gawain*.

471.13 **book of fairytales and some poems** In 1894 Henry and his wife, Maude Wood Henry, published *The Flight of a Pigeon and Other Stories*. Some of Henry's verse had been published in the *Herald* while he and Dreiser still lived in Chicago.

Chapter LXVI

471.34 **Detroit** In a letter to Emma Rector of 4 April 1894, written from Toledo, Dreiser states that he had "been to Detroit and Cincinnati very recently." See Richard W. Dowell, "You Will Not Like Me, I'm Sure," *American Literary Realism* 3(Summer 1970): 268.

472.10 **a river** The Maumee.

475.12 **Tom [Loftin] Johnson** (1854–1911) American manufacturer and politician, U.S. representative from Ohio (1891–95), reform mayor of Cleveland (1901–9), disciple of Henry George, and advocate of honest municipal government.

475.13 **Henry M[orrison] Flagler** (1830–1913) American oil magnate and business promoter; a key associate of John D. Rockefeller (1839–1937) in developing the Standard Oil Company; pioneer developer of Florida resort real estate and railways.

475.16 **All of . . . in Euclid Avenue** Rockefeller and Flagler both had homes on Euclid Avenue, but in 1884 they had moved Standard Oil's base of operations to New York City, where they built homes.

476.25 **The fault was not . . . in ourselves** An echo of *Julius Caesar*, Act 1, sc. 2, lines 140–41.

477.4 **the *Cleveland Leader*** Founded around 1847; purchased by Joseph Medill in 1853; merged with the *Cleveland Plain Dealer* in 1917.

477.9 **small boyish-looking person** James Binkley Morrow (1855–1924). See Charles E. Kennedy, *Fifty Years of Cleveland* (Cleveland: Weidenthal, 1925), pp. 205–6.

478.3 **"Turtleback"** The more customary name was *whaleback*: "A form of steam vessel having sides curving in towards the ends, a spoon bow, and very convex upper deck, much used on the Great Lakes, esp. for carrying grain" (W2).

478.31   **bluff old Lake captain**   Alexander McDougall (1845–1923), Scottish-born mariner and inventor, built the first whaleback in 1888 and founded a successful steel barge company in Duluth, Minnesota, to manufacture this and other types of lake and oceangoing vessels.

479.21   **my story**   See "M'Dougall's Dream," *Cleveland Leader*, 20 April 1894, p. 3; reprinted in *TDJ*, p. 281.

Chapter LXVII

480.30   **Laurence Sterne**   (1713–68) English novelist, best known for *The Life and Opinions of Tristram Shandy* (1760–67); published *A Sentimental Journey through France and Italy* in 1768.

484.16   **of life. I used**   In TS3 the following statement occurs between these sentences: "It was the saloon, not liquor, which brought about the prohibition folly—the American Bar."

485.22   **Alaric**   (370?–410) Gothic king and conqueror; periodically ravaged Italy and in 410 captured and plundered Rome.

485.22   **Attila**   (406?–453) King of the Huns, known as the "Scourge of God," ravaged the Balkans, central Europe, Gaul, and northern Italy.

486.18   **Suspension Bridge**   Completed in 1855, the first major example of such a bridge that employed steel cables; designed and built by John Augustus Roebling (1806–69), who later drew up plans for the Brooklyn Bridge.

486.31   **Blondel**   No swimmer of this name has been identified. Perhaps Dreiser was thinking of the internationally famous French acrobat Blondin (Jean-François Gravelet, 1823?–97), who many times in 1859–60 crossed over the rapids below Niagara Falls on a tightrope.

Chapter LXVIII

488.24   **"foreigners"**   In the page proof of *A Book about Myself*, Dreiser substituted "hunkies" for "foreigners," remembering it, perhaps, as the term of contempt actually used in the 1890s by native-born Americans in general and newspapers and politicians in particular. Although in its original use it probably referred just to Hungarians, it came to be applied indiscriminately to any immigrant laborers from central Europe—Poles, Slovaks, Lithuanians, and others.

489.3   **padrone**   "One that secures employment for immigrant, usually unskilled workers, especially of Italian extraction, and that also acts as banker and commissary for them with the overall purpose of profit by exploitation" (*W3*).

489.4   **breaker children**   Children who worked in coal breakers, separating the slate from the coal.

489.4   **company stockade**   Probably a reference to the management practice of fortifying a company undergoing a strike behind barbed wire and wooden barricades or walls patrolled by armed guards.

489.5   **great steel strike**   Called against the Carnegie Steel Company at Homestead, Pennsylvania, during the summer of 1892.

489.7   **the Olivers**   Henry William Oliver (1840–1904), developer of Minnesota iron-ore deposits; George Tener Oliver (1849–1919), Pittsburgh steel manufacturer.

489.7   **[Henry Clay] Frick**   (1849–1919) Pittsburgh coke manufacturer; chairman of the Carnegie Steel Company; managing head of the company during the Homestead Strike.

489.14   **Alexander Berkman**   (1870–1936) Polish-born anarchist; lover of Emma Goldman, whom he assisted in the publication of the anarchist magazine *Mother Earth.* He served thirteen years in prison for attempting to assassinate Frick.

489.37   **Free Silver campaign and the "gold parades"**   In the 1896 presidential campaign, William Jennings Bryan (1860–1925), the Democratic candidate, advocated the free coinage of silver, whereas his Republican opponent, William McKinley (1843–1901), supported a single, gold standard. Dreiser could probably personally remember a giant rally and parade supporting McKinley that occurred in New York City on 31 October, the Saturday before the election, and lasted for seven and a half hours.

489.38   **"full dinner pail"**   McKinley's campaign slogan in 1900. It was intended to emphasize the prosperity of his first term.

490.3   **Henry George**   (1839–97) American economist who developed a single-tax theory and program; twice a candidate for mayor of New York on a social welfare platform; author of *Progress and Poverty* (1877–79).

490.3   **Father [Edward] McGlynn**   American Roman Catholic clergyman who advocated Henry George's single-tax doctrine and campaigned for him. His excommunication in 1887 and reinstatement in 1892 made national headline news.

490.4   **Herr [Johann] Most**   (1846–1906) German-born anarchist; founded and edited the anarchist journal *Freiheit*, which advocated terrorist activities against the church and state; arrived in the United States in 1882; his treatise *The Science of Revolutionary Warfare* supposedly inspired the Chicago Haymarket anarchists and Alexander Berkman. In the 1880s and 1890s he often lectured before anarchist and labor clubs in Pittsburgh. Conservative American newspapers usually referred to him sneeringly as "Herr Most."

490.4   **Emma Goldman**   (1869–1940) Russian-born anarchist; disciple of Johann Most; edited *Mother Earth*, a revolutionary journal, with Alexander Berkman; imprisoned on Blackwell's Island in 1893 for making inflammatory speeches; imprisoned again in 1916 and 1917 for advocating birth control and obstructing the draft; deported to Russia in 1919. Dreiser became acquainted with her in Greenwich Village around 1910.

490.15 **William Rockefeller** (1841–1922) An associate in the oil business of his brother John D.

490.15 **H[enry] H[uttleston] Rogers** (1840–1909) American financier who became chief executive officer of Standard Oil.

490.18 **William H[enry] Vanderbilt** (1821–85) Son of "Commodore" Cornelius Vanderbilt and president of the New York Central Railroad.

490.18 **Jay Gould** (1836–92) Wall Street speculator and owner of vast railway interests, including the Missouri-Pacific.

490.19 **Mark [Marcus Alonzo] Hanna** (1837–1904) American businessman and politician; guided McKinley into the White House; U.S. senator from Ohio (1897–1904).

Chapter LXIX

492.16 **For to . . . so wide—** From " 'For to Admire' " (1894), by the English poet and writer of fiction Rudyard Kipling (1865–1936).

493.12 **four at least** The Dispatch was founded in 1846, the Leader in 1870; both were bought out by rival dailies in 1923. The Times was founded in 1879, and it united with the Commercial Gazette in 1906 to become the Gazette Times, which continued publication until 1927. Winifred Gregory's American Newspapers 1821–1936 (New York: H. W. Wilson, 1937) does not list a Gazette-Telegraph. Dreiser is probably remembering the Chronicle-Telegraph, which was formed by a merger in 1884 and became in 1927 the Hearst-owned Sun-Telegraph.

495.6 **an individual** Harrison Null Gaither (1860–1952), the city editor. A few years later he became a correspondent for the New York Press during the Spanish-American War and then served as city editor for that paper until his retirement in 1912.

Chapter LXX

500.36 **[Henry] Phipps** (1839–1930) Associate of Andrew Carnegie in the development of the steel industry; director of the U.S. Steel Corporation.

502.17 **Thomsons** A reference to John Edgar Thomson (1808–74), president and developer of the Pennsylvania Railroad; an early financial backer of Carnegie, who named his first big steel plant after him.

Chapter LXXI

506.4 **going on several . . . that had arisen** No stories that fit this general description appear in the Dispatch during Dreiser's period of employment.

Chapter LXXII

510.9   **General [Jacob Sechler] Coxey**   (1854–1951) Businessman and political theoretician; led a large group of men to Washington, D.C., to petition Congress for interest-free loans to communities to be spent on public works that would provide the unemployed with jobs. The title *General* was bestowed on Coxey by the mocking press. His home was in Massillon, Ohio, nine miles west of Canton, from which his group began its trek on 25 March 1894. It moved through the Pittsburgh area shortly before Dreiser began working there, and it assembled in Washington on 1 May. Sympathizing groups from the west coast—Los Angeles, San Francisco, Portland, and Seattle—set out to join Coxey's "army" at the same time that it left Canton.

510.31   **Thomas B[rackett] Reed**   (1839–1902) U.S. representative from Maine (1877–99) and Speaker of the House of Representatives (1889–91 and 1895–99); Reed had come to Pittsburgh to address the Americus Club on its annual celebration of the birthday of General Ulysses S. Grant. He was at this time a strong contender for the next Republican presidential nomination. See "Reed, Just as He Stands," *Pittsburg Dispatch*, 28 April 1894, p. 4; reprinted in *TDJ*, pp. 285–86. Dreiser later interviewed Reed for *Success* 3 (June 1900): 215–16.

512.36   **Allegheny**   The section of Pittsburgh now known as Northside; an independent municipality in 1894 and regarded as Pittsburgh's sister city.

515.15   **Honoré de Balzac**   (1799–1850) The only English version of *The Wild Ass' Skin* (*La Peau de chagrin*, 1831) that Dreiser could have read in 1894 is that made by Katherine Prescott Wormeley, published in Boston in 1888 as *The Magic Skin* and prefaced with a lengthy appreciation by George Frederic Parsons.

515.33   **Raphaël [de Valentin]**   The hero of *The Wild Ass' Skin*. The three other characters figure in several other Balzac novels as well.

516.2   **lady without a heart**   The Countess Foedora, who coldly rejects the suit of the enamored Raphaël.

516.10   **[Eugène de] Rastignac**   One of the central characters in *La Comédie humaine*, who also plays an important role in *Le Père Goriot* (1834).

516.10   **[Lucien] de Rubempré**   The hero of *The Great Man from the Provinces* (*Illusions perdues*, 1837–43).

516.11   **[Dr. Horace] Bianchon**   A medical man who figures as a friend of de Rastignac in several novels beginning with *The Wild Ass' Skin*.

516.14   **Cousin Pons** (1847) and **Cousin Betty** (1846)   Two of Balzac's best-known novels. Taken together they have the title *Les Parents pauvres*.

517.7   **[Jean-Frédéric] Taillefer**   A central character in *The Red Inn* (*L'Auberge rouge*, 1831); has important supporting roles in *The Wild Ass' Skin* and *Le Père Goriot*.

517.7   **[Baron Frédéric de] Nucingen**   Figures notably in *Le Père Goriot* and several other novels in *La Comédie humaine*.

517.20   **Madame Marneffe**   The avaricious siren whom Cousin Betty manipulates into sexual liaisons that will advance her own schemes.

517.22   **another god**   The reference is not clear, but Dreiser may mean one of the English novelists, Thomas Hardy (1840–1928) or George Moore (1852–1933), whose works he greatly admired.

Chapter LXXIII

518.13   **pictures anent . . . news matters**   Dreiser is remembering the following *Dispatch* stories: "After the Rain Storm," 19 May 1894, p. 2; "Reapers in the Fields," 6 July 1894, p. 2; "Hospital Violet Day," 12 May 1894, p. 2; "The Last Fly of Fly Time," 3 October 1894, p. 3; "Confound the Mosquito," 28 July 1894, p. 3. The first four are reprinted in *TDJ*, pp. 286–93, 314–16. No story about an old switchman's dog has been identified.

518.24   **an idle skit**   For a description of how Dreiser's actual story differs from his memory of it, see T. D. Nostwich, "Dreiser's Apocryphal Fly Story," *Dreiser Newsletter* 17 (Spring 1986): 1–8.

523.32   **Library, arriving . . . or the library**   In TS3 this passage has been changed to read "Library, going out on assignments or writing one of these sketches and then going home again or to the Press Club." If this revision is actually Dreiser's, it is significant because it indicates that he carried on regular reportorial duties at the same time he was writing his columns.

524.8   **sent to . . . interview Andrew Carnegie**   See "Talks at a Banquet," *Pittsburg Dispatch*, 21 November 1894, p. 2; reprinted in *TDJ*, pp. 320–24.

Chapter LXXIV

530.12   **census of opinion . . . one greater city**   The results of this canvas were published in sixteen installments in the *Dispatch* between 4 and 17 June 1894.

532.2   **Frick a mansion . . . Fifth Avenue site**   The mansion still stands at 1 East 70th Street and is an art museum known as the Frick Collection.

Chapter LXXV

533.28   **no theatres**   In reality Pittsburgh had at least six theaters at the time Dreiser lived there. Perhaps he means that a "steelworker of the poorer sort" could not afford to attend them.

535.10   **"Pittsburgh stogie"**   A thin, inexpensive cigar manufactured in Pittsburgh when Dreiser lived there.

535.33   **what I have . . . my own attitude**   Dreiser's attitude toward sexuality and vice is more fully set forth in "Neurotic America and the Sex Impulse," written at about the same time as this chapter and published in *Hey Rub-a-Dub-Dub* (New York: Boni & Liveright, 1920), pp. 126–41.

Chapter LXXVI

542.25   **the Standard**   Published under this title between 1894 and 1901; from 1902 to 1913 it was known as *The Standard & Vanity Fair.*

542.36   **Bacchae**   Women who took part in the Bacchanalia, the orgiastic festival in honor of Bacchus.

543.19   **Munsey's**   A monthly magazine published between 1889 and 1929 by Frank Andrew Munsey (1854–1925).

544.1   **Town Topics, [the Journal of Society]**   Regularly published from 1882 to 1932. It specialized in well-crafted, sophisticated fiction and essays and was avidly read for its often scandalous gossip about the doings of high society.

544.3   **C[harles] M[orton] S[tewart] McLellan**   (1865–1916) Best known as a playwright and librettist, his most memorable work being the book for the popular musical *The Pink Lady* (1911). McLellan was probably only an editorial assistant for *Town Topics* because the editor in chief from 1891 to 1920 was Col. William D'Alton Mann (1839–1920).

545.37   **George Du Maurier's Trilby**   The English novelist George Du Maurier (1834–96) published *Trilby* in *Harper's Monthly Magazine* between January and July 1894. Shortly afterward it was published in book form by Harper's.

Chapter LXXVII

549.17   **the small town**   Dreiser probably is referring to Montgomery City, Missouri, for although the White homestead was nearer to the village of Danville, the railroad terminus was at Montgomery City. See Richard Lingeman, *Theodore Dreiser: At the Gates of the City 1871–1907*, p. 135.

551.15   **In The "Genius"**   See Book 1, chapters 17–19.

551.37   **[John] Brown**   American abolitionist who was executed for his 1859 raid on the government arsenal at Harpers Ferry, Virginia.

551.38   **[Robert Edward] Lee**   (1807–70) Commander in chief of the Confederate armies during the American Civil War.

552.1   **[Thomas Jonathan (Stonewall)] Jackson**   (1824–63) The ablest Confederate general serving under Lee, renowned as a battle strategist.

553.14   **The Heavenly Twins**   (1893) A best-seller by the English novelist Sarah Good (pseudonym of Mrs. David C. McFall, née Frances Elizabeth Clarke, 1862–1943).

Chapter LXXIX

561.31   **"Rialto"**   "The district on Broadway frequented by players and playgoers" (W2).

564.33   **Reverend Doctor [Charles Henry] Parkhurst**   (1842–1933) American clergyman who as pastor of the Madison Square Presbyterian Church attacked political corruption and organized vice. The investigations stimulated by his Society for the Prevention of Crime helped defeat Tammany Hall and elect a reform mayor.

564.35   **[Girolamo] Savonarola**   (1452–98) Dominican monk whose fiery denunciations of vice and corruption in Florence led to the expulsion of the de Medici power, to his own installation as virtual dictator of the city-state, and ultimately to his excommunication and execution.

566.1   **George**   His legal name was L. A. Hopkins, and he was sometimes called "Grove" because of his resemblance to Grover Cleveland.

566.14   **two children**   Their names were Gertrude and George.

Chapter LXXX

569.18   **three-days' wonder . . . scandal world**   For the newspaper accounts of Hopkins's theft and elopement with Emma, see the Norton Critical Edition of *Sister Carrie*, pp. 388–93.

570.1   **Lexow Committee**   Appointed in 1894 by the Republican-dominated state legislature to investigate police corruption in New York City and headed by state senator Clarence Lexow.

571.12   **Arnold, Constable and Company**   A large store founded in 1827 that dealt in retail and wholesale dry goods, carpets, and upholstery.

571.33   **Siegel-Cooper**   A Chicago department store that opened a New York City branch in 1896.

571.35   **Altman's**   Founded in 1854, Altman's was a large and widely known quality dry goods store.

572.20   **subsequently he was buried**   Paul, born 23 April 1857, died 30 January 1906 and was buried in Chicago.

573.28   **"On the Sidewalks of New York"**   The lyrics were written by Jim Blake, the music by Charlie Lawlor.

575.16   **Lester [real name John Johnstone] Wallack**   American actor, dramatist, and stage manager. The original Wallack's Theater stood at Broadway and 13th Street (1861–81). It was succeeded by a new Wallack's at Broadway and 30th Street (1882–87). The old Wallack's then became the Star.

575.18   **[Sir Henry] Irving**   (born John Henry Broadribb) (1839–1905) English actor who distinguished himself in Shakespearian roles.

576.12   **Century Company . . . be connected with**   The Century Company published Dreiser's *A Traveler at Forty* in 1913.

576.22   **Park and Tilford**   Founded in 1840, it was the largest retail grocery house in New York City.

576.30   **Madison Square Garden**   Originally an auditorium run by P. T. Barnum, the Garden was rebuilt in 1890 by the well-known architectural firm of McKim, Mead and White. This second Garden was demolished in 1925.

576.31   **Cabildo**   A Spanish-Moorish–style building adjoining the cathedral in the Vieux Carré of New Orleans. Originally it had been the city's seat of government during the Spanish administration of Louisiana. Dreiser and Helen Richardson spent two weeks in New Orleans in October 1919 on their way to California and may have seen the Cabildo on this trip.

576.31 **Diana** This nude, thirteen-foot copper statue, which revolved like a weather vane, was the work of the American sculptor Augustus Saint-Gaudens (1848–1907). The scandal and delight of 1890s New Yorkers, it found a permanent home in the Philadelphia Museum of Art after the second Garden's demolition.

576.36 **Senator [Thomas Collier] Platt** (1833–1910) U.S. representative from New York (1873–77); U.S. senator (1881); resigned from the Senate after a disagreement with President Garfield but remained a power in New York Republican politics. It was at his instigation that the state legislature created the Lexow Committee.

577.25 **Palmer's Theatre (formerly named Wallack's** This theater was again named Wallack's in 1896 and retained that identity until it closed in 1915.

577.29 **Augustin Daly's famous playhouse** Opened in 1879 and named for John Augustin Daly (1839–99), American dramatist and theatrical manager. One of his plays, Under the Gaslight, figured in chapters 17–20 of Sister Carrie. It was demolished in 1920.

577.31 **Weber and Fields'** Joseph Weber (1867–1942) and Lew Fields (1867–1941) were a comedy team specializing in dialect humor and slapstick. Their jointly owned theater was in operation between 1895 and 1904.

578.1 **Manhattan Theatre** Opened as the Eagle in 1875, became the Standard in 1879, and was renamed the Manhattan in 1897. It was demolished to make way for Gimbel's in 1909.

578.5 **Koster and Bial's Music Hall** Established in 1879 by John Koster and Rudolf Bial as a concert hall but soon became a variety or vaudeville house. Originally located on 23rd Street, it reopened in a renovated theater on 34th in 1893. The management introduced films as part of the bill in 1896, thus making Koster and Bial's the first movie house in America. It was demolished in 1901 to make room for Macy's.

578.7 **Oscar Hammerstein** (1847?–1919) German-born impressario and theater builder. Of his many theaters, the most important was probably the Manhattan Opera House, founded in 1906, which competed successfully with the Metropolitan Opera House. Hammerstein managed Koster and Bial's between 1893 and 1895.

578.13 **Garrick, or . . . the Lyceum** Dreiser's memory has merged two different theaters. The Garrick, on 35th Street between Fifth and Sixth avenues, opened as Harrigan's Theater in 1890 and became the Garrick in 1895. It was demolished in 1932. The Lyceum, built in 1885 and managed by American dramatist and producer Steele Mackaye (1842–94), was located on Fourth Avenue between 23rd and 24th streets. It was demolished in 1902, and its successor was opened in 1903 on 45th Street just west of Broadway. Both Lyceums were managed by Daniel Frohman.

578.19 **Knickerbocker Theatre**   Opened in November 1893 with a play starring Sir Henry Irving and continued to present first-rate productions until its demolition in 1930.

578.22 **Casino**   The leading musical-comedy house in New York during its existence (1883–1930).

578.24 **Metropolitan Opera House**   Opened in 1893 on Seventh Avenue between 39th and 40th streets. Ravaged by a fire in 1892, it reopened in November 1893. It was finally demolished in 1967.

578.26 **Empire Theatre**   Built for Charles Frohman in 1893, this theater was the home of many outstanding productions until its demolition in 1953.

578.29 **Browne's Chop House**   Baedeker's 1893 guide to the United States gives this restaurant's address as 31 West 27th Street.

579.38 **ghoulas**   Apparently a Dreiser coinage meaning "ghoulish people." The word occurs also in "Peter" in *Twelve Men*, p. 32.

Chapter LXXXI

581.14 **Roland Burke Hennessy**   (1870–1939) Editor and poet; wrote *Tales of the Heart and Tales of Broadway* (1897); in addition to the *Standard*, he edited *Metropolitan, Broadway, Illustrated American*, and *Stage*, all noted for their pictures of pretty actresses and their rather racy contents.

582.4 **Maude Adams**   (real name Kiskadden) (1872–1953) Famed American actress, remembered especially for her starring roles in *Peter Pan* (1906–7) and other plays by Sir James M. Barrie. If Paul named her as one of Daly's protégées, he was mistaken, because in New York she worked under the aegis of Charles Frohman.

582.5 **Willie (William) Collier**   (1866–1944) American comedian and playwright.

583.23 **Russell Sage's**   (1816–1906) Sage was one of the wealthiest American financiers.

584.23 **Newport [Rhode Island], Lenox [Massachusetts], Bar Harbor [Maine]**   Fashionable summer resorts in the 1890s.

584.25 **[Henry Osborne] Havemeyer**   (1847–1907) Wealthy financier whose fortune was derived from sugar refineries.

587.4 **Gussie L. Davis**   A one-time Pullman porter who picked up a smattering of musical training when he worked as a janitor at the Cincinnati Conservatory of Music. His most popular songs were *The Fatal Wedding* (1893) and *In the Baggage Coach Ahead* (1896).

588.7 **And here they were in number**   Dreiser's memory of the Broadway scene of the summer of 1894 is interestingly confirmed by a newspaper story to the effect that merchants had complained to the police that idle actors were driving away trade by congregating in front of their shops and ogling women patrons. See "Even Loafing's Made Hard," New York *World*, 22 July 1894, p. 6.

Chapter LXXXIII

594.34   ***The House of All Nations***   Located at 117 West 32nd Street and under
the management of a woman identified in newspaper accounts as Madame
Charles. By December 1894 it had gone out of business and been replaced
by the Gotham, a club for rich playboys and men about town. See "For
Gilded Youths and Midnight Suppers," New York *World,* 29 December
1894, p. 17.

599.1   **graveyard . . . river**   Wall Street extends from Trinity Church to the
East River.

599.4   **George [Jay] Gould**   (1864–1923) A less gifted financier than his
father, he lost all of his inherited railroad interests to his rivals.

599.26   **Broad and Wall**   The site of the New York Stock Exchange.

Chapter LXXXIV

600.8   This chapter was omitted from A *Book about Myself* at the urging of Horace
Liveright, who said that it was "dead stuff." A shortened version of it
entitled "A Vanished Seaside Resort" was included in *The Color of a Great
City* (New York: Boni & Liveright, 1923), pp. 119–28.

600.11   **Flatiron Building**   A twenty-three-story skyscraper known officially as
the Fuller Building, designed by Daniel H. Burnham and erected in 1903.

600.18   PAIN'S FIREWORKS   James C. Pain (1837–1923) was an English-born
fireworks manufacturer who regularly provided pyrotechnic displays at
Manhattan Beach, beginning in 1878.

600.20   SEIDL'S GREAT ORCHESTRA   Anton Seidl (1850–98), Hungarian-born
musician, conducted Wagner at the Metropolitan Opera House; he succeeded Theodore Thomas as conductor of the New York Philharmonic
Orchestra (1891).

600.22   MANHATTAN BEACH   A fashionable resort fronting the Atlantic
Ocean at the easternmost end of Coney Island.

601.28   **Asbury Park**   A New Jersey seashore resort.

602.5   **lucky**   In "A Vanished Seaside Resort," a version of this chapter that
appeared in *The Color of a Great City* (New York: Boni & Liveright, 1923),
this word is changed to "mucky."

603.36   **"Washington Post March,"**   Composed by John Philip Sousa in 1889
to promote a student essay contest sponsored by the newspaper.

Chapter LXXXV

607.27   **James Gordon Bennett**   (1841–1918) Inherited the *Herald* from his
father in 1867; resided in Paris beginning in 1877 and in 1887 founded a
Paris edition of the *Herald.*

608.4   **the owner and editor**   Joseph Pulitzer (1847–1911), Hungarian-born journalist, founded the *St. Louis Post-Dispatch* in 1878 and bought the New York *World* in 1883.

609.9   **[Ernst Heinrich] Haeckel**   (1834–1919) German biologist and philosopher.

609.14   **famous playwright**   Augustus Thomas. See note 162.17, chapter XXIII. In chapter XC, 642.3, his brother is identified as Wynne Thomas.

609.23   **the *Recorder***   Frank Luther Mott describes the *Recorder* (1891–96) as "a weak morning paper." See *American Journalism*, p. 521.

609.25   **the *Press***   Founded in 1887, the *Press* was purchased by Frank A. Munsey in 1912 and merged by him with the *New York Sun* in 1916.

609.33   **quondam *Sun***   In the 1890s under the editorship of Charles A. Dana the *Sun* (founded in 1833) was a dominating force in American journalism. By the early 1920s the *Sun* and its sister paper, the *Evening Sun*, had become the property of Frank A. Munsey and had lost much of their onetime force and identity through being merged with other newspapers.

610.19   **[Thomas Henry] Huxley**   (1825–95) English Darwinian scientist who published many works on philosophical and religious subjects.

610.19   **[John] Tyndall**   (1820–93) English professor of natural history who delivered lectures and published works to popularize science.

610.20   ***First Principles***   (1860–62) Published as a preface to Spencer's subsequent studies of the principles of biology, psychology, sociology, and ethics.

610.26   ***Science . . . Christian Tradition***   Both volumes were published in the United States in 1893 and contained various essays written between 1876 and 1891.

610.31   **this too too solid earth**   An echo of *Hamlet*, Act 1, sc. 2, line 129.

611.33   **One of those periodic scandals**   See "Story of a Convict," *Pittsburg Dispatch*, 24 May 1894, p. 2.

612.15   **a humorous article**   See "Fenced Off the Earth," *Pittsburg Dispatch*, 19 July 1894, p. 3; reprinted in *TDJ*, pp. 296–300.

613.8   **"Too . . . mad."**   The source of this quotation is unidentified.

Chapter LXXXVI

613.31   **report the . . . an introduction**   See "General Booth Says Farewell," *Pittsburg Dispatch*, 12 November 1894, pp. 1–2.

618.13   **laughing gas**   An allusion to Dreiser's one-act play "Laughing Gas," the theme of which is the meaninglessness and futility of life. The play was written in 1914 and published in 1916 in *Plays of the Natural and Supernatural* (New York: John Lane Company).

Chapter LXXXVII

622.8   **"The average . . . police-station lawyer."**   This statement occurs in "On Journalism," Mencken's review of Upton Sinclair's *The Brass Check* in

Smart Set 61 (April 1920): 138–44; reprinted in H. L. Mencken, *A Gang of Pecksniffs and Other Comments on Newspaper Publishers, Editors and Reporters* (New Rochelle, N.Y.: Arlington House, 1975), pp. 61–72. Dreiser's quotation differs in some minor points from the original.

624.10 **Arthur Brisbane** (1864–1936) Managing editor of the *World* (1890–97); editor of William Randolph Hearst's *New York Evening Journal* (1897–1921).

625.30 **Alleyne Ireland** (1871–1951) A retired British civil servant who became one of Pulitzer's private secretaries in 1911 and wrote a memoir of the experience called *An Adventure with a Genius* (New York: E. P. Dutton, 1920).

626.4 **he had been horsewhipped** Pulitzer's biographers do not mention such an incident specifically, but Don C. Seitz says that while Pulitzer was editor of the *Post-Dispatch* he "was twice bodily attacked. . . . but treated the incidents as part of his stormy task." See *Joseph Pulitzer: His Life and Letters* (New York: Simon & Schuster, 1924), p. 107.

626.10 **[John Albert] Cockerill** (1845–96) Cited by the *Dictionary of American Biography* as having been "a great fighting editor in the period of the sensational press." For an account of his killing of Alonzo W. Slayback on 13 October 1882, see W. A. Swanberg's *Pulitzer* (New York: Scribner's, 1967), pp. 63–66.

626.20 **William Randolph Hearst** (1863–1951) American newspaper publisher who purchased the *New York Journal* in 1895 and carried on a spectacular circulation war with Pulitzer's *World;* established a nationwide chain of newspapers; one of the early practitioners of yellow journalism.

627.4 **the Harmsworths** A family of British publishers and politicians, the most notable of whom was Alfred Charles William, Viscount Northcliffe (1865–1922), who at various times controlled such London newspapers as the *Evening Mail, Daily Mail, Daily Mirror,* and the *Times.*

627.24 **council of the Secret Ten in Venice** A committee of public safety formed in 1310 to quell rebellions; for many years thereafter it was essentially the governing body of Venice.

628.17 **twice afterwards** Dreiser may be referring to his experiences as editor of *Broadway Magazine* and *The Delineator* (1906–10).

Chapter LXXXVIII

632.5 **presumably the dramatic critic** Charles Henry Meltzer (1853–1936), English-born playwright, opera librettist, and translator of plays; he was dramatic critic for the *World* (1893–96).

632.19 **musical critic** When Dreiser worked for the *World* its regular music critic was Reginald De Koven (1859–1920), the American opera composer best known for *Robin Hood* (1890).

Chapter LXXXIX

634.24   **my friend**   In chapter XLII of the "Yellow Mss" Dreiser identifies this man as Mark Hood, a newspaperman and playwright who had recently been a correspondent for the *Cleveland Plain Dealer.*

636.35   **Newmarket coat**   A long, closely fitting coat (W2).

637.22   **(1) to visit . . . (3) to visit**   The first item is apparently reported in "Canal Boat Victim's Body Found," New York *World,* 30 December 1894, p. 6. The two other stories have not been identified.

638.38   *The Confessions of a Thief*   The existence of a book with this title has not been authenticated.

639.1   **[Thomas F.] Byrnes**   (1842–1910) In his illustrious, not to say notorious, career with the New York City police department, Byrnes rose from patrolman to superintendent. As a detective he was the most famous and successful thieftaker in the country. Although the Lexow Committee proved nothing illegal against him, the bad publicity arising from his testimony in regard to his personal fortune enabled newly appointed police commissioner Theodore Roosevelt to secure his retirement from the force.

639.7   **Old Shakespeare**   Actually a woman named Carrie Brown, an aged prostitute, who was murdered Jack-the-Ripper fashion in a low-class hotel on Water Street, 24 April 1891. Byrnes claimed to have solved the case when he arrested an elderly illiterate Algerian, George Frank (nicknamed Frenchy), and charged him with the crime. Shortly afterward Frank was found guilty of murder in the second degree and sent to prison. The *World* contended that police department detectives under Byrnes's direction had manufactured the evidence against Frank, and after the Lexow investigations it campaigned for his pardon and release. See " 'Frenchy' Says He Is Not a Murderer," New York *World,* 21 January 1895, pp. 1, 3.

640.4   **In later . . . them up."**   Dreiser is probably thinking primarily of "Curious Shifts of the Poor," an article he published first in *Demorest's* 36 (November 1899): 22–26, then incorporated into chapters 45–47 of *Sister Carrie,* and finally reprinted partially in *The Color of a Great City* (New York: Boni & Liveright, 1923) as "The Bread Line" and "The Men in the Storm." The article has been reprinted by Donald Pizer in *Theodore Dreiser: A Selection of Uncollected Prose* (Detroit: Wayne State University Press, 1977), pp. 131–40; in the Norton Critical Edition of *Sister Carrie,* pp. 415–23; and by Yoshinobu Hakutani in *Selected Magazine Articles of Theodore Dreiser* (Rutherford, N.J.: Fairleigh-Dickinson University Press, 1985), 1:170–80.

Chapter XC

643.13   **ridiculous story**   See "Mrs. Moriarity Knocks Out Healy," New York *World,* 24 December 1894, p. 7; reprinted in *TDJ,* p. 332.

644.12   **All . . . the *Herald***   This story has not been identified.

644.22   **"Four Hundred."**   A term coined by New York lawyer and social arbiter Ward McAllister (1827–95) to indicate the limited number of socially acceptable New Yorkers.

644.29   **Goelet**   The name of a wealthy New York City family tracing its lineage to Dutch colonial days.

Chapter XCI

654.36   **James K[eteltas] Hackett**   (1869–1926) A popular American actor who in the 1890s typically assumed gallant roles in romantic dramas such as *The Prisoner of Zenda.*

654.36   **Richard Harding Davis**   (1864–1916) American newspaperman, war correspondent, short-story writer, novelist, and playwright. In 1894–95, when Dreiser worked for the *World,* Davis was a reporter for the *Sun.*

654.36   **Mrs. Humphry Ward**   (née Mary Augusta Arnold) (1851–1920) British novelist and social worker; vigorous opponent of women's suffrage.

656.18   **many short stories and magazine articles**   The standard Dreiser bibliography lists more than one hundred articles published between 1895 and the publication of *Sister Carrie* in 1900 but only one story: "Forgotten," *Ev'ry Month* 2(August 1896): 16–17. In 1901 he published four stories: "When the Old Century Was New," "The Shining Slave Makers," "Nigger Jeff," and "Butcher Rogaum's Door," all republished in *Free and Other Stories* (New York: Boni & Liveright, 1918). See Donald Pizer et al., *Theodore Dreiser: A Primary and Secondary Bibliography.*

Chapter XCII

656.33   **David Graham Phillips**   (1867–1911) American muckraking journalist and novelist; worked for the *New York Tribune* and *New York Sun* as well as for the *World.*

656.34   **James Creelman**   (1859–1915) Canadian-born editor, war correspondent, novelist, and biographer.

657.2   **George Cary Eggleston**   (1839–1911) American journalist, novelist, and historian; editorial writer for the *World* for eleven years.

657.36   **George W[ashington] Cable**   (1844–1925) American short-story writer, novelist, historian; best known for his local color stories about Creoles in pre–Civil War New Orleans, collected as *Old Creole Days* (1879).

657.36   **Thomas Nelson Page**   (1853–1922) American lawyer, short-story writer, novelist, historian; best known for fiction set in his native state of Virginia, for example, *In Ole Virginia* (1887).

657.38   **Charles Dudley Warner**   (1829–1900) Essayist, editor, novelist; remembered especially as Mark Twain's collaborator on *The Gilded Age* (1873).

657.38   **Frank R[ichard] Stockton**   (1834–1902) Novelist, short-story writer, editor; well known in his day for his stories with trick endings, especially "The Lady or the Tiger?" (1882).

659.22   **East 27th Street police station**   Volumes of the *World Almanac* for 1894–96 list no station at this address but do list stations at 24 East 29th Street and 327 East 22nd Street. Perhaps Dreiser meant one of them.

661.18   **frieze**   "A kind of coarse wool cloth or stuff, with a shaggy or tufted (friezed) nap on one side, now mostly of Irish make" (W2).

663.15   **Inspector McCaffrey**   No police department member by this name has been identified.

669.5   **the News**   A New York City daily published between 1855 and 1906. Not to be confused with the *New York Daily News*, which began publication in 1919.

Chapter XCIII

672.2   **story . . . missing girl**   Of all the news items printed in the *World* between 1 January and 1 April 1895, the one that most closely matches Dreiser's description is "Doubtless Susie Martin's Skull," which appeared on p. 12 of the 8 March issue and therefore lends support to the assumption that Dreiser quit the *World* in early March.

673.5   ***Literary Experiences***   Dreiser never wrote this book; however two notes headed "Literary Experiences" in the Dreiser Collection at the University of Pennsylvania list the following topics that presumably he planned to write about: Post N Y World Days; Literary Ideals; Woman who kept bed house; Tramps in Region of Cooper Union; Every Month; Men who came to see me; Bohemia; Arthur Henry; The man on Munseys who said I couldn't write; Magazine World; Sister Carrie; Frank Norris; Street & Smith—Diamond Dick; Butterick—Editorial Days; Greenwich Village; California—1919–22; Success *American Tragedy* Days; "Dr." Klopsch— Christian Herald; Orison Swett Marden—"Success"; B. W. Dodge; Ben B. Hampton; George W. Wilder; Grant Richards "Barfleur"; Mencken— Nathan; Lewis.

TEXTUAL COMMENTARY

The Black Sparrow Press edition reprints the text, historical commentary and notes, appendix, and index of the 1991 University of Pennsylvania Press edition of *Newspaper Days*.

Copy-text for the Pennsylvania edition of *Newspaper Days* is Dreiser's holograph. Into this text have been introduced, as emendations, Dreiser's handwritten revisions from the first and second typescripts. These typescripts derive from the manuscript in a straight line of textual transmission. The first typescript, hereafter TS1, was copied from the holograph and then revised. The second typescript, TS2, was copied from revised TS1, then further revised. In a continuous effort of creativity, Dreiser inscribed the holograph and then put the text through two revised typescripts, polishing it and bringing it to a point of completion insofar as his personal intentions were concerned. All later versions of the text—the typescript that Horace Liveright reworked, the galley and page proofs, the 1922 edition and all subsequent editions based upon it—are essentially expurgated abridgments of Dreiser's original work. They were prepared primarily to avoid giving offense to conservative readers and to the watch-and-ward societies of the early 1920s. These later incarnations of the text result from intentions quite different from those that motivated Dreiser in the creation of the original work. They were produced within strictures imposed by forces that, in effect, had the power to dictate what books could and could not be sold in the United States. One should therefore regard the 1922 edition as an interesting and important historical artifact but not as Dreiser's full autobiography.

Dreiser was unhappy with the expurgation (much of it self-imposed) to which his books had to be subjected to be published. From the early nineteen-teens, his letters contain requests to Mencken and other friends to restore, after his death, what had been cut from the texts of his travel books, memoirs, and novels. The fact that he preserved the holograph and both typescripts of *Newspaper Days* and entrusted them to the University of Pennsylvania strongly suggests that he hoped this book would someday be published in an uncut edition.

Description of the Copy-text

Dreiser's holograph manuscript has been chosen as copy-text for this edition because it represents most fully and accurately what he wanted to say and because it preserves the texture of his style, spelling, and punctuation. With the addition of his revisions from TS1 and TS2, this text becomes the version he brought to completion in May 1920. The holograph has been chosen in preference to TS1 or TS2 because these typescripts are compromised by a very large number of sophistications and errors in transcription, most of which were not caught by Dreiser.

The following passages from alternate texts of *Newspaper Days* are not included in the Pennsylvania edition but contain valuable information on topics in Dreiser's autobiography. One is a passage in the holograph that he deleted when he revised TS1. The rest are in TS3 and enlarge significantly on parallel passages in the holograph. Because they are in typescript, they cannot be incontrovertibly attributed to Dreiser himself, but their presence in TS3 is evidence that at least they had his approval.

The following passage occurs at the beginning of chapter II of TS3.

It may seem a little odd to mingle purely personal and so-called private experiences with those that relate solely to the work of the newspaper profession and my connection with the same, but I propose to do it, for the simple reason that I see no way of indicating the import of the profession to me without indicating the background against which it was shadowing itself in my case, the illusion, the ignorance, the thirst for life. So I may as well state that for years—this was my twentieth—I had been struggling onward, if not upward, via all sorts of cares, courtesies, sympathies and what not on the part of my parents and others, and the previous year, my mother having died and the home being virtually on the edge of dissolution, I had ventured into the world "on my own," as it were. Several sisters, two brothers and my father were still present in the family domicile, but it was a divided and somewhat colorless affair at best. Our mother, the cementing and inspiriting alchemy of this home, as other mothers are of theirs (I trust), was gone. I personally was already wondering, and that in the greatest sadness, how long it could endure, for she had made of it a something as sweet as dreams are at times. That temperament, that charity and understanding and sympathy! We who were left were like fledglings, trying our wings betimes but fearful of the world without because of the shelter and sympathy which she had provided. My practical experience of the world and human contact was so slight that it was scarcely worth talking about, and I may add that I was a creature of slow and uncertain response to anything practical, having almost, as it were, an eye single to color, romance, beauty; truly nothing more. I was but a half-baked poet, romancer, dreamer.

In TS3 the following passage was inserted into chapter III, p. 17, line 26, after "just the same."

Meanwhile, looking here and there and not finding anything, I decided, since I had had ample experience as a collector as well as in several other lines of work and must live while I was making my way into journalism, to return to this one field with which I was most familiar and see if I might not in the meantime secure a place as a reporter by occasionally dropping around. The experiment, as I may as well state beforehand, proved fruitless; for having work it was easier to return to my home and loaf than to use the only convenient hour I had (six o'clock) seeking work in another line.

Having been previously employed by an easy payment instalment house I now sought out another, the Corbin Company, I think it was called, in Lake Street, not very far from the firm with which I had previously worked and from which, I may as well confess, having been hard pressed for a winter overcoat the preceding fall, I had abstracted or held out twenty-five dollars, intending to restore it by degrees. But before I had been able to manage that a slack up in the work occurred, due to the fact that wandering street agents sold less in winter than in summer, I was laid off and had to confess that I was short in my account. The manager and owner, who previous to this had seemed to take a fancy to me, actually said nothing other than that I was making a mistake, taking the path that led to social hell. I do not recall that he even requested that the money be returned, so dishonest and grafting was his own line of work. But so temperamental and nervous was I that I was convinced that some day, unless I returned the sum, I would be arrested and to avoid this I had written him a letter after leaving promising that I would. He never even bothered to answer the letter, and I believe that if I had returned in the spring, paid the twenty-five and asked for work he would have taken me on again. But I had no such thought in mind. I held myself disgraced forever and only wished to be clear of this type of work forever. It was a vulture game at best, selling to the dumb and the inartistic trash worth, say, two or three dollars for as much as twelve and fourteen times its value and pocketing the difference. Now that I was out of it I hated to return. Besides, I had the feeling that if I did so the first thing my new or proposed employer would do would be to inquire of my previous employer and being informed of my stealing would refuse to employ me.

In TS3 the following passage was inserted into chapter XII, p. 78, line 20, after "degradation that preceded it."

In the face of such a scene or picture as this my mind invariably paused in question. I had been reared on dogmatic religious and moral theory, or at least had been compelled to listen to it all my life. Here then was a part of the work or *let* of an omnipotent God, who nevertheless tolerated, apparently, a most industrious devil. Why did He do it? Why did nature, when left to itself, devise such astounding slums and muck heaps as this city then and there could boast? I was wont to gaze with a kind of loathing and sickness of stomach at a very common type of harlot to be found in many doorways or behind windows or under lampposts in these areas, smirking and signalling creatures with the dullest or most fox-like expression and with heavily smeared lips and cheeks and blackened eyebrows, who were ready to give themselves to any and every one for the modest sum of one dollar, or even fifty cents, and this in the heart of this budding and prosperous West, a land presumably flowing with milk and honey. What had brought that about so soon in a new, rich, healthy, forceful land—God? devil? or both working together toward a common end? Near at hand were huge and rapidly expanding industries of every description. The street-cars and trains, morning and evening, were crowded with earnest, careful, saving, seeking, moderately well-dressed people who were presumably anxious to work and "lay aside a competence," as the phrase has it, and own a home. Then why was it that this other element had stepped aside to indulge in such a physical hell as this? Was it the best each could do? Was God to blame? Or society? Or what?

I could not solve it, not being able to take apart and put together the human machine, but there it was, and despite my worthy father and other religionists and moralists in the realm or domain of an omnipotent God. He did nothing about it—that is, not immediately at least. True, the church warred on vice. The politicians, representatives of the people, were supposed not to tolerate such things as this. Yet here it was, and on some days I thought the omnipotent God theory silly. On some other days I blamed the politicians or the inhabitants of these areas. On still other days I half-suspected that all of us, good, bad and indifferent, were helpless victims of uncontrollable superior forces; but I never got the thing straight then or since. This matter of being, with its differences, is permanently above the understanding of man, I am sure.

In TS3 the following passage was added to chapter XX, p. 140, line 1, after "us socially together."

At his home I met his sister, a mere slip of a tow-headed girl, whom I saw in later years in vaudeville as a headliner, and her "act" interested me very much because it was immensely clever. This same Hazard, years later, I encountered once more as a rather blasé correspondent in Washington, representing, if I am not mistaken, a league of papers. He had then but newly completed a wild-West thriller, done in cold blood with an eye to a quick sale. Assuming that I had influence with publishers and editors, he invoked my aid. I gave him such advice and such letters as I could. But only a few months later I read where one Robert Hazard, well-known newspaper correspondent, living with his wife and child in some Washington residence section, had placed a revolver to his temple and ended it all. Why, I have often wondered. He was so much better fitted mentally and physically to enjoy life. . . . Or is it mental fitness that really kills the taste for life?

In TS3 the following passage replaces "So thick was. . . . letter in reply" in chapter XXIV, p. 164, line 10.

These two youths knew this. Hazard, as I now recall, handed it to me with this statement: "Of course a thing like this could never be published over here. We'd have to get it done abroad." Think of that as an atmosphere for budding genius to encounter: the American backwoods puritan with his ruler looking over your shoulder! These two incipient artists had encountered it. They had been overawed to the extent of thinking it necessary to write of French, not American life in terms of fact. Such things as they felt called upon to relate occurred only in France, never here—or at least such things, if done here, were never spoken of. Your Anglo-Saxon Pecksniff at work, you see. I think it was nothing less than tragic that these men, or boys, fresh, forceful, imbued with a burning desire to present life as they saw it, were thus completely overawed by the moral hypocrisy of the American mind and did not even dare to think of sending it to an American publisher.

In TS3 the following passage was added to chapter XXV, p. 171, line 14, following "death in its wake":

I never was and never could be blinded to the obvious and gross favoritism practiced by nature, and this I resented most fiercely, largely, it may be, because it was not, or I thought it was not, practiced in my behalf. Later on in life I began to suspect that a gross favoritism, in regard to certain things at least, was being practiced in my behalf. I was never without friends, never without some one to do me a good turn at a critical moment, never without love and the sacrifice of beauty on the part of some one in my behalf, never without a certain amount of applause or repute. Was I worthy of it? I knew I was not and I felt that the powers that make and control life, the "sightless substances" or chemistries, did not care two whoops whether I was or not. Life, as I had seen and felt from my earliest thinking period, used people, sometimes to their advantage, sometimes not. Occasionally, as I could see, I was used to my advantage as well as to that of some one or something else. Occasionally I was used, as I thought, to my disadvantage. Now and then when I imagined I was being used most disadvantageously I was not so at all, as when for a period I found myself unable to write and so compelled to turn to other things—a turning which resulted in better material later on. It has often been so with me. At this time, however, I felt that whatever the quality of the gifts handed me or the favors done me, they were as nothing compared to some and, again, I was honestly and sympathetically interested in the horrible deprivations inflicted upon others, their weaknesses of mind and body, afflictions of all sizes and sorts, the way so often they helplessly blundered or were driven by internal chemic fires, as in the case of the fascinating and beautiful-minded John T. McEnnis, to their own undoing. That great idealistic soul, that warm, ebullient heart!

Thinking on these things, I would wander here and there, looking into the homes of the big and the little and wondering about them, eating out my own heart at the sight of, presumably, unattainable ease or beauty, wishing that like this one I were handsome; like that one strong; like a third, famous; like a fourth, rich; like a fifth, happy or witty or attractive. This in nowise interfered with the type of work or the specific tasks I was called upon to do; on the contrary, some of the moods evoked by these meditations and contemplations so fired my spirit or altered the atomic rote of my thinking to such an extent that writing or interpretation or exact understanding seemed trebly easy and I returned with enough data on any subject or assignment to write a half dozen times as much as was wanted. It was no trouble for me, as I soon learned, to fascinate the assistant city editor, if not my city editor, with vivid bits which I created out of the whole cloth as being appropriate or took from the pages of fact and gesture which life was constantly placing before me. The motion of a man's or woman's arm, a word he used, the color of the day or the hour, the mood of some one—all these, so easily observed by me, seemed to affect my superior intensely, as when one day, writing of a street-car accident, I described how the raw country motorman, who had killed a little girl, got off his car and appeared to be dying of cramps, holding his waist, sobbing and groaning. My assistant city editor came in and holding the item, simply said: "Gee! But you can put things down all right!" and then went out. For the moment I felt quite set up, not unlike a prize-fighter perhaps who has demonstrated that he has the punch; but a little while later, realizing the hugeness of life and the absolute unimportance and minuteness of our little strengths and honors, I would be as gloomy and as despondent as ever. Praise has never helped me, nor strength, nor the favor of beauty, nor fame. I have never been able to take my eye from the fact of the immense futility of it all, the unimportance of anything save illusion, the gift or littleness of believing that something, however small, is important. Think of a dog growling over the importance of a bone, an ant hugging an ant egg to its breast!

The following passage, which sheds additional light on the character of Rodenberger and on Dreiser's relationship with him, is in the holograph but was excised by Dreiser when he revised TS1. Its place in chapter XXXVIII is on p. 279, line 32, after "never even dreams."

To return to Rodenberger however. He was one such in his modest way. I was too young to grasp the full import of his personality but it was of this order He had such a happy, latitudinarian point of view delightful considering the day in which he flourished and the city Life according to Rody—or as it expressed in this narrow, conventional midwestern world was such a false and meretricious thing. People were all so dull or such victims of astounding illusions. According to him or his paper as I remember it he was having a hard time explaining to himself (if not to a dull public) just why it was that there was such a vast discrepancy between what people professed to believe and what they really believed, or did, here in St. Louis whether they believed it or not. Like myself he was just discovering some of the facts of history, (or had,) some of the anomalies of the social regime in which we were, some of the amazing failures based on reasonably good conduct, some of the huge successes based on the trashiest frauds.

"Well, Theodore"—I can still see him standing in the grateful shade of the La Clede of a warm summer morning contemplating the brisk crowds that turned about these corners and looking at the comfortable Southerners in long coats and big hats sitting in the rockers which graced the front of the hotel for what would be the equivalent of a short New York block. "Whats news? Whose dead? What fortunes have you wrecked since yesterday?"—and then would follow some suave, laughing commentary on the foibles of life, its idiosyncrasies, the fact that some fact that we knew perhaps would never reach the public, until becoming philosophically a little dull or socially a little gay a drink would be proposed and we would adjourn to Hacketts bar inside—(Phil Hackett of cheerful memory) and have something—a beer or a whiskey or a julep.

As I see myself now in connection with all this I was a lank, curious, cynical, sniffling soul—not really believing fully that life was as bad as I sometimes thought, and saw nor as perfect or worthy as some others imagined but a hash of both with myself avoiding the Scylla of failure and the Charybdis of dispair. Rodenberger, charmed as I was by him, as by Dick and Peter, I fancied to be in great danger of not making that material success which I hoped for myself and dreamed so important—then. Above all things life itself—the generality of it—its eating and drinking and dressing and loving was important and health and a taste for it most important Rodenberger with his rosy cheeks, clear blue eyes and stocky vigorous frame, seemed still more or less doomed because of his melancholy, and cynicism whereas I in spite of my being in much the same position mentally still hoped to succeed. He ran with women as much as possible, drank to excess at times, stopped in those house of prostitution which I was always desiring to investigate for myself without having the courage and because he did freely what I wanted to do and argued for it briskly, somewhere back in the puritan depths of my mind, I had a spiritual rod in pickle for him. Free of belief in the rewards of Christianity and the great good to flow from a strict moral behavior, I still had lingering doubts as to the profits of freedom—mental or otherwise—was afraid of it. A kind of sniffing moralist you see, with one hand on the church for safety, and another to take the good of life as I saw it—providing it did not tend to hurt me in any way—to pull me down.

When I think of myself nosing about in this sniffy, fearsome, self gaurding way I wish now that someone would have kindly come forward and given me a good, swift material kick for the sake of my but partially developed common sense.

In TS3 the following passage is inserted into chapter XCIII, p. 672, between lines 35 and 36:

N.B. Four years later, having by then established myself sufficiently to pay the rent of an apartment, secure furniture and romance myself into the belief that I could make a living for two, I undertook that perilous adventure with the lady of my choice—and that, of course, after the first flare of love had thinned down to the pale flame of duty. Need anything more be said? The first law of convention had been maintained, whereas the governing forces of temperament had been overridden—and with what results eventually you may well suspect. So much for romance—in one case anyhow.

INDEX

Printed December 2000 in Santa Barbara &
Ann Arbor for the Black Sparrow Press by
Mackintosh Typography & Edwards Brothers Inc.
Design by Barbara Martin.
This edition is published in paper wrappers
& there are 200 numbered hardcover deluxe
copies published *hors commerce*.

Theodore Dreiser ca. 1915 (Photo by Marceau).

T. D. NOSTWICH is a Professor of English at Iowa State University. He is editor of *"Heard in the Corridors": Articles and Related Writings by Theodore Dreiser* (Iowa State University Press, 1988); *Theodore Dreiser Journalism, Volume 1: Newspaper Writings 1892–1895* (University of Pennsylvania Press, 1988); *Newspaper Days* by Theodore Dreiser (University of Pennsylvania Press, 1991); *Fulfilment and Other Tales of Women and Men* by Theodore Dreiser (Black Sparrow Press, 1992) and *Dawn: An Autobiography of Early Youth* by Theodore Dreiser (Black Sparrow, 1998).